Koren Talmud Bavli
THE NOÉ EDITION

NAZIR

Steinsaltz Center

KOREN

תלמוד בבלי

KOREN TALMUD BAVLI

THE NOÉ EDITION

נזיר

NAZIR

Daf 47a through Daf 66b

COMMENTARY BY

Rabbi Adin Even-Israel Steinsaltz

EDITOR-IN-CHIEF

Rabbi Dr Tzvi Hersh Weinreb

SENIOR CONTENT EDITOR

Rabbi Dr Shalom Z Berger

EXECUTIVE EDITOR

Rabbi Joshua Schreier

STEINSALTZ CENTER

KOREN PUBLISHERS JERUSALEM

MATANEL FOUNDATION
GRANTED TO GIVE

Supported by the Matanel Foundation

Koren Talmud Bavli, The Noe Edition
Vol. 17c: Tractate Nazir, Daf 47a through Daf 66b
Paperback, ISBN, 978-965-7765-82-1

First Hebrew/English paperback edition, 2021

Koren Publishers Jerusalem Ltd.
PO Box 4044, Jerusalem 91040, ISRAEL
PO Box 8531, New Milford, CT 06776, USA
www.korenpub.com

Steinsaltz Center

Steinsaltz Center is the parent organization of institutions established by Rabbi Adin Even-Israel Steinsaltz

PO Box 45187, Jerusalem 91450 ISRAEL
Telephone: +972 2 646 0900, Fax +972 2 624 9454
www.steinsaltz-center.org

This book was published in cooperation with the Israel Institute for Talmudic Publications.

הִנֵּה יָמִים בָּאִים, נְאֻם אֲדֹנָי יֱהוִה, וְהִשְׁלַחְתִּי רָעָב בָּאָרֶץ,
לֹא־רָעָב לַלֶּחֶם וְלֹא־צָמָא לַמַּיִם, כִּי אִם־לִשְׁמֹעַ אֵת דִּבְרֵי יהוה.

Behold, days are coming – says the Lord God – I will send a hunger to the land, not a hunger for bread nor a thirst for water, but to hear the words of the Lord. (AMOS 8:11)

The Noé edition of the Koren Talmud Bavli
with the commentary of Rabbi Adin Even-Israel Steinsaltz
is dedicated to all those who open its covers
to quench their thirst for Jewish Knowledge,
in our generation of Torah renaissance.

This beautiful edition is for the young, the aged,
the novice and the savant alike,
as it unites the depth of Torah knowledge
with the best of academic scholarship.

Within its exquisite and vibrant pages,
words become worlds.

It will claim its place in the library of classics,
in the bookcases of the Beit Midrash,
the classrooms of our schools,
and in the offices of professionals and business people
who carve out precious time to grapple with its timeless wisdom.

For the Student and the Scholar

DEDICATED BY LEO AND SUE NOÉ

Introduction by the Publisher

The Talmud has sustained and inspired Jews for thousands of years. Throughout Jewish history, an elite cadre of scholars has absorbed its learning and passed it on to succeeding generations. The Talmud has been the fundamental text of our people.

Beginning in the 1960s, Rabbi Adin Even-Israel Steinsaltz שליט"א created a revolution in the history of Talmud study. His translation of the Talmud, first into modern Hebrew and then into other languages, as well the practical learning aids he added to the text, have enabled millions of people around the world to access and master the complexity and context of the world of Talmud.

It is thus a privilege to present the *Koren Talmud Bavli*, an English translation of the talmudic text with the brilliant elucidation of Rabbi Steinsaltz. The depth and breadth of his knowledge are unique in our time. His rootedness in the tradition and his reach into the world beyond it are inspirational.

Working with Rabbi Steinsaltz on this remarkable project has been not only an honor, but a great pleasure. Never shy to express an opinion, with wisdom and humor, Rabbi Steinsaltz sparkles in conversation, demonstrating his knowledge (both sacred and worldly), sharing his wide-ranging interests, and, above all, radiating his passion. I am grateful for the unique opportunity to work closely with him, and I wish him many more years of writing and teaching.

Our intentions in publishing this new edition of the Talmud are threefold. First, we seek to fully clarify the talmudic page to the reader – textually, intellectually, and graphically. Second, we seek to utilize today's most sophisticated technologies, both in print and electronic formats, to provide the reader with a comprehensive set of study tools. And third, we seek to help readers advance in their process of Talmud study.

To achieve these goals, the *Koren Talmud Bavli* is unique in a number of ways:

- The classic *tzurat hadaf* of Vilna, used by scholars since the 1800s, has been reset for great clarity, and opens from the Hebrew "front" of the book. Full *nikkud* has been added to both the talmudic text and Rashi's commentary, allowing for a more fluent reading with the correct pronunciation; the commentaries of *Tosafot* have been punctuated. Upon the advice of many English-speaking teachers of Talmud, we have separated these core pages from the translation, thereby enabling the advanced student to approach the text without the distraction of the translation. This also reduces the number of volumes in the set. At the bottom of each *daf*, there is a reference to the corresponding English pages. In addition, the Vilna edition was read against other manuscripts and older print editions, so that texts which had been removed by non-Jewish censors have been restored to their rightful place.
- The English translation, which starts on the English "front" of the book, reproduces the *menukad* Talmud text alongside the English translation (in bold) and commentary and explanation (in a lighter font). The Hebrew and Aramaic text is presented in logical paragraphs. This allows for a fluent reading of the text for the non-Hebrew or non-Aramaic reader. It also allows for the Hebrew reader to refer easily to the text alongside. Where the original text features dialogue or poetry, the English text is laid out in a manner appropriate to the genre. Each page refers to the relevant *daf*.

- Critical contextual tools surround the text and translation: personality notes, providing short biographies of the Sages; language notes, explaining foreign terms borrowed from Greek, Latin, Persian, or Arabic; and background notes, giving information essential to the understanding of the text, including history, geography, botany, archaeology, zoology, astronomy, and aspects of daily life in the talmudic era.
- Halakhic summaries provide references to the authoritative legal decisions made over the centuries by the rabbis. They explain the reasons behind each halakhic decision as well as the ruling's close connection to the Talmud and its various interpreters.
- Photographs, drawings, and other illustrations have been added throughout the text – in full color in the Standard and Electronic editions, and in black and white in the Daf Yomi edition – to visually elucidate the text.

This is not an exhaustive list of features of this edition, it merely presents an overview for the English-speaking reader who may not be familiar with the "total approach" to Talmud pioneered by Rabbi Steinsaltz.

Several professionals have helped bring this vast collaborative project to fruition. My many colleagues are noted on the Acknowledgments page, and the leadership of this project has been exceptional.

RABBI MENACHEM EVEN-ISRAEL, DIRECTOR OF THE STEINSALTZ CENTER, was the driving force behind this enterprise. With enthusiasm and energy, he formed the happy alliance with Koren and established close relationships among all involved in the work.

RABBI DR. TZVI HERSH WEINREB שליט״א, EDITOR-IN-CHIEF, brought to this project his profound knowledge of Torah, intellectual literacy of Talmud, and erudition of Western literature. It is to him that the text owes its very high standard, both in form and content, and the logical manner in which the beauty of the Talmud is presented.

RABBI JOSHUA SCHREIER, EXECUTIVE EDITOR, assembled an outstanding group of scholars, translators, editors, and proofreaders, whose standards and discipline enabled this project to proceed in a timely and highly professional manner.

RABBI MEIR HANEGBI, EDITOR OF THE HEBREW EDITION OF THE STEINSALTZ TALMUD, lent his invaluable assistance throughout the work process, supervising the reproduction of the Vilna pages.

RAPHAËL FREEMAN, EXECUTIVE EDITOR OF KOREN, created this Talmud's unique typographic design which, true to the Koren approach, is both elegant and user friendly.

It has been an enriching experience for all of us at Koren Publishers Jerusalem to work with the Steinsaltz Center to develop and produce the *Koren Talmud Bavli*. We pray that this publication will be a source of great learning and, ultimately, greater *avodat Hashem* for all Jews.

Matthew Miller, Publisher
Koren Publishers Jerusalem
Jerusalem 5772

Contents

Nazir 215

Image Credits 306

For the vocalized Vilna Shas layout, please open as a Hebrew book.

Introduction to **Perek VII**

All the days that he consecrated himself to the Lord he shall not come near to a dead body. He shall not become defiled for his father, or for his mother, for his brother, or for his sister, when they die; because his naziriteship to God is upon his head.

(Numbers 6:7)

And the Lord said to Moses: Speak to the priests the sons of Aaron, and say to them: None shall defile himself for the dead among his people, except for his kin, that is near to him, for his mother, and for his father, and for his son, and for his daughter, and for his brother, and for his sister a virgin, that is near to him, that has had no husband, for her may he defile himself.

(Leviticus 21:1–3)

And the priest that is highest among his brothers, upon whose head the anointing oil is poured, and that is consecrated to put on the garments, shall not let the hair of his head go loose, nor rend his clothes; neither shall he go in to any dead bodies, nor defile himself for his father, or for his mother.

(Leviticus 21:10–11)

This chapter investigates the details of the prohibition against a nazirite becoming ritually impure from a corpse. This restriction is not limited to a nazirite, as it is also incumbent upon common priests and the High Priest to avoid the impurity of corpses. Additionally, one who is impure may not enter the Temple precincts or partake of sacrificial meat. To a certain extent, the discussions in this chapter involve a comparison between the *halakhot* pertaining to a priests and those pertaining to a nazirite.

The phenomenon of impurity from a corpse involves a range of *halakhot* and various measurements with regard to the ritual impurity of different body parts. Furthermore, the methods of contracting impurity from a corpse, i.e., through contact, carrying, and in a tent, are governed by separate *halakhot*.

The chapter addresses the issue of which types of ritual impurity from a corpse cause a nazirite to negate his naziriteship term. The status of a nazirite afflicted with leprosy is also considered.

A comparison between the prohibitions against a nazirite and a priest contracting ritual impurity from a corpse gives rise to certain questions: How should these individuals behave when they come across a corpse with no one available to bury it [*met mitzva*]? Does the sanctity of the priest take precedence over that of the nazirite in this situation, or vice versa? The chapter also discusses other matters concerning impurity from a corpse, including various states of impurity established by rabbinic law.

מתני׳ כֹּהֵן גָּדוֹל וְנָזִיר אֵין מִיטַּמְּאִין לִקְרוֹבֵיהֶן, אֲבָל מִיטַּמְּאִין לְמֵת מִצְוָה. הָיוּ מְהַלְּכִין בַּדֶּרֶךְ וּמָצְאוּ מֵת מִצְוָה, רַבִּי אֱלִיעֶזֶר אוֹמֵר: יִטַּמֵּא כֹּהֵן גָּדוֹל וְאַל יִטַּמֵּא נָזִיר. וַחֲכָמִים אוֹמְרִים: יִטַּמֵּא נָזִיר, וְאַל יִטַּמֵּא כֹּהֵן הֶדְיוֹט.

MISHNA **A High Priest and a nazirite may not become ritually impure** even **to** bury **their** deceased **relatives.**[H] **However, they become impure to** bury **a corpse with no one to bury it** [*met mitzva*].[HB] If one of them comes across the corpse of a Jew, and there is nobody else available to bury it, he must bury the body. If a High Priest and a nazirite **were walking along the way and they found a** *met mitzva*, and one of them can tend to the burial by himself, **Rabbi Eliezer says: Let the High Priest become impure, and do not let the nazirite become impure. And the Rabbis say: Let the nazirite become impure, and do not let** even **a common priest become impure.**[N]

אָמַר לָהֶם רַבִּי אֱלִיעֶזֶר: יִטַּמֵּא כֹּהֵן שֶׁאֵינוֹ מֵבִיא קָרְבָּן עַל טוּמְאָתוֹ, וְאַל יִטַּמֵּא נָזִיר שֶׁהוּא מֵבִיא קָרְבָּן עַל טוּמְאָתוֹ. אָמְרוּ לוֹ: יִטַּמֵּא נָזִיר שֶׁאֵין קְדוּשָּׁתוֹ קְדוּשַּׁת עוֹלָם, וְאַל יִטַּמֵּא כֹּהֵן שֶׁקְּדוּשָּׁתוֹ קְדוּשַּׁת עוֹלָם.

Rabbi Eliezer said to the Rabbis: It is preferable to **let the priest become impure, as he does not bring an offering for his impurity, and do not let the nazirite become impure, as he brings an offering for his impurity.** The **Rabbis said to him:** On the contrary, **let the nazirite become impure, as his sanctity is not permanent, and do not let a priest become impure, as his sanctity is permanent.**[HN]

גמ׳ בִּשְׁלָמָא כֹּהֵן גָּדוֹל וְנָזִיר – הַאי סָבַר: כֹּהֵן גָּדוֹל עֲדִיף, וְהַאי סָבַר נָזִיר עֲדִיף.

GEMARA In light of the mishna's dispute between Rabbi Eliezer and the Rabbis, the Gemara compares the status of various individuals. **Granted,** with regard to **a High Priest and a nazirite,** one can explain the dispute as follows. **This** Sage, the Rabbis, **holds** that it is **preferable** that a **High Priest** remain ritually pure, as his sanctity is permanent. **And this** Sage, Rabbi Eliezer, **holds** that it is **preferable** that **a nazirite** remain ritually pure, as he is obligated to bring an offering for his impurity.

מְשׁוּחַ בְּשֶׁמֶן הַמִּשְׁחָה

Additionally, if the two walking together were a High Priest **anointed with the anointing oil,** as was performed during the First Temple period,

HALAKHA

May not become ritually impure to bury their relatives – **אֵין מִיטַּמְּאִין לִקְרוֹבֵיהֶן**: A High Priest is prohibited from becoming impure to bury any corpse, including those of his relatives. The same applies to a nazirite (Rambam *Sefer Hafla'a*, *Hilkhot Nezirut* 1:1 and *Sefer Shofetim*, *Hilkhot Evel* 3:6).

They become impure to bury a corpse with no one to bury it [*met mitzva*] – **מִיטַּמְּאִין לְמֵת מִצְוָה**: All people must become impure to bury a *met mitzva*. Even a High Priest or a nazirite who encounters a *met mitzva* is obligated to become impure to tend to its burial (Rambam *Sefer Hafla'a*, *Hilkhot Nezirut* 7:12 and *Sefer Shofetim*, *Hilkhot Evel* 3:8; *Shulḥan Arukh*, *Yoreh De'a* 374:1).

A nazirite and a priest – **נָזִיר וְכֹהֵן**: If a nazirite and a High Priest, or even a common priest, encounter a *met mitzva*, it is preferable for the nazirite to become ritually impure and bury the corpse, as his sanctity is considered temporary, while the sanctity of the priest is permanent. This *halakha* applies even to a permanent nazirite (Rambam *Sefer Hafla'a*, *Hilkhot Nezirut* 7:13 and *Sefer Shofetim*, *Hilkhot Evel* 3:9).

BACKGROUND

A corpse with no one to bury it [*met mitzva*] – **מֵת מִצְוָה**: It is an important religious obligation to take part in the burial of the dead. If the deceased has no acquaintances or relatives to bury him, everyone is obligated to assist in his burial. The *halakha* is that a corpse with no one available to bury it acquires its place, i.e., the body must be interred where it was found. This is the *halakha* provided that it is situated in a dignified location. Otherwise, the body must be buried in the nearest cemetery. This religious duty is so important that even priests and nazirites, who are ordinarily prohibited from coming into contact with a corpse, may perform a burial if there is no one else available to do so. Likewise, the obligation to bury this corpse takes precedence over virtually all other religious obligations.

NOTES

And do not let a common priest become impure – **וְאַל יִטַּמֵּא כֹּהֵן הֶדְיוֹט**: Alternative versions of the text, read: High Priest. It is possible to uphold the standard reading, as there is no difference between a common priest and a High Priest with regard to impurity from a corpse. The Rabbis are stressing that it is better for a nazirite rather than a common priest, and certainly a High Priest, to become impure.

As his sanctity is permanent – **שֶׁקְּדוּשָּׁתוֹ קְדוּשַּׁת עוֹלָם**: Naziriteship lasts for a limited period, whereas priesthood status is forever. In the Jerusalem Talmud and the writings of many early commentaries the following question is asked: How does this disagreement resolve the case of a permanent nazirite, whose sanctity also lasts forever? Several answers are offered. Some point out that even this nazirite's sanctity starts only from adulthood, whereas a priest has his status from birth (Rabbi Avraham min HaHar; *Tosefot Yom Tov*). Others claim that the sanctity of a nazirite is always considered temporary, as he can request dissolution of his vow of naziriteship (*Leḥem Mishne*; *Oraḥ Mishor*). In the Jerusalem Talmud it is explained that the term permanent sanctity means that the sanctity is imposed by the Torah itself, as opposed to that of a nazirite, whose sanctity results from a vow (Rabbeinu Azriel). Alternatively, the sanctity of a priest is permanent in that it is transferred from one generation to another, whereas the sanctity of a nazirite is not inherited by his sons (Rashash).

וּמְרוּבֵּה בְגָדִים – מָשׁוּחַ בְּשֶׁמֶן הַמִּשְׁחָה עֲדִיף, דְּאִילּוּ מָשׁוּחַ בְּשֶׁמֶן הַמִּשְׁחָה מֵבִיא פַּר הַבָּא עַל כׇּל הַמִּצְוֹת, וְאִילּוּ מְרוּבֵּה בְגָדִים – אֵין מֵבִיא.

and a High Priest **of many garments,**[NBH] i.e., one who was not anointed with oil but who was sanctified by wearing the eight garments of a High Priest, it is **preferable** that **the one who was anointed with the anointing oil**[N] remain ritually pure. The Gemara explains: **As** a High Priest **anointed with the anointing oil brings the bull**[H] **brought for all the mitzvot,** i.e., if an anointed priest ruled erroneously with regard to a prohibition that if a Jew transgressed it he would be liable to bring a sin-offering, he brings a bull for his sin-offering (see Leviticus 4:3–12), **while** a High Priest **of many garments does not bring** a bull.

מָשׁוּחַ שֶׁעָבַר וּמְרוּבֵּה בְגָדִים – מְרוּבֵּה בְגָדִים עֲדִיף, דִּמְרוּבֵּה בְגָדִים עָבֵיד עֲבוֹדָה, וְאִילּוּ מָשׁוּחַ שֶׁעָבַר לָאו בַּר עֲבוֹדָה הוּא.

In a case where **a former anointed** High Priest, i.e., a priest who had temporarily substituted for a High Priest, is walking together with one of **many garments,**[NH] it is **preferable** that the one who wears **many garments** remain ritually pure. The reason is **that** a High Priest of **many garments** still **performs the service, whereas a former anointed** High Priest **is no** longer **able to** perform **the service.**[H]

עָבַר מֵחֲמַת קִירוּיוֹ וְעָבַר מֵחֲמַת מוּמוֹ – עָבַר מֵחֲמַת קִירוּיוֹ עֲדִיף, דְּאִילּוּ הַאי חֲזֵי לַעֲבוֹדָה לְמָחָר, וְאִילּוּ עָבַר מֵחֲמַת מוּמוֹ לָא חֲזֵי לַעֲבוֹדָה.

In a case where an anointed High Priest who temporarily **left** his role **due to his seminal emission**[H] is walking with a former anointed High Priest who left his role **due to his blemish,** it is **preferable** that the former High Priest who **left due to his seminal emission** remain ritually pure, **as this one,** the High Priest who experienced an emission, **is fit for the** Temple **service the following day, while** the former anointed High Priest who **left due to his blemish is no** longer **fit for the service** at all (see Leviticus 21:16–24).

NOTES

Of many garments – מְרוּבֵּה בְגָדִים: By Torah law, a High Priest must be anointed with the oil prepared by Moses, as commanded by God (see Exodus 30:22–33). However, this oil was hidden by King Josiah toward the end of the First Temple period. Since only it may be used, all subsequent High Priests were not anointed but were appointed High Priest by virtue of wearing the eight garments. Since the garments of a High Priest comprise four more items of clothing than those worn by a common priest, this state is referred to as wearing many garments.

An anointed priest and one of many garments – מָשׁוּחַ וּמְרוּבֵּה בְגָדִים: The early commentaries inquire as to how it is possible that two High Priests could be serving at the same time and only one of them was appointed with the anointing oil. They answer that this ruling is referring to a case where the last High Priest to be anointed with the oil took ill or was exiled, and a replacement was appointed by a common priest donning the additional garments, after which the first High Priest regained his health or returned from exile. In this manner, the two High Priests could be contemporaries (*Tosafot*). Alternatively, the ruling is referring to a High Priest who contracted ritual impurity just before Yom Kippur, so that another had to be appointed quickly in his stead. Since there was no time for him to be anointed, he donned the garments to assume the status of a High Priest (Rabbeinu Todros).

A former anointed High Priest with one of many garments – מָשׁוּחַ שֶׁעָבַר וּמְרוּבֵּה בְגָדִים: The category of a former High Priest typically refers to a case where a High Priest became impure on or just before Yom Kippur and therefore requires an immediate replacement. When the first High Priest is purified, he returns to his office, and the one who filled in for him is called a former High Priest. The Sages ruled that although all the prohibitions of a High Priest apply to a former High Priest, he does not serve in the Temple at all. He does not fulfill the functions of a High Priest, to prevent antagonism between the two priests, but neither does he serve as a common priest, as one does not lower an individual who has been elevated to a higher position.

BACKGROUND

Of many garments – מְרוּבֵּה בְגָדִים:

High Priest wearing vestments

HALAKHA

A High Priest anointed with the anointing oil and a High Priest of many garments – מָשׁוּחַ שֶׁבְּשֶׁמֶן הַמִּשְׁחָה וּמְרוּבֵּה בְגָדִים: A High Priest anointed with the anointing oil takes precedence with regard to all matters over one who was appointed by wearing many garments. Consequently, if they encountered a *met mitzva* together, the one who wore the garments must bury the body and thereby become ritually impure (Rambam *Sefer Avoda, Hilkhot Kelei HaMikdash* 4:19 and *Sefer Shofetim, Hilkhot Evel* 3:9).

A High Priest anointed with the anointing oil brings the bull – מָשׁוּחַ...מֵבִיא פַּר: The only difference between an anointed High Priest and one who wears many garments is that the anointed High Priest brings a bull as a sin-offering for an erroneous ruling involving any of the mitzvot punishable by *karet*. In this regard, a High Priest appointed by donning many garments has the status of a common priest (Rambam *Sefer Avoda, Hilkhot Kelei HaMikdash* 4:14 and *Sefer Korbanot, Hilkhot Shegagot* 15:1–2).

A former anointed High Priest with one of many garments – מָשׁוּחַ שֶׁעָבַר וּמְרוּבֵּה בְגָדִים: A High Priest appointed through the additional garments takes precedence over an anointed High Priest who was removed from his post due to a seminal emission (Rambam *Sefer Avoda, Hilkhot Kelei HaMikdash* 4:19).

A former anointed High Priest is no longer able to perform the service – מָשׁוּחַ שֶׁעָבַר לָאו בַּר עֲבוֹדָה הוּא: A former anointed High Priest who was removed from his office due to the return of the first High Priest does not serve as High Priest during the original High Priest's lifetime. He does not serve as a common priest either, as one does not lower an individual who has been elevated to a higher position (Rambam *Sefer Avoda, Hilkhot Kelei HaMikdash* 4:21 and *Sefer Avoda, Hilkhot Yom HaKippurim* 1:3).

An anointed High Priest who left due to his seminal emission, etc. – עָבַר מֵחֲמַת קִירוּיוֹ וכו׳: A High Priest who was removed because he suffered a seminal emission takes precedence over one who left his office due to a blemish (Rambam *Sefer Avoda, Hilkhot Kelei HaMikdash* 4:19).

איבעיא להו: משוח מלחמה וסגן, הי מינייהו עדיף? משוח מלחמה עדיף – דחזי למלחמה, או דלמא סגן עדיף – דחזי לעבודה?

§ The above cases are all easily resolved and are mentioned merely to introduce the following inquiries, for which there are no obvious answers. **A dilemma was raised before** the Sages. For **which of these** two is it **preferable** that he remain ritually pure: A priest **anointed for war,** who was anointed with oil and appointed to admonish the troops before battle (see Deuteronomy 20:2) **or the deputy** [*segan*][L] High Priest? Is it **preferable** that the priest **anointed for war** remain ritually pure, **as he is fit for war? Or, perhaps** it is **preferable** that the **deputy** High Priest remain ritually pure, **as he is fit for service** in the Temple in place of the High Priest.

תא שמע, דתניא: אין בין משוח מלחמה לסגן, אלא שאם היו מהלכין בדרך ומצאו מת מצוה – יטמא משוח מלחמה ואל יטמא הסגן.

The Gemara suggests: **Come and hear** a resolution, **as it is taught** in a *baraita*: **The difference between** a priest **anointed for war and a** deputy High Priest **is only that if they were walking along the way and found a** *met mitzva*, the ruling is: **Let the one anointed for war become impure,**[H] **and do not let the deputy become impure.**

והתניא: משוח מלחמה קודם לסגן. אמר מר זוטרא: לענין החיותו – משוח מלחמה עדיף, מאי טעמא – דתלו ביה רבים.

The Gemara asks: **But isn't it taught** in a different *baraita*: A priest **anointed for war takes precedence over the deputy**[H] High Priest? **Mar Zutra said:** This is not difficult. **With regard to preserving his life** and rescuing him from captivity or from a dangerous situation, it is **preferable** to preserve **the one anointed for war. What is the reason** for this? The reason is **that the public depends on him** in a time of war.

ולענין טומאה – סגן עדיף. דתניא, רבי חנינא בן אנטיגנוס אומר: למה תקנו סגן לכהן גדול? שאם אירע בו פסול – הרי נכנס ומשמש תחתיו.

But with regard to ritual impurity, it is **preferable** that the **deputy** High Priest remain ritually pure, **as it is taught** in a *baraita* that **Rabbi Ḥanina ben Antigonus says: Why did** the Sages **institute a deputy for the High Priest?** So **that if a disqualification befalls** the High Priest, his deputy **can enter** the Temple **and serve in his stead.** The deputy High Priest cannot fulfill this function if he is allowed to become ritually impure.

עד כאן לא פליגי אלא בכהן גדול ונזיר כי קא אזלי בהדי הדדי, אבל חד חד לחודיה – בר איטמויי אינון. מנא הני מילי?

The Gemara turns its attention to the *halakha* of the mishna. Rabbi Eliezer and the Rabbis **disagree only with regard to a High Priest and a nazirite who are walking together** and find a *met mitzva*, in which case one of them must become impure. **However,** it is evident that if **each of them** is walking **separately, they are able,** i.e., they are required, **to become impure. From where are these matters** derived? From where is it learned that a High Priest and a nazirite, who are prohibited from becoming impure even to bury their relatives, must nevertheless become impure to bury a *met mitzva*?

דתנו רבנן: "על כל נפשות מת לא יבא". במה הכתוב מדבר? אי ברחוקים – קל וחומר הוא: ומה כהן הדיוט שהוא מיטמא לקרובים – אינו מיטמא לרחוקים, כהן גדול שאינו מיטמא לקרובים – אינו דין שאינו מיטמא לרחוקים? אלא בקרובים הכתוב מדבר.

It is **as the Sages taught:** The verse states with regard to a High Priest: **"Neither shall he go in to any dead bodies;** nor defile himself for his father or for his mother" (Leviticus 21:11). **With regard to what** bodies **is the verse speaking? If** it is referring **to distant** people, i.e., non-relatives, **that** *halakha* can be derived by **an** ***a fortiori*** inference: **And if a common priest, who becomes impure to** bury his **close** family members, **may not become impure to** bury **distant** people, then with regard to **a High Priest, who does not become impure** even **to** bury **close** members of his family, **is it not logical that he does not become impure to** bury **distant** people? **Rather, the verse is speaking of close** family members, and it prohibits a High Priest from becoming impure to bury any person, even his relatives.

ולאביו הוא דאינו מיטמא, הא מיטמא הוא למת מצוה.

The Gemara comments: With regard to the rest of the verse: "Nor defile himself for his father or for his mother" (Leviticus 21:11), each of these clauses must serve to teach a novel *halakha*. **And** the phrase "for his father" teaches: **It is to** bury **his father that he may not become ritually impure,** from which it may be inferred that **he becomes impure** to bury **a** ***met mitzva.***

LANGUAGE

Deputy [*segan*] – סגן: This term, which appears in the Bible (see Jeremiah 51:23), is apparently Assyrian in origin. Its principal meaning is an officer, appointee, overseer, and the like. The deputy High Priest [*segan hakohanim*] was the officer in the Temple in charge of the priests. He was responsible for all of the duties of the High Priest in his superior's absence (see Jeremiah 52:24).

HALAKHA

Let the one anointed for war become impure – יטמא משוח מלחמה: If a priest anointed for war and a deputy High Priest encounter a *met mitzva*, it is preferable that the priest anointed for war become impure (Rambam *Sefer Shofetim, Hilkhot Evel* 3:9).

A priest anointed for war takes precedence over the deputy – משוח מלחמה קודם לסגן: A priest anointed for war takes precedence over a deputy High Priest as far as his stature and honor are concerned (Rambam *Sefer Avoda, Hilkhot Kelei HaMikdash* 4:19).

"וּלְאִמּוֹ" – לִגְזֵירָה שָׁוָה, לְכִדְרַבִּי. דְּתַנְיָא, רַבִּי אוֹמֵר: גַּבֵּי נָזִיר, בְּמוֹתָם אֵינוֹ מִיטַּמֵּא אֲבָל מִיטַּמֵּא הוּא לְנִגְעָם וּלְזִיבָתָם. וְאֵין לִי אֶלָּא בְּנָזִיר, בְּכֹהֵן גָּדוֹל מִנַּיִן?

The phrase **"or for his mother"** serves **as a verbal analogy, in accordance with** the opinion of **Rabbi Yehuda HaNasi, as it is taught** in a *baraita*: **Rabbi Yehuda HaNasi says:** It states **with regard to a nazirite:** "He shall not become defiled for them when they die" (Numbers 6:7), which indicates: It is only **when** his relatives **die** that **he may not become impure** for them. **However, he may become impure for their leprosy and for their emission of a *zav*,**[H] i.e., a nazirite is not forbidden to contract those forms of ritual impurity. **And I have** derived **only** that this *halakha* applies **to a nazirite,** the subject of this verse. **From where** do I derive that this applies **to a High Priest** as well?

אָמַרְתָּ: לֹא יֹאמַר "אִמּוֹ" בְּכֹהֵן גָּדוֹל שֶׁאֵין תַּלְמוּד לוֹמַר, שֶׁהֲרֵי קַל וָחוֹמֶר הוּא: וּמָה אִם בְּמָקוֹם שֶׁכֹּהֵן הֶדְיוֹט מִיטַּמֵּא לְאָחִיו מֵאָבִיו – אֵין כֹּהֵן גָּדוֹל מִיטַּמֵּא לְאָבִיו, מָקוֹם שֶׁאֵין כֹּהֵן הֶדְיוֹט מִיטַּמֵּא לְאָחִיו מֵאִמּוֹ – אֵינוֹ דִּין שֶׁאֵין כֹּהֵן גָּדוֹל מִיטַּמֵּא לְאִמּוֹ?

You can say as follows: The verse need **not say "his mother"** with regard **to a High Priest,** as there is no need for **the verse to state** this, **since** this *halakha* is derived ***a fortiori*:**[B] **And if in a case where a common priest becomes impure** to bury **his paternal brother, a High Priest may not become impure** even to bury **his father,** then **in a case where a common priest may not become impure** to bury **his maternal brother,**[H] who is not considered a relative with regard to impurity, **is it not logical that a High Priest may not become impure** to bury **his mother** herself?

אִם זָכִיתָה מֵהַדִּין, מַה תַּלְמוּד לוֹמַר "אִמּוֹ" בְּכֹהֵן גָּדוֹל – מוּפְנֶה לְהַקִּישׁ וְלָדוּן הֵימֶנּוּ גְּזֵירָה שָׁוָה: נֶאֱמַר "אִמּוֹ" בְּנָזִיר וְנֶאֱמַר "אִמּוֹ" בְּכֹהֵן גָּדוֹל,

And if you have successfully derived this *halakha* **from** the *a fortiori* inference, **what** is the meaning when **the verse states "his mother" with regard to a High Priest?** It is **free to** teach a novel *halakha*, and one can **compare and learn a verbal analogy from it** as follows: **It is stated "his mother" with regard to a nazirite** (Numbers 6:7), **and it is stated "his mother" with regard to a High Priest** (Leviticus 21:11).

מָה "אִמּוֹ" הָאָמוּר בְּנָזִיר – בְּמוֹתָם אֵינוֹ מִיטַּמֵּא, אֲבָל מִיטַּמֵּא הוּא לְנִגְעָם וּלְזִיבָתָם, אַף "אִמּוֹ" הָאָמוּר בְּכֹהֵן גָּדוֹל – בְּמוֹתָם אֵינוֹ מִיטַּמֵּא, אֲבָל מִיטַּמֵּא לְנִגְעָם וּלְזִיבָתָם.

The Gemara explains: **Just as** the phrase **"his mother" stated with regard to a nazirite** teaches that in his parents' **death he may not become impure** to bury them **but he may become impure for their leprosy and for their emission of a *zav*,** as a nazirite is not prohibited from contracting these impurities, **so too,** the phrase **"his mother" stated with regard to a High Priest** means that in his parents' **death he may not become impure, but he may become impure for their leprosy and for their emission of a *zav*.**

אַשְׁכַּחַן כֹּהֵן גָּדוֹל, נָזִיר מְנָלַן? דְּתַנְיָא: "כָּל יְמֵי הַזִּירוֹ לַה׳ עַל נֶפֶשׁ מֵת לֹא יָבֹא".

The Gemara clarifies: **We found** a source for the *halakha* that **a High Priest** must become impure for a *met mitzva*; **from where do we** derive that **a nazirite** is likewise obligated? **As it is taught** in a *baraita* that it is stated with regard to a nazirite: **"All the days that he consecrated himself to the Lord he shall not come near to a dead body [*nefesh met*]"** (Numbers 6:6).

שׁוֹמֵעַ אֲנִי אֲפִילּוּ נֶפֶשׁ בְּהֵמָה בְּמַשְׁמַע, כְּעִנְיָן שֶׁנֶּאֱמַר "מַכֵּה נֶפֶשׁ בְּהֵמָה" – תַּלְמוּד לוֹמַר "עַל נֶפֶשׁ מֵת לֹא יָבֹא" – בְּנֶפֶשׁ אָדָם הַכָּתוּב מְדַבֵּר. רַבִּי יִשְׁמָעֵאל אוֹמֵר: אֵינוֹ צָרִיךְ, הֲרֵי הוּא אוֹמֵר "לֹא יָבֹא" – בַּנְּפָשׁוֹת הַמְטַמְּאוֹת בְּבִיאָה הַכָּתוּב מְדַבֵּר.

I would **derive** from this verse that a nazirite is prohibited from coming near all bodies, **including even the body of an animal, similar to that which is stated:** "And he who smites the body [*nefesh*] of an animal" (Leviticus 24:18). Therefore, **the verse states: "He shall not come near to a dead body,"**[N] employing the dual term *nefesh met*, which indicates that **the verse is speaking of the body of a person. Rabbi Yishmael says:** This exposition **is unnecessary,** as the verse **states: "He shall not come near,"** indicating that **the verse is speaking** only **of bodies that render** people and items **ritually impure through going in,** i.e., entering. In other words, the verse is referring solely to corpses. Entering into a tent in which the corpse is contained renders one impure. By contrast, an animal carcass imparts impurity only by means of contact and carrying.

BACKGROUND

A fortiori – קַל וָחוֹמֶר: One of the fundamental principles of rabbinic exegesis, the *a fortiori* inference is included in all of the standard lists of exegetical principles. In essence, it is a principle of logical argumentation by means of which a comparison is drawn between two cases, one lenient and the other stringent. It asserts that if a stringent *halakha* applies in a case where one is usually lenient, it will certainly apply in a more serious case. Likewise, if a lenient *halakha* applies in a case where one is usually not lenient, it will certainly apply in a less serious case.

A fortiori reasoning appears already in the Bible, and the Talmud provides lists of biblical verses containing *a fortiori* inferences. This is one of the most commonly encountered exegetical principles, as *a fortiori* inferences can be drawn even without support from tradition, as opposed to a verbal analogy, for example, which one cannot produce on one's own. Sometimes, the Sages referred to *a fortiori* inferences as logical argumentation.

HALAKHA

He may become impure for their leprosy and for their emission of a *zav* – מִיטַּמֵּא הוּא לְנִגְעָם וּלְזִיבָתָם: It is permitted for priests and nazirites to contract types of impurity other than that of a corpse (Rambam *Sefer Tahara, Hilkhot Tumat Okhalin* 16:9).

To bury his maternal brother – לְאָחִיו מֵאִמּוֹ: A priest may not become ritually impure to bury his maternal brother or sister (Rambam *Sefer Shofetim, Hilkhot Evel* 2:12; *Shulḥan Arukh, Yoreh De'a* 373:4).

NOTES

The verse states…to a dead body – תַּלְמוּד לוֹמַר...עַל נֶפֶשׁ מֵת: The commentaries explain that this is derived from the compound term "dead body," *nefesh met*, which is stated only in reference to humans, as the word dead, *nefesh*, on its own, can refer to animals (see Exodus 21:34). An alternative version of the *baraita* reads: The verse states: "For his father or for his mother," which indicates that the verse is speaking about the body of a person, such as a father or mother, not the body of an animal (Rabbeinu Peretz).

״לְאָבִיו וּלְאִמּוֹ״ אֵינוֹ מִיטַּמֵּא, אֲבָל מִיטַּמֵּא הוּא לְמֵת מִצְוָה.

In any case, once it has been derived that a nazirite is prohibited from becoming impure to bury any person, both relatives and non-relatives, the passage "he shall not become defiled **for his father, or for his mother**" (Numbers 6:7) is available to teach another *halakha*, that it is for only them that a nazirite **may not become impure, but he may become impure to** bury a *met mitzva*.

עַד שֶׁלֹּא יֹאמַר יֵשׁ לִי בַּדִּין: וּמָה כֹּהֵן גָּדוֹל, שֶׁקְּדוּשָּׁתוֹ קְדוּשַּׁת עוֹלָם – מִיטַּמֵּא לְמֵת מִצְוָה, נָזִיר שֶׁאֵין קְדוּשָּׁתוֹ קְדוּשַּׁת עוֹלָם – אֵינוֹ דִּין שֶׁמִּיטַּמֵּא לְמֵת מִצְוָה?

The *baraita* asks: Even **if** the verse **had not stated** this *halakha*, **I have** a way of deriving it **by right**, i.e., logically, with an *a fortiori* inference: **And if a High Priest, whose sanctity is permanent, may become ritually impure to** bury a *met mitzva*, then in the case of **a nazirite, whose sanctity is not permanent, is it not logical that he may become impure to** bury a *met mitzva* as well?

לֹא, אִם אָמַרְתָּ בְּכֹהֵן גָּדוֹל שֶׁכֵּן אֵינוֹ מֵבִיא קָרְבָּן עַל טוּמְאָתוֹ, תֹּאמַר בְּנָזִיר שֶׁמֵּבִיא קָרְבָּן עַל טוּמְאָתוֹ, הוֹאִיל וּמֵבִיא קָרְבָּן עַל טוּמְאָתוֹ – לֹא יִטַּמֵּא לְמֵת מִצְוָה – תַּלְמוּד לוֹמַר ״לְאָבִיו וּלְאִמּוֹ לֹא יִטַּמָּא״. אֲבָל מִיטַּמֵּא לְמֵת מִצְוָה.

The *baraita* rejects this inference: **No; if you say** that this is true **with regard to a High Priest, who does not bring an offering for his impurity, shall you** also **say** that this is the case **with regard to a nazirite, who does bring an offering for his impurity? Since** a nazirite **brings an offering for his impurity,** perhaps he should **not become impure to** bury a *met mitzva*? Therefore, **the verse states: "He shall not become defiled for his father, or for his mother"** (Numbers 6:7). **However,** he does **become impure to** bury a *met mitzva*.

אוֹ אֵינוֹ מִיטַּמֵּא לְאָבִיו וּלְאִמּוֹ, אֲבָל יִטַּמֵּא לִשְׁאָר מֵתִים? אָמַרְתָּ קַל וָחוֹמֶר: וּמָה כֹּהֵן הֶדְיוֹט שֶׁמִּיטַּמֵּא לִקְרוֹבִין אֵינוֹ מִיטַּמֵּא לִשְׁאָר מֵתִים, נָזִיר שֶׁאֵינוֹ מִיטַּמֵּא לִקְרוֹבִין – אֵינוֹ דִּין שֶׁלֹּא יִטַּמֵּא לִשְׁאָר מֵתִים?

The *baraita* suggests: **Or** perhaps one should expound this verse differently: **He may not become impure to** bury **his father or for his mother; however, he may become impure to** bury **other dead people.** The Gemara rejects this suggestion: **You can say** that this argument can be refuted ***a fortiori***: **And if a common priest, who becomes impure to** bury his **relatives,** nevertheless **may not become impure to** bury **other dead people** (see Leviticus 21:1–2), then in the case of **a nazirite, who may not become impure to** bury his **relatives, is it not logical that** also **he should not become impure to** bury **other dead people?**

Perek **VII**
Daf **48** Amud **b**

הָא מַה תַּלְמוּד לוֹמַר ״לְאָבִיו וּלְאִמּוֹ״ – לְאָבִיו וּלְאִמּוֹ הוּא דְּלָא מִיטַּמֵּא אֲבָל מִיטַּמֵּא הוּא לְמֵת מִצְוָה.

If so, **what is** the meaning when **the verse states: "For his father, or for his mother"** (Numbers 6:7)? It emphasizes that **it is** to bury **his father and** to bury **his mother that he may not become impure; however, he may become impure to** bury **a** *met mitzva*.

עַד שֶׁלֹּא יֹאמַר יֵשׁ לִי בַּדִּין: נֶאֶמְרוּ כְּלָלוֹת בְּכֹהֵן גָּדוֹל וְנֶאֶמְרוּ כְּלָלוֹת בְּנָזִיר, מַה כְּלָלוֹת הָאֲמוּרוֹת בְּכֹהֵן גָּדוֹל – לְאָבִיו אֵינוֹ מִיטַּמֵּא אֲבָל מִיטַּמֵּא לְמֵת מִצְוָה, אַף כְּלָלוֹת הָאֲמוּרוֹת בְּנָזִיר – לְאָבִיו אֵינוֹ מִיטַּמֵּא, אֲבָל מִיטַּמֵּא לְמֵת מִצְוָה.

The *baraita* questions the need for this derivation: Even **if** the verse **had not stated** this *halakha*, **I have** a way of deriving it **by right**, i.e., logically, with an *a fortiori* inference: **General** prohibitions **are stated** in the Torah **with regard to a High Priest**[N] contracting impurity from a corpse, i.e., "neither shall he go in to any dead bodies" (Leviticus 21:11), **and** similar **general** prohibitions **are stated with regard to a nazirite:** "He shall not come near to a dead body" (Numbers 6:6). The *baraita* explains: **Just as** the **general** prohibitions **stated with regard to a High Priest** teach that **it is** to bury **his father that he may not become impure, but he may become impure to** bury **a** *met mitzva*, **so too,** the **general** prohibitions **stated with regard to a nazirite** indicate that **it is for his father that he may not become impure, but he may become impure to** bury a *met mitzva*. Accordingly, there is no need for the derivation from the phrase "for his father or for his mother."

NOTES

General prohibitions are stated in the Torah with regard to a High Priest, etc. – **נֶאֶמְרוּ כְּלָלוֹת בְּכֹהֵן גָּדוֹל וכו׳**: The commentaries note that this does not literally mean that one derives from these general prohibitions of a High Priest the prohibitions of a nazirite with regard to a *met mitzva* (*Tosafot*). This comparison can be questioned from both sides, as the High Priest and the nazirite are each bound by certain stringencies that the other lacks. Rather, the general prohibition stated with regard to a High Priest teaches that a nazirite is also prohibited from becoming impure to bury any corpse, whether it is that of a relative or a stranger. Consequently, the verse that states this *halakha* with regard to a nazirite is superfluous and can be used for the case of a *met mitzva*.

NOTES

If someone went, etc. – הֲרֵי שֶׁהָלַךְ וכו׳: Some commentaries explain that the *baraita* is referring to a nazirite who is also a High Priest and who is on his way to slaughter his Paschal offering (Commentary on *Nazir*; *Halakhot Gedolot*). Others maintain that the *baraita* is not referring to a nazirite in particular. Rather, it is speaking of anyone who is on his way to fulfill this mitzva (Rashi on *Berakhot*; *Tosafot*; *Arukh*, citing Rav Hai Gaon).

אוֹ כְּלָךְ לְדֶרֶךְ זוֹ: נֶאֶמְרוּ כְּלָלוֹת בְּכֹהֵן הֶדְיוֹט וְנֶאֶמְרוּ כְּלָלוֹת בְּנָזִיר, מַה כְּלָלוֹת הָאֲמוּרוֹת בְּכֹהֵן הֶדְיוֹט – מִיטַּמֵּא לְאָבִיו, אַף כְּלָלוֹת הָאֲמוּרוֹת בְּנָזִיר – מִיטַּמֵּא לְאָבִיו.

The *baraita* refutes this proof: **Or** perhaps you can **go this way** and accept a different interpretation: **General** prohibitions **are stated with regard to a common priest** contracting impurity imparted by a corpse, i.e., "there shall none defile himself for the dead among his people" (Leviticus 21:1), **and general** prohibitions **are stated with regard to a nazirite. Just as the general** prohibitions **stated with regard to a common priest** teach that he **may become impure to** bury **his father** (Leviticus 21:2), **so too,** the **general** prohibitions **stated with regard to a nazirite** say that he **may become impure to** bury **his father.** Perhaps a nazirite is compared to a common priest, not a High Priest.

תַּלְמוּד לוֹמַר ״לְאָבִיו וּלְאִמּוֹ לֹא יִטַּמָּא״ הָא לְמֵת מִצְוָה מִיטַּמֵּא. הָא מִיבְּעֵי לֵיהּ לוֹמַר שֶׁאֵין מִיטַּמֵּא לְאָבִיו.

Since one cannot learn from the general prohibitions, one must revert to the previous derivation: **The verse states** with regard to a nazirite: **"He shall not become defiled for his father, or for his mother"** (Numbers 6:7), which indicates that **he may become impure to** bury **a *met mitzva*.** The *baraita* raises a difficulty with this last proof: One **requires** this verse for the *halakha* itself, **to say that** a nazirite, unlike a common priest, **may not become impure to** bury **his father.** How, then, can one learn from here that he may become impure to bury a *met mitzva*?

אֶלָּא: ״לְאָבִיו״ – לוֹמַר שֶׁאֵין מִיטַּמֵּא לְאָבִיו. ״לְאָחִיו״ אֵינוֹ מִיטַּמֵּא – הָא לְמֵת מִצְוָה מִיטַּמֵּא: ״וּלְאִמּוֹ״ – לִגְזֵירָה שָׁוָה, לְכִדְרַבִּי.

Rather, the *baraita* explains as follows: The superfluous phrase **"for his father"** serves **to say that he may not become impure to** bury **his father,** and all the more so for his other relatives. The phrase **"for his brother"** teaches that **he may not become impure** to bury his brother but **he may become impure to** bury **a *met mitzva*. "And for his mother"**; this phrase **is for a verbal analogy in accordance with** the opinion of **Rabbi** Yehuda HaNasi, that a nazirite may contract ritual impurity of types other than a corpse.

״וּלְאַחוֹתוֹ״ – לְכִדְתַנְיָא, דְּתַנְיָא: ״לְאַחוֹתוֹ״ מַה תַּלְמוּד לוֹמַר?

As for the phrase **"and for his sister,"** it is used **for that which is taught** in a *baraita*, **as it is taught** in a *baraita*: **"And for his sister"**; **what** is the meaning when **the verse states** this with regard to a nazirite? This detail is apparently superfluous, as the *halakha* that a nazirite may not become impure to bury a relative has already been derived.

הֲרֵי שֶׁהָלַךְ לִשְׁחוֹט אֶת פִּסְחוֹ וְלָמוּל אֶת בְּנוֹ, וְשָׁמַע שֶׁמֵּת לוֹ מֵת – יָכוֹל יִטַּמֵּא? אָמַרְתָּ: לֹא יִטַּמֵּא.

The *baraita* continues: Rather, the term "and for his sister" teaches the following: **If someone went**[N] **to slaughter his Paschal offering or to circumcise his son,** which are particularly stringent positive mitzvot, as their neglect is punished by *karet*, **and he hears that** a relative **of his had died,** one **might** have thought that **he should become impure** to bury his dead relative and abandon his performance of the mitzva. **You can say** in response that **he may not become impure,** as one is not permitted to neglect the obligation of the Paschal offering or circumcision, even to bury a close relative.

יָכוֹל לֹא יִטַּמֵּא לְמֵת מִצְוָה? תַּלְמוּד לוֹמַר ״לְאַחוֹתוֹ״. לְאַחוֹתוֹ הוּא דְּאֵינוֹ מִיטַּמֵּא, הָא לְמֵת מִצְוָה – מִיטַּמֵּא.

The *baraita* continues: One **might** have thought that **he may not become impure** even **to** bury **a *met mitzva*. The verse states: "For his sister."** It is only **for his sister** or another close relative that the nazirite **may not become impure, but he does become impure to** bury **a *met mitzva*.**[H] Since the verse had already taught that a nazirite may not become impure to bury a relative but does become impure to bury a *met mitzva* in an ordinary circumstance, the additional term "and for his sister" teaches that the same *halakha* applies even when he is going to perform an important mitzva.

HALAKHA

He does become impure to bury a *met mitzva* – לְמֵת מִצְוָה מִיטַּמֵּא: It is a mitzva to bury a *met mitzva*, even if one is otherwise prohibited from becoming impure. Even a High Priest, a nazirite, and one who is on his way to slaughter his Paschal offering or circumcise his son must become impure to bury this corpse (Rambam *Sefer Shofetim*, *Hilkhot Evel* 3:8; *Shulḥan Arukh*, *Yoreh De'a* 374:1).

רבי עקיבא אומר: "נפש־ת" - אלו הרחוקין: "מת" - אלו הקרובין: "לאביו ולאמו" אינו מיטמא, אבל מיטמא הוא למת מצוה.

Rabbi Akiva says that this verse dealing with a nazirite should be explained differently. "He shall not come near to a dead body" (Numbers 6:6) teaches the following: **"Body"; these are the distant**[N] people. **"Dead"; these are the close** relatives. The subsequent verse stresses that **"for his father or for his mother" he may not become impure; however, he does become impure to** bury **a *met mitzva*.**

"לאחיו" - שאם היה כהן גדול והוא נזיר, לאחיו אינו מיטמא, אבל מיטמא הוא למת מצוה. "לאחותו" - כדתניא: הרי שהיה הולך לשחוט את פסחו ולמול את בנו כו'.

The next term in the verse, **"for his brother,"** indicates **that** even **if he was a High Priest and he was** also **a nazirite, he may not become impure to** bury **his brother, but he may become impure to** bury **a *met mitzva*.** As for the term **"for his sister,"** this is used to teach **that which is taught** in a *baraita*: **If one was going to slaughter his Paschal offering or to circumcise his son** and encountered a *met mitzva*, the obligation to bury the corpse takes precedence over the other important mitzva.

ולרבי עקיבא, גזירה שוה דרבי מנליה?

The Gemara asks: **And according to** the derivation of **Rabbi Akiva, from where does he** derive the *halakha* of the **verbal analogy of Rabbi** Yehuda HaNasi that a High Priest may contract impurities other than the impurity of a corpse? How does Rabbi Akiva derive this *halakha*?

אמר לך: כיון דאמר מר: אם היה כהן גדול ונזיר, לאחיו אינו מיטמא אבל מיטמא הוא למת מצוה - מה לי כהן גדול לחודיה, מה לי נזיר וכהן גדול.

The Gemara answers: Rabbi Akiva could have **said to you: Since the Master said** that **if** someone **was a High Priest and** also **a nazirite,** it is **to** bury **his brother that he may not become impure but he does become impure to** bury **a *met mitzva*,** one can therefore argue: **What** difference is it **to me** if he was **only a High Priest,** and **what** difference is it **to me** if he was both **a nazirite and a High Priest?** Once the Torah has stated that a nazirite may contract other forms of ritual impurity, the same *halakha* applies equally to a nazirite who is also a High Priest.

ולרבי ישמעאל, כהן גדול והוא נזיר, מנליה? כיון דשרא רחמנא חד לאו גבי מת מצוה - מה לי חד לאו מה לי תרין לאוין.

The Gemara asks: **And according to** the derivation of **Rabbi Yishmael, from where does he** derive that **a High Priest who is** also **a nazirite** must become impure to bury a *met mitzva*? The Gemara answers: **Since the Merciful One permits one prohibition with regard to a *met mitzva*,** either that of a High Priest or that of a nazirite, **what** difference is it **to me** if **one prohibition** is permitted, and **what** difference is it **to me** if **two prohibitions** are permitted? Once the Torah has permitted both a High Priest and a nazirite to contract ritual impurity to bury a *met mitzva*, it makes no difference if a single prohibition or two prohibitions are involved.

"אחותו" למה לי? סלקא דעתך אמינא: כי שרא רחמנא למת מצוה - נזיר וכהן, דאיסור לאוי הוא. אבל מילה ופסח, דכרת - לא יטמא למת מצוה, קא משמע לן.

The Gemara asks further: If so, **why do I** need the term **"his sister"?**[N] The Gemara answers: It might **enter your mind to say** that **when the Merciful One permits** the contracting of impurity **to** bury **a *met mitzva*,** this is in the case of **a nazirite and a priest,** each of which involves **a negative prohibition** not to become impure. **However,** with regard to **circumcision and the Paschal offering,** whose neglect entails the punishment **of *karet*,**[B] perhaps one should **not become impure to** bury **a *met mitzva*.** The verse therefore **teaches us** that one must become impure even if this forces him to neglect a mitzva whose neglect is punishable by *karet*.

NOTES

Body, these are the distant – נפשות, אלו הרחוקין: Rabbi Akiva disagrees with the opinion stated in the *baraita* above (48a), that the word "body" indicates that the verse is referring to people, as an animal is not called a "body," but only the "body of an animal." Furthermore, throughout the Torah (see, e.g., Leviticus 17:15), a dead animal is termed a "carcass" with regard to ritual impurity. It is also possible that Rabbi Akiva accepts Rabbi Yishmael's interpretation that the phrase "he shall not come near to" (Numbers 6:6) is referring to a corpse, which imparts impurity through a person's entrance into a tent (*Tosafot*).

Why do I need "his sister" – אחותו למה לי: Since Rabbi Yishmael does not differentiate between one prohibition and two, as he maintains that the requirement to bury a *met mitzva* overrides several negative prohibitions, one should also be required to neglect the positive mitzvot of the Paschal offering and circumcision for this purpose (Commentary on *Nazir*).

BACKGROUND

Karet – כרת: This is a divine punishment for serious transgressions. The precise definition of the term is a matter of debate among the commentaries. Opinions include premature death, sudden death, barrenness, the death of one's child, and excision of the soul from the World-to-Come. *Karet* is incurred only when one intentionally commits a transgression. If one transgresses a prohibition that is punishable by *karet* in the presence of witnesses, he is subject either to lashes or execution by an earthly court, depending upon the prohibition. Anyone who inadvertently transgresses one of these prohibitions must bring a sin-offering as atonement. Thirty-six transgressions are punishable by *karet*, all of which are violations of prohibitions. The two exceptions are neglecting to sacrifice the Paschal lamb and failure to ensure that one is circumcised.

NOTES

Why do I need, for his father or for his mother – לְאָבִיו וּלְאִמּוֹ לָמָּה לִי: If burying a *met mitzva* overrides both the prohibition against a High Priest becoming impure and the prohibition against a nazirite becoming impure in the case of a High Priest who is a nazirite, it certainly takes precedence over each of these prohibitions separately. Consequently, there is no need for "for his father or for his mother" to be stated with regard to a nazirite at all (Commentary on *Nazir*). Some commentaries maintain that this question is referring to the phrase "for his father and for his mother" stated in connection with a High Priest. Either way, all commentaries agree that the difficulty applies to both cases, as according to the opinion of Rabbi Akiva, both verses are superfluous. Some commentaries state that although the phrase "for his father" is necessary to teach the basic *halakha* that a nazirite must become impure for a *met mitzva*, the question is why the verse specifies both "for his father" and "for his mother" (*Tosafot*). Others similarly say that despite the fact that it was stated above that the term "for his mother" is required for a verbal analogy, it remains unclear why the Torah states "for his father or for his mother" (Rosh).

וּלְרַבִּי עֲקִיבָא, מִכְּדִי לָא שְׁנָא כֹּהֵן גָּדוֹל לְחוּדֵיהּ וְלָא שְׁנָא כֹּהֵן גָּדוֹל וְהוּא נָזִיר, נָפְקָא מִ״לְאָחִיו״. ״לְאָבִיו וּלְאִמּוֹ״ לָמָּה לִי?

The Gemara asks: **And according to** the derivation of **Rabbi Akiva, now consider,** it **is no different** whether the individual was **a High Priest alone, and** it **is no different** if he was **a High Priest who was** also **a nazirite;** the *halakha* that he must become impure to bury a *met mitzva* is **derived from** the phrase **"for his brother,"** stated with regard to a nazirite (Numbers 6:7). But if so, **why do I** need the expression **"for his father, or for his mother"** (Numbers 6:7)?[N] The general prohibition against contracting impurity from any corpse should suffice.

צְרִיכִי, דְּאִי כְּתַב ״אָבִיו״ הֲוָה אָמֵינָא: הַיְינוּ טַעְמָא דְּלָא מִיטַּמֵּא לֵיהּ – מִשּׁוּם דַּחֲזָקָה בְּעָלְמָא הוּא, אֲבָל אִמּוֹ דִּיָדְעִין דִּילֵידְתֵּיהּ – לִיטַּמֵּא לַהּ.

The Gemara answers: Both **are necessary, as had** the verse **written** only "for **his father," I would say** that **this is the reason** that a nazirite **may not become impure for** his father: **Because it is merely a presumption** that he is his father, as one cannot be absolutely sure of the identity of one's father. **However,** with regard to **his mother, whom we know gave birth to him,** perhaps **let him become impure to** bury **her.** The verse therefore states: "His mother."

וְאִי כְּתַב רַחֲמָנָא ״אִמּוֹ״ – הֲוָה אָמֵינָא: אִמּוֹ לָא לִיטַּמֵּא לַהּ – דְּלָאו אָזֵיל זַרְעָהּ בָּתְרַהּ, אֲבָל אָבִיו, כֵּיוָן דְּאָמַר מָר ״לְמִשְׁפְּחוֹתָם לְבֵית אֲבוֹתָם״ – אֵימָא לִיטַּמֵּא לֵיהּ, קָא מַשְׁמַע לַן.

And conversely, **had the Merciful One written** only "for **his mother," I would say** that it is solely to bury **his mother** that **he may not become impure, as her seed does not follow her,** i.e., a man's lineage is determined by his father, not his mother. **However,** with regard to **his father, since the Master said** with regard to the verse **"by their families, by their fathers' house"** (Numbers 1:2) that one's family ancestry follows his father, you might **say: Let him become impure to** bury **him.** The verse therefore **teaches us** that a nazirite may not become impure to bury his father either.

״וְעַל כָּל נַפְשֹׁת מֵת לֹא יָבֹא״ לָמָּה לִי?

The Gemara asks: According to the derivation of Rabbi Akiva, **why do I** need the words **"neither shall he go in to any dead bodies"** (Leviticus 21:11), stated with regard to a High Priest?

״עַל כָּל״ – לְאַפּוֹקֵי רְחוֹקִים. ״מֵת״ – לְאַפּוֹקֵי קְרוֹבִים. ״נַפְשֹׁת״ – לְאַפּוֹקֵי רְבִיעִית דָּם שֶׁיָּצָא מִשְּׁנֵי מֵתִים, שֶׁמְּטַמֵּא בְּאֹהֶל, שֶׁנֶּאֱמַר ״עַל כָּל נַפְשֹׁת מֵת לֹא יָבֹא״.

"In to any" served **to exclude** contracting impurity to bury **distant** people, for whom a High Priest may not become impure; **"dead"** comes **to exclude relatives; "bodies"** comes **to exclude a quarter-***log* **of blood that emerges from two corpses,**[N] **for it renders** people and objects **impure in a tent, as it is stated: "Neither shall he go in to any dead bodies"** (Leviticus 21:11). The plural "bodies" teaches that the blood of two people combines to form the minimum quantity for ritual impurity.

NOTES

A quarter-*log* of blood that emerges from two corpses – רְבִיעִית דָּם שֶׁיָּצָא מִשְּׁנֵי מֵתִים: The quarter-*log* measure, as the minimum measure of blood, is derived from the words "for the blood is the life" (Deuteronomy 12:23). The Sages determined that a person's life is dependent on a quarter-*log* of blood. Although the adult human body contains far more than one quarter-*log* of blood, it is possible that an infant is unable to survive if he loses this amount blood. Another explanation is that a quarter-*log* of blood is the amount contained in the heart.

This quarter-*log* of blood, which transmits ritual impurity, may be comprised from two corpses. The plural form "bodies," in the verse "neither shall he go in to any dead bodies" teaches that even a total of a quarter-*log* of blood from two corpses imparts impurity in a tent.

מתני׳ עַל אֵלּוּ טוּמְאוֹת הַנָּזִיר מְגַלֵּחַ: עַל הַמֵּת, וְעַל כַּזַּיִת מִן הַמֵּת, וְעַל כַּזַּיִת נֶצֶל, וְעַל מְלֹא תַּרְוָוד רָקָב, עַל הַשִּׁדְרָה, וְעַל הַגּוּלְגּוֹלֶת, וְעַל אֵבֶר מִן הַמֵּת וְעַל אֵבֶר מִן הַחַי שֶׁיֵּשׁ עָלָיו בָּשָׂר כָּרָאוּי, וְעַל חֲצִי קַב עֲצָמוֹת, וְעַל חֲצִי לוֹג דָּם,

MISHNA **A nazirite shaves for** having become impure from **these** following **sources of ritual impurity:**[NH] **For** having become impure with impurity imparted by **a corpse; and for** impurity imparted by **an olive-bulk of a corpse; and for** impurity imparted by **an olive-bulk of fluid** [*netzel*][BL] from a corpse; **and for** impurity imparted by **a full ladle** [*tarvad*][L] **of dust** from a corpse; and **for** impurity imparted by **the spine; and for** impurity imparted by **the skull;**[N] **and for** impurity imparted by a **limb from a corpse or for** impurity imparted by **a limb** severed **from a living** person, **upon** either of **which there is a fitting** quantity of **flesh;**[N] **and for** impurity imparted by **a half-*kav***[B] **of bones** from a corpse; **and for** impurity imparted by **a half-*log***[B] **of blood.**[N]

וְעַל מַגָּעָן וְעַל מַשָּׂאָן וְעַל אֲהִילָן. וְעַל עֶצֶם כִּשְׂעוֹרָה, עַל מַגָּעוֹ וְעַל מַשָּׂאוֹ.

And a nazirite shaves in each of these cases for becoming impure **by coming into contact with them; and for** becoming impure by **carrying them;**[H] **and for** becoming impure by **their tent**, i.e., if he was positioned like a tent over them, or if he entered a tent that contains them, or if they served as a tent over him. **And** as **for a bone that is a barley-grain-bulk,**[H] he shaves **for** becoming impure by **coming into contact with it and by carrying it.**[N] However, he is not rendered impure with the impurity imparted in a tent, i.e., by being under the same roof as the bone.

עַל אֵלּוּ הַנָּזִיר מְגַלֵּחַ, וּמַזֶּה בַּשְּׁלִישִׁי וּבַשְּׁבִיעִי, וְסוֹתֵר אֶת הַקּוֹדְמִין, וְאֵינוֹ מַתְחִיל לִמְנוֹת אֶלָּא עַד שֶׁיִּטְהַר וּמֵבִיא אֶת קָרְבְּנוֹתָיו.

For all of **these** occurrences, **a nazirite shaves, and** a priest **sprinkles** the ashes of the red heifer on him **on the third and on the seventh** days[H] to purify him from the impurity imparted by a corpse. **And he negates all the previous** days he counted toward his naziriteship, **and he begins counting** his term of naziriteship again **only after he becomes pure and brings his offerings.**

NOTES

For these following sources of ritual impurity, etc. – עַל אֵלּוּ טוּמְאוֹת וכו׳: As explained in the subsequent mishna, not every item that imparts impurity of a corpse has a degree of impurity severe enough to obligate a nazirite to shave. There are impurities for which a nazirite must purify himself but that do not obligate him to shave or negate any part of his naziriteship.

For the spine and for the skull – עַל הַשִּׁדְרָה וְעַל הַגּוּלְגּוֹלֶת: These two body parts are listed separately, because a special *halakha* applies to them, as they impart impurity even if there is no flesh on them at all. The Gemara discusses whether this *halakha* refers to a spine and a skull together, or each on their own. Many commentaries rule that each of them imparts impurity by itself (Rambam; Meiri).

Upon which there is a fitting quantity of flesh – יֵשׁ עָלָיו בָּשָׂר כָּרָאוּי: The Sages explain that the phrase: A fitting quantity of flesh, refers to that which would develop a scab if it was attached to a living person, i.e., the limb is properly covered with flesh (*Kelim* 1:5). This amount is certainly less than an olive-bulk, as an olive-bulk of flesh from a corpse itself imparts impurity even without a limb (see Commentary on *Nazir*).

A half-*kav* of bones and for a half-*log* of blood – חֲצִי קַב עֲצָמוֹת וְעַל חֲצִי לוֹג דָּם: The commentaries point out that although the *halakha* is that a quarter-*kav* of bones and a quarter-*log* of blood impart impurity in a tent, a nazirite does not shave for these amounts (*Tosafot*). *Tosafot* explain that all these measures are a *halakha* transmitted to Moses from Sinai, for which there is no known justification. Others state that any impurity for which a nazirite is not obligated to shave applies by rabbinic law (Rambam *Sefer Tahara*, *Hilkhot Tumat Met* 3:3).

By coming into contact with it and by carrying it – עַל מַגָּעוֹ וְעַל מַשָּׂאוֹ: This excludes the impurity imparted in a tent. Not only is a nazirite not obligated to shave if he enters a room that contains a bone whose volume is a barley-grain-bulk or greater, but this bone does not impart the impurity of a tent at all (*Tosafot*).

BACKGROUND

Fluid [*netzel*] – נֶצֶל: Certain liquids in the living body, whether lubricants in joints or similar liquids, including products of illness, such as pus, all undergo postmortem coagulation. This is because the processes that kept them fluid while the person was alive shut down sometime after death. Some of these fluids evaporate. Additionally, if a corpse was located in a very warm place, e.g., if the person perished in a fire, the fats of the body first liquefy and later congeal. The fluids from the corpse, both those that flow out of it and those that remain inside and congeal are called *netzel*.

Kav – קַב: This is a basic unit of measurement from which many other small units are derived. It is equivalent to one-sixth of a *se'a*, or twenty-four egg-bulks.

Log – לוֹג: This is the basic liquid measure used by the Sages. It is equivalent to the volume of six egg-bulks, one quarter of a *kav*, or one twenty-fourth of a *se'a*. A range of modern opinions estimates this volume at 300–600 ml.

HALAKHA

A nazirite shaves for these following sources of ritual impurity – עַל אֵלּוּ טוּמְאוֹת הַנָּזִיר מְגַלֵּחַ: For which sources of impurity is a nazirite obligated to shave? A stillborn, even if its limbs have not become joined to its sinews; an olive-bulk of flesh from a corpse; an olive-bulk of fluid from a corpse; the majority of the bones of a single corpse, even if they do not amount to a quarter-*kav*; a half-*kav* of bones from one corpse, even if they do not constitute the majority of the number and the majority of the structure of its bones; the spine of a corpse; the skull of a corpse; a limb from a corpse or a limb from a living person, if these limbs contain enough flesh that would develop a scab on a live person; and a half-*log* of blood. All these impart impurity when they come from a single corpse, as do two handfuls of dust (Rambam *Sefer Hafla'a*, *Hilkhot Nezirut* 7:2).

By coming into contact with them and for carrying them, etc. – וְעַל מַגָּעָן וְעַל מַשָּׂאָן וכו׳: A nazirite must shave for the listed sources of impurity whether he came into contact with or carried them or whether he served as a tent over them, or they were positioned as a tent over him, or if the source of impurity and the nazirite were in the same tent. In all these cases, the nazirite's term of naziriteship is negated, he shaves his hair, and he brings his offerings of impurity. The exception is dust from a corpse, which imparts impurity by carrying and in a tent but not by means of contact (Rambam *Sefer Hafla'a*, *Hilkhot Nezirut* 7:5).

For a bone that is a barley-grain-bulk, etc. – עַל עֶצֶם כִּשְׂעוֹרָה וכו׳: If a nazirite came into contact with a bone from a corpse that is a barley-grain-bulk, he shaves only if he touched or carried it, but it does not impart impurity of a tent (Rambam *Sefer Hafla'a*, *Hilkhot Nezirut* 7:6).

And a priest sprinkles on the third and on the seventh days, etc. – וּמַזֶּה בַּשְּׁלִישִׁי וּבַשְּׁבִיעִי וכו׳: A nazirite who became impure through one of the sources of impurity of a corpse listed in the mishna has his naziriteship negated, performs the shaving of impurity, and brings the offerings for his impurity. He is purified from his impurity through the sprinkling of the purification waters of the red heifer and by bringing his sin-offering. At this point, he begins counting the term of his naziriteship afresh (Rambam *Sefer Hafla'a*, *Hilkhot Nezirut* 6:11–13; 7:1, 5).

LANGUAGE

Fluid [*netzel*] – נֶצֶל: The root of *netzel* is likely connected to *nozel*, fluid, *neitzala* in Syriac. Accordingly, *netzel* is the fluid that flows from a corpse. By halakhic definition, this refers to a portion from the flesh of the corpse that has melted and become watery as a result of heat, illness, or decomposition.

Ladle [*tarvad*] – תַּרְוָוד: This term is also found in Syriac, Aramaic, and Arabic, although it apparently originated from an unidentified language. A *tarvad* is a kind of large spoon that was used to serve food from a pot. Since this utensil has no specific size, it is necessary to define how much a *tarvad* holds for the purposes of this *halakha* (see 50b).

גמ׳ תָּנוּ רַבָּנַן: אַחַר פְּטִירָתוֹ שֶׁל רַבִּי מֵאִיר אָמַר לָהֶן רַבִּי יְהוּדָה לְתַלְמִידָיו: אַל יִכָּנְסוּ תַּלְמִידֵי רַבִּי מֵאִיר לְכָאן מִפְּנֵי שֶׁקַּנְתְּרָנִין הֵן, וְלֹא לִלְמוֹד תּוֹרָה הֵן בָּאִין אֶלָּא לְקַפְּחֵנִי בַּהֲלָכוֹת הֵן בָּאִין. דָּחַק סוּמָכוֹס וְנִכְנַס.

GEMARA **The Sages taught: After Rabbi Meir's death, Rabbi Yehuda**[P] **said to his students: Do not let the students of Rabbi Meir enter here,** into the house of study, **because they are vexatious and they do not come to study Torah, but they come to overwhelm me with their *halakhot*. Nevertheless,** **Sumakhos,**[P] a student of Rabbi Meir, **forced his way and entered** the house of study.

אָמַר לָהֶם, כָּךְ שָׁנָה לִי רַבִּי מֵאִיר: עַל אֵלּוּ טוּמְאוֹת הַנָּזִיר מְגַלֵּחַ – עַל הַמֵּת וְעַל כַּזַּיִת מִן הַמֵּת. כָּעַס רַבִּי יְהוּדָה וְאָמַר לָהֶן: לֹא כָּךְ אָמַרְתִּי לָכֶם: אַל יִכָּנְסוּ תַּלְמִידֵי רַבִּי מֵאִיר לְכָאן, מִפְּנֵי שֶׁקַּנְתְּרָנִין הֵן? עַל כַּזַּיִת מִן הַמֵּת מְגַלֵּחַ, עַל הַמֵּת לֹא כָּל שֶׁכֵּן?!

When they reached the topic of the mishna, Sumakhos **said to them: Rabbi Meir**[P] **taught me like this: A nazirite shaves for** becoming impure from **these** following sources of **ritual impurity: For** impurity imparted by a **corpse and for** impurity imparted by **an olive-bulk from a corpse. Rabbi Yehuda grew angry and said to** his disciples: **Didn't I say to you like this: Do not let the students of Rabbi Meir enter here because they are vexatious?** He explained his annoyance. The clause: For a corpse, is unnecessary, as, if a nazirite **must shave for** impurity imparted by **an olive-bulk from a corpse,** is it **not all the more so** that he must shave **for** impurity imparted by an entire **corpse?**

PERSONALITIES

Rabbi Yehuda – רַבִּי יְהוּדָה: When the Mishna refers to Rabbi Yehuda without any addition, it means Rabbi Yehuda, son of Rabbi Ilai, one of the greatest of the fourth-generation *tanna'im*. Rabbi Yehuda was one of the last five disciples of Rabbi Akiva, while his father, Rabbi Ilai, was a student of Rabbi Eliezer. Rabbi Yehuda studied Rabbi Eliezer's wisdom from his father. In his youth, he studied with Rabbi Tarfon, in whose name he cites *halakhot*, in addition to the other Sages of Yavne: Rabbi Eliezer, Rabbi Yehoshua, Rabban Gamliel, Rabbi Elazar ben Azarya, Rabbi Yishmael, and Rabbi Yosei HaGelili. Nevertheless, Rabbi Yehuda's foremost teacher was Rabbi Akiva, and it was in accordance with his opinion that he laid the foundations for the halakhic exegesis of Leviticus known as the *Sifra*, or *Torat Kohanim*. According to tradition, any unattributed statement in the *Sifra* is authored by Rabbi Yehuda. Rabbi Yehuda was ordained by Rabbi Yehuda ben Bava and is frequently quoted in aggadic statements alongside Rabbi Neḥemya. When there are differences of opinion between Rabbi Yehuda and Rabbi Meir, or between Rabbi Yehuda and Rabbi Shimon, the *halakha* is in accordance with the opinion of Rabbi Yehuda. His disciples included Rabbi Elazar, son of Rabbi Shimon; Rabbi Yishmael, son of Rabbi Yosei; and Rabbi Yehuda HaNasi. His son, Rabbi Yosei, was also a renowned Sage.

Sumakhos – סוּמָכוֹס: This full name of this *tanna* is Sumakhos ben Yosef. He lived in the last generation of *tanna'im*. Sumakhos was the outstanding disciple of Rabbi Meir and transmitted much of Rabbi Meir's knowledge to the subsequent generations. As Rabbi Meir's foremost disciple, Sumakhos made great efforts to explain Rabbi Meir's statements and clarify his opinions after his death. Like his master before him, Sumakhos was known for his fierce intellect, as the Talmud relates that he would provide forty-eight proofs for every *halakha* he discussed. It can be argued that he was the greatest Sage of his generation, as he would dispute even the greatest of *tanna'im*, including Rabbi Meir, Rabbi Yosei, and Rabbi Eliezer ben Ya'akov.

Rabbi Meir – רַבִּי מֵאִיר: Rabbi Meir was one of the greatest *tanna'im* of the generation that preceded the redaction of the Mishna. There is no clear information available concerning Rabbi Meir's parents, although it is told that he descended from a family of converts from the house of the Roman emperors.

Rabbi Meir's exceptional brilliance in Torah study was evident from a very early age, and he was a student of the two greatest scholars of the generation, Rabbi Yishmael and Rabbi Akiva. He was also the lone Sage who continued to study with Elisha ben Avuya, despite the latter's estrangement from Judaism. His primary teacher was Rabbi Akiva, who ordained him at a very young age, for which reason he was ordained a second time by Rabbi Yehuda ben Bava. In recognition of his outstanding scholarship, Rabbi Meir was officially appointed *ḥakham*, literally, wise man, a position third in importance after the *Nasi*, or the head of the Sanhedrin, and the president of the court. The halakhic discussions between him and his colleagues, Rabbi Yehuda, Rabbi Yosei, Rabbi Shimon, and Rabbi Elazar, form one of the most important foundations of the Mishna.

Rabbi Meir's greatest undertaking was apparently a structured, oral redaction of the Oral Law, including the establishment of specific formats for the *halakha*. Rabbi Yehuda HaNasi followed in Rabbi Meir's footsteps and incorporated his work in the Mishna. Consequently, it is a well-known principle that the author of an unattributed statement in the Mishna is Rabbi Meir. Due to his involvement in the attempt to depose the *Nasi* Rabban Shimon ben Gamliel, Rabbi Meir was punished, and for a long period his statements were not cited in his name but were introduced with the words: Others say.

Rabbi Meir's private life was full of suffering. His two sons passed away during his lifetime, and his extraordinary wife Berurya also died in painful circumstances. Nevertheless, it is known that one of his daughters survived. He was eventually forced into exile in Asia Minor, where he died, with the order that his coffin be transferred to Eretz Yisrael and that he be interred temporarily on the shore of the sea whose waves reach the Holy Land.

Rabbi Meir was famous in his lifetime not only for his sharp intellect, which exceeded that of all his peers, but also for his personal attributes, his efforts as a peacemaker, and his willingness to relinquish personal honor for the good of others. He was known as a magnificent public speaker. It is said that following his death, those who composed parables ceased (*Sota* 49a). Several of his animal fables were retold over the course of many generations. He was also renowned as a miracle worker, and for many years a charity fund named after him, Rabbi Meir Ba'al HaNes, literally Rabbi Meir the miracle worker, served as the main source of funding for Jews in Eretz Yisrael.

אָמַר רַבִּי יוֹסֵי: יֹאמְרוּ, מֵאִיר שָׁכַב, יְהוּדָה כָּעַס, יוֹסֵי שָׁתַק, תּוֹרָה מַה תְּהֵא עָלֶיהָ? אָמַר רַבִּי יוֹסֵי: לֹא נִצְרְכָה אֶלָּא לְמֵת שֶׁאֵין עָלָיו כַּזַּיִת בָּשָׂר. וַעֲדַיִין יֹאמַר: עַל אֵבֶר מִמֶּנּוּ מְגַלֵּחַ, עַל כּוּלּוֹ לֹא כׇּל שֶׁכֵּן?!

Rabbi Yosei[P] **said:** Now **they will say: Meir is dead, Yehuda is angry,** and **Yosei remained silent** and did not respond. If so, **what will become of the Torah? Rabbi Yosei** therefore **said:** It is **not necessary** to teach that a nazirite must shave for impurity imparted by a corpse, **but** only that he must shave even **for** impurity imparted by **a corpse upon which there is not an olive-bulk of flesh.** The Gemara asks: **But one could still say:** If he must **shave for** impurity imparted by **a limb from** a corpse, even if it is less than an olive-bulk, as stated in the mishna, is it **not all the more so** that he must shave **for** impurity imparted by **all of** a corpse, even if it does not contain an olive-bulk of flesh?

אֶלָּא כִּדְאָמַר רַבִּי יוֹחָנָן: לֹא נִצְרְכָה אֶלָּא לְנֵפֶל שֶׁלֹּא נִתְקַשְּׁרוּ אֵבָרָיו בְּגִידִין, הָכָא נַמִי – בְּנֵפֶל שֶׁלֹּא נִתְקַשְּׁרוּ אֵבָרָיו בְּגִידִין.

Rather, the mishna should be explained **as Rabbi Yoḥanan said,** with regard to a different issue: It is **necessary only for a miscarried fetus whose limbs had not** yet **become joined** to its **sinews.**[B] **Here too,** one can say that the mishna's statement that a nazirite must shave for impurity imparted by a corpse is referring **to a miscarried fetus whose limbs had not** yet **become joined**[H] **to** its **sinews.** Although it does not impart impurity through one of its limbs, as the limbs lack sinews and bones, this corpse itself does impart impurity.

רָבָא אָמַר: לֹא נִצְרְכָה אֶלָּא לְרוֹב בִּנְיָינוֹ וּלְרוֹב מִנְיָינוֹ שֶׁאֵין בָּהֶן רוֹבַע עֲצָמוֹת.

Rava said a different explanation: This ruling is **necessary only for the majority of the structure or the majority of the number**[BHN] of bones of a very small corpse, despite the fact **that** together **they do not contain a quarter-*kav* of bones.** Since these bones comprise the majority of the structure or the majority of the number of bones of a corpse, they have the status of a whole body. This *halakha* could not have been derived from the measure of impurity of part of the body, as this corpse is very small.

״עַל כַּזַּיִת מֵת וְעַל כַּזַּיִת נֵצֶל״. וְאֵיזֶהוּ נֵצֶל – בְּשַׂר הַמֵּת שֶׁקָּרַשׁ, וּמוֹהַל שֶׁהִרְתִּיחַ.

§ The mishna taught: A nazirite shaves **for** impurity imparted by **an olive-bulk of a corpse and for** impurity imparted by **an olive-bulk of fluid.** The Gemara explains: **And what is fluid?**[H] This is referring to **flesh of the corpse that** liquefied and subsequently **congealed, and liquid** [*mohal*][BL] from the corpse **that** began **to boil** and then hardened.

BACKGROUND

A miscarried fetus whose bones had not formed – נֵפֶל שֶׁלֹּא נִתְקַשְּׁרוּ עַצְמוֹתָיו: The process of bone formation, by which cartilage turns into bone, begins during pregnancy and continues through childhood and adolescence until full adulthood. At certain periods during pregnancy, the fetus already has several bones, mostly in the skull, despite the fact that its muscles and sinews have not yet developed. These bones experience rapid decay upon the death of the fetus.

For the majority of the structure or the majority of the number – לְרוֹב בִּנְיָינוֹ וּלְרוֹב מִנְיָינוֹ: A simple majority of 125 bones in the body might be a collection of especially small bones. The majority of the structure, i.e., large bones that comprise the majority of the skeleton, would be greater than a quarter-*kav* in volume in a full-grown person. Apparently the Gemara here is referring to the remains of a baby or a fetus, in which case the majority of bones in number or size would be less than a quarter-*kav* in volume.

Liquid – מוֹהַל: This might be referring to a corpse that lost a lot of blood, and it drained into one place. In that case, the red and white blood cells sink to the bottom and congeal relatively quickly, whereas the plasma remains in a liquid state for longer. Given enough time, the water in the plasma evaporates, while the remaining plasma congeals as well.

HALAKHA

A miscarried fetus whose limbs had not become joined – נֵפֶל שֶׁלֹּא נִתְקַשְּׁרוּ אֵבָרָיו: A miscarried fetus imparts ritual impurity through contact, through carrying, and in a tent, like the corpse of an adult, even if its limbs are not joined to its sinews. If a nazirite became impure in this manner, he is obligated to shave (Rambam *Sefer Hafla'a, Hilkhot Nezirut* 7:2 and *Sefer Tahara, Hilkhot Tumat Met* 2:1; 3:1).

For the majority of the structure or the majority of the number, etc. – לְרוֹב בִּנְיָינוֹ וּלְרוֹב מִנְיָינוֹ וכו׳: If a nazirite came into contact with bones that constitute the majority of the number of bones in a body or the majority of the structure of a corpse, he becomes impure and must shave on their account, even if they amount to less than a quarter-*kav* (Rambam *Sefer Hafla'a, Hilkhot Nezirut* 7:2 and *Sefer Tahara, Hilkhot Tumat Met* 2: 8–9).

What is fluid [*netzel*] – אֵיזֶהוּ נֵצֶל: *Netzel* is flesh that has softened into a putrefied liquid. For a liquid to be considered *netzel*, it must eventually congeal; otherwise one cannot be sure it comes from the flesh and is not spittle or phlegm (Rambam *Sefer Hafla'a, Hilkhot Nezirut* 7:2 and *Sefer Tahara, Hilkhot Tumat Met* 2:1).

NOTES

For the majority of the structure or the majority of the number – לְרוֹב בִּנְיָינוֹ וּלְרוֹב מִנְיָינוֹ: The phrase: The majority of the structure, means the majority of the five supports for the frame, i.e., the two shins, the two thighs, and the spine. The phrase: The majority of the number, means at least 125 bones, more than half of the 248 limbs in the human body. Some commentaries maintain that these bones need not be whole. If there are parts of bones that come from the majority of the structure or the majority of the number of limbs, this is enough to impart impurity (*Tosafot* on the mishna). Other commentaries disagree.

LANGUAGE

Liquid [*mohal*] – מוֹהַל: The term *mohal*, or *moḥal*, refers to a liquid that flows or seeps out of a solid and that is not the liquid that normally flows from it. The term is used in the case of olives to refer to fluid other than oil that flows from them. Likewise here, the *mohal* of a corpse is a liquid other than blood that seeps out of a corpse.

PERSONALITIES

Rabbi Yosei – רַבִּי יוֹסֵי: This is Rabbi Yosei ben Ḥalafta, one of the greatest of the *tanna'im*. He lived in the generation prior to the redaction of the Mishna, and his influence is evident throughout tannaitic literature. His father, known as Abba Ḥalafta, was also considered one of the great Sages of his generation, while his family, according to one tradition, was descended from Jehonadab, the son of Rechab (see II Kings 10:15).

In addition to studying with his father, Rabbi Yosei was an outstanding student of Rabbi Akiva. Rabbi Yosei and his contemporaries, namely, Rabbi Meir, Rabbi Yehuda, and Rabbi Shimon bar Yoḥai, were students of Rabbi Akiva, and they formed the center of talmudic creativity of that entire generation. In his halakhic approach, as in his way of life, Rabbi Yosei was moderate. He refrained from taking extreme positions on halakhic issues. A well-known principle is that Rabbi Yosei's opinions are based on sound reasoning, and because of his moderation and the logic of his teachings, the *halakha* is in accordance with his opinion in every instance of disagreement with his colleagues.

In addition to being a great master of *halakha*, Rabbi Yosei was also famous for his piety. The Talmud relates many stories about his modesty, humility, and sanctity. It is told that Elijah the prophet would reveal himself to him every day, and several conversations between him and Elijah are related in the Talmud. Rabbi Yosei was apparently the primary redactor of a series on the history of the Jewish people known as *Seder Olam Rabba*. For many years, he lived in Tzippori in the Galilee and earned his living as a tanner.

Many of the prominent Sages of the following generation, including Rabbi Yehuda HaNasi, the redactor of the Mishna, were his students. However, his main students were his five sons, all of whom were Sages in their generation. The most famous of them were Rabbi Eliezer, one of the great masters of *halakha*, and Rabbi Yishmael.

BACKGROUND

His phlegm and his spittle – כִּיחוֹ וְנִיעוֹ: These are discharges principally from the fluids in the lungs that result from the common cold and the like, which people expectorate by coughing or spitting. Since the *halakha* does not regard these fluids as a part of the corpse, they do not impart ritual impurity like flesh. They impart impurity only in the manner of substances that come into contact with a corpse.

HALAKHA

Is there fluid with regard to animals – יֵשׁ נֵצֶל לִבְהֵמָה: If the flesh on a carcass liquefied and congealed, it is uncertain whether it imparts impurity from the size of an olive-bulk, like a carcass, as Abaye's dilemma was left unresolved (Rambam *Sefer Tahara, Hilkhot She'ar Avot HaTumot* 1:13).

A severe impurity until it becomes inedible for a dog – טוּמְאָה חֲמוּרָה עַד לַכֶּלֶב: If the flesh of a carcass putrefied to the extent that it is no longer fit to be eaten by a dog, it is ritually pure. The same applies to the carcass of a pure bird or that of a creeping animal. If it is fit for a dog, it is impure even if it is inedible for humans (Rambam *Sefer Tahara, Hilkhot She'ar Avot HaTumot* 3:11; 4:12 and *Sefer Tahara, Hilkhot Tumat Okhalin* 2:18).

הֵיכִי דָּמֵי? אִילֵימָא דְּלָא יָדְעִינַן דְּדִידֵיהּ הוּא, כִּי קָרַשׁ מַאי הָוֵי? אֶלָּא דְּיָדְעִינַן דְּדִידֵיהּ הוּא – אַף עַל גַּב דְּלָא קָרַשׁ!

The Gemara asks: **What are the circumstances** in which the congealment is a determinative factor in the imparting of impurity? **If we say that we do not know**[N] **that** the substance with which the nazirite came into contact **is** from the corpse, even **if it congealed, what of it? Rather,** you will say **that we know that it** came from the corpse. But then the nazirite should be impure **even though** it has **not congealed.**

אֲמַר רַבִּי יִרְמְיָה: בִּסְתָם, אִי קָרַשׁ – מוֹהַל הוּא, לֹא קָרַשׁ – דִּלְמָא כִּיחוֹ וְנִיעוֹ הוּא.

Rabbi Yirmeya said that this is referring **to an unspecified** substance that is definitely from the corpse but is not necessarily a substance that imparts impurity. One therefore examines the substance: **If** the substance eventually **congeals, it is liquid** from the corpse, which imparts impurity; if it does **not congeal, perhaps it is his phlegm and his spittle,**[BN] which do not impart impurity.

בְּעָא מִינֵּיהּ אַבַּיֵי מֵרַבָּה: יֵשׁ נֵצֶל לִבְהֵמָה אוֹ אֵין נֵצֶל לִבְהֵמָה? מִי אָמְרִינַן: גְּמִירִי נֵצֶל דְּאָתֵי מֵאָדָם, אֲבָל דְּאָתֵי מִבְּהֵמָה – לָא. אוֹ דִּלְמָא לָא שְׁנָא?

§ With regard to the impurity of fluids from a corpse, **Abaye raised a dilemma before Rabba: Is there** the category of **fluid with regard to animals,**[H] **or is there no** category of **fluid with regard to animals?** In other words, does fluid from an animal carcass impart impurity like the animal carcass itself or not? The Gemara explains the two sides of the dilemma: **Do we say** that it **is learned** as a tradition that **fluid that comes from a person** is impure **but** fluid **that comes from an animal** is **not** impure? **Or perhaps** it **is no different,** as fluid from a corpse is always considered like the flesh itself?

הָנִיחָא לְמַאן דְּאָמַר טוּמְאָה חֲמוּרָה עַד לַגֵּר, וְטוּמְאָה קַלָּה עַד לַכֶּלֶב – שַׁפִּיר.

The Gemara comments: **This works out well according to the one who says** that a carcass imparts impurity by **a severe impurity,** through contact and carrying, only **until** the carcass becomes inedible **for a stranger,**[N] i.e., in order impart impurity it must be fit for human consumption. **And** the carcass imparts impurity by **a light impurity** that imparts impurity on food through contact **until** the carcass become inedible **for a dog.** According to this opinion, **it is well,** as the *halakha* of fluid certainly does not apply to an animal, since meat that has liquefied is no longer fit for human consumption.

אֶלָּא לְמַאן דְּאָמַר טוּמְאָה חֲמוּרָה עַד לַכֶּלֶב – מַאי אִיכָּא לְמֵימַר?

However, according to the one who says that a carcass imparts impurity by **a severe impurity until** it becomes inedible **for a dog,**[H] **what is there to say?** Since fluids from an animal carcass are presumably fit to be eaten by a dog, the above dilemma as to whether it is impure remains pertinent.

NOTES

If we say that we do not know – אִילֵימָא דְּלָא יָדְעִינַן: The early commentaries are puzzled by this passage. The situation in which we do not know where the liquid comes from is apparently the same as that involving an unspecified substance. How, then, does Rabbi Yirmeya's answer resolve the problem? It is probably for this reason that some commentaries explain that the phrase: We do not know, means: We know that it is not, i.e., if it is clear that the substance is not from the corpse, it certainly does not impart impurity (Commentary on *Nazir*). Rabbi Yirmeya answers that the substance is unspecified and this is an uncertain case. Many commentaries explain that the Gemara's suggestion that we do not know means that it is unknown whether the liquid came from the corpse itself or was merely found there by chance. In that case, it certainly does not impart impurity merely due to the possibility that it was from the body. According to this opinion, Rabbi Yirmeya answers that the substance definitely came from a corpse. However, we are unaware of its nature, whether it is a substance that imparts impurity or whether it is spittle (*Tosafot*).

His phlegm and his spittle – כִּיחוֹ וְנִיעוֹ: The commentaries explain that spittle is moisture emitted from the mouth by coughing, while phlegm refers to a substance that comes from the body itself, which accumulates in the mouth and throat (Rabbeinu Todros).

Until for a stranger, etc. – עַד לַגֵּר וכו׳: These classifications are derived from two relevant verses. The first states: "You shall not eat any animal carcass; you may give to the stranger who is within your gates, that he may eat it, or sell it to a foreigner" (Deuteronomy 14:21), which indicates that in order to impart impurity a carcass must be edible for a stranger (see Leviticus 11:39–40). The other verse states: "You shall not eat any flesh that is torn [*tereifa*] of beasts in the field; you shall cast it to the dogs" (Exodus 22:30), which teaches that meat that has deteriorated to the extent that it can no longer be eaten by a dog does not impart impurity at all. A *tereifa* animal, i.e., one that will die within twelve months, is considered a *neveila*, an animal carcass, once it is dead. The dispute concerns the impurity of a carcass: Does it lapse when the meat is no longer fit for humans, as the "stranger" mentioned in the verse is a *ger toshav*, a resident alien who has accepted some of the *halakhot* of the Torah but for whom it is not prohibited to eat carcasses? Or, does it retain its status of impurity as long as it is fit to be eaten by dogs?

תָּא שְׁמַע: הַמְחוֹהוּ בָּאוּר – טָמֵא, בַּחַמָּה – טָהוֹר. וְאִי סָלְקָא דַּעְתָּךְ עַד לַכֶּלֶב – אֲפִילּוּ בַּחַמָּה נָמֵי!

The Gemara answers: **Come** and **hear** a resolution from the *Tosefta* (*Zavim* 5:9): The fat of an animal carcass **that** someone **liquefied in fire is** still **impure.**[H] However, if it melted **in the sun,** which impairs its taste, it is **pure. And if it enters your mind** that according to the opinion that a carcass imparts impurity **until** it becomes inedible **for a dog** the impurity of fluids does apply to an animal carcass, if so, **even** fat that dissolved **in the sun** should **also** be impure. Even if its taste is spoiled, it remains edible for a dog.

אֵימַת מְמַחֵי לֵיהּ – בָּתַר דְּאַסְרוּחַ בַּחַמָּה, כֵּיוָן דְּאַסְרַח – הֲוָה לֵיהּ עָפָר.

The Gemara answers: **When does** this fat **liquefy? After it has putrefied,** which is why it was thrown out, at which point it melted **in the sun.** However, **once it putrefied, it had** already **become** like **dust** and lost any status of ritual impurity it once had. Once it has melted, it is no longer edible for a dog. Consequently, this source provides no proof.

תְּנַן: כָּל הַנִּצּוֹק טָהוֹר,

§ The Gemara discusses a related issue. **We learned** in a mishna (*Makhshirin* 5:9): **Anything that is poured** remains **ritually pure.**[H] In other words, if one pours liquid from one vessel into another, the stream of liquid is not considered to connect the two vessels. Consequently, if the upper vessel and its contents are pure, they do not become impure even if the lower vessel into which the liquid is poured is impure. The stream of liquid does not link them in this manner.

חוּץ מִדְּבַשׁ הַזִּיפִים וְהַצַּפִּיחִית.

The mishna adds: This is the case for all liquids **except for *zifim* honey,**[HB] a very thick type of honey, **and batter,**[N] e.g., flour mixed with honey. Since these substances are highly viscous, they are not considered liquids. Rather, they are a kind of soft solid food, which means that they are a single unit that links the two vessels with regard to impurity.

HALAKHA

That someone liquefied in fire is impure, etc. – הַמְחוֹהוּ בָּאוּר טָמֵא וכו׳: If the fat of the carcass of a pure bird was liquefied by fire and someone swallowed it, he is ritually impure. The Meiri writes that the same *halakha* applies in the case of the fat from the carcass of an impure animal. If it melted in the sun he is pure, as it was putrefied by the sun, as stated in the *baraita* (Rambam *Sefer Tahara*, *Hilkhot She'ar Avot HaTumot* 3:10).

Anything that is poured remains ritually pure – כָּל הַנִּיצּוֹק טָהוֹר: A stream of liquid does not connect two items for the purposes of ritual impurity. Consequently, if pure liquid was poured into an impure vessel, the stream remains pure. However, if the lower vessel is hot and the upper one is cold, the hot fumes rise and mingle with the stream and the contents of the upper vessel, thereby imparting impurity (Rambam *Sefer Tahara*, *Hilkhot Tumat Okhalin* 7:1).

Except for *zifim* honey, etc. – חוּץ מִדְּבַשׁ הַזִּיפִים וכו׳: A stream of *zifim* honey or honey batter connects two items with regard to impurity, even if they are cold and are poured into a cold dish. This is because they stretch out like glue (Rambam *Sefer Tahara*, *Hilkhot Tumat Okhalin* 7:4).

NOTES

And batter – וְהַצַּפִּיחִית: According to most commentaries, this refers to a dough of honey and various types of flour. Alternatively, it is honey extracted directly from the hive, which contains a mixture of wax and is therefore very thick (*Tosafot*).

BACKGROUND

Zifim honey – דְּבַשׁ הַזִּיפִים: *Zifim* honey is a certain variety of honey produced in the town of Zif, a biblical settlement identified today as Tel Zif in the area of Hebron. According to Rav Hai Gaon, there are several species of insects that produce honey, including the wild bee and the wasp. The honey they produce is kosher. Apparently, *zifim* honey was thicker than standard bee honey and did not pour as easily.

Tel Zif

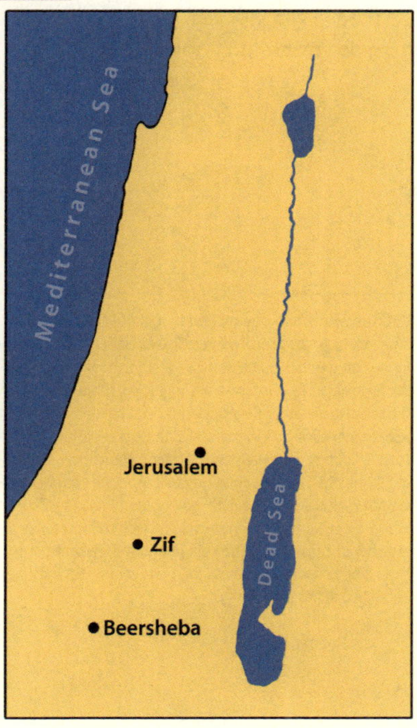

Location of Zif

בֵּית שַׁמַּאי אוֹמְרִים: אַף הַמִּקְפָּה שֶׁל גְּרִיסִין וְשֶׁל פּוֹל, מִפְּנֵי שֶׁהִיא סוֹלֶדֶת לַאֲחוֹרֶיהָ.

Beit Shammai say: Even the stream **of a stew** made **of crushed and broken beans or of whole beans** also connects two items **because it returns backward.** When one stops pouring this stew, part of the dish reverts to its place of origin, and therefore the stream is considered a single unit.

בָּעֵי רָמִי בַּר חָמָא: יֵשׁ נִצּוֹק לָאוֹכָלִין אוֹ אֵין נִצּוֹק לָאוֹכָלִין? מִי אָמְרִינַן מִשּׁוּם דְּאִית בְּהוּ רִירֵי – וְהָנֵי לֵית בְּהוּ רִירֵי, אוֹ דִּלְמָא מִשּׁוּם דִּסְמִיכִין הוּא – וְהָכָא הָא סְמִיכִין?

§ **Rami bar Ḥama raises a dilemma:** According to the opinion of the Rabbis that in general, poured liquid does not serve to connect, **is there a stream for food, or is there not a stream for food?**[H] If one pours melted food into an impure vessel, does the food which one is pouring become impure? The Gemara explains the two sides of the dilemma: **Do we say** that *zifim* honey and batter connect different items **because they have a flow** that returns backward, **and these** regular foods **do not have a flow**[N] that returns backward? **Or, perhaps** the reason why *zifim* honey and batter connect is **because they are viscous, and here** the melted foodstuffs **are also viscous.**

אֲמַר רָבָא, תָּא שְׁמַע: חֵלֶב הַמֵּת שֶׁהוּא שָׁלֵם וְהִתִּיכוֹ – טָמֵא, הָיָה מְפוֹרָד וְהִתִּיכוֹ – טָהוֹר. וְאִי סָלְקָא דַּעְתָּךְ אֵין נִצּוֹק לָאוֹכָלִין, שָׁלֵם וְהִתִּיכוֹ נַמִי לִיטְהַר!

Rava said: Come and hear a resolution from the *Tosefta* (*Oholot* 4:3): If there was **fat of a corpse that was whole**[H] and contained an olive-bulk, **and one melted it,** it is **ritually impure.** If from the outset the fat **was separated** into pieces smaller than an olive-bulk, which do not impart impurity, **and one melted it,**[N] so that it combined into an olive-bulk in its melted state, it is **pure. And if it enters your mind** that **there is no stream for food,** even if it was **whole and one melted it, it should also be pure,**[N] as it became liquid and spread throughout the pan. Consequently, each part should be considered separate, which means the food is not the size of an olive-bulk.

אֲמַר רַבִּי זֵירָא: אֲנָא וּמָר בְּרֵיהּ דְּרָבִינָא תַּרְגִּימְנָא: הָכָא בְּמַאי עָסְקִינַן – כְּגוֹן דְּבַהֲדֵי דְּמַרְתַּח לֵיהּ סָלֵיק עַמּוּדָא דְּנוּרָא לְפוּמֵּיהּ דְּמָנָא וְקָרַשׁ, דְּאִיתֵיהּ כּוּלָּא גַּבֵּי הֲדָדֵי.

Rabbi Zeira said: I and Mar, son of Ravina, explained it: **With what are we dealing here?** With a case **where as he was heating it, the column of fire rose** from under the pan **to the mouth of the vessel, and the fat congealed** there, **so that it was all** present **together,** i.e., there was no stream at all.

אֲמַר לֵיהּ רָבִינָא לְרַב אַשִׁי, תָּא שְׁמַע: בֵּית שַׁמַּאי אוֹמְרִים: אַף הַמִּקְפָּה שֶׁל גְּרִיסִין וְשֶׁל פּוֹל, מִפְּנֵי שֶׁהֵן סוֹלְדִין לַאֲחוֹרֵיהֶן. מִידֵּי אִירְיָא? הָתָם – מִשּׁוּם דִּסְמִיכִין, הָכָא – מִשּׁוּם רִירֵי.

Ravina said to Rav Ashi: Come and **hear** a resolution from the mishna to the question of whether food is considered a stream. **Beit Shammai say: Even** the stream of **a stew made of crushed and broken beans or of whole beans** also connects two items **because it returns backward.** This indicates that the dispute in the mishna is whether or not stew meets the criteria of returning backward, and the Rabbis hold that honey and anything like it, which return backward, are considered a stream. Rav Ashi replied: **Are the cases comparable? There,** in the case of honey, one might suggest it is a stream **because it is viscous.**[N] **Here,** with regard to the stew, the reason Beit Shammai rule stringently is **due to the flow,** which returns backward. The Rabbis do not agree that this is a factor at all.

HALAKHA

Is there not a stream for food – אֵין נִצּוֹק לָאוֹכָלִין: The stream of *zifim* honey and batter connects two items, as these have drippings that stretch out like glue. Consequently, a stream of food does not connect in this manner, even if it is viscous, e.g., beans or melted fat, because it is not held together with a flow of this kind. This ruling is in accordance with the unattributed opinion in the mishna (Rambam *Sefer Tahara, Hilkhot Tumat Okhalin* 7:4).

Fat of a corpse that was whole, etc. – חֵלֶב הַמֵּת שֶׁהוּא שָׁלֵם וכו׳: An olive-bulk of fat from a corpse that was melted down is ritually impure. If the fat separated into small pieces that were melted together, it is pure (Rambam *Sefer Tahara, Hilkhot Tumat Met* 4:6).

NOTES

Because they have a flow, and these do not have a flow, etc. – דְּאִית בְּהוּ רִירֵי וְהָנֵי לֵית בְּהוּ רִירֵי וכו׳: There are conflicting opinions as to whether this question is referring to the unattributed mishna, in which case this means that the *zifim* honey has a flow, or whether the difficulty refers to the opinion of Beit Shammai, and the reference is to the bean stew (see Commentary on *Nazir*). Either way, the issue is whether the stream is considered connected due to its flow or because it is a thick liquid.

If the fat was separated and one melted it – הָיָה מְפוֹרָד וְהִתִּיכוֹ: Since it was separated from the outset, its pieces, which were less than an olive-bulk, do not impart impurity. Admittedly, the parts that were joined together when they were melted in the fire now form a piece larger than an olive-bulk, but an artificial combination is not relevant for ritual impurity. See *Tosafot* for a comparison between this *halakha* and other cases of half-measures that combine with regard to ritual impurity.

If it was whole and one melted it, it should also be pure – שָׁלֵם וְהִתִּיכוֹ נַמִי לִיטְהַר: According to *Tosafot* and one explanation in the Commentary on *Nazir*, this is referring to one who melts the fat in a pan, in which case the liquid flows from one side of the vessel to the other, thereby becoming separated into pieces less than an olive-bulk in size, unless the pieces are considered to be combined by means of the stream. Alternatively, according to the Meiri and a second explanation in the Commentary on *Nazir*, after melting the fat, one poured it into a different vessel. If a stream is not considered connected, the act of pouring should cause its parts to detach from each other, and it should be considered pure, as the parts cannot be artificially combined at this point.

There it is because it is viscous – הָתָם מִשּׁוּם דִּסְמִיכִין: Two interpretations are cited by the Commentary on *Nazir*. According to the first interpretation, Ravina is saying that the dilemma of Rami bar Ḥama as to whether foods have a stream is referring to viscous fluids, whereas Beit Shammai are speaking of lentils that have a flow that returns backward. According to the second interpretation, Ravina is speaking of the unattributed opinion in the mishna, i.e., that honey as opposed to other foodstuffs contains a flow. Other commentaries maintain that Ravina thought that the main reason a stream connects is due to its flow, and that the dispute between Beit Shammai and the unattributed mishna concerns the relevant amount, whether a substantial flow is required, as with honey, or whether the lesser flow of bean stew suffices. The subsequent answer is that this case offers no proof at all, as the ruling of the unattributed mishna might be based on the viscous quality of honey, whereas Beit Shammai maintain that even something less viscous also connects by means of a stream, if it has a lesser flow (*Tosafot*).

״וְעַל מְלֹא תַּרְוָד רָקָב״. וְכַמָּה שִׁיעוּרוֹ? חִזְקִיָּה אָמַר: מְלֹא פִּיסַּת הַיָּד, רַבִּי יוֹחָנָן אָמַר: מְלֹא חׇפְנָיו. תְּנַן: מְלֹא תַּרְוָד רָקָב שֶׁאָמְרוּ יֶשְׁנָן מֵעִיקַּר אֶצְבָּעוֹת וּלְמַעְלָה, דִּבְרֵי רַבִּי מֵאִיר. וַחֲכָמִים אוֹמְרִים: מְלֹא חׇפְנָיו.

§ The mishna taught: **And for** impurity imparted by **a full ladle of dust.** The Gemara inquires: **And how much is** this **measure** of a full ladle of dust? **Ḥizkiyya said: A full palm of the hand. Rabbi Yoḥanan said: His handfuls,**[NHB] i.e., the amount that can be held in the whole hand, including the fingers. The Gemara cites a relevant source. **We learned** in the *Tosefta* (*Oholot* 2:2): **The full ladle of dust that** the Sages **spoke of includes** all that can be contained **from the base** of the **fingers and above;** this is **the statement of Rabbi Meir. And the Rabbis say: His handfuls.**

בִּשְׁלָמָא רַבִּי יוֹחָנָן – הוּא דַּאֲמַר כְּרַבָּנַן. אֶלָּא חִזְקִיָּה כְּמַאן? לָא כְּרַבִּי מֵאִיר וְלָא כְּרַבָּנַן! אָמְרִי: מְלֹא פִּיסַּת הַיָּד וּמְלֹא קִשְׁרֵי אֶצְבְּעוֹתָיו לְמַעְלָה – חַד שִׁיעוּרָא הוּא.

Granted, Rabbi Yoḥanan spoke in accordance with the opinion of **the Rabbis. But** in accordance **with whose** opinion **did Ḥizkiyya** state his opinion? His ruling is **neither in accordance with** the opinion of **Rabbi Meir nor in accordance with** that of **the Rabbis.** The Rabbis require his handfuls, Rabbi Meir refers only to the amount contained in the fingers themselves, while Ḥizkiyya rules that it is the amount that can rest on the palm of a hand. The Sages **say** in response that Ḥizkiyya's amount of **a full palm of** his **hand and** Rabbi Meir's measurement of **a full** amount of **his finger joints** from the palm of the hand **and above are one** and the same **measure.**

אֲמַר לֵיהּ רַב שִׁימִי בַּר אַדָּא לְרַב פַּפָּא: מִמַּאי דְּהַאי מִקִּשְׁרֵי אֶצְבְּעוֹתָיו וּלְמַעְלָה לְרֹאשׁ? דִּלְמָא לְמַטָּה מִדִּידֵיהּ, דַּהֲוָה לֵיהּ מְלֹא פִּיסַּת הַיָּד! תֵּיקוּ.

The Gemara raises a difficulty with regard to the basis of the question directed toward the opinion of Ḥizkiyya. **Rav Shimi bar Adda said to Rav Pappa: From where** do we know **that this** amount specified by Rabbi Meir: **From his finger joints and above,** means **toward the ends** of the fingers? **Perhaps** it is referring **to below it,** toward the arm, **in which** case **it is** exactly the same as Ḥizkiyya's amount: **A full palm of the hand.** If so, this *baraita* presents no difficulty to Ḥizkiyya at all. No answer was found, and the Gemara says that the question **shall stand** unresolved.

NOTES

His handfuls – מְלֹא חׇפְנָיו: Some commentaries maintain that this means the entire amount that can be held in one hand, including the palm and fingers (Commentary on *Nazir*). The Jerusalem Talmud apparently understands this term similarly. Others rule that it is referring to the amount that can be contained in two hands held together (Rambam).

HALAKHA

His handfuls – מְלֹא חׇפְנָיו: If the bones of a corpse have decayed into dust in the grave, a handful of that dust, which is the amount of a full ladle, imparts impurity through carrying and as a tent, and a nazirite must shave on its account. However, it does not impart impurity through touch. The *halakha* is in accordance with the opinion of Rabbi Yoḥanan with regard to the amount of a full ladle (Rambam *Sefer Tahara, Hilkhot Tumat Met* 2:11 and *Sefer Hafla'a, Hilkhot Nezirut* 7:2, 5).

BACKGROUND

His handfuls [*melo ḥofnav*] – מְלֹא חׇפְנָיו: The expression *melo ḥofnav*, the amount that fits into two hands when cupped together, is mentioned in the Torah in reference to the burning of the incense in the Holy of Holies on Yom Kippur (Leviticus 16:12). No precise measurement is stated. Rather, this is the amount that fits into the hands of the High Priest serving on that day. Other measurements are based on parts of the body, e.g., a fingerbreadth and a handbreadth. They were used frequently and became standardized according to the size of an average hand. By contrast, the handfuls mentioned here are a measurement that was not standardized with any precision. In any event, the amount that fits into the cupped hands of an average-sized individual is twice the amount that fits into one open hand.

Perek **VII**
Daf **51** Amud **a**

תָּנוּ רַבָּנַן: אֵיזֶהוּ מֵת שֶׁיֵּשׁ לוֹ רָקָב – מֵת שֶׁנִּקְבַּר עָרוֹם בַּאֲרוֹן שֶׁל שַׁיִשׁ, אוֹ עַל גַּבֵּי רִצְפָּה שֶׁל אֲבָנִים, זֶהוּ מֵת שֶׁיֵּשׁ לוֹ רָקָב. נִקְבַּר בִּכְסוּתוֹ, בַּאֲרוֹן שֶׁל עֵץ, אוֹ עַל גַּבֵּי רִצְפָּה שֶׁל לְבֵינִים – זֶהוּ מֵת שֶׁאֵין לוֹ רָקָב.

§ The mishna taught that one of the sources of ritual impurity for which a nazirite must shave is a full ladle of dust from a corpse. **The Sages taught** (*Tosefta, Oholot* 2:3): **Which is a corpse that has** the *halakha* of **dust,**[H] i.e., whose dust imparts impurity? **A corpse that was buried naked in a marble coffin or on a stone floor; this is a corpse that has** the *halakha* of **dust** that imparts impurity. Any dust found there must have come from the corpse. However, if it was **buried in its cloak, or in a wooden coffin, or on a brick floor, this is a corpse that does not have** the *halakha* of **dust** that imparts impurity. In the latter cases it is assumed that the dust from the corpse includes particles from the clothes, wood, or bricks that disintegrated, and there is a tradition that the impurity of dust applies only to dust that comes solely from the corpse, not to a mixture from different sources.

אָמַר עוּלָּא: אֵין רָקָב אֶלָּא הַבָּא מִן הַבָּשָׂר וּמִן הַגִּידִים וּמִן הָעֲצָמוֹת. אֵיתִיבֵיהּ רָבָא לְעוּלָּא: רָקָב הַבָּא מִן הַבָּשָׂר – טָהוֹר. הָא מִן הָעֶצֶם – טָמֵא, וְאַף עַל גַּב דְּלֵיכָּא בָּשָׂר! אֵימָא הָכִי: רָקָב הַבָּא מִן הַבָּשָׂר – טָהוֹר, עַד שֶׁיֵּשׁ עֶצֶם בַּבָּשָׂר.

With regard to the same issue, **Ulla said: Dust is only that which comes from the flesh and from the sinews and from the bones** of the corpse together, but not if it came from one of these alone. **Rava raised an objection to Ulla** from the following *baraita*: **Dust that comes from the flesh is pure.** It can be inferred from here that if it comes **from the bone it is impure, even though there is no** dust of **flesh** mixed with it. Ulla replied: You **should say** and infer **like this: Dust that comes from the flesh is pure, unless there is bone in the flesh.**

HALAKHA

A corpse that has dust – מֵת שֶׁיֵּשׁ לוֹ רָקָב: The dust of a corpse imparts impurity only if the deceased was buried without clothes in a marble or glass coffin, or one of similar material, and the corpse was not lacking a limb. However, if the corpse was buried in a robe or in a wooden or metal coffin, or if was lacking a limb, its dust does not impart impurity (Rambam *Sefer Hafla'a, Hilkhot Nezirut* 7:3 and *Sefer Tahara, Hilkhot Tumat Met* 3:4).

הָא לֵיכָּא גִּידִים! אִי אֶפְשָׁר לְבָשָׂר וְלַעֲצָמוֹת בְּלֹא גִּידִים.

Rava continued to question Ulla's opinion: Even if one interprets the *baraita* in this manner, **there is no** mention of **sinews** here at all, and Ulla maintains that sinews must also contribute to the makeup of part of the dust. Ulla replied that there is no need to mention sinews explicitly, as **it is impossible for** there to be **flesh and bones without sinews.**[B] Once it is established that the dust is from bones and flesh, it necessarily includes sinews as well.

אָמַר רַב שְׁמוּאֵל בַּר אַבָּא אָמַר רַבִּי יוֹחָנָן: שְׁנֵי מֵתִים שֶׁקְּבָרָן זֶה עִם זֶה – נַעֲשׂוּ גַּלְגַּלִּין זֶה לָזֶה. מְתִיב רַב נָתָן: רָקָב הַבָּא מִשְּׁנֵי מֵתִים טָמֵא!

§ The Gemara continues to discuss the dust of a corpse. **Rav Shmuel bar Abba said** that **Rabbi Yoḥanan said: Two corpses**[H] **that were buried with one another become a mixture** [*galgallin*][NL] **with one another.** Their dust is considered mixed together and does not impart the impurity of the dust from a single corpse. **Rav Natan raises an objection** to this opinion: But it is taught that **dust that comes from two corpses**[H] **is impure.**

אָמַר רָבָא: שֶׁקְּבָרוּ זֶה בִּפְנֵי עַצְמוֹ וְזֶה בִּפְנֵי עַצְמוֹ, וְהִרְקִיבוּ וְעָמְדוּ עַל מְלֹא תַּרְוָוד רָקָב.

Rava said: That *baraita* is referring to a case **where they buried this** corpse **by itself and that** corpse **by itself, and they decayed** separately, **and they** both **stood at,** i.e., yielded the amount of, a **full ladle of dust.** In this situation, the dust imparts impurity despite the fact that it is not from a single corpse, as the status of dust from a corpse initially applied to each corpse. However, if the corpses decayed together they are considered to be mixed together, which means that their dust does not impart impurity.

אָמַר רַבָּה בַּר בַּר חָנָה אָמַר רַבִּי יוֹחָנָן: גָּזַז שְׂעָרוֹ וּקְבָרוֹ עִמּוֹ – נַעֲשָׂה לוֹ גַּלְגַּלִּין. תְּנַן הָתָם: כָּל שֶׁבַּמֵּת – טָמֵא, חוּץ מִן הַשִּׁינַּיִם וְהַשֵּׂעָר וְהַצִּפּוֹרֶן, וּבִשְׁעַת חִיבּוּרָן כּוּלָּן טְמֵאִין.

The Gemara cites a further statement with regard to dust of a corpse. **Rabba bar bar Ḥana said** that **Rabbi Yoḥanan said:** If one **cut the hair** of a corpse[H] **and buried** the hair **with it,** the hair **becomes** part of the **mixture for** the dust, and it does not impart impurity. In relation to the above, the Gemara states: **We learned** in a mishna **there** (*Oholot* 3:3): **Everything that is in a corpse is impure,**[H] **except for the teeth, the hair, and the nails,** which do not impart impurity as part of the body. **But when they are attached** to the corpse, **they are all impure.**

בָּעֵי חִזְקִיָּה: שְׂעָרוֹ הָעוֹמֵד לְגַלֵּחַ, צִפּוֹרֶן הָעוֹמֵד לִיגָּזֵז, מַאי? מִי אָמְרִינַן: כָּל הָעוֹמֵד לִיגָּזֵז כְּגָזוּז דָּמֵי, אוֹ דִּלְמָא הַשְׁתָּא מִיהָא הָא מְחוּבָּרִין?

With regard to this *halakha*, **Ḥizkiyya raised a dilemma:** If **hair** of a corpse **is ready to be shaved,**[N] or its **nail is ready to be cut, what is** the *halakha*? **Do we say** that **anything that is ready to be cut is considered cut,** and therefore these are considered detached from the body and do not impart impurity? **Or, perhaps now, in any event, they are attached,** and therefore they should impart impurity?

וְנִיפְשׁוֹט לֵיהּ מִדְּרַבָּה בַּר בַּר חָנָה; טַעְמָא – מִשּׁוּם דְּגָזַז, הָא לָא גָּזַז – לָא! הָכִי קָאָמַר: גָּזַז – הֲרֵי זֶה גַּלְגַּלִּים, לָא גָּזַז – מִיבָּעֲיָא לֵיהּ.

The Gemara asks: **And let** Ḥizkiyya **resolve** this dilemma **from** the aforementioned statement of **Rabba bar bar Ḥana,** that hair buried with a corpse forms a mixture with the corpse. The inference is as follows: **The reason** that it forms a mixture is **because he cut** the hair, from which it may be inferred if he did **not cut** the hair it would **not** form a mixture, even if it was ready to be cut. The Gemara rejects this argument: One can respond that **this is what** Rabba bar bar Ḥana **is saying:** If he **cut** it, it definitely forms a **mixture;** if he did **not cut** it, Rabba bar bar Ḥana is unsure as to the *halakha* and **he raises** this case **as a dilemma.**[H]

BACKGROUND

It is impossible for there to be flesh and bones without sinews [*gidim*] – אִי אֶפְשָׁר לְבָשָׂר וְלַעֲצָמוֹת בְּלֹא גִּידִים: The word *gidim* is used by the Sages as a general term for all tube-shaped tissues that connect or serve as channels between different parts of the body. Larger parts of various systems that serve very different functions in the body, e.g., veins and arteries in the pulmonary system, visible nerves such as the sciatic nerve in the nervous system, and tissues connecting the bones, are all included in the category of *gidim*. For this reason, it is inconceivable that a bone that is covered with some flesh would not contain at least part of one of these systems. It would often contain a significant amount of them, which is why the Sages said that it is impossible for there to be flesh and bones without sinews.

HALAKHA

Two corpses, etc. – שְׁנֵי מֵתִים וכו׳: The dust of two corpses buried together does not impart impurity, in accordance with the opinion of Rabbi Yoḥanan (Rambam *Sefer Hafla'a, Hilkhot Nezirut* 7:4 and *Sefer Tahara, Hilkhot Tumat Met* 3:5).

Dust that comes from two corpses – רָקָב הַבָּא מִשְּׁנֵי מֵתִים: A double handful of dust from two corpses combine, if the *halakha* of the dust of a corpse applies to both corpses (Rambam *Sefer Tahara, Hilkhot Tumat Met* 4:3).

If one cut the hair of a corpse, etc. – גָּזַז שְׂעָרוֹ וכו׳: If the hair or nails of a corpse is cut and buried with the body, its dust does not impart impurity (Rambam *Sefer Tahara, Hilkhot Tumat Met* 3:5 and *Sefer Hafla'a, Hilkhot Nezirut* 7:4).

Everything that is in a corpse is impure, etc. – כָּל שֶׁבַּמֵּת טָמֵא וכו׳: All parts of a corpse impart ritual impurity, apart from the teeth, hair, and nails, as they are replaced as one grows. This ruling applies only if they were detached from the corpse. However, they do impart impurity when joined to the body. For example, if, at the time of death, the corpse was outside a house but its hair trailed inside, the contents of the house are rendered impure with the impurity of a tent (Rambam *Sefer Tahara, Hilkhot Tumat Met* 3:13).

If he did not cut it, he raises this case as a dilemma – לָא גָּזַז מִיבָּעֲיָא לֵיהּ: It is uncertain whether or not hair of a corpse ready to be cut, and nails ready for removal, are considered part of the body. Consequently, it is uncertain whether one who touches them is impure, as Ḥizkiyya's dilemma remains unresolved (Rambam *Sefer Tahara, Hilkhot Tumat Met* 3:13).

NOTES

Mixture [*galgallin*] – גַּלְגַּלִּין: It is clear from the context that *galgallin* nullifies the *halakha* of the dust of a corpse. However, the early commentaries dispute the meaning and significance of this term. Some explain that *galgallin* means something that rolls [*mitgalgel*], i.e., a foreign substance mingled with the dead matter (Commentary on *Nazir*). Others claim that it refers to a kind of shroud rolled around a corpse (*Arukh*). Yet others state that it means dust [*gal*] mixed with substances from the corpse. Alternatively, is related to *gilgul*, a cause; in other words, *galgallin* is a substance that causes the *halakha* of dust of a corpse to be negated (*Tosafot*, citing *Arukh*; Meiri; *Shita Mekubbetzet*).

Hair is ready to be shaved – שְׂעָרוֹ הָעוֹמֵד לְגַלֵּחַ: The commentaries are unsure as to the meaning of Ḥizkiyya's question. Is he asking about impurity itself, whether hair of this kind imparts impurity like that of a corpse, or is he is referring to the *halakha* of a mixture, i.e., if the hair is not considered part of the body, is the rest of the dust of the corpse pure, as it has another substance mixed with it (*Tosafot*)? The early commentaries dispute whether the discussion in the Gemara lends support to one or the other of these interpretations.

LANGUAGE

Mixture [*galgallin*] – גַּלְגַּלִּין: The commentaries are divided with regard to the correct version and the meaning of this term. Some accept the versions that appear in several manuscripts, of either *gangillin* or *ganginon*. The meaning and derivation of these words is not at all straightforward. It can be argued that they are derived from the Greek γαγγλίον, *ganglion*, which generally means either a small cystic or nerve growth. Others suggest that they come from γάγγραινα, *gangraina*, decayed or gangrenous flesh. Some say they are from the Greek γάγγαμον, *gangamon*, meaning both net and navel, while yet others suggest the Latin cingulum, a belt or sash.

בָּעֵי רַבִּי יִרְמְיָה: רְקַב הַבָּא מִן הֶעָקֵב, מַהוּ? כִּי גָּמְרִינַן – רְקַב הַבָּא מִכּוּלֵּיהּ מֵת, אֲבָל דְּאָתֵי מִן עָקֵב – לָא, אוֹ דִּלְמָא לָא שְׁנָא?

§ **Rabbi Yirmeya raised** another **dilemma** concerning the dust of a corpse: With regard to **dust that comes from the heel,**[BN] **what is** the *halakha*? The Gemara explains the two sides of the dilemma: Do we say that **when we learn** this *halakha* through tradition, is it only in reference to **dust that comes from all of a corpse, but** with regard to dust **that comes from** its **heel, no,** this *halakha* does not apply; **or perhaps** it **is no different?**

תָּא שְׁמַע, דְּתָנֵי רַבִּי נָתָן בְּרַבִּי אוֹשַׁעְיָא: רְקַב הַבָּא מִשְּׁנֵי מֵתִים – טָמֵא. וְאִי סָלְקָא דַּעְתָּךְ הַבָּא מִן הֶעָקֵב לָא, זִיל הָכָא – דִּלְמָא דֶּרֶךְ עָקֵב קָאָתֵי, וְהָכָא – דִּלְמָא דֶּרֶךְ עָקֵב קָאָתֵי!

The Gemara suggests a resolution of this dilemma: **Come** and **hear, as Rabbi Natan, son of Rabbi Oshaya, taught: Dust that comes from two corpses** is **impure. And if it enters your mind** that dust **that comes from the heel** does **not** impart impurity, **go here** and consider that **perhaps** the dust **came from the heel,**[N] **and** go **here** too and consider that **perhaps** it **came from the heel.** The fact that the dust is considered definitely impure shows that dust from the heel imparts impurity as well.

אִי דְּאִירְקִיב כּוּלֵּיהּ מֵת וְקָאָתֵי דֶּרֶךְ עָקֵב – הָכִי נַמִי. אֶלָּא הָכָא כְּגוֹן דְּאִירְקִיב חַד אֵבֶר, וְקָאָתֵי דֶּרֶךְ עָקֵב, מַאי? תֵּיקוּ.

The Gemara rejects this argument: **If the entire corpse decayed and** the dust **came from the heel, so too,** it is all impure, as the dust of the heel is not considered to be a foreign substance. **Rather, here** Rabbi Natan is referring to a case **where one limb decayed**[N] **and** the dust **came from** the **heel.** It was with regard to this situation that Rabbi Yirmeya asked: **What** is its *halakha*? Does this dust impart impurity or not? No answer was found, and therefore the Gemara states that the dilemma **shall stand** unresolved.

בָּעֵי רַבִּי יִרְמְיָה: עוּבָּר בִּמְעֵי אִשָּׁה הָוֵי גַּלְגַּלִּים אוֹ לָא? כֵּיוָן דְּאָמַר מָר עוּבָּר יֶרֶךְ אִמּוֹ – הִלְכָּךְ גּוּפָהּ הוּא, וְלָא הָוֵי גַּלְגַּלִּין. אוֹ דִּלְמָא כֵּיוָן דְּסוֹפוֹ לָצֵאת – מִיפְרַשׁ פָּרֵישׁ מִינָּהּ. וְאִם תִּמְצֵי לוֹמַר עוּבָּר דְּסוֹפוֹ לָצֵאת מִיפְרַשׁ פָּרֵישׁ מִינָּהּ,

§ **Rabbi Yirmeya raised** yet another **dilemma: Does** a dead **fetus in its** dead **mother's womb form a mixture** with regard to her, so that the bodies are considered like two corpses buried together, **or not?** The Gemara explains the two sides of the dilemma: Do we say that **since the Master said** that **a fetus is** considered as **the thigh of its mother, it is therefore** like **her body and it** does **not form a mixture** with it? **Or perhaps** one should maintain: **Since** in most cases a fetus **will ultimately emerge**[H] from the womb at birth, it is already considered **separated from her,** and it is like any other corpse buried with the woman. **And if you say** that **a fetus, which will ultimately emerge,** is considered **separated from her** and is not part of her body, one must still ask this question

BACKGROUND

Dust that comes from the heel – רְקַב הַבָּא מִן הֶעָקֵב: Flesh from the heel and the skin that covers it are different in many ways from other tissues in the body. The quality of the blood vessels and nerves in heels renders them less vulnerable to pain and wounds. This has led some contemporary medical experts to assert that these tissues are fundamentally different from others in the body and have their own form of development. Since they consider the heel a kind of dead zone in their classification of the parts of the body, the Sages ask whether or not the *halakhot* that apply to flesh from other parts of a corpse should apply to the heel as well.

HALAKHA

A fetus will ultimately emerge – עוּבָּר דְּסוֹפוֹ לָצֵאת: If a pregnant woman died and was buried with the fetus in her womb, the dust from both of them does not impart impurity. The Rambam follows his usual principle that the *halakha* is in accordance with the option that forms the basis of the Gemara's ensuing dilemma that opens with: And if you say (Rambam *Sefer Tahara, Hilkhot Tumat Met* 3:5, and *Kesef Mishne* there, and *Sefer Hafla'a, Hilkhot Nezirut* 7:4).

NOTES

Dust that comes from the heel – רְקַב הַבָּא מִן הֶעָקֵב: Many commentaries find this entire discussion problematic, to the extent that the Rid concedes that he does not comprehend the passage and is unable to explain it. There are two broad explanations here. Most early commentaries understand the word heel literally and the heel is singled out because its flesh is callous and dulled even during a person's lifetime (*Tosafot*; Rosh; Rabbeinu Peretz). Consequently, one might think that it should not be considered part of the impure dust of a corpse. Others, based on a different version of the text, maintain that the reference is not to a heel in particular, but to any part of the body that is not vital for existence (Meiri). According to this opinion, the question is referring to a case where that part of the body is removed and buried on its own. The comments in the Jerusalem Talmud indicate that the discussion is understood in a similar manner there, although that Gemara is also problematic (see Meiri). A similar interpretation is that the term heel refers to the lower part of the body, which might not impart impurity as dust because it is not the central part of the corpse (Commentary on *Nazir*). All these explanations have their difficulties, both with regard to the arguments themselves and in terms of how their claims fit in with the text of the Gemara.

From the heel – דֶּרֶךְ עָקֵב: Some commentaries maintain that the phrase from the heel simply means that the dust contains part of the heel (*Tosafot*). According to this opinion, if dust from the heel does not impart impurity, the combined dust of the two corpses would amount to less than the required amount of a full ladle of dust. Other commentaries explain that: From the heel, means that it is possible that the dust from the two corpses is merely from the heel (Commentary on *Nazir*), or that it is considered a mixture with the dust from the rest of the body (Meiri).

Where one limb decayed, etc. – דְּאִירְקִיב חַד אֵבֶר וכו׳: Some commentaries explain that this is referring to a case where the foot decayed, and it is assumed that the heel rotted before the rest of the body did, as a heel decomposes quickly. The *halakha* of dust that imparts impurity does not apply to decomposition of this kind (*Tosafot*). Others maintain, in accordance with their interpretations of the entire passage, that the Gemara is speaking only of the heel, which decayed by itself (Commentary on *Nazir*; Meiri).

שִׁכְבַת זֶרַע בִּמְעֵי אִשָּׁה מַהוּ? מִי אָמְרִינַן: כֵּיוָן דְּלָא אִיתְצַר – כִּי גּוּפָהּ דָּמֵי, אוֹ דִלְמָא כֵּיוָן דְּמֵעָלְמָא קָאָתֵי – לָא?

with regard to **semen in** a dead **woman's womb. What is** the *halakha* in this case? Does it form a mixture with respect to the woman's body? The Gemara explains the two sides of this dilemma: **Do we say** that **since no** fetus **was formed** from the semen, it is **considered like her body? Or, perhaps** one should argue that **since it comes from outside,** it is **not** considered part of her body.

בָּעֵי רַב פָּפָּא: פִּירְשָׁהּ מַהוּ? כֵּיוָן דְּלָא מִקַּיְּימָא בְּדְלָא אָכְלָה – חִיּוּתָא הוּא, אוֹ דִלְמָא הָא נָמֵי מֵעָלְמָא אָתֵי? בָּעֵי רַב אַחָא בְּרֵיהּ דְּרַב אִיקָא: עוֹרוֹ מַהוּ? בָּעֵי רַב הוּנָא בַּר מָנוֹחַ: כִּיחוֹ וְנִיעוֹ מַהוּ?

Rav Pappa raised a similar **dilemma:** With regard to **her excrement,**[H] the food waste that remains in a woman's intestines, **what is** the *halakha*? Once again, the Gemara explains the two sides of this dilemma: Do we say that **since she cannot subsist without food it is** considered **her life,** which means that the food left inside her body is part of her and does not form a mixture with the corpse? **Or perhaps this too comes from outside** and is therefore not part of her body, and does form a mixture with her corpse. Similarly, **Rav Aḥa, son of Rav Ika, raised a dilemma** concerning a corpse: With regard to **its skin,**[N] **what is** the *halakha*? **Rav Huna bar Manoaḥ** likewise **raised a dilemma:** With regard to **its phlegm and its spittle, what is** the *halakha*?

אֲמַר לֵיהּ רַב שְׁמוּאֵל בַּר אַחָא לְרַב פָּפָּא: וְאִי סָלְקָא דַּעְתָּךְ כׇּל הָנֵי דְּקָאָמַר הָוֵי גִּלְגְּלִין, רָקָב דְּמְטַמֵּא הֵיכִי מַשְׁכַּחַתְּ לַהּ? דְּאַשְׁקְיֵיהּ מֵי דְקָלִים, וְסַכְיֵיהּ נַשָּׁא, וּשְׁלָקוֹ בְּמֵי טְבֶרְיָא.

Rav Shmuel bar Aḥa said to Rav Pappa: But if it enters your mind that **all these** cases of **which they spoke** form **a mixture,** under **what circumstances do you find** this case of **dust** that **imparts impurity?** Dust from a corpse will always include some components of the aforementioned elements. The Gemara answers: It is possible. For example, **if** someone **was given palm water** [*mei deka'im*],[L] a powerful laxative, **to drink**[N] before he died, **and was rubbed with a depilatory** agent to remove his hair, **and was boiled** after death **in the** hot **waters of Tiberias**[NB] until the skin came off, this would remove all matter that is not part of the corpse itself.

אָמַר אַבַּיֵי: נְקִיטִינַן, מֵת שֶׁטְּחָנוֹ – אֵין לוֹ רָקָב. אִיבַּעְיָא לְהוּ: טְחָנוֹ וְחָזַר וְהִרְקִיב, מַהוּ? מִידֵּי הוּא טַעְמָא אֶלָּא דְּאִיכָּא בָּשָׂר וְגִידִים וַעֲצָמוֹת – וְהָאִיכָּא, אוֹ דִלְמָא כִּבְרִיָּיתוֹ בָּעֵינַן, וְלֵיכָּא? תֵּיקוּ.

Abaye said: We have a tradition that **a corpse that was ground**[H] into small pieces **has no** *halakha* **of dust. A dilemma was raised before** the Sages: If a corpse **was ground** after death **and** the remains **later decayed,**[H] **what is** the *halakha*? The Gemara clarifies the two sides of the dilemma: **Is the** *halakha* of dust of a corpse **only** due to the fact that **there is flesh and sinews and bones, and** all these **are present** in this case, so it is impure? **Or perhaps, we require** the corpse to have decayed from **its initial state,** before it was ground, **and** this is **not** the situation here. As was the case with regard to the previous inquiries, no answer was found, and the Gemara says that the dilemma **shall stand** unresolved.

HALAKHA

Semen…excrement, etc. – שִׁכְבַת זֶרַע...פִּירְשָׁהּ וכו׳: The Rambam omits these cases in his rulings of *halakhot*. The later authorities claim that the answer to Rav Shmuel bar Aḥa's difficulty is a mere refutation, and that all these combinations are in fact considered a mixture (Rambam *Sefer Hafla'a, Hilkhot Nezirut* 7:4, and *Leḥem Mishna* there; *Arukh HaShulḥan HeAtid, Hilkhot Tumat Met* 8:19).

A corpse that was ground – מֵת שֶׁטְּחָנוֹ: A corpse that was ground into dust does not impart ritual impurity, as it did not become dust of its own accord (Rambam *Sefer Hafla'a, Hilkhot Nezirut* 7:4 and *Sefer Tahara, Hilkhot Tumat Met* 3:6).

If a corpse was ground and it later decayed – טְחָנוֹ וְחָזַר וְהִרְקִיב: If someone ground a corpse and left it until it fully decayed, it is uncertain whether its dust imparts impurity. Consequently, it is uncertain whether one who comes into contact with its dust is impure, as this question was not resolved by the Gemara (Rambam *Sefer Hafla'a, Hilkhot Nezirut* 7:4 and *Sefer Tahara, Hilkhot Tumat Met* 3:7).

LANGUAGE

Palm water [*mei dekalim*] – מֵי דְקָלִים: Based on the context of the Gemara, this apparently is referring to water from the spring at Har HaBarzel, northeast of the Sea of Galilee. This was possibly one of the springs in the area that was used for medicinal purposes. The water of these springs contains many minerals. The high sulfur content in these waters transforms the stomach fluids into a hydrogen sulfide solution, H_2S, which has a purgative effect. Palm water became famous for this quality.

BACKGROUND

Waters of Tiberias – מֵי טְבֶרְיָא: This refers to the hot springs near the city of Tiberias, which can reach temperatures of 60° Celsius and even higher.

Hot springs of Tiberias

NOTES

Its skin [*oro*] – עוֹרוֹ: The notion that a corpse's skin should not be considered part of the body is puzzling, especially in light of the *halakha* that the skin of a corpse imparts ritual impurity. The commentaries disprove the suggestion that the Gemara is referring to skin stripped from a corpse and buried with it (Rabbeinu Peretz). The early commentaries explain that the dilemma concerning the skin is applicable according to the opinion that the impurity of the skin of a corpse applies by rabbinic law. Since, according to this opinion, skin is not considered part of the body by Torah law, it is possible that it might be classified as forming a mixture with the corpse (Rabbeinu Peretz). Some suggest that the word *oro* in this context does not mean its skin. Rather, it is related to the word *me'arer*, meaning to pour, and is referring to saliva found in the mouth, which is not released by coughing like phlegm or through force of effort like spittle but flows out on its own (Commentary on *Nazir*).

Was given palm water to drink – דְּאַשְׁקְיֵיהּ מֵי דְקָלִים: This water is a strong laxative that releases all excrement from the bowels (Commentary on *Nazir*). Others add that it also serves to drain out any moisture, e.g., phlegm or spittle (*Tosafot*).

Boiled in the waters of Tiberias – שְׁלָקוֹ בְּמֵי טְבֶרְיָא: The point of this procedure is to remove the skin and phlegm (Commentary on *Nazir*). The commentaries explain that boiling and removing the skin are insufficient, as the roots of the hair remain attached at the subcutaneous level of the skin. It is therefore necessary to rub a depilatory agent on it afterward to eradicate the roots of the hair as well (*Tosafot*; Meiri). Alternatively, if the head is boiled in hot springs, part of the soft flesh might fall apart as well, which would render the corpse deficient. Consequently, the rest of the body must be boiled, while the head is rubbed with a depilatory agent (see Meiri). Others contend that the Gemara is not referring to successive actions on a single corpse. Rather, each action in this list, i.e., applying palm water, boiling, and rubbing a depilatory agent, is a separate response to the various dilemmas raised by *amora'im* above.

תָּנֵי עוּלָּא בַּר חֲנִינָא: מֵת שֶׁחָסֵר – אֵין לוֹ רָקָב, וְלֹא תְּפוּסָה, וְלֹא שְׁכוּנַת קְבָרוֹת.

§ **Ulla bar Ḥanina teaches: A corpse that lacks** a part[H] **does not have** the *halakha* of **dust,** which imparts ritual impurity in the amount of a full ladle, **nor** the *halakha* of earth that is **caught** [*tefusa*] and considered part of a corpse. If a deficient corpse is moved, the surrounding earth is not considered part of it and need not be moved together with the body, as must be performed for a whole corpse. **Nor** does the *halakha* of **a graveyard**[HN] apply. If three corpses are discovered in close proximity and one of them is deficient in some way, one need not search for more bodies out of concern that the location might have been a cemetery, as must be done if three intact corpses are found. Rather, the bodies are considered isolated corpses.

מֵיתִיבֵי: לֹא, אִם אָמַרְתָּ בַּמֵּת שֶׁיֵּשׁ לוֹ רוֹב וְרוֹבַע, אוֹ מְלֹא תַּרְוָוד רָקָב, תֹּאמַר בַּחַי שֶׁאֵין לוֹ לֹא רוֹב וְלֹא רוֹבַע, וְלֹא מְלֹא תַּרְוָוד רָקָב.

The Gemara **raises an objection** from a mishna (*Eduyyot* 6:3) that addresses the question of whether an olive-bulk of flesh that came from a living person imparts ritual impurity as it would were it to come from a corpse: **No, if you say** that an olive-bulk of flesh imparts impurity **with regard to a corpse, whose** *halakhot* of impurity are stringent, as **the majority** of its structure or the majority of the number of its bones, **or a quarter-***kav* of its bones, **or** even **a full ladle of** its **dust** impart impurity, **shall you** also **say** that it imparts impurity **with regard to a living** person, **who does not have** the *halakha* of **the majority** of structure or the majority of the number of its bones, **nor a quarter-***kav*, **nor a full ladle of dust?**

הֵיכִי דָּמֵי? דְּאִרְקִיב חַד אֵבֶר – דִּכְוָותֵיהּ גַּבֵּי מֵת אֲפִילּוּ חַד אֵבֶר אִיכָּא רָקָב! מִי קָתָנֵי הָא מֵת? הָא קָא מַשְׁמַע לָן: שׁוּם מֵת יֵשׁ לוֹ רָקָב, שׁוּם חַי אֵין לוֹ רָקָב.

The Gemara analyzes this passage: **What are the circumstances** of that mishna that deals with a limb from a living person? If you say **that one limb** of a living person **decayed,** and the mishna is indicating **that in the corresponding** situation **with regard to a corpse, there is dust even** from **one limb.** This shows that the *halakha* of dust applies to a corpse that is missing a limb and not just to a complete corpse. The Gemara rejects this argument: **Did** the mishna **teach that this corpse** in that particular case of an isolated limb has the *halakha* of dust? That is merely an inference, as it is not stated explicitly in the mishna itself. Rather, the mishna **teaches us this: The name,** i.e., the category, **of a corpse has dust.** However, **the name of a living** person **does not have dust.**

בָּעֵי רָבָא: הִרְקִיב כְּשֶׁהוּא חַי, וְחָזַר וּמֵת, מַהוּ? כִּי גְּמִירִי רָקָב – דְּאִירְקִיב כְּשֶׁהוּא מֵת, אוֹ דִּלְמָא הָשְׁתָּא מִיהָא הָא מָיֵית?

Rava raised a dilemma: If a limb of a body **decayed when he was alive,**[H] and that individual **subsequently died, what is** the *halakha*? Do we say that **when this is learned** as a tradition that **dust** imparts ritual impurity, this applies only **if** the body **decayed when he was dead,** but not when he was alive, and therefore this corpse is considered deficient and its dust does not impart impurity? **Or perhaps, now in any event he is dead,** and his whole body has decomposed, and consequently its dust does impart impurity.

תָּא שְׁמַע: לֹא, אִם אָמַרְתָּ בַּמֵּת שֶׁיֵּשׁ לוֹ רוֹב וְרוֹבַע וּמְלֹא תַּרְוָוד רָקָב, תֹּאמַר בַּחַי כו׳.

The Gemara suggests: **Come and hear** the aforementioned mishna: **No, if you say** that an olive-bulk of flesh imparts impurity **with regard to a corpse, whose** *halakhot* of impurity are stringent, as **the majority** of its structure or the majority of the number of its bones, **or a quarter-***kav* of its bones, **or** even **a full ladle of** its **dust** imparts impurity, **shall you** also **say** that this it imparts impurity **with regard to a living** person, who does not have the *halakha* of the majority of structure or the majority of the number of its bones, nor a quarter-*kav*, nor a full ladle of dust.

טַעֲמָא – מִשּׁוּם חַי, הָא מֵת – יֵשׁ לוֹ רָקָב! מִי קָתָנֵי הָא מֵת? הָא קָא מַשְׁמַע לָן: דְּשׁוּם מֵת יֵשׁ לוֹ רָקָב, שׁוּם חַי אֵין לוֹ רָקָב.

The Gemara infers from this passage: **The reason** the olive-bulk of flesh does not impart impurity **is due to** the fact that it is from a **living** person, from which it may be inferred that in a corresponding situation involving **a corpse,** the corpse **has** the *halakha* of **dust,** even if the limb had decomposed during the deceased's lifetime. The Gemara rejects this contention as above: **Did** the mishna **teach that this corpse** in that particular case of an isolated limb has the *halakha* of dust? That is merely an inference, as it is not stated explicitly in the mishna itself. Rather, the mishna **teaches us this: The name,** i.e., the category, **of a corpse has dust.** However, **the name of a living** person **does not have dust.**

HALAKHA

A corpse that lacks a part, etc. – מֵת שֶׁחָסֵר וכו׳: The dust of a corpse that is missing a limb does not impart ritual impurity (Rambam *Sefer Hafla'a, Hilkhot Nezirut* 7:3 and *Sefer Tahara, Hilkhot Tumat Met* 3:4).

Nor the *halakha* of earth that is caught, nor a graveyard – וְלֹא תְּפוּסָה וְלֹא שְׁכוּנַת קְבָרוֹת: If a dead person is missing a limb that would have caused his death had it been removed when he was alive, the *halakhot* of caught earth and a graveyard do not apply to this corpse (Rambam *Sefer Tahara, Hilkhot Tumat Met* 9:5).

Decayed when he was alive, etc. – הִרְקִיב כְּשֶׁהוּא חַי וכו׳: If part of a dead person rotted during his lifetime, it is uncertain whether one who comes into contact with the rest of his dust after his death is impure, as this dilemma was not resolved in the Gemara (Rambam *Sefer Hafla'a, Hilkhot Nezirut* 7:4 and *Sefer Tahara, Hilkhot Tumat Met* 3:7).

NOTES

Nor the *halakha* of a graveyard – וְלֹא שְׁכוּנַת קְבָרוֹת: The commentaries point out that this case is apparently not related to the *halakhot* of ritual impurity. Rather, the issue is factual: Does the discovery of three corpses indicate the presence of an ancient cemetery on the site? If so, what difference does it make if one of the bodies is missing a limb (*Tosafot*)? They suggest that perhaps it is a *halakha* transmitted to Moses from Sinai that this *halakha* of a cemetery applies only to intact corpses (see Rosh). Others propose a logical explanation: If one of the corpses is incomplete, this might indicate that a fight occurred, and the victims were buried at the site. If so, one need not be concerned that more bodies might be found there, as there is no reason to suppose that the area was ever used as a cemetery (Meiri).

בָּעֵי רָבָא: נְמָלָה שֶׁחָסְרָה מַהוּ? שִׁיעוּרָא גְּמִירִין לָהּ – וְהָא חָסֵר, אוֹ בְּרִיָּה גְּמִירִי לָהּ, וְהָאִיכָּא?

§ In relation to the above discussion concerning a body without a limb, **Rava raised a dilemma:** If someone eats an entire ant, even if it is less than an olive-bulk in volume, he is liable for eating a creeping animal because it is a whole creature. Rava's dilemma was as follows: If one eats **an ant that lacks** a part, e.g., a leg, **what is** the *halakha*? Is this individual liable to receive lashes? The two possibilities are as follows: **Is** it **learned** as tradition that **the amount** for which one is liable is a whole ant, **and this one is lacking? Or did we learn** that he is punished for a viable **entity, and there is** a viable entity here, despite the missing limb?

Perek **VII**
Daf **52** Amud **a**

אָמַר רַב יְהוּדָה מִדִּיסְקַרְתָּא, תָּא שְׁמַע: ״בָּהֶם״. יָכוֹל בְּכוּלָּן – תַּלְמוּד לוֹמַר ״מֵהֶם״. אִי ״מֵהֶם״ יָכוֹל מִקְצָתָן – תַּלְמוּד לוֹמַר ״בָּהֶם״.

Rav Yehuda from Diskarta said: Come and **hear** the following halakhic midrash concerning the ritual impurity of creeping animals. The verse states: "Whoever touches **them** when they are dead shall be impure" (Leviticus 11:31). One **might** have thought this *halakha* applies only **to all of them,** i.e., to complete creatures. Therefore, **the verse states:** "And upon whatever any **of them,** when they are dead, fall, it shall be impure" (Leviticus 11:32), which indicates that part of these creatures also imparts impurity. **If the** *halakha* were derived solely from the phrase **"of them,"** one **might** have thought that it applies even to **a small part** of them. **The verse** therefore **states: "Them,"** which means all of them.

הָא כֵּיצַד? עַד שֶׁיִּגַּע בְּמִקְצָתָן שֶׁהוּא כְּכוּלָּן, וְשִׁיעֲרוּ חֲכָמִים בְּכַעֲדָשָׁה, שֶׁכֵּן הַחוֹמֶט תְּחִלַּת בְּרִיָּיתוֹ בְּכַעֲדָשָׁה. שְׁמַע מִינָּהּ: שִׁיעוּרָא גְּמִירִי לָהּ.

How so? How can one reconcile the two verses? He does not become ritually impure **unless he touches** at least **part of them that is** equal in measure **to all of them,** i.e., a large part. **And the Sages calculated** that this is the volume **of a lentil-bulk.**[H] Why is this? **As the start of the formation of a skink,**[B] one of the eight impure creeping animals, is the size **of a lentil-bulk.** This concludes the halakhic midrash. With regard to the issue at hand, one can **learn from here** that it **is learned** as a tradition that **the amount**[N] for a creature to be considered whole is a lentil-bulk. If so, an ant missing a limb should likewise not have the status of a creature.

אָמַר רַב שְׁמַעְיָה: כִּי בָּעֵינַן שִׁיעוּרָא, דִּבְדְלָא הָוְיָא כַּעֲדָשָׁה לָא מְטַמֵּא – דְּלָא נָפְלָה בָּהּ נְשָׁמָה, אֲבָל נָפְלָה בָּהּ נְשָׁמָה – לָא. תִּיבָּעֵי לָךְ.

Rav Shemaya said, in refutation of this argument: **When we require** the above **amount, that if it is not** the volume of **a lentil-bulk it does not impart impurity,** the requirement applies only in a case **where** the creature **does not have** a living **soul** before it grows to the size of a lentil. **However,** if it **does have a soul,**[H] this volume is **not** required. If the creature can survive, perhaps it does impart impurity even if it is lacking a limb. Consequently, with regard to an ant that is missing a limb, **the dilemma remains** unresolved **for you.**

HALAKHA

And the Sages calculated that this is the volume of a lentil-bulk – וְשִׁיעֲרוּ חֲכָמִים בְּכַעֲדָשָׁה: The carcass of a creeping animal imparts ritual impurity if it has the volume a lentil-bulk. All creeping animals combine to form this amount (Rambam *Sefer Tahara, Hilkhot She'ar Avot HaTumot* 4:2).

Does have a soul, etc. – נָפְלָה בָּהּ נְשָׁמָה וכו׳: If someone eats a forbidden creature in its entirety, e.g., if he eats an ant, he is liable to receive lashes regardless of its size. However, if it is missing even a leg, he is liable only if he ate the amount of an olive-bulk. This is because the Gemara's dilemma is left unresolved, and the court does not administer lashes in a case of uncertainty (Rambam *Sefer Kedusha, Hilkhot Ma'akhalot Assurot* 2:22, and *Mishne LaMelekh* there).

BACKGROUND

Skink [*ḥomet*] – חוֹמֶט: The *ḥomet* is one of the eight creeping or swarming animals mentioned in the Torah (Leviticus 11:30). Precise identification of each of these creatures is by no means a simple matter. Throughout the generations, there were two traditions with regard to identification of the *ḥomet*. Some say it is one of the subspecies of snails that lack a shell. This interpretation is supported by the claim that it is as large as a lentil-bulk, which is the size of a small snail. Others identify the *ḥomet* as a species of reptile similar to the chameleon (Rav Se'adya Gaon). Nowadays the *ḥomet* is widely regarded as a species of skink. Dwelling primarily in the sand, narrow and thin skinned, some varieties of the skink have only two working limbs along with two atrophied limbs, while others have no limbs at all.

Legless skink

NOTES

Learn from here that it is learned as a tradition that the amount, etc. – שְׁמַע מִינָּהּ שִׁיעוּרָא גְּמִירִי וכו׳: Some commentaries explain that once it is derived from the verse that the size of a whole creature is required, it is evident that an animal that is missing a limb no longer imparts ritual impurity, and therefore it is not prohibited to consume it either (Commentary on *Nazir*). Others state that a skink in its entirety is the volume of a lentil-bulk, including its legs and other limbs. If part of it is removed, the creature no longer imparts impurity even if the skink can survive without this part, because the remainder is less than the minimum size. This shows that the amount of a whole creature is required (*Tosafot*). Others formulate the argument as follows: If an ant from which a limb has been removed is nevertheless considered a creature, a skink should impart impurity even if it is less than the volume of a lentil (Rosh; Rabbeinu Azriel).

״הַשִּׁדְרָה וְהַגּוּלְגּוֹלֶת״. אִיבַּעְיָא לְהוּ: שִׁדְרָה וְגוּלְגּוֹלֶת תְּנַן, אוֹ דִּלְמָא אוֹ שִׁדְרָה אוֹ גּוּלְגּוֹלֶת? אֲמַר רָבָא, תָּא שְׁמַע: שִׁדְרָה שֶׁגֵּירֵד רוֹב צִילְעִין שֶׁבָּהּ – טְהוֹרָה, וּבַקֶּבֶר אֲפִילּוּ מְשׁוּבֶּרֶת אוֹ מְפוֹרֶקֶת – טְמֵאָה, מִפְּנֵי הַקֶּבֶר.

§ The mishna taught that a nazirite must shave for impurity imparted by **a spine and skull. A dilemma was raised before** the Sages: Did **we learn a spine and** [*ve*] **skull** together? **Or perhaps** the mishna means **either a spine or a skull.** Does the conjunctive *vav* signify: And, or: Or? **Rava said: Come** and **hear** a resolution from a *baraita*: In the case of **a spine, the majority of whose ribs were removed**[H] while the spine itself remained intact, it is **ritually pure. And** if it was **in a grave, even** if it was **broken or disassembled, it is impure, due to the grave,** which joins all the bones together.

טַעְמָא – מִשּׁוּם דְּגֵירֵד, הָא לֹא גֵּירֵד – טְמֵאָה. שְׁמַע מִינָּהּ: אוֹ שִׁדְרָה אוֹ גּוּלְגּוֹלֶת קָתָנֵי. הָא לָא קָתָנֵי, הָא קָא מַשְׁמַע לָן דְּכִי גֵּירֵד – טְהוֹרָה, אִידָּךְ – תִּיבָּעֵי לָךְ.

The Gemara infers from this *baraita*: **The reason** it is ritually pure in the first case **is due to** the fact **that** the ribs **were removed,** from which it may be inferred that if they **were not removed,** it is **impure** on its own, even without the skull. **Learn from this** that the mishna **teaches: Either a spine or a skull.** The Gemara rejects this claim: The *baraita* **does not teach this** explicitly. It does not state that if the ribs were not removed the spine imparts ritual impurity by itself. Rather, the *baraita* **teaches us this, that if** the ribs were **removed** the spine is **pure.** And as to **the other** issue, the impurity of a spine on its own, **the dilemma remains** unresolved **for you.**

תָּא שְׁמַע: רַבִּי יְהוּדָה אוֹמֵר: שִׁשָּׁה דְּבָרִים רַבִּי עֲקִיבָא מְטַמֵּא וַחֲכָמִים מְטַהֲרִין, וְחָזַר בּוֹ רַבִּי עֲקִיבָא. וּמַעֲשֶׂה שֶׁהֵבִיאוּ קוּפָּה מְלֵאָה עֲצָמוֹת לְבֵית הַכְּנֶסֶת שֶׁל טַרְסִיִּים וְהִנִּיחוּהָ בָּאֲוִיר, וְנִכְנַס תּוֹדוֹס הָרוֹפֵא וְכָל הָרוֹפְאִים [עִמּוֹ], וְאָמְרוּ: אֵין כָּאן שִׁדְרָה מִמֵּת אֶחָד.

The Gemara further suggests: **Come** and **hear** a resolution from the *Tosefta* (*Oholot* 4:2). **Rabbi Yehuda says** that **Rabbi Akiva deems six items impure that the Rabbis deem pure, and Rabbi Akiva** later **retracted** his opinion. **And an incident** occurred in **which they brought a box** that was **full of bones to the synagogue of blacksmiths** [*tarsiyyim*],[L] **and they placed it in** an open **airspace,** not under the roof, so that it would not impart ritual impurity. **And Todos the doctor**[P] **entered and all the other doctors** entered **with him, and they said,** after examining the pile: **There is not a** full **spine from one corpse here.**[NB]

טַעְמָא – דְּלֵיכָּא שִׁדְרָה דְּמֵחַדָא, הָא אִיכָּא אוֹ שִׁדְרָה אוֹ גּוּלְגּוֹלֶת דְּמֵחַדָא – נָזִיר מְגַלֵּחַ עָלֶיהָ, שְׁמַע מִינָּהּ: אוֹ שִׁדְרָה אוֹ גּוּלְגּוֹלֶת תְּנַן. לָא מִיבַּעְיָא קָאָמַר; לָא מִיבַּעְיָא שִׁדְרָה וְגוּלְגּוֹלֶת דְּמִמֵּת אֶחָד לֵיכָּא, אֶלָּא אֲפִילּוּ אוֹ שִׁדְרָה מִמֵּת אֶחָד אוֹ גּוּלְגּוֹלֶת מִמֵּת אֶחָד לֵיכָּא.

The Gemara infers from this incident: **The reason** it is ritually pure **is due to** the fact **that there was no spine from one** corpse, from which one can infer that if **there is either a spine or a skull from one** corpse, **a nazirite must shave due to it. Learn from this** that **we learned** in the mishna that a nazirite shaves **either for a spine or a skull.** The Gemara rejects this argument: The *tanna* of the *baraita* **is speaking** utilizing the style of: **It is not necessary,** as follows: **It is not necessary** to state that **there is no spine and skull from one corpse** in the box, **but even** the remains of **either a spine from one corpse or a skull from one corpse,** which together impart impurity, are **not** present. Instead, there are parts of spines and skulls from several bodies.

תָּא שְׁמַע מִמִּנְיָינָא: וּמָה הֵן שִׁשָּׁה דְּבָרִים שֶׁרַבִּי עֲקִיבָא מְטַמֵּא וַחֲכָמִים מְטַהֲרִין: עַל אֵבֶר מִן הַמֵּת שֶׁבָּא מִשְּׁנֵי מֵתִים, וְעַל אֵבֶר מִן הַחַי שֶׁבָּא מִשְּׁנֵי בְּנֵי אָדָם, וְעַל חֲצִי קַב עֲצָמוֹת שֶׁבָּא מִשְּׁנֵי מֵתִים, וְעַל רְבִיעִית דָּם הַבָּא מִשְּׁנַיִם, וְעַל עֶצֶם כִּשְׂעוֹרָה שֶׁנֶּחֱלַק לִשְׁנַיִם, וְהַשִּׁדְרָה וְהַגּוּלְגּוֹלֶת.

The Gemara further suggests: **Come** and **hear from the tally** in the above *baraita*: **And what are those six items that Rabbi Akiva deems ritually impure and the Rabbis deem ritually pure?** They consist **of a limb from a corpse**[H] **that comes from,** i.e., is combined with, **two corpses; and** a severed **limb from a living person that comes from two living people; and half-*kav* of bones that come from two corpses; and a quarter-*log* of blood that comes from two** corpses; **and of a bone that is a barley-grain-bulk,** even from one body, **that was divided into two; and the spine and the skull** from two corpses.

HALAKHA

A spine, the majority of whose ribs were removed – שִׁדְרָה שֶׁגֵּירֵד רוֹב צִילְעִין שֶׁבָּהּ: If the majority of the ribs of a spine were removed, it does not impart impurity in a tent, even if the spine itself remains intact. If it was in a grave, it imparts impurity in a tent even if it was broken into small pieces, as the grave joins them together (Rambam *Sefer Tahara, Hilkhot Tumat Met* 4:7).

A limb from a corpse, etc. – אֵבֶר מִן הַמֵּת וכו׳: A limb from a corpse that is combined from two corpses, a limb combined from two living people, a quarter-*kav* of bones from two corpses, a quarter-*log* of blood from two bodies, spine bones joined from two corpses, and skull bones from two corpses impart ritual impurity through contact or carrying but not in a tent, in accordance with the opinion of the Rabbis (Rambam *Sefer Tahara, Hilkhot Tumat Met* 4:1–2).

PERSONALITIES

Todos the doctor – תּוֹדוֹס הָרוֹפֵא: Todos is a shortened version of the Greek name Θεόδωρος, Theodoros, or, in Hebrew, Mattityahu. It appears that Todos was a prominent doctor in the generation following the destruction of the Second Temple. There are a number of cases recorded in the Talmud in which the Sages relied on his professional advice.

NOTES

There is not a full spine from one corpse here – אֵין כָּאן שִׁדְרָה מִמֵּת אֶחָד: The commentaries ask: Since this was evidently not a whole spine but was broken into its constituent vertebrae, what is the point of the question? After all, a spine of this kind certainly does not impart ritual impurity (*Tosafot*). They answer that these bones were previously in a whole state in a grave, which a nazirite was overlaying. It was therefore necessary to clarify whether or not the grave joined them together to render the nazirite impure (see Rosh and Rabbeinu Peretz).

BACKGROUND

There is not a full spine from one corpse here – אֵין כָּאן שִׁדְרָה מִמֵּת אֶחָד: This determination required medical expertise, as only a doctor could examine the form of each bone and decide whether the collection was from one or several bodies. This became easier when duplicate bones were found in the collection, as two of the same bones could not have come from the same body. Once it was determined that the bones were from more than one body, the investigation would have been painstaking, as separated vertebrae from the spinal column, which in this case were broken, are very similar to each other, and each body contains many of these bones. For this reason, great expertise was required to determine the origin of the bones.

LANGUAGE

Blacksmiths [*tarsiyyim*] – טַרְסִיִּים: From the name of the Greek city Ταρσός, Tarsus. This ancient city, located in Asia Minor, once served as a center of Greek culture and manufacturing. The residents of Tarsus excelled in various crafts, principally the weaving of special textiles and fine metalwork, e.g., inlaying or casting different kinds of metals. Several trades are named after the city. The Sages used the word *tarsiyyim* for a particular kind of weaver, perhaps those who produced the tapestries and linens of Tarsus, as well as a certain type of silversmith.

Already in the Second Temple period, there were synagogues associated with distinct groups of craftsmen, a tradition that has continued until recent generations. Accordingly, it is not surprising that there was a special synagogue for blacksmiths. It is also possible that this was the synagogue of Jews from Tarsus, which had a Jewish community. This would follow the ancient tradition of Jews from a particular town banding together in a new region or country to form their own synagogue.

וְאִי סָלְקָא דַּעְתָּךְ אוֹ שִׁדְרָה אוֹ גוּלְגּוֹלֶת – הָנֵי שִׁבְעָה הָוְיָין! כִּי קָתָנֵי (סימן יחי״ד שהו״א גיל״ח ואח״ד).

And if it enters your mind that the *halakha* applies to **either a spine or a skull** and they are two separate *halakhot*, **these are seven** cases, rather than six. The Gemara rejects this claim: No proof can be brought from here, **as when** the *tanna* **teaches** this tally he lists seven items. However, only six are fully relevant here, and therefore he said they were six. The Gemara inserts **a mnemonic** device for the ensuing suggestions as to which item in the list is not necessary in this context: **An individual**[N] disagrees with him; **that he**; a nazirite **shaves** for it; **and one** quarter-*log*.

כָּל הֵיכָא דִּפְלִיגִי עֲלֵיהּ רַבִּים, לְאַפּוּקֵי עֶצֶם כִּשְׂעוֹרָה דְּיָחִיד הוּא דִּפְלִיג עֲלֵיהּ. דְּתַנְיָא: עֶצֶם כִּשְׂעוֹרָה שֶׁנֶּחְלַק לִשְׁנַיִם, רַבִּי עֲקִיבָא מְטַמֵּא וְרַבִּי יוֹחָנָן בֶּן נוּרִי מְטַהֵר.

The first explanation is: Rabbi Akiva listed the spine and skull as separate items, but the six include **anywhere that many** Sages **disagree with him, to the exclusion of** the case of a bone that is **a barley-grain-bulk,**[H] as here **it is an individual who disagrees with** Rabbi Akiva, **as it is taught** in a mishna (*Oholot* 2:7): **If a bone that is a barley-grain-bulk was divided**[H] **into two, Rabbi Akiva deems** it **impure and Rabbi Yoḥanan ben Nuri deems** it **pure.** In this case, only one Sage disagrees with Rabbi Akiva.

וְאִי בָּעֵית אֵימָא: כִּי קָתָנֵי – אֵבֶר מִן הַמֵּת, אֵבֶר מִן הַחַי לָא קָתָנֵי.

And if you wish, say a different item on the list that is omitted from the tally: **When he teaches** six, he includes a **limb** severed **from a corpse,** but **he does not teach a limb** severed **from a living** person, and that was the case that was not listed.

וְאִיבָּעֵית אֵימָא: כִּי קָתָנֵי – כָּל הֵיכָא דְּנָזִיר מְגַלֵּחַ עַל אֲהִילוֹ, לְאַפּוּקֵי עֶצֶם כִּשְׂעוֹרָה דְּלָא.

And if you wish, say a different item on the list that is omitted from the tally: **When he teaches** six, he mentions **anywhere that a nazirite shaves for his overlaying,** i.e., he formed a tent over the remains of a corpse, **to the exclusion of** the case of **a bone that is a barley-grain-bulk,** as it **does not** impart ritual impurity in a tent. As stated in the mishna, this bone imparts impurity only through contact and carrying.

וְאִיבָּעֵית אֵימָא: כִּי קָתָנֵי – כָּל הֵיכָא דַּהֲדַר בֵּיהּ, לְאַפּוּקֵי רְבִיעִית דָּם דְּלָא הֲדַר בֵּיהּ. דַּאֲמַר לֵיהּ רַבִּי לְבַר קַפָּרָא: לֹא תִּשְׁנֶה רְבִיעִית דָּם בַּחֲזָרָה, שֶׁהֲרֵי לִמּוּדוֹ שֶׁל רַבִּי עֲקִיבָא בְּיָדוֹ,

And if you wish, say a different item on the list that is omitted from the tally: **When he teaches** six, he lists **anywhere that** Rabbi Akiva **retracted** his opinion, **to the exclusion of a quarter-*log* of blood, as he did not retract his** opinion in that case, **as Rabbi** Yehuda HaNasi **said to bar Kappara: Do not teach a quarter-*log* of blood in the** list of Rabbi Akiva's **retractions, as Rabbi Akiva held onto his** opinion[N] in this regard.

וְעוֹד, הַמִּקְרָא מְסַיְּיעוֹ: ״וְעַל כָּל נַפְשֹׁות מֵת לֹא יָבֹא״. רַבִּי שִׁמְעוֹן אוֹמֵר: עַד יָמָיו הָיָה מְטַמֵּא, אִם מִשֶּׁמֵּת חָזַר בּוֹ – אֵינִי יוֹדֵעַ. תָּנָא: הוּשְׁחֲרוּ שִׁינָּיו מִפְּנֵי תַּעֲנִיּוֹתָיו.

And furthermore, the verse supports his opinion, as it states: **"Neither shall he go in to any dead bodies"** (Leviticus 21:11). The plural form "bodies" indicates that two corpses can join together, as stated by Rabbi Akiva. Similarly, **Rabbi Shimon says: All his days,** Rabbi Akiva **would deem** a quarter-*log* of blood from two corpses **ritually impure. Whether he retracted his** opinion **after he died,** this **I do not know.** A Sage **taught:** Rabbi Shimon's **teeth blackened due to his fasts,** which he undertook for uttering this irreverent comment about Rabbi Akiva.

תָּא שְׁמַע: דְּתַנְיָא, בֵּית שַׁמַּאי אוֹמְרִים: רוֹבַע עֲצָמוֹת מִן הָעֲצָמִים, אוֹ מִשְּׁנַיִם אוֹ מִשְּׁלֹשָׁה. וּבֵית הִלֵּל אוֹמְרִים: רוֹבַע מִן הַגְּוִיָּה, מֵרוֹב הַבִּנְיָן אוֹ מֵרוֹב הַמִּנְיָן. אָמַר רַבִּי יְהוֹשֻׁעַ: יָכוֹלְנִי לַעֲשׂוֹת דִּבְרֵי בֵּית שַׁמַּאי וְדִבְרֵי בֵּית הִלֵּל כְּאֶחָד,

§ The Gemara returns to the earlier discussion. **Come** and **hear** an answer to the question of whether a spine and skull must be together to impart ritual impurity, **as it is taught** in a mishna (*Eduyyot* 1:7) that **Beit Shammai say:** The **quarter-*kav* of bones,**[H] which imparts impurity in a tent, can be **from** several **bones** [*ha'atzamim*][NL] **or from two or from three**[N] **bones,** but they cannot be from one bone. **And Beit Hillel say:** The **quarter-*kav*** of bones must come **from the same body,** either **from the majority of the structure** of the skeleton **or from the majority of the number** of 248 bones in the body. **Rabbi Yehoshua said: I can establish the statement of Beit Shammai and the statement of Beit Hillel as one.** In other words, I can explain their opinions so that there is no dispute between them.

NOTES

A mnemonic, an individual, etc. – סִימָן יָחִיד וכו׳: This mnemonic, which does not appear in all manuscripts, is difficult to decipher. Some commentaries explain it as referring to the four options offered in the following discussion for the *halakha* omitted from the tally, with each term representing one option (*Shoshannim LeDavid*).

Rabbi Akiva held onto his opinion – לִמּוּדוֹ שֶׁל רַבִּי עֲקִיבָא בְּיָדוֹ: Some say that Rabbi Akiva was known to have repeated this ruling to his disciples on many occasions, and it is therefore evident that he did not change his mind.

Quarter-*kav* of bones from bones – רוֹבַע עֲצָמוֹת מִן הָעֲצָמִים: Some commentaries suggest that Beit Shammai received a ruling referring to a quarter-*kav* of bones from bones, which they interpreted as referring to two or three bones. Conversely, Beit Hillel's ruling stated: A quarter-*kav* from the body, which they explained as a reference to the majority of the structure or the majority of the number of bones, which has the status of a whole corpse.

Or from two or from three – אוֹ מִשְּׁנַיִם אוֹ מִשְּׁלֹשָׁה: According to most commentaries, this means: From two or three bones. They apparently maintain that a quarter-*kav* from a single bone does not impart ritual impurity (see Meiri). Others explain that Beit Shammai are referring to bones from two or three different people (Rambam's Commentary on the Mishna, *Eduyyot* 1:7). If so, Beit Shammai maintain that bones from several people can combine to the amount of a quarter-*kav*. This means that Rabbi Akiva rules in accordance with the opinion of Beit Shammai. It is stated in one source that Rabbi Akiva was a *Shamuti*, a follower of Beit Shammai.

HALAKHA

To the exclusion of a bone that is a barley-grain-bulk – לְאַפּוּקֵי עֶצֶם כִּשְׂעוֹרָה: A bone from a corpse that has the volume of a barley-grain-bulk imparts impurity by contact and carrying, which means that a nazirite who touches or carries it is obligated to shave. However, it does not render people or items impure in a tent (Rambam *Sefer Tahara*, *Hilkhot Tumat Met* 2:10 and *Sefer Hafla'a*, *Hilkhot Nezirut* 7:6).

A bone that is a barley-grain-bulk was divided – עֶצֶם כִּשְׂעוֹרָה שֶׁנֶּחְלַק: A bone the volume of a barley-grain-bulk that was split in two imparts ritual impurity by carrying, as the *halakha* is in accordance with the opinion of Rabbi Akiva (Rambam *Sefer Tahara*, *Hilkhot Tumat Met* 4:4, and *Kesef Mishne* there).

Quarter-*kav* of bones – רוֹבַע עֲצָמוֹת: A quarter-*kav* of bones imparts impurity even if the bones do not contain the majority of the structure or the majority of the number of the bones of a corpse, nor a spine or whole skull. This quarter-*kav* imparts ritual impurity by touch, carrying, and in a tent (Rambam *Sefer Tahara*, *Hilkhot Tumat Met* 2:9, and *Kesef Mishne* there).

LANGUAGE

Bones [*atzamim*] – עֲצָמִים: Although this plural term usually appears as the feminine *atzamot*, the masculine form *atzamim* is occasionally used (see Ezekiel 24:4).

שבית שמאי אומרים משנים או משלשה – או משני שוקיים וירך אחד, או משני ירכיים ושוק אחד, הואיל ורוב גובהו של אדם מגובה. ובית הלל אומרים: מן הגויה או מרוב בנין או מרוב מנין – הואיל וישנן במפרקי ידים ורגלים. שמאי אומר: אפילו עצם מן השדרה או מן הגולגולת.

How so? As when **Beit Shammai say: From two or three** bones, they mean **either from two shins and one thigh, or from two thighs**[N] **and one shin. Since the majority of a person's height** is contained **in the height** of these limbs, they are considered the majority of the structure of the body. **And Beit Hillel say:** Parts **from the body, or from the majority of the structure, or from the majority of the number** of bones, **since they include the joints of the hands and feet,**[B] which comprise many small bones, impart impurity. **Shammai says:**[N] **Even a bone from the spine or from the skull** imparts impurity. In this source, Shammai explicitly refers to a spine or a skull.

שאני שמאי דמחמיר! ליפשוט מינה: טעמא דבית שמאי דמחמיר, הא רבנן – עד דאיכא שדרה וגולגולת! לא, עד כאן לא פליגי רבנן עליה דשמאי – אלא בעצם אחד דאתי מן השדרה ומן הגולגולת, אבל הכא דאיתיה בעיניה – אפילו חדא מינהון.

The Gemara rejects this proof: One cannot establish a general *halakha* from this source, for **Shammai is different, as he is** invariably **stringent,** whereas the Rabbis might disagree. The Gemara inquires: If so, **let us resolve** the opposite **from this** *baraita*: **The reason** that Shammai spoke of a spine or a skull **is that Beit Shammai are stringent,** from which it may be inferred that according to **the Rabbis** a spine and skull are not ritually impure **unless** both **a spine and skull are present.** The Gemara rejects this proof too: **No, the Rabbis disagree with Shammai only with regard to one bone that comes from the spine or from the skull, but when it is intact, even** if the bone is from **one of them,**[H] either the spine or the skull, they possibly agree that it imparts impurity.

בעי רמי בר חמא: רובע עצמות מן שדרה וגולגולת, מאי? כי קתני חצי קב עצמות – היכא דאיכא משאר אבריו, אבל מן שדרה וגולגולת דחמירי – אפילו רובע עצמות, או דלמא לא שנא?

§ **Rami bar Ḥama raised a dilemma:** With regard to **a quarter-***kav* **of bones from a spine and a skull, what** is the *halakha*? Does a nazirite shave for them? The Gemara explains the two sides of the dilemma: **When** the mishna **teaches** that one shaves for **a half-***kav* **of bones,** does this apply only **when** they **are from his other limbs, but** in the case of bones **from the spine and skull, which are stringent,**[N] as they impart ritual impurity on their own, **even a quarter-***kav* **of bones** imparts impurity? **Or perhaps it is no different.**

אמר רבא, תא שמע: השדרה והגולגולת, ואי סלקא דעתך רובע עצמות דאתי מן שדרה וגולגולת חמיר – ליתני: על רובע עצמות הבא מן השדרה כו'!

Rava said: Come and **hear** a resolution from the mishna, which teaches: **The spine and the skull. And if it enters your mind** that **a quarter-***kav* **of bones that come from a spine and skull is** more **stringent** than other limbs and imparts ritual impurity, **let** the *tanna* **teach** this *halakha* in a manner that presents a greater novelty, by stating: **For a quarter-***kav*[N] **of bones that come from the spine** and the skull.

BACKGROUND

They include the joints of the hands and feet – ישנן במפרקי ידים ורגלים: In tractate *Oholot* (1:8) the Sages count a total of thirty bones in the arms and legs, including hands and feet. Accordingly, the number of bones in these four limbs amounts to 120, close to half the traditional number of 248 bones in the body. Nowadays there are considered to be twenty-seven bones in each arm and twenty-six in each foot. Apparently the Sages also counted the tiny sesamoid bones found in the joints, which is why they arrived at a larger sum. Since the number of sesamoids varies with age and from one individual to another, it follows that in some skeletons the number of bones of the arms and legs could comprise the majority of bones of the entire body in number and size.

HALAKHA

Even from one of them – אפילו חדא מינהון: A whole spine or a whole skull impart impurity by contact, carrying, and in a tent, like an intact corpse, and a nazirite must shave if he is rendered impure by them. Although this dilemma is left unsolved by the Gemara, Shammai clearly rules in this manner, and the wording of the mishna indicates likewise (*Kesef Mishne*). Furthermore, the Gemara goes to great lengths to substantiate this opinion (Rambam *Sefer Hafla'a*, *Hilkhot Nezirut* 7:2 and *Sefer Tahara*, *Hilkhot Tumat Met* 2:8).

NOTES

Or from two thighs – או משני שוקיים: The shin and thigh constitute the majority of the leg, which forms the majority of an individual's height. Some commentaries find Rabbi Yehoshua's statement somewhat problematic, as he lists three bones but not two, whereas Beit Shammai speak of two or three (*Tosafot*). One explanation is that the two thighs do not come from two legs. Rather, they are two bones, one thicker than the other, which together make up the thigh which are considered a single bone. If so, two thighs and a shin are essentially two bones, whereas two shins and a thigh constitute three (*Tosafot*; Rabbeinu Peretz). Others maintain that Beit Shammai's mention of two should not be taken literally, as it is the manner of the Sages to refer to several items by this term (see 10a).

Shammai says, etc. – שמאי אומר וכו': The proof that the spine and skull do not need to both be present to impart ritual impurity is apparently from Shammai's statement, as he explicitly counts the spine and skull separately. Many commentaries claim that the Gemara seeks to prove from Shammai's ruling that the Rabbis agree with him in this regard. Although he disputes the other opinions with regard to one bone, it is unlikely that the opinions are so varied that the Rabbis insist that the spine and skull must be together (*Tosafot*; Rosh). According to this explanation, the answer: Shammai is different as he is stringent, should be understood as follows: Shammai's statement affords no proof, as he is often very stringent, and therefore it is possible that he maintains an extreme opinion in opposition to that of the Rabbis.

The spine and skull, which are stringent – שדרה וגולגולת דחמירי: Some commentaries explain that the stringency is that these bones impart ritual impurity even if they are extremely small, e.g., if they are from babies or miscarried fetuses, as no minimum volume is stated with regard to the spine and skull (Rid). One question is why Rami bar Ḥama doesn't inquire with regard to a quarter-*kav* from the majority of the structure or the majority of the number of bones, which is also a stringency (*Keren Ora*). The *Keren Ora* answers that, unlike the spine and skull, none of these bones is important or particularly stringent on its own, but only when combined together.

Let the ***tanna*** **teach, for a quarter-*****kav*** **– ליתני על רובע:** In other words, the mishna itself should have taught: For a quarter-*kav* of bones from the spine and the skull. The commentaries point out that if this is Rava's inference, he maintains that the spine and skull invariably contain more than a quarter-*kav*, and therefore it is a greater novelty for the mishna to teach: A quarter-*kav* of bones from the spine and skull (*Tosafot*; Rosh).

HALAKHA

With regard to a quarter-*kav* of bones – בְּרוֹבַע עֲצָמוֹת: It is uncertain whether a quarter-*kav* of bones from a spine or skull imparts ritual impurity in a tent. Consequently, a nazirite does not shave after coming into contact with bones of this type. This is because Rami bar Ḥama's dilemma is left unsolved (*Kesef Mishne*). In any case, a nazirite certainly must shave for touching or carrying these bones, as the *halakha* in this case is no more lenient than with regard to a regular bone, which imparts impurity in this manner in the volume of a lentil-bulk (Rambam *Sefer Hafla'a*, *Hilkhot Nezirut* 7:4, and see *Sefer Tahara*, *Hilkhot Tumat Met* 2:9).

וְהָא רָבָא הוּא דְּאָמַר: לֹא נִצְרְכָה אֶלָּא לְשִׁדְרָה וְגוּלְגּוֹלֶת שֶׁאֵין בָּהֶן רוֹבַע עֲצָמוֹת! בָּתַר דִּשְׁמָעָהּ מֵרַבִּי עֲקִיבָא.

The Gemara expresses surprise at this argument: **But wasn't it Rava himself who said:**[N] This statement is **necessary only for** a whole **spine and skull that do not contain a quarter-*kav* of bones?** This indicates that in his opinion a quarter-*kav* of bones from a spine does impart ritual impurity. The Gemara answers: **After he heard** the statement of the *tanna*, he understood **from Rabbi Akiva**[N] that his dispute in the *baraita* (52a) concerns a spine and skull from two corpses, not a quarter-*kav* from a spine and skull. This interpretation led Rava to change his mind.

תָּא שְׁמַע, שַׁמַּאי אוֹמֵר: עֶצֶם אֶחָד מִן שִׁדְרָה אוֹ מִן גּוּלְגּוֹלֶת! שָׁאנֵי שַׁמַּאי דְּמַחְמִיר טְפֵי.

The Gemara further suggests: **Come** and **hear** a resolution from the following: **Shammai says** that **one bone from the spine or from the skull** imparts ritual impurity. Although the Rabbis dispute his ruling, it can be assumed that they do not have a vastly different opinion. Rather, they accept that a quarter-*kav* from a spine imparts impurity and renders a nazirite obligated to shave. The Gemara rejects this proof: **Shammai is different, as he is very stringent,** and therefore nothing at all can be inferred from his opinion with regard to that of the Rabbis.

לִיפְשׁוֹט מִינָּהּ: טַעְמָא דְּשַׁמַּאי – דְּמַחְמִיר, הָא לְרַבָּנַן – עַד דְּאִיכָּא חֲצִי קַב עֲצָמוֹת!

The Gemara counters: If in fact the Rabbis maintain an extremely different opinion from that of Shammai, **let us resolve** the problem in the opposite manner: **The reasoning** here is that **of Shammai, who is** particularly **stringent.** From this it may be inferred that, **according to** the opinion of **the Rabbis,** one is not rendered impure and a nazirite is not required to shave **unless there is a half-*kav* of bones** from the spine and skull.

דִּילְמָא עַד כָּאן לָא פְּלִיגִי רַבָּנַן עֲלֵיהּ דְּשַׁמַּאי אֶלָּא בְּעֶצֶם אֶחָד, אֲבָל בְּרוֹבַע עֲצָמוֹת – אֲפִילּוּ רַבָּנַן מוֹדוּ.

The Gemara rejects this claim as well: **Perhaps** the argument is not that extreme after all, and **the Rabbis disagree with Shammai only with regard to** whether **one bone** from the spine or from the skull imparts impurity. **However, with regard to a quarter-*kav* of bones,**[H] **even the Rabbis** might **concede** that it renders people and items ritually impure, and a nazirite must shave for it.

NOTES

But wasn't it Rava who said, etc. – וְהָא רָבָא הוּא דְּאָמַר וכו׳: The early commentaries dispute the meaning of this question. Some explain that the difficulty is Rava's assumption that a spine and a skull contain more than a quarter-*kav* of bones (*Tosafot*). Others maintain that the difficulty is more fundamental, as Rava's statement indicates that a nazirite must shave for a quarter-*kav* from a spine and skull (Commentary on *Nazir*).

After he heard the statement from Rabbi Akiva – בָּתַר דִּשְׁמָעָהּ מֵרַבִּי עֲקִיבָא: This phrase is difficult for several reasons. It usually refers to a statement of *amora'im*, but here it is referring to the opinion of Rabbi Akiva, a *tanna*. Also, in the context here it is unclear which statement of Rabbi Akiva is being referred to. Furthermore, the relevance of this statement to the issue at hand is not immediately evident.

These difficulties led many commentaries to prefer a different reading, which makes the Gemara easier to understand, although it necessitates an addition to the text. According to this explanation, before the phrase: But wasn't it Rava who said, one should insert the statement: Mar Ukva said here we are dealing with a spine and a skull that do not contain a quarter-*kav*. Accordingly, the novelty in the mishna is that it is referring to this particular spine and skull. In other words, Rava's initial question was based on the assumption that a spine and skull certainly contain a quarter-*kav* of bones, to which Mar Ukva responds that sometimes a spine or a skull can be less than a quarter-*kav* in volume. At this point, the Gemara asks: Doesn't Rava himself agree with that opinion? After all, Rava himself stated the same ruling. The Gemara proceeds to answer that after hearing this reasoning from Mar Ukva, not from Rabbi Akiva, as in the standard text, Rava retracted in accordance with Mar Ukva's explanation (*Tosafot*).

Other commentaries uphold the standard text of the Gemara. They claim that the Gemara's statement is referring to the comment of Rabbi Akiva in *Oholot* 2:4, according to which a spine and skull from two corpses are ritually impure. Rava maintains that it is reasonable to interpret this statement as referring to a spine and skull that contain less than a quarter-*kav*, as a quarter-*kav* of bones is mentioned separately in that same mishna. Even the Rabbis dispute Rabbi Akiva's ruling only with regard to bones from two bodies. However, they accept his opinion in the case of a spine and skull that are not a quarter-*kav* in volume, if they come from a single corpse (*Tosafot*; Rosh). According to this interpretation, the phrase: After he heard it from Rabbi Akiva, must be understood in a rather unconventional manner, as: After he analyzed and understood Rabbi Akiva's opinion. Others agree that the term heard means: Understood from Rabbi Akiva, although they offer a different explanation: The key factor is that Rabbi Akiva and the Rabbis in the *baraita* disagree only with regard to bones from two corpses, but they do not dispute the relevant amount. This indicates that everyone agrees that broken bones do not impart impurity when their volume is less than a half-*kav*, even if they come from the spine and skull (Commentary on *Nazir*). The early commentaries analyze these interpretations at length and attempt to justify the varying explanations (see Rabbeinu Peretz). Later authorities also struggle to explain this passage and suggest various emendations to the text (see *Keren Ora*, Gra, and *Birkat Rosh*).

אָמַר רַבִּי אֱלִיעֶזֶר: זְקֵנִים הָרִאשׁוֹנִים מִקְצָתָן הָיוּ אוֹמְרִים: חֲצִי קַב עֲצָמוֹת וַחֲצִי לוֹג דָּם – לַכֹּל, רוֹבַע עֲצָמוֹת וּרְבִיעִית דָּם – לֹא לַכֹּל. וּמִקְצָתָן הָיוּ אוֹמְרִים: אַף רוֹבַע עֲצָמוֹת וּרְבִיעִית דָּם – לַכֹּל.

§ **Rabbi Eliezer said** that **some of the early Elders would say: A half-*kav* of bones**[H] **and a half-*log* of blood** impart ritual impurity **in all** forms. Their impurity applies by Torah law, and therefore they impart impurity in a tent. But **a quarter-*kav* of bones and a quarter-*log* of blood,**[H] they do **not** impart impurity **in all** forms, i.e., they do not impart impurity in a tent. **And some of** these Elders **would say** that **even a quarter-*kav* of bones and a quarter-*log* of blood** impart impurity **in all** forms. This was the dispute of earlier generations.

בֵּית דִּין שֶׁלְּאַחֲרֵיהֶם אָמְרוּ: חֲצִי קַב עֲצָמוֹת וַחֲצִי לוֹג דָּם – לַכֹּל, רוֹבַע עֲצָמוֹת וּרְבִיעִית דָּם – לִתְרוּמָה וְקָדָשִׁים, אֲבָל לֹא לְנָזִיר וְעוֹשֵׂה פֶסַח.

The **court that followed them said: A half-*kav* of bones and a half-*log* of blood** impart ritual impurity **in all** forms. **A quarter-*kav* of bones and a quarter-*log* of blood** impart impurity only **with regard to *teruma* and offerings,** i.e., the Sages decreed that they impart impurity in a tent to invalidate *teruma* and offerings **but not with regard to a nazirite.** A nazirite is not required to shave or bring offerings for impurity after contact with a quarter-*kav* of bones or a quarter-*log* of blood. **And** similarly, **one who performs** the ritual of **the Paschal offering** may proceed despite the fact that he came into contact with this amount of blood or bones, as the Sages did not apply this decree in cases where one's impurity precludes the performance of a mitzva whose neglect is punishable by *karet*.

מִכְּדִי, אֵין הַכְרָעַת שְׁלִישִׁית מַכְרַעַת! אָמַר רַבִּי יַעֲקֹב בַּר אִידִי: מִפִּי שְׁמוּעָה אָמְרוּ, מִפִּי חַגַּי זְכַרְיָה וּמַלְאָכִי.

The Gemara asks about the ruling of *halakha* in this case. **Now** consider, there is a principle that **the decision** of the **third**[N] opinion is **not** considered **a decision.** A compromise ruling that seeks to resolve a dispute by including factors and cases that were not mentioned in the other two opinions is not considered decisive, so how could the later court make a distinction between a Paschal offering and other cases? **Rabbi Ya'akov bar Idi said:** This ruling was not stated as a compromise. Rather, **they said** it **from tradition, from Haggai, Zechariah, and Malachi,** the last of the prophets. This was not a new attempt to mediate between two earlier opinions but an ancient ruling in its own right.

״עַל אֵלּוּ הַנָּזִיר מְגַלֵּחַ״. ״עַל אֵלּוּ״ דְּרֵישָׁא – לְמַעוּטֵי עֶצֶם כִּשְׂעוֹרָה, דְּעַל מַגָּעוֹ וְעַל מַשָּׂאוֹ – אִין, וְעַל אֲהִילוֹ – לָא. וְ״עַל אֵלּוּ״ דְּסֵיפָא – לְמַעוּטֵי אֶבֶן הַסְּכוּכִית.

§ The mishna taught that **for all these** aforementioned sources of ritual impurity **a nazirite shaves.** The Gemara explains that the phrase: **For these,** in the mishna's **first clause,** serves **to exclude a bone that is a barley-grain-bulk.**[H] **As for touching it and carrying it, yes,** a nazirite shaves, **but for his overlying** it, **no,** he does not shave. **And** the phrase: **For these,** in the mishna's **latter clause,** serves **to exclude an overhanging** [*hasekhukhit*][L] **stone.**[HN] Although a stone that forms a cover over a corpse imparts impurity in a tent, a nazirite is nevertheless not obligated to shave due to this source of impurity.

״וַחֲצִי קַב עֲצָמוֹת״.

§ In its list of sources of impurity for which a nazirite must shave, the mishna taught: **And a half-*kav* of bones.**

HALAKHA

A half-*kav* of bones, etc. – חֲצִי קַב עֲצָמוֹת וכו׳: A half-*kav* of bones from a corpse imparts impurity even if the bones contain less than the majority of the corpse's structure or less than the majority of its bones in number. The same applies to a half-*log* of blood from a single body. Likewise, a nazirite must shave if he comes into contact with either of these and start his term of naziriteship afresh. Furthermore, one is liable to receive the punishment of *karet* for entering the Temple after coming into contact with these bones, and it is also prohibited for him to sacrifice the Paschal offering (Rambam *Sefer Hafla'a, Hilkhot Nezirut* 7:2; *Sefer Avoda, Hilkhot Biat HaMikdash* 3:13; and *Sefer Korbanot, Hilkhot Korban Pesaḥ* 6:2).

A quarter-*kav* of bones and a quarter-*log* of blood, etc. – רוֹבַע עֲצָמוֹת וּרְבִיעִית דָּם וכו׳: If a nazirite contracted impurity in a tent from a quarter-*kav* of bones that do not contain the majority of the number of bones in a body or the majority of its structure, or if he contracted impurity from a quarter-*log* of blood from a single corpse by contact, carrying, or in a tent, although he requires sprinkling and immersion for his purification, he does not void his term of naziriteship and he need not shave. Likewise, one who enters the Temple after contracting impurity from these is not liable to receive the punishment of *karet*. As for the Paschal offering, if the Festival occurred on the seventh day of the nazirite's purification, they slaughter it for him, and he need not wait for the second *Pesaḥ*. The Rambam maintains that these sources of impurity apply by rabbinic law (Rambam *Sefer Hafla'a, Hilkhot Nezirut* 7:6; *Sefer Korbanot, Hilkhot Korban Pesaḥ* 6:2, and see Ra'avad and *Kesef Mishne* there; and *Sefer Tahara, Hilkhot Tumat Met* 3:3).

A bone that is a barley-grain-bulk – עֶצֶם כִּשְׂעוֹרָה: A bone the volume of a barley-grain-bulk imparts ritual impurity by contact and carrying, and a nazirite must shave if he is rendered impure in this manner. However, a bone that is a barley-grain-bulk does not impart impurity in a tent (Rambam *Sefer Hafla'a, Hilkhot Nezirut* 7:6 and *Sefer Tahara, Hilkhot Tumat Met* 2:10; 3:2).

To exclude an overhanging stone – לְמַעוּטֵי אֶבֶן הַסְּכוּכִית: If branches protruding from a tree or stones jutting out from a wall serve as a tent over a nazirite and a corpse, the nazirite need not shave or negate his naziriteship for this impurity (Rambam *Sefer Hafla'a, Hilkhot Nezirut* 7:6).

LANGUAGE

Overhanging [*sekhukhit*] – סְכוּכִית: Although the term *sekhukhit* is usually synonymous with *zekhukhit*, meaning glass, here it is referring to an item that covers or shades. In this context, it means a stone that is not a part of the structure of a grave but is situated over the grave and covers it.

NOTES

The decision of the third, etc. – הַכְרָעַת שְׁלִישִׁית וכו׳: There are two explanations of this principle. According to one opinion, the term decision in this context means the acceptance of a particular opinion by a later generation, and the third decision is referring to the acceptance of a compromise position, which is not based on the logical reasoning of either of the disputing opinions (Commentary on *Nazir*; Meiri). Others maintain that the third opinion is referring to a decision of students, whose ruling is not important enough to be accepted as a novel *halakha*. It is called the third because this expression initially referred to the third generation (see *Pesaḥim* 20b, and Rabbeinu Ḥananel there). Alternatively, third means external, i.e., an insignificant opinion that is not to be taken seriously (see Meiri on *Ḥullin* 132a).

An overhanging stone – אֶבֶן הַסְּכוּכִית: Most early commentaries maintain that this is similar to the hanging branches and projecting stones listed in the next mishna among the items for which a nazirite is not obligated to shave. In other words, this refers to stones that project from a fence over the body. Some commentaries cite a version of the text that says so unambiguously (Meiri). The Commentary on *Nazir* suggests two interpretations. Perhaps this refers to a very heavy stone, i.e., a boulder placed on the corpse, which does not obligate a nazirite to shave although it does render him ritually impure if he sits on it. Alternatively, it means a stone carried by the nazirite on his shoulders, which overlies a grave (see *Nusḥat Rivan*). Some say that an overhanging [*sekhukhit*] stone means one made of glass [*zekhukhit*], i.e., a transparent stone, which does not impart impurity (*Shita Mekubbetzet*).

חֲצִי קַב עֲצָמוֹת – אִין, רוֹבַע עֲצָמוֹת – לָא. הֵיכִי דָמֵי? אִילֵימָא דְּאִית בְּהוֹן עֲצָמוֹת כִּשְׂעוֹרָה – תֵּיפוֹק לֵיהּ מִשּׁוּם עֶצֶם כִּשְׂעוֹרָה! אֶלָּא, דְּאַקְמַח אַקְמוּחֵי.

The Gemara analyzes this ruling of the mishna: **A half-*kav* of bones, yes,** a nazirite must shave if he contracts impurity from them; **a quarter-*kav* of bones, no,** he does not. **What are the circumstances? If we say that they contain**[N] **bones** that are **a barley-grain-bulk, let** the *tanna* of the mishna **derive** the *halakha* that it imparts ritual impurity **due to** the fact that it is **a bone that is a barley-grain-bulk. Rather,** the mishna is referring to a situation **where it has been made like flour.**[H] In that case, a half-*kav* of bones render people and items impure in a tent, although they do not include a bone the volume of a barley-grain-bulk.

״עַל אֵבֶר מִן הַמֵּת וְעַל אֵבֶר מִן הַחַי שֶׁיֵּשׁ עֲלֵיהֶן בָּשָׂר כָּרָאוּי״. אֵין עֲלֵיהֶן בָּשָׂר כָּרָאוּי מַאי? רַבִּי יוֹחָנָן אָמַר: אֵין הַנָּזִיר מְגַלֵּחַ עֲלֵיהֶן, רֵישׁ לָקִישׁ אָמַר: הַנָּזִיר מְגַלֵּחַ עֲלֵיהֶן.

§ The mishna taught that a nazirite shaves **for a limb** severed **from a corpse and for a limb** severed **from a living** person, **upon** either of **which there is a fitting** quantity **of flesh.** The Gemara asks: If **there is not a fitting** quantity **of flesh upon them,**[H] **what** is the *halakha*? **Rabbi Yoḥanan said: The nazirite does not shave for them. Reish Lakish said: The nazirite does shave for them.**

רַבִּי יוֹחָנָן אָמַר: אֵין הַנָּזִיר מְגַלֵּחַ עֲלֵיהֶן, דְּהָא קָתָנֵי בְּרֵישָׁא: עַל אֵבֶר מִן הַמֵּת, וְעַל אֵבֶר מִן הַחַי וכו׳, שֶׁיֵּשׁ עֲלֵיהֶן כְּזַיִת בָּשָׂר – אִין, אֲבָל אֵין עֲלֵיהֶם – לָא.

The Gemara explains their respective opinions. **Rabbi Yoḥanan said: The nazirite does not shave for them, as** the *tanna* **teaches in the first clause** of the mishna in the list of sources of ritual impurity for which a nazirite must shave: **For a limb** severed **from a corpse and for a limb** severed **from a living** person that contains a fitting quantity of flesh. One can infer from this: **Those upon which there is an olive-bulk of flesh, yes,** he must shave for them, **but if there is not** that amount of flesh **upon them, no,** a nazirite need not shave due to them.

וְרַבִּי שִׁמְעוֹן בֶּן לָקִישׁ אוֹמֵר: מְגַלֵּחַ, מִדְּלָא קָתָנֵי בְּסֵיפָא.

And Rabbi Shimon ben Lakish says that **he shaves,** employing the following reasoning: **From** the fact that the mishna **does not teach** the following **in the latter clause,** i.e., the subsequent mishna (54a), in the list of sources of impurity for which a nazirite need not shave: A limb that does not contain a fitting quantity of flesh, one can infer that a nazirite is obligated to shave for a limb of that type.

וְרַבִּי יוֹחָנָן אָמַר לָךְ: כָּל הֵיכָא דְּמַשְׁמַע מִכְּלָלָא – לָא קָתָנֵי בְּסֵיפָא.

And Rabbi Yoḥanan could have **said to you,** in response to Rabbi Shimon ben Lakish's argument: The fact that the mishna omits this case from the list is not proof, as the *tanna* **does not teach in the latter clause anything that can be understood by inference** from the earlier mishna.

NOTES

If we say that they contain, etc. – אִילֵימָא דְּאִית בְּהוֹן וכו׳: The commentaries ask: Since the mishna is dealing with the ritual impurity imparted in a tent, why does the Gemara inquire about the case of a bone the volume of a barley-grain-bulk, which does not impart impurity in a tent (*Tosafot*)? They answer that the basis for the question is the statement of the subsequent mishna (54a), that although a nazirite does not shave for overlying a quarter-*kav* of bones, he is obligated to shave for touching or carrying it. If so, this mishna's statement concerning a half-*kav* of bones, which excludes a quarter-*kav* of bones, likewise is referring to impurity imparted by contact.

HALAKHA

Where it has been made like flour – דְּאַקְמַח אַקְמוּחֵי: A quarter-*kav* of bones from one corpse that does not contain a single bone the volume of a barley-grain-bulk imparts ritual impurity in a tent as though it included a bone of this size. The *halakha* is in accordance with the opinion of the Rabbis (*Kesef Mishne*). The Rambam does not specify whether a nazirite shaves for touching or carrying this quarter-*kav*, but *Tosafot* and the Meiri rule that he is obligated to shave (Rambam *Sefer Tahara*, *Hilkhot Tumat Met* 4:4).

There is not a fitting quantity of flesh upon them – אֵין עֲלֵיהֶן בָּשָׂר כָּרָאוּי: If a nazirite was rendered ritually impure by a limb severed from a living person or by a limb severed from a corpse that was not covered by a fitting quantity of flesh, he requires sprinkling on the third and seventh days. However, he does not shave for his impurity, nor does he bring offerings. He does not negate his earlier period of naziriteship, although his days of impurity do not count toward his term of naziriteship. The *halakha* is in accordance with the opinion of Rabbi Yoḥanan (Rambam *Sefer Hafla'a*, *Hilkhot Nezirut* 7:6–7).

וְהָא חֲצִי קַב עֲצָמוֹת, דְּמַשְׁמַע: חֲצִי קַב עֲצָמוֹת – אִין, רוֹבַע עֲצָמוֹת – לָא, וְקָתָנֵי בְּסֵיפָא רוֹבַע עֲצָמוֹת!

The Gemara raises a difficulty against this claim of Rabbi Yoḥanan: **But** the first clause of the mishna lists the case of **a half-*kav* of bones,** which **indicates: A half-*kav* of bones, yes,** a nazirite must shave for that; **a quarter-*kav* of bones, no,** he is not obligated to shave for that. **And** yet the *tanna* **teaches in the latter clause** that a nazirite does not shave for **a quarter-*kav* of bones.** This shows that the next mishna does not rely on the rulings of this mishna. Rather, it lists all the items for which a nazirite need not shave.

הָתָם, אִי לָאו רוֹבַע עֲצָמוֹת הֲוָה אָמִינָא: אֲפִילּוּ עַל מַגָּעוֹ וְעַל מַשָּׂאוֹ לָא, לְהָכִי אִיצְטְרִיךְ לְמִיתְנֵי רוֹבַע עֲצָמוֹת – דְּעַל אֲהִילָן הוּא דְּאֵין הַנָּזִיר מְגַלֵּחַ.

The Gemara rejects this argument: **There, had** the *tanna* **not** taught **a quarter-*kav* of bones, I would say** that he need **not** shave **even for touching it or carrying it. For this** reason **it was necessary** for the mishna **to teach** the case of **a quarter-*kav* of bones,** to indicate that **it is** only **for their** ritual impurity contracted in **a tent** that **a nazirite does not shave.**

וְהָא חֲצִי לוֹג דָּם, דְּשָׁמְעַתְּ מִינַּהּ: חֲצִי לוֹג דָּם – אִין, רְבִיעִית דָּם – לָא, וְקָתָנֵי בְּסֵיפָא רְבִיעִית דָּם. הָתָם לְאַפּוּקֵי מִדְּרַבִּי עֲקִיבָא, דְּאָמַר רַבִּי עֲקִיבָא: רְבִיעִית דָּם הַבָּא מִשְּׁנֵי מֵתִים – מְטַמֵּא בְּאֹהֶל.

The Gemara raises a further difficulty: **But** the mishna lists **a half-*log* of blood** among those sources of impurity for which a nazirite must shave, **from which you** can **learn** that for **a half-*log* of blood, yes,** he shaves; for **a quarter-*log* of blood, no,** he does not shave. **And** yet **the latter clause** of the mishna **teaches** that he need not shave for **a quarter-*log* of blood.** The Gemara answers: It is also necessary to state this *halakha* unambiguously **there, to exclude** the opinion **of Rabbi Akiva,**[N] **as Rabbi Akiva said: A quarter-*log* of blood that comes from two corpses renders** people and items **impure in a tent,** whereas the mishna simply states: A quarter-*log*, which indicates that all of the blood comes from a single corpse.

הַאי אֵבֶר מִן הַמֵּת, הֵיכִי דָּמֵי? אִי דְּאִית בֵּיהּ עֶצֶם כִּשְׂעוֹרָה – מַאי טַעֲמָא דְּרַבִּי יוֹחָנָן? וְאִי דְּלֵית בֵּיהּ עֶצֶם כִּשְׂעוֹרָה – מַאי טַעֲמָא דְּרֵישׁ לָקִישׁ? אָמַר לָךְ רֵישׁ לָקִישׁ: לְעוֹלָם דְּלֵית בֵּיהּ עֶצֶם כִּשְׂעוֹרָה, וַאֲפִילּוּ הָכִי רַחֲמָנָא רַבְּיֵיהּ,

The Gemara analyzes the dispute between Rabbi Yoḥanan and Reish Lakish: **What are the circumstances** of this **limb** severed **from a corpse** that is not covered by sufficient flesh? **If it contains a bone that is a barley-grain-bulk, what is Rabbi Yoḥanan's reason** for maintaining that a nazirite does not have to shave for this ritual impurity? A bone of this size imparts impurity even if there is no flesh upon it. **And if it does not contain a bone that is a barley-grain-bulk, what is Reish Lakish's reason** for saying that a nazirite must shave due to this bone? The Gemara explains that **Reish Lakish** could have **said to you: Actually** we are dealing with a limb **that does not contain a bone that is a barley-grain-bulk, and even so the Merciful One includes it** as a source of ritual impurity.

דְּתַנְיָא: "וְכֹל אֲשֶׁר יִגַּע עַל פְּנֵי הַשָּׂדֶה בַּחֲלַל חֶרֶב אוֹ בְמֵת". "עַל פְּנֵי הַשָּׂדֶה" – זֶה הַמַּאֲהִיל עַל פְּנֵי הַמֵּת, "בַּחֲלַל" – זֶה אֵבֶר מִן הַחַי וְיֵשׁ לוֹ לְהַעֲלוֹת אֲרוּכָה,

This is **as it is taught** in a *baraita*: **"And whoever in the open field touches one who is slain by the sword, or one who dies on his own,** or a bone of a man, or a grave, shall be unclean seven days" (Numbers 19:16). This verse is expounded by the Sages as follows: **"In the open field"; this** is referring to the *halakha* of **one who overlies a corpse,**[BH] even without touching it. **"One who is slain"; this** is referring to **a limb** slain, i.e., severed, **from a living** person, **that contains**[H] enough flesh **for the limb to heal.**

NOTES

To exclude the opinion of Rabbi Akiva – לְאַפּוּקֵי מִדְּרַבִּי עֲקִיבָא: According to this standard version of the text, the Gemara is saying that emphasis of the mishna is on the phrase a quarter-*log*, which indicates that this volume of blood comes from a single corpse, in contrast to Rabbi Akiva's ruling that blood imparts ritual impurity in this amount even if it comes from two corpses (Commentary on *Nazir*). Most commentaries omit the sentence: As Rabbi Akiva said…from two corpses. They maintain that the reference here is to Rabbi Akiva's argument in the mishna at the end of the chapter (56b) that a nazirite should shave for a quarter-*log* of blood.

BACKGROUND

One who overlies a corpse – הַמַּאֲהִיל עַל פְּנֵי הַמֵּת: The *halakhot* of the ritual impurity imparted by a corpse, including a tent covering a corpse, are discussed in great detail in tractate *Oholot*. The essential *halakhot* of a tent over a corpse are detailed in the Torah (Numbers, chapter 19). The Sages derive that the place in which a corpse is located becomes entirely impure and renders everything in that place impure as well. By Torah law, this *halakha* applies when a corpse is located in a complete tent. However, the Sages concluded that even the smallest area that can be deemed a tent, an item with the size of one square handbreadth that covers one handbreadth of airspace, also falls under the same rubric: The covering itself and what is under it are rendered ritually impure with the impurity imparted by a corpse.

HALAKHA

One who overlies a corpse – הַמַּאֲהִיל עַל פְּנֵי הַמֵּת: A corpse renders one ritually impure for seven days by imparting impurity in a tent, as stated in the Torah. This includes situations where a person or a vessel overlies a corpse (Rambam *Sefer Tahara*, *Hilkhot Tumat Met* 1:1, 10).

A limb from a living person that contains, etc. – אֵבֶר מִן הַחַי וְיֵשׁ לוֹ וכו׳: If a limb severed from a living person is covered with enough flesh for it to heal were it still attached, it imparts ritual impurity via contact, carrying, and in a tent. If any part of the bone itself is missing, it does not render people and items impure. If it lacks sufficient flesh, it imparts impurity by contact and carrying but not in a tent (Rambam *Sefer Tahara*, *Hilkhot Tumat Met* 2:3).

"חרב" – הרי זה כחלל, "או במת" – זה אבר הנחלל מן המת, "או בעצם אדם" – זה רובע עצמות "או בקבר" – זה קבר סתום.

The Sages further derive from the phrase "one who is slain by the sword" that the legal status of a metal **sword** in terms of its degree of ritual impurity **is like** that of **one who is slain**,[NH] i.e., a metal implement, e.g., a sword, that was rendered impure through contact with a corpse is impure to the same degree of severity as a corpse itself. **"Or one who dies on his own"; this is a limb that was slain,** i.e., severed, **from a corpse**[H] and is covered with enough flesh that it would heal if he were alive. **"Or a bone of a man"; this is a quarter-*kav* of bones.**[H] **"Or a grave"; this is a sealed grave,**[NH] which imparts impurity when there is less than a handbreadth between the corpse and its cover.

NOTES

A sword is like one who is slain – חרב הרי זה כחלל: All the commentaries and authorities agree that a special *halakha* applies to a metal vessel rendered ritually impure by a corpse, as it imparts impurity like the corpse itself, so that one who touches it is impure for seven days. This is in contrast to any other vessel that was rendered impure by a corpse. Nevertheless, there are differences of opinion as to whether a sword is like a corpse in all regards, including the impurity imparted in a tent, or whether it imparts impurity only by contact, and some say by carrying as well. Likewise, some authorities maintain that just as it is accepted that the word sword includes all metal implements, the same *halakha* applies to all vessels that can be purified in a ritual bath, including wooden ones and the like.

A sealed grave – קבר סתום: Various *halakhot* apply to a sealed grave, although the details of these *halakhot* are subject to differences of opinion among the early commentaries. The basic *halakha* accepted by everyone is that a sealed grave that lacks the space of a handbreadth between the corpse and its cover imparts ritual impurity in a tent in the manner of a pressed ritual impurity. In other words, it renders impure anything positioned above the grave, even if a stone partition separates the corpse from that which overlies it.

HALAKHA

A sword is like one who is slain – חרב הרי זה כחלל: Some authorities maintain that any vessel rendered ritually impure by a corpse, whether by contact, carrying, or in a tent, imparts impurity via contact like a corpse itself, except for those items that cannot be purified in a ritual bath, e.g., earthenware vessels (Rambam). Others rule that even these implements impart impurity by carrying (Ramban). Yet others contend that this principle applies only to metal vessels, although they rule that these articles render people and items impure even in a tent (Ra'avad; *Tosafot*). Some authorities maintain that a priest is prohibited from contracting impurity from a sword that was rendered impure by a corpse, whereas others are lenient. The custom is not to be stringent in this regard (Rambam *Sefer Tahara, Hilkhot Tumat Met* 5:3; *Shulḥan Arukh, Yoreh De'a* 369:1, and in the comment of Rema).

A limb that was slain from a corpse – אבר הנחלל מן המת: A limb severed from a corpse imparts ritual impurity like a whole corpse, provided it contains flesh, sinews, and bones. If part of the bone is missing, but an olive-bulk of flesh remains, it imparts impurity like a whole body. Some maintain that this bone imparts impurity only via contact and carrying (Ra'avad). If some of the flesh is lacking but enough remains that were this limb attached to a living person it would heal, it imparts impurity like an intact corpse. If it is not covered by sufficient flesh, it is like a regular bone from a corpse (Rambam *Sefer Tahara, Hilkhot Tumat Met* 2:4).

A quarter-*kav* of bones – רובע עצמות: A quarter-*kav* of bones from a corpse imparts ritual impurity by contact, carrying, and in a tent, even if the bones comprise neither the majority of the number of bones in a body nor the majority of its structure, nor a whole spine nor a whole skull. If the bones amount to less than a quarter-*kav*, they do not impart impurity in a tent (Rambam *Sefer Tahara, Hilkhot Tumat Met* 2:9).

This is a sealed grave – זה קבר סתום: If a grave containing a corpse is sealed up, it imparts impurity by contact and in a tent. Consequently, a priest who touches the grave is liable to receive lashes (Rambam *Sefer Tahara, Hilkhot Tumat Met* 2:15 and *Sefer Shofetim, Hilkhot Evel* 3:2).

Perek **VII**
Daf **54** Amud **a**

דאמר מר: טומאה בוקעת ועולה בוקעת ויורדת. ואילו גבי נגיעה, אמר רב יהודה, תניא: "(וכל) הנוגע בעצם או בחלל". "בעצם" – זה עצם כשעורה, "או בחלל" – זה אבר הנחלל מן החי ואין בו להעלות ארוכה,

As the Master said: Ritual impurity in a sealed grave **breaks through and ascends**[H] **and breaks through and descends,** so that the grave imparts impurity like the corpse itself. **While with regard to contact** with these sources of impurity, **Rav Yehuda said** that **it is taught** in a *baraita* that the verse "**and** upon **him that touched a bone, or the slain,** or the dead, or the grave" (Numbers 19:18) is expounded as follows: **"A bone"; this is a bone that is a barley-grain-bulk. "Or the slain"; this is a limb slain,** i.e., severed, **from the living,**[H] **which does not contain** enough flesh **for it to heal.**

"או במת" – זה אבר הנחלל מן המת, "או בקבר" – אמר ריש לקיש: זה קבר שלפני הדיבור.

The *baraita* continues its interpretation of the verse. **"Or the dead"; this is a limb slain from a corpse,** which is not covered by enough flesh for it to heal were he alive. **"Or the grave"; Reish Lakish said: This is a grave** that contained a corpse from **before** the time **the command**[H] of these *halakhot* was given to the Jewish people. These graves render people and items ritually impure by contact, but do not carry the *halakhot* of impurity imparted in a tent.

האי אבר מן המת היכי דמי? אי דאית ביה עצם כשעורה – היינו הנוגע בעצם. אלא – דלית ביה עצם כשעורה, ואפילו הכי רחמנא רבייה!

The Gemara asks: With regard to **this limb from a corpse,** which is listed above as imparting ritual impurity by contact, **what are the circumstances** of the case? **If** the limb **contains a bone that is a barley-grain-bulk, this is** included in the *halakha* of **one who touches a bone,** and it was already taught that a bone imparts impurity by contact. **Rather,** it must be **that it does not contain a bone that is a barley-grain-bulk, and even so the Merciful One includes it** in the *halakhot* of impurity, despite the fact that it does not contain enough flesh. This indicates that a nazirite shaves for a limb of this kind, in accordance with the opinion of Reish Lakish.

HALAKHA

Breaks through and ascends, etc. – בוקעת ועולה וכו׳: If a source of ritual impurity in a tent of a corpse was pressed ritual impurity, i.e., impurity separated from its cover by less than a handbreadth, the impurity breaks through to the sky and down to the depths, even if it is blocked by multiple barriers. However, it does not impart impurity to its surroundings (Rambam *Sefer Tahara, Hilkhot Tumat Met* 7:4–5; see Ra'avad).

A limb slain from the living – אבר הנחלל מן החי: If a limb severed from a living person is not covered by enough flesh for it to heal were it attached, it imparts impurity by contact and carrying but not in a tent (Rambam *Sefer Tahara, Hilkhot Tumat Met* 2:3).

A grave before the command – קבר שלפני הדיבור: Gentiles and their graves do not render people and items impure in a tent (Rambam *Sefer Tahara, Hilkhot Tumat Met* 1:13).

אָמַר לָךְ רַבִּי יוֹחָנָן: לְעוֹלָם דְּאִית בֵּיהּ, וְאִם אֵינוֹ עִנְיָן לְמַגָּעוֹ – תְּנֵהוּ עִנְיָן לְמַשָּׂאוֹ.

The Gemara responds: In answer to this proof of Reish Lakish, **Rabbi Yoḥanan** could have **said to you: Actually,** you should explain **that it does contain**[H] a bone the volume of a barley-grain-bulk, **and if it does not** need to refer to **the matter of its contact,**[N] as the verse explicitly states: "Anyone who touches a bone," **have it refer to the matter of its carrying,**[H] i.e., that one who carries it is also rendered ritually impure.

״וּמַזֶּה בַּשְּׁלִישִׁי וּבַשְּׁבִיעִי וְסוֹתֵר״ וכו׳.

§ The mishna taught with regard to any nazirite who became impure from one of the listed sources of impurity: **And** a priest **sprinkles** the ashes of the red heifer on him **on the third and on the seventh** days, **and he negates** all the previous days he counted toward his naziriteship, and he does not begin counting a fresh term of naziriteship until after he becomes pure and brings his offerings.

אִיבַּעְיָא לְהוּ: הָא דְּקָתָנֵי ״עַד שֶׁיִּטְהַר״ – בַּשְּׁבִיעִי קָאֵי, עַד דְּעָבֵיד הֶעֱרֵב שֶׁמֶשׁ, וּמַנִּי – רַבִּי אֱלִיעֶזֶר הִיא. אוֹ דִּילְמָא: בַּשְּׁמִינִי קָאֵי, וּמַאי ״עַד שֶׁיִּטְהַר״ – עַד שֶׁיָּבִיא קָרְבְּנוֹתָיו, וּמַנִּי – רַבָּנַן הִיא?

A dilemma was raised before the Sages: What is the meaning of **that which is taught** that a nazirite does not start counting **until he is purified?** Does the mishna refer to one who is **standing on the seventh** day of his purification and mean: **Until** he **performs** the requisite waiting for **sunset?**[N] **And whose** opinion is it? **It is** the opinion of **Rabbi Eliezer,** who rules that a nazirite starts counting from the eighth day, even before he brings his offerings. **Or perhaps** it is referring to one who is **standing on the eighth** day. **And** then, **what** is the meaning of: **Until he is purified?** It means: **Until he brings his offerings. And who is** the author of this opinion? **It is the Rabbis,** who maintain that he begins his fresh period of naziriteship only after he has sacrificed his offering of impurity (see 18b).

תָּא שְׁמַע, מִדְּקָתָנֵי סֵיפָא ״מַתְחִיל וּמוֹנֶה מִיָּד״. הָא רֵישָׁא מַאי ״עַד שֶׁיִּטְהַר״ – עַד שֶׁיָּבִיא קָרְבְּנוֹתָיו, וּמַנִּי – רַבָּנַן הִיא, דְּאָמְרִי: נְזִירוּת דְּטָהֳרָה עַד שְׁמִינִי לָא חָיְילָא.

The Gemara answers: **Come and hear** a resolution of this dilemma **from** the fact **that it teaches in the latter clause** of the next mishna that a nazirite who does not have to bring an offering **starts counting immediately** after the conclusion of his seven days of purification. The Gemara infers from this mishna: If so, **what is** the meaning of the different term used in **the first clause: Until he is purified?** It means **until he brings his offerings, and whose** opinion is it? **It is** that of **the Rabbis, who say** that the **naziriteship of purity does not commence until the eighth** day.

מתני׳ אֲבָל הַסְּכָכוֹת, וְהַפְּרָעוֹת, וּבֵית הַפְּרָס,

MISHNA The previous mishna listed the sources of ritual impurity for which a nazirite must shave. This mishna adds: **However,** the nazirite does not shave for these: **The hanging** branches[N] over a corpse, i.e., a tree overhanging a body that a nazirite passes, but it is uncertain which branches are over a corpse; **and the projecting** stones[H] from fences when the place of the impurity is unknown; **and a *beit haperas*,** a place that contained a grave and was plowed. In the latter case, the entire area around the grave is impure from a corpse due to an uncertainty, as it might contain human bones.

NOTES

If it does not refer to the matter of its contact – אִם אֵינוֹ עִנְיָן לְמַגָּעוֹ: The impurity imparted by touching a bone is derived from the words "and upon him that touched a bone" (Numbers 19:18). This includes a bone the volume of a barley-grain-bulk, even when it is not covered by flesh. Since the phrase "or the dead" is superfluous, the Sages learn from it that this bone imparts impurity by carrying as well. According to Rabbi Yoḥanan, this phrase is the main source for the *halakha* of the impurity imparted through carrying a bone the size of a barley-grain-bulk, which is not explicitly stated in the Torah. The commentaries note that Reish Lakish evidently derives this *halakha* from a different verse (Rabbeinu Azriel).

Until he performs the requisite waiting for sunset – עַד דְּעָבֵיד הֶעֱרֵב שֶׁמֶשׁ: Some early commentaries omit this phrase. The key issue is Rabbi Eliezer's opinion. According to some authorities, he maintains that the nazirite does not wait until evening but begins to count from the seventh day itself (*Tosafot*). Others contend that even according to Rabbi Eliezer, he starts counting only from the eighth day (Commentary on *Nazir*; see Rabbi Akiva Eiger on the mishna).

However the hanging branches, etc. – אֲבָל הַסְּכָכוֹת וכו׳: This list of items that do not render a nazirite obligated to shave includes various rabbinic sources of ritual impurity, i.e., hanging branches, projecting stones, and the land of the nations. It is obvious that a nazirite need not shave for these sources of impurity, as the Sages would not impose a decree that nullifies a mitzva of the Torah. However, the mishna also lists other items, including a quarter-*log* of blood and a quarter-*kav* of bones, whose impurity applies by Torah law (see *Tosafot*). Some commentaries maintain that there is a difference between the *halakhot* of a nazirite and the *halakhot* pertaining to standard impurity from a corpse (Rambam's Commentary on the Mishna). With regard to a nazirite, the verse states: "And if any man dies very suddenly beside him" (Numbers 6:9), rather than: If he becomes impure from the body of a person. This indicates that a nazirite shaves only if he was rendered impure from an actual corpse. Others maintain that this verse teaches that the impurity for which a nazirite must shave is that of a whole corpse (Ra'avad). In any case, the Rambam himself states that those sources of impurity for which a nazirite need not shave do not impart impurity by Torah law.

HALAKHA

Actually that it does contain – לְעוֹלָם דְּאִית בֵּיהּ: If a limb severed from a dead body contains a bone the volume of a barley-grain-bulk, but it is not covered with enough flesh that it could heal were it on a living person, it imparts ritual impurity by carrying and contact but not in a tent (Rambam *Sefer Tahara, Hilkhot Tumat Met* 2:4, see Ra'avad).

Have it refer to the matter of its carrying – תְּנֵהוּ עִנְיָן לְמַשָּׂאוֹ: A bone of a corpse the volume of a barley-grain-bulk imparts impurity by carrying as well as by contact (Rambam *Sefer Tahara, Hilkhot Tumat Met* 3:2).

However, the hanging branches and the projecting stones, etc. – אֲבָל הַסְּכָכוֹת וְהַפְּרָעוֹת וכו׳: If a nazirite became ritually impure due to a clod of earth from outside of Eretz Yisrael; or by walking through a *beit haperas*, a field in which a grave was plowed; or if branches of a tree or stones from a fence protruded and served as a tent over both him and a corpse, called hangings and projections by the mishna; or in a tent with a quarter-*kav* of bones that do not contain the majority of the structure or the majority of the number of bones of a corpse; or through a quarter-*log* of blood from a corpse; or by a grave cover or grave walls; or by a limb severed from a corpse or from a living person that was not covered by sufficient flesh; in all of these cases, the nazirite requires sprinkling on the third and seventh days but does not have to shave (Rambam *Sefer Hafla'a, Hilkhot Nezirut* 7:6, 8).

BACKGROUND

Grave cover [*golel*] – גּוֹלֵל: A *golel* was a large stone that was rolled onto a grave or burial cave to seal its entrance. Burial caves of important people were covered with a large, wheel-shaped stone that could be rolled back to allow entrance to the cave.

Burial cave with stone cover in northern Israel

וְאֶרֶץ הָעַמִּים, וְהַגּוֹלֵל וְהַדּוֹפֵק, וּרְבִיעִית דָּם, וְאֹהֶל, וְרוֹבַע עֲצָמוֹת, וְכֵלִים הַנּוֹגְעִים בַּמֵּת, וּבִימֵי סְפָרוֹ וּבִימֵי גְּמָרוֹ – עַל אֵלּוּ אֵין הַנָּזִיר מְגַלֵּחַ.

The mishna continues its list: **And the land of the nations,** i.e., a nazirite left Eretz Yisrael for another land. The Sages decreed that all land outside of Eretz Yisrael is ritually impure. **And the grave cover;**[B] **and the grave walls** upon which the cover rests; **and a quarter-*log* of blood** from a corpse; **and a tent; and a quarter-*kav* of bones**[N] of a corpse; **and vessels that are touching a corpse. And** if the nazirite is **in the days of his counting,** i.e., the seven days a leper must count after purification from his leprosy; **or in his days of full** leprosy, when he is a full-fledged leper, **for these the nazirite does not shave.**[N] This is the case even if he is rendered impure by one of the sources listed in the previous mishna.

וּמַזֶּה בַּשְּׁלִישִׁי וּבַשְּׁבִיעִי,

And in those cases listed that involve ritual impurity from a corpse, **one sprinkles** the purification water upon him **on the third and on the seventh** days of his purification,

NOTES

And a tent, and a quarter-*kav* of bones – וְאוֹהֶל וְרוֹבַע עֲצָמוֹת: Some commentaries infer from the fact that the mishna lists a tent and a quarter-*kav* of bones as distinct items that a nazirite who comes into contact with a tent of a corpse need not shave (Rambam). Others maintain that this should be read as a single item: And the tent of a quarter-*kav* of bones (see Rabbi Ovadya Bartenura and *Tosefot Yom Tov*).

For these the nazirite does not shave – עַל אֵלּוּ אֵין הַנָּזִיר מְגַלֵּחַ: The commentaries note that this statement does not apply to all these cases, as a leper is in fact obligated to shave (*Tosafot*). Others state that although a leper must shave, this differs from the shaving of a nazirite, as a leper shaves all the hair of his body, not merely his head (Rabbeinu Peretz).

Perek **VII**
Daf **54** Amud **b**

HALAKHA

And he does not negate, etc. – וְאֵינוֹ סוֹתֵר וכו׳: A nazirite who was rendered ritually impure by one of the sources of impurity listed in the mishna does not negate his earlier period of naziriteship. He neither shaves for his impurity nor brings the relevant offerings. After his purification, he continues to count the days of his naziriteship. However, the days of his impurity do not count toward his term (Rambam *Sefer Hafla'a, Hilkhot Nezirut* 7:7–9).

Days of the *zav*, etc. – יְמֵי הַזָּב וכו׳: The days of a leper's confinement and the days of the impurity of a *zav* or a *zava* count toward their naziriteship term, despite their impurity. This is a *halakha* transmitted to Moses from Sinai (Rambam *Sefer Hafla'a, Hilkhot Nezirut* 7:9).

Hanging branches and projecting stones – סְכָכוֹת וּפְרָעוֹת: The hangings mentioned in the mishna are boughs that extend from trees, while projections are stones that jut out of fences. These are not strong enough to bear a medium-sized cover without bending inward. If they can bear that weight, they impart ritual impurity by Torah law (Rambam *Sefer Hafla'a, Hilkhot Nezirut* 7:6 and *Sefer Tahara, Hilkhot Tumat Met* 13:2).

וְאֵינוֹ סוֹתֵר אֶת הַקּוֹדְמִים, וּמַתְחִיל וּמוֹנֶה מִיָּד, וְקָרְבָּן אֵין לוֹ. בֶּאֱמֶת אָמְרוּ: יְמֵי הַזָּב וְהַזָּבָה, וִימֵי הֶסְגֵּרוֹ שֶׁל מְצוֹרָע – הֲרֵי אֵלּוּ עוֹלִין לוֹ.

and he does not negate[H] **the earlier** days[N] of his naziriteship, but they are considered part of his naziriteship term. **And he starts counting** the rest of his naziriteship to complete his term **immediately** after his purification, **and he has no** obligation to sacrifice **an offering** of impurity for these sources of ritual impurity. **Actually they said** an ancient tradition that these **days of** the impurity of **the *zav*** (Leviticus 15:1–15)[H] **and the *zava*** (Leviticus 15:25–30) **and the days of the confinement of a leper** before he is confirmed as a full-fledged leper (Leviticus 13:4–5) **count for him** toward the period of his naziriteship.

גמ׳ וְאֵלּוּ הֵן הַסְּכָכוֹת – אִילָן הַמֵּיסַךְ עַל הָאָרֶץ, וּפְרָעוֹת – הַיּוֹצְאוֹת מִן הַגָּדֵר.

GEMARA The Gemara explains the terms hangings and projections by citing a mishna (*Oholot* 8:2). **And these are the hangings: A tree that overhangs the earth.**[N] **And the projections**[N] are stones[H] **that protrude from a fence.**

NOTES

And he does not negate the earlier days – וְאֵינוֹ סוֹתֵר אֶת הַקּוֹדְמִים: Although he does not forfeit the earlier period, these days of purification do not count toward his naziriteship. Rather, after he is purified he resumes counting where he left off.

A tree that overhangs the earth – אִילָן הַמֵּיסַךְ עַל הָאָרֶץ: All commentaries agree that this is referring to a tree whose branches are spread apart so that they do not form one unbroken cover. The disagreements concern the details of the case. Some commentaries maintain that the branches in question are thinner than a handbreadth and are not positioned close together. As a result, they do not form a tent by Torah law, even if the nazirite were to walk under each of the branches (*Tosafot*). Others contend that this is referring to branches that are one handbreadth wide, and the nazirite walked under some, but not all, of them. He is not rendered ritually impure by Torah law because the tree is situated in the public domain, and when there is uncertainty with regard to impurity in the public domain it is considered pure (Rabbeinu Peretz; see Rosh). Others indicate that the tree does not impart impurity by Torah law because the branches are not strong enough, and therefore it is classified as a shaky tent (Rambam).

Projections – פְּרָעוֹת: In this case, it was known that there was a grave of a stillborn or an olive-bulk from a corpse under one of the stones. However, the identity of that stone is unknown. Consequently, a nazirite who passes beneath some of the stones remains pure, as this is a case of uncertainty with regard to impurity in the public domain.

"וְאֶרֶץ הָעַמִּים". אִיבַּעְיָא לְהוּ: אֶרֶץ הָעַמִּים מִשּׁוּם אֲוִירָא גָּזְרוּ עֲלֶיהָ, אוֹ דִילְמָא מִשּׁוּם גּוּשָׁא גָּזְרוּ עֲלֶיהָ?

§ The mishna further taught: **And the land of the nations** does not render a nazirite obligated to shave, despite the fact that it is considered ritually impure. The Gemara inquires with regard to the nature of this impurity. **A dilemma was raised before** the Sages: Did the Sages **decree the land of the nations** impure **with regard to the air,** i.e., is one rendered impure merely by being there? **Or perhaps they decreed** it impure **with regard to the earth,** i.e., one who touches the ground or overlays it becomes impure.

תָּא שְׁמַע: וּמַזֶּה בַּשְּׁלִישִׁי וּבַשְּׁבִיעִי. וְאִי אָמְרַתְּ מִשּׁוּם אֲוִירָא – הַזָּאָה לָמָּה לִי?

The Gemara suggests: **Come** and **hear** a resolution to this question from the mishna, which lists one who enters the land of the nations and states: **And one sprinkles** on him **on the third and on the seventh** days. **And if you say** that the decree was **with regard to the air, why do I** need this **sprinkling?**[H] He neither touched something ritually impure nor overlaid it.

אֶלָּא לָאו מִשּׁוּם גּוּשָׁא. לָא. לְעוֹלָם אֵימָא לָךְ מִשּׁוּם אֲוִירָא, וְכִי קָתָנֵי – אַשְּׁאָרָא.

Rather, is it not with regard to the earth that the land of the nations was decreed impure? The Gemara rejects this proof: **No, actually I** could **say to you** that the decree is **due to the air, and when** the mishna **teaches** that he receives the sprinkling, it is referring **to the other** items listed in the mishna, e.g., the grave cover, the grave walls, and a quarter-*log* of blood.

הָכִי נַמִי מִסְתַּבְּרָא, מִדְּקָתָנֵי: וְכֵלִים הַנּוֹגְעִים בַּמֵּת; הָנֵי כֵּלִים בְּנֵי הַזָּאָה אִינּוּן? אֶלָּא שְׁמַע מִינַּהּ – אַשְּׁאָרָא.

The Gemara comments: **So too, it is reasonable** that this is the case, **from** the fact **that** the mishna also **teaches: And vessels that are touching a corpse.** Now do people who touch **these vessels require sprinkling?**[HN] Does one who touches a vessel that is ritually impure from a corpse require the sprinkling of purification water? This individual is impure only until that evening. **Rather, learn from this** that the *halakha* that he is sprinkled on the third and on the seventh days does not refer to all the cases in the mishna but only **to** some of **the others.**

Perek **VII**
Daf **55** Amud **a**

לֵימָא כְּתַנָּאֵי: הַנִּכְנָס לְאֶרֶץ הָעַמִּים בְּשִׁידָּה תֵּיבָה וּמִגְדָּל, רַבִּי מְטַמֵּא, וְרַבִּי יוֹסֵי בְּרַבִּי יְהוּדָה מְטַהֵר. מַאי לָאו רַבִּי סָבַר מִשּׁוּם אֲוִירָא, וְרַבִּי יוֹסֵי בְּרַבִּי יְהוּדָה סָבַר מִשּׁוּם גּוּשָׁא?

Let us say that this is **parallel to** a dispute between ***tanna'im,*** as it is taught: With regard to **one who enters the land of the nations** not on foot but **in a chest, a box, or a cabinet,**[H] **Rabbi** Yehuda HaNasi **deems** him ritually **impure. And Rabbi Yosei, son of Rabbi Yehuda, deems** him **pure. What, is it not** correct to say that they disagree in this regard: **Rabbi** Yehuda HaNasi, who deems him impure, **holds** that the Sages decreed impurity **with regard to the air, and Rabbi Yosei, son of Rabbi Yehuda, holds** that the Sages decreed impurity **with regard to the earth,** and consequently he is not impure, as the container prevents him from overlying the impurity?

לָא, דְּכוּלֵּי עָלְמָא מִשּׁוּם גּוּשָׁא, מָר סָבַר: אֹהֶל זָרוּק שְׁמֵיהּ אֹהֶל, וּמָר סָבַר: לָא שְׁמֵיהּ אֹהֶל.

The Gemara rejects this suggestion: This is **not** necessarily the correct interpretation of their dispute, as one can say **that everyone** agrees that the decree is **with regard to the earth,** and their dispute concerns only the case of one who enters in a chest, a box, or a cabinet. One **Sage,** Rabbi Yosei, son of Rabbi Yehuda, **holds** that a **moving tent,** an item that serves as a tent as it passes over ritual impurity, **is called a tent,** and therefore a person who enters the land of the nations in a large container is protected from its impurity. **And one Sage,** Rabbi Yehuda HaNasi, **holds** that **a moving tent is not called a tent.** Consequently, nothing separates this individual from the impurity, and he becomes impure by overlying the land of the nations.

HALAKHA

With regard to the air, why do I need this sprinkling – מִשּׁוּם אֲוִירָא הַזָּאָה לָמָּה לִי: The Sages initially decreed ritual impurity on the earth of the lands of the nations, which is imparted by contact and carrying. Later they extended the decree to its air, so that anyone who inserts his head and the majority of his body into those lands contracts impurity. However, the air imparts a lesser degree of impurity. It does not necessitate sprinkling on the third and seventh days; rather, one merely has to immerse and wait for sunset. Similarly, it is not necessary to burn *teruma* and offerings due to this impurity. For this reason, the Rambam rules that the *halakha* of the mishna is referring only to the impurity imparted by contact or carrying the earth of the land of the nations (Rambam *Sefer Hafla'a, Hilkhot Nezirut* 7:6 and *Leḥem Mishne* there; and *Sefer Tahara, Hilkhot Tumat Met* 11:1–2).

Do people who touch these vessels require sprinkling, etc. – הָנֵי כֵּלִים בְּנֵי הַזָּאָה אִינּוּן וכו׳: If a nazirite touched vessels that came in contact with a corpse, he does not require sprinkling on the third and seventh days. This exception applies only to a nazirite, so that these days can count toward his term of naziriteship. Any other individual who becomes ritually impure from these vessels requires sprinkling on the third and seventh days (Rambam *Sefer Hafla'a, Hilkhot Nezirut* 7:8).

NOTES

These vessels require sprinkling – הָנֵי כֵּלִים בְּנֵי הַזָּאָה: Some commentaries cite this as proof that the vessels referred to by the mishna are made of materials other than metal, as metal vessels impart ritual impurity like the corpse itself (Rabbeinu Tam). Others claim that the vessels mentioned in the mishna are of all types, including metal ones (Rabbeinu Ḥayyim HaKohen). A nazirite does not have to shave for them because he shaves only for coming into contact with a corpse itself, not for all items classified as having the impurity of a corpse, as the verse states: "And if any man dies very suddenly beside him" (Numbers 6:9). Some claim that a nazirite does not even need to be sprinkled with water for those sources of impurity (Meiri).

HALAKHA

In a chest, a box, or a cabinet – בְּשִׁידָּה תֵּיבָה וּמִגְדָּל: One who enters the land of the nations in a chest, a box, or a cabinet that does not come in contact with the ground is rendered ritually impure, as a moving tent is not considered a tent. The *halakha* is in accordance with the opinion of Rabbi Yehuda HaNasi (Rambam *Sefer Tahara, Hilkhot Tumat Met* 11:5).

NOTES

But isn't it taught…a box that is full of utensils…is impure – וְהָתַנְיָא...תֵּיבָה שֶׁהִיא מְלֵאָה כֵּלִים...טְמֵאָה: The commentaries explain that this ruling of impurity does not refer to the box itself but to its contents. In other words, the box does not serve as a barrier protecting its contents from impurity (see Rashash). Some say that this *baraita* teaches that a moving tent is not classified as a tent according to the opinion of Rabbi Yosei, son of Rabbi Yehuda. Consequently, it does not block impurity, which means that all the vessels above the corpse are themselves considered to be overlying the corpse and are therefore rendered impure. If so, this *baraita* contradicts the earlier explanation that Rabbi Yosei, son of Rabbi Yehuda, maintains that a moving tent is considered a tent, which leads the Gemara to provide an alternative interpretation of the dispute (Commentary on *Nazir*).

Others explain this in the reverse manner, that the *baraita* offers support for the Gemara's previous interpretation. They maintain that a moving tent refers to a particular category of portable objects and that there is a difference between a moving tent that is thrown in the air and one that is placed on an animal or carried by people whose feet are on the ground. The *baraita* in question proves that according to Rabbi Yosei, son of Rabbi Yehuda, a moving tent that is placed in one spot and tied to the ground has the status of a tent. The same applies to a chest, a box, or a cabinet. Since they are carried on something and connected to the ground, they are treated as a tent positioned in one spot. Consequently, they protect their contents from impurity, despite the fact that they can be moved (*Tosafot*). According to this opinion, the phrase: But isn't it taught, should not be read in the form of a question, but as a confirmation: Indeed it was taught, as in the next usage on this *amud*. Likewise, the subsequent term: Rather, which indicates a rejection of the previous interpretation, must be omitted and replaced by the phrase: If you wish you can say, which introduces an alternative explanation.

And if you wish, say here they disagree with regard to the concern lest he remove – וְאִיבָּעֵית אֵימָא הָכָא שֶׁמָּא יוֹצִיא: Here too, all the commentaries agree that the Gemara retracts its previous answer. However, they dispute the particulars. According to one opinion, both *tanna'im* agree that the decree of impurity on the land of the nations is with regard to its earth, and a moving tent is considered a tent, which means that if one were to remain in the tent he would be pure. However, Rabbi Yehuda HaNasi and Rabbi Yosei, son of Rabbi Yehuda, disagree with regard to the possibility that one might remove his head and the majority of his body from the container and thereby become impure by serving as a tent over the earth of the land of the nations. The Gemara proceeds to cite a proof from the *baraita* that even Rabbi Yosei, son of Rabbi Yehuda, concedes that one who leans his head and the majority of his body into air that overlays the land of the nations is impure (see *Nushat Rivan*).

Other commentaries maintain that the *baraita* is cited to justify the Gemara's distinction between a box on the one hand and a boat or wagon on the other. The question is whether the Sages entertain the likelihood that one might remove his head from the container, in which case he becomes impure due to the air. Rabbi Yosei, son of Rabbi Yehuda, maintains that there is a greater possibility of him doing so on a boat or wagon, whereas it is uncomfortable to jut one's head out of a box or cabinet (*Tosafot*; Rosh).

וְהָתַנְיָא, רַבִּי יוֹסֵי בְּרַבִּי יְהוּדָה אוֹמֵר: תֵּיבָה שֶׁהִיא מְלֵאָה כֵּלִים וּזְרָקָהּ עַל פְּנֵי הַמֵּת בְּאֹהֶל – טְמֵאָה, וְאִם הָיְתָה מוּנַּחַת – טְהוֹרָה.

The Gemara asks: **But isn't it taught** in a *baraita* that **Rabbi Yosei, son of Rabbi Yehuda, says: A box that is full of utensils that one threw over a corpse in a tent,** in such a manner that it overlay the corpse, **is impure,**[N] and everything inside it is also rendered ritually impure, as it does not provide the protection of a tent. **And if it was placed down** and positioned as a tent over a corpse, **it is pure,** and its contents are protected from the impurity. This shows that according to the opinion of Rabbi Yosei, son of Rabbi Yehuda, a moving tent is not considered a tent, which contradicts the above claim.

אֶלָּא, דְּכוּלֵּי עָלְמָא מִשּׁוּם אֲוִירָא, וּמָר סָבַר: כֵּיוָן דְּלָא שְׁכִיחָא – לָא גְּזַרוּ בֵּיהּ רַבָּנַן, וּמָר סָבַר: אַף עַל גַּב דְּלָא שְׁכִיחָא – גְּזַרוּ בֵּיהּ רַבָּנַן.

In light of this argument, the Gemara concedes that the previous explanation of the dispute is incorrect. **Rather,** one must say **that everyone** agrees that the decree of impurity concerning the land of the nations is **with regard to its air, and one Sage,** Rabbi Yosei, son of Rabbi Yehuda, **holds** that **since it is not common** for one to move around in an enclosure, **the Sages did not decree** impurity **with regard to** this case. **And one Sage,** Rabbi Yehuda HaNasi, **holds** that **although it is not common the Sages** nevertheless **decreed** impurity **with regard to it.**

וְהָתַנְיָא: הַנִּכְנָס לְאֶרֶץ הָעַמִּים בְּשִׁידָּה תֵּיבָה וּמִגְדָּל – טָהוֹר, בְּקָרוֹן וּבִסְפִינָה וּבְאִיסְקַרְיָא – טָמֵא.

The Gemara adds: **And it is taught** in the *Tosefta* (*Oholot* 18:5) in accordance with this explanation of the opinion of Rabbi Yosei, son of Rabbi Yehuda: **One who enters the land of the nations in a chest, a box, or a cabinet** is **ritually pure.** If he was **in a wagon** [*karon*],[L] **boat, or raft** [*iskareya*],[L] he is **ritually impure.** The difference is that the latter vessels are commonly used to convey people.

וְאִיבָּעֵית אֵימָא: הָכָא שֶׁמָּא יוֹצִיא רֹאשׁוֹ וְרוּבּוֹ לְשָׁם פְּלִיגִי.

And if you wish, say an alternative explanation of the dispute between Rabbi Yehuda HaNasi and Rabbi Yosei, son of Rabbi Yehuda. Both agree that the ritual impurity of the land of the nations is with regard to the earth, and a moving tent is considered a tent. Therefore, the person in question should be ritually pure according to both opinions. However, **here they disagree** with regard to a different issue, the concern **lest he remove**[N] **his head and the majority of his body** from the chest, box, or cabinet **into there,** i.e., the land of the nations.

וְהָתַנְיָא, רַבִּי יוֹסֵי בְּרַבִּי יְהוּדָה אוֹמֵר: הַנִּכְנָס לְאֶרֶץ הָעַמִּים בְּשִׁידָּה תֵּיבָה וּמִגְדָּל – טָהוֹר, עַד שֶׁיּוֹצִיא לְשָׁם רֹאשׁוֹ אוֹ רוּבּוֹ.

And it is taught likewise in a *baraita* that **Rabbi Yosei, son of Rabbi Yehuda, says: One who enters the land of the nations in a chest, a box, or a cabinet is pure, unless he** actually **removes his head or the majority of his body into** the land of the nations. By contrast, Rabbi Yehuda HaNasi renders him ritually impure due to concern that one's head might protrude from the container.

LANGUAGE

Wagon [*karon*] – קָרוֹן: From the Greek κάρρον, *karron*, meaning a carriage or wagon used for transporting objects or for travel.

Roman stone relief of a carriage

Raft [*iskareya*] – אִיסְקַרְיָא: The *ge'onim* read this as *iskadeya*, from the Greek σχεδιά, *skhedia*, meaning a raft. The source of the present version comes from the Greek ἱστοκεραία, *histokeraia*, which means a mast, a wooden post on which sails are hung.

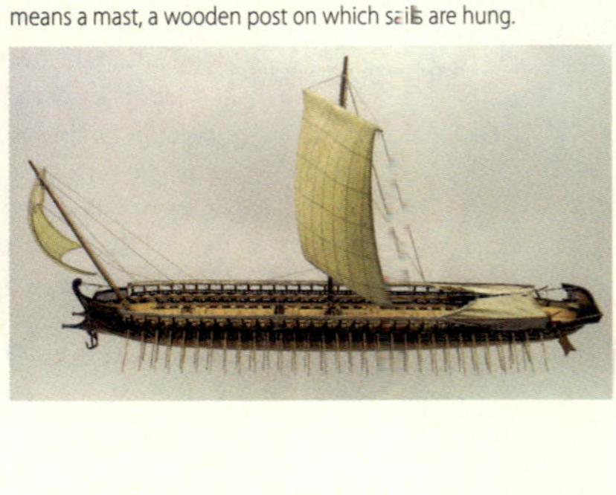

Replica of an ancient Greek ship with a large mast

״וּמַתְחִיל וּמוֹנֶה״. אָמַר רַב חִסְדָּא: לֹא שָׁנוּ אֶלָּא בִּנְזִירוּת מוּעֶטֶת, אֲבָל בִּנְזִירוּת מְרוּבָּה – מִיסְלַק נַמִי סָלְקִין לֵיהּ.

§ The mishna taught that a nazirite who became ritually impure through sources of impurity that do not cause him to forfeit his naziriteship, including his days of leprosy, **starts counting** again from the day of his purification, as his period of impurity does not count toward his naziriteship. **Rav Ḥisda said: They taught** this *halakha* of a leper **only with regard to a short naziriteship** of thirty days, as he shaves his hair for purification from leprosy, and therefore he must count an additional thirty days to allow his hair to grow sufficiently to shave for his naziriteship. **However, with regard to a lengthy naziriteship,** when thirty days or more remain in his naziriteship after having shaved for his leprosy, those days **also count toward his** term, and he need not recount his days as a leper.

מְתִיב רַב שֵׁרֵבְיָא: מַתְחִיל וּמוֹנֶה מִיָּד, וְאֵין מְבַטֵּל בָּהֶן אֶת הַקּוֹדְמִין. בְּמַאי? אִילֵימָא בִּנְזִירוּת מוּעֶטֶת – קָבָעֵי גִּידּוּל שֵׂיעָר!

Rav Sherevya raises an objection from the mishna: **He starts counting immediately, and he does not negate the earlier** days due **to them. To what** case is the mishna referring? **If we say** it is referring **to a short naziriteship, he requires** a thirty-day period of **hair growth,** and as he shaved for purification of his leprosy, he must negate the earlier days as a practical manner, to enable his hair to regrow.

Perek **VII**
Daf **55** Amud **b**

אֶלָּא לָאו בִּנְזִירוּת מְרוּבָּה, וְקָתָנֵי: מַתְחִיל וּמוֹנֶה מִיָּד! הוּא מוֹתִיב לָהּ, וְהוּא מְפָרֵק לָהּ: בִּנְזִירוּת בַּת חֲמִשִּׁים יוֹם, דְּיָתֵיב עֶשְׂרִין וְאִיתְיְלִידָא בֵּיהּ צָרַעַת. מְגַלֵּחַ צָרַעְתּוֹ וַהֲדַר יָתֵיב תְּלָתִין יוֹמִין דְּנָזִיר, דְּהָא אִית לֵיהּ גִּידּוּל שֵׂעָר.

Rather, is it not the case that the mishna is referring **to a lengthy naziriteship, and** nevertheless **it teaches: He starts counting immediately,** which indicates that his time as a leper is not included? Rav Sherevya **raised the objection and he resolved it:** The mishna is referring **to a naziriteship of fifty days,**[N] in a case **where he sat** and observed **twenty** days of his vow, **and** at that point **he developed leprosy.** In that case, he **shaves** for **his leprosy, and he again sits** for **thirty days as a nazirite.** The problem of thirty days' hair growth does not arise in this situation, **as** at the end of this period **there is hair growth** of thirty days.

מְתִיב רָמִי בַּר חָמָא: נָזִיר שֶׁהָיָה טָמֵא בְּסָפֵק וּמוּחְלָט בְּסָפֵק

Rami bar Ḥama raised an objection from a mishna (59b): With regard to **a nazirite who has uncertain impurity** from a corpse **and** whose status as **a confirmed** leper **is uncertain,**

NOTES

A naziriteship of fifty days – נְזִירוּת בַּת חֲמִשִּׁים יוֹם: According to this explanation, the phrase: A short naziriteship, does not refer to the entire length of the vow, which is of no importance with regard to this issue, but to the days remaining for his naziriteship after shaving for his leprosy. If this period is thirty days or less, it is called a short naziriteship, and in practice he will necessarily have to observe more days so that he has thirty days of hair growth. If enough days are left in the naziriteship, he does not have to negate any days for the sake of his hair growth.

Perek **VII**
Daf **56** Amud **a**

אוֹכֵל בְּקָדָשִׁים לְאַחַר שִׁשִּׁים יוֹם,

he eats sacrificial food after sixty days,[N] when the status of uncertain leprosy has passed, and when he has completed all his obligations of naziriteship. He cannot shave for his leprosy right away, as he might be a pure nazirite, and the status of uncertain leprosy does not override naziriteship. Instead, after thirty days he shaves for his uncertain status as a confirmed leper and for his uncertain status as a pure nazirite. Once again, he is not permitted to shave a second time seven days later for the shaving done by a leper as part of his purification process in case he was not a leper but impure. Were that the case, it would mean that the previous shaving was for his impurity, and therefore he would be required observe naziriteship in purity for thirty days. At the conclusion of this period, i.e., the sixtieth day, he shaves and may eat sacrificial food on the following day, as even if he was a full-fledged leper he has now shaved twice.

NOTES

n1**He eats sacrificial food after sixty days – אוֹכֵל בְּקָדָשִׁים לְאַחַר שִׁשִּׁים יוֹם:** He cannot partake of sacrificial food beforehand, as he may be a leper who lacks atonement. Therefore, he must bring his offerings of purification before he can eat sacrificial food. It is important to note that only those lacking atonement whose impurity is inherent, e.g., a leper or a *zav*, are included in this category. However, other people who must bring offerings, e.g., nazirites, may partake of sacrificial food.

וְשׁוֹתֶה יַיִן וּמִיטַּמֵּא לַמֵּתִים לְאַחַר מֵאָה וְעֶשְׂרִים יוֹם.

And he drinks wine and may become impure to bury **a corpse after 120 days.** In other words, this individual has not yet completed his naziriteship vow, as he might have been a confirmed leper, in which case both his acts of shaving would have counted for his leprosy. He therefore waits another thirty days and proceeds to shave on day ninety. Even at that stage, he may not yet drink wine or contract ritual impurity from a corpse, as he might have been impure, which would mean that his third shaving was for his impurity. Consequently, he counts another period of thirty days for his naziriteship of purity, at the end of which he may perform the shaving of purity, drink wine, and become impure from a corpse, 120 days from the start of his naziriteship.

וְתָנֵי עֲלָהּ: בַּמֶּה דְּבָרִים אֲמוּרִים – בִּנְזִירוּת מוּעֶטֶת, אֲבָל בִּנְזִירוּת בַּת שָׁנָה – אוֹכֵל בַּקֳּדָשִׁים לְאַחַר שְׁתֵּי שָׁנִים,

And it is taught in the *Tosefta* (6:1) **with regard to** that mishna: **In what case is this statement said? With regard to a short naziriteship** of thirty days. **However, with regard to a naziriteship of a year, he eats sacrificial food after two years.** He cannot shave until a year has passed, in case he is not a leper, and he may shave the second time only after a second year, in case he was ritually impure, and this was his naziriteship observed in purity. After two years, he may eat sacrificial meat, for if he was a full-fledged leper he has shaved twice.

וְשׁוֹתֶה יַיִן וּמִיטַּמֵּא לַמֵּתִים לְאַחַר אַרְבַּע שָׁנִים.

However, if the first two shavings were for his leprosy, he has not shaved for his naziriteship at all, and therefore he must observe an additional year, shave, and observe another year of naziriteship, as perhaps his third shaving was for impurity and the other for his naziriteship in purity. **And** consequently, **he may drink wine and become impure to** bury **a corpse after four years.**

וְאִי סָלְקָא דַּעְתָּךְ סָלְקִין לֵיהּ יוֹמֵי – תִּיסְגֵּי לֵיהּ בְּשָׁלֹשׁ שָׁנִים וּשְׁלֹשִׁים יוֹם!

And if it enters your mind that the **days** during which he was ritually impure **count toward his** naziriteship, **it should be enough for him to** observe **three years and thirty days.** Due to uncertainty, he cannot shave for his leprosy until a year has passed, in case he was a pure nazirite, and he must wait another year for his second shaving, as he might have been an impure nazirite. However, at that point, if the days of his counting are considered part of his naziriteship, as claimed by Rav Ḥisda, he should be allowed to wait a mere thirty days for hair growth, shave for his impure naziriteship, and then add a final year for his naziriteship in purity. The fact that he is obligated to wait four years proves that his time as a leper does not count toward his naziriteship.

וְעוֹד מְתִיב רַב אַשִׁי: אֵין לִי אֶלָּא יְמֵי טוּמְאָה שֶׁאֵין עוֹלִין לוֹ מִן הַמִּנְיָן, יְמֵי חִלּוּטוֹ מִנַּיִן? וְדִין הוּא: יְמֵי טוּמְאָה מְגַלֵּחַ וּמֵבִיא קָרְבָּן, וִימֵי חִלּוּטוֹ מְגַלֵּחַ וּמֵבִיא קָרְבָּן, מַה יְּמֵי טוּמְאָתוֹ אֵין עוֹלִין לוֹ מִן הַמִּנְיָן – אַף יְמֵי חִלּוּטוֹ אֵין עוֹלִין לוֹ מִן הַמִּנְיָן.

And Rav Ashi raised a further objection from the following halakhic midrash: **I have** derived **only that the days of impurity**[N] **do not count** as part **of his tally** of his naziriteship. **From where** do I derive that **the days of his** status as a **confirmed** leper also do not count toward his naziriteship? **And is this** not **logical: After the days of impurity he shaves and brings an offering, and after his days of confirmed** leprosy **he** likewise **shaves and brings an offering; just as his days of impurity do not count** as part **of his tally, so too, the days of confirmed** leprosy should **not count** as part **of his tally.**

לֹא, אִם אָמַרְתָּ בִּימֵי טוּמְאָתוֹ – שֶׁכֵּן מְבַטֵּל בָּהֶן אֶת הַקּוֹדְמִים, תֹּאמַר בִּימֵי חִלּוּטוֹ שֶׁאֵין מְבַטֵּל בָּהֶן אֶת הַקּוֹדְמִין!

The Gemara rejects this argument: **No, if you say** that this is true **with regard to his days of impurity, which negate the previous** days, **shall you** also **say** that this is the case **with regard to his days of confirmed** leprosy, **which do not negate the previous** ones, as stated in the mishna?

אָמַרְתָּ: קַל וָחוֹמֶר הוּא: וּמַה נָּזִיר בַּקֶּבֶר, שֶׁשְּׂעָרוֹ רָאוּי לְתִגְלַחַת נְזִירוּת – אֵין עוֹלִין לוֹ מִן הַמִּנְיָן. יְמֵי חִלּוּטוֹ, שֶׁאֵין שְׂעָרוֹ רָאוּי לְתִגְלַחַת נְזִירוּת – לֹא כָּל שֶׁכֵּן?!

The Gemara suggests another proof. **You** can **say it is an** ***a fortiori*** inference: **And if a nazirite** who uttered his vow when he was **in** a ritually impure place, e.g., a place of **a grave, whose hair is fit for the shaving**[N] **of naziriteship,** and yet those days when he was impure **do not count** as part **of his tally,** then with regard to **his days of confirmed** leprosy, **when his hair is not fit for the shaving of naziriteship,** as he must first perform the shaving of leprosy, is it **not all the more so** that they should not count toward his naziriteship?

NOTES

I have derived only that the days of impurity – אֵין לִי אֶלָּא יְמֵי טוּמְאָה: These are his days of impurity from a corpse, as the Torah clearly states that they must be completely negated (see Numbers 6:12).

Whose hair is fit for the shaving – שֶׁשְּׂעָרוֹ רָאוּי לְתִגְלַחַת: He does not have to shave this hair at the end of his period as an impure nazirite. Although he must observe thirty days of naziriteship in purity afterward, he shaves the hair that grew in impurity only because he shaves for his naziriteship of purity, as explained above (16b).

וְאֵין לִי אֶלָּא יְמֵי חִלּוּטוֹ, יְמֵי סְפָרוֹ מִנַּיִן? וְדִין הוּא:

And I have derived **only his days of confirmed** leprosy. **From where** do I derive that **his days of counting** for purification from leprosy are not considered part of his term either? **And is this** not **logical:**

Perek **VII**
Daf **56** Amud **b**

מַה יְמֵי חִלּוּטוֹ טְעוּן תִּגְלַחַת – אַף יְמֵי סְפָרוֹ, וּמַה יְמֵי חִלּוּטוֹ אֵין עוֹלִין לוֹ מִן הַמִּנְיָן – אַף יְמֵי סְפָרוֹ.

Just as the days of his confirmed leprosy **require shaving, so too, the days of his counting** require shaving; **and just as the days of his confirmed** leprosy **do not count** as part **of his tally** of naziriteship, **so too, the days of his counting** should not count toward his term of naziriteship?

יָכוֹל אַף יְמֵי הֶסְגֵּרוֹ כֵּן? וְהַדִּין נוֹתֵן: חָלוּט מְטַמֵּא מִשְׁכָּב וּמוֹשָׁב, וִימֵי הֶסְגֵּרוֹ מְטַמֵּא מִשְׁכָּב וּמוֹשָׁב, אִם לָמַדְתָּ לִימֵי חִלּוּטוֹ שֶׁאֵין עוֹלִין לוֹ מִן הַמִּנְיָן – אַף יְמֵי הֶסְגֵּרוֹ אֵין עוֹלִין לוֹ מִן הַמִּנְיָן.

One **might** have thought that **even his days of quarantine** as a leper should share the **same** *halakha* and not be counted. **And it is logical** that those days should not count for him either, as the two states are comparable: **A confirmed** leper **renders** items **ritually impure through lying or sitting,**[H] **and** a leper in **the days of his quarantine** also **renders** items **impure through lying or sitting.** Consequently, **if you learned with regard to the days of confirmed** leprosy **that they do not count** as part **of his tally, so too, the days of quarantine** should **not count** as part **of his tally** either.

אָמַרְתָּ: לֹא, אִם אָמַרְתָּ בִּימֵי חִלּוּטוֹ – שֶׁכֵּן חִלּוּטוֹ טָעוּן תִּגְלַחַת וּמֵבִיא קָרְבָּן – לְפִיכָךְ אֵין עוֹלִין, תֹּאמַר בִּימֵי הֶסְגֵּרוֹ שֶׁאֵין טָעוּן תִּגְלַחַת וְאֵינוֹ מֵבִיא קָרְבָּן – לְפִיכָךְ יַעֲלוּ לְמִנְיָן.

The Gemara rejects this argument: **You can say** in response: **No, if you said** this *halakha* **with regard to the days of confirmed** leprosy, the reason is **that his confirmed** state of leprosy **requires** him to **shave**[H] after he is healed **and to bring an offering** before he can commence his naziriteship. **Therefore,** these days **do not count** toward his naziriteship. However, will **you say** the same **with regard to the days of his quarantine, which do not require shaving and** for which **he does not bring an offering? Therefore,** perhaps they should **count toward** his **tally.**

מִכָּאן אָמְרוּ: יְמֵי סְפָרוֹ וִימֵי גָּמְרוֹ – אֵין עוֹלִין לוֹ מִן הַמִּנְיָן. אֲבָל יְמֵי הַזָּב וְהַזָּבָה, וְהֶסְגֵּרוֹ שֶׁל מְצוֹרָע – הֲרֵי אֵלּוּ עוֹלִין לוֹ.

From here they stated: The days of a leper's **counting**[H] **and the days of his confirmed** leprosy, when he is a full-fledged leper, **do not count** as part **of his tally** of his term of naziriteship. **However, the days** of the impurity **of the** ***zav*** **and the** ***zava***[N] **and the days of a leper's quarantine do count** as part of **his** tally of his term of naziriteship.

קָתָנֵי מִיהַת: לֹא, אִם אָמַרְתָּ בִּימֵי טוּמְאָה שֶׁכֵּן מְבַטֵּל בָּהֶן אֶת הַקּוֹדְמִין, תֹּאמַר בִּימֵי חִלּוּטוֹ. בְּמַאי? אִילֵימָא בִּנְזִירוּת מוּעֶטֶת – הָא בָּעֵינַן גִּידּוּל שֵׂעָר.

With regard to the issue at hand, **in any event** the *baraita* **teaches: No, if you say** that this is true **with regard to his days of impurity, which negate the previous** days, **shall you** also **say** that this is the case **with regard to his days of confirmed** leprosy, which do not negate the previous ones? The Gemara analyzes this argument: **To what** does this statement refer? **If we say** it is referring **to a short naziriteship** of thirty days, this cannot be the case, as **we require hair growth** of thirty days after his purification.

אֶלָּא לָאו – בִּנְזִירוּת מְרוּבָּה, וְקָתָנֵי: שֶׁאֵין עוֹלִין לוֹ מִן הַמִּנְיָן, אַלְמָא: לָא סָלְקִין לֵיהּ, שְׁמַע מִינַּהּ.

Rather, is it not the case that it is referring **to a lengthy naziriteship, and** nevertheless the *baraita* **teaches that they do not count** as part **of his tally. Apparently,** his days as a full-fledged leper **do not count toward** his term of naziriteship, which contradicts Rav Ḥisda's ruling. The Gemara concludes: **Learn from this** that Rav Ḥisda's opinion should be rejected.

HALAKHA

A confirmed leper renders items ritually impure through lying or sitting, etc. – חָלוּט מְטַמֵּא מִשְׁכָּב וּמוֹשָׁב וכו׳: A leper imparts impurity by lying and sitting. This *halakha* applies both to a full-fledged leper and a quarantined leper, as their impurity is similar in all regards (Rambam *Sefer Tahara, Hilkhot Tumat Tzara'at* 10:10–11).

His confirmed state requires him to shave, etc. – חִלּוּטוֹ טָעוּן תִּגְלַחַת וכו׳: A leper who was purified after his quarantine is required to shave and bring birds for his purification. If he was declared pure by a priest after a period of quarantine he does not have to shave or bring an offering (Rambam *Sefer Tahara, Hilkhot Tumat Tzara'at* 10:10).

The days of a leper's counting, etc. – יְמֵי סְפָרוֹ וכו׳: If a nazirite became a confirmed leper, none of his days as a full-fledged leper, or the seven days he counts between his two shavings of leprosy, count toward his term of naziriteship. The *halakha* is in accordance with the ruling of the *baraita*, not the opinion of Rav Ḥisda. Nevertheless, the days of his quarantine are considered part of his term of naziriteship. Similarly, the days of impurity of a *zav* and *zava* count toward their naziriteship terms (Rambam *Sefer Hafla'a, Hilkhot Nezirut* 7:9).

NOTES

The days of the *zav* and the *zava* – יְמֵי הַזָּב וְהַזָּבָה: Although a *zav* and *zava* are obligated to bring an offering upon their purification, they need not shave, and therefore their cases are not comparable to that of a confirmed leper or the days of his counting. One certainly cannot derive the *halakha* of a nazirite from a leper's days of quarantine, as the latter are followed neither by shaving nor by bringing offerings of purity.

מתני׳ אָמַר רַבִּי אֱלִיעֶזֶר מִשּׁוּם רַבִּי יְהוֹשֻׁעַ: כׇּל טוּמְאָה מִן הַמֵּת שֶׁנָּזִיר מְגַלֵּחַ עָלֶיהָ – חַיָּיבִין עָלֶיהָ עַל בִּיאַת מִקְדָּשׁ, וְכׇל טוּמְאָה מִן הַמֵּת שֶׁאֵין הַנָּזִיר מְגַלֵּחַ עָלֶיהָ – אֵין חַיָּיבִין עָלֶיהָ עַל בִּיאַת מִקְדָּשׁ.

MISHNA **Rabbi Eliezer said in the name of Rabbi Yehoshua:** With regard to **any ritual impurity from a corpse for which a nazirite must shave, one is liable due to** the prohibition of **entering the Temple** after contracting that impurity. If someone who became impure from one of those sources of impurity enters the Temple, he violates the prohibition against an impure individual entering the sacred space. **And** with regard to **any impurity from a corpse**[HN] **for which a nazirite does not shave, one is** likewise **not liable due to** the prohibition of **entering the Temple** after contracting it.

אָמַר רַבִּי מֵאִיר: לֹא תְּהֵא זוֹ קַלָּה מִן הַשֶּׁרֶץ.

Rabbi Meir said: This impurity from a corpse that does not obligate a nazirite to shave **should not be more lenient than** the impurity of **a creeping animal.** The Torah clearly states that one rendered impure from a creeping animal is prohibited from entering the Temple (see Leviticus 5:2–3).

גמ׳ וְרַבִּי אֱלִיעֶזֶר מִשּׁוּם רַבִּי יְהוֹשֻׁעַ גְּמַר לַהּ? וְהָא מִשּׁוּם רַבִּי יְהוֹשֻׁעַ בַּר מֶמֶל גְּמַר לַהּ. דְּתַנְיָא, אָמַר רַבִּי אֱלִיעֶזֶר: כְּשֶׁהָלַכְתִּי לְעַרְדַּסְקְיָא מָצָאתִי אֶת רַבִּי יְהוֹשֻׁעַ בֶּן פֶּתֶר רֹאשׁ שֶׁהָיָה יוֹשֵׁב וְדָן לִפְנֵי רַבִּי מֵאִיר בַּהֲלָכָה: כׇּל טוּמְאָה מִן הַמֵּת שֶׁהַנָּזִיר מְגַלֵּחַ עָלֶיהָ – חַיָּיבִין עָלֶיהָ מִשּׁוּם בִּיאַת מִקְדָּשׁ, וְכׇל טוּמְאָה מִן הַמֵּת שֶׁאֵין הַנָּזִיר מְגַלֵּחַ עָלֶיהָ – אֵין חַיָּיבִין עָלֶיהָ מִשּׁוּם בִּיאַת מִקְדָּשׁ. אָמַר לוֹ: אַל תְּהֵא זוֹ קַלָּה מִשֶּׁרֶץ!

GEMARA The Gemara asks: **And did Rabbi Eliezer learn this** *halakha* **in the name of Rabbi Yehoshua** ben Ḥananya? **But didn't he learn it in the name of Rabbi Yehoshua bar Memel?**[P] **As it is taught** in a *baraita* that **Rabbi Eliezer said: When I went to** a place called **Ardaskeya,**[B] **I found Rabbi Yehoshua ben Petter Rosh**[L] **sitting and discussing** the following *halakha* **before Rabbi Meir:** With regard to **any ritual impurity from a corpse for which a nazirite must shave, one is liable due to** the prohibition of **entering the Temple** after contracting it. **And** with regard to **any impurity from a corpse for which a nazirite does not shave, one is not liable due to** the prohibition of **entering the Temple** after contracting it. Rabbi Meir **said to him: This** impurity of a corpse that does not obligate a nazirite to shave **should not be more lenient than** the impurity of **a creeping animal.**

אָמַרְתִּי לוֹ: כְּלוּם אַתָּה בָּקִי בְּרַבִּי יְהוֹשֻׁעַ בַּר מֶמֶל? אָמַר לִי: הֵן. כָּךְ אָמַר לִי רַבִּי יְהוֹשֻׁעַ בַּר מֶמֶל מִשּׁוּם רַבִּי יְהוֹשֻׁעַ: כׇּל טוּמְאָה מִן הַמֵּת שֶׁהַנָּזִיר מְגַלֵּחַ עָלֶיהָ – חַיָּיב עָלֶיהָ מִשּׁוּם בִּיאַת מִקְדָּשׁ, וְכׇל טוּמְאָה מִן הַמֵּת שֶׁאֵין הַנָּזִיר מְגַלֵּחַ עָלֶיהָ – אֵין חַיָּיבִין עָלֶיהָ מִשּׁוּם בִּיאַת מִקְדָּשׁ. הֲוֵי, מִשּׁוּם רַבִּי יְהוֹשֻׁעַ בַּר מֶמֶל גָּמֵיר לַהּ!

Rabbi Eliezer continued: **I said to** Rabbi Meir: **Are you at all familiar with Rabbi Yehoshua bar Memel? He said to me: Yes.** I continued: **Rabbi Yehoshua bar Memel said this to me in the name of Rabbi Yehoshua** ben Ḥananya: With regard to **any ritual impurity from a corpse for which a nazirite must shave, one is liable due to** the prohibition of **entering the Temple** after contracting it. **And** with regard to **any impurity from a corpse for which a nazirite does not shave, one is not liable due to** the prohibition of **entering the Temple** after contracting it. This concludes the *baraita*. The Gemara comments: This **is** proof **that** Rabbi Eliezer **learned** this *halakha* **in the name of Rabbi Yehoshua bar Memel,** not directly from Rabbi Yehoshua ben Ḥananya.

HALAKHA

Any impurity from a corpse, etc. – כׇּל טוּמְאָה מִן הַמֵּת וכו׳: Any ritual impurity from a corpse that obligates a nazirite to shave also renders one liable to receive *karet* for entering the Temple. One does not violate the prohibition against entering the Temple in a state of impurity if he came into contact with those sources of impurity from a corpse for which a nazirite does not have to shave. However, if one touches a person or vessels that were rendered impure in a manner for which a nazirite must shave, he is liable if he subsequently enters the Temple (Rambam *Sefer Avoda, Hilkhot Biat HaMikdash* 3:13 and see Ra'avad and *Kesef Mishne* there).

PERSONALITIES

Rabbi Yehoshua bar Memel – רַבִּי יְהוֹשֻׁעַ בַּר מֶמֶל: This *tanna*, who is mentioned only in the *Tosefta*, was apparently a disciple of Rabbi Yehoshua. Rabbi Meir praised him as a master of *halakhot*.

BACKGROUND

Ardaskeya – עַרְדַּסְקְיָא: Ardaskeya, or Ardaskos, is the name of a village located not far from the town of Tavin, also known as Tivon, in northern Israel near Haifa.

LANGUAGE

Petter Rosh – פֶּתֶר רֹאשׁ: Apparently this is from a Greek name that was Hebraicized. Other versions of the Gemara read: Petora. The Greek name in question is possibly πατρωός, Patroos, meaning of the father, or πάτρως, Patros, meaning one's father's brother.

NOTES

And any impurity from a corpse, etc. – וְכׇל טוּמְאָה מִן הַמֵּת וכו׳: The reason for this *halakha* is unclear. Many commentaries maintain that one should not seek an explanation for it, as it is a *halakha* transmitted to Moses from Sinai. In other words, there is no fundamental connection between the sources of ritual impurity for which a nazirite must shave and those which render one liable due to the prohibition of entering the Temple. The mishna gives the rule comparing the two merely as a kind of mnemonic. It is also possible that this comparison is based on the fact that an offering is brought for entering the Temple in a state of impurity and a nazirite must likewise sacrifice offerings. See the Jerusalem Talmud for a lengthy discussion on this issue.

One extreme opinion is that those items that do not obligate a nazirite to shave are all sources of impurity by rabbinic law (Rambam). However, the Meiri contends that this mishna indicates otherwise, as how could Rabbi Meir suggest that sources of impurity by rabbinic law should be more severe than that of a creeping animal, which is by Torah law? However, as Rabbi Meir's opinion is not accepted by the Rambam as *halakha*, it is possible that he rejects the source of his reasoning as well.

אמרו: שמע מינה, כל שמעתתא דמתאמרה בבי תלתא, קדמאי ובתראי – אמרינן, מציעאי – לא אמרינן.

They said: Learn from this case the following principle: With regard to **any** statement of ***halakha* that was stated** as a tradition **of three** scholars, **we say the first and the last** names in the chain but **we do not say the middle** one. Therefore, the mishna mentions the name of Rabbi Eliezer, the last link in the tradition, and Rabbi Yehoshua ben Ḥananya, the first scholar, but it omits that of Rabbi Yehoshua bar Memel, the middle scholar in the chain.

אמר רב נחמן בר יצחק: אף אנן נמי תנינא, אמר נחום הלבלר: כך מקובלני מרבי מיאשא, שקיבל מאבא, שקיבל מן הזוגות, שקבלו מן הנביאים: הלכה למשה מסיני בזורע שבת וחרדל בשנים ושלשה מקומות, שנותן פאה מכל אחד ואחד.

Rav Naḥman bar Yitzḥak said: We, too, learn in a mishna (*Pe'a* 2:6): **Naḥum the Scribe**[P] [***lavlar***][L] **said: This is** the tradition that **I received from Rabbi Meyasha,**[P] **who received it from father, who received** it **from the pairs** of Sages who served during the period of the Second Temple, **who received** it **from the Prophets:** It is a ***halakha*** transmitted **to Moses from Sinai with regard to one who sows** the plants of **dill**[B] **and mustard**[N] **in two or three** separate **locations** in a single field, **that he leaves a corner**[B] to the poor **for each and every one** of these plots on its own, rather than one corner for all of them.

ואילו יהושע וכלב לא קחשיב, שמע מינה.

The Gemara explains the proof from this source: **And yet** Naḥum the Scribe **does not mention** the names of **Joshua and Caleb,** despite the fact that they were the Elders who passed down this *halakha* from Moses to the Prophets. **Learn from this** that the middle links in a tradition are not necessarily listed.

מתני׳ אמר רבי עקיבא: דנתי לפני רבי אליעזר: מה אם עצם כשעורה שאינו מטמא אדם באהל – הנזיר מגלח על מגעו ועל משאו, רביעית דם שהוא מטמא אדם באהל – אינו דין שיהא הנזיר מגלח על מגעה ועל משאה?

MISHNA The mishna continues to address the sources of ritual impurity for which a nazirite must shave. **Rabbi Akiva said: I discussed** this matter **before Rabbi Eliezer** and suggested the following *a fortiori* inference: **If,** with regard to **a bone that is a barley-grain-bulk, which does not render a person impure in a tent, a nazirite must** nevertheless **shave for touching it or carrying it,** then in the case of **a quarter-*log* of blood, which is** more stringent in that it **renders a person impure in a tent, is it not logical that a nazirite should shave for touching it or carrying it?**

אמר לי: מה זה עקיבא?! אין דנין כאן מקל וחומר. וכשבאתי והרציתי דברים לפני רבי יהושע, אמר לי: יפה אמרת, אלא כן אמרו: הלכה.

Rabbi Eliezer **said to me: What is this, Akiva? One cannot argue by means of an *a fortiori* inference here,** in this particular case. However, Rabbi Eliezer did not provide a reason for this response. Rabbi Akiva continued: **And when I came and presented** these **matters before Rabbi Yehoshua, he said to me: You spoke well,** i.e., your logic is flawless, **but they indeed said** that this is a ***halakha*** transmitted to Moses from Sinai, which cannot be refuted by means of an *a fortiori* inference.

BACKGROUND

Dill – שבת: Dill, *Anethum graveolens*, is a perennial grassy herb from the Apiaceae family. This plant grows to a height of 50–80 cm and has small yellow flowers. Mesh-shaped in appearance, its leaves are trim and form thread-like tongues. Dill has a distinctive, pleasant fragrance. Its seeds and oil are used for medicinal purposes. In the mishnaic period, dill was grown in gardens, and it is still cultivated nowadays in many places. Dill also grows wild in certain parts of the world.

Corner – פאה: The Torah states that a farmer is prohibited from harvesting the produce in the corner of his field. Instead, he must allow the poor to collect this produce for themselves. The Sages decreed that the area of the corner must be at least one-sixtieth of the field. This mitzva appears in the Torah (Leviticus 19:9, 23:22), and tractate *Pe'a* is devoted to discussing its details. By Torah law, fields, vineyards, and olive groves are included in the mitzva.

Field of cultivated dill

PERSONALITIES

Naḥum the Scribe – נחום הלבלר: Naḥum the Scribe was a *tanna* from the Second Temple period. He was a contemporary of Rabban Gamliel the Elder, grandson of Hillel. Naḥum the Scribe is mentioned only once in the Mishna.

Rabbi Meyasha – רבי מיאשא: Rabbi Meyasha was one of the first *tanna'im*. He is listed among the disciples of Hillel and Shammai (*Seder HaDorot*).

LANGUAGE

Scribe [*lavlar*] – לבלר: From the Latin librarius, meaning scribe.

NOTES

With regard to one who sows dill and mustard – בזורע שבת וחרדל: Most early commentaries reject this reading of the text in favor of the version that appears in a different mishna in *Pe'a* (3:2). According to that version, the tradition is referring to one who sows two types of wheat in a field. Their status with regard to *pe'a* depends on whether one brought the grain into one granary or two.

GEMARA **A dilemma was raised before** the Sages with regard to the *halakha* transmitted to Moses from Sinai mentioned in the mishna: Is the *halakha* that a nazirite must shave for **a bone that is a barley-grain-bulk a *halakha*** transmitted to Moses from Sinai, **and** it was the status of a **quarter-*log* of blood** that Rabbi Akiva sought to derive as **an *a fortiori*** inference, **and** with regard to this claim they said: **One does not derive an *a fortiori*** inference **from a *halakha*** transmitted to Moses from Sinai?

גמ׳ אִיבַּעְיָא לְהוּ: עֶצֶם כִּשְׂעוֹרָה – הֲלָכָה, וּרְבִיעִית דָּם – קַל וָחוֹמֶר, וְאֵין דָּנִין קַל וָחוֹמֶר מֵהֲלָכָה.

Or perhaps the ruling that **a quarter-*log* of blood** imparts ritual impurity in a tent is the ***halakha***[N] transmitted to Moses from Sinai, **and** Rabbi Akiva sought to use the case of **a bone that is a barley-grain-bulk** as the source of **an *a fortiori*** inference that a nazirite must shave for a quarter-*log* as well, to which the Sages replied that **one does not derive an *a fortiori*** inference **from a *halakha*** transmitted to Moses from Sinai. The Gemara answers: **Come and hear** the unequivocal statement of a *baraita*: **A bone that is a barley-grain-bulk is a *halakha*,**[H] **and a quarter-*log* of blood is an *a fortiori*** inference, **and one does not derive an *a fortiori*** inference **from a *halakha*.**

אוֹ דִּלְמָא: רְבִיעִית דָּם – הֲלָכָה, וְעֶצֶם כִּשְׂעוֹרָה – קַל וָחוֹמֶר, וְאֵין דָּנִין קַל וָחוֹמֶר מֵהֲלָכָה? תָּא שְׁמַע, עֶצֶם כִּשְׂעוֹרָה הֲלָכָה, וּרְבִיעִית דָּם קַל וָחוֹמֶר, וְאֵין דָּנִין קַל וָחוֹמֶר מֵהֲלָכָה.

הדרן עלך כהן גדול

NOTES

A quarter-*log* of blood is the *halakha* – רְבִיעִית דָּם הֲלָכָה: That is, it is a *halakha* that this amount of blood serves as a source of impurity in a tent. Some commentaries maintain that the traditional *halakha* is that a nazirite does not shave for a quarter-*log* of blood, and it was this *halakha* that Rabbi Akiva attempted to refute by means of an *a fortiori* inference (*Keren Ora*).

HALAKHA

A bone that is a barley-grain-bulk is a *halakha* – עֶצֶם כִּשְׂעוֹרָה הֲלָכָה: The ritual impurity imparted by a single bone through contact or carrying is a *halakha* learned by tradition. This impurity applies by Torah law; it is not a decree of the Sages (Rambam *Sefer Tahara*, *Hilkhot Tumat Met* 2:10, and see Ra'avad on 3:3).

Summary of **Perek VII**

Concerning the *halakhot* of ritual impurity with regard to a nazirite, there is a distinction between situations for which the nazirite's entire term of naziriteship is nullified due to contact with a corpse, and cases where his impurity requires sprinkling of the purification waters and immersion but does not negate the days of naziriteship he has already observed. If one's term of naziriteship is negated due to impurity, then following his purification the individual must bring the offerings of an impure nazirite, after which he starts counting his term of naziriteship afresh. Some Sages suggest that those impurities that do not negate the term of a nazirite are those imposed by rabbinic law or those that are due to uncertainty. Consequently, a nazirite with this type of impurity is not punished for entering the Temple or for eating sacrificial meat. Even those who dispute this opinion concede that the details of these *halakhot* were transmitted to Moses from Sinai, although there is textual support for them in the Torah. These details include the amounts of body material that impart impurity and the ways in which impurity is imparted, i.e., through contact, carrying, and in a tent.

Since the prohibition of a nazirite contracting impurity is limited to that of a corpse, a nazirite's term is not nullified or otherwise affected if he comes into contact with other forms of impurity. The lone exception to this principle is the impurity of a leper, which shares some of the characteristics of that of a corpse. Impurity from a leper does not negate a nazirite's term of naziriteship. However, if a nazirite becomes a confirmed leper, the days during which he is affected are not counted toward the tally of days required to fulfill his term of naziriteship.

Just as a priest, and even a High Priest, who are both prohibited from coming into contact with a corpse, must become ritually impure to tend to a *met mitzva*, the same applies to a nazirite. The Gemara concludes that if only a nazirite and a priest are available to perform the task, the nazirite must bury the corpse, because his sanctity is temporary, whereas that of the priest is permanent. This is the *halakha*, despite the fact that a nazirite must subsequently bring an offering for this impurity and resume the tally of his term of naziriteship from the beginning.

Introduction to **Perek VIII**

All the days of his vow of naziriteship no razor shall come upon his head; until the days are fulfilled in which he consecrated himself to the Lord, he shall be sacred, he shall let the locks of the hair of his head grow long.

(Numbers 6:5)

And if any man dies very suddenly beside him, and he renders impure the head of his naziriteship, then he shall shave his head on the day of his purification, on the seventh day he shall shave it.

(Numbers 6:9)

And this is the law of the nazirite, when the days of his consecration are fulfilled: He shall bring it to the door of the Tent of Meeting; and he shall present his offering to the Lord... And the nazirite shall shave the head of his naziriteship at the entrance to the Tent of Meeting, and he shall take the hair of the head of his naziriteship and put it on the fire that is under the sacrifice of the peace-offering.

(Numbers 6:13–14, 18)

And he shall sprinkle upon him that is to be cleansed from the leprosy seven times, and shall pronounce him clean, and shall let go the living bird into the open field. And he that is to be cleansed shall wash his clothes, and shave off all his hair, and bathe himself in water, and he shall be clean; and after that he may come into the camp, but shall dwell outside his tent seven days. And it shall be on the seventh day, that he shall shave all his hair off his head and his beard and his eyebrows, all his hair he shall shave off; and he shall wash his clothes, and he shall bathe his flesh in water, and he shall be clean.

(Leviticus 14:7–9)

This chapter essentially deals with a single problem: How should a nazirite behave if he might have been rendered impure? Due to this uncertainty, he must accept some of the stringencies of both an impure nazirite and a pure nazirite.

This situation is doubly complex. On the one hand, the impurity nullifies the initial naziriteship, and the nazirite must shave before observing his term of naziriteship anew. On the other hand, if he did not become impure he ought to continue his term without interruption. A second difficulty concerns the nazirite's obligation to bring offerings. Not only do an impure nazirite and a pure nazirite at the completion of their terms bring different sets of offerings, but the possibility that a nazirite may not have any obligation to bring these offerings raises a whole series of problems. These include the order in which the animals are brought, the manner in which they are sacrificed, and the consumption of offerings brought in uncertainty.

This central problem is expressed in two basic cases. The first concerns an uncertainty in which one of two nazirites became impure from a corpse and it is unclear which of them it was. The other case is that of a nazirite who might have been rendered impure from a corpse and who also might be a leper. This second case is especially complicated, as the purification of a leper includes the obligation to shave twice. In addition to the fact that the requirement of a nazirite and a leper to shave do not apply at the same time, there is a conflict between the leper's requirement to shave and the nazirite's prohibition against doing so. An additional question is whether one act of shaving can fulfill the obligation of both conditions. The analyses of these problems comprise the central material of this chapter.

מתני׳ שני נזירים שאמר להן אחד "ראיתי אחד מכם שנטמא, ואיני יודע איזה מכם" – מגלחין, ומביאין קרבן טומאה וקרבן טהרה, ואומר: "אם אני הוא טמא – קרבן טומאה שלי, וקרבן טהרה שלך. ואם אני הוא הטהור – קרבן טהרה שלי, וקרבן טומאה שלך".

MISHNA With regard to **two nazirites,**[H] **where one** other person **said to them: I saw one of you become impure, but I do not know which** one **of you** it was, they must each complete their naziriteship terms, **shave** their hair, and both together **bring an offering of ritual impurity and an offering of purity,** due to the uncertainty. **And** one of them **says** to the other: **If I am the impure** one, **the offering of impurity is mine and the offering of purity is yours; and if I am the** pure one, **the offering of purity is mine and the offering of impurity is yours.**

וסופרין שלשים יום, ומביאין קרבן טהרה, ואומר: "אם אני הוא הטמא – קרבן טומאה שלי, וקרבן טהרה שלך, וזה קרבן טהרתי. ואם אני הוא הטהור – קרבן טהרה שלי, וקרבן טומאה שלך, וזה קרבן טהרתך".

And because of the uncertainty **they** each **count** a further **thirty days** of naziriteship **and** both together **bring an offering of purity. And** one of them **says: If I am the** previously **impure one,** that **offering of impurity** sacrificed earlier was **mine, and the offering of purity** was **yours; and this** offering sacrificed now **is my offering of purity. And if I am the** previously **pure one, the offering of purity** brought earlier was **mine, and the offering of impurity** was **yours; and this** current offering **is your offering of purity.**

גמ׳ קתני: שני נזירים שאמר להם "ראיתי אחד מכם שנטמא, ואיני יודע איזה מכם". ואמאי? כל ספק טומאה ברשות היחיד מהיכא ילפינן לה – מסוטה.

GEMARA The mishna **teaches** with regard to **two nazirites,** that **if one** other person **said to them: I saw one of you become impure, but I do not know which one of you** it was, they must bring an offering of ritual impurity and an offering of purity. The Gemara expresses surprise at this case: **But why** should they be defined as having **uncertain impurity?** After all, the general principle that **any uncertain impurity in a private domain**[H] is considered impure, **from where do we derive this? From** the case of **a** ***sota***.

מה סוטה – בועל ונבעלת, אף כל ספק טומאה ברשות היחיד – כגון דאיכא בי תרי. אבל הכא שני נזירים. והאי דקאי גביהון – הא תלתא, הוה ליה ספק טומאה ברשות הרבים, וכל ספק טומאה ברשות הרבים ספיקו טהור!

Yet this situation is not similar to that of a *sota*, as **just as** the case of **a** ***sota*** involves only **an adulterer and an adulteress, so too any uncertain impurity in a private domain** is considered impure only in a case **where there are** no more than **two** people present. **However,** in the mishna **here** there are **two nazirites and this** other individual **who is standing alongside them,**[HN] who witnessed one of them become impure, which makes a total of **three.** Consequently, **this is an uncertain impurity in the public domain,** as three people are sufficient for the place to be considered a public domain with regard to this *halakha*, **and** the *halakha* with regard to **any uncertain impurity in the public domain** is that **its uncertainty** is considered **pure.**

אמר רבה בר רב הונא: באומר "ראיתי טומאה שנזרקה ביניכם". אמר רב אשי: דיקא נמי,

Rabba bar Rav Huna said that the mishna is referring **to one who says:** From a distance **I saw an impure** item **thrown between you.** Since he was not with them when one of the nazirites became impure, there were only two people present and therefore this is a case of uncertain impurity in a private domain. **Rav Ashi said:** The language of the mishna **is also precise,**

HALAKHA

Two nazirites, etc. – **שני נזירים וכו׳**: How are two nazirites meant to proceed if one of them became impure but they do not know which one contracted the impurity? They complete their naziriteship terms and together bring offerings of purity and impurity. At this point, one of them stipulates: If I am the impure one, the offering of impurity is mine and the offering of purity is yours; and if you are the impure one, the offering of impurity is yours and the offering of purity is mine. They subsequently count another period of naziriteship, at the end of which they together bring an offering of purity. Each of them then says: If I was the impure one, this is my offering of purity, and if you were the impure one, this is your offering of purity (Rambam *Sefer Hafla'a*, *Hilkhot Nezirut* 9:14).

Uncertain impurity in a private domain, etc. – **ספק טומאה ברשות היחיד וכו׳**: Uncertain impurity refers to a case where one is unsure whether or not he was rendered impure. Any uncertain impurity that occurs in a private domain is considered impure. If it occurred in the public domain, it is considered pure (Rambam *Sefer Hafla'a*, *Hilkhot Nezirut* 9:16 and *Sefer Tahara*, *Hilkhot Tumat Met* 2:14 and *Hilkhot She'ar Avot HaTumot* 16:1, 18:1, 20:10).

And this other individual who is standing alongside them – **והאי דקאי גביהון**: If two nazirites standing in a courtyard were informed by another person who is with them that one of them has become impure, but he does not know which one of them contracted the impurity, this is considered an uncertain impurity in the public domain, as there are three people present. Consequently, they are pure. The Ra'avad claims that the fact that they are in one courtyard is not enough to render it a public domain. Rather, the uncertainty must apply to all three individuals (Rambam *Sefer Hafla'a*, *Hilkhot Nezirut* 9:16).

NOTES

And this other individual who is standing alongside them – **והאי דקאי גביהון**: The definition of a public domain with regard to ritual impurity differs from that of other areas of *halakha*, e.g., Shabbat or acquisitions. As far as impurity is concerned, the presence of three people is enough for a place to be considered a public domain, its status with regard to other *halakhot* notwithstanding.

The early commentaries dispute the details of this *halakha*. Some rule that if the three are in the same place, i.e., within four cubits of each other, it is a public domain (Rambam), while others contend that the uncertainty must be applicable to all three for it to be considered a public domain. If the uncertain impurity is relevant to only two of the three, it is considered a private domain (Ra'avad; see also Meiri).

BACKGROUND

Rounding the head – הַקָּפָה:

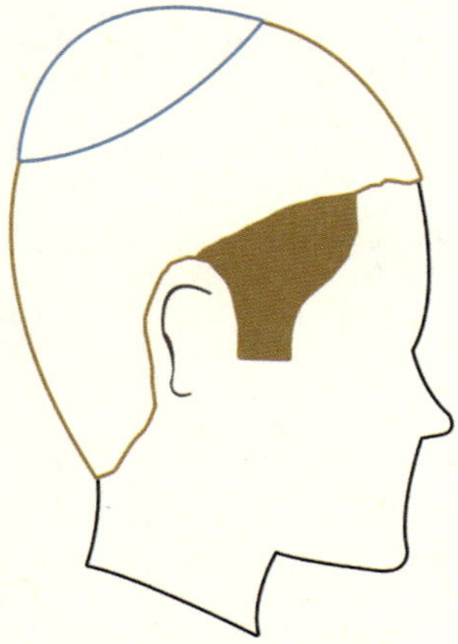

Area included in the prohibition of rounding

דְּקָתָנֵי ״וְאֵינִי יוֹדֵעַ אֵיזֶה מִכֶּם״. שְׁמַע מִינַּהּ.

as it teaches: But I do not know which one **of you.** This indicates that the third individual was too far away to detect which of them became impure. The Gemara says: **Conclude from** the inference from the mishna that it is so.

״מְגַלְּחִין וּמְבִיאִין״. וְאַמַּאי? דִּילְמָא לָאו טְמֵאִין אִינּוּן, וְקָעָבֵיד הַקָּפָה! אָמַר שְׁמוּאֵל: בְּאִשָּׁה וְקָטָן.

§ The mishna taught that the two nazirites **shave** and cut their hair **and bring** an offering of impurity and an offering of purity. The Gemara asks: **But why** are they permitted to shave? **Perhaps** both of **them are not impure, and** therefore one of them **violates** the prohibition against **rounding** the head,[BN] i.e., shaving the hair on the sides of the head (see Leviticus 19:27), when he shaves his hair unnecessarily. Since one of them does not need to shave, he thereby transgresses a mitzva by Torah law. **Shmuel said:** The mishna is referring **to** a case where each nazirite was **a woman,** who is not prohibited from rounding the hair of her head, **or a minor boy,**[H] who is not obligated in the observance of mitzvot.

וְלוֹקְמָא בְּגָדוֹל, וְהַקָּפַת כָּל הָרֹאשׁ לָא שְׁמָהּ הַקָּפָה! מִדְּלָא מוֹקִים לַהּ הָכִי – שְׁמַע מִינַּהּ קָסָבַר שְׁמוּאֵל: הַקָּפַת כָּל הָרֹאשׁ שְׁמָהּ הַקָּפָה.

The Gemara analyzes Shmuel's answer: **And let** Shmuel **establish** the mishna as referring **to a male who reached majority, and** the reason it is permitted is because **rounding the entire head,** not merely its corners, is **not called rounding** as prohibited by the Torah. **From** the fact that **he does not establish** the mishna **in this** manner, **conclude from it** that **Shmuel maintains** that **rounding the entire head**[H] is **called rounding.**

מָר זוּטְרָא מַתְנֵי לַהּ לְהָא שְׁמַעְתָּא דִּשְׁמוּאֵל אַסֵּיפָא: נָזִיר שֶׁהָיָה טָמֵא בְּסָפֵק וּמוּחְלָט בְּסָפֵק – אוֹכֵל בְּקָדָשִׁים לְאַחַר שִׁשִּׁים יוֹם, וּמְגַלֵּחַ אַרְבַּע תִּגְלָחוֹת. וְהָא קָעָבֵיד הַקָּפָה! אָמַר שְׁמוּאֵל: בְּאִשָּׁה וְקָטָן.

Mar Zutra taught this ***halakha*** **of Shmuel** with regard **to the latter clause** of the following mishna (59b): **A nazirite who has uncertain impurity and** whose status as **a confirmed leper is uncertain may eat sacrificial food after sixty days and shaves four times.** One shaving is for his uncertain status as an impure nazirite, one is at the end of his term of naziriteship, and two are due to his status as a leper. A similar problem arose: **But** as he is not definitely obligated to shave, he **violates the** prohibition against **rounding** the head. **Shmuel said:** The mishna is referring **to a woman or a minor boy,**[H] who are not prohibited from rounding their heads.

NOTES

And one of them violates the prohibition against rounding the head – וְקָעָבֵיד הַקָּפָה: The commentaries ask: Isn't it correct to say that either way, the first time he shaves constitutes a mitzva, as the one who is pure performs the shaving of purity, while the impure nazirite shaves for his impurity (Rabbeinu Peretz)? If so, it would not be considered an unnecessary shaving. Rabbeinu Peretz suggests that the witness was watching from a distance, as explained by the Gemara, and therefore it is possible that neither of them is impure. In that case both would violate the prohibition against rounding the head. Others explain simply that as each of them shaves his head twice, the second shaving of the pure nazirite is unnecessary, and therefore it constitutes a violation of the prohibition against rounding the head (Rabbeinu Azriel, cited in *Shita Mekubbetzet*; Meiri; see *Birkat Rosh*).

HALAKHA

The mishna is referring to a woman or a minor boy – בְּאִשָּׁה וְקָטָן: If one of two nazirites became impure but they do not know which one, they do not perform the shaving of impurity due to the uncertainty, as they might transgress the prohibition against rounding the head. If the nazirites were women or minor boys they do shave, in accordance with the opinion of Shmuel (Rambam *Sefer Hafla'a, Hilkhot Nezirut* 9:15).

Rounding the entire head – הַקָּפַת כָּל הָרֹאשׁ: Any man who shaves the corners of his head or his entire head is liable to receive lashes (Rambam *Sefer HaMadda, Hilkhot Avoda Zara* 12:1; *Shulḥan Arukh, Yoreh De'a* 181:2).

Shmuel said, to a woman or a minor boy – אָמַר שְׁמוּאֵל, בְּאִשָּׁה וְקָטָן: A nazirite who has uncertain impurity and whose status as a confirmed leper is uncertain must shave four times to account for all possibilities. This *halakha* applies only to minors and women, as men are not permitted to shave in a case of uncertainty, lest they transgress the prohibition against rounding the corners of the head, in accordance with the opinion of Shmuel (Rambam *Sefer Hafla'a, Hilkhot Nezirut* 10:9).

אָמַר רַב הוּנָא: הַמַּקִּיף אֶת הַקָּטָן הֲרֵי הוּא חַיָּיב. אֲמַר לֵיהּ רַב אַדָּא בַּר אַהֲבָה לְרַב הוּנָא: וְדִידָךְ מַאן מְגַלַּח לְהוֹן? אֲמַר לֵיהּ: חוֹבָה. תִּקְבְּרִינוּן חוֹבָה לְבָנֶיהָ. כּוּלְּהוּ שְׁנֵי דְּרַב אַדָּא בַּר אַהֲבָה לָא אִקַּיַּים לֵיהּ זַרְעָא לְרַב הוּנָא.

With regard to the same issue, **Rav Huna**[P] **said:** An adult **who rounds** the head **of a minor boy**[H] **is liable** to receive lashes, despite the fact that the child himself is not obligated to observe mitzvot. **Rav Adda bar Ahava,**[P] who disputed this ruling, **said to Rav Huna: And** with regard to **your** sons, **who shaves them** and rounds the corners of their heads? After all, you maintain that an adult may not round the head of a minor. Rav Huna **said to him: Ḥova** my wife does it, as she is not prohibited from rounding their heads. Rav Adda bar Ahava exclaimed in anger: **Ḥova should bury her sons**[NH] if she acts in this manner. The Gemara reports: During **the years that Rav Adda bar Ahava** was alive, **Rav Huna's children did not survive.** His children died due to the curse pronounced by Rav Adda.

מִכְּדִי תַּרְוַויְהוּ סְבִירָא הַקָּפַת כָּל הָרֹאשׁ שְׁמָהּ הַקָּפָה, בְּמַאי קָמִיפַּלְגִי? רַב הוּנָא סָבַר: ״לֹא תַקִּפוּ פְּאַת רֹאשְׁכֶם וְלֹא תַשְׁחִית [אֵת] פְּאַת זְקָנֶךָ״. כָּל שֶׁיֵּשׁ לוֹ הַשְׁחָתָה – יֵשׁ לוֹ הַקָּפָה, וְהָנֵי נָשֵׁי, הוֹאִיל וְלֵיתְנְהוּ בְּהַשְׁחָתָה – לֵיתְנְהוּ נַמִי בְּהַקָּפָה.

The Gemara asks: **Since both** Rav Huna and Rav Adda **maintain** that **rounding the entire head is called rounding, with regard to what do they disagree?** What is the reason for their respective rulings? The Gemara explains: **Rav Huna,** who prohibits an adult male from rounding the head of a minor but permits a woman to do so, **maintains** that the association between the two prohibitions in the verse: **"You shall not round the corners of your heads, neither shall you destroy the corners of your beard"** (Leviticus 19:27), teaches: **Whoever has** the prohibition of the **destruction** of the beard also **has** the prohibition of **rounding. And these women, since they are not** included **in** the prohibition of **destruction,**[HB] as they do not have beards, **they are not** included in the prohibition of **rounding either.**[H]

וְרַב אַדָּא בַּר אַהֲבָה סָבַר: אֶחָד הַמַּקִּיף וְאֶחָד הַנִּיקָּף בְּמַשְׁמַע. וְאִיתַּקַּשׁ מַקִּיף לְנִיקָּף; כָּל הֵיכָא דְּנִיקָּף מִיחַיַּיב – מַקִּיף נַמִי מִיחַיַּיב, וְהַאי קָטָן הוֹאִיל וְהוּא גּוּפֵיהּ לָאו בַּר עוֹנָשִׁין הוּא דְּמִיחַיַּיב – מַקִּיף נַמִי לָא מִיחַיַּיב.

And Rav Adda bar Ahava, who permits anyone to shave a minor boy's head, **maintains:** Both **one who rounds and one who is rounded**[NH] **are included** in the phrase "you shall not round," which is stated in the plural. **And** in this manner the verse **juxtaposes one who rounds to one who is rounded: Wherever one who is rounded is liable, the one who rounds is also liable; and** with regard to **this minor boy, since he himself is not liable to be punished** for this transgression, an adult who **rounds** his head **is also not liable** due to this action.

HALAKHA

An adult who rounds the head of a minor – הַמַּקִּיף אֶת הַקָּטָן: One who shaves the corners of a minor boy's head is liable to receive lashes, in accordance with the opinion of Rav Huna (Rambam *Sefer HaMadda, Hilkhot Avoda Zara* 12:1; *Shulḥan Arukh, Yoreh De'a* 181:5).

Ḥova should bury her sons, etc. – תִּקְבְּרִינוּן חוֹבָה וכו׳: Although a woman is permitted to shave the corners of her own head, she may not remove the hair on the corners of the head of a man or a male child. This is evident from Rav Adda bar Ahava's extreme reaction to Rav Huna's statement. Some authorities maintain that this is a rabbinic prohibition (Ra'avad; Rambam according to *Kesef Mishne*). Others claim that the prohibition against rounding the head does not apply to a woman at all, even if she shaves the head of a man (Rif; Rosh). According to this ruling, which the *Shulḥan Arukh* prefers, the *halakha* is in accordance with the opinion of Rav Huna (Rambam *Sefer HaMadda, Hilkhot Avoda Zara* 12:5; *Shulḥan Arukh, Yoreh De'a* 181:6).

They are not included in the prohibition of destruction – לֵיתְנְהוּ בְּהַשְׁחָתָה: If a woman has facial hair she is permitted to shave it all off, as the prohibition against destroying one's beard does not apply to women, as stated by Rav Huna. The same applies to a woman who destroys a man's beard. The *Baḥ* maintains that at the very least a woman is prohibited by rabbinic law from destroying the beard of a man, whereas the *Shakh* claims that the Gemara here proves otherwise (Rambam *Sefer HaMadda, Hilkhot Avoda Zara* 12:7; *Shulḥan Arukh, Yoreh De'a* 181:12).

They are not included in the prohibition of rounding either – לֵיתְנְהוּ נַמִי בְּהַקָּפָה: A woman is permitted to shave the corners of her head, as the prohibition against rounding does not apply to her. If a woman shaved the corners of a man's head she is exempt, as the *halakha* is in accordance with the opinion of Rav Huna. However she is prohibited from doing so, either by rabbinic law or due to the injunction (Leviticus 19:14) "You shall not put a stumbling block before the blind" (Rambam *Sefer HaMadda, Hilkhot Avoda Zara* 12:2; *Shulḥan Arukh, Yoreh De'a* 181:6).

Both one who rounds and one who is rounded – אֶחָד הַמַּקִּיף וְאֶחָד הַנִּיקָּף: It is prohibited to shave the corners of one's head, and one who does so is flogged. One is also liable if another Jew shaves his head with his assistance. It is prohibited to allow one's head to be rounded even without lending any help at all, and therefore one may not allow a gentile to do so (Rambam *Sefer HaMadda, Hilkhot Avoda Zara* 12:1; *Shulḥan Arukh, Yoreh De'a* 181:4).

PERSONALITIES

Rav Huna – רַב הוּנָא: Rav Huna was one of the great second-generation *amora'im* in Babylonia. He served as deputy to his principal teacher, Rav. As the head of the yeshiva in Sura after the death of Shmuel, he was widely regarded as the greatest Sage of his generation. Almost all of the Sages of the next generation were his disciples. Rav Ami and Rav Asi, who studied Torah under him in Babylonia before emigrating to Eretz Yisrael, viewed themselves as subordinate to him. According to a tradition of the *ge'onim* Rav Huna was from the family of the Exilarch. Although in his younger years he was exceedingly poor and studied the Torah amid great hardship, he later became wealthy. Much is related in the Talmud of his piety (see *Ta'anit* 20b), and he was a model of wisdom for generations to follow.

Rav Adda bar Ahava – רַב אַדָּא בַּר אַהֲבָה: A Babylonian *amora*, Rav Adda bar Ahava spanned the first and second generations of *amora'im*. The various talmudic sources referring to Rav Adda bar Ahava indicate that there were at least two, perhaps three, Sages of that name. Apparently the reference in the Gemara here is to the first and greatest Sage to be called by that name. Rav Adda was one of Rav's greatest students. Both Rav and Shmuel appreciated the extent of his righteousness and piety, and would rely on his merit in their belief that they would come to no harm. Future generations would cite his behavior as exemplifying the awe of Heaven. The Talmud tells of his modesty and the painstaking care he took with regard to the honor of Heaven, of his teachers, and of his fellow man. The calculation of the Hebrew calendar, referred to as *tekufat Rav Adda*, is apparently named after this first Rav Adda. Although Shmuel established his own calculation, Rav Adda's far more accurate version serves nowadays as the foundation for the fixed Jewish calendar.

NOTES

Ḥova should bury her sons, etc. – תִּקְבְּרִינוּן חוֹבָה וכו׳: In other words, this does not constitute a prohibition according to my ruling, says Rav Adda; however, according to your opinion she is violating a prohibition (Commentary on *Nazir*; *Tosafot*). Others suggest that she sins even according to the opinion of Rav Adda, albeit by rabbinic law (Meiri). However, the Meiri rejects this explanation, insisting that the question refers only to the ruling of Rav Huna, as his statement indicates that the wife is in violation of a mitzva by Torah law. Yet others contend that Rav Adda was not uttering a curse but posing a question: Does Ḥova want to end up burying her sons for acting this way (Rosh; Rabbeinu Azriel)?

Both one who rounds and one who is rounded – אֶחָד הַמַּקִּיף וְאֶחָד הַנִּיקָּף: Some commentaries explain that Rav Adda derives this *halakha* from the double expressions of: "You shall not round," and: "The corners of your heads." In this manner the verse teaches that the hair of one's head must not be rounded, and also that one must not perform this act upon another man (*Tosafot*). Furthermore, as the two prohibitions are derived from the same phrase, they are dependent on each other. Therefore, one is prohibited from rounding the head only of someone who is bound by this prohibition. The dispute between the *amora'im* can be summarized as follows: Rav Huna maintains that one who rounds the head of a minor boy is liable but a woman who rounds the head of another is exempt; whereas according to Rav Adda one who rounds the hair of a minor boy is exempt, but a woman who rounds the head of an adult is liable (*Tosafot*).

BACKGROUND

Since they are not included in the prohibition of destruction – הוֹאִיל וְלֵיתְנְהוּ בְּהַשְׁחָתָה: A woman who has a beard may shave it with a razor. Although it is extremely rare, a woman may have a beard grow due to a condition referred to as hirsutism, which is the growth of superfluous hair in women resulting from mild androgen excess. Another rare condition which may cause a woman to grow a beard is hypertrichosis, which is abnormal growth of hair that may be local or cover the entire body.

לֵימָא הַקָּפַת כָּל הָרֹאשׁ תַּנָּאֵי הִיא, דְּתָנוּ רַבָּנַן: "רֹאשׁוֹ", מַה תַּלְמוּד לוֹמַר – לְפִי שֶׁנֶּאֱמַר "לֹא תַקִּפוּ פְּאַת רֹאשְׁכֶם",

The Gemara asks: **Shall we say** that the issue of whether one who **rounds the entire head** is considered to have rounded its corners **is a dispute between *tanna'im*? As the Sages taught** in a *baraita*, with regard to a verse that deals with the shaving of a leper: "He shall shave all his hair; **his head** and his beard and his eyebrows, even all his hair he shall shave off" (Leviticus 14:9). **Why must the verse state:** "His head," after it has already stated: "All his hair"? The *baraita* explains that **since it is stated: "You shall not round the corners of your heads"** (Leviticus 19:27),

Perek **VIII**
Daf **58** Amud **a**

יָכוֹל אַף מְצוֹרָע כֵּן – תַּלְמוּד לוֹמַר "רֹאשׁוֹ". וְתַנְיָא אִידָךְ: "רֹאשׁוֹ" מַה תַּלְמוּד לוֹמַר? לְפִי שֶׁנֶּאֱמַר גַּבֵּי נָזִיר "תַּעַר לֹא יַעֲבֹר עַל רֹאשׁוֹ". יָכוֹל אַף נָזִיר מְצוֹרָע כֵּן – תַּלְמוּד לוֹמַר "רֹאשׁוֹ".

one **might** have thought that **even a leper** should **likewise** be prohibited from rounding off his head. **The verse** therefore specifically **states "his head"** to teach that the mitzva for a leper to remove all the hair of his head overrides the prohibition against rounding one's head. **And it was taught in another *baraita*: Why must the verse state: "His head,"** with regard to a leper? **Since it states, with regard to a nazirite: "No razor shall come upon his head"** (Numbers 6:5), one **might** have thought that **even a nazirite leper** should **likewise** be prohibited from shaving upon his purification. Therefore **the verse states: "His head,"** from which it is derived that a nazirite who contracted leprosy must shave his head like any other leper.

מַאי לָאו תַּנָּאֵי הִיא; לְמַאן דְּאָמַר מִנָּזִיר, קָסָבַר: הַקָּפַת כָּל הָרֹאשׁ לָא שְׁמָהּ הַקָּפָה, וְכִי אֲתָא קְרָא – לְמִידְחֵי אֶת לֹא תַעֲשֶׂה וַעֲשֵׂה. וְאִידָךְ סָבַר: הַקָּפַת כָּל הָרֹאשׁ שְׁמָהּ הַקָּפָה, וְכִי אֲתָא קְרָא – לְמִידְחֵי לָאו גְּרֵידָא?

The Gemara explains: **What, is it not** correct to say that this **is a** dispute between *tanna'im*? **According to the one who says** that the additional term "his head" is to counter a possible prohibition derived **from** the case of **a nazirite,** he **holds** that **rounding the entire head is not called rounding,** and therefore there is no need for a verse to teach that a leper can shave all the hair off his head. **And when the verse** "He shall shave all his hair; his head" **comes,** it comes **to override** both the **prohibition**: "No razor shall come upon his head," **and** the **positive mitzva** stated with regard to a nazirite: "He shall be sacred, he shall let the locks of the hair of his head grow long" (Numbers 6:5). **And the other *tanna* holds** that **rounding the entire head is called rounding, and** consequently, **when the verse comes,** it serves **to override only** the **prohibition** against rounding one's head.

אֲמַר רָבָא: דְּכוּלֵּי עָלְמָא הַקָּפַת כָּל הָרֹאשׁ לָא שְׁמָהּ הַקָּפָה, וְכִי אֲתָא קְרָא – כְּגוֹן שֶׁהִקִּיף וּלְבַסּוֹף גִּילֵּחַ; כֵּיוָן דְּאִילּוּ גַּלְחֵיהּ בְּחַד זִימְנָא – לָא מִיחַיַּיב, כִּי הִקִּיף וּלְבַסּוֹף גִּילֵּחַ – נַמִי לָא מִיחַיַּיב.

Rava said in refutation of this proof: No; it is possible **that everyone** agrees that **rounding the entire head is not called rounding,** even the *tanna* who maintains that the purpose of the verse is to permit a leper to round his head. **And when the verse comes,** it serves to address a particular case, **such as** one **in which he rounded** off only the corners of the head **and ultimately shaved** off the rest of his hair. Although shaving only the corners of one's head is prohibited by the Torah, in this instance he is exempt. The reason is that **since if he shaved** his entire head **at one time he would not be liable,** then **if he rounded** off his head **and ultimately shaved he is also not liable.** Since a leper is permitted to shave all of his head, he can do so in any manner he chooses.

וּמִי כְּתַב קְרָא הָכִי? וְהָאָמַר רֵישׁ לָקִישׁ: כָּל מָקוֹם שֶׁאַתָּה מוֹצֵא עֲשֵׂה וְלֹא תַעֲשֶׂה, אִם אַתָּה יָכוֹל לְקַיֵּים אֶת שְׁנֵיהֶם – מוּטָב, וְאִם לָאו – יָבוֹא עֲשֵׂה וְיִדְחֶה אֶת לֹא תַעֲשֶׂה.

The Gemara raises a difficulty with this explanation: **And does the verse write this?** Is it permitted unnecessarily to transgress a prohibition *ab initio*? **But didn't Reish Lakish say: Any place that you find positive mitzvot and prohibitions** that clash with one another, **if you can** find some way to **fulfill both,** that is **preferable; and if** that is **not** possible, **the positive mitzva will come and override the prohibition?** If it is not prohibited to round the entire head, the leper can shave his hair in a permitted manner, and the Torah would not have allowed him to do so in a way that involves the violation of a prohibition.

אֶלָּא, דְּכוּלֵּי עָלְמָא הַקָּפַת כׇּל הָרֹאשׁ שְׁמָהּ הַקָּפָה. וּמַאן דְּמוֹקֵים לִקְרָא לְמִידְחֵי לֹא תַעֲשֶׂה וַעֲשֵׂה – לָאו גְּרֵידָא מְנָלֵיהּ?

Rather, the Gemara retracts its previous explanation and states the opposite. It is **that everyone** agrees that **rounding the entire head is called rounding.** If so, the *baraita* that states that the verse: "He shall shave all his hair; his head" (Leviticus 14:9), comes to permit the rounding of a leper's entire head is easily understood, as it is derived from here that a positive mitzva overrides a prohibition. **But** according to **the one who establishes the verse** "He shall shave all his hair; his head" as coming **to override** the **prohibition and** the **positive mitzva** of a nazirite, **from where does he** derive that a positive mitzva overrides **only a prohibition?**[N]

יָלֵיף מִגְּדִילִים. דְּאָמַר קְרָא ״לֹא תִלְבַּשׁ שַׁעַטְנֵז״. וְתַנְיָא: ״לֹא תִלְבַּשׁ שַׁעַטְנֵז״ – הָא גְּדִילִים תַּעֲשֶׂה לְּךָ מֵהֶם.

The Gemara answers: He **derives** it **from** the case of ritual **fringes.** How so? **As the verse states: "You shall not wear diverse kinds,** wool and linen together" (Deuteronomy 22:11), **and it is taught** in a *baraita* that although the command **"You shall not wear diverse kinds"** applies to most cases, the juxtaposed verse: **"You shall make for you fringes"** (Deuteronomy 22:12), teaches that one may prepare ritual fringes even **from** diverse kinds of wool and linen. This teaches that the positive mitzva of ritual fringes overrides the prohibition of diverse kinds.

וּמַאן דְּנָפְקָא לֵיהּ מֵ״רֹאשׁוֹ״ מַאי טַעְמָא לָא נָפְקָא לֵיהּ מִגְּדִילִים? אָמַר לָךְ: לְכִדְרָבָא הוּא דַּאֲתָא.

The Gemara asks: **And** the *tanna* **who derives** the principle that a positive mitzva overrides a prohibition **from "his head"** stated with regard to a leper, **what is the reason that he does not derive it from** the verse that deals with ritual **fringes?** Why does he require another source? The Gemara answers: He could have **said to you** that the verse concerning ritual fringes does not teach that principle, as **it comes for that which Rava** said.

דְּרָבָא רָמֵי: כְּתִיב ״וְנָתְנוּ עַל צִיצִת הַכָּנָף״ – מִין כָּנָף ״פְּתִיל תְּכֵלֶת״. וּכְתִיב ״צֶמֶר וּפִשְׁתִּים יַחְדָּו״.

As Rava raises a contradiction: It is written: "And that they put on the fringe of each corner a thread of sky blue" (Numbers 15:38). The phrase "the fringe of each corner" indicates that ritual fringes must be of the same **type as the corner**[H] of the robe itself, upon which they must place **"a thread of sky blue." And** yet **it is written:** "You shall not wear diverse kinds, **wool and linen together"** (Deuteronomy 22:11). The juxtaposition of these two verses teaches that ritual fringes must be made from wool and linen.

הָא כֵּיצַד? צֶמֶר וּפִשְׁתִּים – פּוֹטְרִים בֵּין בְּמִינָן בֵּין שֶׁלֹּא בְּמִינָן, שְׁאָר מִינִין – בְּמִינָן פּוֹטְרִין, שֶׁלֹּא בְּמִינָן – אֵין פּוֹטְרִין.

How so? How can ritual fringes be made from the same material as the garment itself and also from wool and linen? The answer is that ritual fringes of **wool and linen exempt**[H] a garment and fulfill the obligation of ritual fringes **whether** the garment is **of their own type,** i.e., wool and linen, or **whether it is not of their own type,** i.e., all other materials. By contrast, with regard to ritual fringes of **other types** of materials, **they exempt** a garment **of their own type;** but **they do not exempt** a garment that is **not of their type.** According to this, the verse juxtaposing ritual fringes to diverse kinds serves to teach that ritual fringes made of wool and linen exempt any garment, not to teach that a positive mitzva overrides a prohibition.

וְהַאי תַּנָּא דְּמַפֵּיק לְ״רֹאשׁוֹ״ לְלָאו גְּרֵידָא, דְּאָתֵי עֲשֵׂה וְדָחֵי אֶת לֹא תַעֲשֶׂה וַעֲשֵׂה מְנָלַן? נָפְקָא לֵיהּ מִ״זְּקָנוֹ״.

The Gemara continues this line of inquiry: **And** according to **this** *tanna,* **who derives from** the term **"his head"** that a positive mitzva overrides **only a prohibition, from where do we** derive the *halakha* **that** the **positive mitzva** of a leper's shaving **comes and overrides** the **prohibition and the positive mitzva** of a nazirite? From where does this **tanna** learn that a nazirite who contracted leprosy is obligated to shave? The Gemara answers: **He derives it from** the verse: "He shall shave all his hair; his head and **his beard"** (Leviticus 14:9).[N]

דְּתַנְיָא: ״זְקָנוֹ״ מַה תַּלְמוּד לוֹמַר? לְפִי שֶׁנֶּאֱמַר ״וּפְאַת זְקָנָם לֹא יְגַלֵּחוּ״. יָכוֹל אַף כֹּהֵן מְצוֹרָע כֵּן – תַּלְמוּד לוֹמַר ״זְקָנוֹ״.

As it is taught in a *baraita:* **Why** must **the verse state: "His beard"?** After all, a beard is already included in the phrase "all his hair." The *baraita* answers: **Since it is stated,** with regard to priests: **"Neither shall they shave off the corners of their beard"** (Leviticus 21:5), one **might** have thought that **even a priest who is a leper is included** in this prohibition against shaving his beard. Therefore, **the verse states: "His beard"** in connection to a leper.

NOTES

From where does he derive that a positive mitzva overrides only a prohibition – לָאו גְּרֵידָא מְנָלֵיהּ: Since this *tanna* learns from the term "his head" that a positive mitzva overrides both a prohibition and a positive mitzva, it is evident that in his opinion it can be derived elsewhere that a positive mitzva overrides a single prohibition. The Gemara is discussing the source of this principle (*Tosafot*; Rosh; Meiri).

He derives it from "his beard" – נָפְקָא לֵיהּ מִזְּקָנוֹ: This *tanna* learns from here that a positive mitzva overrides a prohibition and a positive mitzva if they include a lenient aspect. In the case of a nazirite, the leniency is that prohibitions of naziriteship can be dissolved by a halakhic authority; priestly prohibitions do not apply equally to all Jews but only to male priests. According to this opinion, although a nazirite and a priest are dissimilar, their *halakhot* can be derived from each other, as neither mitzva is an all-encompassing obligation (*Tosafot*).

HALAKHA

Corner, the type of the corner – הַכָּנָף, מִין כָּנָף: The sky-blue threads of ritual fringes must always be of wool. If the garment is a woolen one, the white threads should be of wool as well. The white threads of the fringes of a linen garment must be linen. As for other types of material, the white threads of their ritual fringes can be made from the same fabric as the clothing itself, or of wool or linen (Rambam *Sefer Ahava, Hilkhot Tzitzit* 3:5).

Wool and linen exempt, etc. – צֶמֶר וּפִשְׁתִּים פּוֹטְרִים וכו׳: Ritual fringes of wool or linen can be used to exempt any type of clothing. Today, in the absence of a definitive determination as to the components of the sky-blue dye, one may not attach woolen ritual fringes to a linen garment, as this constitutes diverse kinds in a situation where the mitzva can be performed with the same type, as the white threads need not be of wool. Ritual fringes of other fabrics may be used only in garments of that same type, but not in clothes made of other materials (Rambam *Sefer Ahava, Hilkhot Tzitzit* 3:6; *Shulḥan Arukh, Oraḥ Ḥayyim* 9:2–3).

וּמַאן דְּמַפֵּיק לֵיהּ לְ״רֹאשׁוֹ״ לַעֲשֵׂה וְלֹא תַעֲשֶׂה, לֵילַף מִ״זְּקָנוֹ״! וְלִיטַעֲמִיךְ, דְּקַיְימָא לַן בְּעָלְמָא

The Gemara asks: **And the one who derives** from "his head" that the mitzva of shaving overrides both **the positive mitzva and prohibition** of a nazirite, **let him derive** this principle **from "his beard."** The Gemara refutes this suggestion: **And according to your reasoning,** that the term "his beard" teaches that a positive mitzva overrides the prohibition and positive mitzva of a nazirite, that which **we maintain generally,**

Perek **VIII**
Daf **58** Amud **b**

HALAKHA

A positive mitzva does not come and override, etc. – **לָא אָתֵי עֲשֵׂה וְדָחֵי וכו׳:** In the case of a positive mitzva and a prohibition that involve the same action, if one can fulfill the positive command without violating the prohibition, he should do so. If not, the positive mitzva overrides the prohibition. This applies only if the positive mitzva is in conflict with the prohibition alone; however, it does not override both a prohibition and a positive mitzva. For this reason, priests do not perform the mitzva of burning invalidated offerings on a Festival. Likewise, a widow may not enter into levirate marriage with a High Priest, and a priest may not render himself ritually impure in a cemetery to perform the mitzva of restoring lost property. These are just a few of many examples (Rambam *Sefer Zemanim, Hilkhot Yom Tov* 3:8; *Sefer Nashim, Hilkhot Yibbum VaḤalitza* 6:11; and *Sefer Nezikin, Hilkhot Gezeila VaAveda* 11:18; see *Shulḥan Arukh, Oraḥ Ḥayyim* 586:21 and *Magen Avraham* there).

דְּלָא אָתֵי עֲשֵׂה וְדָחֵי אֶת לֹא תַעֲשֶׂה וַעֲשֵׂה, לֵילַף מִכֹּהֵן דְּדָחֵי!

that a positive mitzva does not come and override[H] **a prohibition and a positive mitzva, let him derive from** the fact that a leprous **priest** must shave **that** this mitzva **does override** a prohibition and another positive mitzva.

אֶלָּא, מִכֹּהֵן לָא יָלְפִינַן; מָה לְכֹהֵן – שֶׁכֵּן לָאו שֶׁאֵינוֹ שָׁוֶה בַּכֹּל. נָזִיר מִכֹּהֵן נַמִי לָא יָלֵיף – שֶׁכֵּן לָאו שֶׁאֵינוֹ שָׁוֶה בַּכֹּל.

Rather, he would explain that **we do not derive** other cases of the Torah **from** the *halakha* **of a priest,** for the following reason: **What is** different about the prohibition **of a priest is that** it is **a prohibition that is not equally** applicable **to all,** i.e., the prohibitions of a priest do not apply to Israelites. For the same reason, the case of **a nazirite also cannot be derived from** that of **a priest, as** the prohibition of a priest is **a prohibition that is not equally** applicable **to all,**[N] in contrast to that of a nazirite. Consequently, the derivation from "his head" is necessary to teach that the shaving of a leper overrides the prohibition stated with regard to a nazirite.

וּמַאן דְּמוֹקֵים לְהַאי ״רֹאשׁוֹ״ בְּנָזִיר, לָמָּה לִי ״זְקָנוֹ״?!

The Gemara turns its attention to the other opinion: **And** according to **the one who establishes this** verse: "He shall shave all his hair; **his head** and his beard" (Leviticus 14:9), as referring **to a nazirite,** i.e., he derives from this verse the principle that in certain cases, including that of a leprous priest, a positive mitzva overrides a prohibition and a positive mitzva, **why do I need** the term **"his beard"?**

מִיבָּעֵי לֵיהּ לִכְדְתַנְיָא: ״זְקָנוֹ״ מַה תַּלְמוּד לוֹמַר? לְפִי שֶׁנֶּאֱמַר ״וּפְאַת זְקָנָם לֹא יְגַלֵּחוּ״. יָכוֹל אַף כֹּהֵן מְצוֹרָע כֵּן – תַּלְמוּד לוֹמַר ״זְקָנוֹ״.

The Gemara answers: **He requires it for that which is taught** in a *baraita* with regard to the shaving of a leper, which must be performed with a razor: **Why** must **the verse state: "His beard,"** as it already stated that he shaves all his hair? **Since it is stated: "Neither shall they shave off the corners of their beard"** (Leviticus 21:5), one **might** have thought that **even a priest** who is **a leper is included** in the prohibition against shaving. **The verse** therefore **states: "His beard,"** to teach that a leprous priest must shave his beard as well.

וּמְנָלַן דִּבְתַעַר? דְּתַנְיָא: ״וּפְאַת זְקָנָם לֹא יְגַלֵּחוּ״. יָכוֹל אַף גִּילְּחוּ בְּמִסְפָּרַיִם יְהֵא חַיָּיב – תַּלְמוּד לוֹמַר ״וְלֹא תַשְׁחִית״. אִי לֹא תַשְׁחִית, יָכוֹל לִיקְּטָן בְּמַלְקֵט וּבִרְהִיטְנִי חַיָּיב.

And from where do we derive that a leper must shave **with a razor?**[N] **As it is taught** in a *baraita*: **"Neither shall they shave off the corners of their beard"** (Leviticus 21:5). One **might** have thought that priests **should be liable even if they shaved** their beards **with scissors. The verse states: "And you shall not destroy** the corners of your beard" (Leviticus 19:27), which teaches that the prohibition applies only to the destruction of the beard from its roots. **If** the sole criterion is the phrase **"you shall not destroy,"** one **might** have thought that **if he extracted** his hair **with tweezers or** removed his hair **with a** carpenter's **plane, he should** likewise **be liable** due to the prohibition against destroying his hair.

NOTES

A prohibition that is not equally applicable to all – **לָאו שֶׁאֵינוֹ שָׁוֶה בַּכֹּל:** Why can one not derive from the case of a nazirite, which is equally applicable to all, that the principle that a positive mitzva overrides a prohibition and a positive mitzva applies to the rest of the mitzvot of the Torah? In other words, just as the positive mitzva of shaving a leper overrides the prohibition and positive mitzva of a nazirite, the same should apply to any positive mitzvot and prohibitions. The answer to this question is stated at the end of the Gemara's discussion: One cannot learn a general principle from the case of a nazirite since the mitzvot of nazariteship are considered lighter than regular ones, as a nazirite vow can be dissolved by a halakhic authority (*Tosafot*). All this represents the opinion of one *tanna*; the other *tanna* maintains that since the mitzvot of a nazirite and a priest are both different from regular mitzvot in that they include a lenient aspect, one can derive the *halakha* of one case from the other.

And from where do we derive that a leper must shave with a razor – **וּמְנָלַן דִּבְתַעַר:** The verse says that a leper shaves off all his hair, but it does not specify the implement he must use. Theoretically, he could apply a depilatory or remove hair in some other way. The obligation to shave with a razor is derived in an indirect manner: Since the Torah found it necessary to permit a priest to shave his beard, the leper's mitzva must involve an implement whose use would otherwise be prohibited.

תַּלְמוּד לוֹמַר ״וּפְאַת זְקָנָם לֹא יְגַלֵּחוּ״. אֵיזוֹ גִּילּוּחַ שֶׁיֵּשׁ בּוֹ הַשְׁחָתָה – הֱוֵי אוֹמֵר זֶה תַּעַר.

The verse therefore states: "Neither shall they shave off the corners of their beard." Together the two verses lead to the following conclusion: **Which is the type of shaving [*giluaḥ*] that involves destruction [*hashḥata*]?**[L] **You must say it is a razor.** The fact that it was necessary for the Torah to permit a leper to shave his beard with a razor, notwithstanding the prohibition against using this implement, proves that the positive mitzva overrides this prohibition, as derived from the term "his beard."

וּמַאן דְּמַפֵּיק לֵיהּ לְהַאי ״רֹאשׁוֹ״ לְלָאו גְּרֵידָא, לָמָּה לִי לְמִיכְתַּב ״רֹאשׁוֹ״ וְלָמָּה לִי לְמִיכְתַּב ״זְקָנוֹ״?

The Gemara continues to inquire: **And** according **to the one who derives from** the term **"his head"** the principle **that** a positive mitzva overrides **only a prohibition, why do I** need the verse **to write: "His head," and why do I** also need the same verse **to write: "His beard"?** Once is it derived from the phrase "his beard" that a positive mitzva overrides a positive mitzva and a prohibition, the same should certainly apply to a prohibition by itself.

מַשְׁמַע לְמִידְחֵי לָאו גְּרֵידָא, וּמַשְׁמַע לְמִידְחֵי לֹא תַּעֲשֶׂה וַעֲשֵׂה, הִילְכָּךְ שָׁקוּל הוּא, וְיָבוֹאוּ שְׁנֵיהֶן.

The Gemara answers: Both the term "his head" and the term "his beard" could come to **teach the overriding of only a prohibition, and** they also could **teach the overriding of a prohibition and a positive mitzva.** Since the verse is formulated in general terms, it includes a priest or a nazirite. **Therefore,** as it cannot be determined to which case the Torah is referring, **it is even,** i.e., equally balanced, **and** consequently **let both** terms **come** and teach this principle, one with regard to a nazirite, and the other with regard to a priest.

כֹּהֵן מִנָּזִיר לָא יָלֵיף – שֶׁכֵּן יֶשְׁנוֹ בִּשְׁאֵלָה, נָזִיר מִכֹּהֵן לָא יָלֵיף – שֶׁכֵּן לָאו שֶׁאֵינוֹ שָׁוֶה בַּכֹּל. וּבְעָלְמָא לָא יָלְפִינַן מִינַּיְיהוּ, מִשּׁוּם דְּאִיכָּא לְמִיפְרַךְ כִּדְאָמְרַן.

The Gemara adds that both terms are necessary, as the *halakha* of a **priest cannot be derived from** that of **a nazirite, as** the case of a nazirite is lenient in that **it is** possible to dissolve naziriteship **by request** from a halakhic authority. Likewise, the *halakha* **of a nazirite cannot be derived from** that of **a priest, as** the case of a priest involves **a prohibition that is not equally** applicable **to all.** The Gemara comments: **And generally,** with regard to other *halakhot*, **we cannot derive from** these two cases that a positive mitzva overrides a prohibition and a positive mitzva, **due to** the fact that this argument **can be refuted as we said** here.

אָמַר רַב: מֵיקֵל אָדָם כׇּל גּוּפוֹ בְּתַעַר. מֵיתִיבֵי: הַמַּעֲבִיר בֵּית הַשֶּׁחִי וּבֵית הָעֶרְוָה – הֲרֵי זֶה לוֹקֶה.

§ **Rav said: A person** who is not a nazirite **may lighten** his burden by removing **all** the hair of **his body with a razor.** One who feels he has too much hair may shave all of it off with a razor, apart from his beard and the corners of his head. The Gemara **raises an objection** against this from a *baraita*: A man **who removes** the hair **of the armpit or the pubic** hair **is flogged** for transgressing the prohibition: "A man shall not put on a woman's garment" (Deuteronomy 22:5), as this behavior is the manner of women.

הָא בְּתַעַר, הָא בְּמִסְפָּרַיִם. וְהָא רַב נַמִי בְּתַעַר קָאָמַר! כְּעֵין תַּעַר.

The Gemara answers: In **this** case he is flogged because he shaved **with a razor,** whereas in **that** case Rav said it is permitted because he was referring to one who removes hair **with scissors,** an act that is not considered a prohibition. The Gemara raises a difficulty: **But Rav said** it is permitted **with a razor as well.** The Gemara answers: He did not mean an actual razor; rather, he said that one may use an implement that is **similar to a razor,**[N] i.e., scissors that cut very close to the skin, in the manner of a razor.

אָמַר רַבִּי חִיָּיא בַּר אַבָּא אָמַר רַבִּי יוֹחָנָן: הַמַּעֲבִיר בֵּית הַשֶּׁחִי וּבֵית הָעֶרְוָה לוֹקֶה. מֵיתִיבֵי: הַעֲבָרַת שֵׂיעָר אֵינָהּ מִדִּבְרֵי תוֹרָה אֶלָּא מִדִּבְרֵי סוֹפְרִים. מַאי לוֹקֶה נַמִי דְּקָאָמַר – מִדְּרַבָּנַן.

Rabbi Ḥiyya bar Abba said that **Rabbi Yoḥanan said:** A man **who removes** the hair **of the armpit**[H] **or the pubic** hair **is flogged.** The Gemara **raises an objection** against this ruling: **The removal of hair is not** prohibited **by Torah law but by rabbinic law.** Why, then, is he liable to receive lashes? The Gemara explains: **What** does it mean **that** Rabbi Yoḥanan **says** that he **is flogged?** This means that he is flogged **by rabbinic law,** a punishment known as lashes for rebelliousness, for disobeying a rabbinic decree.

LANGUAGE

Shaving [*giluaḥ*] and destroying hair [*hashḥata*] – **גִּילוּחַ וְהַשְׁחָתָה**: Although these two terms are often used interchangeably, the Sages distinguished between them with regard to *halakha*. Various languages related to Hebrew indicate that the term *galaḥ* means to smooth a surface. However, based on its usage in both the Bible and rabbinic texts, it apparently refers to cutting hair with a razor-like device or scissors. By contrast, *hashḥata* means the removal of hair in such a manner that nothing remains. This can be done using various substances, such as pumice, a light yet abrasive volcanic rock used during antiquity to remove excess hair; through the use of fire; or by shaving. An act of shaving that also destroys can be performed only with a razor.

Pumice

NOTES

Similar to a razor – **כְּעֵין תַּעַר**: This indicates that it is prohibited to shave one's armpits with a razor; however, one may do so with a razor-like implement. Conversely, the hair that covers other parts of the body may be removed by means of a razor. An alternative version of the text states that it is prohibited to remove armpit hair in any manner, whereas that of other limbs is permitted with scissors alone (Meiri; see *ge'onim*, Rif, and Rambam; see also *Tosafot* on 59a).

HALAKHA

A man who removes the hair of the armpit, etc. – **הַמַּעֲבִיר בֵּית הַשֶּׁחִי וכו׳**: It is prohibited for a man to shave the hair of his armpits and his pubic hair with a razor, or with scissors that remove the hair completely in the manner of a razor. One who does so receives lashes for rebelliousness from the Sages. As for the hair on the rest of his body, it is permitted to remove it with scissors, even if they cut in a manner similar to that of a razor, but not with a razor itself. The *halakha* follows Rav, in accordance with the reading of the *ge'onim*. Rabbeinu Tam, following the standard version of the text, rules that scissors that are similar to razors are prohibited on the rest of the body as well (Rambam *Sefer HaMadda*, *Hilkhot Avoda Zara* 12:9; *Shulḥan Arukh*, *Yoreh De'a* 182:1).

אִיכָּא דְּאָמְרִי, אָמַר רַבִּי חִיָּיא בַּר אַבָּא אָמַר רַבִּי יוֹחָנָן: הַמַּעֲבִיר בֵּית הַשֶּׁחִי וּבֵית הָעֶרְוָה לוֹקֶה מִשּׁוּם ״לֹא יִלְבַּשׁ גֶּבֶר שִׂמְלַת אִשָּׁה״. מֵיתִיבֵי: הַעֲבָרַת שֵׂיעָר אֵינָהּ מִדִּבְרֵי תוֹרָה אֶלָּא מִדִּבְרֵי סוֹפְרִים! הוּא דְּאָמַר כִּי הַאי תַּנָּא, דְּתַנְיָא: הַמַּעֲבִיר בֵּית הַשֶּׁחִי וּבֵית הָעֶרְוָה – הֲרֵי זֶה עוֹבֵר מִשּׁוּם ״לֹא יִלְבַּשׁ גֶּבֶר שִׂמְלַת אִשָּׁה״.

Some say a different version of this statement: **Rabbi Ḥiyya bar Abba said** that **Rabbi Yoḥanan said:** A man **who removes** the hair **of the armpit or the pubic** hair **is flogged, due to** the prohibition: **"A man shall not put on a woman's garment"** (Deuteronomy 22:5). The Gemara **raises an objection** from a *baraita*: **The removal of hair is not** prohibited **by Torah law but by rabbinic law.** How then does Rabbi Yoḥanan say that he is flogged, which by definition is a punishment for individuals who have transgressed a Torah law? The Gemara answers: It was **he who said** this *halakha* **in accordance** with the opinion of **that** *tanna*, **as it is taught** in a *baraita*: A man **who removes** the hair **of the armpit or the pubic** hair **violates** the prohibition of: **"A man shall not put on a woman's garment."**[N]

וְתַנָּא קַמָּא, הַאי ״לֹא יִלְבַּשׁ גֶּבֶר״ מַאי דָּרֵישׁ בֵּיהּ? מִיבָּעֵי לֵיהּ לִכְדְתַנְיָא: ״לֹא יִהְיֶה כְלִי גֶבֶר עַל אִשָּׁה״ מַאי תַּלְמוּד לוֹמַר? אִם שֶׁלֹּא יִלְבַּשׁ אִישׁ שִׂמְלַת אִשָּׁה, וְאִשָּׁה שִׂמְלַת אִישׁ – הֲרֵי כְּבָר נֶאֱמַר ״תּוֹעֵבָה הִיא״ וְאֵין כָּאן תּוֹעֵבָה.

The Gemara asks: **And what does the first** *tanna*, who holds that the prohibition is by rabbinic law, **learn from this verse: "A man shall not put on** a woman's garment"? The Gemara answers: **He requires it for that which is taught** in the *baraita*, where it states: **"A woman shall not wear that which pertains to a man,** and a man shall not put on a woman's garment, for whoever does these things is an abomination to the Lord your God" (Deuteronomy 22:5). **What** is the meaning when **the verse states** this? **If it** teaches only **that a man may not put on**[N] a woman's garment, **and a woman** may not wear **a man's garment, it is already stated** in explanation of this prohibition that **"it is an abomination** to the Lord your God," **and there is no abomination here** in the mere act of wearing a garment.

אֶלָּא, שֶׁלֹּא יִלְבַּשׁ אִישׁ שִׂמְלַת אִשָּׁה וְיֵשֵׁב בֵּין הַנָּשִׁים, וְאִשָּׁה שִׂמְלַת אִישׁ וְתֵשֵׁב בֵּין הָאֲנָשִׁים. רַבִּי אֱלִיעֶזֶר בֶּן יַעֲקֹב אוֹמֵר: מִנַּיִן שֶׁלֹּא תֵּצֵא אִשָּׁה בִּכְלֵי זַיִין לַמִּלְחָמָה – תַּלְמוּד לוֹמַר ״לֹא יִהְיֶה כְלִי גֶבֶר עַל אִשָּׁה וְלֹא יִלְבַּשׁ גֶּבֶר שִׂמְלַת אִשָּׁה״ – שֶׁלֹּא יְתַקֵּן אִישׁ בְּתִיקּוּנֵי אִשָּׁה.

Rather, it means **that a man may not wear a woman's garment** and thereby go **and sit among the women; and a woman** may not wear **a man's garment and sit among the men. Rabbi Eliezer ben Ya'akov says: From where** is it derived **that a woman may not go out with weapons**[H] **to war? The verse states: "A woman shall not wear that which pertains to a man, and a man shall not put on a woman's garment,"** which indicates **that a man may not adorn himself with the cosmetics** and ornaments **of a woman,** and similarly a woman may not go out with weapons to war, as those are for the use of males. Rabbi Yoḥanan's ruling follows this opinion.

אָמַר רַב נַחְמָן: בְּנָזִיר מוּתָּר. וְלֵית הִילְכְתָא כְּוָותֵיהּ. אֲמַרוּ לֵיהּ רַבָּנַן לְרַבִּי שִׁמְעוֹן בַּר אַבָּא: חֲזֵינָא לֵיהּ לְרַבִּי יוֹחָנָן דְּלֵית לֵיהּ. אֲמַר לְהוֹן: מֵחֲמַת זִקְנָה נָשְׁרוּ.

§ **Rav Naḥman said: For a nazirite, it is permitted**[N] to shave armpit hair. The Gemara comments: **And the** *halakha* **is not in accordance with his** opinion. The Gemara reports that **the Sages said to Rabbi Shimon bar Abba: We have** observed **that Rabbi Yoḥanan**[P] **does not have** armpit hairs, despite his own ruling that it is prohibited to shave them. **He said to them: They fell out due to old age.**[B]

NOTES

He violates the prohibition of: A man shall not put on a woman's garment – הֲרֵי זֶה עוֹבֵר מִשּׁוּם לֹא יִלְבַּשׁ גֶּבֶר שִׂמְלַת אִשָּׁה: The *ge'onim* write at length that these issues, including wearing a woman's or a man's adornments, are dependent on time and place. If it is the custom of the gentiles in a certain locale for men to wear a particular item of clothing or to groom themselves in a certain style, e.g., to shave their armpits, Jews are permitted to act likewise. The same applies to the customs of women.

If it teaches that a man may not put on, etc. – אִם שֶׁלֹּא יִלְבַּשׁ אִישׁ וכו׳: This *tanna* maintains that the fact that a woman wears a man's garment or vice versa cannot be termed an "abomination." He therefore explains that wearing these clothes is prohibited only if it is for the sake of performing an abomination and in a manner that enables an action of that kind. By contrast, Rabbi Eliezer ben Ya'akov accepts the straightforward reading of the verse that the very wearing of women's clothing, or grooming oneself in the style of a woman, is prohibited to a man. Rabbi Yoḥanan agrees with this opinion.

For a nazirite it is permitted – בְּנָזִיר מוּתָּר: One explanation of this ruling is that a nazirite is permitted to remove his armpit hair when shaving for his naziriteship, as that is part of the act of shaving, and he is not doing so to improve his appearance (*Tosafot*; see *Meromei Sadeh*). Others maintain that this refers to during his term of naziriteship, as his acceptance of the vow proves that he is not trying to beautify himself, which means he is not acting in the manner of a woman (see *Oraḥ Mishor*). Yet others explain simply that although a nazirite may not shave the hair of his head, he is like other men with regard to armpit hair (*Shita Mekubbetzet*).

HALAKHA

A woman may not go out with weapons, etc. – שֶׁלֹּא תֵּצֵא אִשָּׁה בִּכְלֵי זַיִין וכו׳: A woman may not wear a man's garment, nor may she go to war bearing weapons, even if her garments are those of a woman (Rema, citing *Beit Yosef*). Likewise, a man may not put on a robe or an ornament that is worn only by women, as stated by Rabbi Eliezer ben Ya'akov (Rambam *Sefer HaMadda, Hilkhot Avoda Zara* 12:10; *Shulḥan Arukh, Yoreh De'a* 182:5).

BACKGROUND

Due to old age – מֵחֲמַת זִקְנָה: The same causes of balding, i.e., natural hormonal changes due to age or damage to the hair, also lead to hair loss in other parts of the body. As Rabbi Yoḥanan aged, he apparently experienced hair loss in his armpits.

PERSONALITIES

Rabbi Yoḥanan – רַבִּי יוֹחָנָן: This is Rabbi Yoḥanan bar Nappaḥa, one of the greatest *amora'im*, whose statements are fundamental to both the Babylonian and Jerusalem Talmuds. He resided in Tiberias and lived to an advanced age. Rabbi Yoḥanan was orphaned when he was young and spent virtually all of his resources to enable himself to study Torah. Although his family apparently owned considerable property, he eventually became impoverished. In his youth, he had the privilege of studying under Rabbi Yehuda HaNasi, the redactor of the Mishna, but most of his Torah study was accomplished under Rabbi Yehuda HaNasi's students: Ḥizkiyya ben Ḥiyya, Rabbi Oshaya, Rabbi Ḥanina, and Rabbi Yannai, all of whom lavished praise upon him. In time, Rabbi Yoḥanan became head of the yeshiva in Tiberias, at which point his fame and influence greatly increased.

For a long time Rabbi Yoḥanan was the leading rabbinic Sage in the entire Jewish world, not only in Eretz Yisrael but in Babylonia as well, where he was respected by the Babylonian Sages. Many of these scholars immigrated to Eretz Yisrael to become his students. A master of *halakha* and *aggada*, Rabbi Yoḥanan's statements in both disciplines are found throughout the Babylonian Talmud and the Jerusalem Talmud. As a testament to his intellectual and spiritual stature, the *halakha* is in accordance with his opinion in almost all cases, even when Rav or Shmuel, the preeminent *amora'im* of Babylonia, disagree with him. Only in disputes with his teachers in Eretz Yisrael, e.g., Rabbi Yannai and Rabbi Yehoshua ben Levi, is the *halakha* not in accordance with his opinion.

Rabbi Yoḥanan was renowned for his handsome appearance. Sadly, his life was full of suffering, as ten of his sons died in his lifetime. There is a geonic tradition that one of his sons was the Babylonian *amora* Rabbi Mattana, who did not predecease him. The death of Rabbi Yoḥanan's disciple-colleague and brother-in-law, Reish Lakish, a tragedy for which he considered himself responsible, hastened his own demise.

Rabbi Yoḥanan had many students. In fact, virtually all of the *amora'im* of Eretz Yisrael in succeeding generations were his students and benefited from his wisdom, to the extent that he is considered the author of the Jerusalem Talmud. His greatest students were his brother-in-law Reish Lakish, Rabbi Elazar, Rabbi Ḥiyya bar Abba, Rabbi Abbahu, Rabbi Yosei bar Ḥanina, Rabbi Ami, and Rabbi Asi.

הַהוּא דְּאִיתְחַיַּיב נְגִידָא קַמֵּיהּ דְּרַבִּי אַמִי, אִיגְּלַאי בֵּית הַשֶּׁחִי, חַזְיֵיהּ דְּלָא מְגַלַּח. אֲמַר לְהוֹן רַבִּי אַמִי: שִׁיבְקוּהּ, דִּין מִן חַבְרַיָּא הוּא.

The Gemara relates: There was **a certain** person who committed a transgression and **was found liable to receive lashes before Rabbi Ami.** When they removed his clothes to flog him, his **armpit was exposed,** and Rabbi Ami **saw that he had not shaved** his armpit hair. **Rabbi Ami said to** his attendants: **Leave him; this is one of those who are meticulous in observance of mitzvot.**[H] We can see this is so, as he is particular about prohibitions that ordinary people do not observe.

בְּעָא מִינֵּיהּ רַב מֵרַבִּי חִיָּיא: מַהוּ לְגַלֵּחַ? אֲמַר לֵיהּ: אָסוּר. אֲמַר לֵיהּ: וְהָא קָא גָּדֵל! אֲמַר לֵיהּ: בַּר פָּחְתֵי, זְמַן יֵשׁ לוֹ, כָּל זְמַן שֶׁהוּא גָּדֵל נוֹשֵׁר.

Rav raised a dilemma before Rabbi Ḥiyya: What is the *halakha* with regard **to shaving** armpit hair? **He said to him:** It is **prohibited.** Rav **said to him: But it grows**[HN] and is uncomfortable. Rabbi Ḥiyya **said to him: Son of nobles [*bar paḥtei*],**[L] this hair **has a** limited **time.**[B] **Whenever** a hair **grows** too long **it falls out,** and therefore there is no concern that one's armpit hair will become too long.

בְּעָא מִינֵּיהּ רַב מֵרַבִּי חִיָּיא: מַהוּ לָחוֹךְ? אֲמַר לֵיהּ: אָסוּר. בְּבִגְדּוֹ מַהוּ? אֲמַר לֵיהּ: מוּתָּר. אִיכָּא דְּאָמְרִי: בְּעָא מִינֵּיהּ: בִּתְפִלָּה בְּבִגְדּוֹ מַאי? אֲמַר לֵיהּ: אָסוּר. וְלֵית הִילְכְתָא כְּוָותֵיהּ.

Rav raised another **dilemma before Rabbi Ḥiyya: What is** the *halakha* with regard **to rubbing**[H] armpit hair and thereby removing it manually? Rabbi Ḥiyya **said to him:** It is **prohibited.** Rav continued to ask: **What is** the *halakha* with regard to rubbing armpit hair indirectly **with one's garment?** Rabbi Ḥiyya **said to him:** It is **permitted. Some say** that this was not Rav's question; rather, **he raised** the following **dilemma before him: What** is the *halakha* with regard to rubbing the armpit with **one's garment during prayer?**[HN] Rabbi Ḥiyya **said to him:** It is **prohibited.** The Gemara comments: **And the *halakha* is not in accordance with his** opinion in this case.

BACKGROUND

Has a limited time – זְמַן יֵשׁ לוֹ: Unlike hair on the head, bodily hair usually has a fixed length beyond which it does not grow. The thickness of the hair and its precise length are determined by genetics and general health.

HALAKHA

This is one of those who are meticulous in observance of mitzvot – דִּין מִן חַבְרַיָּא הוּא: Those meticulous in their observance of mitzvot should refrain from grooming themselves in the manner of women, e.g., they may not shave their armpits, even in a place where the custom is for men to do so (*Shulḥan Arukh*, *Yoreh De'a* 182:1, in the comment of Rema; and 156:2, in the comment of Rema).

But it grows – וְהָא קָא גָּדֵל: Although men are prohibited to shave their armpit and pubic hair, one may do so for medical purposes or if it is causing him discomfort, as indicated by Rabbi Ḥiyya's response to Rav (*Shulḥan Arukh, Yoreh De'a* 182:4).

What is the *halakha* with regard to rubbing – מַהוּ לָחוֹךְ: It is prohibited to rub one's armpit or pubic hair manually for the purposes of removal. However, it is permitted to do so by means of a garment, as stated by Rabbi Ḥiyya to Rav. The *Taz* and *Shakh* discuss whether this is permitted only with regard to armpit hair, or if it is permitted with regard to pubic hair as well (*Shulḥan Arukh, Yoreh De'a* 182:3).

With one's garment during prayer – בִּתְפִלָּה בְּבִגְדּוֹ: One may not touch an unclean, sweaty part of his body during prayers, nor may he rub his head. However, it is permitted to clean something off one's body, including the nose or ears, or to rub one's skin with a garment (*Shulḥan Arukh, Oraḥ Ḥayyim* 92:7).

NOTES

But it grows – וְהָא קָא גָּדֵל: Some commentaries explain this comment as follows: Since this hair grows all the time, it will eventually become uncomfortable; shortening it now will prevent future pain, rather than promote beautification. Rabbi Ḥiyya replied that this hair will never grow long enough for it to cause discomfort, and one who removes it is acting to improve his appearance (*Tosafot*).

With one's garment during prayer – בִּתְפִלָּה בְּבִגְדּוֹ: Direct contact with one's armpit is certainly prohibited during prayer, as the armpit is considered unclean. The question is whether it is permitted to touch this spot by means of one's garment, or whether even that is inappropriate during prayer.

LANGUAGE

Son of nobles [*bar paḥtei*] – בַּר פָּחְתֵי: The term *bar paḥtei* is usually translated as: Son of nobles, or: Son of the leaders, with *paḥtei* used in the sense of *peḥa*, meaning governor or pasha. Some commentaries claim that in this context it might be a specific reference to Rav's father, who was the older brother of Rabbi Ḥiyya and a deputy to a major figure in the Parthian government. Some *ge'onim* used the form *bar pa'atei* due to its similarity to: "*Pa'atei Moav*" (Numbers 24:17), which means: The great ones of Moab (Rav Tzemaḥ Gaon). Some suggest that the name signifies an extensive knowledge of *halakha* (*Arukh*).

HALAKHA

If one of them dies, etc. – מֵת אֶחָד מֵהֶן וכו׳: In the case of two nazirites, where it is unknown which of them is impure, and one of them died before they could bring their offerings, the remaining nazirite brings a bird for a sin-offering and an animal for a burnt-offering, and says as follows: If I was the impure one, the sin-offering is for my obligation and the burnt-offering is a gift offering; and if I was pure, the burnt-offering is for my obligation and the sin-offering is brought due to uncertainty. He proceeds to observe another term of naziriteship at the end of which he brings an offering of purity and says: If I was the impure one, the burnt-offering I brought on the first occasion was a gift offering, and this burnt-offering is for my obligation; and if I was the pure one, the first burnt-offering was for my obligation and the one I am bringing now is a gift offering, and I am also sacrificing the rest of my offerings to fulfill my obligation. The *halakha* is in accordance with the opinion of ben Zoma (Rambam *Sefer Hafla'a, Hilkhot Nezirut* 9:15).

מתני׳ מֵת אֶחָד מֵהֶן, אָמַר רַבִּי יְהוֹשֻׁעַ: יְבַקֵּשׁ אֶחָד מִן הַשּׁוּק שֶׁיִּדּוֹר כְּנֶגְדּוֹ בְּנָזִיר,

MISHNA The previous mishna described how two nazirites sacrifice offerings of impurity and purity, in a situation in which one of them has become impure but they do not know which one. This mishna discusses what must be done if **one of them dies**[H] before bringing his offerings. **Rabbi Yehoshua said:** The surviving nazirite **asks someone in the marketplace,** a non-nazirite, **to vow to be a nazirite corresponding to him,** i.e., under the same conditions as his own naziriteship, so that he can bring offerings together with him.

וְאוֹמֵר: ״אִם טָמֵא הָיִיתִי – הֲרֵי אַתָּה נָזִיר מִיָּד, וְאִם טָהוֹר הָיִיתִי – הֲרֵי אַתָּה נָזִיר אַחַר שְׁלֹשִׁים יוֹם״. וְסוֹפְרִין שְׁלֹשִׁים, וּמְבִיאִין קָרְבַּן טוּמְאָה וְקָרְבַּן טׇהֳרָה, וְאוֹמֵר: ״אִם אֲנִי הוּא הַטָּמֵא – קׇרְבַּן טוּמְאָה שֶׁלִּי, וְקׇרְבַּן טׇהֳרָה שֶׁלְּךָ. וְאִם אֲנִי הוּא הַטָּהוֹר – קׇרְבַּן טׇהֳרָה שֶׁלִּי, וְקׇרְבַּן טוּמְאָה בְּסָפֵק״.

And he says to him as follows: **If I was impure, you are hereby a nazirite immediately; and if I was pure, you are hereby a nazirite after thirty days. And they** both proceed to **count thirty days and bring an offering of impurity and an offering of purity. And** the nazirite who was defined as having uncertain impurity **says: If I am the impure** one, **the offering of impurity is mine and the offering of purity is yours; and if I am the pure one, the offering of purity is mine and the offering of impurity** we brought shall be **of uncertain** status.

וְסוֹפְרִים שְׁלֹשִׁים יוֹם, וּמְבִיאִין קָרְבַּן טׇהֳרָה, וְאוֹמֵר: ״אִם אֲנִי הַטָּמֵא – קׇרְבַּן טוּמְאָה שֶׁלִּי וְקׇרְבַּן טׇהֳרָה שֶׁלְּךָ, וְזֶה קׇרְבַּן טׇהֳרָתִי. וְאִם אֲנִי הוּא הַטָּהוֹר – קׇרְבַּן טׇהֳרָה שֶׁלִּי, וְקׇרְבַּן טוּמְאָה בְּסָפֵק, וְזֶהוּ קׇרְבַּן טׇהֳרָתְךָ״.

And they subsequently **count** another **thirty days and bring an offering of purity, and** the first nazirite **says: If I** was **the impure** one, **the offering of impurity** that we sacrificed at the end of the first thirty days was **mine, and the offering of purity** we brought then was **yours; and this** offering I am bringing now is **my offering of purity. And if I** was **the pure** one, and the deceased nazirite was impure, **the offering of purity** we brought thirty days ago was **mine, and the offering of impurity** we brought earlier was **of uncertain** status, **and this is your offering of purity.**

אָמַר לוֹ בֶּן זוֹמָא: וּמִי שׁוֹמֵעַ לוֹ שֶׁיִּדּוֹר כְּנֶגְדּוֹ בְּנָזִיר? אֶלָּא, מֵבִיא חַטַּאת הָעוֹף וְעוֹלַת בְּהֵמָה, וְאוֹמֵר: ״אִם טָמֵא הָיִיתִי – הַחַטָּאת מֵחוֹבָתִי, וְהָעוֹלָה נְדָבָה. וְאִם טָהוֹר הָיִיתִי – הָעוֹלָה מֵחוֹבָתִי, וְהַחַטָּאת מִסָּפֵק״.

Ben Zoma said to Rabbi Yehoshua: **And who will listen to him to vow to be a nazirite corresponding to him?** How can one design a *halakha* on the assumption that a non-nazirite will agree to be a nazirite for a lengthy term? **Rather,** a different procedure is available: After thirty days of naziriteship **he brings a bird sin-offering**[N] **and an animal burnt-offering, and says: If I was impure, the sin-offering is for my obligation** as an impure nazirite **and the burnt-offering** is a regular **gift** offering. **And if I was pure, the burnt-offering is for my obligation** as a pure nazirite, **and the sin-offering** is **of uncertain** status.

וְסוֹפֵר שְׁלֹשִׁים יוֹם, וּמֵבִיא קָרְבַּן טׇהֳרָה, וְאוֹמֵר: ״אִם טָמֵא הָיִיתִי – הָעוֹלָה הָרִאשׁוֹנָה נְדָבָה, וְזוֹ חוֹבָה. וְאִם טָהוֹר הָיִיתִי – הָעוֹלָה הָרִאשׁוֹנָה חוֹבָה, וְזוֹ נְדָבָה. וְזוֹ שְׁאָר קׇרְבָּנִי״.

And he counts another **thirty days, and brings an offering of purity, and says: If I was impure, the first burnt-offering** I brought should be considered **a gift** offering, **and this** one I am bringing now is for my **obligation. And if I was pure, the first burnt-offering** I brought is for my **obligation** as a pure nazirite, **and this** one I am bringing now **is a gift** offering. **And these,** i.e., the sin-offering and peace-offering I am sacrificing now, comprises **the rest of my offerings** that I was obligated to bring earlier.

אָמַר רַבִּי יְהוֹשֻׁעַ: נִמְצָא זֶה מֵבִיא קׇרְבְּנוֹתָיו לַחֲצָאִים. אֲבָל הוֹדוּ לוֹ חֲכָמִים לְבֶן זוֹמָא.

Rabbi Yehoshua said: According to your opinion, **it turns out** that **this** nazirite **brings his offerings in halves,** i.e., in stages. If he was pure, he brings his burnt-offering thirty days before the rest of his offerings. **However, the Rabbis agreed with ben Zoma,** and disregarded the concern about splitting up the offerings.

NOTES

He brings a bird sin-offering – מֵבִיא חַטַּאת הָעוֹף: A bird sin-offering can be brought out in a case of uncertainty, and it is not considered a non-sacred animal in the Temple courtyard, despite the fact that it cannot be eaten (Commentary on *Nazir*). He does not bring a guilt-offering, as this offering is not indispensable to his purification, and it cannot be sacrificed as a gift offering or in a case of uncertainty. Since an impure nazirite is obligated to bring a bird for a burnt-offering in addition to the sin-offering, some commentaries maintain that this nazirite brings his burnt-offering as well, by stipulating that if he is not obligated in this offering it should be considered a gift. The mishna did not find it necessary to mention this offering, as it is well known that a burnt-offering can be voluntary (*Tosafot*; Rabbeinu Peretz). Others claim that he may bring a bird burnt-offering if he wishes, but refraining from bringing this offering does not preclude his purification (see Commentary on *Nazir* and *Shita Mekubbetzet*).

גמ׳ וְלַיְיתֵי! אָמַר רַב יְהוּדָה אָמַר שְׁמוּאֵל: לֹא אָמַר רַבִּי יְהוֹשֻׁעַ אֶלָּא לְחַדֵּד בָּהּ אֶת הַתַּלְמִידִים.

GEMARA The mishna taught that Rabbi Yehoshua countered ben Zoma's opinion by pointing out that his solution would cause the nazirite to bring his offerings in stages. The Gemara asks: What is wrong with that? **And let him bring** the offerings in stages. **Rav Yehuda said** that **Shmuel said: Rabbi Yehoshua said** this comment **only to sharpen** the minds[H] of **the students.** He did not really maintain that it is prohibited to act in this manner; rather, he wanted to test his disciples to see if they were aware of the *halakha*.

אֲמַר רַב נַחְמָן: מַאי לִיעֲבֵיד לֵיהּ רַבִּי יְהוֹשֻׁעַ לְדַקֵּיהּ דְּלָא לִיסְרוּ?

Rav Naḥman said, in a light-hearted vein: **What will Rabbi Yehoshua do with the intestines** of **his** animals so **that they will not spoil?** If he insists that the offerings of purity must all be brought at the same time, the only way to do so is to wait thirty days after slaughtering the burnt-offering before burning its intestines, which is certainly impractical.

מתני׳ נָזִיר שֶׁהָיָה טָמֵא בְּסָפֵק וּמוּחְלָט בְּסָפֵק – אוֹכֵל בְּקָדָשִׁים אַחַר שִׁשִּׁים יוֹם,

MISHNA In the case of **a nazirite who,** on the first day of his naziriteship, **was impure** from a corpse as a matter of **uncertainty and** was also **a confirmed leper** as a matter of **uncertainty,** i.e., it was uncertain whether or not he had leprosy, how can he fulfill the shaving obligations of a pure nazirite and an impure leper? The problem facing this nazirite is that a leper must shave both when he begins his purification process and at the close of it, one week later. However, a nazirite is prohibited from shaving. Additionally, a leper may not partake of sacrificial food, but a nazirite may. Therefore, **he may partake of sacrificial food sixty days after** he may have become impure, when the uncertainty with regard to leprosy will have been clarified. He shaves for the first time for his leprosy after thirty days, and for the second time thirty days later, the shaving of the end of the purification process; at which point he brings the offerings of a purified leper and may partake of sacrificial food.

וְשׁוֹתֶה יַיִן וּמִטַּמֵּא לַמֵּתִים אַחַר מֵאָה וְעֶשְׂרִים יוֹם.

But he **may drink wine and become impure from the dead,** effectively ending his naziriteship, only **after 120 days.** This is because he might have been a full-fledged leper, which means that his shavings count toward his leprosy, not his naziriteship. Consequently, after the first sixty days he must observe another thirty days of naziriteship and shave again. Even then he has yet to fulfill all his obligations, as he might have been impure from a corpse, which means his shaving after ninety days was for his impurity. He must therefore remain a nazirite for another thirty days, before shaving one final time at the end of 120 days to fulfill his naziriteship obligation.

שֶׁתִּגְלַחַת הַנֶּגַע דּוֹחָה תִּגְלַחַת הַנָּזִיר בִּזְמַן שֶׁהוּא וַדַּאי, אֲבָל בִּזְמַן שֶׁהוּא סָפֵק – אֵינוֹ דּוֹחֶה.

The mishna notes: The reason that he cannot shave for his leprosy after seven days and perform the second shaving of a leper seven days later is **because the shaving of leprosy overrides** the prohibition of **the shaving of a nazirite**[H] only **when his** status as **a leper** is **definite. However, when his** status as **a leper** is **uncertain,** the shaving **does not override**[H] his naziriteship, and therefore he must wait thirty days before each of his shavings for leprosy.

HALAKHA

To sharpen the minds – לְחַדֵּד בָּהּ: It is proper for a teacher to mislead his students occasionally through speech or action to test if they recall their studies (Rambam *Sefer HaMadda, Hilkhot Talmud Torah* 4:6; *Shulḥan Arukh, Yoreh De'a* 246:12).

Because the shaving of leprosy overrides the shaving of a nazirite, etc. – שֶׁתִּגְלַחַת הַנֶּגַע דּוֹחָה תִּגְלַחַת הַנָּזִיר וכו׳: A leprous nazirite who was healed during his naziriteship must shave off all his hair, as the positive mitzva of a leper's shaving overrides the prohibition of a nazirite shaving (Rambam *Sefer Hafla'a, Hilkhot Nezirut* 7:15).

When his status as a leper is uncertain, the shaving does not override – בִּזְמַן שֶׁהוּא סָפֵק אֵינוֹ דּוֹחֶה: The shaving of an uncertain leper does not override the prohibition against a nazirite shaving (Rambam *Sefer Hafla'a, Hilkhot Nezirut* 10:1).

NOTES

Birds and a bird sin-offering, etc. – צִפּוֹרִים וְחַטַּאת הָעוֹף וכו׳: He brings the birds in case he is a confirmed leper who requires two birds as part of his purification ritual. The bird of a sin-offering is for the possibility that he is an impure nazirite, while the animal burnt-offering is in case he is neither a leper nor impure, which means he must bring one of the offerings of a pure nazirite to enable him to shave his hair (Commentary on *Nazir*). He is not obligated to bring a bird burnt-offering for his naziriteship of impurity, as this offering is not indispensable to his ritual, and therefore it is not sacrificed in a case of uncertainty. For the same reason he does not bring the peace-offering of a pure nazirite, as it is not certain that he is pure, and therefore he can shave after sacrificing the burnt-offering alone. Consequently, he is not obligated to bring a peace-offering out of uncertainty (*Tosafot*).

גמ׳ תָּנָא: בַּמֶּה דְּבָרִים אֲמוּרִים – בִּנְזִירוּת מוּעֶטֶת, אֲבָל בִּנְזִירוּת בַּת שָׁנָה – אוֹכֵל בְּקָדָשִׁים לְאַחַר שְׁתֵּי שָׁנִים,

GEMARA The Sage **taught: In what case is this statement** of the mishna **said? With regard to a short naziriteship** of thirty days. **However, with regard to a naziriteship of a year,**[H] **he partakes of sacrificial food** only **after two years.** He cannot shave until a year has passed, in case he is not a leper; he may shave the second time only a year later, in case he was impure during the first year and this second year was his naziriteship observed in purity. At this stage he may partake of sacrificial meat, for if he was a full-fledged leper he has shaved twice.

וְשׁוֹתֶה יַיִן וּמִיטַּמֵּא לְמֵתִים לְאַחַר אַרְבַּע שָׁנִים.

Yet if the first two shavings were for his leprosy, he has not shaved for his naziriteship at all, and therefore he must observe a third year of naziriteship and shave. He then must observe another year of naziriteship and shave again, as perhaps his third shaving was for impurity and the fourth will be for his naziriteship in purity. And consequently **he may drink wine and become impure from the dead** only **after four years.**

וְתָנֵי עֲלָהּ: וּמְגַלֵּחַ אַרְבַּע תִּגְלָחִיּוֹת: תִּגְלַחַת רִאשׁוֹנָה – מֵבִיא צִפּוֹרִים,

And it is taught with regard to the *halakha* of the mishna (*Tosefta* 6:1): **And he shaves** with **four** separate acts of **shaving**[H] each time for its own reason. How so? For his **first shaving,** after the thirty days of an unspecified naziriteship or at the end of the period he vowed to observe naziriteship, he **brings** two **birds**[H] of a leper: One is slaughtered over spring water and the other is sent away (Leviticus 14:4–7).

וְחַטַּאת הָעוֹף וְעוֹלַת בְּהֵמָה, שְׁנִיָּה – מֵבִיא חַטַּאת הָעוֹף וְעוֹלַת בְּהֵמָה, שְׁלִישִׁית – מֵבִיא חַטַּאת הָעוֹף וְעוֹלַת בְּהֵמָה, רְבִיעִית – מֵבִיא קׇרְבַּן טׇהֳרָה.

And he also brings **a bird sin-offering**[N] for his shaving of impure naziriteship, as he may have contracted impurity from a corpse, **and an animal burnt-offering** for his shaving of purity, as he may not have contracted impurity from a corpse. For his **second** shaving he **brings a bird sin-offering and an animal burnt-offering.** For his **third** shaving he again **brings a bird sin-offering and an animal burnt-offering.** And for the **fourth** shaving he **brings an offering of purity.**

HALAKHA

However, with regard to a naziriteship of a year, etc. – אֲבָל בִּנְזִירוּת בַּת שָׁנָה וכו׳: If a person who vowed a yearlong term of naziriteship may have contracted both leprosy and impurity from a corpse at the beginning of his term of naziriteship; or if he may have contracted leprosy at the start of his term and contracted impurity from a corpse at the end of the year, his *halakha* is as follows: He counts seven days and is sprinkled with the waters of purification on the third and seventh days. He does not shave on the seventh day. He may not drink wine or become impure to bury a corpse until four years have elapsed, although he may partake of offerings after two years. The Ra'avad holds that in certain cases he does not have to wait the full four years, but only three years and a little more (Rambam *Sefer Hafla'a*, *Hilkhot Nezirut* 10:1, and *Kesef Mishne* there).

He shaves with four acts of shaving, etc. – מְגַלֵּחַ אַרְבַּע תִּגְלָחִיּוֹת וכו׳: If a person who vowed a yearlong term of naziriteship may have contracted both leprosy and impurity from a corpse, he shaves for the first time after a year, on which occasion he removes all his hair, as is required of a leper, and performs the purification ritual of a regular leper, involving cedar wood and the two birds. If it turned out that he was neither impure nor a leper, this shaving will mark the end of his pure naziriteship, but if he was a leper it counts as the first shaving of his purification from leprosy. He proceeds to wait another year before shaving for his leprosy for the second time. He cannot shave after the first seven days in case he was not a leper but was impure, and he is therefore prohibited to shave throughout the second year due to his naziriteship. After these two acts of shaving he is certainly purified from his leprosy, and therefore he may partake of offerings. He subsequently observes naziriteship for another year, at which point he shaves for the third time in case he was a leper in the first year, which would mean that he did not fulfill his naziriteship in the first or second year, as he had not yet been purified from his leprosy. Consequently, this third shaving is for his naziriteship of purity. However, it remains possible that he was impure from a corpse as well as a leper in the first year, and his first two shavings were for his purification from leprosy. That means that the third shaving is for his naziriteship of impurity, and he must therefore remain a nazirite for another year. Only after he shaves at the conclusion of this period may he drink wine (Rambam *Sefer Hafla'a*, *Hilkhot Nezirut* 10:2).

For his first shaving he brings birds, etc. – תִּגְלַחַת רִאשׁוֹנָה מֵבִיא צִפּוֹרִים וכו׳: How does this uncertain nazirite bring his offerings? If he was wealthy he must legally transfer ownership of his property to someone else so that he can bring the offering of a poor leper. He then brings a bird sin-offering and an animal burnt-offering for his first three shavings. He sacrifices the three animals that constitute the conclusion of his naziriteship of purity at his fourth shaving. With regard to the three bird sin-offerings that he brings for his first three shavings, the first is for his uncertain impurity, the second is for his uncertain leprosy, and the third is in case he was a definite leper and must also bring an offering for his impurity. These sin-offerings brought due to uncertainty are not eaten. As for the burnt-offerings, he stipulates at each of the first three shavings that if he is obligated to bring them they are for his naziriteship of purity, and if not they should be considered gift offerings. When he brings the offerings of purity, at the fourth shaving, he stipulates with regard to the burnt-offering that if he is obliged to bring this offering then it is for his obligation, but if not, it should be a gift offering. His condition is as follows: If I was impure, the first burnt-offering is voluntary and this is for my obligation. If I was a full-fledged leper, the first burnt-offering is for my leprosy, this is for my naziriteship obligation, and the two middle ones are gift offerings. Finally, if I was pure and a leper, one of the first two burnt-offerings is for my obligations as a leper, the other is for my naziriteship, while the third and fourth are voluntary. See Ra'avad for a different explanation of the Gemara (Rambam *Sefer Hafla'a*, *Hilkhot Nezirut* 10:4–8, and *Kesef Mishne* there).

אָמְרַתְּ: תִּגְלַחַת רִאשׁוֹן מֵבִיא וכו׳. מִמָּה נַפְשָׁךְ שַׁפִּיר קָמַיְיתִי; דְּאִי וַדַּאי מְצוֹרָע הוּא וְלָאו טָמֵא הוּא – צִיפּוֹרִין חוֹבָתוֹ, וְחַטַּאת הָעוֹף סָפֵק – אָזְלָא לִקְבוּרָה, וְעוֹלָה הָוְיָא נְדָבָה.

The Gemara analyzes the details and reasons for this *halakha*: **You said** in this *baraita* that for the **first shaving he brings** the two birds of a leper, as well as a bird sin-offering and an animal burnt-offering. The Gemara explains: In this manner **he brings** the **proper** offerings **whichever way you** look at it. **As, if his** status as **a leper is definite and he is not impure,** the **birds** he brings are for **his obligation** to purify himself from leprosy. **And as the bird sin-offering** in case he was impure was brought due to **uncertainty, it goes for burial,** like all bird sin-offerings sacrificed in a case of uncertainty, which cannot be eaten. **And** the bird **burnt-offering** that he brought in case he was an impure nazirite **is a gift** offering.

וּלְגַלְּחוֹ תּוֹךְ שִׁבְעָה אִי אֶפְשָׁר, דְּדִילְמָא לָאו מוּחְלָט הוּא, וְרַחֲמָנָא אָמַר ״תַּעַר לֹא יַעֲבֹר עַל רֹאשׁוֹ עַד מְלֹאת״.

The Gemara further explains: **But** it **is not possible to shave him** right **after seven days,** as one usually does when purified from leprosy, **as perhaps he is not a confirmed** leper and has no obligation to shave but is bound by the naziriteship vow, **and the Merciful One says: "No razor shall come upon his head; until** the days are **fulfilled** in which he consecrated himself to the Lord" (Numbers 6:5). This verse teaches that he cannot shave until the end of his naziriteship. Therefore, he shaves only after thirty days.

וְאִי לָאו מְצוֹרָע וַדַּאי הָוֵי, וְהוּא טָמֵא – חַטַּאת הָעוֹף חוֹבָתוֹ, וְצִיפּוֹרִין – אַבָּרָאֵי קָא מִתְעַבְדִין וְלָא הָוֵי חוּלִּין בָּעֲזָרָה, וְעוֹלַת בְּהֵמָה הָוְיָא נְדָבָה.

The Gemara continues to clarify the various uncertainties concerning the first shaving. **And if he is not a definite leper but he is impure** from a corpse, **the bird sin-offering is** for **his obligation** as an impure nazirite, **and** there is no problem with the unnecessary rituals of a leper's **birds,** as **they are performed outside** the Temple, **and are not** subject to the prohibition against bringing **non-sacred** animals **into the** Temple **courtyard.** Therefore, the slaughter of one of the birds outside the Temple is not a transgression. **And** the **animal burnt-offering is** considered **a gift** offering.

וְאִי לָאו מְצוֹרָע הוּא וְלָאו טָמֵא הוּא – צִיפּוֹרִין אַבָּרָאֵי קָא מִתְעַבְדִין, חַטַּאת הָעוֹף לִקְבוּרָה, עוֹלַת בְּהֵמָה הָוְיָא חוֹבָתוֹ. וְהָא בָּעֵי אָשָׁם! רַבִּי שִׁמְעוֹן הִיא, דְּאָמַר: מַיְיתִי וּמַתְנֵי.

And if he is neither a leper nor impure he has also acted correctly, as **the birds are performed outside** the Temple, which means no transgression is committed, while the **bird sin-offering** of uncertain necessity goes **to burial,** and the **animal burnt-offering is** for **his obligation,** like any nazirite who completes his naziriteship. The Gemara asks: **But** isn't a leper **required** to bring **a guilt-offering**[H] to complete his atonement and permit him to partake of sacrificial food? The Gemara answers: **This** ruling is in accordance with the opinion of **Rabbi Shimon, who said** that one **may bring** a guilt-offering **and stipulate** as follows: If I am obligated to bring this offering then it is for my obligation; and if not, it shall be a voluntary peace-offering.

תִּגְלַחַת שְׁנִיָּה וּשְׁלִישִׁית צִיפּוֹרִין לָא צְרִיךְ – דְּהָא עֲבֵיד. מַאי אִיכָּא – דִּילְמָא וַדַּאי מוּחְלָט הוּא, חֲדָא לִסְפֵק סְפָרוֹ,

For the **second and third shavings** he does **not need** to bring **birds** again, **as he has** already **performed** this ritual. **What is** the potential concern? That **perhaps he** was previously **a confirmed** leper of **definite** status. For this reason, **one** of the bird sin-offerings he brings at the second shaving is **for** the days of **his counting** when his status was **uncertain.** After the first purification of a confirmed leper he counts seven days, or thirty days in this case due to the uncertainty, and brings a sin-offering.

וַחֲדָא לִסְפֵק טוּמְאָתוֹ. תִּגְלַחַת רְבִיעִית מֵבִיא קׇרְבַּן טׇהֳרָה וּמַתְנֵי,

And the **one** sin-offering he brings at his third shaving is **for his uncertain impurity.** If he was a leper, the offerings he brought on the previous occasion were for purification of his leprosy, not his naziriteship. This means that, if he was impure, he is still required to bring a sin-offering for his impurity as a nazirite. Furthermore, the animal burnt-offerings he brings for his second and third shavings are for his naziriteship of purity. For his **fourth shaving he brings an offering of purity and stipulates** as follows:

HALAKHA

But isn't he required to bring a guilt-offering, etc. – וְהָא בָּעֵי אָשָׁם וכו׳: The guilt-offering and burnt-offering are not indispensable for the shaving of impurity or for the purification of a leper. The *halakha* is not in accordance with the opinion of Rabbi Shimon that one may stipulate that it is a voluntary offering. Rather, the *halakha* follows the opinion of the Rabbis, who permit one to shorten the time before the invalidation of an offering, as stated in the Jerusalem Talmud (Rambam *Sefer Hafla'a*, *Hilkhot Nezirut* 10:8).

NOTES

Whose status as a confirmed leper was uncertain and who was definitely impure – מוּחְלָט סָפֵק וְטָמֵא וַדַּאי: In this case, the nazirite counts seven days for his purification from the dead, shaves, and then observes another thirty days of naziriteship in purity. At the end of these thirty-seven days, any possibility of the impurity of a confirmed leper has been eliminated, and therefore he may partake of sacrificial food. However, if he was a leper he has yet to shave for his naziriteship, because the first shaving was for his confirmed leprosy and the second for the leper's days of counting. He is therefore required to wait a further seven days so that his hair can grow, at the end of which he shaves in accordance with the *halakha* of an impure nazirite, before commencing his naziriteship of purity. This makes a total of seventy-four days (Commentary on *Nazir*).

וְאִי וַדַּאי נָזִיר הוּא – עוֹלָה הָרִאשׁוֹנָה חוֹבָה, וְזוֹ נְדָבָה. וְאִם טָמֵא וּמוּחְלָט הוּא – עוֹלָה הָרִאשׁוֹנָה נְדָבָה, וְזוֹ חוֹבָה, וְזֶה שְׁאָר קׇרְבָּנוֹ.

And if he was a definite nazirite from the start and was neither impure from a corpse nor a leper, **the first burnt-offering** he brought after his initial shaving was for his **obligation** of pure naziriteship, **and this** one he is bringing now is **a gift** offering. **And if he was impure** from a corpse **and a confirmed** leper, **the first burnt-offering** he brought was **a gift** offering **and this** one he is bringing now is for his **obligation. And these,** the guilt-offering and peace-offering he is currently bringing, are for **the rest of his** obligatory **offerings.** This concludes the Gemara's analysis of the case of the *baraita*.

טָמֵא סָפֵק וּמוּחְלָט וַדַּאי – אוֹכֵל בְּקָדָשִׁים לְאַחַר שְׁמוֹנָה יָמִים, וְשׁוֹתֶה יַיִן וּמִיטַּמֵּא לְמֵתִים לְאַחַר שִׁשִּׁים וְשִׁבְעָה יָמִים.

§ The Gemara addresses similar situations: A nazirite about whom it was **uncertain** if he was **impure** from a corpse, **and** he was a **confirmed** leper whose status was **definite,**[H] **partakes of sacrificial food after eight days.** He counts seven days, after which he is purified from his leprosy. On the following day he brings his offerings and may partake of sacrificial food. **And he may drink wine and become impure from the dead after sixty-seven days.** He is required to count another thirty days for his naziriteship and shave, at which point he must observe another thirty days, in case his first shaving was for his impurity, and his second shaving is for his purity.

מוּחְלָט סָפֵק וְטָמֵא וַדַּאי – אוֹכֵל בְּקָדָשִׁים לְאַחַר שְׁלֹשִׁים וְשִׁבְעָה יָמִים, וְשׁוֹתֶה יַיִן וּמִיטַּמֵּא לְמֵתִים לְאַחַר שִׁבְעִים וְאַרְבָּעָה יָמִים.

The Gemara discusses another case: A nazirite whose status as **a confirmed** leper was **uncertain and** who was **definitely impure**[NH] from a corpse **partakes of sacrificial food after thirty-seven days.** He shaves after seven days for his definite impurity and starts counting thirty days of naziriteship afresh. At the conclusion of this period he shaves again, which renders him pure from any uncertain leprosy, and may partake of sacrificial food. However, **he may drink wine and become impure from the dead** only **after seventy-four days.** Since he might have been a confirmed leper, his first two shavings, after seven and thirty-seven days, count only toward the two stages of his purification from leprosy, for his first shaving and after the days of his counting. He must therefore observe a further thirty days for his naziriteship of purity.

טָמֵא וַדַּאי וּמוּחְלָט וַדַּאי – אוֹכֵל בְּקָדָשִׁים לְאַחַר שְׁמוֹנָה יָמִים, וְשׁוֹתֶה יַיִן וּמִיטַּמֵּא לְמֵתִים לְאַחַר אַרְבָּעִים וְאַרְבָּעָה יָמִים.

The Gemara mentions yet another case: A nazirite who was **definitely impure** from a corpse **and** he was **a confirmed** leper whose status was **definite**[H] **partakes of sacrificial food after eight days.** He immediately shaves his first shaving for his leprosy, then counts seven days and shaves again for his leprosy and partakes of sacrificial food on the following day. **And he may drink wine and become impure from the dead after forty-four days.** He counts a further seven days of hair growth for his shaving of impurity, shaves, and finally observes thirty more days for his naziriteship of purity.

HALAKHA

Uncertain if he was impure from a corpse and he was a confirmed leper whose status was definite – טָמֵא סָפֵק וּמוּחְלָט וַדַּאי: If a nazirite became a confirmed leper and may have contracted impurity from a corpse, after his purification for his leprosy he is sprinkled with the waters of purification on the third and seventh days, starts counting naziriteship again since the uncertain impurity causes him to forfeit his earlier days of naziriteship, and then brings the offering for his naziriteship of purity. At this stage he is permitted to drink wine. Once he has brought the offerings for a leper's purification ritual, he is permitted to eat sacrificial food (Rambam *Sefer Hafla'a, Hilkhot Nezirut* 10:10, and see Radbaz and *Leḥem Mishne* there).

Whose status as a confirmed leper was uncertain and who was definitely impure – מוּחְלָט סָפֵק וְטָמֵא וַדַּאי: With regard to a nazirite who was definitely impure from a corpse and whose status as a confirmed leper is uncertain, he observes a full naziriteship term when he is healed from his uncertain leprosy. He performs the first shaving of a leper, counts the seven days between a leper's two shavings, shaves, and brings his offerings. He may now partake of sacrificial food. Next he is sprinkled with the waters of purification on the third and seventh days to purify himself from his possible impurity from the dead, shaves after seven days for his impurity, and proceeds to complete his naziriteship of purity (Rambam *Sefer Hafla'a, Hilkhot Nezirut* 10:11).

Definitely impure from a corpse and confirmed leper whose status was definite – טָמֵא וַדַּאי וּמוּחְלָט וַדַּאי: A nazirite who was definitely impure from a corpse and is also a confirmed leper becomes ritually pure as follows: He performs the first shaving of a leper once he is healed, is sprinkled with the waters of purification on the third and seventh days, shaves for his leprosy for the second time, and sacrifices his offerings on the eighth day. At that point he may partake of sacrificial food. He then counts seven days and shaves for his impurity, before finally completing his naziriteship in purity (Rambam *Sefer Hafla'a, Hilkhot Nezirut* 10:12).

שָׁאֲלוּ תַּלְמִידָיו אֶת רַבִּי שִׁמְעוֹן בֶּן יוֹחַי: נָזִיר טָהוֹר וּמְצוֹרָע, מַהוּ שֶׁיְּגַלַּח תִּגְלַחַת אַחַת וְעוֹלָה לוֹ לְכַאן וּלְכָאן? אָמַר לָהֶן: אֵינוֹ מְגַלֵּחַ.

§ **The students of** Rabbi Shimon ben Yoḥai **asked Rabbi Shimon ben Yoḥai:**[P] With regard to one who was **a pure nazirite and a leper,**[N] **what is the** *halakha* concerning the possibility **that he may shave one shaving and it will count for him**[H] both **for this and for that?** In other words, can it serve for his shaving of leprosy as well as for his naziriteship? **He said to them: He may not shave** once for both requirements.

אָמְרוּ לוֹ: לָמָּה? אָמַר לָהֶן: אִילּוּ זֶה לְגַדֵּל וְזֶה לְגַדֵּל, וְזֶה לְהַעֲבִיר וְזֶה לְהַעֲבִיר – יָפֶה אַתֶּם אוֹמְרִים. עַכְשָׁיו, נָזִיר – לְהַעֲבִיר, וּמְצוֹרָע – לְגַדֵּל.

They said to him: Why not? He said to them: If the aim of both shavings were the same, **this one to grow** hair **and that one to grow** hair, **or this one to remove** hair **and that one to remove** hair, **you** would have **spoken well. Now** in actual fact the two shavings have different functions: **A nazirite** shaves **to remove** his hair, **and a leper** shaves **to grow** hair, so that he can shave again after the days of his counting.

וְלֹא תַּעֲלֶה לוֹ לִימֵי חִלּוּטוֹ, וְתַעֲלֶה לוֹ לִימֵי סְפָרוֹ. וְאָמַר לָהֶן אִילּוּ זֶה לִפְנֵי זְרִיקַת דָּמִים וְזֶה לִפְנֵי זְרִיקַת דָּמִים – יָפֶה אַתֶּם אוֹמְרִים, אֶלָּא מְצוֹרָע לִפְנֵי זְרִיקַת דָּמִים וְנָזִיר לְאַחַר זְרִיקַת דָּמִים.

His students posed another question: **But** even if his shaving of naziriteship does **not count for him as** the shaving of the completion of **his days of confirmed** leprosy, **let it** at least **count for him** as the shaving at the end of the **days of his counting,** which is not followed by another act of shaving, and therefore is performed only for the purpose of removing his hair. **And** Rabbi Shimon ben Yoḥai **said to them: If this one** were performed **before the sprinkling of blood and that one before the sprinkling of blood, you** would have **spoken well. However, a leper** shaves **before the sprinkling of** his offering's **blood, and a nazirite** does so **after the sprinkling of the blood.** Therefore, the two shavings are not equivalent.

וְלֹא תַּעֲלֶה לוֹ לִימֵי צָרַעְתּוֹ וּנְזִירוּתוֹ, וְתַעֲלֶה לוֹ לִימֵי צָרַעְתּוֹ וְטוּמְאָתוֹ. אָמַר לָהֶן: אִילּוּ זֶה לִפְנֵי בִּיאַת מַיִם וְזֶה לִפְנֵי בִּיאַת מַיִם – יָפֶה אַתֶּם אוֹמְרִים, אֶלָּא טָמֵא לְאַחַר בִּיאַת מַיִם מְצוֹרָע לִפְנֵי בִּיאַת מַיִם.

Rabbi Shimon ben Yoḥai's students asked him yet another question: **And** granted that his shaving does **not count for his days of leprosy and his naziriteship, let it** at least **count for his days of leprosy and his** shaving of naziriteship of **impurity,** both of which are performed before the sprinkling of the blood. **He said to them: If this one** shaved **before** his **immersion in water, and that one before immersion in water, you would have spoken well. However, an impure** nazirite shaves **after immersion in water,** whereas **a leper** shaves **before immersion in water.**

אָמְרוּ לוֹ: יָפֶה אָמַרְתָּ שֶׁלֹּא תַּעֲלֶה לוֹ לִימֵי סְפָרוֹ וְלִנְזִירוּתוֹ. וְתַעֲלֶה לוֹ לִימֵי חִלּוּטוֹ וְטוּמְאָתוֹ – דְּזֶה לְגַדֵּל וְזֶה לְגַדֵּל הוּא!

They said to Rabbi Shimon ben Yoḥai: **You have spoken well,**[N] and convinced us **that** one shaving **should not count for** the **days of his counting and for his naziriteship. But** why not say that it should at least **count for his days of confirmed** leprosy **and his** naziriteship of **impurity, as** the purpose of **this** shaving is **to grow** hair **and** the purpose of **that one** is **to grow** hair.

אָמַר לָהֶן: נָזִיר טָהוֹר וְהוּא מְצוֹרָע – זֶה לְגַדֵּל וְזֶה לְהַעֲבִיר, וְאִם נָזִיר טָמֵא וְהוּא מְצוֹרָע – זֶה לִפְנֵי בִּיאַת מַיִם וְזֶה לְאַחַר בִּיאַת מַיִם.

He said to them: Here too the acts of shaving for naziriteship and leprosy are not exactly the same: If he is **a pure nazirite and he is** also **a leper,** the difference is that the aim of **this** one, the shaving of a leper, is **to grow** hair, **and** the aim of **that** one, the shaving of the pure nazirite, is **to remove** his hair. **And if** he is **an impure nazirite and he is** also **a leper,** the difference is that **this** shaving, of a leper, occurs **before immersion in water, and that** one, the shaving of an impure nazirite, is performed **after immersion in water.**

NOTES

A pure nazirite and a leper, etc. – נָזִיר טָהוֹר וּמְצוֹרָע וכו׳: Later authorities write that this cannot be referring to one who contracted leprosy during his term as a nazirite, as those days do not count toward his naziriteship, and therefore there is no situation in which he is obligated to perform both shavings. Rather, this refers to one who has finished his naziriteship but has yet to bring his offerings. With regard to this case, the students asked why four acts of shaving are necessary when two can serve for both leprosy and naziriteship (*Meromei Sadeh*; *Keren Ora*).

They said to him, you have spoken well, etc. – אָמְרוּ לוֹ יָפֶה וכו׳: Some early commentaries claim that this entire passage, until the end of the *amud*, should be omitted, as it merely repeats the previous arguments without adding anything. Some commentaries suggest that it should be read as a different version of the discussion between Rabbi Shimon ben Yoḥai and his students (*Tosafot*; see also the *Tosefta*).

HALAKHA

What is the ***halakha*** **that he may shave one shaving and it will count for him – מַהוּ שֶׁיְּגַלַּח תִּגְלַחַת אַחַת וְעוֹלָה לוֹ:** One may not count a single shaving toward his obligations of both leprosy and naziriteship, as explained by Rabbi Shimon (Rambam *Sefer Hafla'a, Hilkhot Nezirut* 10:ה).

PERSONALITIES

Rabbi Shimon ben Yoḥai – רַבִּי שִׁמְעוֹן בֶּן יוֹחַי: Rabbi Shimon ben, or bar, Yoḥai, was among the greatest *tanna'im* of the generation prior to the redaction of the Mishna. Rabbi Shimon was the preeminent student of Rabbi Akiva. Rabbi Shimon's greatness was manifest in his mastery of both *halakha* and *aggada*, and his statements can be found on all topics in every tractate of the Talmud. Although *halakha* is not always ruled in accordance with Rabbi Shimon ben Yoḥai's opinion, especially in disputes with Rabbi Yosei and Rabbi Yehuda, with regard to several core issues, the *halakha* is in accordance with his opinion. Rabbi Shimon had his own unique method of deriving *halakha* from the Torah: He factored in the rationale of the verse and inferred halakhic conclusions from the Bible based on the spirit and purpose of the *halakha*.

Rabbi Shimon traveled to Rome as an emissary of the Jewish people but he harbored profound enmity toward the Romans. Because he made no attempt to conceal his feelings, he was sentenced to death in absentia by the Romans and forced into hiding for many years. He was an ascetic by nature who was very exacting, and was famous in his generation for his righteousness and his performance of miracles. There are many anecdotes related in the Talmud about miraculous acts that he performed.

The *Sifrei*, a collection of halakhic derivations from the books of Numbers and Deuteronomy, was developed in his study hall. He is also the primary figure in the fundamental book of kabbala, the *Zohar*. His greatest students were Rabbi Yehuda HaNasi; Rabbi Shimon ben Yehuda; and his son, Rabbi Elazar ben Rabbi Shimon, who was also among the most prominent *tanna'im*.

תָּנֵי רַבִּי חִיָּיא: זֶה לִפְנֵי בִּיאַת מַיִם (חַיִּים) וְזֶה לְאַחַר בִּיאַת מַיִם, זֶה לִפְנֵי זְרִיקַת דָּמִים וְזֶה לְאַחַר זְרִיקַת דָּמִים.

Rabbi Ḥiyya teaches the same *halakha*: The shaving of a leper does not count for the shaving of naziriteship, as **this** one, a leper, shaves **before immersion in water, and that** one, an impure nazirite, shaves **after immersion water. This** one, the leper, shaves **before** the **blood is sprinkled, and that** one, the pure nazirite, shaves **after** the **blood is sprinkled.**

״שֶׁתִּגְלַחַת הַנֶּגַע״ וכו׳. בָּעֵי רָמִי בַּר חָמָא: הָנֵי אַרְבַּע תִּגְלָחִיּוֹת דְּקָאָמַר, מִשּׁוּם מִצְוָה אוֹ מִשּׁוּם אַעְבּוּרֵי שֵׂיעַר טוּמְאָה?

§ The mishna taught **that the shaving of leprosy** overrides the shaving of a nazirite only when he is a confirmed leper. **Rami bar Ḥama raises a dilemma: Those four shavings about which the** *tanna* **spoke,** the four that a nazirite performs for his leprosy and impurity, are they all **due to the mitzva**[N] of shaving, **or** are some of them not performed for the sake of a mitzva, but **for the sake of removing hair** that grew in **impurity,** so that other hair can grow?

לְמַאי נָפְקָא מִינָּהּ – לְעַבּוּרֵי בְּנָשָׁא. אִי אָמְרַתְּ מִשּׁוּם מִצְוָה – לְעַבּוּרֵי בְּנָשָׁא לָא, וְאִי אָמְרַתְּ מִשּׁוּם אַעְבּוּרֵי שֵׂיעַר טוּמְאָה – אֲפִילּוּ סָכֵיהּ נָשָׁא נַמִי.

The Gemara asks: **What** is the **difference** whether he shaves for one reason or another? The Gemara explains: It is relevant with regard **to removing** hair **with a depilatory. If you say** that the reason is **due to a mitzva, removing with a depilatory** is **not** an option, as the mitzva is specifically to shave. **But if you say** the reason is **due to the removal of hair of impurity, even if he rubs it with a depilatory** that is **also** effective.

מַאי? אֲמַר רָבָא, תָּא שְׁמַע: וּמְגַלֵּחַ אַרְבַּע תִּגְלָחִיּוֹת; אִי סָלְקָא דַּעְתָּךְ מִשּׁוּם עַבּוּרֵי שֵׂיעַר טוּמְאָה – אֲפִילּוּ בְּשָׁלֹשׁ נַמִי סַגְיָא לֵיהּ, שְׁמַע מִינָּהּ: מִשּׁוּם מִצְוָה, שְׁמַע מִינָּהּ.

What then is the *halakha*? **Rava said: Come and hear** a resolution from a *baraita* (*Tosefta* 6:1): **And he shaves** with **four** acts of **shaving.** Now **if it should enter your mind** that the reason is **for the sake of removing hair of impurity, even three** shavings should **be enough for him,** two for his leprosy, and the last one for his naziriteship of purity. Since the third shaving is performed only to remove his hair of impurity so that he can start his pure naziriteship afresh, why is it included? **Conclude from** the *baraita* that all four shavings are **due to the mitzva** of shaving. The Gemara says: **Conclude from** the *baraita* that this is the case.

הדרן עלך שני נזירים

NOTES

Due to the mitzva, etc. – מִשּׁוּם מִצְוָה וכו׳: The commentaries explain that this question does not arise in the case of the four shavings of the nazirite discussed in the mishna, as each of those might be his shaving of purity, which must be performed with a razor (see 40a). The difficulty concerns the four shavings of a nazirite who may be a leper and impure from a corpse and similar cases, when one of the shavings is certainly for his impurity (*Tosafot*). The question could have been posed with regard to the shaving of impurity in general, but it happened to have been asked in the course of the discussion of this particular case.

Summary of **Perek VIII**

To resolve the predicament of a nazirite who might have become impure, the individual in question is required to observe two full naziriteship terms. At the end of the first period he brings the offerings of a nazirite who has become impure, while adding the stipulation that if he was in fact not impure the offerings should be considered those of a pure nazirite or as gift offerings. He then begins a conditional naziriteship term in purity: If he was impure, the new period is obligatory, whereas if he was not impure it is an additional voluntary term. With regard to an uncertainty that involves two nazirites, at the end of the first term they bring offerings of impurity and offerings of purity and stipulate that the offerings for impurity should satisfy the obligation of the individual who was impure, while the other should be for the pure nazirite. At the end of the second term they bring offerings of purity for the one who was impure in the first term, while issuing a corresponding stipulation.

If a nazirite might have become impure from a corpse and might be a leper, he observes four periods of naziriteship. This is because one act of shaving does not count toward both the obligation of naziriteship and that of a leper. After the first term has been completed, he performs the first shaving of a leper; after the second, he undergoes the second shaving for his leprosy; following the third term he shaves as an impure nazirite; and when the fourth term is over he performs the shaving for the completion of naziriteship in purity.

Since some of the offerings are sacrificed only due to uncertainty, e.g., those of an impure nazirite and a leper, this individual does not bring a guilt-offering but only a bird sin-offering brought for uncertainty, and other offerings that can be stipulated as voluntary.

The Gemara analyzed the issue of why one cannot satisfy the obligation of a leper to shave and the shaving of a nazirite with the same act. The Gemara also discussed the tangential issue of the prohibitions against rounding one's head and shaving one's beard. A more in-depth study concerned the relationship between a positive mitzva and a prohibition with regard to the order of preference when two or more mitzvot conflict.

Introduction to **Perek IX**

Speak to the children of Israel and say to them: When a man or woman shall clearly utter a vow, the vow of a nazirite, to consecrate himself to the Lord.

(Numbers 6:2)

Speak to the children of Israel and say to them: When a man shall clearly utter a vow of persons to the Lord, according to your valuation.

(Leviticus 27:2)

And if any man shall die very suddenly beside him, and he defile his consecrated head, then he shall shave his head in the day of his cleansing, on the seventh day shall he shave it.

(Numbers 6:9)

This chapter completes the various topics associated with naziriteship and incidentally addresses issues of a similar halakhic nature. The first topic concerns individuals who are unable to become full-fledged nazirites, e.g., gentiles, who may not adopt any measure of naziriteship. It also addresses those who are under another's authority and are therefore incapable of adhering to the strictures of this vow, e.g., women, Canaanite slaves, and minors. The Gemara seeks textual support for these *halakhot* and contrasts the rulings that apply to these different individuals.

Another topic addressed is the procedure of a nazirite who contracted ritual impurity from a corpse but discovered that fact only after he completed his term of naziriteship. The *halakhot* of impurity of a nazirite depend on the degree of one's awareness of the source of impurity, and therefore this chapter considers various uncertainties involving different sources of impurity. The Gemara discusses when one must search for unknown graves and when one must be concerned for a possible plague of leprosy or the discharge of a *zav*. In addition, the chapter examines *halakhot* concerning a source of impurity that is not fixed in place but is floating.

מתני׳ הַגּוֹיִם אֵין לָהֶם נְזִירוּת, נָשִׁים וַעֲבָדִים יֵשׁ לָהֶן נְזִירוּת, חוֹמֶר בְּנָשִׁים מִבַּעֲבָדִים: שֶׁהוּא כּוֹפֶה אֶת עַבְדּוֹ, וְאֵינוֹ כּוֹפֶה אֶת אִשְׁתּוֹ.

MISHNA **Gentiles do not have naziriteship,**[H] i.e., the *halakhot* of naziriteship do not apply to gentiles. They are not subject to the prohibitions of a nazirite, nor does one accept their offerings at the end of naziriteship. However, **women and** Canaanite **slaves**[H] **do have naziriteship.** The mishna adds: There is a greater **stringency in** the case of **women than in** the case of **slaves, as a** master **may force his slave**[NH] to drink wine, shave his hair, or become ritually impure from a corpse, despite the slave's vow of naziriteship, **but** a husband **cannot force his wife** to transgress her naziriteship.

גמ׳ קָתָנֵי: הַגּוֹיִם אֵין לָהֶם נְזִירוּת. מְנָא הָנֵי מִילֵּי? דְּתָנוּ רַבָּנַן: ״דַּבֵּר אֶל בְּנֵי יִשְׂרָאֵל״ – וְלֹא לַגּוֹיִם: ״וְאָמַרְתָּ אֲלֵיהֶם״ לְרַבּוֹת אֶת הָעֲבָדִים. לָמָּה לִי קְרָא? הָאָמַרְתְּ: כׇּל מִצְוָה שֶׁהָאִשָּׁה חַיֶּיבֶת בָּהּ עֶבֶד חַיָּיב בָּהּ.

GEMARA The mishna **teaches** that **gentiles do not have naziriteship,** whereas women and slaves can be nazirites. The Gemara asks: **From where are these matters** derived? It is **as the Sages taught,** that the beginning of the passage about naziriteship, which states: **"Speak to the children of Israel"** (Numbers 6:2), serves to emphasize that these *halakhot* apply to Jews, **but not to the gentiles.** Furthermore, the continuation of the verse: **"And say to them,** when a man or woman shall clearly utter a vow," serves **to include slaves.** The Gemara asks: **Why do I need a verse** to include slaves? **Haven't you said** the following principle: **Any mitzva that a woman is obligated in** its performance,[H] **a slave is** also **obligated in** its performance? Since the *halakhot* of naziriteship apply to a woman, they should likewise apply to slaves.

אֲמַר רָבָא: שָׁאנֵי הָכָא, דְּאָמַר קְרָא ״לֶאְסֹר אִסָּר עַל נַפְשׁוֹ״ – בְּמִי שֶׁנַּפְשׁוֹ קְנוּיָה לוֹ, יָצָא עֶבֶד שֶׁאֵין נַפְשׁוֹ קְנוּיָה לוֹ; הוֹאִיל וְאֵין נַפְשׁוֹ קְנוּיָה לוֹ, אֵימָא גַּבֵּי נָזִיר נַמִי לָא – קָמַשְׁמַע לַן.

Rava said: Here it is **different,** as with regard to vows **the verse states: "To bind his soul with a bond"** (Numbers 30:3), and the Sages expounded that this is referring only **to one whose soul is in his possession,** i.e., who is under his own jurisdiction. This **excludes a slave, whose soul is not in his possession,** but who is under his master's control. The verse from Leviticus is necessary, lest you say that **since** a slave's **soul is not in his possession,** one should **say** that **with regard to** the *halakhot* of **a nazirite as well,** he **cannot** undertake this vow notwithstanding the principle that slaves have similar *halakhot* to women with regard to obligations, who can become nazirites. The aforementioned verse **teaches us** that a slave can in fact take a vow of naziriteship.

אָמַר מָר: ״דַּבֵּר אֶל בְּנֵי יִשְׂרָאֵל״ – וְלֹא לַגּוֹיִם. וְכׇל הֵיכָא דִּכְתִיב ״יִשְׂרָאֵל״ גּוֹיִם לָא? וְהָא גַּבֵּי עֲרָכִין, דִּכְתִיב ״דַּבֵּר אֶל בְּנֵי יִשְׂרָאֵל״. וְתַנְיָא: בְּנֵי יִשְׂרָאֵל מַעֲרִיכִין, וְאֵין הַגּוֹיִם מַעֲרִיכִין.

The Gemara returns to the earlier exposition of the verse. **The Master said** in the *baraita* that the verse specifies: **"Speak to the children of Israel," but not to the gentiles.** The Gemara asks: **And anywhere that "Israel" is written,** are **gentiles not** included in that verse? **But** there is a counterexample in the verse written **with regard to** the *halakhot* of **valuations,**[B] **as it is written: "Speak to the children of Israel"** (Leviticus 27:2), **and it was taught** in a *baraita*: **The children of Israel can take a valuation vow**[H] **but gentiles cannot take a valuation vow.** If a gentile declares: I undertake to donate the value of so-and-so, his vow does not take effect.

HALAKHA

Gentiles do not have naziriteship – הַגּוֹיִם אֵין לָהֶם נְזִירוּת: The *halakhot* of naziriteship do not apply to gentiles, as the Torah begins the passage dealing with these *halakhot* (Numbers 6:2) with the phrase: "Speak to the children of Israel" (Rambam *Sefer Hafla'a, Hilkhot Nezirut* 2:16).

Women and slaves – נָשִׁים וַעֲבָדִים: Women and Canaanite slaves can become nazirites (Rambam *Sefer Hafla'a, Hilkhot Nezirut* 2:17).

As he may force his slave, etc. – שֶׁהוּא כּוֹפֶה אֶת עַבְדּוֹ וכו׳: A father or a husband can nullify the naziriteship of a daughter or wife, respectively, just as with her other vows. If he failed to nullify the naziriteship, he may not force her to transgress her vow. However, if upon hearing her vow, he acts in a manner that indicates his desire to nullify the vow, it serves as nullification. By contrast, a master may force his slave who has undertaken naziriteship to drink wine and to contract impurity imparted by a corpse (Rambam *Sefer Hafla'a, Hilkhot Nezirut* 2:17; *Shulḥan Arukh, Yoreh De'a* 234:39).

Any mitzva that a woman is obligated in its performance – כׇּל מִצְוָה שֶׁהָאִשָּׁה חַיֶּיבֶת בָּהּ: A Canaanite slave is immersed in a ritual bath and is then obligated in those mitzvot that a woman must observe. Likewise, he is exempt from those mitzvot from which a woman is exempt (Rambam *Sefer Korbanot, Hilkhot Ḥagiga* 2:1; *Shulḥan Arukh, Yoreh De'a* 267:17).

The children of Israel can take a valuation vow – בְּנֵי יִשְׂרָאֵל מַעֲרִיכִין: Jews can take a valuation vow, but gentiles cannot. If a gentile says: I am obligated to give my value, or: I am obligated to give the value of so-and-so the Jew, his statement is of no consequence. However, a gentile's value may be used in a Jew's valuation vow, i.e., if a Jew declares: I am obligated to give the value of so-and-so the gentile, he must donate the gentile's value in accordance with the latter's gender and age.

This issue is the subject of a dispute between Rabbi Yehuda and Rabbi Meir, as Rabbi Yehuda claims that a gentile can valuate others but he cannot be valuated himself. The Rambam rules in accordance with the opinion of Rabbi Meir, because the Gemara states that his opinion is more reasonable. This consideration outweighs the principle that the *halakha* follows the opinion of Rabbi Yehuda in his disputes with Rabbi Meir (Rambam *Sefer Hafla'a, Hilkhot Arakhin VaḤaramim* 1:6).

NOTES

Force his slave – כּוֹפֶה אֶת עַבְדּוֹ: Even if a slave has taken a vow of naziriteship, his master may force him to drink wine, shave, or become ritually impure, and thereby to violate the terms of his vow. By contrast, if one fails to nullify his wife's vow at the appropriate time, he may not force her to transgress it at a later stage.

BACKGROUND

Valuations – עֲרָכִין: The *halakhot* of valuations are outlined in the Torah (Leviticus 27:1–8) and are clarified in tractate *Arakhin*. An *erekh*, valuation, is a special type of consecration, by which a fixed sum is given to the Temple treasury in accordance with the age and gender of the subject of the vow, and without regard for his importance or actual monetary worth as a slave. Valuation applies only to a whole person. Consequently, one who says: I am obligated in the valuation of my hand, has not said anything of consequence. However, one can vow and consecrate the monetary value of a hand or foot in and of itself to the Temple treasury, but this is not an aspect of the passage in the Torah addressing valuations. Notwithstanding the above distinction, if one valuates a part of the body upon which life depends, e.g., if he says: I am obligated in the valuation of my head, it is as though he valuated the entire individual, as one cannot live without a head.

NOTES

The verse states, when a man – **תַּלְמוּד לוֹמַר אִישׁ**: Some commentaries explain that just as the term "man" serves to include gentiles with regard to one aspect of valuations, i.e., that they can be valuated like Jews, perhaps the term "man" stated with regard to a nazirite likewise serves to include a gentile in certain aspects of naziriteship, i.e., the prohibitions, even if his nazirite offerings are not accepted (Commentary on *Nazir*; *Tosafot*).

Is it written, honor – **מִי כְּתִיב כַּבֵּד**: The *halakhot* of inheritance are not connected to naziriteship either, and yet the Gemara did not raise this point when it discussed the issue of inheritance. The commentaries explain that paternity is inherently connected to inheritance, whereas honoring one's father is a special mitzva imposed by the Torah (*Tosafot*; Rosh).

HALAKHA

A gentile inherits the estate of his father – **גּוֹי יוֹרֵשׁ אֶת אָבִיו**: A gentile inherits his father's property by Torah law. As for the other *halakhot* of inheritance, gentiles may follow their own customs (Rambam *Sefer Mishpatim, Hilkhot Naḥalot* 6:9; *Shulḥan Arukh, Ḥoshen Mishpat* 283:1).

יָכוֹל לֹא יְהוּ נֶעֱרָכִין – תַּלְמוּד לוֹמַר "אִישׁ"!

The *baraita* continues: One **might** have thought that this means that gentiles **cannot be** the subject **of a valuation** either, i.e., if a Jew says: I am obligated to give the value of so-and-so the gentile, his vow would not take effect. Therefore, **the verse states** the inclusive expression: "When **a man**[N] shall clearly utter a vow of persons to the Lord, according to your valuation" (Leviticus 27:2), to teach that in this regard, every "man," even a gentile, is included in *halakhot* of valuations. Inasmuch as the Torah also states with regard to a nazirite: "When a man or woman shall clearly utter a vow, the vow of a nazirite" (Numbers 6:2), perhaps one should include gentiles in the *halakhot* of naziriteship as well.

שָׁאנֵי הָכָא, דְּאָמַר קְרָא "לְאָבִיו וּלְאִמּוֹ לֹא יִטַּמָּא" – בְּמִי שֶׁיֵּשׁ לוֹ אָב, יָצָא גּוֹי שֶׁאֵין לוֹ אָב. לְמַאי? אִילֵימָא לְעִנְיַן יְרוּשָּׁה – וְהָאָמַר רַבִּי חִיָּיא בַּר אָבִין אָמַר רַבִּי יוֹחָנָן: גּוֹי יוֹרֵשׁ אֶת אָבִיו דְּבַר תּוֹרָה, שֶׁנֶּאֱמַר "כִּי יְרֻשָּׁה לְעֵשָׂו נָתַתִּי אֶת הַר שֵׂעִיר".

The Gemara answers: **Here,** in the case of naziriteship, it is **different, as the verse states: "For his father, or for his mother,** for his brother, or for his sister, **he shall not defile himself"** (Numbers 6:7). From here it is derived that this mitzva applies only **to one who has a father.** This **excludes a gentile, who does not have a father.** The Gemara asks: With regard **to what** *halakha* does a gentile lack a father? **If we say it is with regard to inheritance, but didn't Rabbi Ḥiyya bar Avin say that Rabbi Yoḥanan said: A gentile inherits** the estate of **his father**[H] **by Torah law, as it is stated: "Because I have given Mount Seir to Esau as an inheritance"** (Deuteronomy 2:5)?

אֶלָּא: בְּמִי שֶׁמּוּזְהָר עַל כִּיבּוּד אָבִיו. מִי כְּתִיב "כַּבֵּד אָבִיךָ" גַּבֵּי נָזִיר? אֶלָּא, אָמַר קְרָא "לְאָבִיו וּלְאִמּוֹ לֹא יִטַּמָּא" – בְּמִי שֶׁיֵּשׁ לוֹ טוּמְאָה,

Rather, this mitzva of naziriteship applies **to one who is warned concerning the honor of his father,** and as the mitzva to honor one's father does not apply to a gentile, it is as though he has no father. The Gemara asks: **Is it written: Honor**[N] **your father, in the context of a nazirite?** What is the connection between these two issues? **Rather, the verse states** with regard to a nazirite: **"For his father, or for his mother,** for his brother, or for his sister, **he shall not defile himself"** (Numbers 6:7), and it should be understood as referring **to one who has** the potential to become **ritually impure,**

Perek **IX**
Daf **61** Amud **b**

HALAKHA

A gentile, who has no potential to become ritually impure – **גּוֹי שֶׁאֵין לוֹ טוּמְאָה**: A gentile cannot become ritually impure nor impart impurity of any kind to others. However, the Sages decreed that in certain cases gentiles are considered impure, to ensure that Jews will avoid them with regard to those matters (Rambam *Sefer Tahara, Hilkhot Tumat Met* 1:13–14 and *Hilkhot Metamei Mishkav UMoshav* 2:10).

NOTES

Anyone who does not have the possibility of purity – **וְכׇל שֶׁאֵין לוֹ טׇהֳרָה**: The *halakhot* of ritual impurity do not apply to anyone who cannot be purified in a ritual bath or through the sprinkling of the ashes of the red heifer. Although the Gemara does not state how it is derived that ritual purity in general does not apply to a gentile, the early commentaries explain that this is learned from a verse that deals with the waters of purification: "And it shall be kept for the congregation of Israel for a water of sprinkling; it is a purification from sin" (Numbers 19:9). This verse indicates that the *halakha* of the waters of purification applies only to Jews, and the same applies to other methods of purification (*Tosafot*; Rosh).

יָצָא גּוֹי שֶׁאֵין לוֹ טוּמְאָה. מְנָלַן דְּלֵית לְהוּ טוּמְאָה? דְּאָמַר קְרָא "וְאִישׁ אֲשֶׁר יִטְמָא וְלֹא יִתְחַטָּא וְנִכְרְתָה הַנֶּפֶשׁ הַהִיא מִתּוֹךְ הַקָּהָל" – בְּמִי שֶׁיֵּשׁ לוֹ קָהָל, יָצָא זֶה שֶׁאֵין לוֹ קָהָל.

which **excludes a gentile, who has no** potential to become **ritually impure.**[H] A gentile is not rendered impure even if he touches a corpse. An individual of this kind cannot become a nazirite. The Gemara asks: **From where do we** derive **that** gentiles **do not have** the ability to become **ritually impure?** It is **as the verse states** with regard to one who enters the Temple in a state of impurity: **"But the man who shall be impure and shall not purify himself, that soul shall be cut off from the midst of the assembly"** (Numbers 19:20). This indicates that the *halakhot* of ritual impurity apply only **to one who has** membership in the **assembly** of the Jewish people and **excludes this** gentile, **who has no** membership in the **assembly,** i.e., he is not part of the Jewish people.

מִמַּאי? דִּלְמָא כָּרֵת הוּא דְּלָא מִיחַיַּיב, אֲבָל אִיטַּמּוֹיֵי מִיטַּמּוּ. אָמַר קְרָא "וְהִזָּה הַטָּהוֹר עַל הַטָּמֵא". כׇּל שֶׁיֵּשׁ לוֹ טׇהֳרָה יֵשׁ לוֹ טוּמְאָה, וְכׇל שֶׁאֵין לוֹ טׇהֳרָה – אֵין לוֹ טוּמְאָה.

The Gemara asks: **From where** is it derived that this verse teaches that ritual impurity does not apply to a gentile at all? **Perhaps** the verse **is** referring merely to **excision from the World-to-Come** [*karet*], i.e., it is teaching **that he is not liable** to receive *karet* for entering the Temple when impure, **but** that perhaps a gentile **does become impure.** The Gemara answers that **the previous verse states: "And the pure** person **shall sprinkle upon the impure"**; this indicates that **anyone who has** the possibility of attaining **ritual purity** by means of the waters of purification also **has** the potential for **ritual impurity, and anyone who does not have** the possibility of attaining **purity**[N] by means of the waters of purification **does not have** the potential for **impurity** either.

וְאֵימָא: טָהֳרָה הוּא דְּלָא הָוְיָא לֵיהּ, טוּמְאָה הָוְיָא לֵיהּ. אָמַר קְרָא "וְאִישׁ אֲשֶׁר יִטְמָא וְלֹא יִתְחַטָּא".

The Gemara asks: **But** one can **say** that **it is** only **purity** by means of the waters of purification **that he does not have,** but **he does have** the potential for **impurity.** The Gemara answers: It is for this reason that **the verse states: "But the man who shall be impure and shall not purify himself"** (Numbers 19:20), to teach that these two statuses are interdependent. One who cannot be purified by the waters of purification cannot become impure in the first place.

רַב אַחָא בַּר יַעֲקֹב אָמַר: שָׁאנֵי הָכָא, דְּאָמַר קְרָא "וְהִתְנַחַלְתֶּם אֹתָם לִבְנֵיכֶם אַחֲרֵיכֶם".

Rav Aḥa bar Ya'akov said a different reason why a gentile cannot become a nazirite, despite the fact that the term "man" does include gentiles in the case of valuations. **Here,** with regard to naziriteship, it **is different,**[N] **as** the verse prohibits a nazirite from becoming impure for his father and mother. This prohibition is not relevant for gentiles because **the verse states: "And you shall make them an inheritance for your children after you"** (Leviticus 25:46). This verse establishes a child as one to whom a person can bequeath his slaves, the subject of this verse.

כָּל שֶׁיֵּשׁ לוֹ נַחֲלָה – יֵשׁ לוֹ טוּמְאָה, וְכָל שֶׁאֵין לוֹ נַחֲלָה – אֵין לוֹ טוּמְאָה. אִי הָכִי עֲבָדִים נַמִּי לָא.

Rav Aḥa bar Ya'akov explains: This verse teaches that **anyone who has inheritance,** i.e., he has the ability to bequeath his slaves to his children, also **has** the status of a father with regard to **impurity,** and the verse prohibiting a nazirite from becoming impure to bury his father can be addressing him. **But anyone who does not have inheritance does not have** the status of a father with regard to **impurity.** Since a gentile cannot bequeath slaves to his child (see *Gittin* 38a), the status of a father with regard to impurity also does not apply to him. Consequently, the verse prohibiting a nazirite from becoming impure to bury his father cannot be addressing him. The Gemara asks: **If so, slaves should also not** be included in the *halakhot* of ritual impurity or naziriteship, as they too cannot bequeath slaves to their children.

אֶלָּא אָמַר רָבָא: בִּשְׁלָמָא גַּבֵּי עֲרָכִין, שֶׁנֶּאֱמַר "בְּנֵי יִשְׂרָאֵל" – בְּנֵי יִשְׂרָאֵל מַעֲרִיכִין, וְאֵין הַגּוֹיִם מַעֲרִיכִין. יָכוֹל לֹא יְהוּ נֶעֱרָכִין – תַּלְמוּד לוֹמַר "אִישׁ".

Rather, Rava said a different reason why a gentile cannot become a nazirite, even though he is included in the *halakhot* of valuations, and despite the fact that the term "man" appears in both passages. **Granted, with regard to valuations, as it is stated:** "Speak to **the children of Israel"** (Leviticus 27:2), one can derive that **the children of Israel can take a valuation vow but gentiles cannot take a valuation vow.** One **might** have thought that gentiles **cannot be valuated** either. Therefore, **the verse states: "Man"** (Leviticus 27:2), so as to include a gentile in only one aspect of the *halakhot* of valuations, i.e., that a gentile can be the subject of a valuation. This does not negate the derivation from "the children of Israel" that gentiles are generally excluded.

הָכָא, בְּנֵי יִשְׂרָאֵל נוֹזְרִין וּמְבִיאִין קָרְבָּן, וְאֵין הַגּוֹיִם נוֹזְרִין וּמְבִיאִין קָרְבָּן. יָכוֹל אַף לֹא יְהוּ נְזִירִין כְּלָל – תַּלְמוּד לוֹמַר "אִישׁ"?

Rava continues his explanation: However, **here,** in the case of naziriteship, there is no possibility of interpreting the word "man" to include a gentile in only one aspect of the *halakhot* of naziriteship. Rava explains: If one would suggest the following derivation: From the phrase "the children of Israel" (Numbers 6:2) derive that **the children of Israel can** both **take a vow** of **naziriteship and bring** the nazirite **offering, but gentiles cannot** both **take a vow** of **naziriteship and bring** the nazirite **offering,** one **might** have thought that gentiles **cannot be nazirites at all;** therefore, **the verse states: "Man,"** which includes gentiles in one aspect of the *halakhot* of naziriteship, i.e., that they can become nazirites.

אָמְרִי: אִי מִשּׁוּם קָרְבָּן – לָאו מֵהָכָא נָפְקָא לֵיהּ, אֶלָּא מֵהָתָם: "לְעוֹלָה", פְּרָט לִנְזִירוּת, דִּבְרֵי רַבִּי יוֹסֵי הַגְּלִילִי!

Rava continues his explanation: However, the Sages would **say** in response to this suggestion: **If** the phrase "the children of Israel" is written **due to** the need to exclude a gentile from bringing a nazirite **offering, one does not** need to **derive** this *halakha* **from here, and** this is because it is already derived **from there,** as a *baraita* teaches that the verse: "Any man from the house of Israel, or of the strangers in Israel, who sacrifices his offering, whether it be any of their vows, or any of their gift offerings, which are sacrificed to the Lord **as a burnt-offering"** (Leviticus 22:18), **excludes** a gentile from the offering of **naziriteship;** this is **the statement of Rabbi Yosei HaGelili.** Therefore, the phrase "the children of Israel" must exclude gentiles from the entire passage of naziriteship, and not just from bringing the offerings.

NOTES

Here it is different, etc. – **שָׁאנֵי הָכָא וכו׳**: The commentaries explain that the statement of Rav Aḥa bar Ya'akov refers back to the earlier claim that naziriteship does not apply to a gentile because he does not have a father with regard to inheritance. Although the Gemara already refuted this suggestion by pointing out that a gentile does inherit from his father, Rav Aḥa maintains that the fact that Jews alone can bequeath their slaves shows that the inheritance of a gentile is not a full inheritance. Some commentaries note that the reason why gentiles cannot bequeath their slaves is because they do not have full ownership of them, i.e., they do not own their bodies but merely maintain rights over them. Consequently, it might have been thought that this *halakha* has no bearing on their status with regard to inheritance. Nevertheless, the fact that the verse links this *halakha* to the issue of inheritance in general indicates that the concept of inheritance does not apply in full to gentiles (Rabbeinu Azriel, cited in *Shita Mekubbetzet*).

אֵימָא: בְּנֵי יִשְׂרָאֵל נוֹזְרִין נְזִירוּת עוֹלָם, וְאֵין הַגּוֹיִם נוֹזְרִים נְזִירוּת עוֹלָם. יָכוֹל לֹא יְהוּ נְזִירִים – תַּלְמוּד לוֹמַר ״אִישׁ״. אָמַר רַבִּי יוֹחָנָן: מִי כְּתִיב נְזִיר עוֹלָם?

The Gemara asks: But it can still be argued that "the children of Israel" is excluding a gentile from only some aspects of naziriteship, as one can **say** that this phrase teaches that **the children of Israel can take a vow of permanent naziriteship, but gentiles cannot take a vow of permanent naziriteship,** and one **might** have thought that gentiles **cannot be nazirites** at all. **The verse** therefore **states: "Man,"** to teach that they can become nazirites. The Gemara answers: **Rabbi Yoḥanan said: Is it written: A permanent nazirite?** Since the verse does not specify a particular type of naziriteship, it excludes gentiles from all types.

אֵימָא: בְּנֵי יִשְׂרָאֵל מַדִּירִין בְּנֵיהֶם בְּנָזִיר, וְאֵין הַגּוֹיִם מַדִּירִין בְּנֵיהֶם בְּנָזִיר. יָכוֹל לֹא יְהוּ נְזִירִים – תַּלְמוּד לוֹמַר ״אִישׁ״. הָאָמַר רַבִּי יוֹחָנָן: הֲלָכָה הִיא בְּנָזִיר.

The Gemara offers another suggestion: But it can still be argued that "the children of Israel" is excluding a gentile from only some aspects of naziriteship, as one can **say** that this phrase teaches that **"the children of Israel" can vow** that **their** minor **sons be nazirites, but gentiles cannot vow** that **their** minor **sons be nazirites;** and one **might** have thought that gentiles **cannot be nazirites** at all. **The verse** therefore **states: "Man,"** to teach that they can become nazirites. The Gemara answers: **Didn't Rabbi Yoḥanan say** that the fact that a father can take a vow that his minor son will be a nazirite **is a *halakha*** transmitted to Moses at Sinai **with regard to a nazirite?** Since this *halakha* is not stated in the Torah, it cannot be excluded by a verse.

אֵימָא: בְּנֵי יִשְׂרָאֵל מְגַלְּחִין עַל נְזִירוּת אֲבִיהֶן, וְאֵין הַגּוֹיִם מְגַלְּחִין עַל נְזִירוּת אֲבִיהֶן.

The Gemara offers another suggestion: But it can still be argued that "the children of Israel" is excluding a gentile from only some aspects of naziriteship, as one can **say** that this phrase teaches that **"the children of Israel" can shave**[N] and cut their hair **by** means of the offerings of **their fathers' naziriteships, but gentiles cannot shave** and cut their hair **by** means of **their fathers' naziriteships.** In other words, if the father of a nazirite, who was himself a nazirite, died after having separated his nazirite offerings, the son is able to bring those offerings at the close of his own naziriteship.

NOTES

Say that the children of Israel can shave, etc. – אֵימָא בְּנֵי יִשְׂרָאֵל מְגַלְּחִין וכו׳: The suggestion of the Gemara that a gentile is excluded only from using his late father's offerings for his own naziriteship is puzzling, as everyone agrees that regardless of whether he can accept naziriteship upon himself, a gentile certainly cannot bring naziriteship offerings (see Rosh). Later authorities explain that although a gentile cannot bring nazirite offerings, he can bring voluntary offerings at the end of his period of naziriteship. It is therefore not unreasonable to suggest that the verse might be excluding a gentile from using his late father's offerings (see *Birkat Rosh* and *Meromei Sadeh*).

Perek **IX**
Daf **62** Amud **a**

יָכוֹל לֹא יְהוּ נְזִירִין – תַּלְמוּד לוֹמַר ״אִישׁ״! הָאִיתְּמַר, אָמַר רַבִּי יוֹחָנָן: הֲלָכָה הִיא בְּנָזִיר.

One **might** have thought that gentiles **cannot be nazirites** at all. **The verse** therefore **states: "Man,"** to teach that they can become nazirites. The Gemara answers: **Wasn't it stated** that **Rabbi Yoḥanan said** that the *halakha* that a son may use his father's nazirite offerings **is a *halakha*** transmitted to Moses at Sinai **with regard to a nazirite?** Since this *halakha* does not appear in the Torah, the verse cannot be coming to exclude it.

אִי הָכִי: ״אִישׁ כִּי יַפְלִא נֶדֶר בְּעֶרְכְּךָ״ בַּעֲרָכִין לָמָּה לִי? מִכְּדִי, הָאִיתְקַשׁ עֲרָכִין לִנְדָרִים, דְּאָמַר קְרָא ״אִישׁ כִּי יַפְלִא נֶדֶר בְּעֶרְכְּךָ״. וְהָתַנְיָא גַּבֵּי נְדָרִים: ״אִישׁ״ מַה תַּלְמוּד לוֹמַר ״אִישׁ אִישׁ״, לְרַבּוֹת אֶת הַגּוֹיִם שֶׁהֵן נוֹדְרִים נְדָרִים וּנְדָבוֹת כְּיִשְׂרָאֵל.

§ The Gemara asks: **If so, why do I** need the verse: **"When a man shall clearly utter a vow** of persons to the Lord, **according to your valuation"** (Leviticus 27:2), stated **with regard to valuations,** from which it is derived that gentiles are included in the *halakhot* of valuations? **After all, aren't valuations juxtaposed to vows, as the verse states: "When a man shall clearly utter a vow** of persons to the Lord, **according to your valuation." And isn't it taught** in a *baraita* **with regard to** a verse dealing with vows: "Any man [*ish*] from the house of Israel, or of the strangers in Israel, who sacrifices his offering, whether it be any of their vows, or any of their gift offerings, which are sacrificed to the Lord as a burnt-offering" (Leviticus 22:18), **what** is the meaning when **the verse states** the extra emphasis: **"Any man [*ish ish*]"?** The *baraita* explains: This serves **to include the gentiles, that they can take a vow**[H] for **vow offerings and gift offerings like a Jew.** It can be derived from this juxtaposition that gentiles are included in the *halakhot* of valuations.

HALAKHA

Gentiles, that they can take a vow, etc. – הַגּוֹיִם שֶׁהֵן נוֹדְרִים וכו׳: Even idolatrous gentiles can vow and bring burnt-offerings to the Temple. However, they may not bring obligatory burnt-offerings or any other obligatory offering, e.g., sin-offerings or guilt-offerings, and also may not bring peace-offerings (Rambam *Sefer Avoda, Hilkhot Ma'aseh HaKorbanot* 3:2).

"אִישׁ כִּי יַפְלִא" בַּעֲרָכִין לָמָּה לִי? אֶלָּא, הַאי "אִישׁ" מִיבָּעֵי לֵיהּ לְאִיתוּיֵי מוּפְלָא סָמוּךְ לְאִישׁ.

The Gemara now restates its question: In that case, **why do I** need the phrase **"when a man shall clearly utter** a vow" stated **with regard to valuations? Rather, this** term, **"man,"** does not include gentiles, but is **necessary to include a minor one year before** he or she **reaches majority.**[H] If a minor takes a vow one year before coming of age, and shows a clear understanding of his statement, the vow takes effect. This individual is included in the *halakhot* of valuations as well.

הָנִיחָא לְמַאן דְּאָמַר מוּפְלָא סָמוּךְ לְאִישׁ דְּאוֹרַיְיתָא, אֶלָּא לְמַאן דְּאָמַר דְּרַבָּנַן: "אִישׁ כִּי יַפְלִיא" לָמָּה לִי? לְאִיתוּיֵי מוּפְלָא סָמוּךְ לְאִישׁ דְּגוֹי.

The Gemara comments: **This works out well according to the one who says** that **a minor one year before** he or she **reaches majority** must fulfill his or her vows **by Torah law,**[H] because the verse serves as the source for this *halakha*. **However, according to the one who says** that this *halakha* applies **by rabbinic law,**[N] **why do I** need the verse **"when a man shall clearly utter** a vow"? The Gemara answers: The verse serves **to include a minor one year before** he or she **reaches majority who is a gentile,** that this *halakha* applies to gentiles by Torah law.

הָנִיחָא לְמַאן דְּאָמַר בְּנֵי יִשְׂרָאֵל נֶעֱרָכִין וְאֵין הַגּוֹיִם נֶעֱרָכִין, יָכוֹל לֹא יְהוּ מַעֲרִיכִין – תַּלְמוּד לוֹמַר "אִישׁ". שַׁפִּיר.

The Gemara comments: **This works out well according to the one who says** that it is inferred from the phrase: "The children of Israel" (Leviticus 27:2), that **Jews can be valuated but gentiles cannot be valuated;** and one **might** have thought that gentiles **cannot take a valuation vow.** Therefore, **the verse states: "Man."** According to this opinion it is **fine,** as the phrase "when a man shall clearly utter a vow" can teach that if a gentile close to adulthood grasps the meaning of vows, he can take a valuation vow.

אֶלָּא לְמַאן דְּאָמַר בְּנֵי יִשְׂרָאֵל מַעֲרִיכִים, וְאֵין הַגּוֹיִם מַעֲרִיכִים, יָכוֹל לֹא יְהוּ נֶעֱרָכִין – תַּלְמוּד לוֹמַר "אִישׁ". אֲפִילּוּ תִּינוֹק בֶּן חֹדֶשׁ בַּר עֵירוּכֵי הוּא: "כִּי יַפְלִיא" לָמָּה לִי?

However, according to the one who says that **the children of Israel can take a valuation vow but gentiles cannot take a valuation vow,**[H] one **might** have thought that gentiles **cannot be valuated;** therefore, **the verse states** the additional term: **"Man,"** to teach that anyone, **even a month-old baby,**[H] **can be valuated** according to the assigned value stated in the Torah. According to this opinion, it is of no importance how old the subject of the vow is, and therefore the verse clearly cannot be including a gentile on the verge of adulthood. Consequently, the question remains: **Why do I** need the phrase **"when a man shall clearly utter** a vow"?

אָמַר רַב אַדָּא בַּר אַהֲבָה: לְאִיתוּיֵי גּוֹי גָּדוֹל, דְּאַף עַל גַּב דְּגָדוֹל הוּא אֵינוֹ יוֹדֵעַ לְהַפְלוֹת.

Rav Adda bar Ahava said: The verse is referring to all vows, and serves **to include,** i.e., to teach, the *halakha* of a type of **adult gentile, who although he is an adult he does not know** how to **clearly utter** a vow. The verse teaches that his vows are invalid, as derived from the phrase "when a man shall clearly vow." Vows of a gentile are valid only if he can express them clearly.

אֶלָּא "כִּי יַפְלִיא" דִּכְתַב רַחֲמָנָא גַּבֵּי נְזִירוּת, לָמָּה לִי? מִכְּדִי הָאִיתְקַשׁ נְזִירוּת לִנְדָרִים: "כִּי יַפְלִיא" לָמָּה לִי?

Having clarified the verse concerning valuations, the Gemara asks: **However,** concerning the verse: **"When** a man or woman **shall clearly utter** a vow" (Numbers 6:2), **which the Merciful One writes with regard to naziriteship, why do I need it? After all, isn't** the *halakha* of **naziriteship juxtaposed to vows; why do I** need the verse **"when** a man or woman **shall clearly utter"?**

HALAKHA

A minor one year before he or she reaches majority – מוּפְלָא סָמוּךְ לְאִישׁ: The vows and consecrations of a boy or girl who is in the year before reaching majority and who understands the nature of vows are valid, as are those of one who has reached the age of adulthood who lacks this understanding, even if he or she has not reached maturity through the appearance of two pubic hairs. Such people are obligated to fulfill all their vows, including vows of naziriteship. They can also separate *terumot* and tithes from produce. Similarly, their dedications to the Temple treasury take effect and they are obligated to give any valuations they undertake (Rambam *Sefer Hafla'a, Hilkhot Nedarim* 11:1–4, *Hilkhot Nezirut* 2:13, and *Hilkhot Arakhin VaḤaramim* 1:15; *Sefer Zera'im, Hilkhot Terumot* 4:5; *Shulḥan Arukh, Yoreh De'a* 233:1).

A minor one year before he or she reaches majority, by Torah law – מוּפְלָא סָמוּךְ לְאִישׁ דְּאוֹרַיְיתָא: The vows and consecrations of a minor one year before he or she reaches majority are valid by Torah law. *Amora'im* engage in a dispute with regard to this issue in tractate *Nidda* (46b), and the *halakha* is in accordance with the opinions of Rabbi Yoḥanan and Reish Lakish (Rambam *Sefer Hafla'a, Hilkhot Nedarim* 11:1 and *Sefer Zera'im, Hilkhot Terumot* 4:5).

But gentiles cannot take a valuation vow – וְאֵין הַגּוֹיִם מַעֲרִיכִים: A gentile can be valuated but cannot take a valuation vow. How so? If a gentile said: I am obligated to give my value, or: I am obligated to give the value of this Jew, his statement is of no consequence. However, if a Jew said: I am obligated to give the value of this gentile, he must give the gentile's value according to his age and gender, as specified in the Torah. The *halakha* is in accordance with the opinion of Rabbi Meir, as the Gemara considers his explanation the more reasonable one. The Ra'avad rules that a gentile can take a valuation vow but cannot be valuated, in accordance with the opinion of Rabbi Yehuda rather than that of Rabbi Meir (Rambam *Sefer Hafla'a, Hilkhot Arakhin VaḤaramim* 1:6 and *Kesef Mishne* there).

Even a month-old baby, etc. – אֲפִילּוּ תִּינוֹק בֶּן חֹדֶשׁ וכו׳: The value of a male between the ages of thirty-one days and five years is five *sela*, while a female of the same age group is valuated at three *sela*, as specified in the Torah (Rambam *Sefer Hafla'a, Hilkhot Arakhin VaḤaramim* 1:3).

NOTES

However, according to the one who says this applies by rabbinic law, etc. – אֶלָּא לְמַאן דְּאָמַר דְּרַבָּנַן וכו׳: The conclusion of this discussion is that even according to those who maintain that a Jew one year before he or she reaches majority can take a vow by rabbinic law, a gentile in the same age category must observe his vows by Torah law. The early commentaries ask how a gentile could be obligated by Torah law in a situation where a Jew is exempt. The Commentary on *Nazir* explains that there are in fact many cases in which the Torah is more stringent with gentiles than with Jews, e.g., with regard to the *halakhot* of damages (see *Bava Kamma* 37b).

Others explain that the vow of a minor Jew does not take effect because the prohibition against delaying the fulfillment of one's vow does not apply to a Jew until he reaches the age of maturity. By contrast, this prohibition does not apply to gentiles at all, and therefore there is no reason to distinguish between an adult and a minor gentile (*Tosafot*; Rosh).

There is another opinion that the entire difference between an adult and a minor applies only to Jews, as the Torah imposed special *halakhot* that go into effect only when one comes of age. However, with regard to gentiles the change from being a minor to being an adult depends only on the intellectual capacity of the individual in question. Since an intelligent person who is almost an adult understands what he is doing, his vow is effective (*Keren Ora*).

לְאִיתּוּיֵי יָדַיִם שֶׁאֵינָן מוֹכִיחוֹת. דְּאִיתְּמַר, יָדַיִם שֶׁאֵינָן מוֹכִיחוֹת; אַבַּיֵי אָמַר: הָוְיָין יָדַיִם, רָבָא אָמַר: לָא הָוְיָין יָדַיִם. לְאַבַּיֵי – נִיחָא, אֶלָּא לְרָבָא מַאי אִיכָּא לְמֵימַר?

The Gemara answers: This verse serves **to include** the case of one who vowed by means of **ambiguous intimations**,[N] i.e., he expressed only part of the formula of the vow, so that his meaning is unclear. **As it was stated** that *amora'im* had a dispute with regard to this issue: With regard to **ambiguous intimations**,[H] **Abaye said** that **they are** considered **intimations** to vows, and the vows take effect, and **Rava said** that **they are not** considered **intimations** to vows, and the vows do not take effect. **According to** the opinion of **Abaye**, this answer **works out well**, as the phrase "when a man shall clearly utter," serves to include all pronouncements indicative of vows, even ambiguous intimations. **However, according to** the opinion of **Rava, what is there to say?**

אֶלָּא: ״כִּי יַפְלִיא״ מִיבְּעֵי לֵיהּ לְכִדְרַבִּי טַרְפוֹן. דְּתַנְיָא, רַבִּי יְהוּדָה אוֹמֵר מִשּׁוּם רַבִּי טַרְפוֹן: אֵין אֶחָד מֵהֶן נָזִיר, לְפִי שֶׁלֹּא נִיתְּנָה נְזִירוּת אֶלָּא לְהַפְלָאָה. הָנִיחָא לְרַבִּי טַרְפוֹן, אֶלָּא לְרַבָּנַן מַאי אִיכָּא לְמֵימַר?

Rather, the Gemara explains that the phrase **"when** a man or woman **shall clearly utter"** is **necessary for that** which was stated **by Rabbi Tarfon, as it is taught** in the *Tosefta* (3:19) that **Rabbi Yehuda said in the name of Rabbi Tarfon:** If several people took a vow of naziriteship as part of a wager with regard to an uncertain occurrence, **not one of them is a nazirite, as naziriteship is imposed** upon someone **only if** his vow is **explicitly** enunciated. That is, one is a nazirite only if he vows in a definitive manner, not if there was any uncertainty involved. The Gemara asks: **This works out well according to** the opinion of **Rabbi Tarfon. However,** according **to the** opinion of **the Rabbis,** who disagree with his ruling, **what is there to say?**

אֶלָּא, מִיבְּעֵי לֵיהּ לְכִדְתַנְיָא: הֶיתֵּר נְדָרִים פּוֹרְחִין בָּאֲוִיר וְאֵין לָהֶן עַל מַה שֶּׁיִּסְמוֹכוּ.

Rather, the phrase "when a man or woman shall clearly utter" is **necessary for that which is taught** in a *baraita*: The *halakhot* of **dissolution of vows,** namely that one may request from a halakhic authority to dissolve them, **fly in the air**[H] **and have nothing to lean upon,** i.e., these *halakhot* are not mentioned explicitly in the Torah.

רַבִּי אֱלִיעֶזֶר אוֹמֵר: יֵשׁ לָהֶם עַל מַה שֶּׁיִּסְמוֹכוּ, שֶׁנֶּאֱמַר ״אִישׁ כִּי יַפְלִא״ ״כִּי יַפְלִא״ שְׁתֵּי פְעָמִים, אֶחָד הַפְלָאָה לְאִיסּוּר, וְאֶחָד הַפְלָאָה לְהֶיתֵּר.

Rabbi Eliezer says: The *halakhot* of dissolution of vows **have** a basis **upon which to lean, as it is stated: "When a man shall clearly utter** a vow" (Leviticus 27:2) and: **"When** a man or woman **shall clearly utter** a vow" (Numbers 6:2), **twice. One explicit utterance is for prohibition,**[N] i.e., when one takes a vow, he is bound to keep it, **and one explicit utterance is for dissolution,**[NH] i.e., in the event that he provides a halakhic authority with a reason why the vow should no longer apply, the vow can be dissolved and he will no longer be bound by it. This is an allusion in the Torah for the dissolution of vows.

NOTES

To include…intimations, etc. – לְאִתּוּיֵי יָדַיִם וכו׳: According to some commentaries, the verse teaches that even vows with ambiguous intimations are nevertheless considered vows. If so, the phrase "when a man shall clearly utter a vow" indicates that provided that one pronounces a vow, even if his meaning is ambiguous, it still takes effect. Others explain this in the opposite manner. They claim that the term: To include, is a term of exclusion. Consequently, ambiguous intimations are not considered intimations to vows, because they do not constitute the requisite clear enunciation of a vow (*Tosafot*). To a great extent this issue depends on the different versions of the opinions of Abaye and Rava, as discussed by the early commentaries.

One explicit utterance is for prohibition – אֶחָד הַפְלָאָה לְאִיסּוּר: This refers to someone who does not regret his vow, whose vow is therefore not dissolved (Commentary on *Nazir*). Alternatively, it means that one is required to express his vow clearly, so that it accords with his intention (Meiri).

And one explicit utterance is for dissolution – וְאֶחָד הַפְלָאָה לְהֶיתֵּר: This refers to one who regrets having uttered the vow (Commentary on *Nazir*). The idea is that if he regrets his vow it is not considered to be clearly expressed, as his intentions no longer correspond to his vow. Some commentaries state that this explicit utterance refers to the clarification of one's vow in the presence of a halakhic authority, when the one who took the vow requests its dissolution (*Shita Mekubbetzet*).

HALAKHA

Ambiguous intimations – יָדַיִם שֶׁאֵינָן מוֹכִיחוֹת: With regard to the intimations of vows, i.e., incomplete expressions whose meaning can be inferred from the context, if one's intention is somewhat evident from the statement itself, it is a valid vow. If the meaning of the words is ambiguous, the vow does not take effect, in accordance with the opinion of Rava. The early commentaries dispute the precise meaning of the concept of ambiguous intimations (Rambam *Sefer Hafla'a*, *Hilkhot Nedarim* 1:23; *Shulḥan Arukh*, *Yoreh De'a* 206:1).

***Halakhot* of dissolution of vows fly in the air** – הֶיתֵּר נְדָרִים פּוֹרְחִין בָּאֲוִיר: The *halakha* that vows can be dissolved by halakhic authorities has no explicit source in the Torah, but is a *halakha* transmitted to Moses from Sinai. However, the Sages find an allusion to this *halakha* in the verse (Numbers 30:3): "He shall not profane his word" (Rambam *Sefer Hafla'a*, *Hilkhot Shevuot* 6:2).

And one explicit utterance is for dissolution – וְאֶחָד הַפְלָאָה לְהֶיתֵּר: One may request the dissolution of valuations and dedications to the Sanctuary, just like other vows (Rambam *Sefer Hafla'a*, *Hilkhot Arakhin VaḤaramim* 1:17).

מתני׳ חוֹמֶר בַּעֲבָדִים מִבְּנָשִׁים, שֶׁהוּא מֵפֵר נִדְרֵי אִשְׁתּוֹ וְאֵינוֹ מֵפֵר נִדְרֵי עַבְדּוֹ. הֵפֵר לְאִשְׁתּוֹ – הֵפֵר עוֹלָמִית, הֵפֵר לְעַבְדּוֹ – יָצָא לְחֵירוּת וּמַשְׁלִים נְזִירוּתוֹ.

MISHNA The previous mishna taught that the naziriteship of women includes a stringency that does not apply to slaves. This mishna adds: There is a greater **stringency in the case of slaves**[N] **than in the case of women, as a** man **can nullify the vows of his wife**[H] **but he cannot nullify the vows of his slave,**[H] despite the fact that he can prevent him from fulfilling them in practice. Similarly, if **he nullified** the naziriteship **of his wife it is permanently nullified,**[H] and it remains nullified even if she is later divorced or widowed. Conversely, if **he nullified** the naziriteship **of his slave** by forcing him to violate the terms of his vow of naziriteship, when the slave **is emancipated he completes his naziriteship.**[H]

גמ׳ תָּנוּ רַבָּנַן: לְמָה רַבּוֹ כּוֹפוֹ – לִנְזִירוּת, אֲבָל לֹא לִנְדָרִים וְלַעֲרָכִין.

GEMARA The Sages taught (*Tosefta* 6:4): With regard **to what** matter can **his master force** a slave? **With regard to naziriteship. However,** he **cannot** force his slave in the case **of** other **vows and valuations.** This *baraita* is apparently saying that a master cannot prevent his slave from fulfilling the terms of a vow.

מַאי שְׁנָא גַּבֵּי נָזִיר – דְּאָמַר רַחֲמָנָא ״לֶאְסֹר אִסָּר עַל נַפְשׁוֹ״ – בְּמִי שֶׁנַּפְשׁוֹ קְנוּיָה לוֹ, יָצָא עֶבֶד שֶׁאֵין נַפְשׁוֹ קְנוּיָה לוֹ. אִי הָכִי אֲפִילּוּ גַּבֵּי נְדָרִים נַמִי!

The Gemara asks: **What is different with regard to a nazirite** that a master can force his slave to transgress his naziriteship, **as the Merciful One states: "To bind his soul with a bond"** (Numbers 30:3), from which it is inferred that the Torah is referring only **to one whose soul is in his possession,** i.e., who is not owned by another; this **excludes a slave, whose soul is not in his possession** because he is under his master's control. **If so,** then **even with regard to vows** that same *halakha* should apply **as well,** as that verse is written in the context of vows in general, not specifically vows of naziriteship. Why is a master unable to compel his slave to break a vow?

אָמַר רַב שֵׁשֶׁת: הָכָא בְּמַאי עָסְקִינַן – כְּגוֹן שֶׁהָיָה אֶשְׁכּוֹל שֶׁל עֲנָבִים מוּנָּח לְפָנָיו; גַּבֵּי נְדָרִים, דְּכִי מִיתְסַר בְּהַאי לָא מִיתְּסַר בְּאַחֲרִינֵי – לָא מָצֵי כָּפֵי לֵיהּ.

Rav Sheshet said: With what are we dealing here? With a case **where a cluster of grapes was placed before** the slave and he vowed not to derive benefit from it. **With regard to vows, when** he **is prohibited from** eating **this** cluster he **is not rendered prohibited from** eating **others;** therefore, the master **cannot force him**[N] to eat it, as he has no reason to insist that the slave consume this particular cluster of grapes.

גַּבֵּי נְזִירוּת, דְּכִי מִיתְסַר בְּהַאי אִיתְּסַר בְּכוּלְּהוּ – מָצֵי כָּפֵי לֵיהּ. וְגַבֵּי נְדָרִים, מִי לָא עָסְקִינַן דְּלֵיכָּא אֶלָּא הַאי אֶשְׁכּוֹל, דְּאִי לָא אָכֵיל לֵיהּ חָלֵישׁ?

By contrast, **with regard to naziriteship, when** he **is prohibited from** eating **this** cluster he **is rendered prohibited from** consuming **all others;** therefore, the master **can force him** to eat. This is because the lack of food weakens the slave, who is the property of his master. The Gemara asks: **And with regard to vows, are we not dealing** even with a situation **where he has** only **this cluster** before him and he vows not to eat it, in which case **if he does not eat it he is weakened?** Why can't the master compel him to eat the grapes in this case?

אֶלָּא אֲמַר רָבָא: כְּגוֹן שֶׁהָיָה חַרְצָן מוּנָּח לְפָנָיו; גַּבֵּי נְדָרִים – בְּהַאי הוּא דְּמִיתְסַר, לָא מָצֵי כָּפֵי לֵיהּ. גַּבֵּי נָזִיר, דְּאִיתְּסַר נַמִי בְּאַחֲרִינֵי – מָצֵי כָּפֵי לֵיהּ.

Rather, Rava said that the difference between vows of naziriteship and other vows concerns a case **where there was a grape seed,** which provides only negligible nourishment, that was **placed before** the slave, and he vowed not to eat it. **With regard to vows,** concerning **which he is prohibited to** eat only **this** one seed, the master **cannot force him** to eat it, as refraining from eating a grape seed would not weaken him. **With regard to a nazirite, who is prohibited from** consuming **other** grape products **as well,** the master **can force him.**

וְגַבֵּי נְדָרִים, מִי לָא עָסְקִינַן דְּלֵיכָּא אֶלָּא הַאי חַרְצָן, דְּאִי לָא אָכֵיל לֵיהּ חָלֵישׁ?

The Gemara again asks: **And with regard to vows, are we not dealing** even with a situation **where he has only this grape seed** in front of him, in which case **if he does not eat it he would be weakened?** Why, then, can the master compel him to violate only his naziriteship vow but not a regular vow?

NOTES

A stringency in the case of slaves – חוֹמֶר בַּעֲבָדִים: The commentaries state that this mishna can be explained in two ways. It is possible that its second part serves to explain the first statement. A husband can nullify his wife's vows so that they no longer exist, even if she later leaves his jurisdiction. In the case of a slave, however, the fact that a master can force his slave to break his vow does not mean he has nullified it; he has merely suspended its observance temporarily. Consequently, if the slave is emancipated he must fulfill his vow. According to this interpretation, the mishna repeats some information, at least with regard to a wife.

Alternatively, one can explain that the first part of the mishna is not referring to naziriteship after the wife or slave leaves his jurisdiction, but while they are still under his authority. If so, the mishna is teaching that a husband cannot reinstate his wife's naziriteship after he has nullified it, whereas in the case of a slave the master can always stop requiring the slave to violate his naziriteship, which would again render the slave obligated in naziriteship (Rosh).

Cannot force him – לָא מָצֵי כָּפֵי לֵיהּ: Likewise, a husband cannot nullify a vow of this kind uttered by his wife, as it is not in the category of vows of affliction (see *Nedarim* 79a); she could eat some other cluster of grapes (Commentary on *Nazir*).

HALAKHA

As he can nullify the vows of his wife – שֶׁהוּא מֵפֵר נִדְרֵי אִשְׁתּוֹ: A father can nullify the vows of his daughter, and a husband can nullify those of his wife, including vows of naziriteship (Rambam *Sefer Hafla'a, Hilkhot Nedarim* 12:1 and *Hilkhot Nezirut* 2:17; *Shulḥan Arukh, Yoreh De'a* 234:2, 37).

But he cannot nullify the vows of his slave – וְאֵינוֹ מֵפֵר נִדְרֵי עַבְדּוֹ: A master cannot nullify the vows of his slave (Rambam *Sefer Hafla'a, Hilkhot Nezirut* 2:17–18).

If he nullified the naziriteship of his wife, it is permanently nullified – הֵפֵר לְאִשְׁתּוֹ הֵפֵר עוֹלָמִית: A husband can nullify vows of affliction taken by his wife. If he does so they are permanently nullified, and she does not have to observe them even after she has left his jurisdiction. By contrast, while he can also nullify those vows of his wife that impinge on their personal relationship, such vows are nullified only for the duration of their marriage (Rambam *Sefer Hafla'a, Hilkhot Nezirut* 12:2, 3; *Shulḥan Arukh, Yoreh De'a* 234:55).

If he nullified the naziriteship of his slave, when he is emancipated he completes his naziriteship – הֵפֵר לְעַבְדּוֹ, יָצָא לְחֵירוּת וּמַשְׁלִים נְזִירוּתוֹ: According to the Rambam, if a slave took a vow of naziriteship and his master said to him: It is nullified for you, the slave is emancipated and he must complete his naziriteship. However, the Ra'avad maintains that the declaration itself does not emancipate the slave, and he must complete his vow in the event that he does gain his freedom (Rambam *Sefer Hafla'a, Hilkhot Nezirut* 2:18, and *Kesef Mishne* there, and *Sefer Kinyan, Hilkhot Avadim* 8:17; *Shulḥan Arukh, Yoreh De'a* 267:72).

אֶלָּא אֲמַר אַבַּיֵי: לְמָה רַבּוֹ צָרִיךְ לְכוֹפוֹ – לִנְזִירוּת, וְאֵין צָרִיךְ לְכוֹפוֹ לִנְדָרִים, וְאֵינוֹ צָרִיךְ לְכוֹפוֹ לִשְׁבוּעָה.

Rather, Abaye said that the *baraita* does not in fact list cases in which a master can compel his slave to violate his vow, but rather means the following: **With regard to what** situation **is a master** who wants to negate his slave's vow **required to force** his slave to violate his vow by stating explicitly that he does not want him to fulfill it? It is the case **of a vow of naziriteship.**[H] **But he is not required to force him** in the case of other **vows**[N] **and he is not required to force him in the** case of **an oath,**[H] as these do not take effect at all.

מַאי טַעֲמָא – דְּאָמַר קְרָא ״לְהָרַע אוֹ לְהֵיטִיב״ מָה הֲטָבָה רְשׁוּת – אַף הֲרָעָה רְשׁוּת, יָצָא לְהָרַע לַאֲחֵרִים שֶׁאֵין הָרְשׁוּת בְּיָדוֹ.

What is the reason for this? It is **as the verse states** with regard to oaths: "Or if anyone swear clearly with his lips **to do evil, or to do good**" (Leviticus 5:4). **Just as** the **"good"** mentioned in this verse is referring to **a voluntary** action, **so too the "evil" is voluntary,** e.g., if he takes an oath not to derive benefit from an item. This **excludes** a slave, whose oath or vow **would cause evil to others, as it is not in his power** to affect his master adversely. Therefore, his statement is invalid. Here too, as the owner will suffer if his slave's diet is restricted, a slave may not accept a vow or an oath upon himself.

מתני׳ עָבַר מִכְּנֶגֶד פָּנָיו, רַבִּי מֵאִיר אוֹמֵר: לֹא יִשְׁתֶּה, וְרַבִּי יוֹסֵי אוֹמֵר: יִשְׁתֶּה.

MISHNA In a case where a slave took a vow of naziriteship but was prevented by his master from fulfilling the terms of his vow, the Sages engaged in a dispute what the *halakha* would be if he permanently **left his** master's **presence,**[H] i.e., he ran away without being emancipated. **Rabbi Meir says: He may not drink** wine. Since the slave is free in practice, his vow goes into effect. **And Rabbi Yosei says: He may drink** wine, as he is not emancipated.

גמ׳ לֵימָא בְּדִשְׁמוּאֵל קָמִיפַּלְגִי, דְּאָמַר שְׁמוּאֵל: הַמַּפְקִיר עַבְדּוֹ – יָצָא לְחֵירוּת, וְאֵין צָרִיךְ גֵּט שִׁיחְרוּר.

GEMARA The Gemara suggests: **Shall we say** that Rabbi Meir and Rabbi Yosei **disagree with regard to** the following statement **of Shmuel? As Shmuel said:** With regard to one **who renounces ownership of his slave,**[H] the slave **is emancipated, and he does not require a bill of manumission.** This *halakha* indicates that if a slave is free in practice, he no longer requires a bill of manumission but is automatically considered a freeman.

רַבִּי מֵאִיר – אִית לֵיהּ דִּשְׁמוּאֵל, רַבִּי יוֹסֵי – לֵית לֵיהּ דִּשְׁמוּאֵל?

The Gemara asks: If so, should one say that **Rabbi Meir is of** the opinion that the ruling is in accordance with the opinion **of Shmuel,** and therefore the slave is obligated in naziriteship as soon as he runs away, like any other freed slave, and **Rabbi Yosei is of** the opinion that the ruling is **not** in accordance with the opinion **of Shmuel?**

לָא, דְּכוּלֵּי עָלְמָא אִית לְהוּ דִּשְׁמוּאֵל. אֶלָּא, מַאן דְּאָמַר יִשְׁתֶּה – סָבַר: סוֹף סוֹף מִיהֲדַר הָדַר וְאָתֵי גַּבֵּיהּ, לִישְׁתֵּי חַמְרָא כִּי הֵיכִי דְּלָא לִיכְחוֹשׁ. וּלְמַאן דְּאָמַר לֹא יִשְׁתֶּה – סָבַר: לֶיהֱוֵי לֵיהּ צַעֲרָא, כִּי הֵיכִי דְּלִיהֲדַר גַּבֵּיהּ.

The Gemara rejects this suggestion: **No,** it is possible **that everyone is of** the opinion that the ruling is in accordance with the opinion **of Shmuel. Rather,** the mishna is referring to a case where the master refused to declare the runaway ownerless, and was intent on recovering him. Consequently, the slave is not in fact a freeman at all, and the *tanna'im* disagree with regard to the following: Rabbi Yosei, the **one who says** that **he may drink** wine, **maintains** that the slave **will ultimately return and come back to** his master, and therefore it is preferable for him **to drink wine so that he should not be weakened** by the time he returns. **And according to** Rabbi Meir, **the one who says** that **he may not drink** wine, he **maintains** that it is better that the slave **should suffer** by being deprived of wine, **so that he will return to** his master, as the desire to drink wine will spur him to return.

HALAKHA

A master required to force him, it is the case of a vow of naziriteship – רַבּוֹ צָרִיךְ לְכוֹפוֹ לִנְזִירוּת: If a slave took a vow of naziriteship, his master may force him to drink wine or become impure to bury a corpse, and his vow is thereby negated. If the slave uttered any other vow of affliction or took a vow that would cause him to neglect his work, or if he vowed to give the value of another, the master does not have to compel him to violate its terms. The reason is that vows of this kind are automatically canceled (Rambam *Sefer Hafla'a, Hilkhot Nezirut* 2:17–18).

And he is not required to force him in the case of an oath – וְאֵינוֹ צָרִיךְ לְכוֹפוֹ לִשְׁבוּעָה: If a slave takes an oath, his master need not force him to transgress it, as the oath is automatically nullified (Rambam *Sefer Hafla'a, Hilkhot Shevuot* 12:6).

If he left his presence – עָבַר מִכְּנֶגֶד פָּנָיו: If a slave took a vow of naziriteship and permanently left his master's presence, it is prohibited for him to drink wine, so that his discomfort will cause him to return to his master. This *halakha* is in accordance with the opinion of Rabbi Meir. The Ra'avad disagrees, in keeping with the principle that the *halakha* is in accordance with the opinion of Rabbi Yosei in his disputes with Rabbi Meir (Rambam *Sefer Hafla'a, Hilkhot Nezirut* 2:19).

One who renounces ownership of his slave – הַמַּפְקִיר עַבְדּוֹ: One who renounces ownership of his slave has emancipated him, but the slave requires a bill of manumission before he can marry a Jew. The *halakha* is in accordance with the opinions of Rav and Rabbi Yoḥanan in tractate *Gittin* (39a) and not in accordance with the opinion of Shmuel (Rambam *Sefer Kinyan, Hilkhot Avadim* 8:13; *Shulḥan Arukh, Yoreh De'a* 267:64).

NOTES

But he is not required to force him in the case of other vows – וְאֵין צָרִיךְ לְכוֹפוֹ לִנְדָרִים: The vows and oaths of a slave do not go into effect at all, and his master need not even register an objection. *Tosafot* maintain that the *baraita* does not include valuations because a master cannot in fact cancel them. The reason is that whether the slave owns the money now or intends to pay it after his release, the master loses nothing by his valuation (see Commentary on *Nazir*).

The early commentaries discuss why there should be any difference between naziriteship and other vows, in light of the fact that the verses that serve as the basis for this *halakha* speak of vows in general. Some contend that naziriteship is an especially powerful vow, as it is effective even with regard to matters that are not optional. For example, if one takes an oath to drink wine, thereby obligating himself to do so, and then takes a vow of naziriteship, the vow of naziriteship overrides the oath. Consequently, naziriteship takes effect even for a slave, unless the master objects (*Tosafot*). The early commentaries also point out that the vows and oaths of a slave are automatically canceled only if they are vows of affliction or would lead him to neglect his work. A master may not compel his slave to transgress any other kind of vow.

מתני׳ נָזִיר שֶׁגִּילַּח וְנוֹדַע לוֹ שֶׁהוּא טָמֵא, אִם טוּמְאָה יְדוּעָה – סוֹתֵר, וְאִם טוּמְאַת תְּהוֹם – אֵינוֹ סוֹתֵר. אִם עַד שֶׁלֹּא גִּילֵּחַ – בֵּין כָּךְ וּבֵין כָּךְ סוֹתֵר.

MISHNA With regard to **a nazirite who shaved** for the conclusion of his nazariteship, **and it** later **became known to him that** during his naziriteship **he was ritually impure**[H] from a corpse, **if it was a known impurity**, i.e., people were aware of the impurity when he became impure, **he negates** his entire naziriteship. **And if it was ritual impurity** imparted by a grave **in the depths**,[B] one that was unknown at the time, **he does not negate** his naziriteship. **If** he discovered he was impure **before he shaved, he negates** his naziriteship **in either case.**

כֵּיצַד? יָרַד לִטְבּוֹל בִּמְעָרָה וְנִמְצָא מֵת צָף עַל פִּי הַמְּעָרָה – טָמֵא. נִמְצָא מְשׁוּקָּע בְּקַרְקַע הַמְּעָרָה;

The mishna asks: **How** does one differentiate between a known and an unknown impurity? If a nazirite **descended to immerse in a cave, and a corpse was found floating at the mouth of the cave,** he is **impure**, as an openly visible corpse is a known impurity. What, then, is an impurity of the depths? This is referring to a case where the corpse **was found sunk into the ground of the cave** in such a manner that it was unknown.

יָרַד לְהָקֵר – טָהוֹר, לִיטָּהֵר בְּטוּמְאַת מֵת – טָמֵא, שֶׁחֶזְקַת טָמֵא – טָמֵא, וְחֶזְקַת טָהוֹר – טָהוֹר. שֶׁרַגְלַיִם לַדָּבָר.

However, even here the circumstances of the case must be taken into account. If one **descended** not descend to immerse himself in the water, as he was ritually pure, but **to cool** himself, he remains **pure.** If he was impure and entered the water **to purify himself from the impurity from a corpse,** he is **impure.** The reason is that something **that** has **the presumptive status of impurity** remains **impure, and** something that has **the presumptive status of purity** is **pure, as there is a basis for the matter.**[N] It is reasonable that items or people retain their presumptive status.[H]

גמ׳ מְנָא הָנֵי מִילֵּי? אָמַר רַבִּי אֱלִיעֶזֶר: דְּאָמַר קְרָא ״וְכִי יָמוּת מֵת עָלָיו בְּפֶתַע פִּתְאֹם״. ״עָלָיו״ – בִּמְחוּוֶּרֶת לוֹ.

GEMARA The Gemara asks: **From where are these matters** derived, that there is a difference between known and unknown impurity? **Rabbi Eliezer said that the verse states** with regard to a nazirite: **"And if any man shall die very suddenly beside him"** (Numbers 6:9). The emphasis provided by the term **"beside him"** indicates **that** it is **clear to him** that he has become impure. However, one is not impure if the presence of the corpse is unknown.

רֵישׁ לָקִישׁ אָמַר: אָמַר קְרָא ״כִּי יִהְיֶה טָמֵא לָנֶפֶשׁ אוֹ בְדֶרֶךְ רְחֹקָה״ – כִּי דֶּרֶךְ, מַה דֶּרֶךְ בְּגָלוּי – אַף כָּל בְּגָלוּי.

Reish Lakish said a different source: **The verse states** with regard to the Paschal offering: "Any man of you **who shall be ritually impure due to a corpse or on a road far away"** (Numbers 9:10). The word "road" is juxtaposed in the verse to the term "ritually impure," indicating that the impurity is **like a road. Just as a road is in the open, so too, every** impurity is **in the open.** It must be a known impurity.

וְאֶלָּא הָדִתְנַן: אֵיזוֹהִי טוּמְאַת הַתְּהוֹם – כָּל שֶׁאֵינוֹ מַכִּירָהּ אֶחָד בְּסוֹף הָעוֹלָם, אֲבָל מַכִּירָהּ אֶחָד בְּסוֹף הָעוֹלָם – אֵין זוֹ טוּמְאַת הַתְּהוֹם.

The Gemara objects: **But** consider **that which we learned** in the *Tosefta* (*Zavim* 2:9): **Which is the ritual impurity** imparted by a grave **in the depths?**[H] It is impurity imparted by **any** corpse **of which no one is aware,** even **at the end of the earth.** This type of impurity is permitted for both a nazirite and one who sacrifices the Paschal offering. **However,** if even **one** person **is aware of it,** even **at the end of the earth, this is not impurity** imparted by a grave **in the depths.**

HALAKHA

A nazirite who shaved and it became known to him that he was ritually impure – נָזִיר שֶׁגִּילַּח וְנוֹדַע לוֹ שֶׁהוּא טָמֵא: In the case of a nazirite who discovered after shaving for his purity that he had contracted impurity during his naziriteship, if the impurity was known he negates his entire term of naziriteship, brings the offerings of impurity, counts his naziriteship afresh, and again brings his offerings of purity. If he became impure from impurity of the depths he does not negate his naziriteship (Rambam *Sefer Hafla'a, Hilkhot Nezirut* 6:16).

Impurity of the depths – טוּמְאַת הַתְּהוֹם: If a nazirite who descended to immerse himself found a corpse floating in the place of his immersion, he is impure, as he is presumed to have come into contact with the corpse.

If he immersed himself, shaved for his impurity, counted his naziriteship of purity, and was then informed that there was a body sunk in the place of his immersion, he negates the entire period. The reason is that he retains the presumptive status of impurity he had before immersing. However, if he was ritually pure and descended only to cool off, he does not negate his naziriteship, as he retains his presumptive status of purity (Rambam *Sefer Hafla'a, Hilkhot Nezirut* 6: 20).

Which is the ritual impurity in the depths – אֵיזוֹהִי טוּמְאַת הַתְּהוֹם: Ritual impurity imparted by a grave in the depths is impurity that is not known to anyone in the world (Rambam *Sefer Hafla'a, Hilkhot Nezirut* 6:18).

NOTES

As there is a basis for the matter – שֶׁרַגְלַיִם לַדָּבָר: Some commentaries explain that it is reasonable to establish each item in accordance with its presumptive status (Commentary on *Nazir*). Others add that the *halakha* learned by tradition of impurity of the depths is only with regard to one who was ritually pure (*Tosafot*).

BACKGROUND

Ritual impurity imparted by a grave in the depths – טוּמְאַת תְּהוֹם: This is a *halakha* that applies to a grave found in a place where people had no previous knowledge of its existence. If a nazirite passes over a grave of this kind unknowingly and becomes aware of its existence only after his nazirite vow is completed, he is not considered to have contracted ritual impurity. The same *halakha* applies if one on his way to perform the ritual of the Paschal offering traverses such a grave and becomes aware of it only after sacrificing his offering. It is a *halakha* transmitted to Moses from Sinai that the frontplate worn by the High Priest on his forehead atones for this unwitting transgression.

בִּשְׁלָמָא לְמַאן דְּאָמַר כִּי דֶּרֶךְ – שַׁפִּיר, אֶלָּא לְמַאן דְּאָמַר בְּמַחֲוֶורֶת לוֹ – כִּי מַכִּירָהּ אֶחָד בְּסוֹף הָעוֹלָם מַאי הָוֵי?

The Gemara states its question: **Granted, according to the one who says** that this *halakha* is derived from the verse that states that ritual impurity is **like a road,** it is **fine,** as an item known to someone in the world can be compared to a road. **However, according to the one who says** that this *halakha* is derived from the term "beside him," i.e., it is referring **to** an impurity that is **clear to him, if one** person **at the other end of the earth is aware of** this impurity, **what of it?** It was unknown to the nazirite himself.

וְתוּ, הָא דְּתַנְיָא: הַמּוֹצֵא מֵת מוּשְׁכָּב לְרׇחְבָּהּ שֶׁל דֶּרֶךְ, בִּתְרוּמָה – טָמֵא, בְּנָזִיר וּבַעֲשִׂיַּית פֶּסַח – טָהוֹר, מַאי שְׁנָא? אֶלָּא: טוּמְאַת הַתְּהוֹם גְּמָרָא גְּמִירִי לַהּ.

And furthermore, consider **that which is taught** in another *baraita* (*Tosefta, Zavim* 2:8): In the case of **one who finds a corpse lying** across **the width of a road,**[H] i.e., it had been buried there in such a way that it was impossible for the passerby to avoid becoming impure by passing over the corpse, then **with regard to** *teruma*, the passerby is **impure.** Therefore, if he is a priest, he may not eat *teruma*. However, **with regard to** both being **a nazirite and** being **one performing** the ritual of **the Paschal offering,** the passerby is **pure. What is different** about these situations? **Rather,** it must be that the *halakha* of **impurity** imparted by a grave **in the depths is learned as a tradition**[H] and not from the verses, which are cited merely in support.

״אִם עַד שֶׁלֹּא גִּילֵּחַ״ וכו׳. מַאן תַּנָּא? אָמַר רַבִּי יוֹחָנָן: רַבִּי אֱלִיעֶזֶר הִיא, דְּאָמַר: תִּגְלַחַת מְעַכֶּבֶת.

§ The mishna taught that **if** a nazirite discovered he was ritually impure **before he shaved,** he negates his naziriteship even if he was rendered impure by impurity of the depths. The Gemara asks: **Who is the** *tanna* who **taught** this opinion? **Rabbi Yoḥanan says: It is Rabbi Eliezer, who says** that **shaving is indispensable**[H] to the completion of one's naziriteship. Consequently, if he discovered he was impure before he shaved, he became impure during his naziriteship, and he negates the period he has observed.

בָּעֵי רָמִי בַּר חָמָא: נִטְמָא בְּתוֹךְ מְלֹאת, וְנוֹדַע לוֹ לְאַחַר מְלֹאת, מַהוּ? בָּתַר יְדִיעָה אָזְלִינַן – וִידִיעָה אַחַר מְלֹאת הִיא, אוֹ לָא? וּלְמַאי – לְמִיסְתַּר.

Rami bar Ḥama raised a dilemma: What is the *halakha* with regard to one who **became impure during the full term** of the regular days of his naziriteship **but** his impurity **became known**[N] **to him** only **after the full term** but before he shaved? Perhaps **we go** according to his **knowledge, and it is** a case of **knowledge after the full term, or** perhaps the *halakha* is **not** determined by the time of his awareness but by the actual time of the impurity, which occurred during his naziriteship. The Gemara adds: **And with regard to what** issue was this dilemma raised? It was **with regard to** his possible **negation** of the period he observed as a nazirite: Does he negate his naziriteship, or is he considered to have contracted impurity after the completion of his term, in which case he need not start his naziriteship afresh?

Perek **IX**
Daf **63** Amud **b**

אָמַר רָבָא, תָּא שְׁמַע: אִם עַד שֶׁלֹּא גִּילֵּחַ – בֵּין כָּךְ וּבֵין כָּךְ סוֹתֵר. הֵיכִי דָּמֵי? אִי דְּאִיתְיְדַע לֵיהּ בְּתוֹךְ מְלֹאת – צְרִיכָא לְמֵימַר? אֶלָּא לָאו – לְאַחַר מְלֹאת, שְׁמַע מִינַּהּ.

Rava said: Come and hear a resolution to this dilemma from the mishna: **If** he discovered he was impure **before he shaved,** he **negates** the days of his naziriteship **in either case.** The Gemara seeks to clarify this: **What are the circumstances** of this case? When exactly did he find out about the impurity? **If it became known to him during the full term** of his naziriteship, **need this be said,** that he negates the previous days? After all, he has yet to complete his naziriteship vow. **Rather, is it not** referring to a case when the impurity was discovered **after the full term** of his naziriteship? **Conclude from** the mishna that he negates the days of his naziriteship even if he discovered the impurity after the completion of his term.

HALAKHA

One who finds a corpse lying across the width of a road – הַמּוֹצֵא מֵת מוּשְׁכָּב לְרׇחְבָּהּ שֶׁל דֶּרֶךְ: With regard to one who crossed a path and later discovered that a corpse lay buried across its width, if this was a case of impurity of the depths he is pure with regard to the Paschal offering, even if the body is stretched over the entire width of the path. Consequently, he may slaughter the Paschal offering and eat it, unless it became known that he had definitely touched the corpse. However, his status is that of uncertain impurity with respect to partaking of *teruma*.

If the individual is a nazirite, he is pure even if the impurity was known, as it is a case of uncertain impurity in the public domain, unless it was impossible for him to have traversed the path without coming into contact with the corpse (Rambam). Some authorities maintain that even a nazirite is pure only in the case of an impurity of the depths (Ra'avad; see Radbaz). The *Kesef Mishne* claims that the Rambam had a different version of the Gemara here (Rambam *Sefer Hafla'a*, *Hilkhot Nezirut* 9:18 and *Sefer Korbanot*, *Hilkhot Korban Pesaḥ* 6:11).

Learned as a tradition – גְּמָרָא גְּמִירִי לַהּ: The ruling that a nazirite who contracts ritual impurity imparted by a grave in the depths does not negate his naziriteship is a *halakha* learned by tradition (Rambam *Sefer Hafla'a*, *Hilkhot Nezirut* 6:16).

It is Rabbi Eliezer who says shaving is indispensable – רַבִּי אֱלִיעֶזֶר הִיא דְּאָמַר תִּגְלַחַת מְעַכֶּבֶת: If the blood of a nazirite's offerings was sprinkled and then he discovered he had been rendered impure by impurity of the depths, it does not negate his naziriteship, even if he has yet to shave. The *halakha* is in accordance with the opinion of the Rabbis that shaving is not an indispensable part of the ritual, and contrary to the opinion of Rabbi Eliezer cited here (Rambam *Sefer Hafla'a*, *Hilkhot Nezirut* 6:17).

NOTES

Became impure during the full term but it became known, etc. – נִטְמָא בְּתוֹךְ מְלֹאת וְנוֹדַע וכו׳: Some commentaries maintain that this inquiry refers only to impurity of the depths, which is why the Gemara asks whether he negates his naziriteship at all. If so, Rami bar Ḥama was unaware of the ruling of the mishna (Commentary on *Nazir*). Most commentaries claim that the question refers to all types of impurity, known or otherwise (see *Tosafot*). According to this opinion, Rami bar Ḥama does not entertain the possibility that the individual in question might not have to negate his naziriteship at all, as no one accepts that ruling. Rather, this passage serves as an opening to the ensuing discussion of the Gemara as to whether Rabbi Eliezer rules that he negates thirty days or merely seven, like one who became impure after the completion of his term.

וַעֲדַיִין תִּיבָּעֵי לָךְ: כּוּלּוֹ סוֹתֵר אוֹ שִׁבְעָה סוֹתֵר? לְמַאן? אִילֵימָא לְרַבָּנַן - פְּשִׁיטָא דְּכוּלּוֹ סוֹתֵר, וְאִי לְרַבִּי אֱלִיעֶזֶר, כָּל אַחַר מְלֹאת - שִׁבְעָה סוֹתֵר.

The Gemara continues to analyze the aforementioned case. **And you can still raise the dilemma:** Does **he negate the entire** period of his naziriteship **or** does **he negate** just **seven** days? The Gemara asks: **According to whom** is this dilemma raised? **If we say** this dilemma is referring **to** the opinion of **the Rabbis** (see 16b), **it is obvious that** he **negates it all,** as they maintain that even a nazirite who becomes impure after the completion of his naziriteship must observe another thirty days. **And if** it is referring **to** the opinion of **Rabbi Eliezer,** his ruling with regard to **any** impurity **after the full term** of his term is that one **negates** only **seven** days.

אָמַר לָךְ: הָנֵי מִילֵּי כִּי נִטְמָא אַחַר מְלֹאת, וְהַאי לִפְנֵי מְלֹאת הוּא. אוֹ דִּילְמָא שָׁאנֵי הָכָא, דִּידִיעָה אַחַר מְלֹאת הִיא?

The Gemara responds: The one who raised this dilemma could have **said to you: This statement** of Rabbi Eliezer that a nazirite negates a mere seven days applies only **if he became impure after the full term** of his naziriteship, **but this one** became impure **before** the end of **the full term,** and therefore he negates the entire period. **Or perhaps it is different here, as it is** a case of **knowledge** that came to light **after the full term** of his naziriteship.

וּמִינָּהּ, קָתָנֵי: בֵּין כָּךְ וּבֵין כָּךְ סוֹתֵר, וְלָא קָמִיפַּלְגִי.

The Gemara answers: **And** one can resolve the dilemma **from this**[N] mishna itself. The mishna **teaches** that if the nazirite discovered he was impure before he shaved **he negates** his naziriteship **in either case. And it does not distinguish** between cases where this happened before the end of the full term or after it. This indicates that in any case he negates only seven days.

תָּנוּ רַבָּנַן: הַמּוֹצֵא מֵת מוּטָּל לְרׇחְבָּהּ שֶׁל דֶּרֶךְ, לִתְרוּמָה - טָמֵא, וּבְנָזִיר וּבְעוֹשֵׂה פֶסַח - טָהוֹר. בַּמֶּה דְּבָרִים אֲמוּרִים - שֶׁאֵין לוֹ מָקוֹם לַעֲבוֹר,

§ **The Sages taught** (*Tosefta, Zavim* 2:8): In the case of **one who finds a corpse lying** across **the width of a road, with regard to** ***teruma*** the passerby is **impure. But with regard to** both **a nazirite and one performing** the ritual of **the Paschal offering,** the passerby is **pure,** as it is considered impurity imparted by a grave in the depths. **In what** case **is this statement said,** that one is impure with regard to partaking of *teruma*? It is said in a case **where he does not have space to pass by**[H] on the road without passing over the corpse.

אֲבָל יֵשׁ לוֹ מָקוֹם לַעֲבוֹר - אַף לִתְרוּמָה טָהוֹר.

But if he has space to pass by, then **even with regard to** ***teruma*** he **is pure.** This is because it is possible that the passerby did not become ritually impure, and there is a principle that if an uncertainty arises concerning the ritual purity of a person or item in the public domain, the person or item is considered pure.

בַּמֶּה דְּבָרִים אֲמוּרִים - שֶׁמְּצָאוֹ שָׁלֵם, אֲבָל מְשׁוּבָּר אוֹ מְפוֹרָק, אֲפִילּוּ אֵין מָקוֹם לַעֲבוֹר - חָיְישִׁינַן שֶׁמָּא בֵּין פְּרָקִין עָבַר. וּבַקֶּבֶר - אֲפִילּוּ מְשׁוּבָּר וּמְפוֹרָק טָמֵא, מִפְּנֵי שֶׁקֶּבֶר מְצָרְפוֹ.

Similarly, **in what** case **is this statement said?** It is said in a case **where one finds** the corpse **whole. However,** if it is **broken or dismembered** he is pure, **even if there is no space to pass by.** The reason is that **we suspect**[N] that **perhaps he passed between the parts** of the corpse and did not touch or pass over any of them. This applies when he finds the corpse out in the open. **But** if he finds it **in a grave, even** if it is **broken** or **dismembered,** he is **impure.** This is **because the grave joins** the parts into one unit and renders him impure if he passed over any part of the grave, even if he did not pass over part of the corpse.

בַּמֶּה דְּבָרִים אֲמוּרִים - בִּמְהַלֵּךְ בְּרַגְלָיו, אֲבָל טָעוּן אוֹ רָכוּב - טָמֵא, לְפִי שֶׁמְּהַלֵּךְ בְּרַגְלָיו אֶפְשָׁר לוֹ שֶׁלֹּא יִגַּע וְשֶׁלֹּא יָסִיט וְשֶׁלֹּא יַאֲהִיל, טָעוּן אוֹ רָכוּב - אִי אֶפְשָׁר שֶׁלֹּא יִגַּע וְשֶׁלֹּא יָסִיט וְשֶׁלֹּא יַאֲהִיל.

The *baraita* adds: **In what** case **is this statement said,** i.e., that if the corpse was dismembered the passerby is pure? It is said **with regard to** a passerby who **travels by foot.**[N] **However,** if he was **loaded** with a heavy burden **or** was **riding** an animal, he is **impure.** This is **because** in the case of **one who travels by foot, it is possible that he will not touch** the corpse **and will not move** it **and will not pass over** it, whereas in the case of one who is **loaded** with a heavy burden and therefore does not walk in a straight line, **or** one **riding** an animal, **it is impossible that he will not touch** the corpse **and will not move** it **and will not pass over** it.

בַּמֶּה דְּבָרִים אֲמוּרִים - בְּטוּמְאַת הַתְּהוֹם, אֲבָל טוּמְאָה יְדוּעָה - שְׁלׇשְׁתָּן טְמֵאִים.

In what case **is this statement said,** that a nazirite and one bringing a Paschal offering are considered pure? It is said **with regard to impurity** imparted by a grave **in the depths. However,** if the source of **impurity** was **known** to others but not to the individual who became impure, all **three of them,** i.e., a nazirite, one performing the ritual of the Paschal offering, and the one who wishes to partake of *teruma*, are **impure.**

NOTES

And from this – וּמִינָּהּ: The dilemma can be resolved from the mishna itself, which simply states that he negates, without further specification. This indicates that he negates only seven days, like a nazirite who becomes impure after the completion of his term. Most commentaries explain in this manner (see Meiri). Others suggest a different explanation: The fact that no alternative opinion of the Rabbis is recorded here indicates that Rabbi Eliezer agrees in this case that the nazirite negates the entire period, as the impurity occurred before the completion of his term (Commentary on *Nazir*).

Some commentaries are puzzled by this answer of the Gemara, according to which the *halakha* follows the time of his discovery that he was impure. The Rosh explains that this is problematic because the first clause of the mishna teaches that if a nazirite found out after shaving that he was definitely impure he negates the entire period, which indicates that one follows the time that he became impure rather than the time of his discovery that he was impure. He answers that there is a difference between the two cases: If the nazirite discovered his impurity only after shaving, then he cannot possibly follow the time of his discovery, as in that case his naziriteship is over and he would not negate anything. Instead, as he has discovered that he was impure, his offerings are invalid and he must count again. However, if he finds out on the day of the completion of his term, there is room for debate with regard to how many days he negates.

We suspect – חָיְישִׁינַן: The commentaries note that although this phrase usually means: We are concerned, denoting a stringency, it can occasionally refer to a possible leniency, as it does here (Meiri; Rashash).

In what case is this statement said? With regard to a passerby who travels by foot – בַּמֶּה דְּבָרִים אֲמוּרִים, בִּמְהַלֵּךְ בְּרַגְלָיו: In the case of a dismembered corpse, one is pure with regard to partaking of *teruma* only if he was traveling by foot. However, a nazirite and one who was bringing a Paschal offering are not considered impure from impurity of the depths even if they were riding an animal. This is the explanation accepted by the Commentary on *Nazir*, which holds that the *halakha* concerning impurity of the depths that a nazirite and one who is performing the ritual of the Paschal offering are considered pure even if they later become aware that they had definitely been rendered impure is a *halakha* transmitted to Moses from Sinai.

Others maintain that this ruling involving one who was carrying a load or riding an animal applies even to the impurity of the depths. The reason is that a nazirite and one who was performing the ritual of the Paschal offering are pure only if there was merely a presumption of impurity, but not if there was no doubt about the impurity at all (Rambam and Meiri).

HALAKHA

Where he does not have space to pass by – שֶׁאֵין לוֹ מָקוֹם לַעֲבוֹר: In the case of a corpse positioned across the width of a path, if the corpse was whole, all those who pass along that route are impure with regard to *teruma* and offerings, as they are presumed to have touched it. If it was in pieces, a passerby is pure. If it was in a grave dug across the path he is impure. However, if he was on the way to perform the ritual of the Paschal offering and it was an impurity of the depths, he it is not considered impure, provided he was traveling by foot; if he was riding an animal or carrying a load he is impure. The same *halakha* applies to a nazirite (Rambam *Sefer Hafla'a, Hilkhot Nezirut* 9:18, 19; *Sefer Korbanot, Hilkhot Korban Pesaḥ* 6:11; and *Sefer Tahara, Hilkhot She'ar Avot HaTumot* 18:3).

HALAKHA

If it was concealed in hay, etc. – הָיָה טָמוּן בְּתֶבֶן וכו׳: A corpse that was concealed by hay or pebbles is considered to impart impurity of the depths. If it was in water or a dark place or in rocky crevices, it does not impart impurity of the depths (Rambam *Sefer Hafla'a*, *Hilkhot Nezirut* 6:19).

The impurity imparted by a grave in the depths applies only with regard to a corpse – טוּמְאַת הַתְּהוֹם...לְמֵת בִּלְבַד: The *halakha* of the impurity of the depths applies only to one who died without human interference, but not if he was murdered, as the killer is aware of the body's presence, as can be inferred from the Gemara's use of the term *met*, corpse, and not *harug*, meaning one who was killed. The Ra'avad disagrees, maintaining that the Gemara here is simply stating that the concept of impurity of the depths refers solely to the impurity imparted by a corpse, not to any other type of impurity (Rambam *Sefer Hafla'a*, *Hilkhot Nezirut* 6:18).

Uncertain impurity that was floating – סְפֵק טוּמְאָה צָפָה: If the carcass of a creeping animal was floating on the surface of water, whether the water was contained in a vessel or in the ground, an individual who enters that place remains pure, even if there is room only for him and the carcass of the creeping animal, unless it is known for certain that he was rendered impure through contact with the carcass. This is in accordance with the opinion of the first *tanna*. *Tosafot* claim that the same *halakha* applies to all floating objects that impart impurity by contact, in a situation where there is uncertainty as to whether one touched it (Rambam *Sefer Tahara*, *Hilkhot She'ar Avot HaTumot* 14:3).

NOTES

Only with regard to a corpse – אֶלָּא לְמֵת בִּלְבַד: The Commentary on *Nazir* adds: But not for a *zav* or a *zava*. It is explained at length in the Jerusalem Talmud that according to this opinion the impurity of the depths applies, based on an *a fortiori* inference, to other types of impurities as well, e.g., an animal carcass. This *halakha* is relevant only for one who is performing the ritual of the Paschal offering, as in any case a nazirite negates his naziriteship only for the impurity of a corpse. The statement of the *baraita*: Only with regard to a corpse, excludes an impurity transmitted by lying and sitting, namely that of a *zav* and a *zava*.

וְאֵיזוֹ הִיא טוּמְאַת הַתְּהוֹם – כָּל שֶׁאֵין מַכִּירָהּ אֶחָד בְּסוֹף הָעוֹלָם, מַכִּירָהּ אֶחָד בְּסוֹף הָעוֹלָם – אֵין זוֹ טוּמְאַת הַתְּהוֹם.

The *baraita* continues: **And which** corpse is considered to impart **impurity of the depths? Any** corpse **of which no one is aware,** even **at the end of the earth.** But if even **one** individual **is aware** of it, even if that person is **at the end of the earth, this is not** considered **impurity** imparted by a grave **in the depths.**

הָיָה טָמוּן בְּתֶבֶן אוֹ בִּצְרוֹרוֹת – הֲרֵי זוֹ טוּמְאַת הַתְּהוֹם. בַּמַּיִם וּבָאֲפֵילָה וּבִנְקִיקֵי הַסְּלָעִים – אֵין זוֹ טוּמְאַת הַתְּהוֹם.

The *baraita* continues: To ascertain whether anyone ever knew about the corpse, its condition is taken into account. If the body **was concealed in hay**[H] **or in pebbles,** so the person might have died in an avalanche, it is likely that the corpse had never been found; **this is impurity** imparted by a grave **in the depths.** However, if it was found **in water, or in a dark** place, **or in the clefts of the rocks, this is not impurity** imparted by a grave **in the depths.** Although these are places where people do not often go, with the passage of time the corpse is likely to be discovered, and it is quite possible that someone already passed by and saw it.

וְלֹא אָמְרוּ טוּמְאַת הַתְּהוֹם אֶלָּא לְמֵת בִּלְבַד.

The *baraita* concludes: **And** the Sages **said** that the leniency of **impurity** imparted by a grave **in the depths** applies **only with regard to a corpse,**[NH] but not with regard to other sources of impurity.

״כֵּיצַד יָרַד״. צָפָה אֵינָהּ מְטַמְּאָה לְעִנְיַן שֶׁרֶץ, דְּתַנְיָא: סְפֵק טוּמְאָה צָפָה, בֵּין בְּכֵלִים בֵּין בְּקַרְקַע – טְהוֹרָה. רַבִּי שִׁמְעוֹן אוֹמֵר: בְּכֵלִים – טְמֵאָה, בְּקַרְקַע – טְהוֹרָה.

§ The mishna taught: **How** does one differentiate between a known and an unknown impurity? If a nazirite **descended** to immerse in a cave, and a corpse was found floating at the mouth of the cave, he is impure. The Gemara comments: **A floating** impurity **does not render** a person or item **impure in the case of** a carcass of **a creeping animal. As it is taught** in a *baraita* (*Tosefta*, *Teharot* 5:6): With regard to the case of **uncertain impurity,** where an item might have touched something impure that was **floating,**[H] **either** in water **in a vessel or** in water **in the ground,** e.g., a well, the item is **pure. Rabbi Shimon says:** If the impurity was floating in water that was **in a vessel,** the item is **impure;** if the impurity was in water **in the ground,** it is **pure.**

Perek **IX**
Daf **64** Amud **a**

NOTES

Where it swarms – שֶׁהוּא שׁוֹרֵץ: That is, any place where it can swarm, including water (Rosh).

מַאי טַעֲמָא דְּתַנָּא קַמָּא? אָמַר רַבִּי יִצְחָק בַּר אֲבוּדִימִי: כְּתִיב ״בְּכָל הַשֶּׁרֶץ הַשּׁוֹרֵץ״ – כָּל מָקוֹם שֶׁהוּא שׁוֹרֵץ, וּכְתִיב ״עַל הָאָרֶץ״. הָא כֵּיצַד? וַדַּאי מַגָּעוֹ – טָמֵא, סְפֵק מַגָּעוֹ – טָהוֹר.

What is the reason of the first ***tanna*** for declaring that in all uncertain cases of floating impurity the person or item remains pure? **Rabbi Yitzḥak bar Avudimi says:** In the passage dealing with the impurity of creeping animals and the prohibition of eating them **it is written: "With any swarming thing that swarms"** (Leviticus 11:43), indicating that a carcass of a creeping animal renders items impure in **any place where it swarms.**[N] **And it is written:** "All swarming things that swarm **upon the earth"** (Leviticus 11:42), indicating that it transmits impurity only if it is on the earth. **How so?** How can one reconcile these two verses? **Definite contact** with **it** renders one **impure;** one who has **uncertain contact** with **it,** e.g., the impurity is floating, remains **pure.**

וְרַבִּי שִׁמְעוֹן מַאי טַעֲמָא? אֲמַר עוּלָּא: כְּתִיב ״אַךְ מַעְיָן״ וּכְתִיב ״יִטְמָא (עַד הָעָרֶב)״, הָא כֵּיצַד? צָפָה בְּכֵלִים – טָמֵא, בְּקַרְקַע – טָהוֹר.

The Gemara asks: **And Rabbi Shimon, what is the reason** for his opinion? **Ulla said** that as **it is written: "Nevertheless a fountain** or a cistern in which there is a gathering of water shall be pure" (Leviticus 11:36), this indicates that a creeping animal found in one of these places does not impart impurity. **And it is written** in the same verse: "He who touches their carcass **shall be impure** until evening," which indicates that it does render one impure. **How so?** If the impurity was **floating** in water contained **in vessels,** the item it touched **is** rendered **impure,** but if the water was **in the ground** itself, e.g., in a spring or pit, the item it touched is **pure.**

תָּנוּ רַבָּנַן: כָּל הַנִּיטָּלִין וְהַנִּגְרָרִין – סְפֵיקָן טָמֵא, מִפְּנֵי שֶׁהֵן כְּמוּנָּחִין. וְהַנִּזְרָקִין – סְפֵיקָן טָהוֹר.

The Sages taught (*Tosefta, Teharot* 3:13): **All** items that impart impurity **that are carried** by human hand **or that are dragged**[NH] along are not considered floating impurities, despite the fact that they are in motion. Rather, in a case where there is **uncertainty** whether a carried or dragged item affected a person, the individual is rendered **impure,** because the items are considered **as though** they were **at rest. And** in the case of items **that are thrown** by people, in **uncertain** cases that pertain to them, the individual remains **pure.**[H]

חוּץ מִן כְּזַיִת הַמֵּת, וְהַמַּאֲהִיל עַל פְּנֵי טוּמְאָה, וְכָל דָּבָר שֶׁמְּטַמֵּא מִלְמַעְלָה כִּלְמַטָּה, לְאֵיתוּיֵי זָב וְזָבָה.

This is the *halakha*, **except for an olive-bulk** from **a corpse,**[H] which transmits impurity through uncertain contact even if it was thrown; **and that which overlies impurity**[N] when thrown, i.e., an item that might have been positioned over a corpse when it was thrown; **and anything that renders** items **above** it **impure like** it renders those **below** it impure.[N] To what does this last clause refer? It comes **to include a *zav* and a *zava*,**[H] who render items placed above and below them impure even without contact. If something thrown or floating might have come into contact with a *zav* or *zava*, it is impure.

בָּעֵי רָמִי בַּר חָמָא: מֵת בִּכְלִי, וּכְלִי צָף עַל פְּנֵי הַמַּיִם, מַהוּ? בָּתַר כְּלִי אָזְלִינַן אוֹ בָּתַר מֵיתָא אָזְלִינַן?

With regard to this *halakha* of a floating impurity, **Rami bar Ḥama raises a dilemma:** If there is **a corpse in a vessel**[N] **and the vessel is floating**[H] **on water,** and one did not overlie it but might have touched it, **what is the** *halakha*? Do **we go according to** the floating **vessel or do we go according to the corpse,** which is resting on a solid surface?

אִם תִּמְצֵי לוֹמַר בָּתַר כְּלִי אָזְלִינַן, מֵת עַל גַּבֵּי שֶׁרֶץ מַהוּ? כֵּיוָן דְּהַאי טוּמְאַת עֶרֶב וְהַאי טוּמְאַת שִׁבְעָה – כְּמַאן דְּמַחְתָּא טוּמְאָה בִּכְלִי דָּמְיָא, אוֹ דִילְמָא טוּמְאָה סְמִיכְתָּא הִיא?

If you say that **we go according to the vessel** and one is rendered ritually impure, the following question arises: If **a corpse** is placed **on top of** the carcass of **a creeping animal,** which is floating on water, **what is the** *halakha*? Do we say that **since this** impurity of a creeping animal is **an impurity for an evening,** i.e., it lasts one day, **and this** impurity imparted by a corpse is **an impurity for seven** days, **it is considered as though the impurity** imparted by a corpse **were placed in a vessel,** and he is impure? **Or, perhaps** the fact that both a corpse and a creeping animal impart impurity means that **it is** one **solid impurity,** and because the creeping animal is floating he is pure.

NOTES

That are carried or that are dragged – הַנִּיטָּלִין וְהַנִּגְרָרִין: Because these items are tied to the individual, who transfers them from one place to another, they are considered placed on the ground, despite the fact they are not entirely stationary. Some commentaries maintain that anything dragged or carried is considered fixed in place, whether it is in a person's hand or not (Commentary on *Nazir*). Others explain this to mean that items that are dragged and carried through water do not have the status of floating impurities (*Tosafot*).

And that which overlies impurity – וְהַמַּאֲהִיל עַל פְּנֵי טוּמְאָה: Whether the impurity, e.g., an olive-bulk of a corpse, overlies a pure item, or whether the pure item overlies the impurity, both a floating impurity and the item thrown over it contract impurity imparted in a tent. This is because the leniency of a floating impurity is derived from the *halakha* of a creeping animal, and therefore even those who accept this ruling can apply it only to a case similar to that of a creeping animal, i.e., impurity through contact, but not impurity imparted in a tent (Rabbeinu Peretz).

That renders items above it impure like it renders those below it impure – שֶׁמְּטַמֵּא מִלְמַעְלָה כִּלְמַטָּה: Some commentaries explain that this refers to a heavy stone upon which a *zav* is sitting. This stone transmits impurity to items above and below it even without direct contact (Commentary on *Nazir*). According to *Tosafot*, it refers to the impurity of a *zav*, imparted by him lying, sitting, or moving an item, as a *zav* can impart impurity to an item in these ways even without directly touching it.

A corpse in a vessel – מֵת בִּכְלִי: The standard version of the text is somewhat problematic, as the mishna explicitly states that a floating corpse imparts impurity even in a case of uncertainty. The commentaries explain that this refers to a situation where it is clear that one had not overlaid the corpse, and the uncertainty concerns only the possibility of impurity through contact. In this regard, the *halakha* of all impurities, including that imparted by a corpse, is derived from the case of a creeping animal, in which a floating impurity does not render items impure through contact. Some early commentaries read: A creeping animal in a vessel (see Rabbeinu Peretz and Meiri). Accordingly, this is not connected to the *halakha* of the mishna, which discusses a corpse.

HALAKHA

All those that are carried or that are dragged – כָּל הַנִּיטָּלִין וְהַנִּגְרָרִין: All items that are carried or dragged are considered at rest, and therefore people or items that have possibly come into contact with them are impure (Rambam *Sefer Tahara, Hilkhot She'ar Avot HaTumot* 14:3).

And in the case of items that are thrown by people, in uncertain cases the individual remains pure – וְהַנִּזְרָקִין סְפֵיקָן טָהוֹר: If one threw a creeping animal among loaves, or a pure loaf among impure ones, and it is uncertain whether the impurity touched the pure loaf, they are pure, as the individual did not see the pure loaf touching the impurity. In a case of this kind of uncertainty, the item is pure (Rambam *Sefer Tahara, Hilkhot She'ar Avot HaTumot* 15:6).

Except for an olive-bulk from a corpse – חוּץ מִן כְּזַיִת הַמֵּת: If an olive-bulk of a corpse in the mouth of a raven possibly overlaid a person in a private domain, he is impure due to uncertainty. If the uncertain impurity involves a vessel, it is pure, as there is a difference in this regard between people and items (Rambam *Sefer Tahara, Hilkhot She'ar Avot HaTumot* 17:1).

To include a *zav* and a *zava* – לְאֵיתוּיֵי זָב וְזָבָה: One who is uncertain if he touched a floating impurity is pure only if the impurity is from a creeping animal. Similarly, in a case of uncertain impurity involving a thrown item, the *halakha* that the person is pure applies only to a creeping animal, as stated by the *baraita*. The *Or Same'aḥ* notes that this opinion is also recorded in the Jerusalem Talmud (Rambam *Sefer Tahara, Hilkhot She'ar Avot HaTumot* 14:3, 15:6).

An impurity in a vessel and the vessel was afloat – טוּמְאָה בִּכְלִי וּכְלִי צָף: If a creeping animal was in a vessel that was floating on water, or if the creeping animal was placed on a carcass or on a corpse, even if the carcass or the flesh of the corpse had decomposed, or if the creeping animal was located on semen, and the substance the creeping animal was placed on was floating on water, the creeping animal is considered to be on the ground. Consequently, in cases of uncertain contact in a private domain, the item that was in contact with the creeping animal is rendered impure. It seems that the Rambam had a different version of the text of the Gemara (Rambam *Sefer Tahara, Hilkhot She'ar Avot HaTumot* 14:4).

HALAKHA

A creeping animal atop a creeping animal – שֶׁרֶץ עַל גַּבֵּי שֶׁרֶץ: If one creeping animal was positioned atop another creeping animal that was floating on water, it is considered like a single floating impurity, and therefore one remains pure in the case of any uncertain contact. Apparently, the Rambam's text of the Gemara differed from the standard version, which accounts for his lenient ruling (Rambam *Sefer Tahara, Hilkhot She'ar Avot HaTumot* 14:4 and see *Kesef Mishne* there).

A creeping animal atop waters of purification – שֶׁרֶץ עַל גַּבֵּי מֵי חַטָּאת: If a creeping animal was positioned atop waters of purification that was floating on regular water, it is uncertain whether it renders one impure. The Rambam rules leniently, as the *halakha* is lenient in uncertain cases with regard to rabbinic law (Rambam *Sefer Tahara, Hilkhot She'ar Avot HaTumot* 14:4).

וְאִם תִּמְצֵי לוֹמַר כְּמַאן דְּמַחְתָא טוּמְאָה בִּכְלִי דָּמְיָא, וְטָמֵא וַדַּאי, שֶׁרֶץ עַל גַּבֵּי נְבֵלָה וּנְבֵלָה צָפָה מַהוּ? כֵּיוָן דְּתַרְוַיְיהוּ טוּמְאַת עֶרֶב אִינּוּן – טוּמְאָה סְמִיכְתָּא הִיא, אוֹ דִּילְמָא הַאי כְּזַיִת וְהַאי כַּעֲדָשָׁה?

And if you say that due to their different levels of impurity **it is considered as though the impurity were placed in a vessel and** therefore one is **definitely impure,** one can raise an additional dilemma. If a **creeping animal** is **atop** an unslaughtered **animal carcass and the animal carcass is floating,** then **what is the** *halakha*? Do we say that **since they are both** examples of **an impurity for an evening, it is** considered a single **solid impurity, or perhaps** here too they are different, as **this** one, the carcass, renders items impure when it is the amount of **an olive-bulk, and this** one, the creeping animal, does so when it is the amount **of a lentil-bulk.** In that case, the animal carcass and the creeping animal should be considered separate items, and it is as though the impurity is placed in a vessel, and he is impure.

שֶׁרֶץ עַל גַּבֵּי שֶׁרֶץ מַהוּ? הָנֵי וַדַּאי חַד שִׁיעוּרָא נִינְהוּ, אוֹ דִּילְמָא כֵּיוָן דְּמִפְסְקִי מֵהֲדָדֵי לָא?

If in that case they are considered separate, then one can also ask: If **a creeping animal** is positioned **atop** another **creeping animal,**[H] **what is the** *halakha*? Do we say that **these certainly** have the **same measurement** with regard to transmitting impurity, and that they consequently should be viewed as a single floating items, which means he is pure? **Or, perhaps, since** they **are separate from each other** and are not in fact a single item, they are **not** considered as one unit.

וְאִם תִּמְצֵי לוֹמַר שֶׁרֶץ עַל גַּבֵּי שֶׁרֶץ, כֵּיוָן דְּמִפְסְקִי מֵהֲדָדֵי – כְּמַאן דְּמַנְחָא בִּכְלִי דָּמֵי, שֶׁרֶץ עַל גַּבֵּי נְבֵלָה שֶׁנִּימּוֹחָה מַהוּ? כֵּיוָן דְּנִימּוֹחָה הָוְיָא לֵיהּ מַשְׁקֶה, אוֹ דִּלְמָא הַאי אוֹכְלָא הוּא?

And if you say that in the case of **a creeping animal atop a creeping animal, since** they **are separate from each other, it is considered as though** the impurity **were placed in a vessel** and is not floating, one can raise an additional dilemma. If a **creeping animal** was placed **atop an animal carcass that has dissolved,**[N] **what is** the *halakha*? Do we say that **since it has dissolved it has become** like **liquid,** and therefore it is as though the creeping animal were floating on liquid? **Or, perhaps this** carcass is still considered **food,** rather than a liquid, and the creeping animal is on a solid surface.

וְאִם תִּמְצֵי לוֹמַר דְּאוֹכְלָא הוּא, שֶׁרֶץ עַל גַּבֵּי שִׁכְבַת זֶרַע מַהוּ? וְאִם תִּמְצֵי לוֹמַר כֵּיוָן דְּמִיתְעַקְרָא הָוְיָא לָהּ כִּי אוֹכְלָא, שֶׁרֶץ עַל גַּבֵּי מֵי חַטָּאת וּמֵי חַטָּאת צָפִין עַל גַּבֵּי הַמַּיִם, מַהוּ? לָא יָדְעִינַן, תֵּיקוּ.

And if you say that a dissolved animal carcasses **is** considered **food,** one can raise an additional dilemma. If **a creeping animal** was placed **on top of semen,** which is certainly liquid, **what is the** *halakha*? Is this creeping animal considered a floating impurity? **And if you say** that **once** semen **is ejaculated** from the body **it is considered like food** rather than drink, as it is viscous, one can raise an additional dilemma. If **a creeping animal** was placed **atop waters of purification,**[HN] i.e., the water into which the ashes of the red heifer are mixed, which becomes highly viscous, **and the waters of purification are floating on water, what is** the *halakha*? The Gemara responds: **We do not know** the answer to any of these questions, and therefore the dilemmas **shall stand** unresolved.

NOTES

Atop an animal carcass that has dissolved – עַל גַּבֵּי נְבֵלָה שֶׁנִּימּוֹחָה: This question concerns the status of the carcass itself: Does one go according to its current, liquefied state, in which case the creeping animal is on a liquid, or does one follow its original solid form? Some commentaries maintain that in this dilemma and in the subsequent dilemma pertaining to semen, the question is if the dissolved carcass or semen is disregarded, thereby causing the creeping animal to be considered as though it is directly on the water (Rambam; Rosh).

Atop waters of purification – עַל גַּבֵּי מֵי חַטָּאת: According to most commentaries, the dilemma is whether the presence of the ashes in the water means that it is no longer considered liquid, or whether it nevertheless retains the status of liquid. Some commentaries note that this dilemma specifically refers to the waters of purification, not to ordinary water mixed with ashes, because waters of purification have the unique characteristic of rendering a pure person impure (see Numbers 19:7). Consequently, one might have thought that it should form one solid, impure entity with the creeping animal atop it (*Tosafot*).

אָמַר רַב הַמְנוּנָא: נָזִיר וְעוֹשֵׂה פֶסַח שֶׁהָלְכוּ בְּקֶבֶר הַתְּהוֹם בַּשְּׁבִיעִי שֶׁלָּהֶן – טְהוֹרִים. מַאי טַעְמָא – דְּלָא אַלִּימָא טוּמְאַת הַתְּהוֹם לְמִיסְתַּר.

Rav Hamnuna says: In the case of **a nazirite and one performing** the ritual of **the Paschal** offering **who walked by a grave in the depths,** i.e., an unknown grave, **on their seventh** day of **their** purification, i.e., seven days after they were sprinkled with the purification waters after having contracted ritual impurity imparted by a corpse, **they are pure.** If the nazirite shaved for his impurity and completed his naziriteship in purity or if the one performing the ritual of the Paschal offering sacrificed his offering, then when he eventually discovers the impurity, it is considered as though he were pure all along. **What is the reason** for this lenient ruling? It is **because the ritual impurity** imparted by a grave **in the depths is not strong** enough **to negate** their actions, i.e., the nazirite offerings or the Paschal offering.

מְתִיב רָבָא: יָרַד לִיטָּהֵר מִטּוּמְאַת הַמֵּת – טָמֵא, שֶׁחֶזְקַת טָמֵא – טָמֵא, שֶׁחֶזְקַת טָהוֹר – טָהוֹר!

Rava raised an objection to this ruling from the statement of the mishna that if there is one whose impurity imparted by a grave in the depths is uncertain and he **descended to purify himself from the ritual impurity** imparted by **a corpse,** he is **impure,** as a person or item **that has the presumptive status of impurity** remains **impure, and** one that has **the presumptive status of purity** remains **pure.** Here too, the nazirite and the one performing the ritual of the Paschal offering people had not completed their purification at the time, as the seventh day following their being sprinkled had not ended. As their presumptive status is impure, they are retroactively rendered impure, even by an impurity of the depths.

אֲמַר לֵיהּ: מוֹדֵינָא לָךְ בְּנָזִיר, שֶׁמְּחוּסַּר תִּגְלַחַת.

Rav Hamnuna **said to** Rava: **I agree with you with regard to a nazirite** who descended to purify himself and **who is lacking** the act of **shaving.**[N] He has yet to shave his head for his impurity and is therefore not completely pure. Consequently, he follows his prior presumptive status of impurity.

אֲמַר לֵיהּ רָבָא: אַף אֲנָא מוֹדֵינָא לָךְ בְּעוֹשֵׂה פֶסַח, דְּלָא מְחוּסָּר וְלָא כְּלוּם. אֲמַר לֵיהּ אַבַּיֵי: וְהָא מְחוּסַּר הֶעֱרֵב שֶׁמֶשׁ! אֲמַר לֵיהּ: שִׁמְשָׁא מִמֵּילָא עָרְבָא.

Rava said to him: I, too, agree with you with regard to one performing the ritual of **the Paschal offering**[H] that he is pure, **as he is not lacking anything.** Since he does not have to perform any action on his body before he can bring an offering, one can say that he already has a presumptive status of purity on the seventh day. **Abaye said to him: But** he **is** still **lacking sunset,**[B] i.e., he is not fully pure until the sun sets on the seventh day. Rava **said to** Abaye: **The sun sets by itself,** and therefore this cannot be seen as a deficiency involving an action.

וְאַף אַבַּיֵי הֲדַר בֵּיהּ. דְּתַנְיָא:

The Gemara comments: **And even Abaye** accepted Rava's answer and **retracted, as** can be seen from that which **is taught** in a *baraita*. By Torah law, a woman who gives birth to a boy is ritually impure for seven days, and a woman who gives birth to a girl is impure for fourteen days. At that point, the woman immerses in a ritual bath and is purified. Any blood that emerges from the woman during her days of purity, i.e., for forty days following the birth of a male and eighty days following the birth of a female, does not render her impure. She cannot bring the offering brought by a woman who has given birth or miscarried until she has immersed at the end of these days (see Leviticus, chapter 12). The *baraita* discusses a case where a woman who had given birth became pregnant and miscarried before she had brought her offering for the first birth.

יוֹם מְלֹאת – תָּבִיא, תּוֹךְ מְלֹאת – לֹא תָּבִיא.

The *baraita* teaches: If a woman miscarried on **the day of the fulfillment** of her purity, on the eighty-first day after a female, **she must bring**[H] a separate offering for the miscarried fetus, as she was obligated to bring one offering before her miscarriage. If she miscarried **during the fulfillment,** i.e., before the conclusion of the eighty days for the birth of a daughter, **she does not bring**[H] two offerings but only one, just as is the *halakha* in the case of one who gives birth to twins.

NOTES

I agree with you with regard to a nazirite who is lacking shaving – מוֹדֵינָא לָךְ בְּנָזִיר שֶׁמְּחוּסַּר תִּגְלַחַת: Rav Hamnuna points out that this is the case mentioned in the mishna, when it refers to a nazirite who descended to immerse himself for his impurity (*Tosafot*).

HALAKHA

I…agree with you with regard to one performing the Paschal offering – מוֹדֵינָא לָךְ בְּעוֹשֵׂה פֶסַח: With regard to one who contracted impurity imparted by a corpse, received the sprinkling on the third and seventh days, performed the ritual of the Paschal offering, and then later discovered that on the seventh day he was rendered impure by an impurity of the depths, he is not obligated in the offering of the second *Pesaḥ*. However, if he was rendered impure on the sixth day or earlier, he must bring the second *Pesaḥ*. This is because one who has the presumptive status of purity remains pure until proven otherwise, while one who has the status of impurity remains impure until proven otherwise. The Ra'avad writes that if one was rendered impure on the seventh day before the sprinkling, he is obligated in the second *Pesaḥ*, as there was an action that had yet to be performed (Rambam *Sefer Korbanot, Hilkhot Korban Pesaḥ* 6:13).

On the day of the fulfillment she must bring, etc. – יוֹם מְלֹאת תָּבִיא וכו׳: In the case of a woman who gave birth or miscarried many times in succession, if these events were within the days of purity of each other, she brings only one offering for all of them. Accordingly, if she gave birth to a female, any miscarriages that occur within eighty days of each birth or miscarriage are all considered a single birth. If she miscarried from the eighty-first day onward, she is obligated to bring a separate offering (Rambam *Sefer Korbanot, Hilkhot Meḥusrei Kappara* 1:8).

During the fulfillment she does not bring – תּוֹךְ מְלֹאת לֹא תָּבִיא: If a woman who gave birth brought her offering during her days of purity, she has not fulfilled her obligation (Rambam). Some commentaries are puzzled by this ruling, as an impure person is generally allowed to send his offerings with one who is pure (Ra'avad). One explanation is that the Rambam derives this *halakha* from the verse: "And when the days of her purity are fulfilled" (Leviticus 12:6), which indicates that she brings the offering only upon the completion of her days of purity, but not earlier (*Kesef Mishne*). The wording of the *baraita* suggests a similar conclusion (Rambam *Sefer Korbanot, Hilkhot Meḥusrei Kappara* 1:5).

BACKGROUND

Sunset – הֶעֱרֵב שֶׁמֶשׁ: The concept of sunset is relevant for the *halakhot* of ritual impurity. If an impure person immersed himself in a ritual bath, he remains impure with regard to the eating of *teruma* until the sun has set and the stars are visible on the evening following his immersion. After the stars are visible he may eat *teruma*. However, certain types of ritually impure people who have already immersed themselves in a ritual bath are not allowed to enter the Temple or to come into contact with sacrificial offerings until they bring expiatory offerings on the day after their immersion.

HALAKHA

One who finds a corpse for the first time – הַמּוֹצֵא מֵת בַּתְּחִילָּה: With regard to one who was digging and found a corpse buried in the proper manner, he removes it and the surrounding earth, i.e., the loose dirt underneath it, and up to three fingerbreadths of uncultivated earth. Similarly, if he discovers two bodies, he removes both of them, and the entire field is assumed to be pure (Rambam *Sefer Tahara*, *Hilkhot Tumat Met* 9:3).

He found three, etc. – מָצָא שְׁלֹשָׁה וכו׳: The Rambam states that if three bodies were found in the usual position of burial, and each was separated from the next by no fewer than four cubits and no more than eight, one must take into account the possibility that he has encountered a graveyard, and he must therefore examine twenty cubits from the outermost corpse. Some claim that he measures twenty cubits from the first grave, as stated in tractate *Bava Batra* 102a (Ra'avad). Others state that the Rambam probably had a different version of that Gemara (Rambam *Sefer Tahara*, *Hilkhot Tumat Met* 9:3 and *Kesef Mishne* there).

BACKGROUND

Graveyard – שְׁכוּנַת קְבָרוֹת:

Burial cave from Hasmonean era discovered near Modi'in, Israel

יָכוֹל לֹא תָּבִיא עַל לֵידָה שֶׁלִּפְנֵי מְלֹאת, אֲבָל תָּבִיא עַל לֵידָה שֶׁלְּאַחַר מְלֹאת, וְתִיפָּטֵר מִשְּׁתֵּיהֶן,

The *baraita* continues: One **might** have thought that **she should not bring** an offering **for her childbirth,** i.e., miscarriage, **that** occurred **before the fulfillment** of the days of her purity **but she should bring for her childbirth that** occurred **after** its **completion.** In other words, if she had yet another miscarriage, after the days of her purity for her initial birth but within the eighty days of purity following her first miscarriage, she should bring an extra offering **and** thereby **discharge both** obligations, of her birth and her final miscarriage.

תַּלְמוּד לוֹמַר ״וּבִמְלֹאת יְמֵי טָהֳרָה״. בְּיוֹם מְלֹאת – תָּבִיא, תּוֹךְ מְלֹאת – לֹא תָּבִיא.

Therefore, to counteract this possibility, **the verse states: "And when the days of her purity are fulfilled…** she shall bring" (Leviticus 12:6). This teaches that it is only if she miscarried **on the day of the fulfillment** itself that **she must bring** an offering for a miscarriage, but if she miscarried **before the fulfillment** of the days of her purity of the earlier miscarriage, even if this occurred more than eighty days after the first birth, **she does not bring** another offering.

אָמַר רַב כָּהֲנָא: שָׁאנֵי הָכָא דִּמְחַסְּרָא קׇרְבָּן, הָתָם נָמֵי מְחַסְּרָא הֶעֱרֵב שֶׁמֶשׁ!

Rav Kahana said in explanation: **Here it is different. The** reason why she does not bring an offering for a miscarriage during her days of purity is **that she lacks** the possibility of bringing her **offering.** Since she cannot bring her offering until the end of her term of purity, she cannot incur another obligation during this period, no matter how many births occur within eighty days of the previous one. However, this leads Rav Kahana to ask: **There too,** if she had a miscarriage on the day of the completion of her term, she cannot bring her offering either, as she **lacks sunset.**[N] Why, then, must she bring an additional offering?

אָמַר לֵיהּ אַבָּיֵי: שִׁמְשָׁא מִמֵּילָא עָרְבָא.

Abaye said to Rav Kahana: **The sun sets by itself**[N] and is not considered a deficiency with regard to her purity. This discussion shows that Abaye accepted Rava's reasoning, as he submitted the same argument himself in a different context.

מתני׳ הַמּוֹצֵא מֵת בַּתְּחִילָּה, מוּשְׁכָּב כְּדַרְכּוֹ – נוֹטְלוֹ וְאֶת תְּפוּסָתוֹ,

MISHNA One who finds a corpse[N] **for the first time,**[H] i.e., he discovers a single corpse in a place that was not previously established as a cemetery, if the corpse is **lying in the usual manner** of Jewish burial, **he removes it**[N] from there **and** also **its surrounding** earth. It is assumed that this corpse was buried there alone. There is no concern that this area is a cemetery and therefore the corpse may not be moved, nor does one take into account the possibility that another corpse may be buried in the vicinity.

שְׁנַיִם – נוֹטְלָן וְאֶת תְּפוּסָתָן. מָצָא שְׁלֹשָׁה, אִם יֵשׁ בֵּין זֶה לְזֶה מֵאַרְבַּע אַמּוֹת וְעַד שְׁמוֹנֶה – הֲרֵי זוֹ שְׁכוּנַת קְבָרוֹת.

Similarly, if he found **two** corpses, **he removes them and their surrounding** earth. In a case where he **found three**[H] corpses, **if there is** a space **between this** corpse **and that** corpse **of four to eight cubits,** in a standard design, **this is a graveyard.**[NB] There is a concern that this might be an ancient cemetery.

NOTES

There too she lacks sunset – הָתָם נָמֵי מְחַסְּרָא הֶעֱרֵב שֶׁמֶשׁ: Therefore, she should not be obligated to bring an offering even if she had a miscarriage on the night of the eighty-first day, as she still requires immersion and sunset before she can bring her offering in a state of purity on the following day. The early commentaries offer different explanations as to why this woman is lacking sunset, which applies to one who has immersed in a ritual bath. *Tosafot* explain that the *baraita*, by not specifying to the contrary, includes the case of a woman who did not immerse after fourteen days, and is immersing only before she brings her offerings. Other commentaries, based upon tractate *Ḥagiga* (21a), claim that she must immerse before bringing her offerings in any case, so that she can partake of the offerings (*Shita Mekubbetzet*; Rosh).

The sun sets by itself – שִׁמְשָׁא מִמֵּילָא עָרְבָא: Her forthcoming immersion is not cited as a factor that prevents her from sacrificing the offering, as a ritual bath is always available, and therefore this is not considered a bodily deficiency. The novelty is that even sunset, which is not dependent upon her, is not a deficiency either, as it is a natural event.

One who finds a corpse – הַמּוֹצֵא מֵת: This mishna is not connected to the subject matter of the chapter, or even that of the tractate as a whole. Rather, this mishna and the subsequent one, each of which also appears elsewhere, are cited because they share the key phrase: As there is a basis for anticipating the matter. These diverse topics are linked by this recurring expression (Rabbi Ovadya Bartenura).

He removes it – נוֹטְלוֹ: Although a corpse acquires its place by rabbinic decree, i.e., it is not moved from its burial site, it is assumed that this corpse was buried here on a temporary basis, with the intention of removing it at a later stage. For this reason, it may be transferred to a cemetery, and the site of the temporary burial may be used afterward without concern for impurity.

Graveyard – שְׁכוּנַת קְבָרוֹת: In this scenario it is prohibited to remove the bodies, as they were initially buried with the aim of leaving them in that place permanently. One must also examine the surrounding areas in case the graveyard extends farther, or if a similar burial cave is in close vicinity.

בּוֹדֵק הֵימֶנּוּ וּלְהַלָּן עֶשְׂרִים אַמָּה, מָצָא אֶחָד בְּסוֹף עֶשְׂרִים אַמָּה – בּוֹדֵק הֵימֶנּוּ וּלְהַלָּן עֶשְׂרִים אַמָּה, שֶׁרַגְלַיִם לַדָּבָר, שֶׁאִילּוּ תְּחִילָּה מְצָאוֹ – נוֹטְלוֹ וְאֶת תְּפוּסָתוֹ.

One must therefore **examine from that spot**[NH] **outward for twenty cubits.**[N] If one **finds** another corpse **at the end of twenty cubits,** he **examines** from that spot **outward twenty cubits, as there is a basis for** anticipating **the matter.** It is likely that he has stumbled upon an ancient gravesite. He is not permitted to relocate the corpses, despite the fact **that if he had found** the single corpse by itself **at first**[N] he could have **removed it and its surrounding** earth.

גמ׳ אָמַר רַב יְהוּדָה: מָצָא – פְּרָט לְמָצוּי, מֵת – פְּרָט לְהָרוּג, מוּשְׁכָּב – פְּרָט לְיוֹשֵׁב, כְּדַרְכּוֹ – פְּרָט לְשֶׁרֹאשׁוֹ מוּנָּח בֵּין יְרֵכוֹתָיו.

GEMARA **Rav Yehuda said** the following inferences from the mishna: The phrase: He **found, excludes** a corpse **that** already had **been found.**[NH] If it was known that there was one corpse buried in a certain place, the discovery of two previously unknown corpses does not raise the concern that perhaps it is a forgotten graveyard. Similarly, the term **corpse** [*met*] **excludes a killed** [*harug*] person. Even if there were three corpses found, if there are signs that these people were killed, the area is not assumed to be a graveyard, as they may have been buried where they were found killed. Likewise, the term **lying excludes a sitting** person,[H] as Jews were not generally buried in a seated position. The phrase: **In the** usual **manner, excludes** one **whose head was placed between his thighs,**[B] as that is not the way Jews are buried.

תָּנֵי עוּלָּא בַּר חֲנִינָא: מֵת שֶׁחָסֵר – אֵין לוֹ תְּפוּסָה, וְלֹא שְׁכוּנַת קְבָרוֹת. וְכׇל הָנֵי, מַאי טַעְמָא לָא? אָמְרִינַן דִּילְמָא גּוֹי הוּא.

Ulla bar Ḥanina taught a *baraita* (*Tosefta, Oholot* 16:2): **A corpse that is lacking**[NH] a part of his body indispensable to life **has no** *halakha* of **surrounding** earth, i.e., there is no need to remove the nearby earth along with the corpse. **Nor** does it have the *halakha* of **a graveyard,** i.e., it does not join with two other corpses to establish this site as a cemetery. The Gemara asks: **And** with regard to **all these** listed above, i.e., a corpse that was buried in a sitting position or with its head between its thighs, **what is the reason** that they are **not** considered part of a graveyard? The Gemara answers: **We say** that **perhaps** the deceased **was a gentile,**[H] as Jews are not usually buried in these ways.

NOTES

Examine from that spot – בּוֹדֵק הֵימֶנּוּ: Some commentaries state that one examines twenty cubits from the last grave (Rambam). Others maintain that it refers to the first grave, based on the Gemara in *Bava Batra* (102a), which explains that the concern is that there may be another burial cave adjacent to it (Ra'avad). The interpretation of the Ra'avad fits the Gemara in *Bava Batra*, at least according to the standard version of the Gemara there (*Kesef Mishne*; see Meiri).

Twenty cubits – עֶשְׂרִים אַמָּה: The commentaries explain, based on the Gemara in *Bava Batra* (102a), that if these caves were six by eight cubits, then in accordance with the opinion of Rabbi Shimon, one must examine the length of two caves, sixteen cubits, and the intervening courtyard of six cubits. The amount stated here is less than that because it might be a smaller cave for children or stillborn babies.

The Rabbis, however, claim that a cave measures four by six cubits, which means that the two caves and the courtyard amount to only eighteen cubits. According to their opinion, there is a concern that one cave might have been positioned at a diagonal from the other, and therefore the extra space for the diagonal must be taken into account. The entire area of the twenty cubits must be searched, as the second cave might be alongside the other, which would mean that the space between the grave is less than twenty cubits.

As there is a basis for anticipating the matter, that if he had found the single body by itself at first, etc. – שֶׁרַגְלַיִם לַדָּבָר שֶׁאִילּוּ תְּחִילָּה כְּצָאוֹ וכו׳: If one found only a single body in his search of those twenty cubits, it may be moved, in accordance with the *halakha* of an isolated corpse. In the case in the mishna, however, since the twenty cubits were examined due to the discovery of three graves, there is a basis to anticipate that there was an ancient cemetery there. Consequently, further examination is required.

He found, excludes a corpse that had been found – מָצָא, פְּרָט לְמָצוּי: Most commentaries maintain that this refers to the second *halakha* of the mishna: If he found three…this is a graveyard, and explain that if one body was known to be buried there, it is permitted to move all three. The problem with this explanation is that it is unclear why the first body itself should be moved, as a corpse acquires the place of its burial. Therefore, some commentaries add that it was also known that this body was interred there only on a temporary basis, which is why one may move it (Rabbi Avraham min HaHar; Meiri; see Commentary on *Nazir*).

Others state that the Gemara is referring to the first *halakha* of the mishna: One who finds a corpse must remove it and its surrounding earth. It is from this statement that Rav Yehuda inferred that one may remove it only if he discovered the body, but if its presence was known it is prohibited to remove it (*Tosafot*; *Shita Mekubbetzet*). An entirely different interpretation is that the phrase: Excluding one that had been found, is referring to a corpse discovered that was not buried at all lying in a field (Rambam). According to this explanation, the exclusion is referring to the entire mishna, as one is permitted to remove this body without taking its surrounding earth. Additionally, three corpses of this kind would not constitute a graveyard.

A corpse that is lacking – מֵת שֶׁחָסֵר: *Tosafot* inquire into the reason for this *halakha* and conclude that it is apparently a *halakha* learned by tradition, for which no justification is provided. The *Tosefta* in tractate *Oholot* defines the word: Lacking, in this context as missing a part whose absence would cause the death of a living person.

HALAKHA

Examine from that spot, etc. – בּוֹדֵק הֵימֶנּוּ וכו׳: If one finds three corpses lying in the usual manner for burial, which necessitates the examination of twenty cubits, and he subsequently finds another body at the end of twenty cubits, he must check a further twenty cubits. This is because there is a basis to anticipate that this is a graveyard (Rambam *Sefer Tahara, Hilkhot Tumat Met* 9:3).

Excludes a corpse that had been found – פְּרָט לְמָצוּי: The *halakhot* of a graveyard and the surrounding earth do not apply to corpses found lying in an open field. One merely collects all of the bones to bury elsewhere, and the rest of the area is pure (Rambam *Sefer Tahara, Hilkhot Tumat Met* 9:5).

Excludes a killed person…excludes a sitting person – פְּרָט לְהָרוּג...פְּרָט לְיוֹשֵׁב: If one was digging and discovered a corpse of one who was killed, or a corpse buried in a sitting position or with its head between its thighs, not in the manner of Jewish burial, then he need not be concerned that this might be a cemetery, even if the body was one of three within the proper distance for a gravesite. Instead, he removes the bodies and their surrounding earth, and the rest of the field remains pure (Rambam *Sefer Tahara, Hilkhot Tumat Met* 9:1; 3).

A corpse that is lacking – מֵת שֶׁחָסֵר: If a body is missing a vital limb, the *halakhot* of the surrounding earth and a graveyard do not apply to it, as stated in the *Tosefta* in tractate *Oholot* (Rambam *Sefer Tahara, Hilkhot Tumat Met* 9:5).

Perhaps he was a gentile – דִּילְמָא גּוֹי הוּא: The ritual impurity of graves does not apply to gentiles, as the impurity of their corpses is not imparted in a tent. Consequently, one who touches their graves remains pure, unless he came into contact with or carried the corpse itself. This *halakha* is indicated by the Gemara here (Rambam *Sefer Tahara, Hilkhot Tumat Met* 9:4 and *Kesef Mishne* there).

BACKGROUND

Whose head…between his thighs – רֹאשׁוֹ...בֵּין יְרֵכוֹתָיו: In the Jewish tradition, it is customary for the body to be buried face up in the grave. A burial that differed from the custom in any manner was considered disgraceful and termed the burial of a donkey. In later generations, the custom developed for the grave to be pointing in a specific direction determined by local custom. By contrast, many graves have been found in Eretz Yisrael dating from prehistoric times or from the later Canaanite period in which the body was buried sitting upright or with the head situated between the thighs. One can safely assume that a corpse buried in this fashion is not the body of a Jew.

מָצָא שְׁנַיִם, רֹאשׁוֹ שֶׁל זֶה בְּצַד מַרְגְּלוֹתָיו שֶׁל זֶה, וְרֹאשׁוֹ שֶׁל זֶה בְּצַד מַרְגְּלוֹתָיו שֶׁל זֶה – אֵין לָהֶן תְּפוּסָה, וְלֹא שְׁכוּנַת קְבָרוֹת. מָצָא שְׁלֹשָׁה, הָאֶחָד יָדוּעַ וּשְׁנַיִם תְּחִילָּה, אוֹ שְׁנַיִם תְּחִילָּה וּשְׁנַיִם יְדוּעִים – אֵין לָהֶם תְּפוּסָה, וְאֵין לָהֶם שְׁכוּנַת קְבָרוֹת.

The *baraita* further states: If one **found two** corpses, with **the head of this one**[H] **by the feet of that one and the head of that** one **by the feet of this one, they do not have** the *halakha* of **surrounding earth, nor** do they have the *halakha* of **a graveyard.** This is not the way Jews are buried, as corpses in a Jewish cemetery always face the same direction. If one **found three** corpses, **one** of which was previously **known,**[H] **while** the other **two** were found **for the first** time now, **or** if one found **two for the first** time **and two** that were **known, they do not have** the *halakha* of **surrounding earth,**[N] **and** they also **do not have** the *halakha* of **a graveyard.** One does not view these corpses as connected.

מַעֲשֶׂה בְּרַבִּי יְשֵׁבָב שֶׁבָּדַק וּמָצָא שְׁנַיִם יְדוּעִין וְאֶחָד תְּחִילָּה, וּבִיקֵּשׁ לַעֲשׂוֹתָן שְׁכוּנַת קְבָרוֹת. אָמַר לוֹ רַבִּי עֲקִיבָא: כׇּל שֶׁיָּגַעְתָּ – לָרִיק יָגַעְתָּ, לֹא אָמְרוּ שְׁכוּנַת קְבָרוֹת אֶלָּא לִשְׁלֹשָׁה יְדוּעִין, אוֹ לִשְׁלֹשָׁה תְּחִילָּה.

The *baraita* relates: **An incident** occurred **involving Rabbi Yeshevav,**[P] **who examined and found two known** corpses **and one** corpse discovered **for the first** time, **and he wished to deem** the three corpses **a graveyard. Rabbi Akiva said to him: All your toil is in vain. They said** it is **a graveyard only**[N] **in** a case **of three known** corpses buried in one spot **or three** corpses found **for the first** time. However, if some were known and others were discovered for the first time, one does not combine them.

״נוֹטְלָן וְאֶת תְּפוּסָתָן״. הֵיכִי דָּמֵי תְּפוּסָה? אָמַר רַב יְהוּדָה: אָמַר קְרָא ״וּנְשָׂאתַנִי מִמִּצְרַיִם״ – טוֹל עִמִּי.

§ The mishna taught that **he removes them and their surrounding earth.** The Gemara asks: **What are the circumstances** of **surrounding earth? Rav Yehuda said: The verse states** with regard to Jacob's instruction to Joseph to transfer his remains to Eretz Yisrael: **"You shall carry me out from Egypt"** (Genesis 47:30), which indicates: **Take** some earth out from Egypt **with me,** i.e., take the earth that is near the corpse.

וְכַמָּה שִׁיעוּר תְּפוּסָה? פֵּירֵשׁ רַבִּי אֶלְעָזָר (בְּרַבִּי צָדוֹק): נוֹטֵל עֲפַר תִּיחוּחַ, וְחוֹפֵר בַּבְּתוּלָה שָׁלֹשׁ אֶצְבָּעוֹת.

The Gemara further asks: **And what is the measure of surrounding earth? Rabbi Elazar, son of Rabbi Tzadok, explained: One takes loose dirt** from near the corpse, as it is assumed it has been loosened by the blood and moisture from the corpse, **and digs virgin,** uncultivated, ground to a depth of **three fingerbreadths,** in case this earth has absorbed the blood.

מֵיתִיבֵי: וְכַמָּה שִׁיעוּר תְּפוּסָה? פֵּירֵשׁ רַבִּי אֶלְעָזָר בְּרַבִּי צָדוֹק: נוֹטֵל אֶת הַקִּיסְמִין וְאֶת הַקְּסָסוֹת,

The Gemara **raises an objection** to this ruling from a different *baraita*: **And what is the measure of surrounding earth? Rabbi Elazar, son of Rabbi Tzadok, explained: One takes wood chips**[N] found nearby, which might have been part of the coffin, **and lumps** of earth[N] that might have absorbed the blood and moisture from a corpse.

וְזוֹרֵק אֶת הַוַּדָּאִין, וּמַנִּיחַ אֶת הַסְּפֵיקוֹת, וְהַשְּׁאָר מִצְטָרֵף לְרוֹב בִּנְיָנוֹ שֶׁל מֵת, וּלְרוֹבַע עֲצָמוֹת, לִמְלֹא תַרְוָד רָקָב!

And he discards that which is **certainly** not from the corpse, e.g., stones. And **he sets aside the** items with regard to which it is **uncertain**[N] if they have a connection with the corpse. **And the rest,** i.e., anything that is apparently from the corpse, **combine to** reach the amount **of the majority of the structure of a corpse, or of a quarter-*kav* of bones,** or **of a full ladle of dust**[N] from a corpse. The remains of a corpse impart ritual impurity in a tent only if they meet one of those three qualifications. Anything which is apparently the remains of the corpse is considered dust of a corpse with regard to this *halakha*. In any event, it is clear that this *baraita* presents a different definition of surrounding earth.

NOTES

If one found three…they do not have the *halakha* of surrounding earth – מָצָא שְׁלֹשָׁה...אֵין לָהֶם תְּפוּסָה: This *halakha* is puzzling, as the *baraita* is referring to Jewish corpses. Why should the *halakha* of surrounding earth not apply to these corpses? Some commentaries cite an alternative version of the text, which states: They have surrounding earth and they do not have a graveyard. This follows the ruling of the *Tosefta*.

They said a graveyard only, etc. – לֹא אָמְרוּ שְׁכוּנַת קְבָרוֹת אֶלָּא וכו׳: Some commentaries explain that there is a tradition to this effect (Commentary on *Nazir*; *Tosafot*, citing Rashbam). Others maintain that if the place was recently designed to serve as a cemetery, all the corpses would be known, and if it was an ancient cemetery none of them would have been known. Since only two of the corpses are known or were discovered for the first time, they are simply considered two corpses found together, not part of a graveyard. As for the other corpses, it is possible that by chance they were buried in the same spot where others were interred.

One takes wood chips – נוֹטֵל אֶת הַקִּסְמִין: One explanation is that these splinters might be part of a rotted coffin. Some commentaries maintain that they might come from fragrant pieces of wood that were sometimes placed on graves (see *Tosafot* and Commentary on *Nazir*).

Lumps of earth – קְסָסוֹת: The concern is that these lumps might have been formed by the earth absorbing blood from the corpse (Commentary on *Nazir*). Alternatively, this term is referring to a worn-out piece of clothing or to spices placed alongside a corpse (*Tosafot*).

And he sets aside the uncertain – וּמַנִּיחַ אֶת הַסְּפֵיקוֹת: However, one must set them aside in a protected place (Commentary on *Nazir*) so that others do not contract uncertain impurity (*Tosafot*). Some commentaries maintain that one may discard the aforementioned items that certainly did not absorb any part of the blood, e.g., wood chips, whereas one may leave the uncertain items together with the body in the fresh grave (Meiri; see Gra).

A full ladle of dust – מְלֹא תַרְוָד רָקָב: The commentaries are puzzled by this ruling, as it was taught earlier (51a) that the *halakha* of a ladleful of dust applies only to a marble coffin, which is clearly not the case here. The Commentary on *Nazir* answers that the prior Gemara is referring to a single body buried in a wooden coffin, whereas here the Gemara is dealing with the question of whether the dust of one corpse can combine with that of another.

Others claim that this *halakha* refers to a marble coffin that broke, revealing dirt underneath it. In this situation, it is uncertain if the dirt is impure, while the remaining dust inside the marble coffin is considered a definite ladleful of dust from a corpse (Rosh). Yet others contend that there is no need to explain this case in such a contrived manner, as one can simply say that the Gemara here follows an alternative opinion with regard to the *halakha* of a ladleful of dust, one that is not accepted as *halakha* (Meiri; see Gra).

PERSONALITIES

Rabbi Yeshevav – רַבִּי יְשֵׁבָב: Rabbi Yeshevav was a third-generation *tanna* and scribe who was a disciple of Rabbi Yehoshua and a contemporary of Rabbi Akiva. He was exceedingly generous, to the extent that Rabbi Akiva criticized him for giving too much of his money to charity. Rabbi Yeshevav was one of the ten martyrs who were killed by the Romans during the bar Kokheva rebellion, and according to tradition, in his last message the ninety-year-old Sage told his disciples to support each other and uphold justice and peace. He was then thrown to the dogs and was denied burial (*Midrash Eleh Ezkera*).

HALAKHA

The head of this one, etc. – רֹאשׁוֹ שֶׁל זֶה וכו׳: If bodies were found lying one atop the other or in a row, the surrounding earth is removed, but one need not be concerned that a graveyard has been discovered (Rambam *Sefer Tahara*, *Hilkhot Tumat Met* 9:1).

If one found three, one of which was known, etc. – מָצָא שְׁלֹשָׁה, הָאֶחָד יָדוּעַ וכו׳: If one discovered two corpses, and one more corpse whose presence was previously known, the *halakha* of surrounding earth does apply to them, but the *halakha* of a graveyard does not apply (Rambam). This is in accordance with the ruling of Rabbi Akiva that all three corpses must have been previously unknown for the *halakha* of a graveyard to go into effect. The Rambam's text of the Gemara evidently read: They have surrounding earth (*Kesef Mishne*). The Rambam further indicates that if all three were known, the *halakha* of a graveyard does not apply, in accordance with the *Tosefta* rather than with the Gemara here (Rambam *Sefer Tahara*, *Hilkhot Tumat Met* 9:6).

הוּא דְּאָמַר כִּי הַאי תַּנָּא, דְּתַנְיָא: וְכַמָּה שִׁיעוּר תְּפוּסָה? אָמַר רַבִּי יוֹחָנָן מִשּׁוּם בֶּן עַזַּאי: נוֹטֵל עָפָר תִּיחוּחַ וְחוֹפֵר בִּבְתוּלָה שָׁלֹשׁ אֶצְבָּעוֹת.

The Gemara answers: With regard to the first statement of Rabbi Elazar, it was **he who said in accordance with** the opinion of **that** *tanna*, ben Azzai, **as it is taught** in a *baraita*: **And how much is the measure of surrounding** earth? **Rabbi Yoḥanan says in the name of ben Azzai: One takes loose earth**[H] **and digs virgin** ground to a depth of **three fingerbreadths.**

״בּוֹדֵק הֵימֶנּוּ״.

§ The mishna taught that one must **examine** the ground for up to twenty cubits **from that** spot where a corpse was found.

HALAKHA

One takes loose earth, etc. – נוֹטֵל עָפָר תִּיחוּחַ וכו׳: One who finds a corpse must take all the loose earth from beneath it and dig a further three fingerbreadths into the uncultivated ground. All this dirt is called the surrounding earth of a corpse, in accordance with the opinion of Rabbi Yoḥanan in the name of ben Azzai (Rambam *Sefer Tahara, Hilkhot Tumat Met* 9:1).

Perek **IX**
Daf **65** Amud **b**

אֲמַר רָבָא: בָּדַק וּפִנָּה, בָּדַק פִּנָּה, בָּדַק וְאַשְׁכַּח – לָא הַאי מְפַנֵּי לֵיהּ גַּבֵּי הָנָךְ תְּרֵי, וְלָא הָנֵי תְּרֵי לְגַבֵּי הַאי חַד.

Rava said: With regard to one who **examined,** found a corpse, **and removed** it from its place, and again **examined** nearby, found another corpse, **and removed** it from its place as well, if he **examined** yet again **and discovered** a third corpse, **he does not move this** third one **alongside these two** he has already moved, as he now knows that this was a graveyard and the corpses were buried there intentionally. **And he does not** return **these two alongside this one** either, as he is not obligated to restore the corpses to their prior locations after they have been reburied.

אִיכָּא דְּאָמְרִי, אֲמַר רָבָא: כֵּיוָן שֶׁנִּתְּנָה רְשׁוּת לְפַנּוֹת – מְפַנֶּה לְהוֹן. וְלִישַׁוְינְהוּ שְׁכוּנַת קְבָרוֹת! אֲמַר רֵישׁ לָקִישׁ: עִילָּא מָצְאוּ וְטִיהֲרוּ אֶרֶץ יִשְׂרָאֵל.

There are those **who say** that **Rava said: Since permission was granted to move** the first and second corpses, one may therefore **move them** all, including the third one. The Gemara asks: **And let us deem them** part of **a graveyard.** Since three corpses were found buried together, there might be others in the vicinity. **Reish Lakish said: They found a pretext and deemed Eretz Yisrael ritually pure.** Since at that point there was just one corpse, the Sages were lenient and were not concerned about any further impurity. The Sages wished to avoid uncertain impurity because people were careful to observe the *halakhot* of ritual purity in Eretz Yisrael, and additional cases of uncertain impurity would be complicated to observe.

בָּדַק מֵעֶשְׂרִים אַמָּה וְלֹא מָצָא, מַאי? אָמַר רַב מְנַשְּׁיָא בַּר יִרְמְיָה אָמַר רַב: שְׁכוּנַת קְבָרוֹת. מַאי טַעְמָא? אֲמַר רֵישׁ לָקִישׁ: עִילָּא מָצְאוּ וְטִיהֲרוּ אֶת אֶרֶץ יִשְׂרָאֵל.

The Gemara asks another question: If one **examined twenty cubits** from the location of those corpses **and did not find**[H] anything, **what is the** *halakha*?[N] **Rav Menashya bar Yirmeya says** that **Rav says:** This is **a graveyard.**[N] Those three corpses compose the graveyard and there is no concern for others. The Gemara asks: **What is the reason** for this ruling? Why is there no concern that there might be many more corpses in the surrounding area? Once again **Reish Lakish said: They found a pretext and deemed Eretz Yisrael ritually pure.** Eretz Yisrael is deemed pure in a case of uncertainty.

HALAKHA

If one examined…and did not find – בָּדַק...וְלֹא מָצָא: If one found three corpses and examined twenty cubits around the bodies without finding additional corpses, those twenty cubits are pure, despite the fact that the corpses he discovered formed a graveyard (Rambam *Sefer Tahara, Hilkhot Tumat Met* 9:3, and see Ra'avad and *Kesef Mishne* there).

NOTES

If one examined…and did not find, what is the *halakha* – בָּדַק...וְלֹא מָצָא מַאי: One explanation is that this refers to someone who examined the earth in one direction without finding anything, and the question is whether he can assume that his search in other directions will produce similar results. Other commentaries maintain that the inquiry is whether one must dig into the ground until he reaches uncultivated turf or rock (*Tosafot*). Some are unsatisfied with both of these interpretations, as there is no logical reason why one should not check the other directions just because one search yielded no corpses. Similarly, the Rosh notes that it is already taught elsewhere that digging up earth is an essential part of the investigation. He therefore explains that the question refers to a situation when one examined all sides properly and found no other bodies. The Gemara is asking whether this is an indication that this site was not a cemetery at all, but merely a place where three corpses happened to be interred together (see Commentary on *Nazir* and Meiri).

Graveyard – שְׁכוּנַת קְבָרוֹת: According to most commentaries, this is meant as a leniency, i.e., one does not have to search farther or be concerned that his investigation was inadequate. Reish Lakish's statement with regard to ritual purity in Eretz Yisrael is cited in support of this lenient ruling. Some explain that it is assumed that this was the town's gravesite, and therefore there is no concern about locations on the other sides (Commentary on *Nazir*).

By contrast, the Rosh claims that this is a stringent ruling: Despite the failure to find an additional corpse the site is nevertheless considered a graveyard, from which a corpse may not be moved. He also omits the rest of the passage. Yet others suggest that this refers to a situation where a single corpse was discovered at the end of twenty cubits, and the Gemara's ruling is that this corpse may be relocated, as this is merely a graveyard, not a proper cemetery (*Birkat Rosh*).

מתני׳ כָּל סְפֵק נְגָעִים בַּתְּחִילָּה טָהוֹר – עַד שֶׁלֹּא נִזְקַק לְטוּמְאָה. מִשֶּׁנִּזְקַק לְטוּמְאָה – סְפֵקוֹ טָמֵא.

MISHNA Any case of uncertainty with regard to **leprous sores is initially** deemed **pure**[H] **until it is established** that it is a case **of ritual impurity. Once** it **has been determined** to be a case **of impurity, uncertainty** concerning **it is** deemed **impure.**[H]

גמ׳ מְנָא הָנֵי מִילֵּי? אֲמַר רַב יְהוּדָה אֲמַר רַב: אָמַר קְרָא ״לְטַהֲרוֹ אוֹ לְטַמְּאוֹ״. הוֹאִיל וּפָתַח [בּוֹ] הַכָּתוּב בְּטָהֳרָה תְּחִילָּה. אִי הָכִי, אֲפִילּוּ מִשֶּׁנִּזְקַק לְטוּמְאָה נַמִּי סְפֵקוֹ טָהוֹר!

GEMARA The Gemara asks: **From where are these matters** derived? **Rav Yehuda said** that **Rav said: The verse states:** "This is the law of the plague of leprosy… **to pronounce it pure or to pronounce it impure"** (Leviticus 13:59). **Since the verse opened with purity first,** this teaches that any case of uncertainty concerning leprous sores is deemed pure. The Gemara asks: **If so,** if the *halakha* is based on this verse, then **even once it has been determined**[N] to be a case **of impurity, uncertainty** concerning **it** should be deemed **pure as well,** as this interpretation of the verse should apply to all cases of uncertainty with regard to leprosy.

אֶלָּא, כִּי אִיתְּמַר דְּרַב יְהוּדָה אֲמַר רַב – אַהָא אִיתְּמַר: אִם בַּהֶרֶת קָדְמָה לְשֵׂעָר לָבָן – טָמֵא, וְאִם שֵׂעָר לָבָן קוֹדֵם לְבַהֶרֶת – טָהוֹר. סָפֵק – טָמֵא. וְרַבִּי יְהוֹשֻׁעַ אָמַר: כֵּיהָה.

Rather, when this statement, **that Rav Yehuda** said that **Rav said, was stated, it was stated with regard to the following** dispute in a mishna concerning an uncertain leprous sore (*Nega'im* 4:11): **If** the **snow-white leprous sore** [*baheret*], which is one sign of leprosy, **preceded**[H] the **white hair,** which is another sign, **he is impure.** This *halakha* is stated in the Torah (see Leviticus 13:3). **And if** the **white hair preceded** the ***baheret*** he is **pure,** as this is not considered a sign of impurity. If there is **uncertainty** as to which came first, he is **impure.**[H] **And Rabbi Yehoshua said: *Keiha.***[N]

מַאי כֵּיהָה? אָמַר רַב יְהוּדָה: כֵּיהָה וְטָהוֹר. וְדִילְמָא כֵּיהָה וְטָמֵא? אֲמַר רַב יְהוּדָה אֲמַר רַב: אָמַר קְרָא ״לְטַהֲרוֹ אוֹ לְטַמְּאוֹ״ – הוֹאִיל וּפָתַח בּוֹ הַכָּתוּב בְּטָהֳרָה תְּחִילָּה.

The Gemara asks: **What is** the meaning of ***keiha*****? Rav Yehuda said:** Rabbi Yehoshua **pronounced** the matter **unsolvable and** ruled it is **pure.** The Gemara further asks: **And perhaps** this means that he **pronounced** the matter **unsolvable and** ruled it **is impure? Rav Yehuda said** that **Rav said: The verse states: "To pronounce it pure or to pronounce it impure"** (Leviticus 13:59); **since the verse opened with purity first,** any case of uncertainty concerning leprous sores is deemed pure.

NOTES

If so, even once it has been determined, etc. – אִי הָכִי אֲפִילּוּ מִשֶּׁנִּזְקַק וכו׳: This proves that the verse cited by the Gemara does not serve as the source for this *halakha*. The simplest explanation for this *halakha* is that it is based on the principle of a presumptive status: As long as one has a particular status, this status continues until it is definitively changed. The fact that the *halakha* of this mishna is based upon this principle concerning presumptive status connects it to the previous mishna, which also invokes this principle by employing the phrase: There is a basis for anticipating the matter (*Shita Mekubbetzet*).

He said *keiha* – אָמַר כֵּיהָה: Most commentaries explain the word *keiha* as a verb, i.e., an action performed by Rabbi Yehoshua, and have a version of the text that omits the word: Said. Various interpretations have been offered for the meaning of this term. Early commentaries read the word as *kiha*, with the letter *kuf*, as opposed to *kaf* in the text here, meaning that he was persistent in his opinion. Alternatively, following the Aramaic root of the word, it means that he gathered or collected all the evidence he could muster for his ruling (Rabbeinu Azriel, cited in *Shita Mekubbetzet*). Others explain that he could not arrive at a conclusive ruling on the matter, and yet others explain that Rabbi Yehoshua brought his students together to vote on it (*Shita Mekubbetzet*).

Some accept the standard reading of *keiha* and explain it as an expression of rebuke, i.e., he reprimanded his disciples and refused to accept their opinion. A very different explanation is that *keiha* is referring to the affliction itself, and it indicates that the uncertain leprous sore is pure, in accordance with the verse (Leviticus 13:6): "And behold if the plague is dim [*keiha*]…then the priest shall pronounce him pure" (see Rosh).

HALAKHA

Any case of uncertainty with regard to leprous sores is initially deemed pure – כָּל סְפֵק נְגָעִים בַּתְּחִילָּה טָהוֹר: If any uncertain signs of leprous sores appear while the afflicted person is pure, he remains pure. For example, two people came before a priest; one had a possible leprous sore the size of a bean, while the other's sore was larger, the size of a *sela* coin. The priest confined them for a week, at which point they each had a sore the size of a *sela*, and they do not remember who began the week with the smaller sore, so it is unknown whose affliction has spread. In this case, they are both pure due to the uncertainty (Rambam *Sefer Tahara, Hilkhot Tumat Tzara'at* 6:5).

Once it has been determined to be a case of impurity, uncertainty concerning it is deemed impure – מִשֶּׁנִּזְקַק לְטוּמְאָה סְפֵקוֹ טָמֵא: After one has been rendered impure, his uncertain leprous sore is impure, as in the following example: Two people with leprous sores came before a priest, one with a sore the size of a bean and the other with a sore the size of a *sela* coin. The priest confined them for a week, at the end of which he found that both sores had spread, and were now larger than a coin, and he declared them both impure. If they do not remember who began the week with the smaller sore, then even if their sores later decreased in size to that of a *sela*, i.e., one of their sores reverted to its initial size, they both remain impure until both sores decrease to the size of a bean. The fact that they are both impure means that they remain impure in uncertain cases (Rambam *Sefer Tahara, Hilkhot Tzara'at* 5:6).

If the snow-white leprous sore [*baheret*] preceded, etc. – אִם בַּהֶרֶת קָדְמָה וכו׳: The presence of white hair is a definitive sign of impurity only if its development came after the appearance of a *baheret*. If the white hair was present first, the *baheret* is not considered to be a definitive sign of impurity, and the afflicted individual is quarantined for a week (Rambam *Sefer Tahara, Hilkhot Tzara'at* 2:6).

If there is uncertainty, he is impure – סָפֵק טָמֵא: If there is uncertainty as to whether the *baheret* preceded the white hair or vice versa, the afflicted individual is impure. The Rambam writes that he is inclined to rule that this is merely an uncertain impurity (Rambam *Sefer Tahara, Hilkhot Tumat Tzara'at* 2:9).

מתני׳ בְּשִׁבְעָה דְּרָכִים בּוֹדְקִין אֶת הַזָּב עַד שֶׁלֹּא נִזְקַק לְזִיבָה: בְּמַאֲכָל, וּבְמִשְׁתֶּה, בְּמַשָּׂא, וּבִקְפִיצָה, וּבְחוֹלִי, וּבְמַרְאֶה, וּבְהִירְהוּר.

MISHNA This mishna discusses another case that includes the statement: There is a basis to anticipate the matter. **One examines a man who experienced a gonorrhea-like discharge** [*zav*][B] **in seven ways,**[H] **as long as he has not been confirmed** as having **a gonorrhea-like discharge** [*ziva*.] With regard to an individual's second such discharge, before he has been established as a greater *zav*, one examines to see whether there may have been a particular trigger of his discharge. One examines him **with regard to food and with regard to drink,** in case the discharge might have been the result of overeating or excess drinking; **with regard to a burden,** as it might have been caused by the weight of a heavy burden; **and with regard to jumping,** in case he jumped and this led to the discharge; **and with regard to sickness; and with regard to** an arousing **sight; and with regard to** the **thought**[N] of a woman.

מִשֶּׁנִּזְקַק לְזִיבָה – אֵין בּוֹדְקִין אוֹתוֹ. אוֹנְסוֹ, וּסְפֵיקוֹ, וְשִׁכְבַת זַרְעוֹ – טְמֵאִים, שֶׁרַגְלַיִם לְדָּבָר.

Once he has been confirmed as having **a** *ziva*,[H] after two definite discharges of *ziva*, **one** no longer **examines him** in this way, as any discharge is deemed impure. If one experiences three discharges of *ziva*, he is obligated to bring an offering following his purification. Accordingly, **his** discharge that was due to **circumstances beyond his control,** i.e., for one of the seven reasons listed above, **and his** discharge about which it is **uncertain** if it is *ziva*, **and** even **his semen,**[H] which is not usually considered the discharge of a *zav*, **are** all **impure.** Why is this so? It is **because there is a basis for** anticipating **the matter.** Once he has the status of a *zav*, it can be assumed that subsequent discharges are of *ziva* as well.

הַמַּכֶּה אֶת חֲבֵירוֹ וַאֲמָדוּהוּ לְמִיתָה וְהֵיקֵל מִמַּה שֶּׁהָיָה, לְאַחַר מִכָּאן הִכְבִּיד וּמֵת – חַיָּיב, רַבִּי נְחֶמְיָה אוֹמֵר: פָּטוּר, שֶׁרַגְלַיִם לְדָּבָר.

The Sages similarly taught: With regard to **one who strikes another**[H] with heavy blows, **and** doctors **assessed** that **he would die** as a result of the beating, **but his** health **improved from what it was,** so that they then determined that he would not die from his injuries, and **afterward** his condition **worsened and he died,** the one who struck him is **liable** to receive court-imposed capital punishment, as it is assumed that the victim's death was caused by the assault. **Rabbi Neḥemya says:** He is **exempt, because there is a basis for** anticipating **the matter.** Since the victim began to recover during his illness, it is reasonable to assume that his death was caused by a factor other than the assault.

גמ׳ מְנָא הָנֵי מִילֵּי. אָמַר רַבִּי נָתָן: אָמַר קְרָא ״וְהַזָּב אֶת זוֹבוֹ״ – לִרְאִיָּה שְׁלִישִׁית אִיתְּקַשׁ לִנְקֵיבָה.

GEMARA The Gemara asks: **From where are these matters** derived, that one examines a *zav* before he has been confirmed as having a *ziva*, but not after? **Rabbi Natan says** that **the verse states: "And the** ***zav*** **who has an issue** [***zav et zovo***], whether it is a man or a woman" (Leviticus 15:33). This teaches that after two discharges, corresponding to the words *zav* and *zovo*, with regard **to the third sighting,** when one is already a *zav*, the verse **juxtaposes** the *halakha* of a male to that **of a female:** Just as it makes no difference in the case of a female whether her discharge of menstrual blood was triggered by an external factor, as she is ritually impure regardless, once a male *zav* has the status of impurity, one no longer examines him to see if his discharge was triggered by an external factor.

BACKGROUND

Zav – זָב: The laws relating to the severe ritual impurity of a *zav* appear in Leviticus, chapter 15, and in tractate *Zavim*. The *zav* becomes ritually impure as a result of the secretion of a white, pus-like discharge from his penis. A man who experiences a discharge of this kind on one occasion becomes ritually impure for one day, like a man who experienced a seminal emission. If he experiences a second discharge on the same day or the following day, or if he experiences a prolonged initial discharge, he contracts the more severe ritual impurity of a *zav*, which lasts seven days. If he experiences a third discharge within the next twenty-four hours he is obligated to bring an offering as part of his purification process.

In the laws governing secretions of a *zav*, the cause and frequency of the discharge are halakhically significant. Before definitely determining a man as a *zav*, an effort is made to determine if the discharge can be attributed to some other physical or mental condition. Although the Sages distinguished between semen and discharge of a *zav*, this distinction is not always obvious. For this reason, it is possible that a particular discharge might not be that of a *zav* but an unintentional discharge, whose causes are listed in the mishna. A discharge is not considered a sign of a *zav* until it has been established as such by a repeated occurrence.

A *zava* is a woman who experiences a discharge of blood at a time other than her normal menstrual period. The *halakhot* of a *zava* are similar to those of a *zav*.

HALAKHA

One examines a ***zav*** **in seven ways – בְּשִׁבְעָה דְּרָכִים בּוֹדְקִין אֶת הַזָּב:** One who experienced a discharge due to sickness or a similar factor is not impure as a *zav*, as the impurity of a *zav* must not be triggered by an external factor. The Sages said that one examines a *zav* in seven ways: To see whether he overate or he drank too much, or he ate or drank a substance that leads to a seminal emission; or he carried a heavy load; or he jumped from one place to another or had his body jarred in another manner; or he was sick; or he saw a woman and lusted after her; or he thought about sexual intercourse. If any of these happened before his discharge, it is assumed to be the cause, and he is not impure (Rambam *Sefer Korbanot, Hilkhot Meḥusrei Kappara* 2:2).

Once he has been confirmed as having a ***ziva***, **etc. – מִשֶּׁנִּזְקַק לְזִיבָה וכו׳:** A person experiencing a discharge that might be a *ziva* is examined after the first and second times. While he is impure for one day after the first discharge regardless of the cause, he is examined in order to determine whether it should count as the first of a potential three discharges. After the second discharge, the examination will determine whether he is impure for only one day, in the event that it was triggered by an external cause, or for seven days, in the event that it was not. If one who had been determined to be a *zav* impure for seven days experiences a third discharge, one no longer checks to see if it was triggered by an external factor, as he has already been declared a *zav* due to his second discharge, and therefore he is liable to bring an offering for the third discharge regardless (Rambam *Sefer Korbanot, Hilkhot Meḥusrei Kappara* 2:5).

And his semen – וְשִׁכְבַת זַרְעוֹ: The semen of a *zav* is a primary source of ritual impurity by Torah law (Rambam *Sefer Tahara, Hilkhot Metamei Mishkav UMoshav* 1:14).

One who strikes another, etc. – הַמַּכֶּה אֶת חֲבֵירוֹ וכו׳: If one strikes another and doctors assess that the assault will result in the victim's death, but the victim's health improved before it subsequently deteriorated and he died, the one who struck him is liable to receive court-imposed capital punishment. The court does not reassess the case when the victim's health improves, as there is a basis to assume that the beating caused his death. The Rambam rules in this manner because he had a version of the mishna that read: And the Rabbis render him liable as there is a basis for anticipating the matter, and the *halakha* is in accordance with the majority opinion (Rambam *Sefer Nezikim, Hilkhot Rotze'aḥ UShmirat HaNefesh* 4:5).

NOTES

And with regard to thought – וּבְהִירְהוּר: The commentaries explain that the difference between sight and thought is that sight refers to arousal precipitated by visual stimulation, while thought refers to arousal without precipitation by visual stimulation (Rambam; Rosh). Some explain that sight refers to arousal precipitated by actually seeing a man and woman engaged in sexual intercourse (Rabbeinu Todros). Alternatively, sight refers to becoming frightened through seeing something, thereby causing the discharge (Commentary on *Nazir*).

NOTES

For the fourth – ברביעית: If a *zav* has another discharge after he started counting his seven clean days of purification, one does not examine him, as this is also considered *ziva*.

והתניא, רבי אליעזר אומר: בשלישית – בודקין אותו, ברביעית – אין בודקין אותו! אלא באתים קמיפלגי, רבי אליעזר דריש אתים ורבנן לא דרשי אתים.

The Gemara asks: **But isn't it taught** in a mishna (*Zavim* 2:2) that **Rabbi Eliezer says: For the third** discharge **one** still **examines him; for the fourth**[N] discharge **one does not examine him.** Where does the verse allude to the fourth discharge? The Gemara answers: **Rather, they disagree with regard to** instances of the word "*et*," i.e., whether or not the word "*et*" teaches an additional *halakha*, or whether it is written purely for syntactical reasons. **Rabbi Eliezer expounds** instances of the word "*et*," and therefore he counts the phrase "*zav et zovo*" as three words referring to three discharges. **And the Rabbis do not expound** instances of the word "*et*," which means that in their opinion this verse alludes to only two discharges.

"אונסו וספיקו".

§ The mishna taught that **his** discharge that was due to **circumstances beyond his control, and his** discharge about which it is **uncertain** if it is *ziva*, are considered impure.

Perek **IX**
Daf **66** Amud **a**

NOTES

Do not say that it is uncertain whether he saw – לא תימא ספק חזא: One would not declare him a full-fledged *zav* based on an uncertainty of this kind, and he would not be obligated to bring an offering nor to negate the clean days he had counted. Rather, the uncertainty concerns the nature of his discharge (Commentary on *Nazir*). It is stated in the Jerusalem Talmud that Rava's explanation is the correct one.

Uncertain whether it was due to, etc. – ספק מחמת וכו׳: It is indicated in the Jerusalem Talmud that the uncertainty is whether it is a seminal emission or a *ziva*. Others explain that it refers to one who saw both substances, but it is unclear whether he saw the *ziva* and the seminal emission separately, in which case he is impure for seven days, or whether they were mixed together, which would mean that his impurity lasts only one day (*Tosafot*). Some commentaries explain that he saw both of them but is unsure which came first. If the seminal emission occurred first then the *ziva* is discounted, whereas if the *ziva* was first he is an impure *zav* (Rosh).

אמר רבא: לא תימא ספק חזא ספק לא חזא. אלא ודאי חזא, ספק מחמת שכבת זרע ספק מחמת ראייה, כיון שנזקק לטומאה – ספיקו טמא.

Rava said: Do not say that it is **uncertain** whether he **saw**[N] a discharge and **uncertain** whether he **did not see** one. The uncertainty is not with regard to whether he experienced a discharge at all. **Rather, he certainly saw a** discharge, but it is **uncertain** whether the discharge was **due to,**[N] i.e., defined as, an emission of **semen,** and it is **uncertain** whether the discharge was **due to** the **sighting** of *ziva*. In this case, **once he has been confirmed as being ritually impure** as a *zav*, **his uncertain** case is also **impure.**

"שכבת זרעו טמאה". למאי? אילימא למגע, מי גרע משכבת זרע דטהור? אלא זרעו של זב מטמא במשא.

§ The mishna taught that **his semen is impure.** The Gemara asks: With regard **to what** *halakha* is the mishna stating that the semen of a *zav* is impure? **If we say** that this is referring **to** the impurity **of contact,** i.e., this semen renders one who touches it impure, there is no need to teach this *halakha*. **Is it** any **worse than the semen of a pure** man, which also imparts impurity through contact? **Rather,** the mishna is teaching that **the semen of a *zav* renders** people **impure** even **by carrying,** like the impurity of *ziva*.

מאן שמעת להא דאמר שכבת זרע של זב מטמא במשא? אילימא האי תנא, דתניא, רבי אליעזר אומר: שכבת זרעו של זב אינו מטמא במשא, ורבי יהושע אומר: מטמא במשא, לפי שאי אפשר לה בלא ציחצוחי זיבה. אפילו רבי יהושע לא אמר אלא משום ציחצוחי זיבה, אבל בעיניה – לא אמר!

The Gemara asks: **Who did you hear that said that** the **semen of a *zav* renders** one **impure by carrying? If we say** it is **this *tanna*, as it is taught** in a *baraita* that **Rabbi Eliezer says: The semen of a *zav***[H] **does not render** one **impure by carrying, and Rabbi Yehoshua says: It** does **render** one **impure by carrying, because it is impossible for** his semen **to be without droplets of *ziva***; yet this source is no proof, as **even Rabbi Yehoshua said** that this semen imparts impurity by carrying **only due to the droplets of *ziva*** it contains. **However, he did not say** that semen **in its unadulterated** form renders people impure.

אלא אמר רב אדא בר אהבה: לומר שאין תולין בה.

Rather, Rav Adda bar Ahava said: The mishna does not mean that the semen of a *zav* itself renders one impure by carrying. Rather, it comes **to say that one does not attribute** the *ziva* **to it.** Even if the man experienced a discharge within twenty-four hours of his ejaculation of semen, one does not say his discharge was triggered by a general weakening as a result of his seminal emission. Once the man has experienced two discharges of a *zav* he is an impure *zav*, and this third discharge is also considered *ziva*.

HALAKHA

The semen of a *zav* – שכבת זרעו של זב: The semen of a *zav* imparts impurity as a primary source of impurity by contact and carrying, as it inevitably contains droplets of *ziva*. The *halakha* is in accordance with the opinion of Rabbi Yehoshua (Rambam *Sefer Tahara, Hilkhot Metamei Mishkav UMoshav* 1:14).

סָבַר רַב פָּפָּא קַמֵּיהּ דְּרָבָא לְמֵימַר: אַיְּידֵי חוּלְשָׁא הוּא דַּחֲזֵי. אֲמַר לֵיהּ רָבָא: וְהָתְנַן, גֵּר שֶׁנִּתְגַּיֵּיר – מְטַמֵּא מִיָּד בְּזִיבָה! אֲמַר לֵיהּ: אֵין לְךָ חוֹלִי גָּדוֹל מִזֶּה.

When he was **before Rava, Rav Pappa thought to say** the following explanation for this *halakha*: **Since he sees** his discharges **out of the weakness**[N] brought about from his previous *ziva*, it can be assumed that any later discharge, even one that follows a seminal emission, is *ziva*. **Rava said to him: But didn't we learn** in a mishna (*Zavim* 2:3): **A convert who** has just **converted**[H] **can immediately become impure as a *zav*.** Even if he had a seminal emission as a gentile, subsequently converted, and then experienced the discharge of a *zav*, one does not associate the discharge of a *zav* with the earlier emission of semen. Rather, it is treated as the first discharge of a *zav*. In this case there is no prior weakness of a *zav* to speak of, and nevertheless the convert is impure as a *zav*. Rav Pappa **said to** Rava: **There is no greater illness than this.**[N] The very acceptance of mitzvot can be considered an illness, as the burden of mitzvot is a weighty matter. For this reason, one does not ascribe a discharge of a *zav* to the earlier emission of semen.

אֶלָּא, תַּנָּאֵי הִיא. דְּתַנְיָא: שִׁכְבַת זֶרַע שֶׁל זָב מְטַמֵּא בְּמַשָּׂא כׇּל מֵעֵת לְעֵת, וְרַבִּי יוֹסֵי אוֹמֵר: יוֹמוֹ.

The Gemara comments: **Rather,** the possibility rejected earlier, that the mishna means that semen of a *zav* imparts impurity by carrying, **is a dispute between *tanna'im*,**[N] **as it is taught** in a *baraita*: **The semen of a *zav* renders** one **impure by carrying** like the regular discharge of a *zav* **for** a twenty-four hour **period.** In other words, if a *zav* experienced a seminal emission within twenty-four hours of a *ziva*, the seminal emission does not impart impurity only through contact in the manner of the semen of a pure individual, but by carrying as well. **And Rabbi Yosei says** that it imparts impurity by carrying only on **its day,** i.e., if the seminal emission was before the evening of the day of the *ziva*. As opposed to Rabbi Eliezer and Rabbi Yehoshua cited earlier, these *tanna'im* both maintain that the semen of a *zav* imparts impurity by carrying like *ziva* does.

בְּמַאי קָמִיפַּלְגִי – בִּדְשְׁמוּאֵל. דִּשְׁמוּאֵל רָמֵי: כְּתִיב "כִּי יִהְיֶה בְךָ אִישׁ אֲשֶׁר לֹא יִהְיֶה טָהוֹר מִקְּרֵה לָיְלָה" וּכְתִיב "לִפְנוֹת עֶרֶב יִרְחַץ בַּמָּיִם".

The Gemara asks: **With regard to what do** the first *tanna* and Rabbi Yosei **disagree?** What is the basis of their dispute? The Gemara answers: They disagree **with regard to** the following issue discussed **by Shmuel, as Shmuel raises a contradiction: It is written: "If there be among you any man who is not pure, by reason of that which chances him by night,** then shall he go abroad out of the camp, he shall not come within the camp" (Deuteronomy 23:11). This verse is applied to a *zav* who experienced a seminal emission. **And it is written: "When evening comes on, he shall bathe himself in water,** and when the sun is down, he may come within the camp" (Deuteronomy 23:12).

מַאן דְּאָמַר מֵעֵת לְעֵת – דָּיֵיק מִ"לִּפְנוֹת עֶרֶב". וְאִידַּךְ דָּיֵיק "מִקְּרֵה לָיְלָה".

The Gemara explains the dispute. **The one who says** that the semen of a *zav* imparts impurity by carrying **for** a twenty-four hour **period** after experiencing a *ziva* **infers from** the phrase **"when evening comes on"**[N] that the period can involve two evenings, as "comes on" indicates another evening. If so, the semen imparts impurity by carrying for a full twenty-four hour period. **And the other** Sage, Rabbi Yosei, **infers** from the expression **"by reason of that which chances him by night"**[N] that the seminal emission imparts impurity by carrying only until that night, i.e., until the end of the day on which the man experienced the *ziva*.

וּמַאן דְּאָמַר מִ"לִּפְנוֹת עֶרֶב". הָכְתִיב "מִקְּרֵה לָיְלָה"! אָמַר לָךְ: אוֹרְחָא דְּקֶרִי לְמֶתְיָא בְּלֵילְיָא.

The Gemara asks: **But** according to **the one who says** that this *halakha* is derived from **"when evening comes on," isn't it written: "By reason of that which chances him by night"?** The Gemara answers: He could have **said to you** that this verse affords no proof, as it is referring to the usual case and **it is the manner of a seminal emission to occur at night.** Consequently, one cannot derive a *halakha* from this expression.

HALAKHA

A convert who just converted, etc. – גֵּר שֶׁנִּתְגַּיֵּיר וכו׳: One who experiences a seminal emission cannot become impure as a *zav* for the next twenty-four hours, as any ensuing discharge is attributed to weakness following his seminal emission. However, if a gentile had a seminal emission and then converted, he can immediately become impure as a *zav*. If he was circumcised before his conversion, one attributes his discharge to his circumcision, as long as he is still recovering from it (Rambam *Sefer Korbanot*, *Hilkhot Meḥusrei Kappara* 2:3–4 and *Kesef Mishne* there).

NOTES

Since he sees out of weakness – אַיְּידֵי חוּלְשָׁא הוּא דַּחֲזֵי: The early commentaries have several different versions of this passage, which are reflected in their interpretations. The Meiri cites four possible readings of this text. According to some commentaries, Rav Pappa is explaining that the reason why the semen of a *zav* renders one impure is that there is a basis to assume that the weakened state of a *zav* is the cause of all his discharges (Commentary on *Nazir*). Others maintain that Rav Pappa is referring to the *halakha* that the discharge of a *zav* that follows a seminal emission is considered the result of an external factor. His reasoning is that the body is weak after a seminal emission, and this causes the discharge of a *zav* (*Tosafot*).

There is no greater illness than this – אֵין לְךָ חוֹלִי גָּדוֹל מִזֶּה: The convert's incorporation into the Jewish people and his acceptance of the burden of mitzvot that accompanies it is as great a transformation and psychological upheaval as any illness, and can be powerful enough to have a physical effect. In keeping with the standard version of the text, some commentaries maintain that this is Rav Pappa's response to Rava's question: It is the conversion itself that causes his weakness, not the seminal emission, and therefore it is assumed that the discharge was that of a *zav* (Commentary on *Nazir*). Others read: But why? There is no greater illness than this. According to this version, this statement is a continuation of Rava's difficulty against the opinion of Rav Pappa: If weakness is accepted as a causative factor, nothing causes greater weakness than this change of identity, and one should therefore consider the discharge to be the result of illness (*Tosafot*; Rosh).

Rather it is a dispute between *tanna'im* – אֶלָּא תַּנָּאֵי הִיא: The term: Rather, indicates a retraction from the previous explanation. Some commentaries maintain that the Gemara here reverts to its initial assumption that the semen of a *zav* imparts impurity by carrying. Although their opinion contradicts that of Rabbi Eliezer and Rabbi Yehoshua, the *tanna'im* in the subsequent *baraita* maintain that this semen imparts impurity through carrying by Torah law (Commentary on *Nazir*). Others contend that this is part of Rava's statement, i.e., Rava is claiming that the reason one does not attribute the discharge of this *zav* to his earlier seminal emission is not due to weakness but is derived from a verse from which various details of these *halakhot* are learned (*Tosafot*; Rosh). However, these commentaries also agree that, according to this opinion, the mishna is referring to the *halakha* that the semen of a *zav* renders items impure by carrying, which is not in accordance with Rav Adda bar Ahava's explanation.

Infers from, when evening comes on – דָּיֵיק מִלִּפְנוֹת עֶרֶב: The Commentary on *Nazir* explains that the term "comes on" in and of itself signifies the end of the day (see Jeremiah 6:4). By adding the term "evening," the verse must be speaking both of the end of the day and of the evening, which together compose a twenty-four-hour period.

And the other infers from, by reason of that which chances him by night – וְאִידַּךְ דָּיֵיק מִקְּרֵה לָיְלָה: Rabbi Yosei learns from here that this impurity extends only until nightfall (Commentary on *Nazir*). The Gemara does not address the question of how Rabbi Yosei interprets "when evening comes on." Some commentaries state that he expounds this phrase as referring to the related *halakha* of a seminal emission that occurs before a *ziva*. This emission is considered to be the cause for any *ziva* that occurs in the next twenty-four hours (*Tosafot*). Alternatively, just as the first *tanna* maintains that the phrase "which chances him by night" is referring to the usual case, so too, Rabbi Yosei contends that the phrase "when evening comes on" is merely ordinary speech, from which nothing can be inferred (Rabbi Shimshon of Saens on *Zavim* 2:3).

מתני׳ נָזִיר הָיָה שְׁמוּאֵל, כְּדִבְרֵי רַבִּי נְהוֹרַאי, שֶׁנֶּאֱמַר ״וּמוֹרָה לֹא יַעֲלֶה עַל רֹאשׁוֹ״. נֶאֱמַר בְּשִׁמְשׁוֹן ״וּמוֹרָה״ וְנֶאֱמַר בִּשְׁמוּאֵל ״וּמוֹרָה״. מַה מּוֹרָה הָאֲמוּרָה בְּשִׁמְשׁוֹן – נָזִיר, אַף מוֹרָה הָאֲמוּרָה בִּשְׁמוּאֵל – נָזִיר.

MISHNA The tractate concludes with an aggadic statement about nazirites. **Samuel** the prophet **was a nazirite,**[H] **in accordance with the statement of Rabbi Nehorai, as it was stated** that when Hannah, his mother, prayed for a son, she vowed: **"And no *mora* shall come upon his head"** (I Samuel 1:11). How is it derived that *mora* is an expression of naziriteship? **It is stated with regard to Samson: "And no razor [*mora*]**[L] shall come upon his head, for the child shall be a nazirite to God" (Judges 13:5), **and it is stated: "And no *mora*," with regard to Samuel. Just as the term "*mora*" that is stated with regard to Samson** means that he was **a nazirite, so too the term "*mora*" that is stated with regard to Samuel** indicates that he was **a nazirite.**

אָמַר רַבִּי יוֹסֵי: וַהֲלֹא אֵין מוֹרָה אֶלָּא שֶׁל בָּשָׂר וָדָם! אֲמַר לֵיהּ רַבִּי נְהוֹרַאי: וַהֲלֹא כְּבָר נֶאֱמַר ״וַיֹּאמֶר שְׁמוּאֵל אֵיךְ אֵלֵךְ וְשָׁמַע שָׁאוּל וַהֲרָגָנִי״ – שֶׁכְּבָר הָיָה עָלָיו מוֹרָא שֶׁל בָּשָׂר וָדָם.

Rabbi Yosei said: But doesn't the word **"*mora*"** mean **nothing other** than the fear **of flesh and blood?** The word should be read as though it were written with an *alef*, and not a *heh*, so that it means fear. **Rabbi Nehorai said to him: But isn't it already stated: "And Samuel said: How can I go; if Saul hears it he will kill me"** (I Samuel 16:2). This verse indicates **that there was fear of flesh and blood upon** Samuel. Consequently, the term *mora* must be understood in accordance with its plain meaning of a razor. If so, Samuel was indeed a nazirite.

גמ׳ אֲמַר לֵיהּ רַב לְחִיָּיא בְּרֵיהּ:

GEMARA **Rav said to his son Ḥiyya:**[P]

HALAKHA

Samuel was a nazirite – נָזִיר הָיָה שְׁמוּאֵל: The prophet Samuel was a permanent nazirite. Consequently, if one says: I am hereby like Samuel the Ramathite, or: I am hereby like the son of Hannah, or: Like the son of Elkanah, or: Like the one who killed Agag in Gilgal, all of which refer to Samuel, he is a permanent nazirite (Rambam *Sefer Hafla'a, Hilkhot Nezirut* 3:16).

LANGUAGE

Razor [*mora*] – מוֹרָה: From the Septuagint onward, most biblical commentaries interpret *mora* as referring to iron or a razor. However, Targum Yonatan translates *mora* in a similar manner as *marut*, meaning authority or control. Some commentaries interpret *mora* as though it were written with the letter *alef* at the end, meaning fear or awe.

PERSONALITIES

Ḥiyya bar Rav – חִיָּיא בַּר רַב: Ḥiyya bar Rav was a second-generation Babylonian *amora*. Although Rav had additional descendants, only Ḥiyya followed in his footsteps and became one of the prominent Sages of his generation.

It is known that during Rav's lifetime as well as after his death, his students looked after Ḥiyya. Even Rav's close friend, Shmuel, treated Ḥiyya fondly, due to his relationship with his father. Rav loved his son dearly and took great pleasure in his son's wisdom, even when the latter was a child. Since Ḥiyya suffered from ill health, Rav gave him medical advice at various times. Ḥiyya's son, Rav Shimi bar Ḥiyya, was one of the great *amora'im* of the next generation.

Perek **IX**
Daf **66** Amud **b**

חֲטוֹף וּבְרֵיךְ. וְכֵן אֲמַר לֵיהּ רַב הוּנָא לְרַבָּה בְּרֵיהּ: חֲטוֹף וּבְרֵיךְ.

Seize the opportunity **and** quickly **recite a blessing**[H] over the cup of blessing for the Grace after Meals. **And similarly, Rav Huna said to his son, Rabba:**[P] **Seize** the opportunity **and recite a blessing.**

לְמֵימְרָא דִּמְבָרֵךְ עֲדִיף? וְהָתַנְיָא, רַבִּי יוֹסֵי אוֹמֵר: גָּדוֹל הָעוֹנֶה ״אָמֵן״ יוֹתֵר מִן הַמְבָרֵךְ. וְאָמַר לוֹ רַבִּי נְהוֹרַאי: הַשָּׁמַיִם! כָּךְ הוּא. תֵּדַע, שֶׁהֲרֵי גּוּלְיָירִים מִתְגָּרִין בַּמִּלְחָמָה וְגִבּוֹרִים נוֹצְחִין!

The Gemara asks: **Is this to say that one who recites a blessing is preferable** to one who answers amen? **But isn't it taught** in a *baraita* that **Rabbi Yosei says: The one who answers amen is greater**[N] **than the one who recites the blessing? And Rabbi Nehorai said to him: By Heavens, it is so. Know** that this is true, **as the military assistants [*gulyarim*]**[L] descend to the battlefield and **initiate the war and the mighty** follow them and **prevail.** The amen that follows a blessing is compared to the mighty who join the war after the assistants, illustrating that answering amen is more significant than reciting the initial blessing.

LANGUAGE

Military assistants [*gulyarim*] – גּוּלְיָירִים: Possibly from Greek or from the Latin galearius, meaning a soldier's servant. Its imagery is based on the strategy of ancient armies, which would first dispatch light regiments to harass the enemy and then deploy heavy battalions comprised of legions of mighty warriors who would determine the outcome of the battle. In the Roman army, the first line of soldiers, referred to as the Histati, were generally the weaker soldiers who were not as well equipped as the rest of the legion. The army would allow this line to be penetrated, after which the stronger soldiers would attack.

Reenactment of the first line of Roman soldiers on the attack

HALAKHA

Seize the opportunity and recite a blessing – חֲטוֹף וּבְרֵיךְ: It is appropriate to make an effort to be designated to receive the cup of blessing in order to lead the *zimmun* before the Grace after Meals, in accordance with Rav Huna's advice to his son (*Shulḥan Arukh, Oraḥ Ḥayyim* 201:4).

PERSONALITIES

Rabba bar Rav Huna – רַבָּה בַּר רַב הוּנָא: Rabba bar Rav Huna, a third-generation Babylonia *amora*, was old enough to learn Torah from Rav, in whose name he transmitted several *halakhot*. Rabba bar Rav Huna was a preeminent disciple of his father, Rav Huna, and there are several instances in the Talmud where Rav Huna gives practical halakhic guidance to his son. A judge in the city of Sura after the death of his father, Rabba bar Rav Huna was a disciple-colleague of Rav Ḥisda and a colleague of Rava and Rav Naḥman.

NOTES

The one who answers amen is greater – גָּדוֹל הָעוֹנֶה אָמֵן: Some commentaries explain that one who answers amen listens carefully to the entire blessing, and therefore he sometimes pays greater attention than the one who actually recites the blessing (Meiri). Alternatively, the reason he is considered greater is because he completes the blessing (*Shita Mekubbetzet*). Yet others suggest that one who answers amen fulfills two mitzvot, as according to the *halakha* one who listens is considered to have pronounced the blessing itself; consequently, he has recited a blessing and added amen as well (*Birkat Rosh*).

תַּנָּאֵי הִיא, דְּתַנְיָא: אֶחָד הַמְבָרֵךְ וְאֶחָד הָעוֹנֶה "אָמֵן" בְּמַשְׁמַע, אֶלָּא שֶׁמְּמַהֲרִין לַמְבָרֵךְ תְּחִילָּה.

The Gemara responds: This **is** a dispute between ***tanna'im*****, as it is taught** in a *baraita*: **Both the one who recites a blessing and the one who answers amen**[H] **are included** among those who "stand up and bless" (Nehemiah 9:5), **but one hurries to first** reward **the one who recites the blessing.** This *baraita* apparently holds that reciting the blessing is greater than answering amen.

אָמַר רַבִּי אֶלְעָזָר אָמַר רַבִּי חֲנִינָא: תַּלְמִידֵי חֲכָמִים מַרְבִּים שָׁלוֹם בָּעוֹלָם, שֶׁנֶּאֱמַר "וְכָל בָּנַיִךְ לִמּוּדֵי ה׳ וְרַב שְׁלוֹם בָּנָיִךְ".

Rabbi Elazar said that **Rabbi Ḥanina said: Torah scholars increase peace in the world, as it is stated: "And all your children [*banayikh*] shall be taught of the Lord, and great shall be the peace of your children"** (Isaiah 54:13). The Sages interpreted this verse homiletically: Do not read it as: "Your children [*banayikh*]," but as: Your builders [*bonayikh*]. Torah scholars are those who build peace for their generation.

הדרן עלך הגוים אין להם נזירות
וסליקא לה מסכת נזיר

HALAKHA

Both the one who recites a blessing and the one who answers amen – אֶחָד הַמְבָרֵךְ וְאֶחָד הָעוֹנֶה אָמֵן: Whoever answers amen to the recitation of a blessing is considered to have said the blessing himself. Some authorities (*Magen Avraham*) state that although the one who answers amen does as important an act as the one who recites the blessing and receives an equal reward, nevertheless, the one who recites the blessing is rewarded first (Rambam *Sefer Ahava, Hilkhot Berakhot* 1:11; *Shulḥan Arukh, Oraḥ Ḥayyim* 201:4).

Summary of **Perek IX**

In this chapter, the Gemara concluded that gentiles cannot undertake a vow of naziriteship, although it is permitted for them to sacrifice some of the offerings associated with it. Canaanite slaves are categorized as Jews with respect to naziriteship obligations. However, their masters can prevent them from observing this vow in practice, in which case the Canaanite slave must wait until he is emancipated before he can fulfill it. A married woman can accept naziriteship upon herself, but under certain circumstances her husband can nullify the vow and thereby absolve her from any obligation to fulfill it.

A case can arise where a nazirite discovers his impurity only after the completion of his term. If the impurity in this situation was imparted by a grave in the depths, i.e., if the grave was unknown to anyone, the nazirite's term is not negated. However, if the impurity could have been known, whether or not one can determine it was known in practice, his term is negated, and he must restart his naziriteship once he is purified. The leniency of the *halakha* of impurity imparted by a grave in the depths applies both to a nazirite, in that his term is not negated, and to an individual on his way to bring a Paschal offering, in that he need not bring an offering on the second *Pesaḥ*.

This topic led to discussion in the Gemara about other cases involving uncertain impurity. With regard to impurity imparted by a corpse, the chapter addressed the issue of how to relocate a grave that has been discovered, including the size of the radius that must be examined outward from the grave to ascertain if there are other graves nearby.

On a separate note, if an individual has not yet been determined to be a leper or a *zav*, the *halakha* is generally lenient in a situation where he might have been rendered impure. However, once one is definitely a leper or a *zav*, cases of uncertainty are treated stringently. In light of this ruling, the chapter examines a case where an individual beat another and the victim was diagnosed as fatally injured. If the victim improves but subsequently deteriorates and dies, one attributes his death to the beating and not to another factor.

The chapter and the tractate as a whole end with aggadic statements praising a nazirite and a discussion as to whether the great prophet Samuel was a nazirite.

Image **Credits**

All images are copyright © Koren Publishers Jerusalem Ltd., except:

p218 © courtesy of the Temple Institute; **p229** left image © Tzilamti ; **p234** © fabcom; **p236** © Benny Trapp; **p246** © Ian Scott; **p248** left image © Johann Jaritz; **p248** right image © Matthias Kabel; **p253** © Matt Lavin; **p265** © Norbert Nagel; **p294** © Government Press Office; **p302** © Matthias Kabel.

My Notes

My Notes

My Notes

My Notes

The following paragraph is recited three times:

הַדְרָן עֲלָךְ מַסֶּכֶת נָזִיר וְהַדְרָךְ עֲלָן, דַּעְתָּן עֲלָךְ מַסֶּכֶת נָזִיר וְדַעְתָּךְ עֲלָן, לָא נִתְנְשֵׁי מִנָּךְ מַסֶּכֶת נָזִיר וְלָא תִתְנְשֵׁי מִנָּן, לָא בְּעָלְמָא הָדֵין וְלָא בְּעָלְמָא דְאָתֵי.

The following paragraph is recited three times:

הַדְרָן We shall return to you, tractate *Nazir,* and your glory is upon us. Our thoughts are upon you, tractate *Nazir,* and your thoughts are upon us. We will not be forgotten from you, tractate *Nazir,* and you will not be forgotten from us; neither in this world nor in the World-to-Come.

יְהִי רָצוֹן מִלְּפָנֶיךָ יהוה אֱלֹהֵינוּ וֵאלֹהֵי אֲבוֹתֵינוּ, שֶׁתְּהֵא תּוֹרָתְךָ אֻמָּנוּתֵנוּ בָּעוֹלָם הַזֶּה, וּתְהֵא עִמָּנוּ לָעוֹלָם הַבָּא. חֲנִינָא בַּר פָּפָּא, רָמֵי בַּר פָּפָּא, נַחְמָן בַּר פָּפָּא, אֲחַאי בַּר פָּפָּא, אַבָּא מָרִי בַּר פָּפָּא, רָפְרָם בַּר פָּפָּא, רָכִישׁ בַּר פָּפָּא, סוּרְחָב בַּר פָּפָּא, אַדָּא בַּר פָּפָּא, דָּרוּ בַּר פָּפָּא.

יְהִי רָצוֹן May it be Your will, Lord our God and God of our ancestors, that Your Torah will be our avocation in this world and will accompany us to the World-to-Come. Ḥanina bar Pappa, Ramei bar Pappa, Naḥman bar Pappa, Aḥai bar Pappa, Abba Mari bar Pappa, Rafram bar Pappa, Rakhish bar Pappa, Surḥav bar Pappa, Adda bar Pappa, Daru bar Pappa.

הַעֲרֶב נָא יהוה אֱלֹהֵינוּ אֶת דִּבְרֵי תוֹרָתְךָ בְּפִינוּ וּבְפִי
עַמְּךָ בֵּית יִשְׂרָאֵל, וְנִהְיֶה אֲנַחְנוּ וְצֶאֱצָאֵינוּ (וְצֶאֱצָאֵי
צֶאֱצָאֵינוּ) וְצֶאֱצָאֵי עַמְּךָ בֵּית יִשְׂרָאֵל, כֻּלָּנוּ יוֹדְעֵי
תהלים קיט שְׁמֶךָ וְלוֹמְדֵי תוֹרָתְךָ לִשְׁמָהּ. מֵאֹיְבַי תְּחַכְּמֵנִי מִצְוֹתֶךָ
כִּי לְעוֹלָם הִיא־לִי: יְהִי־לִבִּי תָמִים בְּחֻקֶּיךָ לְמַעַן לֹא
אֵבוֹשׁ: לְעוֹלָם לֹא־אֶשְׁכַּח פִּקּוּדֶיךָ כִּי־בָם חִיִּיתָנִי:
בָּרוּךְ אַתָּה יהוה לַמְּדֵנִי חֻקֶּיךָ: אָמֵן אָמֵן אָמֵן סֶלָה
וָעֶד.

הַעֲרֶב נָא Please, Lord our God, make the words of Your
Torah sweet in our mouths and in the mouths of Your
people, the house of Israel, so that we, our descendants
(and their descendants), and the descendants of Your
people, the house of Israel, may all know Your name and
study Your Torah for its own sake. Your commandments Psalms 119
make me wiser than my enemies, for they are ever with
me. Let my heart be undivided in Your statutes, in order
that I may not be put to shame. I will never forget Your
precepts, for with them You have quickened me. Blessed
are You, O Lord; teach me Your statutes. Amen, Amen,
Amen, Selah, Forever.

מוֹדִים אֲנַחְנוּ לְפָנֶיךָ יהוה אֱלֹהֵינוּ וֵאלֹהֵי אֲבוֹתֵינוּ
שֶׁשַּׂמְתָּ חֶלְקֵנוּ מִיּוֹשְׁבֵי בֵּית הַמִּדְרָשׁ, וְלֹא שַׂמְתָּ
חֶלְקֵנוּ מִיּוֹשְׁבֵי קְרָנוֹת. שֶׁאָנוּ מַשְׁכִּימִים וְהֵם
מַשְׁכִּימִים, אָנוּ מַשְׁכִּימִים לְדִבְרֵי תוֹרָה, וְהֵם מַשְׁכִּימִים
לִדְבָרִים בְּטֵלִים. אָנוּ עֲמֵלִים וְהֵם עֲמֵלִים, אָנוּ עֲמֵלִים
וּמְקַבְּלִים שָׂכָר, וְהֵם עֲמֵלִים וְאֵינָם מְקַבְּלִים שָׂכָר. אָנוּ
רָצִים וְהֵם רָצִים, אָנוּ רָצִים לְחַיֵּי הָעוֹלָם הַבָּא, וְהֵם
תהלים נה רָצִים לִבְאֵר שַׁחַת, שֶׁנֶּאֱמַר: וְאַתָּה אֱלֹהִים תּוֹרִדֵם
לִבְאֵר שַׁחַת אַנְשֵׁי דָמִים וּמִרְמָה לֹא־יֶחֱצוּ יְמֵיהֶם
וַאֲנִי אֶבְטַח־בָּךְ:

מוֹדִים We give thanks before You, Lord Our God and
God of our ancestors, that You have placed our lot
among those who sit in the study hall and that you have
not given us our portion among those who sit idly on
street corners. We rise early and they rise early. We rise
early to pursue matters of Torah and they rise early to
pursue frivolous matters. We toil and they toil. We toil
and receive a reward and they toil and do not receive a
reward. We run and they run. We run to the life of the
World-to-Come and they run to the pit of destruction,
as it is stated: But You, God, will bring them down into Psalms 55
the pit of destruction; men of blood and deceit shall not
live out half their days; but as for me, I will trust in You.

יְהִי רָצוֹן מִלְּפָנֶיךָ יהוה אֱלֹהַי, כְּשֵׁם שֶׁעֲזַרְתַּנִי לְסַיֵּם
מַסֶּכֶת נָזִיר כֵּן תְּעַזְרֵנִי לְהַתְחִיל מַסֶּכְתּוֹת וּסְפָרִים
אֲחֵרִים וּלְסַיְּמָם, לִלְמֹד וּלְלַמֵּד לִשְׁמֹר וְלַעֲשׂוֹת
וּלְקַיֵּם אֶת כָּל דִּבְרֵי תַלְמוּד תּוֹרָתְךָ בְּאַהֲבָה, וּזְכוּת
כָּל הַתַּנָּאִים וְאָמוֹרָאִים וְתַלְמִידֵי חֲכָמִים יַעֲמֹד לִי
וּלְזַרְעִי שֶׁלֹּא תָמוּשׁ הַתּוֹרָה מִפִּי וּמִפִּי זַרְעִי וְזֶרַע זַרְעִי
משלי ו עַד עוֹלָם, וְיִתְקַיֵּם בִּי: בְּהִתְהַלֶּכְךָ תַּנְחֶה אֹתָךְ בְּשָׁכְבְּךָ
משלי ט תִּשְׁמֹר עָלֶיךָ וַהֲקִיצוֹתָ הִיא תְשִׂיחֶךָ: כִּי־בִי יִרְבּוּ יָמֶיךָ
משלי ג וְיוֹסִיפוּ לְךָ שְׁנוֹת חַיִּים: אֹרֶךְ יָמִים בִּימִינָהּ בִּשְׂמֹאולָהּ
תהלים כט עֹשֶׁר וְכָבוֹד: יהוה עֹז לְעַמּוֹ יִתֵּן יהוה יְבָרֵךְ אֶת־עַמּוֹ
בַשָּׁלוֹם:

יְהִי רָצוֹן May it be Your will, Lord my God, just as you
have assisted me in completing tractate *Nazir* so assist
me to begin other tractates and books and conclude
them to learn and to teach, to observe and to perform,
and to fulfill all the teachings of Your Torah with love.
And may the merit of all the *tanna'im* and *amora'im* and
Torah scholars stand for me and my descendants so that
the Torah will not move from my mouth and from the
mouths of my descendants and the descendants of my
descendants forever. And may the verse: When you Proverbs 6
walk, it shall lead you, when you lie down, it shall watch
over you; and when you awaken, it shall talk with you
be fulfilled in me. For in the Torah your days shall be Proverbs 9
multiplied, and the years of your life shall be increased.
Length of days is in her right hand; in her left hand are Proverbs 3
riches and honor. May the Lord give strength to His Psalms 29
people; the Lord will bless His people with peace.

תלמוד בבלי

— מהדורת נאה —

נזיר חלק ג

Steinsaltz Center

KOREN

Please note that the number ranges that appear at the bottom of each daf of the Vilna pages indicate the corresponding pages of the Koren Talmud Bavli translation and commentary.

תלמוד בבלי

הוצאת קורן ירושלים

— מהדורת נאה —

מסכת נזיר

דף מז. עד דף סו:

COMMENTARY BY

Rabbi Adin Even-Israel Steinsalz

EDITOR-IN-CHIEF

Rabbi Dr Tzvi Hersh Weinreb

EXECUTIVE EDITOR

Rabbi Joshua Schreier

•

STEINSALTZ CENTER

KOREN PUBLISHERS JERUSALEM

קיג א מיי' פ"ו מהל' נזירות הלכה ד:
א ב מיי' פ"ג מהל' אבל הל' ו סמג לאוין רלו:
ב ג מיי' שם הלכה ח ופ"ז מהל' נזירות הל' יא יב:
ג ד ה מיי' פ"ו מהל' נזירות הל' יג ופ"ג מהל' אבל הל' ט:

מתני' מִי שֶׁנִּזְרַק עָלָיו אֶחָד מִן הַדָּמִים וְנִטְמָא, *רַבִּי אֱלִיעֶזֶר אוֹמֵר: סוֹתֵר אֶת הַכֹּל, וחכ"א: אעיבִיא שְׁאָר קָרְבְּנוֹתָיו וְיִטְהַר. אָמְרוּ לוֹ: מַעֲשֶׂה בְּמִרְיָם הַתַּרְמוֹדִית שֶׁנִּזְרַק עָלֶיהָ אֶחָד מִן הַדָּמִים, וּבָאוּ וְאָמְרוּ לָהּ עַל בִּתָּהּ שֶׁהָיְתָה מְסוּכֶּנֶת, וְהָלְכָה וּמְצָאָהּ שֶׁמֵּתָה, וְאָמְרוּ חֲכָמִים: תָּבִיא שְׁאָר קָרְבְּנוֹתֶיהָ וְתִטְהַר.§ גמ' קָתָנֵי: ר' אֱלִיעֶזֶר אוֹמֵר סוֹתֵר אֶת הַכֹּל, *וְהָאָמַר ר' אֱלִיעֶזֶר: כָּל אַחַר מְלֹאת — שִׁבְעָה סוֹתֵר! אָמַר רַב: מַאי "סוֹתֵר" נַמִי דְּקָאָמַר ר' אֱלִיעֶזֶר — סוֹתֵר קָרְבְּנוֹתָיו. הָכִי נַמִי מִסְתַּבְּרָא, דְּקָתָנֵי: וחכ"א: (א) תָּבִיא שְׁאָר קָרְבְּנוֹתֶיהָ וְתִטְהַר, ש"מ. וּמַעֲשֶׂה נַמִי בְּמִרְיָם הַתַּרְמוֹדִית שֶׁנִּזְרַק עָלֶיהָ אֶחָד מִן הַדָּמִים וּבָאוּ וְהוֹדִיעוּהָ עַל בִּתָּהּ שֶׁהָיְתָה מְסוּכֶּנֶת, וְהָלְכָה וּמְצָאָהּ שֶׁמֵּתָה, וְאָמְרוּ חֲכָמִים: תָּבִיא שְׁאָר קָרְבְּנוֹתֶיהָ וְתִטְהַר, ש"מ.§

הדרן עלך שלשה מינין

כֹּהֵן גָּדוֹל וְנָזִיר (ב) באֵין מִיטַּמְּאִין לִקְרוֹבֵיהֶן, גאֲבָל מִיטַּמְּאִין לְמֵת מִצְוָה. הָיוּ מְהַלְּכִין בַּדֶּרֶךְ וּמָצְאוּ מֵת מִצְוָה, רַבִּי אֱלִיעֶזֶר אוֹמֵר: יִטַּמֵּא כֹּהֵן גָּדוֹל וְאַל יִטַּמֵּא נָזִיר. וַחֲכָמִים אוֹמְרִים: דיִטַּמֵּא נָזִיר, וְאַל יִטַּמֵּא כֹּהֵן *הֶדְיוֹט. אָמַר לָהֶם רַבִּי אֱלִיעֶזֶר: יִטַּמֵּא כֹּהֵן שֶׁאֵינוֹ מֵבִיא קָרְבָּן עַל טוּמְאָתוֹ, וְאַל יִטַּמֵּא נָזִיר שֶׁהוּא מֵבִיא קָרְבָּן עַל טוּמְאָתוֹ. אָמְרוּ לוֹ: היִטַּמֵּא נָזִיר שֶׁאֵין קְדוּשָּׁתוֹ קְדוּשַּׁת עוֹלָם, וְאַל יִטַּמֵּא כֹּהֵן שֶׁקְּדוּשָּׁתוֹ קְדוּשַּׁת עוֹלָם.§ גמ' בִּשְׁלָמָא כֹּהֵן גָּדוֹל וְנָזִיר — הַאי סָבַר: כֹּהֵן גָּדוֹל עָדִיף, וְהַאי סָבַר נָזִיר עָדִיף. מָשׁוּחַ בְּשֶׁמֶן הַמִּשְׁחָה וּמְרוּבֵּה

רש"י

מתני' בְּמִרְיָם הַתַּרְמוֹדִית. מִתַּרְמוֹד, שֵׁם מָקוֹם. שֶׁהִיא מְסוּכֶּנֶת וְהָלְכָה וּמָצְאָה שֶׁמֵּתָה. וְנִטְמֵאת עָלֶיהָ, וְאָמְרוּ חֲכָמִים כו' א). גמ' קָתָנֵי. בְּמַתְנִי', ר' אֱלִיעֶזֶר אוֹמֵר: סוֹתֵר אֶת הַכֹּל. וְהָא שָׁמְעִינַן לֵיהּ דְּאָמַר דְּכָל אַחַר מְלֹאת שִׁבְעָה סוֹתֵר, וְתוּ לָא. וְהָא הָכָא אַחַר מְלֹאת הוּא! אָמַר רַב מַאי סוֹתֵר נַמִי דְּקָאָמַר ר"א סוֹתֵר קָרְבְּנוֹתָיו. וְהָכִי קָאָמַר: יָבִיא כָּל קָרְבְּנוֹתָיו לְאַחַר שֶׁיִּטְהַר, וְאוֹתוֹ זֶבַח רִאשׁוֹן שֶׁנִּזְרַק דָּמוֹ לֹא עָלָה לוֹ. וּלְעוֹלָם הַז' הוּא דְּסוֹתֵר וְתוּ לָא, לְדִבְרֵי הַכֹּל. וּבְהָא פְּלִיגִי: ר' אֱלִיעֶזֶר סָבַר אוֹתוֹ זֶבַח רִאשׁוֹן לֹא עָלָה לוֹ, וְיָבִיא אַחֵר בִּמְקוֹמוֹ עִם שְׁאָר קָרְבְּנוֹתָיו שֶׁהִפְרִישׁ, לִכְשֶׁיִּטְהַר לְאַחַר ז'. וְהָכִי נַמִי מִסְתַּבְּרָא. דְּאַקָּרְבְּנוֹתָיו קָאֵי, מִדְּקָתָנֵי: וַחֲכָמִים אוֹמְרִים יָבִיא שְׁאָר קָרְבְּנוֹתָיו וְיִטְהַר — מִכְּלָל דְּלְרַבִּי אֱלִיעֶזֶר סְבִירָא לֵיהּ דְּאַף רִאשׁוֹן לֹא עָלָה לוֹ, וְצָרִיךְ לְהָבִיא אַחֵר ב): עִנְיָן אַחֵר: אָמַר רַב מַאי סוֹתֵר נַמִי דְּקָאָמַר ר' אֱלִיעֶזֶר — סוֹתֵר אֶת קָרְבְּנוֹתָיו. וְלָא מִיבַּעְיָא זֶבַח רִאשׁוֹן דְּאֵינוֹ עוֹלֶה לוֹ, אֶלָּא ג) אוֹתוֹ שֶׁהִפְרִישׁ תְּחִלָּה צָרִיךְ לְהַחֲלִיף, וְיָבִיא אַחֵר בִּמְקוֹמוֹ. וַחֲכָמִים אוֹמְרִים: אוֹתוֹ רִאשׁוֹן בִּלְבַד לֹא עָלָה לוֹ, וְצָרִיךְ לְהָבִיא אַחֵר בִּמְקוֹמוֹ. אֲבָל שְׁאָר קָרְבָּנוֹת שֶׁהִפְרִישׁ — אֵינוֹ צָרִיךְ לְהַחֲלִיף, אֶלָּא לִכְשֶׁיִּטְהַר יָבִיא אוֹתָם. ה"נ מִסְתַּבְּרָא דְּאַקָּרְבָּנוֹת פְּלִיגִי, מִדְּקָאָמְרִי רַבָּנַן דְּיָבִיא שְׁאָר קָרְבָּנוֹת וְיִטְהַר, אַלְמָא דְּשָׁמְעִי מִינֵּיהּ דְּרַבִּי אֱלִיעֶזֶר דַּאֲפִי' אוֹתָן קָרְבָּנוֹת שֶׁהִפְרִישׁ תְּחִלָּה אֵינוֹ יָכוֹל לְהָבִיא לְקָרְבְּנוֹתָיו, וַאֲמַרוּ לֵיהּ רַבָּנַן: מֵבִיא, וּמַעֲשֶׂה נַמִי כו'.

הדרן עלך שלשה מינין

כֹּהֵן גָּדוֹל וְנָזִיר אֵין מִיטַּמְּאִין לִקְרוֹבֵיהֶן. וּכְדִמְפָרֵשׁ דְּהָנֵי קְרָאֵי לְטוּמְאָה, לְקַמָּן בַּגְּמָ'. גמ' בִּשְׁלָמָא כֹּהֵן וְנָזִיר. שָׁמְעִינַן ד) לְהוּ הֵי מִינַּיְיהוּ לִיטַּמֵּא תְּחִלָּה, דְּרַבָּנַן סָבְרֵי כֹּהֵן גָּדוֹל (ג) שֶׁקְּדוּשָּׁתוֹ קְדוּשַּׁת עוֹלָם, וְרַבִּי אֱלִיעֶזֶר סָבַר נָזִיר עָדִיף, שֶׁכֵּן מֵבִיא קָרְבָּן עַל טוּמְאָתוֹ, וְיִטַּמֵּא כ"ג שֶׁאֵינוֹ מֵבִיא קָרְבָּן עַל טוּמְאָתוֹ וְאַל יִטַּמֵּא נָזִיר. מָשׁוּחַ

תוספות

ונטמא ר' אליעזר אומר סותר את הכל. ולא כל הימים, כדמפרש בגמ', דהא ר' אליעזר הוא דאמר [לעיל] בפ"ג (דף טז:) נטמא לאחר מלאת – סותר ז'. א] אלא סותר הקרבנות קאמר, ור' אליעזר לטעמיה, דאמר בגמ': אחר המעשים כולם מותר לשתות יין ב] ומגלח. הרי כשנזרק אחד מן הדמים עד [שיביא שאר הקרבנות – אינו ראוי] לתגלחת, והואיל ונטמא [קודם] שהקריב כולם – כנטמא שחרית לפני הקריבו אף אחד מהן דמי, ולא ראוי לתגלחת כל היום, והוי קרבן ראשון שהביא כאילו הביאו תוך מלאת, בימים שלא ראוי כלל לתגלחת דמי. וחכ"א יביא שאר קרבנותיו ויטהר. פי': לכשיטהר. כך מפרש בירושלמי: שתם מעשה ג] דטהרה, ואחר כך יביא קרבנות. ודאי אותו הזבח שהיה בהכשר לא יחזור ויביא. ורבנן לטעמייהו, דאמרי: אחר מעשה יחידי מותר לשתות יין ומגלח, הרי הוא קודש שנטמא [ראוי] לתגלחת, ולמה יסתור אותו? [אבל] הזבחים שהקריב משנטמא – יסתור, דהא קפיד קרא שיביא קרבנות נזיר בטהרה. ואח"כ כשיטהר ויהיה לו הזאת ג' וז' יביאם [למנין ספירה] ד].

במרים התרמודית. מתרמוד. והאמר. לעיל בפ"ק (דף ו:) ובפ' ג' (דף טז:) דטומאה דלאחר מלאת סותר [ז'] ולרבנן [ל']. ובפ"ק פירשתי דמדרבנן הוא, דמן התורה בספירה הבא מספק, דמשמע הואיל ובהדא ראוי לתגלחת, שנזרק א' מן הדמים – לרבנן [נמי דיו] בספירת ז'. סותר קרבנות. כדפי' במתני', דייק נמי בברייתא דבקרבנות איירי, מדאייתו רבנן ראייה לדבריהם שאמרו חכמים "שאר קרבנות".

הדרן עלך שלשה מינין

כהן גדול ונזיר אינן מיטמאין לקרוביהם. ה] בספרי היא, אבל מיטמא למת מצוה, ולא גרסינן ליה כדמוכח בגמ'. כהן גדול הלכותיו בפרשת "אמור אל הכהנים" ונזיר בפרשת "נשא". ואל יטמא נזיר. שקדושתו עדיפא, כיון שהזקיקתו תורה להביא קרבן על טומאתו. מה שאין כן בכהן, ו] למאן דאמר דיטמא נזיר ואל יטמא כהן ואפי' כהן הדיוט. יטמא כהן. ואפילו כהן גדול. נזיר קדושתו קדושת שעה. ואפי' אמר נזיר עולם, מכל מקום סתם נזירות הוי שלשים יום (לעיל ה.). בשלמא כהן גדול ונזיר האי סבר כהן גדול עדיף והאי סבר נזיר עדיף. וטעמא דמ"ד במתניתין. וכן משוח בשמן המשחה. כ"ג שנמשח בשמן המשחה ומרובה בגדים קרי משנגנז שמן המשחה. דיאשיהו גנז שמן המשחה שעשה משה, כדאיתא בפ' "הוציאו לו" (יומא נב:), ואחריו לא היה כהן משוח בשמן המשחה אלא מרובה בגדים בלא שמן, שהיו ממלאים ידיו בח' בגדים. ולא היו יכולין לעשות שמן המשחה אחר למשוח בו, כדכתיב (שמות ל) "שמן משחת קדש יהיה זה לי לדורותיכם", זה – ולא אחר, וכדאיתא בפ' קמא דכריתות (דף ה:): וכי נס א' בשמן המשחה היה? והלא הרבה נסים נעשו בו, שמתחלה לא היה אלא י"ב לוג, ובו נמשח המשכן וכל כליו ואהרן ובניו כל ז' ימי המלואים, ובו נמשחו כהנים גדולים ומלכים, וכולו קיים לעתיד לבא, שנאמר "משחת קדש יהיה זה לי לדורותיכם". והא דאמר התם (דף ה.): המפטם השמן ללמוד בו או למוסרו לצבור – פטור, הא דקתני למוסרו לצבור (ללמדם שידעו לעשותו) היינו בימי משה, אם עשאו פטור. אי נמי: למוסרו לצבור ללמדם שידעו לעשותו, ולא שימשחו ממנו. והשתא אחרי יאשיהו לא היה כהן נמשח בשמן המשחה אלא עובד בח' בגדים, וכשר בכך בלא משיחה. דת"ר בפ"ק דמגילה (דף ט:): "משוח" – אין לי אלא בשמן המשחה, מרובה בגדים מנלן? ת"ל "הכהן המשיח". והשתא משוח ומרובה בגדים משכחת לה בדור א', כגון שנמשח א' לכ"ג ובתוך כך נגנז שמן המשחה, ואירע בו קרי בכהן המשוח ומינו אחר תחתיו, מרובה בגדים, לעשות עבודה ביה"כ. ז] וקשה: דא"כ הל"ל משוח חזי לעבודה, ומרובה בגדים לא חזי לעבודה, דראשון חוזר לעבודתו, כדקאמר גבי משוח שעבר! ונראה לומר: כגון שכהן גדול גלה, ומינו אחר תחתיו ברבוי בגדים, כגון שנגנז השמן כבר, ושימש כמה שנים. שאם אף הראשון שב – אינו חוזר לעבודתו, שהרי שימש זה תחתיו כמה שנים. והרי שניהם מהלכין בדרך כו'.*) (ה"ג) דאילו משוח מביא פר הבא על כל המצות, כדכתיב "אם הכהן המשיח יחטא לאשמת העם והביא פר" וגו', ומרובה בגדים לא, דכתיב בפ' הכהן המשיח דוקא משוח. וליכא לפרושי: משוח מביא פר העלם דבר של צבור – כלומר שכהן משוח מקריבו ולא מרובה בגדים, כדכתיב גביה ח] "ולקח הכהן המשיח מדם הפר" – והא ליתא, דבתורת כהנים מוכח בהדיא דאף כהן הדיוט מקריבו. ט] (ה"ג) וא"ת: אי מיירי אחר יה"כ לא היה לו לקרותו לזה "מרובה בגדים" אלא "שעבר", ואי מצאו מת מצוה ביה"כ – והא קבורת מת מצוה, לא דחי י"ט, וכ"ש שבת ויה"כ! וי"ל: לעולם ביה"כ עצמו איירי, ולא לקברו, אלא לטלטלו מחמה לצל, דשרי אפי' בשבת. והא קאמר דמשוח בשמן עדיף, ומטמא המרובה בגדים מחמה לצל. דמשוח עדיף, דמייתי פר הבא על כל המצות אם הכהן המשיח הורה וטעה בהוראתו. אבל מרובה בגדים אינו מביא פר על כל המצות, ד"משיח" דוקא כתיב, אלא מביא כשבה או שעירה כיחיד. ובהוריות (דף יא:) עיקר הדבר ופירושו. ופר הבא על כל המצות – היינו בפר שהוא עצמו מביא, שהורה בעצמו ועשה כהוראתו, שהוראת כהן משיח לעצמו כהוראת ב"ד לציבור.

*) שייך לע"ב

מרובה

פי' הרא"ש

ותיפוק לי מאחר כל המעשים. ואם באנו לומר דאינו חושש מואת א"כ גם ההיא דיש לו כפים א' למי' דכר"א אתיא: זאת אומרת קסבר ר"ש נזיר שגלח על שלמי נדבה יצא השלמי נזיר ששחטן שלא לשמן לא עלה לשם חובה והרי הן כשלמי נדבה: דאמר קרא אשר תחת זבח השלמים ולא כתיב שלמיו משמע כל שלמים ויס"ג דאמר קרא (על) [ובשר] זבח תודת שלמיו ולא כתיב שלמים. ופי' הר' משה דמהאי קרא דרשי' בפ' התודה [דף ע"ח] לרבות שלמים נזיר ליום ולילה א). ומקשינן נמי שלמי תודה לשלמי נזיר שאם גילח עליהם יצא: מי שנזרק עליו א' מן הדמים ונטמא. ר"א או' סותר את הכל. לא כל הימים קאמר כדמפרש בגמ' דר"א סבר נטמא אחר מלאת סותר שבעה. אלא סותר כל הקרבנות קאמר. ר"א לטעמיה דאמר אחר כל המעשים כולם שאינו מותר לשתות יין עד אחר הבאת כל קרבנותיו. נמצא כשנזרק א' מן הדמים עדיין אינו ראוי לתגלחת וכיון דס"ל לר"א שאין א' מן הקרבנות מתירו בתגלחת עד שיקריב את כולם א"כ כל קרבנותיו חשובים כקרבן [אחד] וכשנטמא קודם שהקריב כולו הוי כאילו נטמא שחרית קודם שהקריב אפי' א' מהם והוי הקרבן שהביא כאילו הקריבו תוך מלאת. וחכ"א יביא שאר קרבנותיו ויטהר פי' לכשיטהר. וכן מפ' בירושלמי בהאי מתני' יטהר ואח"כ יביא קרבנותיו ואותו הזבח שהביא בטהרה לא יחזור ויביאנו. רבנן לטעמייהו דאמרי אחר מעשה יחידי מותר לגלח. הרי האדם שנטמא נראה לתגלחת ולמה יסתור אותו זבח אבל שאר זבחים שהקריב משנטמא ודאי סותר דהא קפיד קרא בסתירות ז' לבר פדא. ואיכא לספוקי הכא הואיל ונראה להגלחת משנזרק א' מן הדמים אולי די בסתירת ז'. ולי נראה דלרבנן אין כאן סתירה כלל דכיון שנזרק א' מן הדמים מותר לשתות יין ולישמא למתים ולגלח יצא מכלל נזיר ולא שייך ביה סתירה. מרים התרמודית. מתמרוד היתה. הכי נמי מסתברא דסותר קרבנותיו קאמר מדמייתו

נוסחת הריב"ן

א) כו' ובגמ' מפרש לה: ב) אחר תחתיו: ג) אלא אף אותן שהפריש כו' ויביא אחרים במקומן: ד) שמעינן הי מינייהו ס' כה"ג עדיף ויטמא נזיר ואל יטמא כ"ג שקדושתו כו' שכן מביא קרבן על טומאתו ולא יטמא נזיר הס"ד:

ס"א גדול

הגהות הב"ח

(א) גמ' וחכ"א יביא שאר קרבנותיו ויטהר ומעשה נמי כצ"ל ותיבות שמע מינה נמחק: (ב) במשנה כהן גדול ונזיר אינן מיטמאין: (ג) רש"י ד"ה בשלמא וכו' סברי כ"ג עדיף שקדושתו:

הגהות מהר"ב רנשבורג

א] תוד"ה ונטמא וכו' סותר ז' נבר אלא כצ"ל: ב] בא"ד מותר לשתות יין ולגלח וכו' מן הדמים עדיין [אינו ראוי] לתגלחת וכו' כצ"ל: ג] ד"ה וחכ"א וכו' מעשה דטהרה. תיבת דטהרה נמחק ונ"ב תטהר ואח"כ תביא קרבנותיה וכו': ד] בא"ד ואח"כ כשיטהר וכו' יביאם [למנין ספירה]. ונ"ב ותימה דהאמר לעיל בפ"ק דף ו' ופ"ג דף טז דטומאה דלאחר מלאת סותרת שלשים לרבנן ובפ"ק פירשתי דהוא מדרבנן גזירה אטו סתירה דמן התורה כסתירה הבא בסתם נזירות. ושמא הואיל וחזי לתגלחת שנזרק אחד מן הדמים די לרבנן נמי בסתירת ז' כצ"ל והד"א ודלא כדפוס פפד"מ שחלקוהו לשני דיבורים וטעות הוא. עכ"ל א"מ וישוע"ה ודו"ק: ה] ד"ה כ"ג וכו' בספרים הוא וכו' כנ"ל: ו] ד"ה ואל וכו' מש"כ בכהן כאן הס"ד ואח"כ מה"ד למ"ד יטמא וכו' תיבת למ"ד נמחק ונ"ב וחכ"א יטמא כנ"ל. א"מ: ז] ד"ה וכן משוח וכו' עבודה ביוה"כ. נ"ב כאן שייך קושיית וא"ת וכו' האמורה בסוף הדיבור: ח] בא"ד ולא מרובה וכו' גביה ולקח תיבת ולקח נמחק ונ"ב והביא: ט] בא"ד דבת"כ מוכח וכו' ה"ג. פי' ה"ג נמחק ונ"ב הגה"ה כנ"ל א"מ וישוע"ה לקושיא זאת מקומה לעיל:

א) בס' הגה"ה כאן חסר איזה תיבות ונ"ל וכו' גורסין ובשר זבח ט' וכעו שכ' הרא"ש כאן.

מסורת הש"ס

[לעיל יד: וש"נ]

לעיל טז: לג: [לקמן סג:]

וּמְרוּבֵּה בְּגָדִים — אמָשׁוּחַ בְּשֶׁמֶן הַמִּשְׁחָה עֲדִיף, בדְּאִילּוּ מָשׁוּחַ בְּשֶׁמֶן הַמִּשְׁחָה מֵבִיא פַּר הַבָּא עַל כָּל הַמִּצְוֹת, וְאִילּוּ מְרוּבֵּה בְגָדִים — אֵין מֵבִיא. מָשׁוּחַ שֶׁעָבַר וּמְרוּבֵּה בְּגָדִים — גמְרוּבֵּה בְּגָדִים עֲדִיף, דִּמְרוּבֵּה בְּגָדִים עָבֵיד עֲבוֹדָה, דוְאִילּוּ מָשׁוּחַ שֶׁעָבַר לָאו בַּר עֲבוֹדָה הוּא. עָבַר מֵחֲמַת קֵירוּיוֹ וְעָבַר מֵחֲמַת מוּמוֹ — העָבַר מֵחֲמַת קֵירוּיוֹ עֲדִיף, דְּאִילּוּ הַאי חֲזֵי לַעֲבוֹדָה לְמָחָר, וְאִילּוּ עָבַר מֵחֲמַת מוּמוֹ לָא חֲזֵי לַעֲבוֹדָה. *אִיבַּעְיָא לְהוּ: מְשׁוּחַ מִלְחָמָה וּסְגָן, הֵי מִינַּיְיהוּ עֲדִיף? מְשׁוּחַ מִלְחָמָה עֲדִיף — דַּחֲזֵי לְמִלְחָמָה, אוֹ דִּלְמָא סְגָן עֲדִיף — דַּחֲזֵי לַעֲבוֹדָה? ת"ש, דְּתַנְיָא: *אֵין בֵּין מְשׁוּחַ מִלְחָמָה לַסְּגָן, אֶלָּא שֶׁאִם הָיוּ מְהַלְּכִין בַּדֶּרֶךְ וּמָצְאוּ מֵת מִצְוָה — ויִטַּמֵּא מְשׁוּחַ מִלְחָמָה וְאַל יִטַּמֵּא הַסְּגָן. וְהָתַנְיָ': זמְשׁוּחַ מִלְחָמָה קוֹדֵם לַסְּגָן! אָמַר מָר זוּטְרָא: חלְעִנְיַן הַחֲיוֹתוֹ — מְשׁוּחַ מִלְחָמָה עֲדִיף, מַאי טַעְמָ' — דְּתָלוּ בֵּיהּ רַבִּים. וּלְעִנְיַן טוּמְאָה — סְגָן עֲדִיף. דְּתַנְיָא, *רַבִּי חֲנִינָא בֶּן אַנְטִיגְנוֹס אוֹמֵר: לָמָּה תִּקְּנוּ סְגָן לְכֹהֵן גָּדוֹל? שֶׁאִם אֵירַע בּוֹ פְּסוּל — הֲרֵי נִכְנָס וּמְשַׁמֵּשׁ תַּחְתָּיו. עַד כָּאן לָא פְּלִיגִי אֶלָּא בְּכֹהֵן גָּדוֹל וְנָזִיר כִּי קָא אָזְלִי בַּהֲדֵי הֲדָדֵי, אֲבָל חַד חַד לְחוּדֵיהּ — בַּר אִיטַּמּוּיֵי אִינּוּן. מְנָא הָנֵי מִילֵּי? דת"ר: °"עַל כָּל נַפְשֹׁת מֵת לֹא יָבֹא", בַּמֶּה הַכָּתוּב מְדַבֵּר? אִי בִּרְחוֹקִים — קַל וָחוֹמֶר הוּא: וּמָה כֹּהֵן הֶדְיוֹט שֶׁהוּא מִיטַּמֵּא לִקְרוֹבִים — אֵינוֹ מִיטַּמֵּא לִרְחוֹקִים, כֹּהֵן גָּדוֹל שֶׁאֵינוֹ מִיטַּמֵּא לִקְרוֹבִים — אֵינוֹ דִּין שֶׁאֵינוֹ מִיטַּמֵּא לִרְחוֹקִים? אֶלָּא בִּקְרוֹבִים הַכָּתוּב מְדַבֵּר. וּלְאָבִיו הוּא דְּאֵינוֹ מִיטַּמֵּא, הָא מִיטַּמֵּא הוּא לְמֵת מִצְוָה. וּלְאִמּוֹ

ויקרא כא

תורה אור

רש"י

א) מָשׁוּחַ בְּשֶׁמֶן הַמִּשְׁחָה וּמְרוּבֵּה בְּגָדִים. כְּלוֹמַר, וְהָא פְּשִׁיטָא לָן דְּכ"ג שֶׁנִּמְשַׁח בְּשֶׁמֶן הַמִּשְׁחָה קוֹדֶם שֶׁנִּגְנַז לִגְלֶגֶת הַמָּן וּמַקְלוֹ שֶׁל [אַהֲרֹן] וְשֶׁמֶן הַמִּשְׁחָה בִּימֵי יֹאשִׁיָּהוּ, וְכֹהֵן גָּדוֹל שֶׁלֹּא נִמְשַׁח בְּשֶׁמֶן הַמִּשְׁחָה שֶׁעוֹמֵד בִּכְהוּנָּתוֹ לְאַחַר שֶׁנִּגְנַז שֶׁמֶן הַמִּשְׁחָה, אֲפִילּוּ בְּבַיִת רִאשׁוֹן, וְאֵין בֵּינוֹ לְבֵין כֹּהֵן הֶדְיוֹט אֶלָּא שֶׁהוּא מְרוּבֵּה בְגָדִים — שֶׁמְּשַׁמֵּשׁ בְּח' בְּגָדִים בְּבִגְדֵי לָבָן וּבִגְדֵי זָהָב, וְכֹהֵן הֶדְיוֹט אֵינוֹ מְשַׁמֵּשׁ אֶלָּא בְּד' — הָא נַמִי פְּשִׁיטָא, שֶׁאִם הָיוּ מְהַלְּכִין בַּדֶּרֶךְ וּמָצְאוּ מֵת מִצְוָה דְּמִיטַּמֵּא מְרוּבֵּה בְגָדִים ב) וְלֹא יִטַּמֵּא מָשׁוּחַ בְּשֶׁמֶן הַמִּשְׁחָה, מִשּׁוּם דְּאִיהוּ עָדִיף, שֶׁכֵּן מֵבִיא פַּר הֶעְלֵם עַל כָּל הַמִּצְוֹת כְּמוֹ לְצִבּוּר, כִּדְכְתִיב (ויקרא ד) "וְאִם הַכֹּהֵן הַמָּשִׁיחַ" וגו', כְּלוֹמַר שֶׁהוּא מֵבִיא קָרְבָּן עַל אַשְׁמָתוֹ כְּמוֹ לְצִבּוּר עַל אַשְׁמָתָן. אֲבָל מְרוּבֵּה בְגָדִים אֵינוֹ (א) דִּינוֹ אֶלָּא כְּיָחִיד. וּמָשׁוּחַ שֶׁעָבַר. כְּלוֹמַר, קוֹדֶם שֶׁנִּגְנַז שֶׁמֶן הַמִּשְׁחָה, וְאֵירַע קֶרִי בְּכ"ג, וּמִינּוּ אַחֵר תַּחְתָּיו וּמְשָׁחוּהוּ, וְאַחַר כָּךְ כְּשֶׁנִּטְהַר כ"ג — חוֹזֵר לַעֲבוֹדָתוֹ, וְשֵׁנִי עוֹבֵר לוֹ. וּמָשׁוּחַ שֶׁעָבַר לָאו בַּר עֲבוֹדָה הוּא. אֶלָּא אוֹתוֹ יה"כ, ג) כִּדְאָמְרִי' בְּמַסֶּ' יוֹמָא (דף יב:): רִאשׁוֹן חוֹזֵר לַעֲבוֹדָתוֹ, וְשֵׁנִי אֵינוֹ רָאוּי לֹא לְכ"ג ד) וְלֹא לְכֹהֵן הֶדְיוֹט, מִשּׁוּם דְּמַעֲלִין בַּקּוֹדֶשׁ וְלֹא מוֹרִידִין. כֹּהֵן מְשׁוּחַ מִלְחָמָה לָא חֲזֵי לַעֲבוֹדָה. כִּדְאָמְרִינַן בְּמַסֶּ' הוֹרָיוֹת. וְהָתַנְיָא מְשׁוּחַ מִלְחָמָה קוֹדֵם לַסְּגָן. דְּמַשְׁמַע: לְכָל דָּבָר קוֹדֵם לוֹ, דְּאִיהוּ עָדִיף טְפֵי. בְּמַסֶּ' הוֹרָיוֹת קָאֵי. דְּתָלוּ בֵּיהּ רַבִּים. דְּעָבֵיד מִלְחָמָה בִּשְׁבִיל רַבִּים. עַד כָּאן לָא פְּלִיגִי. ר' אֱלִיעֶזֶר וְרַבָּנַן אֶלָּא בְּכ"ג וְנָזִיר דְּקָאָזְלֵי בַּהֲדָדֵי וְאַשְׁכְּחוּ מֵת מִצְוָה, הֵי מִינַּיְיהוּ לִיטַּמֵּא בְּרֵישָׁא. אֲבָל חַד לְחוּדֵיהּ כו'. עַל כָּל נַפְשׁוֹת מֵת לֹא יָבֹא. לֹא בָּא אֶלָּא לִקְרוֹבִין, דְּאִי לִרְחוֹקִים — הֲרֵי כְּבָר לָמַדְנוּ מִכֹּהֵן הֶדְיוֹט. וְהוֹאִיל וְלֹא בָּא הַכָּתוּב ה) לְהַזְהִיר עַל כָּל נַפְשׁוֹת מֵת אֶלָּא מִשּׁוּם קְרוֹבִין, מַה ת"ל ו) "לְאָבִיו"? לֹא בָּא אֶלָּא לוֹמַר לְךָ: לְאָבִיו אֵינוֹ מִיטַּמֵּא, אֲבָל מִיטַּמֵּא הוּא לְמֵת מִצְוָה. וּלְאִמּוֹ. הָאָמוּר בְּכֹהֵן גָּדוֹל, מַה ת"ל? לג"ש

תוספות

מרובה בגדים ומשוח שעבר. וה"ה דמצי למינקט משוח ומשוח שעבר, או מרובה בגדים ומרובה בגדים שעבר. אלא רבותא נקט, דאפי' אותו שעבר משוח – מרובה בגדים עדיף ממנו. הכי גרים: מרובה בגדים ומשוח שעבר. לכאורה משמע מרובה בגדים – כגון שכבר נגנז שמן המשחה, והיה כ"ג מרובה בגדים, ואירע בו קרי ומינו אחר תחתיו ומשחוהו, ועבר יום הכפורים, ושוב הראשון שהוא מרובה בגדים חוזר לעבודתו. והשתא יש לפנינו מרובה בגדים ומשוח שעבר. ואי אפשר לומר כן, דאיך נעשה זה שמשחו השני ולא משחו הראשון? אלא יש לפרש: כגון שיש כאן כ"ג משוח (שעבר), ואירע בו קרי ומשחו אחר תחתיו, ועבד יה"כ אחד, ושוב המשוח הראשון חזר לעבודתו ועבד כמה שנים אחרי כן, ומשוח השני עבר (עבודתו), ובין כך ובין כך נגנז שמן המשחה. וזה המשוח ראשון שחזר לעבודתו גלה עם יכניה, ומינו אחר תחתיו מרובה בגדים. אבל משוח שעבר אינו מתמנה תחתיו כל ימי חייו של הראשון אף כי יצא בגולה, משום איבה. ולהכי ליכא למימר דמת המשוח – דא"כ משוח שעבר יתמנה תחתיו. אלא גלה, ומינו מרובה בגדים תחתיו. והשתא המשוח שעבר קודם למרובה בגדים בזמן שעדיין היה שמן המשחה. והשתא שניהם, המרובה בגדים והמשוח שעבר, מרובה בגדים עדיף – שעבד עבודה, שראוי לעבודה, ואילו משוח שעבר – לאו בר עבודה הוא, כדאמרינן פרק קמא דיומא (דף יב:) דלכהן גדול אינו ראוי משום איבה, ולא לכהן הדיוט דמעלין בקדש ולא מורידין, כשמעתיה דר' יוסי, דאמר: אינו ראוי לא לכה"ג ולא לכהן הדיוט. **עבר** מחמת קריו ועבר מחמת מומו. בין מום קבוע בין מום עובר – מחמת קריו עדיף דחזי לעבודה למחר, ומחמת מומו לא [עביד] עד שיתרפא מומו. **משוח** מלחמה וסגן הי מינייהו עדיף. כלומר, כל הני פשיטא לי, והא מיבעיא לי: משוח מלחמה עדיף דחזי למלחמה, שנתמנה לכך לצאת עם העם למלחמה ותלו ביה רבים. או דלמא סגן עדיף דהא חזי לעבודה. פירוש: ביום הכפורים, שנתמנה לכך שאם יארע קרי בכ"ג שיכנס הוא תחתיו, ונקרא סגן. נמצא כי עיקר מינויו לשמש בעבודה, ועיקר מינוי משוח מלחמה – למלחמה.

ת"ש דתניא אין בין משוח לסגן אלא שאם היו מהלכין בדרך ומצאו מת מצוה יטמא משוח מלחמה. וקשה: דטובא איכא בינייהו, כדאיתא בשילהי "בא לו" (יומא עב:): בבגדים שכ"ג משמש משוח מלחמה משמש, (משמע) וסגן עובד בבגדים כמו הדיוט, כמו שעובד ביה"כ נמי תחת כ"ג. ותו: כל החמשה דברים האמורים בפרשה: לא פורע, ולא פורס, מצווה על הבתולה, ואסור באלמנה – דאין נוהגין בסגן ונוהגין במשוח מלחמה, כדמרדינן בפרק בתרא דהוריות (דף יב:) מקראי! ואומר הרמ"ר: דודאי טובא מילי איכא דמשוח מלחמה חמור מסגן. ותנא קולי קולי קתני, דאין קולא שנוהגת במשוח מלחמה שלא תנהוג בסגן [אלא] הך – שיטמא משוח מלחמה ולא יטמא סגן. והכי נמי אמרינן פרק "מקום שנהגו" (פסחים נה.) תנא קולי קולי קתני. **והתניא** משוח מלחמה קודם לסגן. וקא ס"ד דקדים לכל מילי קאמר. אלא בקונט' פי' דידע שפיר המקשה דבהוריות (דף יג.) מתניא לענין להחיותו, לפקח עליו את הגל – קודם לסגן, דאם נפל גל על שניהם. ומכל מקום פריך, דאי סגן עדיף לענין טומאה – הוה לן לפקח את הגל תחלה על הסגן. ומשני מר זוטרא, דודאי לעניין להחיותו לפקח עליו את הגל – משוח מלחמה עדיף, דתלו ביה רבים. ולענין טומאה סגן עדיף, דנתמנה לעבודה. ומיהו, גם בהוריות מוקי לה התלמוד לענין להחיותו כי הכא, משמע דבברייתא לא נשנית בהדיא הך לענין להחיותו. **למה** תקנו סגן לכ"ג. ובפרק "טרף בקלפי" (יומא לט.) גרסינן: למה סגן מימינו, פי' לימינו. **עד** כאן לא פליגי אלא בכ"ג ונזיר כי אזלי בהדי הדדי אבל חד חד לחודיה בני איטמויי אינון. פי': למת מצוה. מכאן מוכח שאין לגרוס במשנתנו בפי' "ומיטמאין למת מצוה" ברישא, דא"כ למה לו לדקדק בפלוגתייהו? ישאל על המשנה להדיא: מנלן. **מנא** הני מילי. דכהן ונזיר מיטמא למת מצוה? דתנו רבנן: "על כל נפשות מת לא יבא לאביו ולאמו לא יטמא", בכ"ג כתיב בפרשת "אמור". **אי** ברחוקים ק"ו מהדיוט ומה כהן הדיוט שמיטמא לקרובים. כדכתיב קרא, אינו מיטמא לרחוקים, כ"ג שאינו מיטמא לקרובים, כדכתיב "לאביו ולאמו לא יטמא" – אינו דין שלא יטמא לרחוקים? אלא ע"כ קרא ד"על כל נפשות מת לא יבא" בקרובים הכתוב מדבר, ואייתר לאביו למידרש: לאביו אינו מיטמא, אבל מיטמא הוא למת מצוה. וא"ת: היכי מייתר "לאביו"? והא ק"ו אין שייך לומר אם לא שנאמר הכתוב לאביו, שכך מסיים הדין: כ"ג שאינו מיטמא לקרובים, ומנלן הא אם לא נכתב "לאביו"? וי"ל: דק"ו דקאמר לאו דוקא, ואינו אלא לרווחא דמילתא, כאילו היה אומר כן: על כרחיך דקרא "על כל נפשות מת לא יבא" בקרובים, דאי על רחוקים בא להזהיר – הרי הוא מוזהר ועומד משהיה כהן הדיוט, שהוזהר על הרחוקים, דאטו משנעשה כהן גדול פקעה קדושת כהן הדיוט? וקדושתו להיכא אזלא? אלא על כרחיך על הקרובים בא להזהירו, דכהן הדיוט שרי בהן, אייתר לו "לאביו ולאמו" לדרשא, לומר: לאביו אינו מיטמא, אבל מיטמא הוא למת מצוה.

ולאמו

עין משפט נר מצוה

ד א מיי' פ"ג מהל' אבל הל' ט ופ"ד מהל' כלי המקדש הל' יט:
ה ב מיי' פ"ד מהל' כלי המקדש הל' יד ופ"ט מהל' שגגות הל' י:
ו ג מיי' פ"ד מהל' כלי המקדש הל' יט:
ז ד מיי' פ"א מהל' עבודת יום הכפורים הלכה ג:
ח ה מיי' פ"ד מהל' כלי המקדש הל' יט:
ט ו מיי' פ"ג מהל' אבל הל' ט:
י ז ח מיי' פ"ד מהל' כלי המקדש הל' יט ופ"ח מהל' מתנות עניים הל' יח:

פי' הרא"ש

מדמייתו רבנן ראיה לדבריהם ממה שאמרו חכמים תביא שאר קרבנותיה:

סליק פירקא

ומרובה בגדים. לאחר (שנתנה) [שנגנז] שמן המשחה ולא יכלו לעשות אחר כדדריש פ"ק דכריתות. שמן משחת קודש יהיה זה לי זה ולא אחר ולא נמשחו הכהנים אלא היה משמש בח' בגדים. ואמרינן פ"ק דמגילה דכהן מרובה בגדים כשר לכל עבודת כ"ג כמו כהן משוח ואין ביניהם אלא פר הבא על כל המצות שמרובה בגדים מביא כשבה או שעירה כמו שאר כל אדם. וכהן משוח מביא פר. וי"מ א) דבעבודת פר העלם דבר של צבור וכתי' בפר' ויקרא שהכהן המשיח היה מקריב אותו. ואתא למי' שמרובה בגדים לא יקריבנו. וליתא דבת"כ מוכח דאף כהן הדיוט מקריבו. הלכך אם היו שניהם מהלכין בדרך ומצאו מת מצוה יטמא מרובה בגדים ואל יטמא משוח. וא"ת היאך היו ב' כהנים גדולים כאחד וי"מ שאירע קרי בכ"ג שנמשח אחר שנגנז שמן המשחה ומינו מרובה בגדים לשמש תחתיו. ולא נהירא דא"כ הול"ל כדקאמר בסמוך משוח עדיף דחזי לעבודה ומרובה בגדים לא חזי לעבודה לפי שהראשון חוזר לעבודתו. והשני אינו משמש בח' בגדים משום איבת כ"ג. ולא בד' בגדים דמעלין בקדש ולא מורידין. ופי' הר' משה כגון שחלה כ"ג או גלה ומינו אחר תחתיו וכיון ששימש ימים רבים בכהונה מסתמא אין מעבירין אותו אף כשב הראשון או נתרפא דדוקא באירע קרי והשני אינו משמש אלא לפי שעה הראשון חוזר לעבודתו. והמרובה בגדים ומשוח שעבר כגון שאירע קרי לכ"ג ומינו אחר תחתיו קודם שנגנז שמן המשחה ומת כ"ג ומינו אחר תחתיו אחר שנגנז שמן המשחה. ומה שלא מינו משוח שעבר אפשר שהאחר ב) נתחר' ונתעלה אחר או שמא על פי מלך מנוהו כמו שמצינו שהיו עושים בימי בית שני שהיו מתמנים על פי המלך בתוספת דמים. משוח שעבר לאו בר עבודה הוא. היינו כר' יוסי והתם פסק כוותיה. והוה מצי למימר מרובה בגדים ומרובה בגדים שעבר או משוח ומשוח שעבר אלא לרבותא נקט אעפ"י שזה משוח אפ"ה מרובה בגדים עדיף שראוי לעבודה. עבר מחמת קריו ועבר מחמת מומו. כגון שאירע בכ"ג מום ומינו אחר תחתיו ואירע בו קרי עבר מחמת קריו עדיף דחזי לעבודה למחר כשיטהר ואילו האי לא חזי לעבודה עד שיתרפא. וה"ה בשני כהנים הדיוטים א' בעל מום וא' בעל קרי. מי אמרינן דמשוח מלחמה וסגן. משוח מלחמה עדיף לפי שנמשח בשמן המשחה או דלמא סגן עדיף (שנתמנה) [דחזי לעבודה] והתניא משוח מלחמה קודם לסגן. פ' בתוספתא דהוריות מיתניינא. לענין להחיותו כגון להקדים לו מזונות או לפקח עליו את הגל משוח מלחמה עדיף דתלו ביה רבים. כל ערך המלחמה נעשה על פיו. על כל

א) נראה דל"ל וי"מ דלענין עבודת פר והעלם דבר של צבור מיירי דכתיב וכו'. ב) נ"ל אפשר שהמשוח שעבר נחלה או אירע בו אונס ונתמנה אחר או שמא וכו'.

מסורת הש"ס

הוריות יג. [כ"ש שינויים רבים]

שם

[יומא לט. ע"ש סוטה מב. ע"ש]

נוסחת הריב"ן

א) ומשוח בשמן כו' והא נמי פשיטא כו' ומקלו של משה כו' שעמד בכהונה: ב) ואל יטמא: ג) אותו יום בלבד: ד) משום איבה: ה) להחזיר להזהיר: ו) לאח"כ לאביו:

הגהות הב"ח

(א) רש"י ד"ה משוח בשמן וכו' אינו נידון אלא כיחיד:

"וּלְאִמּוֹ" — לִגְזֵירָה שָׁוָה, לְכִדְרַבִּי. דְּתַנְיָא, *רַבִּי אוֹמֵר: גַּבֵּי נָזִיר, "בְּמוֹתָם" אֵינוֹ מִיטַּמֵּא [א]אֲבָל מִיטַּמֵּא הוּא לִנְגָעִם וּלְזִיבָתָם. וְאֵין לִי אֶלָּא בְּנָזִיר, בְּכֹהֵן גָּדוֹל מִנַּיִן — אָמַרְתָּ: לֹא יֹאמַר "אִמּוֹ" בכ"ג שֶׁאֵין ת"ל, שֶׁהֲרֵי ק"ו הוּא: וּמָה אִם בְּמָקוֹם שֶׁכֹּהֵן הֶדְיוֹט מִיטַּמֵּא לְאָחִיו מֵאָבִיו — אֵין כֹּהֵן גָּדוֹל מִיטַּמֵּא לְאָבִיו, מָקוֹם שֶׁאֵין כֹּהֵן הֶדְיוֹט מִיטַּמֵּא לְאָחִיו מֵאִמּוֹ — אֵינוֹ דִּין שֶׁאֵין כ"ג מִיטַּמֵּא לְאִמּוֹ? אִם זָכִיתָה מֵהַדִּין, מַה ת"ל "אִמּוֹ" בְּכֹהֵן גָּדוֹל — מוּפְנֶה לְהַקִּישׁ וְלָדוּן הֵימֶנּוּ גְּזֵירָה שָׁוָה: נֶאֱמַר "אִמּוֹ" בְּנָזִיר וְנֶאֱמַר "אִמּוֹ" בכ"ג, מָה "אִמּוֹ" הָאָמוּר בְּנָזִיר — בְּמוֹתָם אֵינוֹ מִיטַּמֵּא, [ב]אֲבָל מִיטַּמֵּא הוּא לִנְגָעִם וּלְזִיבָתָם, אַף "אִמּוֹ" הָאָמוּר בכ"ג — בְּמוֹתָם אֵינוֹ מִיטַּמֵּא, אֲבָל מִיטַּמֵּא לִנְגָעִם וּלְזִיבָתָם. אַשְׁכַּחַן כ"ג, נָזִיר מְנָלַן? דְּתַנְיָא: °"כָּל יְמֵי הַזִּירוֹ לַה' עַל נֶפֶשׁ [א] מֵת לֹא יָבֹא", ⊕שׁוֹמֵעַ אֲנִי אֲפִי' נֶפֶשׁ בְּהֵמָה בְּמַשְׁמַע, כְּעִנְיָן שֶׁנֶּאֱמַר °"מַכֵּה נֶפֶשׁ בְּהֵמָה" — ת"ל "עַל נֶפֶשׁ מֵת לֹא יָבֹא" — בְּנֶפֶשׁ אָדָם הַכָּתוּב מְדַבֵּר. ר' יִשְׁמָעֵאל אוֹמֵר: אֵינוֹ צָרִיךְ, הֲרֵי הוּא אוֹמֵר "לֹא יָבֹא" — בַּנְּפָשׁוֹת הַמְטַמְּאוֹת בְּבִיאָה הַכָּתוּב מְדַבֵּר. "לְאָבִיו וּלְאִמּוֹ" אֵינוֹ מִיטַּמֵּא, אֲבָל מִיטַּמֵּא הוּא לְמֵת מִצְוָה. עַד שֶׁלֹּא יֹאמַר יֵשׁ לִי בַּדִּין: וּמַה כ"ג, שֶׁקְּדוּשָּׁתוֹ קְדוּשַּׁת עוֹלָם — מִיטַּמֵּא לְמֵת מִצְוָה, נָזִיר שֶׁאֵין קְדוּשָּׁתוֹ קְדוּשַּׁת עוֹלָם — אֵינוֹ דִּין שֶׁמִּיטַּמֵּא לְמֵת מִצְוָה? לֹא, אִם אָמַרְתָּ בכ"ג שֶׁכֵּן אֵינוֹ מֵבִיא קָרְבָּן עַל טוּמְאָתוֹ, תֹּאמַר בְּנָזִיר שֶׁמֵּבִיא קָרְבָּן עַל טוּמְאָתוֹ; הוֹאִיל וּמֵבִיא קָרְבָּן עַל טוּמְאָתוֹ — לֹא יִטַּמֵּא לְמֵת מִצְוָה — ת"ל "לְאָבִיו וּלְאִמּוֹ לֹא יִטַּמָּא", אֲבָל מִיטַּמֵּא לְמֵת מִצְוָה. אוֹ אֵינוֹ מִיטַּמֵּא לְאָבִיו וּלְאִמּוֹ, אֲבָל יִטַּמֵּא לִשְׁאָר מֵתִים? אָמַרְתָּ ק"ו: וּמַה כֹּהֵן הֶדְיוֹט שֶׁמִּיטַּמֵּא לַקְּרוֹבִין אֵינוֹ מִיטַּמֵּא לִשְׁאָר מֵתִים, נָזִיר שֶׁאֵינוֹ מִיטַּמֵּא לַקְּרוֹבִין — אֵינוֹ דִּין שֶׁלֹּא יִטַּמֵּא לִשְׁאָר מֵתִי'?

הָא

Margin: לעיל מג. · במדבר ו · ויקרא כד

רש"י

לִגְזֵירָה שָׁוָה לְכִדְרַבִּי א) דְּתַנְיָא רַבִּי אוֹמֵר. "לְאָבִיו וּלְאִמּוֹ לְאָחִיו וְלַאֲחוֹתוֹ לֹא יִטַּמָּא לָהֶם בְּמוֹתָם כִּי נֵזֶר" וגו', וְהַאי קְרָא בְּנָזִיר כְּתִיב. אֵין לִי. שֶׁמִּיטַּמֵּא לְאָבִיו וּלְאִמּוֹ בִּנְגָעִם וּבְזִיבָתָם אֶלָּא נָזִיר, כ"ג מִנַּיִן? אָמַרְתָּ לֹא יֹאמַר אִמּוֹ בְּכ"ג. שֶׁיֵּשׁ לָנוּ לִלְמוֹד מִן הַדִּין שֶׁאֵינוֹ מִיטַּמֵּא, ב) שֶׁהֲרֵי ק"ו הוּא כו'. אֵין כֹּהֵן הֶדְיוֹט מִיטַּמֵּא לְאָחִיו אֶלָּא אִם כֵּן יֶשְׁנוֹ אָחִיו מֵאָבִיו. אֵין כ"ג מִיטַּמֵּא לְאָחִיו מֵאִמּוֹ, וְלֹא מֵאָבִיו, וְלֹא אֲפִי' לְאָבִיו. אע"פ שֶׁאֵין כֹּהֵן הֶדְיוֹט מִיטַּמֵּא לְאָחִיו אֶלָּא בִּשְׁבִיל שֶׁבָּא מִכֹּחַ אָבִיו. אִם זָכִיתָה מִן הַדִּין. אִם לָמַדְתָּ מִן הַדִּין שֶׁאֵין כ"ג מִיטַּמֵּא לְאִמּוֹ, מַה תַּלְמוּד לוֹמַר "אִמּוֹ"? אֶלָּא מוּפְנֶה כו'. אַשְׁכַּחַן כ"ג. דְּמִיטַּמֵּא לְמֵת מִצְוָה, נָזִיר מְנָלַן? ת"ל עַל (כָּל) נֶפֶשׁ מֵת בְּנֶפֶשׁ אָדָם הַכָּתוּב מְדַבֵּר. שֶׁלֹּא מָצִינוּ שֶׁנִּקְרָא "נֶפֶשׁ מֵת" אֶלָּא אָדָם בִּלְבָד. בְּנֶפֶשׁ הַמְטַמְּאָה לוֹ לְאָדָם בְּבִיאָה. כֵּיוָן שֶׁנִּכְנַס עִמָּהֶם בְּאֹהֶל הַכָּתוּב מְדַבֵּר, וְאֵיזוֹ זוֹ — נֶפֶשׁ אָדָם וְלֹא נֶפֶשׁ בְּהֵמָה. וְכֵיוָן דְּ"עַל נֶפֶשׁ מֵת לֹא יָבֹא" מְדַבֵּר בְּנֶפֶשׁ אָדָם, ג) וּמַשְׁמַע בֵּין קְרוֹבִי' בֵּין רְחוֹקִים, וְלָמָּה חָזַר הַכָּתוּב וְאָמַר "לְאָבִיו וּלְאִמּוֹ"? אֶלָּא לְאָבִיו הוּא ד) דְּלָא מִיטַּמֵּא כו'. עַד שֶׁלֹּא יֹאמַר. שֶׁמִּיטַּמֵּא לְמֵת מִצְוָה, הָיִיתִי מְבִיאוֹ מִן הַדִּין, שֶׁנָּזִיר מִיטַּמֵּא לְמֵת מִצְוָה מַה כ"ג כו' (א)ה). *נֶאֶמְרוּ כְּלָלוֹת בְּכ"ג. "עַל כָּל נַפְשׁוֹת מֵת לֹא יָבֹא", וְנֶאֱמַר כְּלָל בְּנָזִיר "עַל נֶפֶשׁ מֵת", דְּכָל נֶפֶשׁ בְּמַשְׁמַע בֵּין קְרוֹבִים בֵּין רְחוֹקִים. מַה כְּלָל הָאָמוּר בְּכ"ג כו' — אַף כְּלָל הָאָמוּר בְּנָזִיר, לְאָבִיו וּלְאִמּוֹ אֵינוֹ מִיטַּמֵּא, אֲבָל מִיטַּמֵּא לְמֵת מִצְוָה.

Margin: שייך לע"ב

תוספות

ולאמו שנכתב בכ"ג לגזירה שוה. לנזיר, דכתיב בנזיר "לא יטמא להם במותם" ודרשינן "במותם" יתירא, דהא כתיב ברישיה דקרא "על כל נפשות מת", למה לי "במותם" – לומר לך: במותם הוא דאינו מיטמא, אבל מיטמא הוא לנגעם ולזיבתם. נראה דעיקר קרא לנגעם איצטריך, דס"ד אמינא דמצורע חשיב כמת, ולזיבתם נקט אגב נגעם. **ואין** לי אלא בנזיר. שמותר ליטמא לנגעם ולזיבתם, כ"ג מנין? אמרת: לא יאמר "אמו" בכ"ג דאינו צריך; ומה במקום שכהן הדיוט מיטמא לאחיו מאביו – דכתיב "לאחיו", וסבירא ליה דגמר אחוה אחוה מבני יעקב, כי היכי דילפינן לענין יבום ביבמות (דף יז:), הרי עדיפא משפחת אב ממשפחת אם לגבי כהן הדיוט – אין כ"ג מיטמא לאביו, [מקום] שאין כהן הדיוט מיטמא לאחיו מאמו – אינו דין שאין כ"ג מיטמא לאמו? אם זכיתה מן הדין, א"כ מה ת"ל "אמו" בכ"ג? וא"ת: ומה צריך קל וחומר? הרי כבר אמר ד"על כל נפשות מת" אזהר רחמנא אקרובים, ועל כרחך כדפרישי', ואמו נמי בכלל כל הקרובי', א"כ למה כתיב אמו בפירוש? על כרחך מייתרא לג"ש! וי"ל: דאי לאו ק"ו הוה אמינא: אע"ג דאסר קרובים מ"על כל נפשות מת" וכתיב נמי "לאביו" – לאו למעוטי מת מצוה, אלא למעוטי אם דמיטמא לה. דהוה אמינא: דווקא קרובים דמצד האב דגריעי טפי, משום דאינה קורבא ודאית אלא חזקה בעלמא, אבל אמו דודאי ילדתו, ליטמא לה, כדאמר לקמן האי סברא, ע"כ איצטריך קל וחומר ללמד דאין זו סברא, שהרי בכהן הדיוט אנו מחשיבים קורבא דאב טפי מן האם. ומהשתא אייתר אביו ואמו בכהן גדול, "אביו" לומר דמיטמא למת מצוה, "ואמו" לגזירה שוה. ואם תאמר: אכתי מנלן דאביו בא למת מצוה? הא איצטריך לגופיה, דלא לימא ד"לאמו" למעוטי לאביו, דיטמא לאביו, דקורבא דאב עדיפא, דמתייחס אחריו, כדלקמן! ונראה לומר: דהתנא תפס לדין ק"ו לרווחא דמלתא, כק"ו דלעיל. והך ברייתא כרבי ישמעאל דבסמוך, ולית ליה האי צריכותא דלקמן. דאמו ודאי ילדתו דלקמן – אליבא דר"ע קאמר ליה, אבל לר' ישמעאל בלאו ק"ו אייתר "לאמו" שהיא בכלל שאר קרובים. דאפי' אי נכתב "לאביו" לא הוה אמינא דלמעוטי אמו קאתי משום דודאי ילדתו, דלית ליה הנך סברות דלקמן. הלכך, כי כתיב "על כל נפשות מת" – כולהו קרובים במשמע, אייתר "לאביו" למת מצוה, ואייתר "לאמו" לגזירה שוה, וקל וחומר לרווחא דמילתא. **הכי** גרסינן: אשכחנא כהן גדול דמיטמא למת מצוה נזיר מנלן. תימה: תיפוק ליה מגזירה שוה ד"אמו" "אמו", כמו שאנו לומדים כהן גדול מנזיר לענין נגעם וזיבתם – ה"נ ניהדר ונילף נזיר מכהן גדול לענין מת מצוה, דאין גזירה שוה למחצה! נראה למהר"ף: אי לאו דנפקא לן מת מצוה בנזיר מקרא אחרינא, הוה אמינא דכולה גזירה שוה ד"אמו" "אמו" אתיא למת מצוה. אבל לענין למעוטי נגעם וזיבתם, בין בכהן הדיוט ובין בכהן גדול, כיון דמצורע איתקש למת, דהוה ליה כעוקר קרא ממשמעותיה ע"י ג"ש – להכי איצטריך למילף מת מצוה בנזיר מקרא אחרינא. **כל** ימי הזירו לה' על (כל) נפש מת **לא יבא שומע אני נפש בהמה במשמע**. אי לא כתיב "מת" אלא "נפש", שנאמר "ומכה נפש בהמה ישלמנה" – ת"ל "נפש מת" – בנפש אדם הכתוב מדבר, דבהמה לא איקרי מת. אע"ג דכתיב (שמות כא) "והמת יהיה לו" – "מת" סתמא איקרי, "נפש מת" לא איקרי. **ר'** ישמעאל **אומר אין צריך**. למעוטי בהמה מנפש מת, דהא הוא אומר "לא יבא" – בנפש המטמא בביאה, היינו באהל, הכתוב מדבר. ואילו נבילה לא מטמאה באוהל. **לאביו** ולאמו. בנזיר כתיב ד' פרטי: "לאביו ולאמו לאחיו ולאחותו לא יטמא להם במותם" לאביו ולאמו אינו מיטמא – אבל מיטמא למת מצוה. מסקנא דברייתא זו ד"לאביו" בא לגלויי על "נפש מת" דאיירי בקרובין, ו"לאמו" – לגזירה שוה לכדרבי, ו"לאחיו" – למת מצוה. א] ומפיק ליה האי סברא כמו שנושא ונותן בברייתא עד דיליף ליה מ"אחיו". אי נמי: התנא ידע בטוב דלא נפיק מת מצוה אלא מ"לאחיו", והאי דקאמר "לאביו ולאמו" – הוי כמו [וגו'], ולעולם סומך א"לאחיו". **עד** שלא יאמר. קרא בנזיר דמיטמא למת מצוה, יש לי בדין, בקל וחומר, למשמע מיניה דנזיר מיטמא למת מצוה: ומה כהן גדול שקדושתו קדושת עולם מיטמא למת מצוה, מקרא כדלעיל. **או** אינו. אלא לכך כתיב "לאביו ולאמו" – לומר לך דמותר ליטמא לשאר מתים רחוקים. וטעמא איכא למימר, דשמא אקרובים אזהריה רחמנא מפני [שמיצר] עליהם, וזהו זילותא דנזיר דאיקרי קדוש. אבל רחוקים, שאינו נעצב עליהם – לא אזהריה רחמנא. אמרת ק"ו *מכהן גדול, דעל כרחיך סברא זאת לא אמיתית היא, שהרי ב] [בכ"ג] הוא איפכא. *ו**עד** שלא יאמר יש לי בדין נאמרו כללות בכ"ג. "על כל נפשות מת לא יבא", ונאמר כללות בנזיר "על (כל) נפש מת לא יבא"; מה כללות האמורות בכ"ג וכו'. תימה: והיכי בעי למילף נזיר מכ"ג לענין מת מצוה? והא איכא למיפרך: מה לכ"ג – שכן אינו מביא קרבן על טומאתו, כדפרכינן לעיל! ופי' הר"ס: דלאו לענין מת מצוה בעי למילף, אלא בא לומר ד"לאביו ולאמו" בנזיר מייתר. דאגופיה לא איצטריך, דלכתוב כללות לחודייהו "על נפש מת לא יבא", וממילא ידעינן דהיינו קרובים נמי, דילפינן להו מכללות דכ"ג. ג] או כלך לדרך זו: נאמר כלל בכהן הדיוט "לנפש לא יטמא בעמיו" כו', ושפיר איצטריך לגופיה. והאי דקאמר: אף כללות דאמרינן בנזיר מיטמא למת מצוה – היינו כלומר מיתורא ד"אביו", דלא איצטריך לגופיה, וכן מוכח בתר הכי. **האי** מיבעי ליה לאביו ולאמו ממש. שאינו מיטמא

לאביו

Margin: גי' א"מ מכהן הדיוט · שייך לע"ב

עין משפט נר מצוה

יא א ב מיי' פי"ז מהל' טומאת אוכלין הל' ט סמג עשין רמ:

פי' הרא"ש

כל נפשות מת לא יבא בכ"ג כתיב: מטמא לקרובים כדכתי' לאמו ולאביו וגו' לה יטמא: לנגעם ולזיבתם להני אצטריך דסד"א מצורע חשוב כמת ולזיבתם אגב נגע נקט. שכהן הדיוט מטמא לאחיו מאביו. דילפינן אחוה אחוה מבני יעקב כי היכי דילפינן לענין יבום ביבמות. נמצא דעדיפא משפחת אב ממשפחת אם. א"כ כיון דגלי קרא שאינו מטמא לאביו כ"ש שאינו מטמא לאמו: אשכחן כ"ג נזיר מנלן. הוה מצי למימר מג"ש דאמו אמו אלא (ניחה) [ניחא] ליה לאשכחיה בגופיה. ת"ל נפש מת ובהמה לא אקרי נפש מת. בנפשות המטמאות בביאה. באהל: לאביו ולאמו אינו מטמא אבל מטמא הוא למת מצוה. לאמו כדי נקטי' דדרשי' ליה לקמן לג"ש. עד שלא יאמר שיטמא למת מצוה יש לי בדין. אבל מטמא הוא לשאר מתים משום דכתיב נזר אלהיו על ראשו הלכך לרחוקים שאינו עציב עליהם כ"כ יטמא. אמרת קל וחומר ומה כ"ג שמטמא לקרובים אינו מטמא לשאר מתים הרי גלה הכתוב שדין הוא שיטמא לקרובים יותר מלרחוקים ומחמת סברא כל דהו אין לנו שיטמא לרחוקים אף על פי שאינו מטמא

נוסחת הריב"ן

א) לגזרה שוה לכדרבי משום האמור בנזיר דתניא כו': ב) לה שהרי: ג) ומשמעו: ד) דאי: ה) ועדיין עד שלא יאמר יש לי בדין דנזיר מטמא למת מצוה דנאמר כלל בכ"ג על כל נפשות מת כו':

הגהות הב"ח

(א) רש"י ד"ה עד שלא וכו' כ"ג כו' הס"ד ואח"כ מ"ה ועד שלא יאמר יש לי בדין דנזיר מיטמא למת מצוה דנאמר כלל בכ"ג על כל:

הגהות הגר"א

[א] גמ' (מת) תז"מ (ועי' תוס'):

גליון הש"ס

גמ' שומע אני אפי' נפש בהמה. עי' ביצה דף כח ע"א:

הגהות מהר"ב רנשבורג

א] תוד"ה לאביו וכו' ומפיק ליה האי סברא כמו. מן תיבת ומפיק עד כמו נמחק ונ"ב ולא מסיק ליה עדיין האי סברא כיון שטעא וכו' כנ"ל א"מ: ב] ד"ה או אינו וכו' שהרי בכה"ג. תיבת בכה"ג נמחק ונ"ב בכהן הדיוט. א"מ: ג] ד"ה ועד שלא יאמר כו' דכ"ג או כלך. נ"ב עיין א"מ דמוחק כל זה מן או כלך וכו' עד ע"כ אוקמי' אכללא דכ"ג ועושה מן הכל דבור אחד:

יב א ב מיי' פ"ג מהל' אבל הל' ח טוש"ע י"ד סי' שעד סעיף א:

הָא מַה ת"ל "לְאָבִיו וּלְאִמּוֹ" — לְאָבִיו וּלְאִמּוֹ הוּא דְּלָא מִיטַּמֵּא, אֲבָל מִיטַּמֵּא הוּא לְמֵת מִצְוָה. עַד שֶׁלֹּא יֹאמַר יֵשׁ לִי בַּדִּין: נֶאֶמְרוּ כְּלָלוֹת בכ"ג וְנֶאֶמְרוּ כְּלָלוֹת בְּנָזִיר, מַה כְּלָלוֹת הָאֲמוּרוֹת בכ"ג — לְאָבִיו אֵינוֹ מִיטַּמֵּא אֲבָל מִיטַּמֵּא לְמֵת מִצְוָה, אַף כְּלָלוֹת הָאֲמוּרוֹת בְּנָזִיר — לְאָבִיו אֵינוֹ מִיטַּמֵּא, אֲבָל מִיטַּמֵּא לְמֵת מִצְוָה. אוֹ כְּלָךְ לְדֶרֶךְ זוֹ: נֶאֶמְרוּ כְּלָלוֹת בְּכֹהֵן הֶדְיוֹט וְנֶאֶמְרוּ כְּלָלוֹת בְּנָזִיר, מַה כְּלָלוֹת הָאֲמוּרוֹת בְּכֹהֵן הֶדְיוֹט — מִיטַּמֵּא לְאָבִיו, אַף כְּלָלוֹת הָאֲמוּרוֹת בְּנָזִיר — מִיטַּמֵּא לְאָבִיו! ת"ל "לְאָבִיו וּלְאִמּוֹ לֹא יִטַּמָּא" הָא לְמֵת מִצְוָה מִיטַּמֵּא. הָא מִיבָּעֵי לֵיהּ לוֹמַר שֶׁאֵין מִיטַּמֵּא לְאָבִיו! אֶלָּא: "לְאָבִיו" — לוֹמַר שֶׁאֵין מִיטַּמֵּא לְאָבִיו, "לְאָחִיו" אֵינוֹ מִיטַּמֵּא — הָא לְמֵת מִצְוָה מִיטַּמֵּא, "וּלְאִמּוֹ" — לִגְזֵרָה שָׁוָה, לְכִדְרַבִּי. "וּלְאַחוֹתוֹ" — לְכִדְתַנְיָא, *דְּתַנְיָ': "לַאֲחוֹתוֹ" מַה ת"ל? הֲרֵי שֶׁהָלַךְ לִשְׁחוֹט אֶת פִּסְחוֹ וְלָמוּל אֶת בְּנוֹ, וְשָׁמַע שֶׁמֵּת לוֹ מֵת — יָכוֹל יִטַּמֵּא? אָמַרְתָּ: לֹא יִטַּמֵּא. יָכוֹל לֹא יִטַּמֵּא לְמֵת מִצְוָה? ת"ל "לַאֲחוֹתוֹ", לַאֲחוֹתוֹ הוּא דְּאֵינוֹ מִיטַּמֵּא, אהָא לְמֵת מִצְוָה — מִיטַּמֵּא. *ר"ע אוֹמֵר: (א)*"נַפְשׁוֹת" — אֵלּוּ הָרְחוֹקִין, "מֵת" — אֵלּוּ הַקְּרוֹבִין, "לְאָבִיו וּלְאִמּוֹ" אֵינוֹ מִיטַּמֵּא, אֲבָל מִיטַּמֵּא הוּא לְמֵת מִצְוָה. "לְאָחִיו" — בשֶׁאִם הָיָה כ"ג וְהוּא נָזִיר, לְאָחִיו אֵינוֹ מִיטַּמֵּא, אֲבָל מִיטַּמֵּא הוּא לְמֵת מִצְוָה. "לַאֲחוֹתוֹ" — כִּדְתַנְיָא: הֲרֵי שֶׁהָיָה הוֹלֵךְ לִשְׁחוֹט אֶת פִּסְחוֹ וְלָמוּל אֶת בְּנוֹ כו'. וּלְרַבִּי עֲקִיבָא, גְּזֵירָה שָׁוָה דְּרַבִּי מְנָלֵיהּ? אָמַר לָךְ: כֵּיוָן דְּאָמַר מָר: אִם הָיָה כ"ג וְנָזִיר, לְאָחִיו אֵינוֹ מִיטַּמֵּא אֲבָל מִיטַּמֵּא הוּא לְמֵת מִצְוָה — מַה לִּי כֹּהֵן גָּדוֹל לְחוּדֵיהּ, מַה לִּי נָזִיר וכ"ג. וּלְרַבִּי יִשְׁמָעֵאל, כֹּהֵן גָּדוֹל וְהוּא נָזִיר, מְנָלֵיהּ? כֵּיוָן דִּשְׁרָא רַחֲמָנָא חַד לָאו גַּבֵּי מֵת מִצְוָה — מַה לִּי חַד לָאו מַה לִּי תְּרֵין לָאוִין. "אֲחוֹתוֹ" לָמָּה לִי? סָלְקָא דַּעְתָּךְ אָמִינָא: כִּי שְׁרָא רַחֲמָנָא לְמֵת מִצְוָה — נָזִיר וְכֹהֵן, דְּאִיסּוּר לָאוֵי הוּא. אֲבָל מִילָה וּפֶסַח, דְּכָרֵת — לֹא יִטַּמֵּא לְמֵת מִצְוָה, קמ"ל. ולר"ע

ומה ת"ל (ג) אביו. א) שאם אתה אומר מן הכלל – הייתי אומר לך: עד שאתה דן כו'. או כלך לדרך זו: נאמר כלל בכהן הדיוט "לנפש לא יטמא" כו', אף כלל האמור בנזיר יהא מיטמא, לכך הוצרך לומר בנזיר ב) דלאביו לא יטמא. והא מיבעי ליה לאביו. כלומר, ועכשיו נמצאת אתה דן שצריך לומר בנזיר שלא יטמא לאביו ממש, והואיל ואינו מיותר לכך – מהיכן אתה דן דנזיר מיטמא למת מצוה? אלא. ג) מהיכן אתה לומד – ממה שאמר "לאחיו", שאינו צריך, דהשתא לאביו אינו מיטמא – לשאר קרובין לא כ"ש? "ולאחיו" מה ת"ל? אלא לומר דלאחיו הוא דאינו מיטמא, אבל מיטמא הוא למת מצוה. ולאמו אתא ליה לג"ש. למילף מינה אמו האמורה בכהן גדול לכדרבי, וכדלעיל. וגבי כ"ג ליכא למימר דהא דכתיב ביה "ולאביו", דלאביו ממש הוא דקאתי, [דלא] יטמא לו. דכיון ד"על כל נפשות מת לא יבא" לא אתא אלא בקרובים, כדפירש ברישא דשמעתא – שמע מינה ד"לאביו" מייתר ליה, וקאתא למימר דלאביו הוא דאינו מיטמא, אבל מיטמא הוא למת מצוה. ולאחותו. דכתיב גבי נזיר, למה ליה? לכדתניא הרי שהיה נזיר והולך למול את בנו ולשחוט את פסחו. והאי דנקיט להו אהדדי היינו משום דמילת זכריו ועבדיו מעכבין את פסחו. ת"ל ולאחותו. וקאתא לאשמועינן, דאע"ג דאזיל לדבר מצוה – למצות מילה ופסח דאית בהו כרת – אפי' הכי יניח מצות מילה ופסח, ומיטמא למת מצוה. ר"ע אומר. כשהוא אומר "על נפש" – הרי רחוקין אמורין, וכשהוא אומר "מת" – הרי קרובין אמורין, "לאביו ולאמו" מה ת"ל? אלא: לאביו ולאמו אינו מיטמא כו'. ור"ע לא משמע ליה מ"אמו" כלום, אלא אגררא דאמר "מאביו" נסביה קרא. ולאחיו מה ת"ל שאם היה כ"ג ונזיר כו'. דסד"א: היכא דלא הוה ליה אלא נזיר או כהן – ליטמא למת מצוה. אבל היכא דהוה נזיר וכ"ג, דאית ביה תרי – אימא לא, קמ"ל. ולאחותו לכדתניא הרי שהיה הולך לשחוט את פסחו כו'. ולר"ע ג"ש לכדרבי מנא ליה. דכ"ג מיטמא בנגעו ובזיבתו של אביו. דאילו לדידיה לא משמע ליה מ"לאמו" כלל, הא קאמר דאגררא נסביה קרא. אמר לך כיון דאמינא שאם היה כ"ג ונזיר לאחיו אינו מיטמא ד) אבל מיטמא הוא למת מצוה. וכתיב ביה בכ"ג ונזיר "לא יטמא להם במותם" אבל מיטמא בנגעם ובזיבתם. מה לי כ"ג לחודיה מה לי כ"ג כשהוא נזיר. דמיטמא בנגעו ובזיבתו של אביו, כ"ש דכ"ג לחודיה מותר ליטמא בנגעם ובזיבתם. מה לי חד לאו מה לי תרי לאוין. דכיון דמישתרי ליה לגבי מת מצוה חד לאו – אישתרי ליה נמי בתרי לאוי, כגון כ"ג ונזיר. ולאחותו למה לי. כלומר, א"כ דלר' ישמעאל נפקא ליה כ"ג ונזיר משום מה לי חד לאו מה לי תרי לאוי, ה) "אחותו" למה לי למישרי פסח ומילה? (ג) אהכי איצטריכא "ולאחותו"; ס"ד כו'. ולרבי

לאביו ממש. אין ה"ג, דאיצטריך לאביו, וכיון דאפיקתיה מכללא דכהן הדיוט שמיטמא לאביו – אוקמיה אכללא דכ"ג א] שאינו מיטמא לקרובים, ואייתר לו "לאמו ולאחיו ולאחותו". "לאמו" – לג"ש. תימה: כיון דאמו דכהן גדול מופנה, כדאמרינן לעיל, למה לי תו (למופנה) הפנאה מ"אמו" דנזיר? וי"ל: אליבא דר' ישמעאל קיימא (לן) דאית ליה פרק "המפלת" (נדה כב:): מופנה מצד אחד – למדין ומשיבין. והכא יש להשיב: דמה לנזיר שאין קדושתו קדושת עולם, וישנו בשאלה.

לאחיו אינו מיטמא אבל מיטמא למת מצוה. לג"ש לא מצי למידרשיה, דלא כתיב "לאחיו" בכ"ג. וכ"ת: אמאי לא קאמר התלמוד הדרשות על סדר הכתוב, ולומר "לאמו" לגזירה שוה, שהיא מוקדמת בקרא, ו"לאחיו" – לאחיו אינו מיטמא, אבל מיטמא למת מצוה! אלא לפי מה שפירשתי לעיל, דאי לאו דידעינן מת מצוה מקרא אחרינא לא הוה מוקמי' גזירה שוה ד"אמו" לכדרבי, לנגעם ולזיבתם, אלא הוה ממעטינן מ"אמו" מת מצוה – להכי קאמר דמת מצוה ידעינן מ"לאחיו" לגבי נזיר, אייתר ליה "אמו" על כרחיך לג"ש. **ולאחותו** מה תלמוד לומר הרי שהיה הולך לשחוט את פסחו וכו' אמרת לא יטמא. אף בעושה פסח ומילה [גרידא], בלא נזיר וכ"ג, משום דלא אתי עשה דטומאה שאין בה כרת ודחי עשה דפסח ומילה שיש בהם כרת. כך פי' בקונטרס בזבחים פרק "טבול יום" (דף ק.). ובסנהדרין (דף לה.) ובברכו' (דף כ.) מפורש באורך. **ר"ע** אומר נפש אלו הרחוקין. דסברא הוא לאוקמיה קרא קמא ברחוקים. ו"מת" הכתוב אחרי כן מייתר לאוסרן אף בקרובים, דסבירא ליה לר"ע דאפילו לא כתיב "מת" – "בנפש" ליכא למיטעי לאוקמי בבהמה, אי משום דרשא ד"לא יבא" דמטמא באהל משמע, אי משום דאע"ג דאיקרי "נפש בהמה" – ב] "נפש" סתמא לא איקרי. ועוד: דלא מצינו בהמה מוזכרת גבי טומאה רק בלשון נבילה. **לאביו** ולאמו לא מיטמא אבל מיטמא הוא למת מצוה. לקמן קעביד צריכותא בין "אביו" ובין "אמו", וצריכי תרוייהו למיכתב למעוטי מת מצוה. "לאחיו" – שאם היה כ"ג ונזיר דמיטמא למת מצוה. דכולהו פרטי מיותרים לר"ע, הלכך כולהון צריכי. אבל לא מצריך קרא לכהן הדיוט, דכהן הדיוט מיטמא לקרובים – דין הוא דטופיינא דכהן הדיוט דקדושתו קדושת עולם אינו מעלה ומוריד לגבי מת מצוה, ולא איצטריך קרא [אלא] ג]לכהן גדול ונזיר.

ולאחותו כדתניא וכו' ור"ע ג"ש דרבי מנא ליה. פי': דהא ליכא הפנאה כלל, דהנהו פרטי דנזיר דרשי' לכולהו. ו"לאביו ולאמו" דכ"ג נמי ד] (כדאמרינן) דאיצטריכו למת מצוה תרוייהו, כי היכי דצריכי תרוייהו בנזיר למת מצוה! ומשני: כיון דאמר מר, היינו ר"ע: "לאחיו" דאם היה כ"ג ונזיר לאחיו אינו מיטמא, אבל מיטמא הוא למת מצוה – מהשתא תיפוק לן מהכא דכ"ג ואפי' נזיר מיטמא למת מצוה, וכ"ש כ"ג גרידא. ומהשתא מייתר לן אביו *ואביו בכ"ג לגזירה שוה. וצריך למכתב שניהם "אביו ואמו" בכ"ג, כדעביד לקמן צריכותא בנזיר לר"ע מאביו ואמו דנזיר – ה"נ בעי למיעבד צריכותא מאביו ואמו דכ"ג. וא"ת: ואכתי איט מופנה אלא מצד כ"ג, דאילו בנזיר צריך למת מצוה! וי"ל: דסבירא ליה לר"ע מופנה מצד אחד למידין ואין משיבין, אבל לר' ישמעאל לעיל – ודאי צריך להפנותן משני לצדדין, דאיהו לטעמיה בפרק "המפלת" (נדה כב:) דסבירא ליה למידין ומשיבין, כדפירש' לעיל. **ולר'** ישמעאל כ"ג והוא נזיר מנא ליה. היכא דאית ביה שתי קדושות. דלדידיה לא אייתר "לאחיו" דנזיר לכ"ג שהוא נזיר, כיון דלית ליה "מת" אלו הקרובין – א"כ איצטריך "אביו" לגופיה, לאשמועינן אפילו לקרובין לא יטמא, ו"לאמו" – לגזירה שוה, ו"לאחיו" – למישרי מת מצוה, ו"לאחותו" – כדתניא! ומשני: כיון דשרי רחמנא חד לאו במת מצוה בנזיר לחודיה, או בכ"ג לחודיה – מה לי חד לאו מה לי תרי לאוין.

ולאחותו למה לי. פירוש: לרבי ישמעאל. דבשלמא לר"ע, כיון דצריך קרא להיכא דאית ביה קדושת כ"ג והוא נזיר, ולא אמר מה לי חד לאו מה לי תרי לאוין – ה"נ איצטריך קרא מיותר ד"אחותו" שידחה מ"מ עשה דפסח ומילה, אע"ג שיש בהן כרת. אלא לרבי ישמעאל, דאין לו חילוק בין חד לאו לשני לאוין – היה סבור נמי דאין לו חילוק בכרת. ומשני: דבהא ודאי מודה רבי ישמעאל, דסד"א כי שרא רחמנא למת מצוה נזיר וכהן ה] דחד לאו הוא, כלומר לית ביה כרת, אבל פסח ומילה דכרת – לא יטמא למת מצוה, קמ"ל "אחותו". ולרבי

פי' הרא"ש

לקרובים: נאמרו כללות בכ"ג על כל נפשות מת לא יבא. כללות בנזיר על כל נפש מת. כללות בכהן הדיוט לנפש לא יטמא. לאביו מבעי ליה לגופיה דלא נילף מכהן הדיוט שמטמא לאביו. ולאחותו מה ת"ל. הרי שהיה הולך ישראל ואינו נזיר. יכול יטמא דאתי עשה דטומאת קרובים דכתיב בכהן הדיוט לה יטמא ודחי עשה דפסח ומילה. אמרת לא יטמא. דחמור עשה דידהו דאית בהו כרת: ר"ע אומר נפש אלו הרחוקים דסברא הוא לאוקמה מידי דהוה אבכהן הדיוט. מת אלו הקרובים לאוסרו אף בקרובים. לאביו ולאמו וכו' אבל מטמא הוא למת מצוה ותרוייהו צריכי להך דרשא כדמצריך לה לקמן בשמעת'. לאחיו שאם היה כ"ג ונזיר וכו' ולא מצריך קרא לכהן הדיוט ונזיר. כיון דקדושת כהן הדיוט דמטמא לקרובים לא בעי קרא אם נתוספה קדושתו על נזירות. ולאחותו לכדתניא הרי שהיה הולך וכו'. מה לי כ"ג ומה לי כ"ג ונזיר דכיון דכ"ג ונזיר מטמא למת מצוה כ"ש כ"ג לחודיה. ולא איצטריך אמו דכ"ג להתירו במת מצוה ומופנה הוא לג"ש: ולר' ישמעאל כ"ג ונזיר מנא ליה דלאביו מבעי ליה לגופיה לאמו לג"ש שמטמא למת מצוה: ולאחותו לכדתניא ולא אייתר ליה קרא לכ"ג שמטמא למת מצוה: כיון דשרא רחמנא חד לאו (א) לאביו מת מצוה. כ"ג לחודיה או כשישנו יחד דמה לי חד לאו מה לי תרי לאוי. א"כ דלא בעי קרא להך להולך לשחוט פסחו ולמול בנו. אבל מילה ופסח דכרת. בדמילה נמי איכא כרת הגדול מחייה כרת.

א) נראה דצ"ל דקרא דלא אמי גבי מת מצוה מקרא דלאביו גבי כה"ג לחודיה.

מגילה ג: סנהדרין לה. ברכות יט: זבחים ק.

[זבחים ק. ע"ש בהס"]

נ"ל נפש

נוסחת הריב"ן

א) אביו בנזיר: ב) לאביו דלאביו: ג) מכלן אתה דן ממה שאמר כו'. ד) אינו מיטמא ומכתיב ביה: ה) תרי לאוי לנזיר ולפסח אלפני אילטריכא כו'.

הגהות הב"ח

(א) גמ' ר"ע אומר על נפש אלו הרחוקים: (ב) רש"י ד"ה ומה ת"ל לאביו הס"ד ואח"כ מ"ה: או כלך כו' שאם אתה אומר כלל שאתה דן כו' נאמר כלל כל"ל ותיבות או כלך לדרך זו נמחק: (ג) ד"ה ולאחותו וכו' ומילה ואשני אלמא:

גליון הש"ס

תוס' ד"ה ולאחותו וכו' למדין ומשיבין. לפנינו הגירסא שם בנדה לר"י ס"ל למדין ואין משיבין:

נ"ל ולאמו

הגהות מהר"ב רנשבורג

א] תוד"ה (מעבר לדף) האי וכו' אכללא דכ"ג א) ע"כ מוחק בא"מ ושונה הכל דיבור אחד כמ"ש לעיל: ב] ד"ה ר"ע אומר וכו' דאיקרי נפש בהמה וכו'. נ"ב והא דכבילה לא ע"ב אמר ר"ע אפילו נפש בהמה במשמע שאני התם שהכתוב לכל נפש והכי משמעות הברייתא עם דקאמרה משמעות שנאמר לכל נפש שהוא מלא אפי' נפש בהמה וכו' אך קשה לי מהא דכתב בפ' אמור וכהן כי יקנה נפש קנין כספו דקי"ל אפי' נפש בהמה במשמע וכמ"ש הכ"ב פי"א דתרומות משנה ט ולע"ע: ג] ד"ה לאביו וכו' אלא לכהן הדיוט וכו' לכ"ג נמי כל"ל. א"מ: ד] ד"ה ולאחותו וכו' דכ"ג נמי כדאמרי'. היכא דאמרינן נמחק ונ"ב סלקא דעתך. א"מ: ה] ד"ה ולאחותו נ"ל וכו' נזיר וכהן דלאיסור לאו וכו' כצ"ל:

תורה אור

ולר"ע, מכדי לא שנא כהן גדול לחודיה ולא שנא כ"ג והוא נזיר, נפקא מ"לאחיו", "לאביו ולאמו" למה לי? צריכי, דאי כתב "אביו" הוה אמינא: היינו טעמא דלא מיטמא ליה — משום דחזקה בעלמא הוא, אבל אמו דידעין דילידתיה — ליטמא לה. ואי כתב רחמנא "אמו" — הוה אמינא: אמו לא ליטמא לה — דלאו אזיל זרעה בתרה, אבל אביו, כיון דאמר מר °"למשפחותם לבית אבותם" (במדבר א) — אימא ליטמא ליה, קא משמע לן. (א) °"ועל כל נפשות מת לא יבא" (ויקרא כא) למה לי? על

ולרבי עקיבא מכדי לא שנא כהן גדול לחודיה ול"ש כהן גדול ונזיר. איכא למשמע מ"ולאחיו", דהשתא כהן גדול והוא נזיר מיטמא למת מצוה, כל שכן כהן גדול לחודיה. ולאביו נמי דאינו מיטמא משמע ליה מ"על כל נפשות מת" כדלעיל, הא דכתב רחמנא "לאביו ולאמו" לבתר הכי למה ליה? הא קא (ב) משמע לן מ"על כל נפשות מת"! צריכי דאי כתב רחמנא לאביו. ולא א) לאמו, הוה אמינא: לאביו הוא דאינו מיטמא משום דלא ברירא מילתא אי אבוה הוא, ב) דחזקה בעלמא הוא. אבל אמו דודאי ילידתיה — ליטמא לה, קמשמע לן. למשפחותם לבית אבותם. (ב"ב קט:) משפחת אב קרויה משפחה, ולא משפחת אם קרויה משפחה. ולרבי עקיבא דאמר גבי נזיר: "נפש" אלו רחוקים, "מת" אלו קרובים, האי "על כל נפשות מת" דכתיב גבי כהן גדול למה ליה? אמר לך: צריכא.

ולרבי עקיבא ל"ש כהן גדול לחודיה ול"ש כ"ג והוא נזיר נפקא ליה מלאחיו. דנזיר, דאפילו יש בו שתי קדושות, "לאביו ולאמו" דנזיר ל"ל? וא"ת: והא צריכי למת מצוה! וי"ל, דהכי פירושא: למה לי תרווייהו? לכתוב חד למת מצוה. והוא הדין נמי דיש להקשות: "לאביו ולאמו" דכ"ג למה לי תרווייהו! לא לכתוב אלא "לאמו" לגזרה שוה, ד"אביו" לא איצטריך לגופיה בכ"ג לקרובים, א] [דלעיל] דריש ר"ע מ"על כל נפשות" — רחוקים, "מת" — קרובים. ב] והצריכותא דקעביד על תרין קראי — בין בנזיר בין בכ"ג. ומשני דצריכי. דאי כתב אביו ולא "לאמו" הוה אמינא: דווקא לאביו אינו מיטמא, משום דקורבא דאביו חזקה בעלמא הוא, משום דרוב בעילות אחר הבעל. אבל אמו דודאי ילידתיה — אימא דמיטמא לה. לכך אי הוה כתב "לאביו" לחודיה הוה אמינא דאתי יתורא ד"אביו" למעוטי "לאמו" מהאי טעמא. ואי הוה כתיב ל"אמו" בלא לאביו הוה אמינא: דוקא לאמו אינו מיטמא, דלא אזיל זרעה בתרה, כדכתיב "למשפחותם לבית אבותם", והלכך אי הוה כתיב "לאמו" ולא כתיב "לאביו" — הוה אמינא ד"אמו" מייתרא למעוטי "אביו". ו"על כל נפשות מת לא יבא" דמוקי ליה לקרובים מיותרא, אע"ג דכתיב סתמא, דאי לא כתיב "אביו" בפי' הוה מוקמינן ליה בקורבא דלד אם דוקא מסברא, דקאמר ג] בודאי ילידתיה. ואי כתיב "אביו" ולא "אמו" (כו') בפי', אע"ג דמרבינן קרובים מ"מת" דמיותר הוא, הוה מוקמינן ליה דוקא בקורבא דלד אב, מטעמא דקאמר התלמוד ד] שזרעו מתייחס אחריו. וא"ת: ואפי' אי כתיב "אביו" ולא "אמו", היכי תיסק אדעתין דלאמו יטמא? ותיפוק ליה מק"ו מאביו מק"ו דלעיל: ומה במקום שכהן הדיוט מיטמא לאחיו מאביו, כדאמרינן לעיל! ה] והוא גופא [*תימא], דק"ו ניתן למידרש! ונראה למהר"ף: דלר"ע דדריש מ"נפש מת" דנזיר, וכן מ"על כל נפשות מת לא יבא" דכ"ג, דבקרובים איירי — א"כ הוי כללא לכל הקרובים, הלכך כי פרט בתר הכי חד מן הקרובים, אביו או אמו הוה אמינא אין בכלל אלא מה שבפרט אביו אין, אמו לא. או איפכא, כיון שיש טעם לחלק ביניהם. וכיון דהוי מטעם כלל *או פרט, דאין בכלל אלא מה שבפרט — א"כ אפילו בק"ו נמי לא אתי אמו מאביו. כמו כלל ופרט דעלמא, דאין לרבות יותר מן הפרט, לא בק"ו ולא בשום דרשא אחרת, כדפרישית בריש "שלשה מינין" (לעיל דף לה.). וא"ת: כיון דמטעם כלל ופרט הוא, א"כ למה לי טעמא שנותן לאביו מטעם חזקה, וכן לאמו משום דלא אזיל זרעה בתרה? תיפוק ליה מהאי טעמא דאין בכלל אלא מה שבפרט, כמו בעלמא! ועוד קשה: דמשמע כאן מדכתיב "ואמו" הוה ידעינן כולהון קרובים, כגון אחיו ואחותו, ואמאי? נימא לעולם אין בכלל אלא מה שבפרט! וי"ל: שאני איסור טומאה, דגלי קרא בכהן הדיוט שמטמא לקרובים ולא לרחוקים, א"כ בסברא דקורבא היתה תליא מילתא, והלכך צריך ליתן טעמא באביו ובאמו מה לד קורבא יש בזה יותר מבזה. וניחא נמי דמאביו ואמו ידעינן אחיו ואחותו, שהרי אין לך עוד טעם לחלק בקרובים יותר רק מב' טעמים — מלד האב ומלד האם, כדקא מפרש בצריכותא. והלכך, כיון דגלי אביו ואמו — ה"ה אחיו ואחותו, ואין לנו לומר תו: אין בכלל אלא מה שבפרט. ותדע דהכי הוא, שהרי לעיל במילתיה דרבי ישמעאל דקאמר מעיקרא: או אינו אומר "לאביו" [אלא] למעוטי אחרים רחוקים, ו] ופירשו בתוספות לעיל — מטעמא דכלל ופרט, [וסתר] ליה משום דגלי בכהן הדיוט שסברא הוא ליטמא לקרובים יותר מלרחוקים — ש"מ דגבי איסור טומאה, גם כי דיינינן ליה בכלל ופרט, צריך טעם וסברא לדבר. והשתא ניחא, דלר"ע צריך למיכתב תרווייהו "לאביו ולאמו" ולא אתיא אמו בק"ו מאביו, כדפרישית. ולא דמי לר' ישמעאל דיליף ליה מק"ו אמו מאביו, דלרבי ישמעאל כללא דנזיר "על כל נפשות מת לא יבא" — לא בקרובים כתיב, וכיון דברחוקים כתיב — אינך יכול לומר כלל ופרט, אא"כ תאמר דלמעוטי רחוקים קאתי, וזה אינך יכול לומר, כדאיתא לעיל [ק"ו] מכהן הדיוט. הלכך תו ליכא למידייניה בכלל ופרט למעוטי קרובים אחרים, כגון אמו, כמו לר"ע, דהא כללא לאו בקרובים כתיב כמו לר"ע. והלכך אתיא אמו שפיר בק"ו מאביו. ומ"מ צריכינן לק"ו משום סברא דצריכותא, כדפרישית לעיל. וא"ת: הא תינח גבי נזיר, אבל גבי כ"ג הא כללא הויא בקרובים גם לר' ישמעאל, כדאמר לעיל: "על כל נפשות מת לא יבא" — בקרובים, או אינו אלא ברחוקים — אמינא ק"ו מכהן הדיוט. וא"כ נידייניה בכלל ופרט! וי"ל: כיון דגבי נזיר לא מצי למידייניה בכלל ופרט, ואתיא אמו בק"ו מאביו כדפרישית, א"כ גבי כ"ג נמי הכי הוא, דהא ילפינן מהדדי מגזרה שוה ד"אמו". ועוד י"ל: דשמא לא חשיב ליה כללא, כיון דהא דאוקימנא ליה להאי דכ"ג בקרובים אינו מכח [הפסוק] עצמו דכ"ג, אלא מכהן הדיוט ב"או אינו" כדפרישית לעיל. ולא דמי לדר"ע, דר"ע מוקי קרא מטעמא דנפשיה, מכח הפסוק עצמו, הלכך חשיב כלל גמור. וצריך עיון: דהא ר"ע דריש ריבה ומיעט פ"ג דשבועות (דף כו.)! וי"ל: דגם בריבה ומיעט ממעטינן מיהא דבר אחד, ואין מועיל ק"ו או מדה אחרת לרבות. והלכך, אי הוה כתיב "אביו" הוה ממעטינן אמו, ולא אתיא בק"ו, ותו לא מידי. כל זה לשון מהר"ף. וא"ת: וכיון דצריכי לגופייהו אביו אמו, א"כ מהיכא תיתי [מת מצוה] בנזיר? וגם לא מייתרי לג"ש בכ"ג, כיון דמילרך צריכי! וי"ל: דעל כרחיך מיותרים הם למת מצוה בנזיר, ולג"ש בכ"ג, דאל"כ לישתוק קרא מתרוייהו, דהא ר"ע דריש מייתורא [ד"מת"] קרובים בין בנזיר בין בכ"ג, ועל כרחיך מקרא מלא דבר הכתוב בכולהו קרובים, ולא מפליג בין אביו לאמו בשום סברא, למה נכתבו שניהם כל עיקר? אלא בנזיר — לאיתויי מת מצוה, ובכ"ג — לג"ש. ומיהו, אי לא כתיב אלא חד "לאביו" או "לאמו" — אז הוה אמינא דאע"ג דמקרא מלא דבר הכתוב, מ"מ הוה אמינא דלהכי כתיב חד — למעוטי אידך, ולאפוקי מקרא מלא כדפרישית. וא"ת: מי מזקקין לומר את הצריכותא לר"ע בין אמו לאביו? אדרבה, נאמר דאין שום סברא לחלק ביניהם, ומייתרי תרווייהו "לאביו ולאמו" בין בנזיר בין בכ"ג, ונדרוש "אביו" למת מצוה, "ואמו" לג"ש שבשניהם. ואע"ג דברייתא מזכיר שניהם במילתיה דר"ע "לאביו ולאמו" תרווייהו למת מצוה — מה בכך? מ"מ נימא דלאו דווקא נקט, אלא מ"אביו" לחודיה נפקא, דהכי נמי אמרינן לעיל לר' ישמעאל, דאע"פ שהזכיר בברייתא "לאביו ולאמו" גבי מת מצוה, אפ"ה אסיקנא דלא אתי כלל אביו ואמו למת מצוה, אלא אביו לגופיה, ואמו לג"ש, ומת מצוה מ"לאחיו" הוא דנפקא לן, כדאמרינן לעיל — אלמא לאו דווקא — הכי נמי נימא דלאו דווקא נקט "אמו", אלא מ"אביו" לחודיה נפקא! וי"ל: דלא דמי, דודאי לר' ישמעאל לא הזכיר לדרשת מת מצוה כי אם "אמו", דהא "לאביו" איצטריך לגופיה, לקרובים, כדאמרינן לעיל. הלכך, אע"ג דלמסקנא מת מצוה מ"לאחיו" הוא דנפקא לן ולא מ"אמו", מ"מ שפיר הזכיר "לאמו" לגבי מת מצוה, משום דאי לא הוה כתיב "לאחיו" — הוה דרשינן ומוקמינן "לאמו" למת מצוה, ולא לג"ש. דלעולם אית לן לאוקמי קודם למת מצוה דדמי לגופיה, מלגזרה שוה למילף לעלמא. הלכך, "לאמו" שנכתב קודם הוה מוקמינן לדרשה דמת מצוה, אי לא כתיב "לאחיו" אחרי כן. ומיהו, למסקנא דמצינן למדרש למת מצוה מ"לאחיו" — מוקמי לן לאמו לג"ש. אבל הכא, במילתיה דר"ע דנפקא לן קרובים מ"על כל נפשות" כדאמרינן לעיל, מ"לאביו ולאמו" לא אצטרכינן כלל לגופייהו, הלכך על כרחין מה שהזכיר בברייתא גבי מת מצוה "לאביו ולאמו" דהא תרווייהו מייתרי כדפרישית — תרווייהו נקט משום מת מצוה. דאי "לאביו" משום מת מצוה "ולאמו" משום ג"ש — למה הזכיר כלל "לאמו" לגבי מת מצוה, דכיון דכתיב "לאביו" קודם בקרא, וקרא קמא לאוקמי למת מצוה כדפרישית, ואם כן הכא ליכא למימר כמו לר' ישמעאל. אלא ש"מ דוקא הזכיר שניהם למת מצוה, ומילרך צריכי, כדמסיק במסקנא כל זה לשון מהר"ף. מקשינן: דבסוגיא דידן דריש לר"ע "לאביו ולאמו" דנזיר מתרווייהו למת מצוה, ובפ' "טבול יום" בזבחים (דף ק.) דריש לר"ע "לאביו" לחודיה למת מצוה, ו"לאמו" — הרי שהיה כהן הדיוט והוא נזיר, דגם הוא מיטמא למת מצוה, "לאחיו" — הרי שהיה כ"ג והוא נזיר, שגם הוא מיטמא למת מצוה. ומאי שנא? ועוד קשה: היכי דריש סתמא שתי דרשות מ"אביו ואמו"? והא צריכי "אביו ואמו" כדקאמר הכא, וא"כ ליכא למידרש מינייהו כי אם דרשא אחת, כדפרישית לעיל! מיהו בתוספת' דסוגיא דפ' "טבול יום" פליגא אהך דהכא, ולית ליה צריכותא דהכא, הלכך "לאביו ולאמו" לשתי דרשות קאתו. וא"ת סוגיא דידן, אמאי לא מצריך נמי קרא לכהן הדיוט ונזיר כי התם? וי"ל: דסברא, דכיון דכהן הדיוט מיטמא לקרובים — לא מהניא טופיינא דכהן הדיוט בקרא דקדושתו קדושת עולם בהדי נזיר להצריך פסוק, דכיון דבטומאת עצמו קיל מנזיר. אבל כ"ג, דגם הוא אינו מיטמא לקרובים — ההוא ודאי הוה אמינא דמהניא טופיינא דידיה, דקדושתו קדושת עולם, שלא יטמא למת מצוה. ולהכי איצטריך קרא דנזיר ד"לאחיו" לכ"ג והוא נזיר. וסוגיא דהתם סברה דאף לטופיינא דכהן הדיוט ונזיר צריך קרא מיותר. ומיהו ק': דכיון דהתם בפ' "טבול יום" לית ליה צריכותא ד"אביו ואמו", א"כ אביו ואמו דכ"ג ל"ל? בשלמא דנזיר — כולהו [מפורש] התם, כדפריש'. אבל בכ"ג קשיא, דתסגי *בהך לגזירה שוה! וליכא למימר דסוגיא דהתם ידרוש גבי כ"ג מ"לאביו" מת מצוה, "ולאמו" לג"ש — דהא ידעינן מת מצוה בכ"ג מלאחיו

כ"א לימא

נ"ל ופרט

נ"ל בחד

ולר"ע מכדי ל"ש כ"ג לחודיה ול"ש כ"ג ונזיר נפקא ליה מלאחיו לאביו ולאמו דכ"ג למה לי נהי דלאמו צריך לג"ש לאביו למה לי וה"ה דמצי למבעי לאביו ולאמו דנזיר אמאי צריך תרוייהו למת מצוה: משום דחזקה בעלמא הוא דרוב בעילות אחר הבעל אבל אמו דודאי ילידתי' אימא ליטמא לה והאי דדרשי' מת אלו הקרובים הוה מוקמי' לה בקרובים מצד האב דמדכתיב לאביו הוה ממעטינן אמו וקרוביה שיטמא להם כיון שהם ודאים: כיון דכתיב למשפחותם לבית אבותם ודרשי' מינה פ' יש נוחלין משפחת אב קרויה משפחה הוה אמינא דלאמו אתא למעוטי אב וקרובים דידיה שיטמא להם ומת אלו הקרובים הוה מוקמי' בקרובי האם אבל השתא דכתיב תרוייהו מעל כל נפשות מת דכ"ג ומנפש מת דנזיר שמעי' כל קרובים ולאמו דכ"ג הוצרך לכתוב לג"ש וכיון דהוצרך לכתוב לאמו הוצרך לכתוב [לאביו] למדרש מיניה דמטמא למת מצוה ואצטריך נמי למכתב לאמו דלא תימא מאביו ממעטי' אמו ואית ליה לר"ע מופנה מצד א' למדים ואין משיבין א"נ כיון דגלי קרא גבי כ"ג דאביו ואמו שקולים הם ה"ה גבי נזיר ואייתר לאמו דנזיר להפנות ג"ש מב' צדדים: על כל נפשות מת למה לי אגב דדריש נפש מת דנזיר בעי נמי למדרש קרא דכהן גדול

נוסחת הריב"ן

א) כתב לאמו: ב) אלא חזקה:

הגהות הב"ח

(א) גמ' קמ"ל ולר"ע על כל נפשות: (ב) רש"י ד"ה ולר"ע וכו' לבתר הכי למה לי הא קא משמעינן לה מעל נפש מת הס"ד ותיבת כל נמחק:

הגהות מהר"ב רנשבורג

א] תוס' ד"ה ולר"ע וכו' בכ"ג לקרובים דלעיל תיבת דלעיל נמחק וכ"ב דלקמן א"מ ויעו"ש: ב] בא"ד דריש ר"ע וכו' קרובים נ"ב דלקמן קאי על כ"ג אבל לעיל בדברי ר"ע נפש אלו הרחוקים מת אלו קרובים זה איירי בנזיר כנ"ל א"מ: ג] ד"ה ומשני וכו' דקאמר בודאי ילידתיה תיבות בודאי ילידתיה נמחקו וכ"ב דלא אזיל זרעה בתרה ואי כתיב אביו ולא אמו בפי' כנ"ל א"מ: ד] בא"ד מטעמא דקאמר הש"ס שזרעו מתייחס אחריו. תיבות שזרעו מתייחס אחריו נמחקו וכ"ב משום דחזקה בעלמא הוא א"מ: ה] בא"ד כדאמרינן לעיל והוא גופא תימא תיבות והוא גופא תימא נמחקו וכ"ב והוי כמו דכתיב אמו בהדיא א"מ: ו] בא"ד אחרים רחוקים ופירשו בתוס' וכו' על כל נפשות מת לא יבא וכו' דברחוקים כתיב אינך יכול לומר וכו' ומ"מ צריכינן לק"ו משום סברא דצריכותא עי' בכ"ז באורח מישור:

עין משפט
נר מצוה

יג א מיי׳ פ״ז מהלכות נזירות הלכה ב סמג עשין קכז:
יד ב מיי׳ שם הלכה א והלכה ה ופ״ו שם הלכה ג:

"עַל כָּל" — לְאַפּוּקֵי רְחוֹקִים, "מֵת". לְאַפּוּקֵי קְרוֹבִים, "נַפְשׁוֹת" — לְאַפּוּקֵי *רְבִיעִית דָּם שֶׁיָּצָא מִשְּׁנֵי מֵתִים, שֶׁמְּטַמֵּא בְּאֹהֶל, שֶׁנֶּאֱמַר "עַל כָּל נַפְשֹׁת מֵת לֹא יָבֹא".§ **מתני׳** *א"עַל אֵלּוּ טוּמְאוֹת הַנָּזִיר מְגַלֵּחַ: עַל הַמֵּת, וְעַל כַּזַּיִת מִן הַמֵּת, וְעַל כַּזַּיִת, וְעַל מְלֹא תַּרְווֹד רָקָב, עַל הַשִּׁדְרָה, וְעַל הַגּוּלְגּוֹלֶת, וְעַל אֵבֶר מִן הַמֵּת וְעַל אֵבֶר מִן הַחַי שֶׁיֵּשׁ עָלָיו בָּשָׂר כָּרָאוּי, וְעַל חֲצִי קַב עֲצָמוֹת, וְעַל חֲצִי לוֹג דָּם, וְעַל מַגָּעָן וְעַל מַשָּׂאָן וְעַל אֲהִילָן. וְעַל עֶצֶם כִּשְׂעוֹרָה, עַל מַגָּעוֹ וְעַל מַשָּׂאוֹ. בעַל אֵלּוּ הַנָּזִיר מְגַלֵּחַ, וּמַזֶּה בַּשְּׁלִישִׁי וּבַשְּׁבִיעִי, וְסוֹתֵר אֶת הַקּוֹדְמִין, וְאֵינוֹ מַתְחִיל לִמְנוֹת אֶלָּא עַד שֶׁיִּטְהַר וּמֵבִיא אֶת קָרְבְּנוֹתָיו.§ **גמרא** *תָּנוּ רַבָּנַן: אַחַר פְּטִירָתוֹ שֶׁל רַבִּי מֵאִיר אָמַר לָהֶן רַבִּי יְהוּדָה לְתַלְמִידָיו: אַל יִכָּנְסוּ תַּלְמִידֵי רַבִּי מֵאִיר לְכָאן מִפְּנֵי שֶׁקַּנְתְּרָנִין הֵן, וְלֹא לִלְמוֹד תּוֹרָה הֵן בָּאִין אֶלָּא לְקַפְּחֵנִי בַּהֲלָכוֹת הֵן בָּאִין. דָּחַק סוּמָכוֹס וְנִכְנַס. אָמַר לָהֶם, כָּךְ שָׁנָה לִי רַבִּי מֵאִיר: עַל אֵלּוּ טוּמְאוֹת הַנָּזִיר מְגַלֵּחַ — עַל הַמֵּת וְעַל כַּזַּיִת מִן הַמֵּת. כָּעַס רַבִּי יְהוּדָה וְאָמַר לָהֶן: לֹא כָּךְ אָמַרְתִּי לָכֶם: אַל יִכָּנְסוּ תַּלְמִידֵי רַבִּי מֵאִיר לְכָאן, מִפְּנֵי שֶׁקַּנְתְּרָנִין הֵן? עַל כַּזַּיִת מִן הַמֵּת מְגַלֵּחַ, עַל הַמֵּת לֹא כ"ש?! אָמַר

עַל כָּל לְאַפּוּקֵי רְחוֹקִים. דְּלָא לִיטַמֵּא. מֵת לְאַפּוּקֵי קְרוֹבִים. נַפְשׁוֹת. שֶׁאִם יָצָאת רְבִיעִית דָּם מִב׳ מֵתִים אֵינוֹ מִטַּמֵּא לָהֶם. **מתני׳** נֵצֶל. מְפָרֵשׁ בַּגְּמָרָא. וְעַל אֵבֶר מִן הַחַי וְעַל אֵבֶר מִן הַמֵּת שֶׁיֵּשׁ עֲלֵיהֶם בָּשָׂר כָּרָאוּי. דְּהַיְינוּ כְּדֵי שֶׁיָּכוֹל לִחְיוֹת וּלְהַבְרִיא, אַף עַל פִּי שֶׁאֵין עֲלֵיהֶן בָּשָׂר כַּזַּיִת. חֲצִי לוֹג דָּם. שְׁתֵּי רְבִיעִיּוֹת. עַל עֶצֶם כִּשְׂעוֹרָה עַל מַגָּעוֹ וְעַל מַשָּׂאוֹ. אֲבָל לֹא עַל אֲהִילוֹ. **גמ׳** קַנְתְּרָנִין. טירטוריו"ש. לְקַפְּחֵנִי. לְנַצְּחֵנִי. כָּעַס רַבִּי יְהוּדָה. וְאָמַר: זוֹ א) אֵינוֹ מִשְׁנָה. וַעֲדַיִין

מ"לְאָחִיו" דנזיר, כדקאמר התלמוד, מה לי כ"ג לחודיה, מה לי כ"ג ונזיר? לכך נראה דהתם נמי בפ׳ "טבול יום" אית ליה צריכותא לגבי כ"ג, אלא סבר כיון דגלי לן תרוייהו בכ"ג, דאין חילוק בין זה לזה בין אב לאם, כי אם גילוי מילתא בעלמא הוא, ויליף נזיר מיניה, הלכך דריש תרוייהו גבי נזיר סתם. מיהו, צריך לומר דסוגיא דהכא חלוקה, דמצריך גם לגבי נזיר תרוייהו, לכך לא דריש מ"לאמו" כהן הדיוט והוא נזיר כי התם. ועוד יש ליישב גם הך דהכא, דסברה כי ההיא ד"טבול יום", דדוחק הוא לפלוגי סוגיא דשמעתין אההיא דפ׳ "טבול יום", דהא אידי ואידי ר"ע היא, ואין סברא לומר דתרי תנאי נינהו אליבא דר"ע, מדלא קאמר התלמוד בהדיא. ואף על גב דסוגיא דידן עביד צריכותא מאביו ומאמו, והתם דריש תרתי מאביו ומאמו — נאמר דמקרא דכ"ג עביד צריכותא, ולגלויי מילתא בעלמא אנזיר הוא. ומעתה גם בנזיר שוין, ואייתר לן בנזיר תרוייהו לדרשא כדדריש התם. וא"ת: א"כ אמאי דריש הכא מ"לאביו ולאמו" דנזיר תרוייהו למת מצוה לר"ע? הא בחדא סגי! וי"ל: דאין הכי נמי, דהכא נמי נימא "לאביו" לחודיה למת מצוה, ו"לאמו" משום כהן הדיוט והוא נזיר, כדדריש התם. ומיהו, לא חש לפרושי כל הדרשות הכא, משום דסמיך אסוגיא דהתם דפרק "טבול יום". וכן דרך התלמוד שמקצר במקום אחד ומאריך במקום אחר. וא"ת: א"כ למה הזכיר לר"ע כאן דרשא דכ"ג ונזיר כדדרשינן, *בסמוך נמי אסוגיא דהתם, כמו שסומך בדרשא דכהן הדיוט ונזיר דדרשינן מ"לאמו", שלא הביאה כאן לאותה הדרשא? ויש לומר: היינו משום דאיצטריך ליה להביא דרשא דכהן גדול ונזיר מ"לאחיו", ולמימר: *למה לי כ"ג ונזיר כו׳ כדי לאפנויי ההוא לאביו ולאמו דכ"ג לגזירה שוה, ומה שנכתבו שניהם אביו ואמו — היינו משום הצריכותא שביניהם. וגם מיניה מקשינן לר׳ ישמעאל כ"ג ונזיר א] עליה, ו"לאחותו" נמי מפרש לר"ע דכתיב בתר "לאחיו", הואיל והתחיל לדרוש "לאחיו" כדפרישית, שצריך לו ב] לגמור הפסוק עד סופו. אי נמי: משום דלר"ע איצטריך טפי "לאחותו" יותר מלרבי ישמעאל, משום (*דאית) ליה לר"ע מה לי חד לאו כו׳. כל זה לשון מהר"ף. **על** כל לאפוקי רחוקים. הנך "לאפוקי" הוי פירושא כמו: נפקא ליה מהאי קרא. כלומר, שמפסוק זה יוצאה הדרשא שלהם. משמע דמ"על כל" לחודיה דריש רחוקים, מדדריש בסמוך "נפשות" לרביעית דם הבאה משני מתים. ודוחק הוא, דהא ג] גבי נזיר נמי כתיב "על כל נפש", ואפ"ה לא דריש מיניה רחוקים כי אם מ"נפש"! לכך נראה דהכא נמי דריש רחוקים מ"על כל נפשות", ומ"מ דריש נמי מיניה רביעית דם משני מתים, מדכתיב "נפשות" לשון רבים, ולא "נפש". ויש לתמוה: למה ליה לר"ע גבי כ"ג קרא דרחוקים? תיפוק ליה מק"ו מכהן הדיוט, כמו לתנא דריש פרקין, או משום איסור שהיה עליו בהדיוטותו להיכא אזל, כדפרישית לעיל, דזה עיקר הטעם לעיל! ופי׳ בתוס׳: לעבור עליו בשני לאוין. ותימה קצת: דהתלמוד לא הזכירו כלל, וצריך עיון. לשון מהר"ף. **מתני׳** על אלו טומאות הנזיר מגלח על המת ועל כזית מן המת. בין במגע בין במשא בין באהל. ומפרש בגמרא, דהשתא על כזית מן המת מגלח, על מת שלם לא כ"ש? **נצל.** מוהל מן המת, כדמפרש בגמ׳. **ועל** מלא תרווד רקב. רקבון ועפרורית הבא מן המת. ובגמרא מפרש שיעורא. תרוד = כף. **ועל** השדרה ועל הגולגולת. ואע"פ שאין עליה בשר כלל. ובגמ׳ בעי אי על תרוייהו או על חדא מנהון. **ועל** אבר מן המת ואבר מן החי שיש עליהם בשר כראוי. בפרק "העור והרוטב" (חולין דף קכח:) מפרש שזהו בשר שיוכל האבר לחיות ממנו אם היה מחובר לאדם חי, שיוכל להעלות ארוכה. ואע"פ שאין בו כזית בשר. **ועל** חצי קב עצמות. ומיירי שבאו מרוב מנייני או מרוב בנייני. כגון שיש ד] בקב עצמות שנשתברו וחצי קב עצמות זה מהן מעט מכל עצם ועצם — והיינו מרוב מנייני. ורוב בנייני — מפרש לקמן: שני שוקים וירך אחד או איפכא. ואע"פ שמטמא באהל ברובע הקב, כדאיתא בהדיא במתניתין *בפ"ק דאהלות: אלו מטמאין באהל, וקחשיב רובע עצמות הבא מרוב מניינו או מרוב בניינו, מ"מ הלכה הוא דאין הנזיר מגלח אלא על חצי קב. וליכא לפרושי חצי קב משאר עצמות, שאינו מרוב בניינו ולא מרוב מניינו, דהא באהל נמי לא מטמא, מדלא קתני להו בפ"ק דאהלות בהדי הנך דמטמא באהל. **ועל** חצי לוג דם. ואע"פ שמטמא באהל ברביעית, כדאיתא במתניתין דאהלות — מ"מ אין הנזיר מגלח אלא על חצי לוג. ושיעורין הלכה למשה מסיני. **על** משאו ועל מגעו ועל אהילו. דכל הני דחשיב לעיל — מטמא בין במגע בין במשא בין באהל. ועצם כשעורה על מגעו ועל משאו מגלח, אבל באהל — אפילו טמויי לא מטמא. **על** אלו הנזיר מגלח. בגמ׳ מפרש "על אלו" דרישא, ו"על אלו" דסיפא למעוטי מאי. **ומזה** בשלישי ובשביעי וסותר את הקודמין. דכתיב "והימים הראשונים יפלו", ואין מתחיל למנות נזירות דטהרה עד שיטהר. ול"ג במשנה "ויביא קרבנותיו". וכן מוכח בגמ׳, דאיבעיא מיבעיא ליה: מתניתין מני, דא"כ — פשיטא דרבנן היא. **אלא** לקפחני בהלכות. לצערני. **כך** שנה לי רבי מאיר. במשנה: על המת ועל כזית מן המת. ורבי יהודה לא היה שונה "על המת" במשנתנו, משום דכל שכן דמכזית מן המת וכו׳. *עדיין. יכול להקשות ולומר: על אבר ממנו מגלח, כדתנן במתניתין, ומיירי דאפילו אין עליו כזית בשר, כדתנן פ"ק דאהלות שהאברים אין להם שיעור — כל שכן על מת שלם, ואכתי מאי קמשמע לן "על המת"? **אלא** כדאמר ר׳ יוחנן לא נצרכה אלא לנפל שלא נתקשרו אבריו בגידין. ה] [ואית] בו כזית בשר. ואבר מאותו נפל אינו מטמא באהל, כיון שאין בו גידין, דלא מיקרי אבר אלא עצם ובשר וגידין. ועל כל המת מגלח אע"פ שאין לו עדיין גידין. והא דקאמר הכא "כדאמר ר׳ יוחנן", פי׳ רבינו יצחק דאמתניתין דאהלות אמרה, דקתני: המת וכזית מן המת דמטמא באהל — מוקי לה רבי יוחנן בנפל שלא נתקשרו אבריו בגידין*.

רבא

פי׳ הרא"ש

על כל לאפוקי רחוקים ולעבור עליו בב׳ לאוין דבלאו האי קרא ידעי׳ ליה דלא גרע מכהן הדיוט נפשות לאפוקי רביעית דם הבאה מב׳ מתים שאסור ליטמא להם דדרשינן נפשות מת ב׳ נפשות משום מת א׳ דהיינו רביעית א׳ דאין אדם יכול להיות בפחות מרביעית דם: כך כתוב במקצת ספרים לאפוקי רביעית דם וכו׳ והצריכו המפרשים לפרושי לאפוקי שלא יטמא לה וברוב ספרים כתיב לאיתויי וניחא הך גיר׳ טפי לאיתויי שמטמא באוהל: אלא לקפחני בהלכות. לצערנא: כך שנה לנו רבי מאיר ור׳ יהודה לא היה שונה

נ"ל מה לי

גליון הש"ס

תום׳ ד"ה על כל. גבי נזיר נמי כתיב על כל נפש. בנזיר לא כתיב כל ע׳ א"מ:

הגהות מהר"ב רנשבורג

א] בא"ד (המתחיל מעבר לדף) ולמימר מה לי וכו׳ כהן גדול ונזיר עליה תיבת עליה נמחק ונ"ב מגליה: ב] בא"ד כדפרישית שצריך לו לגמור תיבת לגמור נמחק ונ"ב גומר: ג] ד"ה על כל וכו׳ דהא גבי נזיר נמי כתיב על כל נ"ב עי׳ א"מ ביאור דבריהם בזה דתמוהים דבנזיר לא כתיב כל: ד] ד"ה ועל חצי וכו׳ כגון שיש בקב תיבת בקב נמחק ונ"ב רוב א"מ: ה] ד"ה אלא וכו׳ נתקשרו אבריו בגידין ואית תיבת ואית נמחק ונ"ב ואין א"מ:

מסורת הש"ס

[לעיל לח וש"נ]

חולין פט: ק:

קדושין נב:

נוסחת הריב"ן

א) אינה צריכה תלמוד:

נ"ל נסמוך

דלית כל"ל

נ"ל בפרק שני

שייך לדף נ.

[וע"ע תוס׳ חולין פט: ד"ה ואמר]

וַעֲדַיִין יֹאמַר עַל אֵבֶר מִמֶּנּוּ מְגַלֵּחַ, עַל כּוּלּוֹ לֹא כָּל שֶׁכֵּן?!

*אָמַר ר' יוֹסֵי: יֹאמְרוּ, מֵאִיר שָׁכַב, יְהוּדָה כָּעַס, יוֹסֵי שָׁתַק, תּוֹרָה מַה תְּהֵא עָלֶיהָ? א"ר יוֹסֵי: לֹא נִצְרְכָה אֶלָּא לְמֵת שֶׁאֵין עָלָיו כַּזַּיִת בָּשָׂר. וַעֲדַיִין יֹאמַר: עַל אֵבֶר מִמֶּנּוּ מְגַלֵּחַ, עַל כּוּלּוֹ לֹא כָּל שֶׁכֵּן?! אֶלָּא *כִּדְאָמַר רַבִּי יוֹחָנָן: לֹא נִצְרְכָה אֶלָּא [א]לְנֵפֶל שֶׁלֹּא נִתְקַשְּׁרוּ אֵבָרָיו בְּגִידִין, הָכָא נַמִּי – בְּנֵפֶל שֶׁלֹּא נִתְקַשְּׁרוּ אֵבָרָיו בְּגִידִין. רָבָא אָמַר: *לֹא נִצְרְכָה [ב]אֶלָּא לְרוֹב בִּנְיָינוֹ וּלְרוֹב מִנְיָינוֹ שֶׁאֵין בָּהֶן רוֹבַע עֲצָמוֹת.§ "עַל כַּזַּיִת מֵת וְעַל כַּזַּיִת נֵצֶל".§ וְאֵיזֶהוּ נֵצֶל – [ג]בְּשַׂר הַמֵּת שֶׁקָּרַשׁ, וּמוֹהַל שֶׁהִרְתִּיחַ. הֵיכִי דָּמֵי? אִילֵימָא דְּלָא יָדְעִינַן דְּדִידֵיהּ הוּא, כִּי קָרַשׁ מַאי הָוֵי? אֶלָּא דְּיָדְעִינַן דְּדִידֵיהּ הוּא – אע"ג דְּלָא קָרַשׁ! אֲמַר ר' יִרְמְיָה: [ד]בִּסְתָם, אִי קָרַשׁ – מוֹהַל הוּא, לֹא קָרַשׁ – דִּלְמָא כִּיחוֹ וְנִיעוֹ הוּא. [ה]בְּעָא מִינֵּיהּ אַבַּיֵי מֵרַבָּה: יֵשׁ נֵצֶל לִבְהֵמָה אוֹ אֵין נֵצֶל לִבְהֵמָה? מִי אָמְרִינַן: (א) גְּמִירִי נֵצֶל דְּאָתֵי מֵאָדָם, אֲבָל דְּאָתֵי מִבְּהֵמָה לָא. אוֹ דִּלְמָא לָא שְׁנָא? הָנִיחָא לְמ"ד *טוּמְאָה חֲמוּרָה עַד לַגֵּר, וְטוּמְאָה קַלָּה עַד לַכֶּלֶב – שַׁפִּיר. אֶלָּא לְמ"ד [ו]טוּמְאָה חֲמוּרָה עַד לַכֶּלֶב – מַאי אִיכָּא לְמֵימַר? תָּא שְׁמַע: *[ז]הִמְחוּהוּ בָּאוּר – טָמֵא, בַּחַמָּה – טָהוֹר. וְאִי ס"ד עַד לַכֶּלֶב – אֲפִי' בַּחַמָּה נַמִּי! אֵימַת מְמַחֵי לֵיהּ – בָּתַר דְּאַסְרוּחַ בַּחַמָּה, כֵּיוָן דְּאַסְרַח – הֲוָה לֵיהּ עָפָר. *תְּנַן: [ח]כָּל הַנִּצּוֹק טָהוֹר, [ט]חוּץ מִדְּבַשׁ הַזִּיפִים וְהַצַּפִּיחִית.

ב"ש

רש"י

וַעֲדַיִין (א) יֹאמַר עַל אֵבֶר מִמֶּנּוּ מְגַלֵּחַ. וּבִלְבַד שֶׁיְּהֵא עָלָיו בָּשָׂר כָּרָאוּי, וְאע"פ שֶׁאֵין עָלָיו כַּזַּיִת בָּשָׂר, עַל מֵת כּוּלּוֹ לֹא כ"ש? (ג) ב) כִּי אָמַר ר"מ דְּעַל מֵת מְגַלֵּחַ כִּי הַהִיא דַּאֲמַר ר' יוֹחָנָן לֹא נִצְרְכָה אֶלָּא ג) לְנֵפֶל כו'. וּכְמַאן' חוּלִּין קָאֵי. וְה"נ בְּנֵפֶל שֶׁלֹּא נִתְקַשְּׁרוּ אֵבָרָיו בְּגִידִין יָפֶה יָפֶה קָאָמַר ר"מ דְּמִיטַּמֵּא, וְאע"פ שֶׁאֵין עָלָיו בָּשָׂר. וְרָבָא אָמַר. כִּי קָאָמַר ר"מ – ד) בְּרוֹב בִּנְיָינוֹ שֶׁל מֵת אוֹ בְּרוֹב מִנְיָינוֹ שֶׁאֵין עֲלֵיהֶן כַּזַּיִת בָּשָׂר וְאֵין בֵּין ה) כּוּלּוֹ רוֹבַע הַקַּב עֲצָמוֹת. דְּאע"ג דִּבְעָלְמָא לָא הָוֵי חָשִׁיב לְעִנְיַן טוּמְאַת אֹהֶל אא"כ שֶׁיְּהֵא בָּהֶן רוֹבַע עֲצָמוֹת, גַּבֵּי נָזִיר הָוֵי חָשׁוּב כְּמֵת שָׁלֵם, הוֹאִיל דְּאִית בֵּיהּ רוֹב בִּנְיָינוֹ אוֹ רוֹב מִנְיָינוֹ שֶׁהוּא מִיטַּמֵּא עָלָיו וּמְגַלֵּחַ עֲלֵיהֶם. שֶׁקָּרַשׁ. שֶׁנִּימּוֹחַ וְאַחַ"כ קָרַשׁ. וּמוֹהַל שֶׁהִרְתִּיחַ. שֶׁיָּצָא מִבְּשַׂר הַמֵּת כְּמִין מַיִם וְהִרְתִּיחַ ו) לִיקָּרֵשׁ ע"י רְתִיחוֹת שֶׁהִרְתִּיחַ. דְּכָל הָנֵי נֵצֶל כִּבְשַׂר הַמֵּת דָּמֵי וְנָזִיר מְגַלֵּחַ עָלָיו. נֵצֶל. לְשׁוֹן הֶפְרֵשׁ, כְּמוֹ "וַיַּצֵּל אֱלֹהִים" (בראשית לא). הֵיכִי דָּמֵי אִילֵימָא דְּלָא יָדְעִינַן. אִי הַהִיא מַשְׁקֶה דְּקָרַשׁ הָוֵי מִן הַמֵּת, כְּלוֹמַר דְּיָדְעִינַן וַדַּאי דְּלָאו מִמֵּת הוּא. כִּי קָרַשׁ אַמַּאי מִיטַּמֵּא. הָא יָדְעִי' דְּלָאו מִמֵּת הוּא. וְאִי מִן הַמֵּת הוּא. בְּוַדַּאי, אֲפִילּוּ לֹא קָרַשׁ אַמַּאי לָא מְטַמֵּא? א"ר יִרְמְיָה בִּסְתָם. כְּלוֹמַר, סְפֵיקֵי מְסַפְּקָא לָן אִי דְּמֵת הָוֵי אִי לָא. הִלְכָּךְ, אִי קָרַשׁ – וַדַּאי ז) מִגּוּפֵיהּ שֶׁל מֵת הוּא וְלָא כִּיחוֹ וְנִיעוֹ, וְאִי לָא קָרַשׁ – דִּלְמָא כִּיחוֹ וְנִיעוֹ הוּא, דְּהָא לֵיכָּא כִּיחוֹ וְנִיעוֹ בְּמֵת טָמֵא, דְּכָל הַמַּשְׁקִים הַיּוֹצְאִים מִמֵּת טְהוֹרִין, חוּץ מִן הַדָּם. כִּי גְּמִירִי. דְּנֵצֶל מְטַמֵּא – הַהוּא דְּאָתֵי מֵאָדָם, אֲבָל נֵצֶל דְּאָתֵי מִבְּהֵמָה לָא מְטַמֵּא כִּנְבֵלָה. אוֹ דִּלְמָא לָא שְׁנָא וְהָנִיחָא. דְּלָא אִיצְטְרִיךְ לֵיהּ לְמִיבְּעֵי אִית לֵיהּ נֵצֶל אוֹ לָא – אַלִּיבָּא דְּמ"ד דְּטוּמְאָה חֲמוּרָה, כְּלוֹמַר דְּטוּמְאַת נְבֵלָה הָוֵי לְעוֹלָם כָּל זְמַן דַּחֲזֵי לַאֲכִילָה לְגֵר, הִלְכָּךְ כֵּיוָן דְּנֵצֶל הוּא ח) לָא חֲזֵי לַאֲכִילַת אָדָם לָא מְטַמֵּא. אֶלָּא לְמ"ד דְּטוּמְאָה חֲמוּרָה לְעוֹלָם ט) הוּא עַד דְּמִיפְּסַל מֵאֲכִילַת כֶּלֶב הָכָא מַאי. מִי אָמְרִי': כֵּיוָן דַּאֲכַתִּי חֲזֵי לַאֲכִילַת כֶּלֶב – אֲכַתִּי מְטַמֵּא כַּזַּיִת נְבֵלָה, אוֹ דִּלְמָא כֵּיוָן דְּנִימּוֹחַ – כְּעַפְרָא בְּעָלְמָא דָּמֵי, וְלָא מְטַמֵּא טוּמְאָה קַלָּה. עַד לַכֶּלֶב. כָּל זְמַן שֶׁלֹּא תִּיפָּסֵל מֵאֲכִילַת כֶּלֶב, שֶׁאֵינָהּ מוּסְרַחַת כָּל כָּךְ שֶׁהַכֶּלֶב אֵינוֹ רוֹצֶה לְאוֹכְלָהּ. ת"ש. חֵלֶב נְבֵלָה שֶׁהִמְחָהוּ בָּאוּר = שֶׁהִתִּיכוֹ בָּאוּר. טָמֵא. דַּעֲדַיִין אוֹכֶל רָאוּי הוּא. הִמְחָהוּ בַּחַמָּה טָהוֹר. דְּפָרְחָה טוּמְאָתוֹ. וְאִי ס"ד. דְּיֵשׁ נֵצֶל לִבְהֵמָה, אֲפִי' הִמְחָהוּ בַּחַמָּה לֶיהֱוֵי טָמֵא כִּי חָזַר וְקָרַשׁ. לְעוֹלָם אֵימָא לָךְ דְּיֵשׁ נֵצֶל לִבְהֵמָה. וְהָכָא הַיְינוּ טַעְמָא דְּכִי הִמְחָהוּ בַּחַמָּה טָהוֹר, דְּאֵימַת קָא מְמַחֵי לֵיהּ חַמָּה – לְבָתַר דְּאַסְרַח, וְכֵיוָן דְּאַסְרַח – תּוּ לָא חֲזֵי אֲפִי' לַאֲכִילַת כֶּלֶב, וּמִשּׁוּם הָכִי טָהוֹר, וְאֵינוֹ מְטַמֵּא אֲפִי' בְּטוּמְאָה קַלָּה. תְּנַן הָתָם כָּל הַנִּיצּוֹק טָהוֹר. כָּל מַשְׁקִין שֶׁמְּרִיקִין מִכְּלִי אֶל כְּלִי, אע"פ שֶׁנִּטְמָא תַּחְתּוֹן וְקִילּוּחַ יוֹרֵד מִשָּׂפָה לְשָׂפָה – לֹא נַעֲשָׂה חִיבּוּר כְּדֵי לְטַמֵּא הָעֶלְיוֹן. חוּץ מִדְּבַשׁ הַזִּיפִים. מֵאוֹתוֹ דְּבַשׁ שֶׁהוּא עָבֶה, וִיכוֹלִין לְזַיְּיפוֹ לְעָרֵב בּוֹ מַשְׁקִין אֲחֵרִים. וְ"זִיפִים" מַשְׁמַע לְשׁוֹן זִיּוּף, כִּדְמְפָ' בְּמַסֶּ' סוֹטָה בְּפֶ' בַּתְרָא (דף מח:). וְהַצַּפִּיחִית. כְּמוֹ "כְּצַפִּיחִית בִּדְבָשׁ" (שמות טז) = בריסקרי"ש בְּלַעַ"ז. וְהוֹאִיל וְהֵן עָבִין, נַעֲשָׂה הַתַּחְתּוֹן כְּמוֹ מְחוּבָּר לָעֶלְיוֹן, שֶׁהַקִּילּוּחַ הַיּוֹרֵד לְמַטָּה לְמַשְׁקִין טְמֵאִין (ג) י) נַעֲשָׂה כּוּלּוֹ טָמֵא, וַאֲפִילּוּ הָעֶלְיוֹן. אֲבָל דְּבַשׁ שֶׁלָּנוּ, שֶׁאֵינוֹ עָב, הוֹאִיל וְזָלוּל הוּא – נִיצּוֹק שֶׁבּוֹ טָהוֹר, כְּכָל הַמַּשְׁקִין.

בש"א

תוספות

רבא אמר לא נצרכה אלא לרוב בנינו ולרוב מנינו שאין בהם רובע עצמות. והיינו "על המת" דקתני דמתני', דליכא אבר שלם. ולרבותא נקט "שאין בהם רובע עצמות", דשיעורא דנזיר הוא בחצי קב, (אלא לרבותא) דאע"פ שאין בו רובע עצמות הוא מגלח כיון שיש בו רוב הבנין או רוב המנין, אבל אם אין בו רוב הבנין או רוב המנין אינו מגלח אא"כ יש בו חצי קב, כדאמרינן במתני' דאין מגלח על אהל רובע עצמות. ואית ספרים דגרסי: לא נצרכה אלא לשדרה וגולגולת שאין בו רובע עצמות. והכי נמי בפרקין לקמן (דף נג. ושם) פריך: והאמר רבא לא נצרכה אלא לשדרה וגולגות שאין בו רובע עצמות. ולא מצינו שאמר רבא בעלמא אם לא כאן, ולכך הגיהו בספרים כן. ולא גרסי' ליה, דהיכי מצינן למימר ד"על המת" דמתני' איירי בשדרה וגולגולת? והא קתני במתני' בהדיא: ועל השדרה ועל הגולגולת! לכך יש לגרוס: [אלא] לרוב בנין, דלא תניא במתני' בפירוש. ומהאי טעמא נמי ניחא אמאי לא משני רבא אמתני' דאהלות כדמשני הכא "על המת" דקתני התם לרוב בנינו או לרוב מנינו, משום דבמתני' דאהלות קתני בהדיא: על רוב בנין או על רוב מנין דמטמא באהל. הלכך ליכא לפרושי התם "על המת" אלא כר' יוחנן. וא"כ לר' יוחנן תנא ושייר במתני' רוב בנינו ורוב מנינו, אי ס"ל דנזיר מגלח עלייהו.

ת"ר איזהו נצל בשר המת שקרש. כן היא ברייתא: בשר המת שקרש – שנימוח הבשר מתחלה ואח"כ קרש. וכן מוהל שהרתיח – מוהל היוצא מן המת, והרתיחו באור, והעלה רתיחות – היינו נצל, וכזית – מטמא באהל.

היכי דמי אי לא ידעי' דדידיה הוא. כלומר, שאין אנו יודעים אם המוהל הזה מבשר המת שנימוח, או מכיחו וניעו שהן טהורים, כי קריש מאי הוי? היכי מגלח על הספק? ואי דידעינן דדידיה הוא – ואע"ג דלא קריש נמי, ול"ל דקריש, כיון דידעינן שהוא מבשר המת? **א"ר** ירמיה בסתם. כלומר, דידעינן דבא מזה המת, אבל לא ידעינן מוהל זה מבשרו או מכיחו. קירש – ודאי מוהל הוא הבא מבשר המת, ואי לא קירש – כיחו וניעו הוא. וה"נ יש לפרש גבי הרתיח, דלא ידעינן, וכי הרתיח והעלה רתיחות – ודאי מוהל הבא מהמת הוא, וזהו נצל, לא הרתיח – כיחו וניעו הוא. **יש** נצל לבהמה. כזית מן הנבלה שנרקב מאליו ונימוח, מי מטמא במגע ובמשא או לאו? ולא לענין גילוח דנזיר קבעי. **טומאה** חמורה. היינו טומאת נבילות, לטמא אדם במגע ובמשא. **עד** לגר. עד שתפסל מלאכול לגר, כדכתיב (דברים יד) "לגר אשר בשעריך תתננה ואכלה" – הראויה לגר קרויה נבילה לטמא במגע ובמשא. והכא, כיון שאינה ראויה – לא מטמא. וליכא למיבעי מידי אי יש נצל, דאפילו אם תימצי לומר דיש נצל לבהמה – הכא טהורה, כיון דכבר נפסלה מאכילת גר. **וטומאה** קלה. פי': שאר אוכלין, שאינן מטמאין אלא כביצה לשאר אוכלין ומשקין, ומטמאין טומאת אוכלין עד שיפסלו מאכילת כלב. ומהאי סיומא לא נפקא מידי לסוגיא דידן, אלא אגב רישא נקטיה. **אלא** למ"ד טומאה חמורה עד לכלב מאי. כלומר, לדידיה איכא למיבעי: מי הוי א] של בהמה חשיב כבשר נבלה, ומטמאה לאדם במגע ובמשא, שהרי אכתי ראוי לכלב הוא. או לא גמירי נצל בהמה להחשב כבשר, ואע"ג דראוי לכלב – עפרא בעלמא הוי, ואינו מטמא. **ת"ש** המחהו באור טמא. גבי נבלת עוף טהור מיתניא (חולין דף קכ.): המחהו לשומן של נבלת עוף טהור באור טמא, דמשום הכי לא נפסל מלאכול לכלב כדמעיקרא, דדרך להמחות שומן באור. **בחמה** טהור. דכשנימוח בחמה הוא מסריח מחום השמש ואינו ראוי לאכילת אדם, ולכך הוא טהור. ואי ס"ד יש נצל לבהמה, וה"ה לנבלת עוף טהור – אפילו בחמה נמי ליטמא, דאכתי הוא ראוי לכלב. אלא ש"מ דאין נצל, ולכך הוא טהור. אבל באור מיהא, כיון שהמחהו בידים – עדיף מנצל, דלא הוי אלא כשנרקב ונמחה מעלמו. ומשני: אימת קא ממחו – לבתר דקא מסרח, ובתר דאסרח מכח החמה – מבאיש למאד, דה"ל כעפרא, דאף לכלב אינו ראוי. ולא דמי לנצל דבהמה שנמחה בלא חמה, וראוי אכתי לכלב. **תנן** התם. בפרק [חמישי] דמכשירין: כל הנצוק טהור, שאם יצק ועירה משקין טהורים לתוך משקין טמאין מלמעלה למטה – לא נטמאו הטהורים, דנצוק אינו חיבור לא לטומאה ולא לטהרה. **חוץ** מן דבש הזיפים. בפרק בתרא דסוטה (דף מח:) מפרש רבי יוחנן: מאי זיפים – דבש שמזייפין אותו, לפי שהוא עב יותר מדאי, ומשימין בו מים ואינו ניכר. רשב"ל אומר: על שם מקומו, שנאמר "זיף וטלם ובעלות". וצפיחית – כמו כצפיחית בדבש, כלומר שרודה אותו מן הכוורת מעורב עם השעוה. ובערוך פירש: עיסה שמטוגנת בדבש. באלו נצוק טמא, דמתוך שהוא עב [הרבה] – חשיב אוכל, וכאילו העליון והתחתון מעורבין יחד זה בזה, ולכך הנצוק הוי חיבור.

בית

פי' הרא"ש

אלא כזית מן המת ונפל שלא נתקשרו אבריו בגידין. דעל אבר ממנו אינו מגלח כיון דאין בו גידין דאמרינן דאינו מטמא באהל עד שיהא בו משהו בשר וגידין ועצמות: לרוב בנינו ורוב מנינו. רוב בנינו מפרש לקמן שני שוקים ויירך א' ורוב מנינו היינו קכ"ב אברי' אע"פ שאין בהם רובע עצמות אבל אם לא היה רוב הבנין או רוב המנין אינו מגלח עד שיהיה בהם חצי קב: וים"ג כדאמר רבא לא נצרכה וכו' ור' יוחנן ורבא אמרי למלתייהו אמתני' דאהלות דקתני אלו מטמאין באהל המת וכזית מן המת ואיכא למפרך כדפריך הכא כזית ממנו מטמא באהל כולו לכ"ש וא"א לגרוס כן דהא באהלות קתני בהדיא רובע עצמות מרוב הבנין או מרוב המנין וים"ג לא נצרכה אלא לשדרה וגלגולת דהא לקמן פריך והא רבא הוא דאמר לא נצרכה אלא לשדרה ולגלגולת שאין בהם רובע עצמות ולא מצינו בשום מקום שאמר רבא אם לא שאמרה בכאן וליתא להך גירסא דהא תנא במתני' שדרה וגלגולת והא דפריך לקמן והא רבא פשיטא ליה דרבא לא מצריך רובע לשדרה וגלגולת כי היכי דלא מצריך לרוב בנינו ולרוב מנינו ולא נהירא לי דאי פריך משום דנראה לו להשוות השדרה וגלגולת לרוב בנינו מאי פריך והאמר רבא מתני' היא באהלות רוב בנינו ורוב מנינו שאין בהם רובע וי"ל דהתם לענין אהל מתניא אבל הכא מייתי ראיה מגלוח נזיר אגילוח נזיר ואע"ג דלרבא נמי מיבעי ליה לשנויי מתני' דאהלות כדתרצה רבי יוחנן מ"מ מסתברא לי' דנזיר מגלח על רוב בנין ורוב מנין ולהכי אוקי מתני' דהכא לאיתויי רוב בנין ורוב מנין: בשר המת שהקריש. שנימוח הבשר תחלה ואח"כ הקריש: ומוהל שהרתיח. מוהל שנמצא אצל המת ואינו יודע אם מבשר המת הוא או כיחו וניעו אם מעלה רתיחות כשמשימין אותו על האור בידוע שהוא מבשר המת: היכי דמי בשר המת אי דלא ידעינן שבא מבשר המת כי קריש מאי הוי. היאך הנזיר מגלח עליו מספק שמא מכיחו וניעו הוא ואי דידעינן דדידיה שמבשרו בא אפילו לא קרש נמי א"ר ירמיה בסתם כגון שנמצא אצל המת וידוע הוא שבא מן המת אבל אין ידוע אם מבשר המת שנימוח או מכיחו וניעו אי קריש ודאי מוהל הוא וכו': יש נצל לבהמה. בשר נבלה שנימוח מי מטמא במגע ובמשא או לא: טומאה חמורה טומאת נבלות לטמא אדם וכלים עד לגר עד שתפסל מאכילת הגר שנאמר לגר אשר בשעריך תתננה הראויה לגר קרויה נבלה ושאינה ראויה לגר אינה קרויה נבלה: טומאה קלה כלומר לבטלה מתורת אוכל שאם תגע בשרץ לא תקבל טומאה אחר שנפסל מאכילת הגר עד לכלב כל זמן שראויה לכלב תורת אוכל יש עליה ומקבלת טומאה וכן דין כל אוכל: שפיר. לדידיה ודאי אין נצל לבהמה דכבר נפסל מאכילת הגר כשנימוח אלא למ"ד טומאה חמורה עד לכלב מאי מי הוי (של) כבשר שעדיין הוא ראוי לכלב: המחהו באור גבי נבלת עוף טהור מתניא המחהו באור טמא דעדיין ראוי לאדם בחמה טהור דכשנימוח בחמה הוא מסריח מחום החמה ואינו ראוי לאכילת אדם (ואף אם) [ואי ס"ד] יש נצל לבהמה ואפילו לכלב לא חזי: דכיון דאסרח מחמת חמה הוי עפרא ואפילו לכלב לא חזי: כל הנצוק טהור. משנה היא פ"ה דמכשירין כל הנצוק טהור אם משקים טהורים לתוך משקים טמאים העליונים טהורים ואין הנצוק מחברם חוץ מדבש הזיפים והצ' [ובפ'] בתרא דסוטה מפרש ר' יוחנן מאי זיפים שמזייפין אותו לפי שהוא עב ביותר ומשימים בו מים ואינו ניכר רשב"ל אומר על שם מקומו דכתיב זיף וטלם וכו' וצפחית כמו כצפיחית בדבש ומפ' (במדות) [בערוך] בעיסה שמטוגנת בדבש ומתוך שהוא עב הנצוק מחברן

עין משפט נר מצוה

טו א ב ג מיי' פ"ב מהלכות נזירות הל' ב ופ"ב מהלכות טומאת מת הלכה א:
טז ד מיי' פ"ג מהלכות טומאת מת הל' א:
יז ה מיי' פ"ג מהלכות אבות הטומאות הלכה יג:
יח ו מיי' שם ופ"ג שם הלכה יא ופ"ד הל' יב סמג עשין רמג:
יט ז מיי' שם פ"ג הל' ו:
כ ח מיי' פ"ז מהלכות טומאת אוכלים הל' ח:
כא ט מיי' שם הל' ז:

מסורת הש"ס

[קדושין נב:]
חולין פט.
[לקמן נג.]
בכורות נג: [חולין עח.]
תוספתא סוף זבים חולין קכ. כילה ז.
סוטה מח: מכשירין פ"ה מ"ט

נוסחת הריב"ן

א) יאמרו: ב) אלא כי אמר: ג) לשובר: ד) לצריכה תלמוד כרוב: ה) כולן: ו) וקרש: ז) הלכך אי קרש ודאי דמת הוא ולא כיחו כו' ואי לא קרש כו' המשקים: ח) ולא חזי: ט) הוא: י) כשעשה שהוא פוסק מתוך עב נעשה כתוב ושולה במשקים טמאים שבתחתון למעלה ונעשה כולו טמא כו':

הגהות הב"ח

(א) גמ' מי אמרינן כי גמירי: (ב) רש"י ד"ה ועדיין וכו' לא כל שכן הס"ד ואח"כ מ"ה אלא כלאו"ר כי אמר ר"מ דעל מת: (ג) ד"ה והצפיחית וכו' טמאין עושה כולו טמא:

הגהות מהר"ב רנשבורג

א] תוס' ד"ה אלא וכו' לדידיה איכא למיבעי מי הוי נצל וכו' כצ"ל ומ"נ:

כב א מיי' פ"ז מהלכות טומאת אוכלין הל' ד:
כג ב מיי' פ"ב מהל' טומאת מת הלכה ו:
כד ג מיי' שם פ"ב הל' יא ופ"ג שם הלכה ח והלכה טו ופ"ו מהל' מזרות הלכה כ:

ב"ש אוֹמְרִים: אַף הַמִּקְפָּה שֶׁל גְּרִיסִין וְשֶׁל פּוֹל, מִפְּנֵי שֶׁהִיא סוֹלֶדֶת לַאֲחוֹרֶיהָ. בָּעֵי רָמִי בַּר חָמָא: יֵשׁ נִצּוֹק לָאוֹכָלִין אוֹ אאֵין נִצּוֹק לָאוֹכָלִין? מִי אָמְרִינַן מִשּׁוּם דְּאִית בְּהוּ רִירֵי — וְהָנֵי לֵית בְּהוּ רִירֵי, אוֹ דִּלְמָא מִשּׁוּם דִּסְמִיכִין הוּא — וְהָכָא הָא סְמִיכִין? אֲמַר רָבָא, ת"ש: *בחֵלֶב הַמֵּת שֶׁהוּא שָׁלֵם וְהִתִּיכוֹ — טָמֵא, הָיָה מְפוֹרָד וְהִתִּיכוֹ — טָהוֹר. וְאִי סָלְקָא דַּעְתָּךְ אֵין נִצּוֹק לָאוֹכָלִין, שָׁלֵם וְהִתִּיכוֹ נַמִי לִיטַהֵר! א"ר זֵירָא: אֲנָא וּמָר בְּרֵיהּ דְּרָבִינָא תַּרְגִּימְנָא: הָכָא בְּמַאי עָסְקִינַן — כְּגוֹן דִּבַהֲדֵי דְּמַרְתַּח לֵיהּ סָלֵיק עַמּוּדָא דְּנוּרָא לְפוּמֵּיהּ דְּמָנָא וְקָרֵשׁ, דְּאִיתֵיהּ כּוּלָּא גַּבֵּי הֲדָדֵי. א"ל רָבִינָא לְרַב אַשִׁי, ת"ש: ב"ש אוֹמְרִים: אַף הַמִּקְפָּה שֶׁל גְּרִיסִין וְשֶׁל פּוֹל, מִפְּנֵי שֶׁהֵן סוֹלְדִין לַאֲחוֹרֵיהֶן. מִידֵּי אִירְיָא? הָתָם — מִשּׁוּם דִּסְמִיכִין, הָכָא — מִשּׁוּם רִירֵי. § "וְעַל מְלֹא תַּרְוָוד רָקָב". § וְכַמָּה שִׁיעוּרוֹ? חִזְקִיָּה אָמַר: מְלֹא פִּיסַּת הַיָּד, רַבִּי יוֹחָנָן אָמַר: גמְלֹא חָפְנָיו. *תְּנַן: *מְלֹא תַּרְוָוד רָקָב שֶׁאָמְרוּ יֶשְׁנָן [א] מֵעִיקַּר אֶצְבָּעוֹת וּלְמַעְלָה, דִּבְרֵי ר"מ. וחכ"א: מְלֹא חָפְנָיו. בִּשְׁלָמָא ר' יוֹחָנָן — הוּא דַּאֲמַר כְּרַבָּנַן. אֶלָּא חִזְקִיָּה כְּמַאן? לָא כר"מ וְלָא כְּרַבָּנַן! אָמְרִי: [ב] מְלֹא פִּיסַּת הַיָּד וּמְלֹא קִשְׁרֵי אֶצְבְּעוֹתָיו לְמַעְלָה — חַד שִׁיעוּרָא הוּא. אֲמַר לֵיהּ רַב שִׁימִי בַּר אַדָּא לְרַב פַּפָּא: מִמַּאי דְּהַאי מִקִּשְׁרֵי אֶצְבְּעוֹתָיו וּלְמַעְלָה לְרֹאשׁ? דִּלְמָא לְמַטָּה מִדִּידֵיהּ, דַּהֲוָה לֵיהּ מְלֹא פִּיסַּת הַיָּד! [ג] תֵּיקוּ. §

ת"ר

בית שמאי אומרים אף מקפה של גריסין. שנכתשו בריחים של גרוסות ושל פול שלמים, ועושה מהם תבשיל, כמו כן חשיב אוכל והוי חיבור מפני שהיא סולדת לאחוריה — ב] כשנהפך התבשיל של מקפה ופוסק מלשפוך העמוד — סולד וחוזר לאחוריו, מתוך שהתבשיל עב [ולית] ביה רירי, והם מחברים האוכל להיות יחד.

יש נצוק לאוכלין. כגון המחה שומן ועירהו לתוך אוכלין טמאים. ולרבנן קמיבעיא ליה. מי אמרי' אינון משום דאית בהו רירי — פירוש: דבש הזיפים והצפיחית אמרו חכמים דהוו חיבור משום דאית בהו רירי, כלומר שהן סולדים לאחוריהם. ואע"ג דפליגי אמקפה של גריסין דאית להו רירי — לא חשיב לת"ק. וב"ש סברי אע"ג דלית להו כולי האי רירי, חשיבי לחבר העליון לתחתון, ושאר אוכלין לית בהו רירי, והלכך לא שייך בהו נצוק. או דלמא: טעמא דת"ק משום דסמיכין — משום שהם עבים, ושאר אוכלים נמי סמיכין. אבל לב"ש לא קא מיבעיא ליה, דמדקאמר: מפני שהן סולדין לאחוריהן — אם כן טעמייהו משום רירי. ת"ש חלב המת שהוא שלם. פי': כזית שלם, והתיכו — טמא. התיכו — כמו: איתכו, שהמחהו באור. טמא — כדמעיקרא, דמעיקרא היה בו כזית שלם, ועדיין ישנו כולו ביחד כדמפרש בסמוך, או משום דנצוק הוי חיבור. הלכך אפילו כי התיכו, ב] אפי' שאם לא היה מחובר ביחד [אלא] ע"י נצוק, ואי משום שלא נפרד מעולם זה מזה, כדמפרש בשינויא: היה מפורר. פירורין של חלב המת, שלא היה מעיקרא זית שלם, אע"ג דהתיכן באור ונעשה הכל חתיכה אחת — טהור, כדמסיים בתוספ' דאהלות פרק רביעי: מפני שחיבור אדם אינו חיבור. וקודם שהתיכו לא היה כזית מחובר יחד, ולא היה מטמא הנוגע במקלת, [או] אפילו הנוגע בכולו למאן דלית ליה נוגע וחוזר ונוגע. לכך, כי התיכו — נמי לא חשיב זית שלם, כיון שחיבור זה בא ע"י אדם. ואע"ג דרביעית דם הבאה משני מתים מטמא למאן דאית ליה [יש אם למקרא, דכתיב "על כל נפשות מת"] (סנהדרין דף ד.), וכן שני חצאי זיתים משני מתים, דטמא, במס' אהלות (בתוספתא פ"ד) — י"ל: דהיינו דוקא לענין אהל, לפי שראוי להאהיל על שני החצאין יחד, אבל בנגיעה — לא מטמא. והא דאמרי' בפ' [שלישי] דאהלות [מ"ג]: הנוגע בשני חצאי זיתים מן הנבלה טמא! י"ל: דהתם מיירי שיש בשר מרודד ביניהן המחברם יחד. וכי האי גוונא משני בפרק "העור והרוטב" (חולין דף קכד:). וא"ת: תפשוט מהכא דחיבורי אדם אינו חיבור! וי"ל: היינו דוקא בטומאת מת, שהטומאה באה ממנו לצרפו לכזית לטמא אחרים, ואפשר להיות שכן הקבלה. אבל לצרף האוכלין לקבל טומאה בכבילה מעלמא — התם חיבור אדם הוי חיבור, כי הך דכל האוכלין מצטרפין לכביצה.

ואי ס"ד אין נצוק לאוכלין שלם והתיכו נמי ליטהר. כזית חלב כשנותנין על האש א"א שלא נפרדה טפה אחת ממקום חיבורה מחמת ההתכה, אי נצוק אין חיבור. דאי אפשר שאותה טפה אינה מחוברת לשאר החלב ע"י נצוק. דאי לא חשיב חיבור — הרי נפרדה הטפה, ואין כאן כזית. כגון בהדי דמרתח ליה סליק עמוד לפומיה דמנא וקירש דאיתיה כוליה גבי הדדי. כשנתן ע"ג האש והרתיח — עלה כזית לפומא דמנא בבת אחת מכח האש וקירש, דהשתא איתיה כוליה גבי הדדי. וצ"ל דקירש אפומא דמנא, דאילו לא קרש אלא חזר ונפל למקומו — אין נופל יחד, אלא דרך נצוק, שאין כח האש מסייע ליפול כמו שמעלהו, וכי סליק — סליק בבת אחת, וכי נפיל — נפיל דרך נצוק. ת"ש אף מקפה של גריסין ושל פול מפניג] (שידים) [שהן] סולדים לאחוריהם. [אלמא] טעמא דשמאי משום רירי. הכי נמי מסתברא טעמא דת"ק משום רירי, אלא דת"ק בעי רירי טובא. ותפשוט לשאר אוכלין דאין להם רירי — אין נצוק. מידי איריא התם משום דסמיכי. דבש של זיפים וצפיחית דהוי חיבור לרבנן — היינו משום דסמיכי, ולא משום רירי. ובהא פליגי; דבית שמאי סברי: אף כי לא סמיכי הוי חיבור, כיון דאיכא רירי, כגון מקפה של גריסין. ולת"ק רירי לא מעלה ולא מוריד. מלא פיסת יד. מתחילת פיסוק האצבעות עד הזרוע. ישנן מעיקר אצבעות ולמעלה. עד ראשי האצבעות. חד שיעורא הוא. כך מחזיק באצבעות כמו בפיסת ידו. אמר ליה רב שימי. שנויא הוא, ממאי דהאי מקישרי אצבעותיו ולמעלה היינו לראשי אצבעותיו, דפרכת מינה? דלמא "למטה" דקרי — עיקר אצבעות מקום שמחוברין לה ליד, ו"למעלה" דקאמר — היינו לצד הגוף עד פרק הזרוע, דהיינו ממש פיסת ידו! לא גרסי' "תיקו".

איזהו

בש"א אַף נִצּוֹק מִקְפָּה שֶׁל גְּרִיסִין. פּוֹלִין שֶׁנִּכְתְּשׁוּ בְּמַכְתֵּשׁ וְנֶחְלְקוּ לִשְׁנַיִם. [וְשֶׁל פּוֹל]. א) שֶׁל פּוֹלִין שְׁלֵמוֹת. סוֹלֶדֶת לַאֲחוֹרֶיהָ. שֶׁבְּשָׁעָה שֶׁמְּרִיקִין אוֹתוֹ מִכְּלִי אֶל כְּלִי וּפוֹסֵק אֶת הַנִּצּוֹק — חוֹזֵר רֹאשׁ הַנִּצּוֹק וְעוֹלֶה לוֹ לְמַעְלָה כְּלַפֵּי אֲחוֹרָיו, וּכְחוֹזֵר וְנוֹגֵעַ לָעֶלְיוֹנִים דָּמֵי, ב) וְהָווּ טְמֵאִין. יֵשׁ נִצּוֹק לָאוֹכָלִין. הָיָה מֵרִיק מִקְפָּה שֶׁל עֲדָשִׁים אוֹ שֶׁל אֲפוּנִים בִּמְקוֹם מִדְרוֹן (א) ג) לְמַעְלָה, וְנִטְמְאוּ תַּחְתּוֹנִי' בִּשְׁעַת שְׁפִיכָה, מִי הָוְיָין הָעֶלְיוֹנִי' טְמֵאִין אוֹ לֹא? גַּבֵּי דְּבַשׁ הַזִּיפִים וְצַפִּיחִית מ"ט אִית בְּהוּ נִצּוֹק — מִשּׁוּם דְּאִית בְּהוּ רִירֵי, דְּסוֹלְדוֹת. וְהָנֵי אוֹכָלִין — לֵית בְּהוּ רִירֵי, וְהָוְיָין עֶלְיוֹנִים טְהוֹרִים. אוֹ דִּלְמָא גַּבֵּי זִיפִים וְצַפִּיחִית מ"ט נִצּוֹק שֶׁלָּהֶן טָמֵא — מִשּׁוּם דִּסְמִיכִין, שֶׁהֵן עָבִים, וְהָנֵי נַמִי סְמִיכִין, וְלֶיהֱוֵי נִצּוֹק שֶׁלָּהֶן טָמֵא. ת"ש חֵלֶב שֶׁל מֵת (ב) ד) טָמֵא. וְיֵשׁ בּוֹ כַּזַּיִת, וְהִתִּיכוֹ בְּמַחֲבַת. אע"פ שֶׁנִּתְגַּלְגֵּל בְּמַחֲבַת — לֹא נַעֲשָׂה מְפוֹרָד, וְטָמֵא. הָיָה מְפוֹרָד. אוֹתוֹ כַּזַּיִת מִן הַמֵּת, וְהִתִּיכוֹ, אע"פ שֶׁנִּתְחַבֵּר בְּיַחַד — טָהוֹר. כֵּיוָן דְּה"ל מְפוֹרָד מֵעִיקָּרָא — פָּרְחָה מִינֵּיהּ טוּמְאָה, וְהַאי דַּהֲדַר חִבְּרוֹ בְּיַחַד לָא הָוֵי חִיבּוּר, דְּחִיבּוּר בִּידֵי אָדָם לָא ה) הָוֵי חִיבּוּר. וְאִי ס"ד אֵין נִצּוֹק לָאוֹכָלִין. כִּי (ג) ו) הֲוָה שָׁלֵם וְהִתִּיכוֹ בְּמַחֲבַת נַמִי לִיטַּהֵר, דְּכֵיוָן דְּמִגַּלְגֵּל לֵיהּ מִזָּוִית זוֹ לְזָוִית זוֹ — נִפְרָד זֶה מִזֶּה, וְלָא הָוֵי בֵּיהּ כַּזַּיִת בִּמְכוּנָּס. אִי נַמִי, לִכְשֶׁהִתִּיכוֹ וֶהֱרִיקוֹ מִכְּלִי אֶל כְּלִי — לֶיהֱוֵי כִּמְפוֹרָד וְלִיטַּהֵר. אֶלָּא לָאו ש"מ דְּיֵשׁ נִצּוֹק, וְחִיבּוּר הוּא. א"ר זֵירָא. לְעוֹלָם אֵימָא לָךְ אֵין נִצּוֹק לְאוֹכָלִין, וְהָא מַתְנִי' (ד) דְּהָכָא — אֲנָא וּמָר בְּרֵיהּ דְּרָבִינָא תַּרְגְּמִינָא דְּהָכָא בְּמַאי עָסְקִינַן — כְּגוֹן שֶׁלֹּא הוּרַק מִכְּלִי אֶל כְּלִי, וּמֵעוֹלָם לֹא נִעְנְעוֹ בִּכְלִי כְּלָל. דִּבַהֲדֵי דְּמַרְתַּח לֵיהּ. שֶׁהִתִּיכוֹ בְּמַחֲבַת ז) בְּמָקוֹם אֶחָד וְלֹא נִעְנְעוֹ כְּלָל, וְהַהוּא חֵלֶב לְבַהֲדֵי דְּקָא מְהַתֵּךְ לֵיהּ סָלֵיק עַמּוּדָא דְּנוּרָא לְפוּמֵּיהּ דְּמָנָא, וְלֹא א] ח) [מַגִּיעַ] לָא לְהָכָא וְלָא לְהָכָא, וְלָא הָוֵי נִצּוֹק כְּלָל, דְּכוּלֵּיהּ הֲוָה בַּהֲדֵי הֲדָדֵי, וְקָרֵשׁ בִּמְקוֹמוֹ וְלֹא נִתְפַּזֵּר ט) לְכָאן וְלֹא לְכָאן, מִשּׁוּם הָכִי טָמֵא. ת"ש בש"א אַף מִקְפָּה שֶׁל גְּרִיסִין. אַלְמָא דְּיֵשׁ נִצּוֹק לְאוֹכָלִין. מִידֵּי אִירְיָא. כְּלוֹמַר, לְעוֹלָם אֵימָא לָךְ אֵין נִצּוֹק, וְהָכִי הוּא דְּקָא מִיבַּעְיָא י) לֵיהּ: מִי אָמְרִי' דְּגַבֵּי שְׁאָר אוֹכָלִין כְּגוֹן עֲדָשִׁים, (ה) כ) (מִי אָמְרִינַן) כֵּיוָן דִּסְמוּכוֹת כְּגוֹן מִקְפָּה שֶׁל גְּרִיסִין — הָוֵי חִיבּוּר. אוֹ דִּלְמָא, הָתָם לָא הֲוָה טַעְמָא אֶלָּא מִשּׁוּם דְּאִית לֵיהּ רִירֵי בְּמִקְפָּה שֶׁל גְּרִיסִין, אֲבָל בִּשְׁאָר אוֹכָלִין דְּלֵית בְּהוּ רִירֵי — לָא הֲוֵה נִצּוֹק. לִישָּׁנָא אַחֲרִינָא: ת"ש ב"ש אוֹמְרִים כו' מִפְּנֵי שֶׁהֵן סוֹלְדִין לַאֲחוֹרֵיהֶן — אַלְמָא דְּלָא הֲוֵה טַעְמָא דְּנִצּוֹק אֶלָּא מִשּׁוּם דְּאִית בֵּיהּ רִירֵי, וְגַבֵּי שְׁאָר אוֹכָלִין הוֹאִיל דְּלֵית בְּהוּ רִירֵי — לָא הָוֵי נִצּוֹק. מִידֵּי אִירְיָא? לְעוֹלָם אֵימָא לָךְ יֵשׁ נִצּוֹק לְאוֹכָלִין, וְכִי קָא מִיבַּעְיָא לָן — אַלִּיבָּא דְּרַבָּנַן, וְהָכִי קָמִיבָּעְיָא לָן: טַעֲמַיְיהוּ דְּרַבָּנַן דְּאָמְרִי דְּהָוֵי נִצּוֹק גַּבֵּי דְּבַשׁ הַזִּיפִים — טַעְמָא מִשּׁוּם דִּסְמִיכִין, וְהִלְכָּךְ כָּל אוֹכָלִין דִּסְמִיכִין, כְּגוֹן עֲדָשִׁים — אִית לְהוּ נִצּוֹק. אֲבָל אַלִּיבָּא דְּב"ש לָא מִיבַּעְיָא לָן, דְּאִינְהוּ לָא אָמְרִי דְּהָוֵי נִצּוֹק אֶלָּא מִשּׁוּם רִירֵי, וְאִילּוּ שְׁאָר אוֹכָלִין דְּלֵית לְהוּ רִירֵי — לָא אִיצְטְרִיךְ לָן לְמִישְׁאַל. תַּרְוָוד. כַּף. מְלֹא פִּיסַּת יָד. בְּלֹא ל) אֶצְבָּעוֹת. מְלֹא חָפְנָיו. בַּהֲדֵי אֶצְבְּעוֹתָיו. וּמִמַּאי דְּהַאי קִשְׁרֵי אֶצְבְּעוֹתָיו וּלְמַעְלָה. דְּקָאָמַר כְּלַפֵּי רֹאשׁ אֶצְבְּעוֹתָיו קָאָמַר, וּמִשּׁוּם הָכִי מוֹתְבַתְּ מִינֵּיהּ לְחִזְקִיָּה? דִּלְמָא לְמַטָּה מִיַּד — דִּלְמָא כְּלַפֵּי פִּיסַּת יָד הוּא דְּקָאָמַר, כְּווֹתֵיהּ דְּחִזְקִיָּה, וְחִזְקִיָּה כר"מ.

אֵיזֶהוּ

תוספתא דאהלות פ"ד

[תוספתא אהלות פ"ד]

[עי' חולין פז: מש"ש על הגליון ובתוס' שם ד"ה תנן]

פי' הרא"ש

מחברן: מפני שהיא סולדת לאחוריה. המערה אותן מכלי אל כלי לאחר שפסק הקלוח העמוד סולד וכווץ מפני שהוא עב: יש נצוק לאוכלין. לדברי חכמים קא בעי הני טעמא מאי משום דאית בהו רירי כלומר שהם סולדים לאחוריהם או דלמא משום דסמיכי ואה"נ אוכלים אבל לב"ש לא קא מיבעיא ליה משום דמפרשי טעמייהו בהדיא מפני שהיא סולדת לאחוריה אבל לרבנן מיבעיא ליה אי טעמא משום רירא ופליגי בהא דרבנן בעי רירא טובא כדבש הזיפים וב"ש אמרי אף מקפה של גריסין דלית בה רירי כולי האי או דלמא טעמא דרבנן משום דסמיכי ולאו משום רירי: ת"ש כזית חלב מן המת והתיכו טמא. פי' המחהו כמו חלב מהותך טמא אם נשאר בו כזית: היה מפורד פירורין מן חלב המת והתיכן טהור כדמסיים בתוספתא דאהלות פ"ד מפני שחיבורי אדם אינו חבור. וקודם שהתיכו לא היה מטמא הנוגע במקצתו או אפילו בכולו למאן דלית ליה נוגע וחוזר ונוגע הלכך כי התיכו וחברו בידי אדם לא יטמא ואף על גב דדרשינן רביעית דם הבא מב' מתים למאן דאית ליה [יש אם למקרא] וכן ב' חצאי זיתים מתים במס' אהלות פ"ד היינו לענין אהל אבל במגע לא מטמא והא דאמר ברפ"ב דאהלות הנוגע

נוסחת הריב"ן

א) מקפה של פולין שלמות שסולדת לאחוריה: ב) והוי טמאין: ג) מלמעלה: ד) של מת שהוא שלם ויש ה) שמיה חיבור: ו) הוה: ז) כגון: ח) במקום: ט) לא לכאן ולא: י) לא מיבעיא: כ) דסמיכין: ל) אלבעותיו:

הגהות הב"ח

(א) רש"י ד"ה יש נצוק וכו' מדרון ונטמאו מלמעלה: (ב) ד"ה ת"ש חלב של מת שהוא שלם והתיכו טמא יש בו כזית שלם והתיכו במחבת: (ג) ד"ה ואי ס"ד וכו' כי הוה שלם והתיכו: (ד) ד"ה א"ר זירא וכו' והא מתניתין אנא כצ"ל ותיבת הכא נמחק: (ה) ד"ה מידי איריא וכו' כגון עדשים כיון דסמוכות כצ"ל ותיבות מי אמרינן נמחק:

הגהות הגר"א

[א] גמ' מעיקר. נ"ל מקשרי (וכמ"ש לקמן ממאי דהאי מקשרי כו'. אבל בתוספתא דאהלות ובכלים ב"מ פ"ז איתא מעיקר: [ב] גמ' אמרי מלא פיסת כו'. נ"ב בתוספתא דכלים פ"ב דב"מ דקתני גבי מכתב (דמשמע שם דלא שוו שיעורייהו): [ג] שם (תיקו) תז"מ (וכמ"ש התוס' דל"ג לה):

הגהות מהר"ב רנשבורג
א] רש"י ד"ה כבהדי וכו' לפומיה דמנא ולא מגיע תיבה מגיע נמחק וצ"ב מגלי. א"מ: ב] תוד"ה ב"ש וכו' מפני שהיא סולדת לאחוריה כשנהפך תיבת כשנהפך נמחק וצ"ב כשנפסך כצ"ל: ג] ד"ה ת"ש וכו' הלכך אפילו כי התיכו אפילו נמחק וצ"ב לא. ח"מ: ד] ד"ה ת"ש וכו' ושל פול מפני שידים סולדים תיבות שידים סולדים נמחקו וצ"ב שידם סולדים.

בב' חצאי נבלה טמא י"ל דמיירי כגון שיש בשר מרודד המחברן יחד ובבה"ג משני פ' העור והרוטב: ואי ס"ד אין ניצוק לאוכלין כזית שלם והתיכו נמי ליטהר. דכשנתנו כזית שלם על האור א"א שלא נפרדה טפה א' ממקום חבורה מחמת ההתכה ואי ניצוק אין חבור דאי לא חשיב חבור ע"י ניצוק הרי נפרדה הטפה ואין כאן כזית: כגון בהדי דמרתח ליה סליק עמוד לפומיה דמנא וקירש דאיתיה כוליה בהדי הדדי ולא נפרד ממנו א) כלומר אבל אם לא קרש אלא חזר ונפל למקומו אינו נופל יחד דאין כח האש מסייעתו ליפול כמו שמעלהו וכי סליק סליק בבת אחת וכי נפיל נפיל דרך ניצוק: ת"ש אף מקפה של גריסין ושל פול מפני שהם סולדים לאחוריהן. אלמא דבית שמאי משום רירי הוא ושמאי סבר דאפילו לא סמכי חבור. מידי איריא התם משום דסמיכי הכא משום רירי. מעיקר אצבעותיו ולמעלה קס"ד ממקום שמתחילין האצבעות להתפצל לפי שבאדם משתמש בידיו ומגביה ראשי האצבעות הם כלפי מעלה: מלא פסת היד מסוף היד עד הזרוע דהיינו מלא חפניו: ממאי דהאי מקשרי אצבעותיו ולמעלה לראש האצבעות דלמא למטה לצד הגוף היינו מלא פסת היד:
איזהו
א) נ"ל דקירש לפומא דמנא אבל אם לא קרש וכו'.

*ת"ר: [א]איזהו מת שיש לו רקב – מת שנקבר ערום בארון של שיש, או על גבי רצפה של אבנים, זהו מת שיש לו רקב. נקבר בכסותו, בארון של עץ, או על גבי רצפה של לבנים – זהו מת שאין לו רקב. אמר עולא: *אין רקב אלא הבא מן הבשר ומן הגידים ומן העצמות. איתיביה רבא לעולא: רקב הבא מן הבשר – טהור. הא מן העצם – טמא, ואע"ג דליכא בשר! אימא הכי: רקב הבא מן הבשר – טהור, עד שיש עצם בבשר. הא ליכא גידים! אי אפשר לבשר ולעצמות בלא גידים. אמר רב *שמואל בר אבא א"ר יוחנן: [ב]שני מתים שקברן זה עם זה – נעשו גלגלין זה לזה. מתיב (א) רב נתן: רקב הבא מב' מתים טמא! אמר רבא: שקברו זה בפני עצמו וזה בפני עצמו, והרקיבו ועמדו על מלא תרווד רקב. אמר רבה בר בר חנה א"ר יוחנן: [ג]גזז שערו וקברו עמו – נעשה לו גלגלין. *תנן התם: [ד]כל שבמת – טמא, חוץ מן השינים והשער והצפורן, ובשעת חיבורן כולן טמאין. °בעי חזקיה: שערו העומד לגלח, צפורן העומד ליגזז, מאי? *מי אמרינן: כל העומד ליגזז כגזוז דמי, או דלמא השתא מיהא הא מחוברין? וניפשוט ליה מדרבה בר בר חנה; טעמא – משום דגזז, הא לא גזז – לא! הכי קאמר: גזז – הרי זה גלגלים, לא גזז – [ה]מיבעי ליה. בעי ר' ירמיה: רקב הבא מן העקב, מהו? כי גמרינן – רקב הבא מכוליה מת, אבל דאתי מן עקב – לא, או דלמא לא שנא? ת"ש, דתני ר' נתן ברבי אושעיא: רקב הבא משני מתים – טמא. ואי ס"ד הבא מן העקב לא, זיל הכא – דלמא דרך עקב קאתי, והכא – דלמא דרך עקב קאתי! (ב) אי דאירקיב כוליה מת וקאתי דרך עקב – הכי נמי. אלא הכא כגון דאירקיב חד אבר, וקאתי דרך עקב, מאי? תיקו. בעי רבי ירמיה: עובר במעי אשה הוי גלגלים או לא? כיון *דאמר מר עובר ירך אמו – הלכך גופה הוא, ולא הוי גלגלין. או דלמא כיון דסופו לצאת – מיפרש פריש מינה. ואת"ל [ו]עובר דסופו לצאת מיפרש פריש מינה,

שכבת

איזהו מת שיש לו תורת רקב נקבר ערום כו'. אבל אם נקבר בכסותו, אפי' בארון של שיש – אין לו תורת רקב, לפי שכסותו שנרקבת עמו נעשית לו תערובות, ואנו אין לנו הלכה למשה מסיני שיהא רקב מטמא אלא רקב הבא מן המת עצמו בלא תערובות. וכן אם נקבר בארון של עץ, ואפי' ערום, או על גבי רצפה של לבנים, הואיל והארון של עץ והטבן של לבנים עשוין לירקב – נעשין לו תערובות, ואין לו תורת רקב. נעשו גלגלים זה לזה. נעשה כמי שנתערבו זה בזה, ואין זה רקב גמור. גלגלין – כלומר המגלגל זה לזה, ונתערב זה עם זה. (ג) וכשנתערב עמו כסות או רקבון אחר דמי, ואפילו נקברו ערומים בארון של שיש, הואיל דלא הוי רקב א) דמת אחד. אמר רבא. כי קתני התם דרקב הבא מב' מתים טמא – כגון שקברו ב) זה בפני עצמו וזה בפני עצמו, והרקיבו כל אחד בפני עצמו, ועמד על מלא תרווד רקב – ממת זה חצי תרווד, וממת זה חצי תרווד – מצטרפין למלא תרווד, הואיל ולא נעשו גלגלין זה לזה מתחילה, בשעה שהרקיבו. אבל היכא ג) דנקברו זה עם זה – לעולם אימא לך דנעשו גלגלין זה לזה, ואין לו תורת רקב. גזז שערו וקברו עמו נעשה לו גלגלין. ד) אבל כי לא גזז, והניחו מחובר כמו שהוא – לא נעשה לו גלגלין. שערו העומד ליגזז. קודם מיתה, כגון שהכביד עליו שערו – כגזוז דמי, ונעשה לו גלגלין, ואין לו רקב. הא לא גזז לא. ואע"ג דעומד ליגזז. לא ה"ק גזז הוי גלגלין. כלומר, מדרבה בר בר חנה ליכא למשמע מידי, דהא דרבה בר בר חנה אמר דכי גזז הוי גלגלין, אבל לא גזז – לא אמר ביה ולא מידי, ואכתי תיבעי לך. מן העקב. מן מרגלותיו, כלומר מִמָּתְנַיִם ולמטה. כי קאמר דמלא תרווד רקב טמא – היכא דאתי מכוליה מת מכלפי גוייה שלמעלה, דעיקר הגוף בו. ואי ס"ד. רקב הבא מן העקב לא הוי טמא, כי בא משני מתים אמאי טמא להאי רקב? [זיל] להכא – ה) איכא למימר דדילמא דרך עקב קאתי, וכן נמי להכא, גבי אידך מת – דילמא דרך עקב קאתי, ואין לו תורת רקב! אלא מדלא אמר הכי – ש"מ דרקב הבא מן העקב יש לו תורת רקב. ה"ד אי דאירקיב כוליה מת. כלומר, לעולם אימא לך דרקב ו) שבא מן העקב טהור. והכי קבעינא מינך: (*תרווד) אי דאירקיב כוליה מת, והיינו מלא [תרווד] רקב דשקלית מיניה אתא ליה דרך עקב עד כלפי הראש, על פני כולו של מת – הכי נמי דאיכא למיפשט מהיא דרב נתן בר אושעיא דהוי טמא. אלא כי קא מיבעיא ליה הכא כגון דארקיב חד אבר, והיינו אבר עצמו דארקיב אתא ליה דרך עקב בלבד. והכי קמיבעיא לן: מי אמרינן כי גמירי רקב – כגון דאתי מכל גוף דמת, אבל היכא דאתי מן עקב לחודיה – לא, או דלמא לא שנא?

שכבת

איזהו מת שיש לו רקב. מלא תרווד רקב מטמא באהל, ונזיר מגלח עליו. **שנקבר** ערום בארון של שיש או על גבי רצפה של אבנים. שאינה נשחקת, ואין להסתפק בעפר אחר, כי אם ברקב גוף של מת. **נקבר** בכסותו ואפילו בארון של שיש או ערום בארון של עץ או על גבי רצפה של לבנים. שנוחות לישחק וליכתש מאליהן – זהו מת שאין לו רקב. ואפילו לקח ארבע או חמש תרוודין מן רקב שלו, שבודאי יש כאן מלא תרווד מגוף המת – טהור. כדאמרינן בפ' "המפלת" (נדה כז:): מה תחילתו דבר אחר נעשה לו גלגלין, משמע דבהא ליכא מאן דפליג, שאם נתערב דבר אחר עמו בתחילתו – אינו מטמא. **אמר** עולא אין רקב אלא הבא מן הבשר ומן הגידין ומן העצמות. מכולם צריך שיהא הרקב. **הא** מן העצם. לחוד, טמא. **והא** ליכא גידין. ולא הוה מצי לשנויי דהכי קאמר: ומן הבשר לחודיה טהור עד שיהא רקב עצם וגידין בהדי בשר. דא"כ ליתני: מן הבשר ועצם טהור, ודייקינן עד דאיכא גידין בהדייהו. **א"א** לבשר ועצמות בלא גידים. ועולא שהזכיר גידים – אצטריך לאפוקי נפל שלא נתקשרו אבריו בגידים. וברייתא לא איירי בהכי, אלא בולד נגמר. **שני** מתים שנקברו זה עם זה נעשו גלגלין זה לזה. ובפרק "המפלת" (שם כז:) גרסינן בכל הספרים: גנגילאן. וגם בערוך *פי': גלגלים – עפר הוא שמעורב ממקום אחר, לשון דבר המתגלגל. ועוד פירש בערוך: גלגלין = קוטריימ"א בלע"ז. דלא גמירי רקב אלא של מת אחד, ולא שיש מת אחר מעורב בו. **מתיב** רב נתן רקב הבא משני מתים טמא. וקא ס"ד דמיירי שנקברו יחד.

ונרקבו ועמדו על מלא תרווד. אחר שאכלן עש, ולא נשאר בכל אחד אלא חצי תרווד. וכיון שהיה כל אחד יחידי כשנקברו – יש להן דין רקב. ויש תימה: למה נקט ועמדו על מלא תרווד רקב אחד, שלא נשתייר? וי"ל: דלרבותא נקטיה, [דאפילו] כי אין בשניהם אלא תרווד אחד, דאיכא השתא רקב מן העקב – אפ"ה הוי שיעור כתרווד. דלקמן פשטינן מינה בעיא דרקב הבא מן העקב מהו, דגם לפי הדיחוי שמעי' דמת דארקיב כוליה מיהא מצטרף רקב העקב לשאר רקבובית לתרווד. **תנן** התם במס' אהלות (פ"ג מ"ג): כל שבמת טמא, וגם העור. ופליגי בה בפ' "דם נדה" (נדה נה.), איכא למ"ד דרבנן, ואיכא למ"ד דאורייתא. **חוץ** מן השינים והשער והצפורן. שטהורין אף מדרבנן. ובשעת חיבורן למת כולן טמאין, שהנוגע או מאהיל עליהם [א]הוא נוגע או מאהיל על המת דהוו יד לטומאת המת. **בעי** חזקיה שערו העומד ליגזז מהו. מי הוי [ב][כשאר] חיבורין למת וטמא, או כגזוז דמי ולא מטמא במת אף במחובר למת, או דלמא מטמא בעודו מחובר בו? ויש מפרשים דלענין גלגלין קא מיבעיא ליה; כגזוז דמי ונעשה גלגלין או לא? ומיהו, [כפי'] קמא מסתברא, דקאי אמתניתין ד"כל שבמת טמא". **טעמא** דגזז. אז הוי גלגלין, הא לא גזז – לא, ומיירי בכל ענין, אף משער העומד ליגזז. וקאמר דלא גזז דלא הוי גלגלין – הכי נמי נימא דבשעת חיבורו טמא, דהוי כגופו. **לא** גזז תיבעי לך. כלומר, לרבה בר בר חנה גופיה קא מיבעיא ליה היכא דלא גזז, ולהכי נקט גזז, דבגזוז דוקא הוא דפשיטא ליה.

רקב הבא מן העקב מהו. לפי שבעקבו של אדם יש בו עובי בשר שאין בו חיות, ומיבעיא ליה אי גמירי ביה רקב או לא. **הבא** מכוליה מת. כלומר, מכל הבשר שיש בו חיות. **רקב** הבא משני מתים טמא. ולעיל אוקמיה רבא כגון שעומד על מלא תרווד, שלא נשאר משניהם כי אם מלא תרווד. ואי סלקא דעתך הבא מן העקב לא, כלומר (לא) שאינו מטמא – זיל הכא דלמא דרך עקב קאתי, כלומר שמא יש בו מן העקב. ולהכי נקט "דלמא" – שאין בזה [ודאי], דשמא מן העקב אכלן עש, וזה הרקב נשאר מן שאר הגוף: היכי דמי. כלומר, היכי הוי [בעיין]? ודאי אי דארקיב כוליה מת ואתי דרך עקב – ה"נ דיש לו רקב, דבהכי מיירי הא דתני רב נתן – כשנרקב כל המת ונרקב גם העקב, שיש בו דין רקב. אלא [בעיין] היכא דארקיב חד אבר – הרגל, ואתי דרך העקב. דאיכא למימר לפי שאין חיות בבשר העקב [מיהר] להרקיב, בכי האי גוונא לא גמירי רקב. **עובר** במעי אשה מי הוי גלגלין. כשני מתים שקברן זה עם זה.

כיון

פי' הרא"ש

איזהו מת שיש לו רקב. שמלא תרווד מעפר (רקבו ביתו) [רקב גופו] מטמא באהל נקבר בארון של שיש. שלא נתערב רקבון אחר בעפרו. אבל אם נקבר בכסותו או בארון של עץ או על גבי רצפה של (אבנים) [לבנים] אין לו דין רקב: אין רקב אלא הבא מן הבשר ומן הגידין ומן העצמות מכולם צריך שיהיה ברקב: הא מן העצם טמא אע"ג דליכא בשר. ולא מצי לשנויי דה"ק מן הבשר לבדו טהור עד שיהיה עמו עצמות וגידין דא"כ הול"ל מן הבשר ומן העצם טהור והוה דייקנא עד דאיכא גידים בהדייהו: אי אפשר לבשר ועצמות בלא גידים. ועולא שהזכיר גידים איצטרך לאפוקי נפל שלא נתקשרו איבריו זה לזה: [נעשו גלגלין זה לזה] בערוך גרס גלגילין ופי' עפר מעורב ממקום אחר לשון דבר שמתגלגל ועוד פי' גלגילין קונטריימא דלא גמירי רקב אלא במת שנקבר לבדו. והרקיבו ועמדו על מלא תרווד. שאכלו עש ולא נשאר בכל א' כי אם חצי תרווד. וצ"ע למה נקט שעמדו על מלא תרווד רקב ולא נשאר מהם יותר. תנן התם פ"ד דאהלות כל שבמת טמא ואף העור טמא איכא מאן דאמר מדרבנן ואיכא מ"ד מדאורייתא: חוץ מן השינים והשער והצפורן. בפ' דם הנדה מפ' טעמא משום דבעי' דומיא דעצם מה עצם שנברא עמו ואין גזעו מחליף אף כל שנברא עמו ואין גזעו מחליף יצאו השינים שלא נבראו עמו יצאו שער וציפורן שאע"פ שנבראו עמו גזעו מחליף ובשעת חבורן הכל טמא והנוגע בהם כנוגע בבשר המת: בעי חזקיה שערו העומד ליגזז וכו' גבול היה להם לגידול שער מתי היה עומד ליגזז ומיבעיא ליה אי מטמא בשעת חבורן למת. וי"מ דמבעי ליה אם נעשה גלגלין כאילו היה גוזז וקברו עמו. ולא נהירא דא"כ אמאי מייתי הך מתני' דאהלות הכא. ותפשוט ליה מדרבה בב"ח טעמא דגזז וכו' משמע ליה דרבה בב"ח איירי בכל עניין אפי' עומד ליגזז וקאמר דוקא גזז. ולא גזז תבעי לך לרבה בב"ח מיבעי ליה היכא דלא גזז ולהכי נקט גזז דבגזז דוקא הוה פשיטא ליה: רקב מן העקב מהו לפי שיש בעקבו של אדם עובי בשר שאין בו חיות ולהכי מיבעי ליה אם רקבובתו מטמא שהוא אינו חשוב כגוף המת כי גמירי רקב הבא (מן שלא) [מכוליה] מת. כלומר שבא מן דבר שמת שבשעת מיתה מת הכל יחד אבל דאתי דרך עקב לא. לפי שמתחיים הוי כבשר המת. רקב הבא מב' מתים טמא [illegible]

ת"ר: נדה כז: תוספתא דאהלות פ"ב
[עי' תוס' נדה כז: ד"ה למעוטי]
נ"א שמן
נדה נה. אהלות פ"ג מ"ג
[סנהדרין טו.]
ב"ק מז. חולין נח. תמורה לא.
נ"א דודאי

נוסחת הריב"ן
א) רקב כולו: ב) שקברן: ג) דקברן: ד) ואבל כי כו' גלגלין ליתא בכ"י: ה) זיל להכא לגבי חד מת איכא למימר: ו) [illegible]

הגהות הב"ח
(א) גמ' מתיב רבי נתן ברבי אושעיא רקב הבא: (ב) שם דלמא דרך עקב קאתי הכי דאי דאירקיב: (ג) רש"י ד"ה נעשו וכו' עם זה וכמו שנתערב עמו כסות:

גליון הש"ס
גמ' בעי חזקיה שערו העומד לגלח. עי' גיטין דף לט ע"א:

עין משפט נר מצוה
כה א מיי' פ"ז מהל' נזירות הלכה ג ופ"ג מהל' טומאת מת הלכה ד סמג עשין קכז:
כו ב ג מיי' פ"ז מהל' נזירות הלכה ד ופ"ג מהל' טומאת מת הלכה ה סמג עשין קכו:
כז ד ה מיי' פ"ג מהל' טומאת מת הלכ' יג סמג עשין רלא:
כח ו מיי' שם הלכה ה ופ"ז מהל' נזירות הלכה ז:

הגהות מהר"ב רנשבורג
א] תוס' ד"ה חוץ וכו' או מאהיל עליהם הוא נוגע. תיבות הוא נוגע נמחקו ונ"ב הוי כנוגע: ב] ד"ה בעי וכו' מי הוי כשאר תיבת כשאר נמחק ונ"ב בשעת חיבורן וכו' כצ"ל:

[בערך גלגל ע' ובערך גנגיליון]

שכבת זרע במעי אשה מהו? מי אמרי': כיון דלא איתצר – כי גופה דמי, או דלמא כיון דמעלמא קאתי – לא? בעי רב פפא: פירשה מהו? כיון דלא מקיימא בדלא אכלה – חיותא הוא, או דלמא הא נמי מעלמא אתי? בעי רב אחא בריה דרב איקא: עורו מהו? בעי רב הונא בר מנוח: כיחו וניעו מהו? א"ל רב שמואל בר אחא לרב פפא: ואי ס"ד כל הני דקאמר הוי גלגלין, רקב דמטמא היכי משכחת לה? דאשקייה מי דקלים, וסכיא נשא, ושלקו במי טבריא. אמר אביי: אנקטינן, מת שטחנו – אין לו רקב. איבעיא להו: טחנו וחזר והרקיב, מהו? מידי הוא טעמא אלא דאיכא בשר וגידים ועצמות – והאיכא, או דלמא כברייתו בעינן, וליכא? תיקו. *תני עולא בר חנינא: מת שחסר – אין לו רקב, ולא תפוסה, ולא שכונת קברות. מיתיבי: *לא, אם אמרת במת שיש לו רוב ורובע, או מלא תרווד רקב, תאמר בחי שאין לו לא רוב ולא רובע, ולא מלא תרווד רקב. היכי דמי? דארקיב חד אבר – דכוותיה גבי מת אפי' חד אבר איכא רקב! מי קתני הא מת? הא קמ"ל: שום מת יש לו רקב, שום חי אין לו רקב. בעי רבא: הרקיב כשהוא חי, וחזר ומת, מהו? כי גמירי רקב – דאירקיב כשהוא מת, או דלמא השתא מיהא הא מיית? ת"ש: לא, אם אמרת במת שיש לו רוב ורובע ומלא תרווד רקב, תאמר בחי כו'; טעמא – משום חי, הא מת – יש לו רקב! מי קתני הא מת? הא קא משמע לן: דשום מת יש לו רקב, שום חי אין לו רקב. בעי רבא: נמלה שחסרה מהו? שיעורא גמירין לה – והא חסר, או בריה גמירי לה, והאיכא? אמר

כיון דלא איתצר. שלא נוצר הולד עדיין בגופה, שהרי אין סופה לפרוש ממנה. פירשה מהו. פרש שלה שבתוכה מי הוי גלגלין, כיון דלא מיקיימא בדלא אכלה חיותא היא, ולא הוי גלגלין. ואגב שאל עובר במעי אשה בנקבה, שאל נמי בפירשה, וה"ה בזכר.

עורו מהו שיעשה גלגלין, כיחו וניעו מהו – שיעשה גלגלין. כל הני דקאמר הוי גלגלין. פרש וניעו וכיחו כו', היכי משכחת לה? דאשקייה מי דקלין. דאמרי' בפ' "שמונה שרצים" (שבת קי.): מאי מי דקלים – תרי דקלי איכא במתא מחסיא, ונפיק מעיינא דמיא מבינייהו, כסא קמא מרפי, ואידך משלשל, ואידך – כי היכי דעייל הכי נפק. משלשל את הגוף ומנקה את הגוף ביותר, ובכך העביר הפרש וכיחו וניעו. וסכיא נשא. פי' רש"י: להסיר השער. ושלקו במי טבריא תחלה, קודם שסכו בנשא להסיר שער הראש ושער הגוף. ע"י שסכו נשא נשרו (השער) עקרי השערות. דאי סכו מעיקרא בנשא – אכתי שרשי השער העוברים דרך העור לבשר לא היו עוד נושרים א] מן הנשא, משום דשער הלחולי מתחלחל, ומחובר לבשר הראש שתחת העור, כדאמרינן בפרק "העור והרוטב" (חולין קיט:). ונראה דלא סברא הך סוגיא הא דאמר לעיל: שערו העומד ליגזז מהו, משמע דאותו שאינו עומד ליגזז – לא הוי גלגלין. ושמא ס"ל כרבה, דאמר: גזז שערו – הוי גלגלין, ולא גזז – תיבעי ליה, בין שעומד ליגזז, ובין שאינו עומד ליגזז ועלה קאי. מת שטחנו אין לו רקב. דוקא רקבות גמירי, ולא עפרורית דטחינה.

כברייתו בעינן. כלומר שירקב כמו שהיה, שלא נשתנה מברייתו. מת שחסר אין לו רקבון. א) שנקבר חסר. ולא תפוסה. לקמן בפ' ב) ["הכותים"] (דף סד:): המוצא מת בדרך כדרכו – נוטלו עם תפוסתו, ודריש לה מקרא. ומפרש ליה שנוטל כל עפר התיחוח, ושלשה אצבעות מקרקע בתולה. ולא שכונת קברות. לקמן בפרק בתרא (דף סד:) אמרינן: מצא שלשה מתים, אם יש בין זה לזה מארבע אמות עד שמנה אמות – הרי זה שכונת קברות, ובודק הימנו ולהלן, כי יש לחוש שמא יש שם בית הקברות. ואם מצא שנים שלמים ואחד חסר – אין זה שכונת קברות. וצריך עיון: למה? אם טעם שכונת קברות משום חששא דדילמא היה שם בית הקברות – אף כי אחד חסר נמי ניחוש. ואם הוא הלכה למשה מסיני – מוטב. מיתיבי לא אם אמרת במת כו'. במס' עדיות (פ"ו מ"ג) תנן לה, דאיפלגו על כזית בשר [הפורש] מן האבר מן החי, דאיכא למאן דמטהר, ואיכא למאן דמטמא ויליף לה מבשר הפורש מאבר מן המת. ומותיב: לא אם אמרת באבר מן המת – שכן במת יש בו כמה חומרות: רוב, ורובע, ומלא תרווד. ברוב – פירוש: רוב בנין או רוב מנין. ג) ורובו[ע] – רובע קב עצמות דמטמא באהל. וכן מלא תרווד רקב מן המת שמטמא באהל, כדתני באהלות. והיכי דמי דאין לו רקב לחי – כמו דארקיב חד אבר, דכוותה גבי מת אפי' ארקיב חד אבר, אם חתך האבר ממנו – יש לו רקב. ואמאי? והא מת חסר הוא! ומשני: מי קתני הא מת? הא קמ"ל: שום מת יש לו רקב – ובמת שאינו חסר, שום חי אין לו רקב – וכדאיתא שחתך אבר מן החי ונרקב. טעמא משום חי. פי': כל זמן שהוא חי אין לו רקב, אבל מת יש לו רקב, כגון מת אדם אחד שנרקב בעודו חי אחד מאבריו – יש לו רקב לאותו אבר, אע"פ שהרקיב בעודו חי. ומשני: מי קתני [הא מת]? הא קמ"ל דשום מת יש לו רקב – כשנרקב לאחר שמת, ושום חי אין לו רקב – אפי' כי מת אחרי כן אין האבר שנרקב בעודו חי מטמא ג] כדין רקב.

נמלה שחסרה מהו. דאמר בפ' "אלו הן הלוקין" (מכות יג.): האוכל נמלה חייב עליה בכל שהוא, אע"פ שאין בה כזית, ומיבעיא ליה אם נקצצו רגליה, שעדיין היא יכולה לחיות, ועדיין שם בריה עליה. מי אמרינן שיעורא גמירי. כלומר, שלימה בבריה – והא חסרה. או דלמא בריה גמירי לה, והויא לה שרץ, הואיל ועדיין ראויה לחיות. ת"ש

א) נ"ל שנרקב. ב) נ"ל ורובע.

א) שכבת זרע במעי אשה מהו. כגון שמתה (א) שהיתה בת בנים, דסתם אשה בת בנים אית לה שכבת זרע במעיה. או שנבעלה סמוך למיתתה. מאי מי אמרינן כיון. דאכתי בשעת מיתתה לא נוצר עובר כי גופה הוא, ולא הוי גלגלין. או דלמא ש"ז מעלמא אתי לה, והוי גלגלין. ובאשה לעולם אין רקב עד דהויא בתולה, או זקנה דלאו בת בנים. פירשה. פרש שבתוך הגוף, דהיינו ריעי, מי נעשה ב) גלגלין? מי אמרינן: כיון דלא מקיימה בחייה אי לא אכלה – חיותא נמי דידה היא, וכגופה דמי, ולא הוי גלגלין. וה"ה לפרש דאיש, אלא איידי דקאי במילי דאשה מסיק לה נמי להא על שם אשה. בעי רב אחא בריה דרב איקא עורו מהו. רוק היוצא לו לאדם שלא ע"י טורח, אלא כיון שמתערערו לתוך פיו וגרונו – יוצא, מי הוי ליה גלגלין? ואית ג) דמפרשי: עורו – עור האדם ממש. כיחו וניעו. אינו יוצא אלא ע"י הדחק. היכי משכחת לה. דלית ליה פירשא קודם שמת. כגון דאשקייה מי דקלים. כדמפ' במס' שבת, בפ' "שמונה שרצים" (דף קי.): מאי מי דקלים – תרי דיקלי איכא במערבא, ונפיק מעיינא דמיא מבינייהו, כסא קמא מרפי, ואידך משלשל, ואידך – כי היכי דעייל הכי נפיק. וסבייה נשא. וסך גופו נשא שקורין טהרה, והעביר השיער העומד ליגזז. ושלקי במי טבריא. שהן חמים, והופשט עורו, ויצא כיחו וניעו. נקטינן מת שטחנו. בריחים, או ששחקו דק הרבה – אין לו תורת רקב, משום דרקב בעינן, והא לא אירקיב. מידי הוא טעמא. דרקב ד) מטמא, אלא משום דאיכא רקב בשר גידים ועצמות, כדאמר עולא לעיל – ה"נ איכא רקב של בשר גידין ועצמות, ויש לו תורת רקב. או דלמא. רקב הבא ממידי דכברייתו בעינן, והא ליכא – שהרי טחנו כבר, ואין לו תורת רקב. תיקו. מת שחסר. אבר כל שהוא, אין לו תורת רקב. ולא תפוסה. כההיא דתנן לקמן (דף סד:): המוצא מת מושכב כדרכו – נוטלו ואת תפוסתו. ואילו הכא, כיון דחסר – אין צריך ליטול תפוסתו עמו. ולא שכונת קברות. כי ההיא דתנן לקמן (שם): מצא שלשה – הרי זו שכונת קברות, וקנה מקומו. ואילו היכא דחסר אבר אחד מהן – אינו שכונת קברות, ולא קנה מקומו. איתיביה. ה) בסיפא קאי. לא, אם אמרת במת שהוא מטמא באהל – שיש לו רוב בניינו, מטמא באהל, ורובע הקב עצמות. תאמר באבר מן החי כו'. שאין רקב שלו טמא. והיכי דמי בחי, דאין לו תורת רקב – כגון דארקיב ביה חד אבר. אבל במת כי האי גוונא יש לו תורת רקב, ושמע מינה, דאע"ג דלא אירקיב בו אלא אבר אחד – יש ו) רקב. מי קתני הא דכוותיה במת. אלא לעולם לא קשיא, והא קמ"ל: דשום מת יש לו רקב כשהוא שלם ולא כשהוא חסר. ושום חי אין לו רקב. דאי אירקיב כוליה – ה"ל מת ולא חי, ואי אירקיב חד אבר, השתא י"ל במת אין לו תורת רקב, בחי לא כ"ש. בעי ז) רבא הרקיב. חד אבר כשהוא חי, בין שמיטפל עמו בין שאינו מיטפל, ולאח"כ חזר והרקיב כולו, מהו? כי מטמא היכא דהרקיב כולו כשהוא מת. והאי כשהוא חי הרקיב מקצתו, ואין לו תורת רקב. או דלמא הא מיית. וכהרקיב כולו כשהוא מת דמי. הא מת. לאחר כך יש לו רקב, ח) דאע"ג דהרקיב במקצת כשהוא חי. מי קתני הא מת. לאח"כ, אע"ג דנרקב מחיים, דיש לו רקב? לא, הכי קאמר: ט) דשום מת יש לו רקב, שום חי אין לו רקב. בעי רבא נמלה שחסרה. כל שהו, ואכלה, מהו? שיעור נמלה שלימה גמירי י) לה, דכי אכיל חייב, ואילו היכא דחסרה – הוי פטור. או דלמא בריה גמירי לה, דכי אכיל בריה מיחייב, וכי חסרה – נמי חייב, דהאיכא בריה, ואמרינן רובו ככולו. אמר

עין משפט נר מצוה

כט א מיי' פ"ז מהל' נזירות הלכ' ד ופ"ג מהל' טומאת מת הלכה ו:

ל ב מיי' פ"ז מהל' נזירות שם ופ"ג מהל' טומאת מת הלכה ז:

לא ג מיי' פ"ז מהל' נזירות הלכה ג ופ"ג מהל' טומאת מת הל' ז:

לב ד ה מיי' פ"ט מהל' טומאת מת הלכה ה:

לג ו מיי' שם פ"ג הלכ' א ופ"ז מהל' נזירות הלכה ב סמג עשין רלח:

פי' הרא"ש

כב' מתים שנקברו יחד: א) כיון דלא איתי שלא נולד עדיין העובר שסופו לצאת: פירשה הפרש שבמעיו: עורו מהו (מסתברה לי) [משכחת לה] דאשקיה מי דקלים אמרי' במסכת שבת פ' ח' שרצים תרי תאלתא איכא במערבא ונפיק עינא דמייא מבינייהו כסא קמא מרפי ואידך משלשל ואידך כי היכי דעייל הכי נפיק והשקהו ממנו ג' פעמים ובזה העביר הפרש וכיחו וניעו וסכיא נשא. סם שהעביר השער ושלקיה נמי במי טבריה להעביר עורו: מת שטחנו אין לו רקב דעפר רקבון גמירי ולא עפר טחינה ולא תפוסה לקמן בפ"ב מפ' לה דהמפנה המת מקברו צריך ליטול תפוסתו עמו ג' אצבעות מקרקע בתולה סביב המת: ולא שכונת קברות לקמ' פ' בתרא מפרש מצא ג' מתים אם יש בין זה לזה מד' אמות ועד [כ']. ה"ז שכונת קברות ובודק ממנו ולהלן כ' אמה כי יש לחוש שמא היה שם בית הקברות ואם מצא ב' מתים שלימים וא' חסר אין זה שכונת הקברות וא"צ לבדוק. ויראה שכל אלו הדברים הלכה למשה מסיני הם: לא אם (גמרה) [אמרת] במת וכו' במסכת עדיות תני לה ופליגי בכזית בשר הפורש מאבר מן החי אם מטמא ובא ללמדינו שמטמא מבשר הפורש מאבר מן המת. ומתיב לא אם אמרת במת שיש לו רוב שרוב בנינו או רוב מנינו מטמא באהל וכן רובע קב עצמות ומלא תרווד רקב מה שאין כן בחי: היכי דמי דאין לו רקב לחי דארקב חד אבר. דכוותה גבי מת אפי' הרקיב חד אבר אית ליה רקב ומשני מי קתני הא מת [הא] קמ"ל שום מת יש לו רקב שלא חסר ממנו יש לו רקב. אבל שום חי אין לו [רקב] טעמא משום דחי הא מת יש לו רקב אפי' אותו אבר שהרקיב בחייו מטמא במותו. שום מת יש לו רקב. כשהרקיב אחרי מותו. שום חי אין לו רקב דאם הרקיב בחייו אפי' אחרי מותו טהור בעי רבה נמלה שחסרה מהו דאמר פ' אלו הן הלוקין האוכל נמלה כל שהוא חייב אעפ"י שאין בה (כעדשה) [כזית] וכן לענין טומאה נמי ומיבעי ליה אם נקצצו רגליה שעדיין יכולה לחיות או שם בריה עליה מי אמר' שיעורה גמירי בריה שלימה עומדת עדיין במקום שיעור כעדשה. וכמו שאם חסר משיעור עדשה כל שהוא טהור בריה נמי בעי' שתהא שלימה או דילמא בריה גמירי והא איכא כבריה שיכולה לחיות ת"ש

א) נראה דצ"ל כיון דלא איתצר. שלא נוצר עדיין העובר ואין סופו לצאת וכ"ה בתוס':

מסורת הש"ס

[לקמן סה. ע"ש]

עדיות פ"ו מ"ג

נוסחת הריב"ן

א) (שכתב זרע בו' או זקנה דלאו בת בנים) ליתא בכ"י והכי איתא כיון דלא איתצר שעדיין לא נעשית הימנו כי גופו דמי ולא נעשה לה גלגלין תעטרכות. או דלמא כיון דמזדווגי דעלמא קא אתי לה הוי גלגלין ואין לה תורת רקב: ב) מי נעשה לה גלגלין כו' חיותא דידה נמי היא: ג) דגרסי: ד) דרקב במת מטמא כו' ועצמות וכדאמר: ה) בספרי קאי כו' שיש לו רוב רוב בינו כו' ורובע רובע הקב: ו) יש לו רקב: ז) רבה: ח) ואע"ג: ט) ה"ק לית לן למגמר ממידי דגמרי הלכתא אלא ממידי דהכי בה והכא קמ"ל דשום מת יש לו רקב הא חי אין לו רקב: י) גמירי דהאוכל חייב כו' בריה מקום דאמרינן רובו ככולו:

הגהות הב"ח

(א) רש"י ד"ה שכבת וכו' שמתה כשהיא בת בנים:

הגהות מהר"ב רנשבורג

א] תוס' ד"ה וסכיא וכו' לא היו עוד נושרים מן. תיבת מן נמחק ונ"ב מכח: ב] ד"ה ולא תפוסה. לקמן בפ' הכותים. תיבת הכותים נמחק. ונ"ב בתרא: ג] ד"ה טעמא וכו' מטמא כדין רקב כל:

אמר רב יהודה מדיסקרתא, ת"ש: *"בהם", יכול בכולן – ת"ל "מהם". אי "מהם" יכול מקצתן – ת"ל "בהם". הא כיצד? עד שיגע במקצתן שהוא ככולן, [א]ושיערו חכמים בכעדשה, שכן החומט תחלת ברייתו בכעדשה. ש"מ: שיעורא גמירי לה. אמר רב שמעיה: כי בעינן שיעורא, דבדלא הויא כעדשה לא מטמא – דלא נפלה בה נשמה, [ב]אבל נפלה בה נשמה – לא. תיבעי לך.§ "השדרה והגולגולת". איבעיא להו: שדרה וגולגולת תנן, [ג]או דלמא או שדרה או גולגולת? אמר רבא, ת"ש: *[ד]שדרה שנגרד רוב עילעין שבה – טהורה, ובקבר אפילו משוברת או מפורקת – טמאה, מפני הקבר. טעמא – משום דגירד, הא לא גירד – טמא. ש"מ: או שדרה או גולגולת קתני. א] הא לא קתני, הא קמ"ל דכי גירד – טהורה, אידך – תיבעי לך. תא שמע: *רבי יהודה אומר: ששה דברים ר' עקיבא מטמא וחכמים מטהרין, וחזר בו ר' עקיבא. ומעשה שהביאו קופה מלאה עצמות לבהכ"נ של טרסיים והניחוה באויר, ונכנס תודוס הרופא וכל הרופאים [עמו], ואמרו: אין כאן שדרה ממת אחד. טעמא – דליכא שדרה דמחדא, האיכא או שדרה או גולגולת דמחדא – נזיר מגלח עליה, ש"מ: או שדרה או גולגולת תנן. לא מיבעיא קאמר; לא מיבעיא שדרה וגולגולת דממת אחד ליכא, אלא אפי' או שדרה ממת אחד או גולגולת ממת אחד ליכא. תא שמע ממניינא: ומה הן ששה דברים שרבי עקיבא מטמא וחכמים [ה]מטהרין: *[ו]על אבר מן המת שבא משני מתים, [ז]ועל אבר מן החי שבא משני בני אדם, [ח]ועל חצי קב עצמות שבא משני מתים, ועל רביעית דם הבא משנים, ועל עצם כשעורה שנחלק לשנים, והשדרה והגולגולת. ואי

רש"י

אמר רב יהודה מדסקרתא ת"ש. "אלה הטמאים לכם בכל השרץ, כל הנוגע בהם במותם" וגו' (ויקרא יא), אי "בהם" יכול בכולם, דכי נגע בכולם יהא טמא, אבל לא א) במקצתו – ת"ל "וכל אשר יפול עליו מהם במותם" כו'. ושיערו חכמים. שמגע עדשה יטמא, שהוא כעדשה ב) שהוה כולו. שכן החומט תורה אור כו'. ומדקא בעי שיעור בריה כעדשה – ש"מ שיעורא דבריה כולה בעינן, ואי חסרה שיעורא – נפקא לה מכלל טומאתה, וה"ה לענין אכילה. אמר ר' שמעיה כי בעינן שיעורא. דבריה, במידי דכל ברייתו בכעדשה. אבל גבי נמלה, ג) בפחות מכעדשה הויא בה נשמה, דהא שלימה נמי לא הויא כולה כעדשה – לא בעינן שיעורא, ואכתי תבעי לך. אמר רבא ת"ש [שדרה] שנגרד רוב צלעות שבה. שעקר רוב צלעות שבה – טהורה, ואע"ג שהן מונחות בלדה. ובקבר כו'. מפני שהקבר מצרפה להיות ד) כמו שלמה. הא לא גירד – טמאה, ואע"ג דליכא גולגולת בהדה. וש"מ דשדרה או גולגולת תנן. אידך. לא גירד, עדיין תיבעי לך. ששה דברים. לקמן קחשיב להו. של טרסיים. צורפי נחשת. ואמרי לה: של אותה אומה. ואמרי לה: אורגים. ודומה לו במסכת ע"ז (דף יז:) במעשה דרבי אליעזר כשנתפס למלכות, דאמר להו: רבם של טרסיים אני. והניחוה באויר. כדי שלא יהיו מיטמאין באותן עצמות. ונכנס תודוס הרופא. שהיה בקי ומומחה אם הן ממת אחד או משני מתים. ואמרו אין כאן שדרה ממת אחד. ואין הנזיר מגלח על אהילו. ואפילו לר"ע, שהיה אומר בתחלה שאפי' היא באה משני מתים מטמא על אהילו – חזר בו ר"ע. טעמא משום דליכא ביה שדרה ממת אחד. קאמר דאין הנזיר מגלח. הא איכא (א) חדא דמת אחד – מטמא באהל, ואין מועיל הנחתו באוירא כלום, והנזיר מגלח עליו. ותפשוט דאו שדרה או גולגלת. לא, לעולם אימא לך דשדרה וגולגולת ממת אחד בעינן. והאי דקאמר להו ה) הרופאים דקא מטהר להו – לא מיבעיא קאמר; לא מיבעיא שדרה וגלגולת דמת אחד כדי שיעור טומאת אהל, דליכא, אלא אפילו שדרה ממת אחד וגולגולת ממת אחד, דלדברי ר"ע הוה מטמא – לא איכא. ת"ש ממניינא. דששה דברים. על אבר מן המת הבא מב' מתים – כגון הזרוע או השוק שיש בו שתי עצמות, והאחד בא ממת אחד והאחר בא ממת שני, וקרויין הן אבר אחד. ר"ע מטמא וחכמים מטהרים. לפי שלא אמרו שיהא מטמא באהל אלא באבר ממת אחד, ואבר מן החי הבא מאדם אחד, וחצי קב עצמות הבא ממת אחד, ורביעית דם הבא ממת אחד, במגע ולא באהל. ולדברי ר"ע אפי' באהל. ועצם כשעורה ממת אחד. ובכל אלו ו) אומר ר' עקיבא שאפי' הן באין משני מתים הרי אלו מטמאין. לעולם

תוספות

ת"ש בהם יכול בכולן. גבי שרצים כתיב "אשר יפול מהם אל תוכו" ובמקום אחר כתיב "אשר יגע בהם במותם", הא כיצד נייסב שני המקראות הללו? וכו' ושיערו חכמים בכעדשה, דמיקריא "מהם" – שזהו במקצת שרץ אחד, ומיקריא "בהם" – לפי שהחומט תחילת בריתו בכעדשה. וש"מ שיעורא גמירי, מדבעינן כעדשה. שהרי החומט גם כי הוי תחילתו בכעדשה – היינו עם רגליו וקרניו, ומ"מ אי חתיך מיניה פורתא, דמיפחתי' מכעדשה – אפ"ה חיה, ואפ"ה בעינן כעדשה ממש כברייתה, וש"מ שיעורא גמירי. ודחי, א"ר שמעיה: כי בעינן שיעורא בכעדשה – היכא דלא נפלה ביה נשמה, כגון חומט, שאם נפחת מעט תחילה – אז ודאי אין לנו להחשיבו בריה בפחות, הואיל ולעולם לא יפול בו נשמת חיים בפחות מכן. אבל היכא דנפלה ליה, כגון נמלה חיה – חשובה היא, כי אף קיצץ רגליה או שום דבר ממנה – יכולה עדיין לחיות הרבה, שאין חייה תלוין בדבר שקצץ. **איבעיא** להו שדרה וגולגולת תנן. דדוקא על שניהם מגלח, או דלמא או שדרה או גולגולת תנן. והוא הדין דאמתניתין דאהלות (פ"ב מ"א) נמי מיבעיא ליה, וכן משמע בסמוך דמייתי מתניתין דאהלות למיפשט בעיין. **ת"ש** שדרה שנגרד רוב עלעולין שבה. פי': שיבר רוב צלעות שבה. תרגום של צלעות – עלעולין. **טהורה.** בעלמא [אמרינן] כמה חסרון בשדרה וכו' ולא תטמא, אמר שמואל בפ' "אלו טרפות" (חולין מב:): וכן לטרפה. וגם כאן נראה לרבינו יצחק דיש להשוות, דאם נשתברו רוב צלעותיה טרפה, וכדאמר בפ' "אלו טרפות" (שם נב.): נשתברו ברוב שני צדדין – טרפה, נעקרו – אפילו ברוב צד אחד. **ובקבר** אפי' משוברת או מפורקת טמאה מפני שהקבר מצרפה. דהכי גמירי. **טעמא** דגירד הא לא גירד טמא. וקס"ד דאיירי בלא גולגולת, ואפ"ה טמאה, וש"מ דאו שדרה או גולגולת תנן. ומשני: מי קתני: הא לא גירד טמאה? הא קמ"ל דכי גירד טהורה ואידך תיבעי לך. פירוש: מי קתני הא לא גירד טמאה בלא גולגולת? דלמא כשיש עמה גולגולת איירי, ואע"פ [כן] כי גירד רוב צלעות שבה – טהורה. ואידך תיבעי לך, כלומר: בלא גירד, ואין שם אלא השדרה בלא גולגולת, תיבעי לך. **תא** שמע רבי יהודה אומר ששה דברים ר"ע מטמא. בסמוך קא חשיב להנך ששה דברים. וחכמים מטהרין, וחזר בו ר"ע. **מעשה** שהביאו קופה מלאה עצמות לבית הכנסת של טרסיים. פירוש: צורפי נחשת. והניחוה באויר במקום שאין גג עליו, פן יטמאו באהל הנכנסין שם. נכנס תודוס הרופא וכל הרופאים עמו, ואמרו: אין כאן שדרה ממת אחד. ובפירוש משניות מצאתי דהכי איתא בסיפרי: אמרו, הואיל ויש כאן מטהרין [ומטמאין] נעמוד למנין. פירוש: ר"ע וחכמים שנחלקו בשדרה ובגולגולת הבאים משני מתים, ובסמוך מייתי לה. ובמס' אהלות פ"ב (מ"ו) נמי תנן פלוגתייהו, התחילו מר' עקיבא תחילה וטיהר, אמרו לו: הואיל ואתה הוא שהיית מטמא, טיהרת – יהו טהורין. **טעמא** דליכא שדרה ב] דמת חדא. פי': ממת חדא, הא איכא שדרה או גולגולת דמת חדא – נזיר מגלח עליה. וש"מ: או שדרה או גולגולת תנן. ודחי: דלמא לא מיבעיא קאמר, לא מיבעיא שדרה וגולגולת דממת אחד ליכא. ל"ע: מה היו צריכין להראות לרופאים אם השדרה ממת אחד או לא? והא מסתמא היתה מפורקת ומשוברת, ואמרינן לעיל דאף ממת אחד טהורה! ואומר רבינו יצחק: דאיירי כגון דעל אותן עצמות האהיל האדם בעודן בקבר, ואמר לעיל הקבר מצרפו. **ת"ש** ממניינא מה הן ששה דברים שר"ע מטמא וחכמים מטהרין על אבר מן המת שבא משני מתים, ועל אבר מן החי שבא משני בני אדם, ועל חצי קב עצמות שבא מב' מתים. ומדלא קאמר הכא "ועל רובע עצמות הבא משני מתים" כדתנן במסכת אהלות (פ"ב מ"ו) בפלוגתא דר"ע ורבנן – יש להוכיח דהכא לענין תגלחת נזיר איירי, דאינו מגלח על פחות מחצי קב. ולהכי נקט חצי קב, דעל רובע הקב דאתי ממת אחד אינו מגלח, כדתנן במתניתין, והתם לענין טומאת אהל גרידא קתני. ג] **שבא** משני מתים. דאילו בא ממת אחד לר"ע מגלח, כדתנן במתני' לר"ע, ופליגי רבנן עליה. והכא תנן דר"ע הדר ביה. ודין הוא דמיבעי ליה למינקט לרבנן "על חצי לוג דם הבא משני מתים", אלא איידי דלר"ע דאף ברביעית מגלח נקט הכי. הר"ף. **ועל** עצם כשעורה ד]ועל רביעית דם כו' ועל עצם כשעורה שנחלק לשנים. אף כי הוא ממת אחד. והשדרה וגולגולת – במסכת אהלות (פ"ג מ"ו) תניא בהדיא בפלוגתא דר"ע ורבנן: השדרה וגולגולת משני מתים. *ואי ס"ד או שדרה או גולגולת הני שבעה הויין. פי': דנחלקו בו ר"ע ורבנן, ובריש תנא ששה דברים. אלא ודאי שדרה וגולגולת חד, דלא מטמא הא בלא הא. ומשני: לעולם שדרה וגולגולת כתרי חשיב להו, וסמי עצם כשעורה מחושבנא דששה דברים. דכי קתני ששה דברים דפליגי על ר"ע – לאפוקי עצם כשעורה, דיחיד הוא דפליג עליה, דתניא עצם כשעורה כו'. ואיבעית

פי' הרא"ש

ת"ש בהם יכול בכולן בשרצים כתיב וכל אשר יגע בהם. דמשמע שיגע בשרץ שלם ת"ל כל אשר יפול מהם דמשמע אפי' מקצתן: הא כיצד יתקיימו ב' מקראות הללו: ושיערו בכעדשה. דהיינו מקצתו וקרינן ביה בהם לפי שהחומט תחלת בריתו בכעדשה והוא שלם: ש"מ שיעורא גמירי. דאי אמרת דנמלה שנקצצו רגליה קרויה בריה (ואכתי) [ואף דעתה] אין בו כעדשה דתחילת ברייתו כשהוא שלם אין בו אלא כעדשה ונילף מיניה דפחות מכעדשה [נמי] מטמא. ודחי כי בעי' שיעורא בכעדשה היכא דלא נפלה ביה נשמה כמו חומט בתחי' (דמקומו) ודאי אין לנו להחשיבו בריה בפחות מכעדשה הואיל ולא תפול בי' נשמה בפחות מכאן: אבל היכא דנפלה ביה נשמה. כגון נמלה חיה חשובה ברי' אפילו חסרה הואיל ועדיין יכולה לחיות: איבעיא להו שדרה וגולגולת תנן. דוקא תרוייהו. או דלמא [או שדרה כו'] ועל מתני' דאהלות דתנן ואלו מטמאין באוהל השדרה והגולגולת שייך נמי למבעי הך בעיא. וכן מוכח בשמעתין דמייתי הך בעיא ממתני' דאהלות. ת"ש שדרה שנגידר. פי' חותך כמו גודו אילנא. רוב עלעין שבה. צלעות תרגומו עילעין ובפ' אלו טרפות מפ' נשתברו ברוב ב' צדדים נתפרקו ברוב צד א: טהורה. שביטל שם שדרה ממנה ובקבר אפי' נשברה או נפרקה טמאה שהקבר מצרפם דהכי גמירי. הא לא גידר טמאה השדרה לבדה. מי קתני הא לא גדרה טמאה דלמא כי גדר טהורה אידך תבעי לך. מי קתני הא לא גדר טמאה בלא גולגולת. דלמא עם גולגולת מיירי ואעפ"כ אם גדר טהורה אידך. כלומר אם לא גידר תיבעי לך אי מטמא שדרה לבדה. ת"ש ר' יהודה (דברי) [אומר ששה דברים] ר"ע מטמא בסמוך קא חשיב להו: של טרסיים צורפי נחושת והגיחוה באויר מקום שאין עליה אוהל שלא יטמאו הנכנסים שם וכל הרופאים אמרו שהיו בקיאים להכיר בעצמות שהם משדרה וגולגולת ולהשוות עצם לעצם ולידע אם הם מב' מתים או ממת א' ואמרו אין כאן שדרה ממת א' ולא גולגולת ממת אחד והנזיר שהאהיל עליהם בעודם בקבר א) אינו מגלח. דאי משום טומאת אוהל אפילו היה שם שדרה ממת א' לא היה מגלח כיון דאין השדרה שלימה כדאמרי' לעיל גדר רוב עילעין שבה טהורה. ת"ש ממניינא ומה הן ז' דברים וכו' ועל חצי קב עצמות וכו' מדלא קתני ועל רובע עצמות הבא מב' מתים כדאיתא בפלוגתא דר"ע ורבנן במסכת אהלות אלמא דלענין תגלחת נזיר איירי הכי ועל עצם כשעורה שנחלק לשנים אעפ"י שהוא ממת א'. והשדרה והגולגולת במס' אהלות קתני בהדיא בפלוגתא דר"ע ורבנן השדרה והגולגולת מב' מתים כי קתני אבר

א) נראה דל"ל והכל לפי' שם שדרה ממת אחד היה מגלח דאי משום וכו'.

עין משפט נר מצוה

לד א מיי' פ"ד מהל' אבות הטומאות הלכ' ב סמג עשין רמג:
לה ב מיי' פ"ב מהלכות מאכלות אסורות הל' כב סמג לאוין קלב:
לו ג מיי' פ"ב מהל' טומאת מת הלכה ח ופ"ז מהל' נזירות הלכ' ב וע"ש בכ"מ סמג עשין רלא:
לז ד מיי' פ"ד מהלכות טומאת מת הלכה ז:
לח ה ו מיי' שם הלכ' ב ופ"ז מהל' נזירות הלכה ב:
לט ז מיי' פ"ז מהלכות נזירות שם ופ"ד מהלכות טומאת מת הלכה ג:
מ ח מיי' שם הלכה ה:

מסורת הש"ס

(חגיגה יא. נדה נו.)
תוספתא דאהלות פ"ב
שם פ"ד
(אהלות פ"ב)
שייך לע"ב

נוסחת הריב"ן

א) במקלתו: ב) שהוה: ג) בפחות: ד) להיות שלמה: ה) הרפא וקא מטהר להו: ו) היה אומר:

הגהות הב"ח

(א) רש"י ד"ה טעמא וכו' הא איכא שדרה דמת אחד:

הגהות מהר"ב רנשבורג

א] גמ' הא לא קתני. נ"ב עי' תוס' ד"ה טעמא דגירד וכו': ב] תוס' ד"ה טעמא דליכא שדרה דמת חדא. תיבות דמת חדא נמחקו ונ"ב כ"ה: ג] ד"ה רביעית דם שבא משני מתים וכו' כצ"ל: ד] ד"ה ועל עצם כשעורה. ועל רביעית דם וכו' ועל עצם כשעורה. מן תיבות ועל רביעית עד כשעורה נמחק.

ואי ס"ד או שדרה או גולגולת – הני שבעה הויין! כי קתני (סימן יחיד שהוא גילח ואחד) כל היכא דפליגי עליה רבים, לאפוקי עצם כשעורה דיחיד הוא דפליג עליה. *דתני': *עצם כשעורה שנחלק לשנים, ר"ע א מטמא ורבי יוחנן בן נורי מטהר. ואי בעית אימא: כי קתני – אבר מן המת, אבר מן החי לא קתני. ואיבעית אימא: כי קתני – כל היכא דנזיר מגלח על אהילו, ב לאפוקי עצם כשעורה דלא. ואיבעית אימא: כי קתני – כל היכא דהדר ביה, לאפוקי רביעית דם דלא הדר ביה. דאמר ליה רבי לבר קפרא: לא תשנה רביעית דם בחזרה, שהרי למודו של ר' עקיבא בידו, ועוד, המקרא מסייעו: "ועל כל נפשות מת לא יבא". *ר"ש אומר: עד ימיו היה מטמא, אם משמת חזר בו – איני יודע. תנא: *הושחרו שיניו מפני תעניותיו. ת"ש: *דתניא, *בש"א: ג רובע עצמות מן העצמים, או משנים או משלשה. ובה"א: רובע מן הגויה, מרוב הבנין או מרוב המנין. אמר רבי יהושע: יכולני לעשות דברי ב"ש ודברי ב"ה כאחד; שב"ש אומרים משנים או משלשה – או משני שוקיים וירך אחד, או משני ירכיים ושוק אחד, הואיל ורוב (א) גובהו של אדם *מגובה. וב"ה אומרים: מן הגויה או מרוב בנין או מרוב מנין – הואיל וישנן במפרקי ידים ורגלים. שמאי אומר: אפילו עצם מן השדרה או מן הגולגולת. *שאני שמאי דמחמיר! (ב) ליפשוט מינה: טעמא דבית שמאי דמחמיר, הא רבנן – עד דאיכא שדרה וגולגולת! לא, עד כאן לא פליגי רבנן עליה דשמאי – אלא בעצם אחד דאתי מן השדרה ומן הגולגולת, אבל היכא דאיתיה בעיניה – אפילו חדא מינהון. בעי רמי בר חמא: רובע עצמות מן שדרה וגולגולת, מאי? [א] כי קתני חצי קב עצמות – היכא דאיכא משאר אבריו, אבל מן שדרה וגולגולת דחמירי – אפי' רובע עצמות, או דלמא לא שנא? אמר רבא, ת"ש: השדרה והגולגולת, ואי סלקא דעתך רובע עצמות דאתי מן שדרה וגולגולת [ב] חמיר – ליתני: על רובע עצמות הבא מן השדרה כו'! והא

[לקמן נג.]

לעולם או שדרה או גולגולת תנן. כי קתני דששה דברים הן – בהנהו דפליגי עליה רבים. אבל בעצם כשעורה, דלא פליגי עליה רבים, אלא יחיד – לא חשיב ליה מתנייתא, ולעולם או שדרה או גולגולת תנן, וחשיב להו תרי, וליכא בהו אלא ששה, דסמי (ג) מכאן שעורה. ואיכא דאמרי: כשעורה הוא מתנייתא משום דאתיי' לה מן המת, אבל אבר מן החי סמי מכאן. ואיבעית אימא כי קתני כל היכא דנזיר מגלח על אהילו א) לאפוקי עצם כשעורה. דלדברי הכל לא מיטמא נזיר על אהילו. וא"ת: רביעית דם דלא מיטמא באהילו, וקתני! לר"ע מיטמא נזיר באהילו, דאיהו משמע ליה מ"על כל נפשות מת לא יבא" כדאמרינן לעיל (דף לח.): מנין לרביעית דם שמטמא באהל כו'. לא תשנה רביעית דם בחזרה. שחזר בו ר"ע. דודאי לא חזר בו, שלעולם היה סבור שרביעית דם הבאה מב' מתים מטמא באהל. שהרי ב) למודו בידו. (ד) למודו ערוך כך שהוא מטמא, והנזיר מגלח. ותכ"א: כשהוא בא ממת א' ה"ז מטמא באהל, אבל אין הנזיר מגלח עליו עד שיהא בו א] ג) רביעית לוג. עד ימיו. כלומר, כל ימיו היה מטמא ר"ע. ד) שמא משמת חזר בו. הושחרו שיניו. של ר"ש. מפני תעניותיו ה). לפי שדרך גנאי היה משתעי עליה דר"ע, ואמר: אם משמת חזר בו. ת"ש ב"ש אומרים רובע עצמות מן העצמות. שאמרו שמטמאין באהל, ומזה עליהן בשלישי ו) – כגון שבא משני עצמות או משלשה עצמות. אבל לא מעצם אחד. וב"ה אומרים. רובע עצמות שאמרו מן הגויה – בזמן שהוא בא מרוב הבנין או מרוב המנין. אבל משאר איברים שאין רוב בנין או רוב מנין – אינו מטמא באהל. משני שוקים וירך אחד. ז) ג' איברים (ה) כב"ש, ויהא בהן רוב בניינו. וב"ה אומרים: מרוב המנין אבל לא משאר אברים, הרי הוא יכול להתקיים דברי ב"ה – כמו במפרקי ידים ורגלים, שיהא בהן רוב מנין וג' אברים כב"ש. שמאי אומר. רובע עצמות שאמרו – אפילו הבא מעצם אחד מטמא באהל, ומאי מעצם אחד – כגון דאתי מן השדרה או מגולגולת. מאי. מי הוי נזיר מגלח עליו או לא? דחמירי. דאית בהו חומרא טפי משאר אברים. ליתני. בא בהדיא: ועל רובע עצמות הבא מן השדרה של שני מתים ומן הגולגולת של ב' מתים, שר' עקיבא מטמא וחכמים מטהרין ח)! והא

ואיבעית אימא כי קתני מידי דמת מידי דחי לא קתני. ולא תחשוב בהנך ששה דברים אבר מן החי. ואיבעית אימא: כי קתני מילי דנזיר מגלח על אהילו – לאפוקי עצם כשעורה דאינו מגלח אלא על מגעו ועל משאו. ואיבעית אימא: מידי דהדר ביה, שחזר ר"ע, כדקתני לעיל שחזר בו ר"ע – לאפוקי רביעית דם הבאה מב' מתים דלא הדר. וששה דברים דקא חשיב מהנך דהדר ביה, ולעולם שדרה וגולגולת בתרי חשיב להו: דא"ל רבי לבר קפרא תלמידיה לא תשנה דם רביעית בחזרה שהרי למוד ערוך הוא בפיו של ר"ע. דעל רביעית הבאה מב' מתים דנזיר מגלח. ועוד, המקרא מסייעו. ובא להכחיש דברי האומר שר"ע חזר. ב] ובא ר"ש לומר כרבי, דר"ע לא חזר בו. אלא שאמר דרך קנתור כלפי ר"ע, שאמר: אם משמת חזר בו איני יודע. [אמר ר"ש עד יום מותו של ר"ע היה מטמא. כלומר לא חזר בו]. תנא הושחרו שיניו. של ר"ש מפני תעניותיו, מפני שאין דרך ארץ לדבר על רבו בלשון זה. וישב והתענה ימים רבים.

ת"ש דתני' ב"ש אומרים רובע עצמות מן העצמים מן השנים מן הג'. פירוש: או משנים או משלשה אברים, יטמא רובע עצמות באהל. ובית הלל אומרים מן הגויה. פירוש: מעיקר הגויה, מרוב הבנין או מרוב המנין. שרמ"ח אברים יש באדם, כדתניא בריש מסכת אהלות, וקכ"ה הם רוב מנין, ואם תפש קכ"ה עצמות וקילה מעט מן כל אחד ואחד עד שהעמיד על רובע – יטמאו באהל. אמר ר' יהושע יכולני לעשות דברי ב"ש ודברי ב"ה אחד שב"ש אומרים משנים או מג' או מב' שוקים וירך אחד או משני ירכים ושוק אחד. נמצא רוב בנינו של אדם. ג] תנינא במס' אהלו' (פ"א מ"ח) דקחשבינן רמ"ח אברים, וחשיב מלמטה למעלה פרסות הרגל, וחשיב: שנים בשוק, חמשה בארכובה, ואחד בירך. לכאורה משמע ממתני' דהתם דשוק למטה מן הארכובה, וירך למעלה: משני שוקים וירך אחד או משני ירכים ושוק אחד, הואיל והוא רוב בנינו של אדם מגובה. ומב' או משלשה דקאמרי ב"ש – לאו דווקא, אלא כלומר רובע עצמות הבא מרוב הבנין ורוב ד] המנין הוי לגובה האדם, ירך ע"ג שני שוקים. ויש מפרשים דשני שוקים וירך אחד קרי שנים, לפי שהשוקים דקים ביותר והוו כחד, ועם ירך אחד נחשבים כשני עצמות, ושני ירכים ושוק אחד – הרי שלשה, לפי שהירכים עבים וגדולים נחשבין כשנים, והשוק עמהם הרי שלשה. וב"ה אומרים מן הגויה מרוב המנין. הואיל וישנו ברוב המנין, דהיינו מפרקי ידים ורגלים. וב"ש איירו ברובע הבא מרוב הבנין, וב"ה איירו ברובע הבא מרוב המנין. ומר אמר חדא ומר אמר חדא ולא פליגי. ומפרקי ידים ורגלים ה] תנינא רוב המנין בלא רוב הבנין, כדמפרש במסכת אהלות (פ"א מ"ח) דפרסת הרגלים יש ל' – ששה בכל אצבע, ובפיסת היד שלשים – ששה בכל אצבע – הרי ק"כ אברים בידים וברגלים. שמאי אומר אפי' עצם אחד מן השדרה או מן הגולגולת. וקס"ד: מדקאמר שמאי עצם אחד מן השדרה או מן הגולגולת מטמא באהל, מכלל דלרבנן, דקאמרי: לא עצם אחד מן השדרה או מן הגולגולת מטמא – הא שדרה גופה או גולגולת גופה מטמא אפי' האי לחודיה והאי לחודיה. דמשמע ליה דלא פליגי [אלא] על האי, ו] ב"ש עצם אחד משדרה, ולב"ה בעינן שדרה וגולגולת. ודחי: שמאי דמחמיר, אבל לרבנן בעינן תרוייהו. וליפשוט מינה. לאידך גיסא, דטעמא (דמחמיר) שמאי דמחמיר ז] דטמאות דעצם משדרה לבד או בעצם מגולגולת לבד, כדקתני "או" "או", הא לרבנן דלא תנן "או" "או", אלא "השדרה והגולגולת" – ש"מ תרוייהו בעו! ודחי: עד כאן לא פליגי רבנן עליה דשמאי אלא בעצם אחד משדרה או מגולגולת. אבל היכא דאיתא בעיניה, שהשדרה שלימה – אפי' חד מנהון. ומשום דלא קתני במילתייהו דרבנן "או" "או" לא ניחוש לדקדק, דב"ה לא חשו לפרש מילתייהו. או דקיימי אמילתא דב"ש, דקאמרי "או" ומדב"ש נשמע לב"ה דבעו למימר "או". מהרפ"ש. בעי רמי בר חמא רובע עצמות משדרה או מגולגולת מאי. מי אמרי': כי קתני במתני' דחצי קב עצמות דנזיר מגלח – כגון דאתי משאר אברים, כגון מרוב הבנין או המנין, אבל משדרה וגולגולת דחמירי טפי – אפי' רובע עצמות הבא מהן מגלח עליהן נזיר, או דלמא לא שנא? אמר רבא ת"ש השדרה והגולגולת. דקתני במתני' דנזיר מגלח עליהן. וקס"ד דליכא שדרה וגולגולת דלית בהן רובע עצמות, ואי לא הויא בהן רובע עצמות לא מגלח. ולהכי פריך: ואי ס"ד רובע עצמות דאתי משדרה וגולגולת חמיר, ליתני במתני': רובע עצמות הבא מן השדרה וגולגולת, ולמה לי דתני במתניתין "השדרה והגולגולת", דמשמע דווקא כשהן שלמין? הא

שמאי או' אפי' עצם א' מן השדרה מן הגולגולת. וקס"ד מדקאמר שמאי אפי' עצם א' מן השדרה או מהגולגולת מטמא באוהל מכלל דרבנן דפליגי אמרי שדרה או גולגולת דאי לאו הכי מפלגת פלוגתיהו יותר מדאי: ומשני שמאי דמחמיר. אבל רבנן לעולם תרוייהו בעו. לפשוט מיניה. טעמא דשמאי דמחמיר לטמא בעצם משדרה לבד או מגלגולת לבד כדקתני או הכי רבנן דלא תנו או אלא השדרה והגולגולת עד דאיכא שדרה וגולגולת אבל היכא דאיתיה בעיניה חד מנהון. ושמאי דמחמיר לטמא אפי' בעצם הוצרך למתני או דלא תימא כולי האי לא מחמיר אלא בעי עצם מכל חד מנייהו אבל לרבנן דמצריכי שדרה שלימה או גולגולת שלימה לא צריך למתני או: היכא דאיכא משאר איברים מרוב בניינו או מרוב מניינו. ליתני על רובע עצמות הבא מן השדרה ומן הגולגולת וכ"ש שדרה וגולגולת דקס"ד דליכא שדרה וגולגולת שאין בהם רובע עצמות. א) אלמא דיש שדרה וגולגולת בלא רובע וא"כ היכי בעי למפשט מדקתני שדרה וגולגולת ולא קתני רובע עצמות הבא מן השדרה או מן הגולגולת אלמא דרובע לא מטמא הא איצטריך למתני שדרה וגולגולת לגופיה אע"פ שאין בה רובע ולעולם אימא לך דרובע הבא [משדרה וגולגולת] טמא ולא אתפרש היכא אמר רבא וי"מ דדייק לה מהך דאמר רבא לעיל בפרקי' לא נצרכה אלא לרוב בניינו או לרוב מניינו שאין בהם רובע קב עצמות וכו' נמי על שדרה וגולגולת. בתר דשמעה מר' עקיבא לא אתפרש והר' יעקב מפ' דרבא אמרה למתני' על מתני' דאהלות דקא חשיב ו' דברים שר"ע מטמא וקא חשיב שדרה וגולגולת מב' מתים ורובע עצמות מב' מתים. ואי אין שדרה וגולגולת פחות מרובע אמאי איצטריך לשנותן. ותריץ רבא לא נצרכה אלא לשדרה וגולגולת שאין בהם רובע אבל מקמי דשמעה לר"ע הוה ס"ד דאין שדרה וגולגולת פחות מרובע וקשיא לכו אמאי קאמר בתר דשמעה מר"ע הא מקמי הך דר"ע קתני במתני' ואלו מטמאין באהל וקתני השדרה והגולגולת ורובע עצמות ועלה נמי בעי לשנויי לא נצרכה אלא לשדרה וגולגולת שאין בהם רובע:

ת"ש

א) אולי צ"ל דאמר לא נצרכה אלא וכו' אלמא דיש שדרה וכו'.

הגהות מהר"ב רנשבורג א] רש"י ד"ה שהרי וכו' עד שיהא בו רביעית. תיבת רביעית נמחק ונ"ב חצי: ב] תוד"ה ואי בעית אימא וכו' שר"ע חזר וכו'. תיבת וכו' נמחק. ונ"ב וכן ר"ש בא לומר כנ"ל: ג] ד"ה אמר ר"י וכו' (וכו') של אדם תנינא. תיבת תנינא נמחק ונ"ב מגובה: ד] בא"ד הבא מרוב הבנין ורוב הבנין כנ"ל: ה] ד"ה וב"ה וכו' ומפרקי ידים ורגלים תנינא. תיבת תנינא נמחק ונ"ב מליט. א"מ ויעו"ש: ו] ד"ה שמאי אומר וכו' דלא פליגי אלא על כ"ש נמחק תיבת ב"ש ונ"ב דב"ש אומרים: ז] ד"ה וליפשוט וכו' דמחמיר לטמאות בעצם וכו' כנ"ל:

מא א מיי' פ"ד מהלכ' טומאת מת הלכה ד:
מב ב מיי' פ"ו מהלכות נזירות הלכה ו:
מג ג מיי' שם הלכה ב ופ"ב מהלכ' טומאת מת הלכה ט ו ופ"ג שם הלכה א ועיין שם כס"מ סמג עשין רלה:

[תוס' דאהלות פ"ד]

[מילתא דרבי יהושע ליתא במשנה ולכך שפיר גרסי' דתניא]

פי' הרא"ש

אבר מן המת וכו' פי' כי קתני (בכלל) אבר מן המת ובכללו אבר מן החי הלכך בכללא קא מני ו' ובפרטא קא מני ז'. לאפוקי עצם כשעורה דאין הנזיר מגלח אלא על מגעו ועל משאו ולא על רביעית דם דקתני ס"ל לר"ע דנזיר מגלח על אהלו וקשה דבמתני' מוכח דר"ע דנזיר מגלח על רביעית דם מק"ו דעצם כשעורה ודין לבא מן הדין להיות כנדון. וצ"ל לפי הך שינויא בודאי ר"ע נמי אמר דנזיר מגלח על רביעית דם ואף על אהילו ובמתני' לדבריו דר"א קאמר: מידי דהדר ביה ר"ע כדקאמר לעיל ורביעית דם לא חזר בו: הושחרו שיניו מפני תעניותיו משום שלא דבר כבוד על רבו בלשון דקאמר אם משמת חזר בו: ב"ש או' רובע עצמות הבא מן העצמות מב' או ג' וב"ה או' הבא מן הגויה מרוב הבנין או מרוב המנין הבנין ואם קצע מכולן רובע עצמות. יכולני לעשות דברי ב"ש וב"ה שלא נחלקו בדבר זה. מב' שוקים וירך א' ובמב' שוקים וירך א' דקאמרי ב"ש לאו דוקא דלעולם מתלתא נמי. וי"מ ב' שוקים וירך א' לא חשיב כי אם לב' לפי שהשוק הוא קטן מן הירך ושוק אחד שהוא קטן מן הירך שהוא למטה מן הארכובה והירך הוא למעלה מן הארכובה ובמס' אהלות דחשבינן אברי האדם ממטה למעלה קא חשיב ב' בשוק ו' בארכובה וא' בירך:

[נ"ל דתנן אהלות פ"ב מ"ז]

[חגיגה כב:]

עדיות פ"א מ"ז ופ"ו משנה ג

נוסחת הריב"ן

א) דנזיר מגלח על אהילו וא"ת רביעית דם לא מטמא כו' וקתני מיהו לר"ע מיטמא: ב) תלמודו בידו תלמוד ערוך בפיו כך: ג) חצי לוג: ד) היה מטמא ר"ע בכלן ו' דברים ולא חזר בו הס"ד: ה) מפני תעניותיו משום דאמר דברים שאינן כדי כבוד ר"ע שאמר אם משמת חזר בו הס"ד: ו) ובשביעי: ז) שיהא בהן ג' אברים כב"ש רוב בניינו וב"ה כו' הרי הן יכולים להתקיים דברי ב"ה כו': ח) מטהרין עד שיהא בהן רובע עצמות וגולגולת של מת אחד אלא מדלא קתני הכי ש"מ דהאי רובע גמירי ואפילו בשדרה וגולגולת ומי אמר רבא הכי דכרוב עצמות לא מגי בשדרה וגולגולת הס"ד:

הגהות הב"ח

(א) גמ' הואיל ורוב בנינו של אדם מגובה: (ב) שם שמאי דמחמיר לא ליפשוט מינה טעמא דשמאי דמחמיר: (ג) רש"י ד"ה לעולם וכו' דסמי מכאן שעורה וכו': (ד) ד"ה שהרי וכו' תלמוד ערוך היה כך בידו שהוא מטמא וכו': (ה) ד"ה משני וכו' וג' אברים כב"ש:

הגהות הגר"א

[א] גמ' (כי קתני חצי כו' עד לא שנא) תא"מ (ועיקר הבעיא קאי על טומאת אהל דאם רובע עצמות מרוב בנין או מרוב מנין כו' ה"ה רובע כו' ע"ש): [ב] שם חמיר נ"ל טמא:

וְהָא *רָבָא הוּא דְּאָמַר: לֹא נִצְרְכָה אֶלָּא לְשִׁדְרָה וְגוּלְגּוֹלֶת שֶׁאֵין בָּהֶן רוֹבַע עֲצָמוֹת! [א] בָּתַר דִּשְׁמָעָהּ מר"ע. ת"ש, שַׁמַּאי אוֹמֵר: עֶצֶם אֶחָד מִן שִׁדְרָה אוֹ מִן גּוּלְגּוֹלֶת! *שָׁאנֵי שַׁמַּאי דְּמַחְמִיר טְפֵי. לִיפְשׁוֹט מִינָּהּ: טַעֲמָא דְּשַׁמַּאי – דְּמַחְמִי', הָא לְרַבָּנַן – [ב] עַד דְּאִיכָּא חֲצִי קַב עֲצָמוֹ'! דִּילְמָא עַד כָּאן לָא פְּלִיגִי רַבָּנַן עֲלֵיהּ דְּשַׁמַּאי אֶלָּא בְּעֶצֶם אֶחָד, אֲבָל בְּרוֹבַע עֲצָמוֹת – אֲפִילּוּ רַבָּנַן מוֹדוּ. אָמַר רַבִּי אֱלִיעֶזֶר: זְקֵנִים הָרִאשׁוֹנִים מִקְצָתָן הָיוּ אוֹמְרִים: חֲצִי קַב עֲצָמוֹת וַחֲצִי לוֹג דָּם – לַכֹּל, רוֹבַע עֲצָמוֹת וּרְבִיעִית דָּם – לֹא לַכֹּל. וּמִקְצָתָן הָיוּ אוֹמְרִים: אַף רוֹבַע עֲצָמוֹת וּרְבִיעִית דָּם – לַכֹּל. ב"ד שֶׁלְּאַחֲרֵיהֶם [א]אָמְרוּ: חֲצִי קַב עֲצָמוֹת וַחֲצִי לוֹג דָּם – לַכֹּל, [ב]רוֹבַע עֲצָמוֹת וּרְבִיעִית דָּם – לִתְרוּמָה וְקָדָשִׁים, אֲבָל לֹא לְנָזִיר וְעוֹשֵׂה פֶסַח. מִכְּדִי, *אֵין הַכְרָעַת שְׁלִישִׁית מַכְרַעַת! אָמַר רַבִּי יַעֲקֹב בַּר אִידִי: *מִפִּי שְׁמוּעָה אָמְרוּ, מִפִּי חַגַּי זְכַרְיָה וּמַלְאָכִי.§ "עַל אֵלּוּ הַנָּזִיר מְגַלֵּחַ".§ "עַל אֵלּוּ" דְּרֵישָׁא – לְמַעוּטֵי עֶצֶם כִּשְׂעוֹרָה, [ג]דְּעַל מַגָּעוֹ וְעַל מַשָּׂאוֹ – אִין, וְעַל אֲהִילוֹ – לָא. וְ"עַל אֵלּוּ" דְּסֵיפָא – [ד]לְמַעוּטֵי אֶבֶן הַסְּכוּכִית.§ "וַחֲצִי קַב עֲצָמוֹת".§ חֲצִי

רש"י

וְהָא רָבָא הוּא דְּאָמַר. לְעֵיל (דף נ.): א) הָא דְּקָתָנֵי (א) מִן הַמֵּת – לֹא נִצְרְכָה אֶלָּא לְרוֹב בִּנְיָינוֹ אוֹ לְרוֹב מִנְיָינוֹ, אע"פ שֶׁאֵין בָּהֶן רוֹבַע עֲצָמוֹת, וְאע"פ שֶׁאֵין עָלָיו בָּשָׂר – שֶׁהַנָּזִיר מְגַלֵּחַ עָלָיו. וְה"ה לְשִׁדְרָה וְגוּלְגּוֹלֶת שֶׁאֵין בָּהֶן רוֹבַע עֲצָמוֹת, דְּהָא חֲשִׁיבִי כִּי הֲדָדֵי. אַלְמָא [כ"ש] דִּסְבִירָא לֵיהּ לְרָבָא דְּהֵיכָא דְּאִיכָּא רוֹבַע עֲצָמוֹת מִשִּׁדְרָה וְגוּלְגּוֹלֶת – דְּנָזִיר מְגַלֵּחַ עָלֶיהָ: אִין הָכִי נַמִּי דְּמֵעִיקָּרָא סְבִירָא לֵיהּ דְּרוֹבַע עֲצָמוֹת גְּמִירִי. אֶלָּא בָּתַר דִּשְׁמָעָהּ מר"ע, דְּאָמַר: הַשִּׁדְרָה וְהַגּוּלְגּוֹלֶת, וְלֹא אָמַר בָּהּ רוֹבַע עֲצָמוֹת, ב) דַּהֲוָה אָמִינָא לְרַבִּי עֲקִיבָא דְּאע"ג דְּמִשְּׁנֵי מֵתִים בָּאִים אִית בְּהוּ טוּמְאָה, וּלְרַבָּנַן עַד דְּאָתֵי מִמֵּת א', וּמִדְּלָא תָּנֵי הָכִי – ש"מ דִּלְכוּלֵּי עָלְמָא חֲצִי קַב עֲצָמוֹת בָּעֵינַן, בֵּין בִּשְׁאָר עֲצָמוֹת, בֵּין בְּרוֹב בִּנְיָינוֹ וְרוֹב מִנְיָינוֹ, בֵּין בְּשִׁדְרָה וְגוּלְגּוֹלֶת. ת"ש שַׁמַּאי אוֹמֵר. רוֹבַע עֲצָמוֹת שֶׁאָמְרוּ – אֲפִי' בִּזְמַן שֶׁבָּא מֵעֶצֶם אֶחָד, אוֹ מִשִּׁדְרָה אוֹ מִגּוּלְגּוֹלֶת. אַלְמָא דִּבְרוֹבַע סַגִּי, וְהוּא שֶׁיְּהֵא ג) מִשִּׁדְרָה וְגוּלְגּוֹלֶת. אָמַר רַבִּי אֱלִיעֶזֶר זְקֵנִים הָרִאשׁוֹנִים מִקְצָתָן הָיוּ אוֹמְרִים חֲצִי קַב עֲצָמוֹת וַחֲצִי לוֹג דָּם לַכֹּל. מְטַמֵּא בְּאֹהֶל, בֵּין לִתְרוּמָה וְקָדָשִׁים בֵּין לְנָזִיר וְעוֹשֵׂה פֶסַח. רוֹבַע וּרְבִיעִית דָּם לֹא לַכֹּל ד). מְטַמֵּא, כְּלוֹמַר: אֲפִי' א' מִכּוּלָּם אֵינוֹ מְטַמֵּא. וּמִקְצָתָן הָיוּ אוֹמְרִים אַף רוֹבַע עֲצָמוֹת וּרְבִיעִית דָּם מְטַמְּאִים אֶת הַכֹּל. וּב"ד שֶׁל אַחֲרֵיהֶן אוֹמְרִים חֲצִי קַב כו'. אֲבָל רוֹבַע עֲצָמוֹת וּרְבִיעִית דָּם, לְעִנְיַן ה) אֲכִילַת תְּרוּמָה וְקָדָשִׁים – מְטַמְּאִין בְּאֹהֶל, אֲבָל לֹא לִיסְתּוֹר יְמֵי נָזִיר, וְעוֹשֵׂה פֶסַח – לְטַמֵּא שֶׁלֹּא לַעֲשׂוֹתוֹ, דִּבְמָקוֹם כָּרֵת לֹא הֶעֱמִידוּ דִּבְרֵיהֶם. מִכְּדִי אֵין הַכְרָעַת שְׁלִישִׁית מַכְרַעַת. מִכְּדִי כָּל הַכְרָעָה שֶׁהִיא בְּמִקְצָת כְּדִבְרֵי זֶה וּמִקְצָת כְּדִבְרֵי זֶה – אֵינָהּ הַכְרָעָה עַד שֶׁתְּהֵא כּוּלָּהּ ו) כְּדִבְרֵי א' מֵהֶן. דְּהַכְרָעָה לְשׁוֹן שִׁיקּוּל, שֶׁשּׁוֹקֵל דִּבְרֵי שְׁנַיִם יוֹתֵר מֵאֶחָד, וּמָה רָאָה ר' אֱלִיעֶזֶר לוֹמַר כָּךְ: ב"ד שֶׁל אַחֲרֵיהֶן כָּךְ הָיוּ אוֹמְרִים? אָמַר ר' יַעֲקֹב בַּר אִידִי. לוֹמַר שֶׁעִיקָּר הוּא, שֶׁהוּא מִפִּי שְׁמַעְיָה וְאַבְטַלְיוֹן. וְאִית דְּאָמְרִי: שֶׁאָמְרוּ מִפִּי חַגַּי זְכַרְיָה וּמַלְאָכִי ז). עַל אֵלּוּ דְּרֵישָׁא לְמַעוּטֵי עֶצֶם כִּשְׂעוֹרָה. שֶׁאֵין הַנָּזִיר מְגַלֵּחַ עַל אֲהִילוֹ. דְּסָלְקָא דַּעְתָּךְ אָמִינָא: הוֹאִיל וְאִיתָא בְּטוּמְאָה לְעִנְיַן מַגָּע – לִיטַמֵּא נַמִּי בְּאֹהֶל, קָא מַשְׁמַע לָן דְּלָא. וְאע"ג דַּהֲדַר תָּנֵי לְהוּ בְּהֶדְיָא בְּסֵיפָא – לָא תֵּיקְשֵׁי וְלָא מִידֵּי, מִשּׁוּם דְּתָנֵי וַהֲדַר מְפָרֵשׁ. וּצְרִיכִי לְפָרוּשֵׁי, דְּאִי לָא מְפָרֵשׁ לָהּ – הֲוָה אָמִינָא דַּאֲפִי' עַל מַגָּעוֹ וְעַל מַשָּׂאוֹ לֹא יְהֵא ח) מְגַלֵּחַ. לְמַעוּטֵי אֶבֶן הַסְּכוּכִית. אֶבֶן מְסַמָּא. וְזוֹ הִיא אֶבֶן שֶׁמּוּטֶּלֶת עַל גַּבֵּי הַמֵּת בְּרה"ר, כִּדְמְפָרֵשׁ בְּמַסֶּ' שַׁבָּת בְּפֶרֶק "אָמַר ר' עֲקִיבָא" (דף פב:), שֶׁאִם הַנָּזִיר יוֹשֵׁב עָלֶיהָ, אע"פ שֶׁמְּטַמְּאָתוֹ – אֵינוֹ מְגַלֵּחַ עָלֶיהָ. אֶבֶן ט) מְסַמָּא – אֶבֶן שׁוּמָא, וְלִישָּׁנָא דִּקְרָא נָקַט, דִּכְתִיב: "וְשׂוּמַת עַל פּוּם גּוּבָּא" (דניאל ו) כְּתִיב. לָשׁוֹן אַחֵר: אֶבֶן הַסְּכוּכִית – אֶבֶן הַמְסַכֶּכֶת י) עַל הַקֶּבֶר, דְּקיי"ל *) כָּל הַמִּטַּלְטְלִין מְבִיאִין אֶת הַטּוּמְאָה בְּעוֹבִי הַמַּרְדֵּעַ, חוּץ מִכְּלֵי גְלָלִים וּכְלֵי אֲבָנִים וּכְלֵי אֲדָמָה.

*) [שבת טז:]

תוספות

הא אפי' שבורין ומפורקין בעיא למימר אם יש בהן רובע עצמות דנזיר מגלח עליהן! ותיפשוט דמדקתני במתני' השדרה והגולגולת שלמים מסתמא אית בהון רובע עצמות, מכלל דעל עצמות שבורין ומפורקין שיש בה רובע, ובאו (השדרה) משדרה וגולגולת – לא מגלח. ופריך: והא הוא דאמר, פירוש: רבא, לא נצרכה אלא לשדרה וגולגולת שאין בהן רובע עצמות. אלמא דרבא גופיה סבירא ליה דאיכא שדרה וגולגולת דלית בהון רובע עצמות, ולעולם אימא לך דאפי' על רובע עצמות הבא מן השדרה והגולגולת נזיר מגלח, ומתני' דקתני "שדרה וגולגולת" דמשמע שלמים – איצטריך לאשמועינן דאפילו אין בהן רובע – נזיר מגלח. ולא איתפרש היכא איתמר דרבא. ויש ספרים דגרסי לעיל (דף נ.): אמר רבא לא נצרכה אלא לשדרה וגולגולת שאין בהן רובע עצמות, מכח סוגיא דהכא. [ולעיל פירשתי] דאי אפשר לקיים אותה גירסא. **בתר** דשמעה מר"ע. כך כתוב בכל הספרים, ולא איתפרש. מהר"ל, וגימגו"ם. ואי לא מסתפינא מרבוותא הוה אמינא שיש חסרון בספרים, וגרסינן מקמי פירכא דקאמר רבא לא נצרכה: אמר מר עוקבא: הכא בשדרה וגולגולת שאין בהן רובע עסקינן. פירוש: מר עוקבא בא לדחות התשובה שהביא רבא, מחמת שהיה סבור רבא דסתם שדרה וגולגולת יש בהן רובע, ודחי לה מר עוקבא דמיירי בשדרה וגולגולת שאין בהן רובע. ופריך התלמוד: ורבא ל"ל האי סברא דאפשר לשדרה וגולגולת בלא רובע? והאמר רבא לא נצרכה וכו'? ומשני: בתר דשמעה ממר עוקבא לההוא שינויא דשני מר עוקבא הכא דמוקי לה בשדרה וגולגולת שאין בהן רובע, וכי האי גוונא הגיה רש"י בזבחים בפרק שני (דף כא:) שהיה כתוב בספרים [הקושיא] וחסר הסוגיא מן הספרים, והגיה רש"י [התירוץ] גבי שמעתין דקידוש ידים. והכי נמי בשמעתין שיש הקושיא בלא התירוץ – יש להגיה התירוץ. ובעלמא נמי אשכחנא שהיה רבא בימי מר עוקבא, ע"כ לשון מהרפ"ש. והרב רבי יעקב מקינון דחק ליישב גירסת הספרים "בתר [דשמעה מרבי עקיבא]", וה"פ: א] דהא רבא לא נצרכא כו', כלומר: והיכי תסיק אדעתיה דרבא לאיתויי ממתני'? והא איהו גופיה הוא דמוקי לה בשדרה וגולגולת שאין בה רובע עצמות! ומשני: בתר דשמעה [מרבי עקיבא] – רבא לא אמר על מתני', אלא על משנה דאהלות (פ"ב מ"ו), דקחשיב רובע ב] ורביעית הבא משני מתים ושדרה וגולגולת משני מתים, ועלה איצטריך ליה לשנויי הכי. [אבל] מקמי דשמעה [מר' עקיבא] – סבירא ליה שאין שדרה וגולגולת שלא יהא בהן רובע עצמות, ומשום הכי הוה מייתי רבא ממתני' שפיר, דאכתי לא שמעה [מר"ע]. **ת"ש** שמאי אומר אפי' עצם אחד משדרה או מגולגולת. ומדלא בעי שמאי אלא עלם משדרה – מכלל דרבנן דפליגי עליה סגי להו בשיעור דרובע עצמות הבא מן השדרה, כדקתני ברישא דרובע מטמא באהל כי בא מעיקר הגוייה, וכי בא רובע מן השדרה – אפי' מגלח עליה הנזיר, דאין סברא לומר דפליגי כולי האי, דלרבנן ליבעי חצי קב ולשמאי סגי בעלם אחד. ודחי: שאני שמאי דמחמיר, אבל רבנן [חצי] קב עצמות בעו אף משדרה ג]. ליפשוט מינה לאידך גיסא דלרבנן בעינן חצי קב, דמדשמאי דמחמיר לא בעי אלא עלם אחד – מכלל דלרבנן שיעורא ד] דבית הלל בעו, דהיינו חצי קב, דאי לא בעו אלא רובע קב – הוה להו לפרושי חומרייהו, כמו שפירש שמאי חומריה! ודחי: דילמא לא פליגי אלא בעלם אחד, דלא מטמא באהל לרבנן, אבל רובע מטמא, ולא חשו לפרושי מילתייהו. **זקנים** הראשונים מקצתן היו אומרים חצי קב עצמות וחצי לוג דם לכל. שאם האהיל עליהם – טמא ה] לתרומה ולקדשים, ופליגי אמתניתין דמסכת אהלות. ומקצתם היו אומרים אף רביעית דם ורובע עצמות לכל, אף לנזיר, ופליגי אמתניתין [דהכא]. **בית** דין שלאחריהם אמרו חצי קב עצמות וחצי לוג דם לכל. אף לנזיר כדתנן במתני'. רובע עצמות ורביעית דם לתרומה ולקדשים – דהמאהיל עליהם טמא, כדתנן במתניתין דמסכת אהלות (פ"ב מ"א ומ"ב). אבל לא לנזיר ועושה פסח – והכי גמירי להו, וסברי להו כמתניתין דאין הנזיר מגלח עליו כלל, וסברו נמי כמתניתין דאהלות, דתנן התם דמטמא באהל בעלמא לתרומה וקדשים, כי ב"ד אחרון סברי כתנא דמתניתין וכתנא דאהלות ו]. י"מ: הכרעה שלישית. היינו תלמידים, שב"ד אחרון היו תלמידים לזקנים הראשונים. ופריך: והא אין הכרעת שלישית מכרעת ז] בתרא, ומדמתני' דהכא ומתני' דהתם דאהלות כב"ד אחרון סבירא – מכלל דהכי הילכתא. ומשום דהוו להו מכריע. ח] והא אין דעת שלישית מכרעת – שדעת שלישית טעם בפני עצמו הוא, כי הראשונים לא גילו דעתם שיהא ראוי לחלק בין נזיר ועושה פסח לתרומה וקדשים! ומשני, אמר רבי יעקב בר אידי: מפי שמועה אמרוה מפי חגי זכריה ומלאכי, ועל כן סברי ב"ד של אחרונים לסמוך על שמועתם ולקבוע הלכה כמותם. **על** אלו דרישא למעוטי עצם כשעורה. ואע"ג דבהדיא קתני על עלם כשעורה על מגעו ועל משאו, דמשמע: אבל על אהילו לא! י"ל: תני והדר מפרש. ועל אלו דסיפא למעוטי אבן הסככות – אבן המיסך על הארץ, ויש שני אבנים או ג' יוצאין מן הגדר וטומאה תחת אחת מהן, ועבר תחת אחת מהן, ואינו יודע אם האהיל על הטומאה. וקצת קשה: דהא תנא ליה סיפא: אבל סככות ופרעות אין מגלח! וי"ל: דה"נ תני והדר מפרש כמו עלם כשעורה. מהרפ"ש.

חצי

עין משפט נר מצוה

מד א מיי' פ"ז מהל' נזירות הלכה ב ופ"ג מהל' ביאת מקדש הל' יג יד ופ"ו מהל' קרבן פסח הלכה ב סמג עשין ל קכז רכד ולאוין סד:

מה ב מיי' פ"ז מהל' נזירות הלכה ו ופ"ו מהלכות קרבן פסח שם ופ"ג מהל' ביאת מקדש שם ופ"ג מהל' טומאת מת הלכה ג סמג שם ועשין רלא:

מו ג מיי' פ"ז מהלכות נזירות הל' ו ופ"ג מהלכות טומאת מת הלכה ב:

מז ד מיי' פ"ז מהלכות נזירות הלכה ו:

פי' הרא"ש

ת"ש שמאי אומר אפי' עצם א' מן השדרה או מן הגולגולת מכלל דרבנן פליגי עליה אית להו דרובע עצמות הבא מהם טמא דאי לאו הכי קא מפלגת לפלוגתייהו טובא: ומשני שאני שמאי דמחמיר. אבל רבנן לעולם אימא לך חצי קב: תימה היכי בעי למפשט לתגלחת נזיר א) מהקדש מהאי דמתני' לענין טומאת אהל. ועוד תימה מנ"ל לרמי בר חמא דשדרה וגלגולת חמירי מרוב בניינו ורוב מניינו דשדרה וגלגולת איברי' גדולים הם ואפשר שיש בהם כ"כ עצמות כמו רוב בניינו או רוב מניינו. ונראה דבעיא דרמי בר חמא תליא בהך דמבעיא לן לעיל אי שדרה וגלגולת תנן או שדרה או גלגולת תנן דפשיטא ליה לרמי בר חמא אי שדרה וגלגולת תנן דבעי חצי קב דהא לא חמירי ואי שדרה או גלגולת תנן פשיטא ליה דעל רובע מהם מגלח כיון דחמירי והיא גופא קא מיבעיא לרמי בר חמא שדרה או גלגולת תנן ונזיר מגלח על רובע כיון דחמירי. או דלמא שדרה וגלגולת תנן ולא חמירי ובעי' חצי קב והשתא מייתי שפיר ממתניתין דאהלות דמשמאי מטמא בעצם א' מן השדרה או מן הגלגולת. מכלל דרבנן מטמו בשדרה או בגלגולת אלמא חמירי: ליפשוט מינה טעמא דשמאי דמחמיר הא רבנן עד דאיכא קב עצמות. כלומר הא רבנן בעו שדרה וגלגולת לענין טומאה ולתגלחת נזיר [וא"כ] נמי בעי חצי קב: חצי קב עצמות וחצי לוג דם לכל. פי' לכל דבר בעי' שיעור גדול אף לתרומה וקדשים. ופחות משיעור זה אינו מטמא באהל המת ופליגי אמתני' דאהלות. ומקצתן היו אומרים רובע עצמות ורביעית דם לכל ואף הנזיר מגלח על אהלן ופליגי אמתני' דהכא: מכדי אין הכרעת שלישית מכרעת. פי' דב"ד של אחריהן פי' למ"ש במתני':

א) אולי צ"ל לתגלחת נזיר מהאי מתני' דמיירי בטומאת אוהל לענין תרומה וקדשים ועוד תימה.

[לעיל נ.] [לעיל נב:] פסחים כח. חולין קלז. [חולין שם: בכורות נח. ע"ש בתוס' ד"ה מפי]

נוסחת הריב"ן

א) לעיל לא נצרכה אלא לרוב בניינו ולרוב מניינו דהיינו נמי כשדרה וגולגלת דכי הדדי [illegible] שאין בהן רובע עצמות [illegible] ב) [illegible] ג) [illegible] ד) לא מטמא: ה) לענין תרומה וקדשים: ו) כדברי אחד מהן: ז) [illegible] מפי חגי זכריה ומלאכי הס"ד: ח) יהא מגלח: ט) משנה: י) [illegible]

הגהות הב"ח

(א) רש"י ד"ה והא רבא וכו' הא דקתני על המת וכו' [illegible] דסבירא ליה לרבה:

הגהות הגר"א

[א] גמ' בתר דשמעה מר"ע [illegible] [ב] שם עד דאיכא חצי קב עצמות [illegible]

הגהות מהר"ב רנשבורג א] תוד"ה בתר וכו' וה"פ דהאמר כצ"ל. ב] בא"ד דקחשיב רובע עלמות הבא כצ"ל: ג] ד"ה ת"ש וכו' אף משדרה ופריך ליפשוט כצ"ל: ד] בא"ד מכלל דלרבנן שיעורא דב"ה. תיבת דב"ה נמחק ונ"ב רבה. א"מ: ה] ד"ה זקנים וכו' שאם האהיל עליהם טמא בין לנזיר בין לתרומה כצ"ל: ו] ד"ה בית דין וכו' וכתנא דאהלות. נ"ב כאן שייך ד"ה והא אין דעת שלישית וכו' הנאמר לקמן: ז] בא"ד וי"מ וכו' הכרעת שלישי מכרעת בתרא. תיבת בתרא נמחק. ח] בא"ד ומשום דהוו להו מכריע. כאן הס"ד. ומכאן ואילך שייך לעיל בתר וכתנא דאהלות כאמור לעיל:

חֲצִי קַב עֲצָמוֹת — אִין, רוֹבַע עֲצָמוֹת — לָא. הֵיכִי דָּמֵי? אִילֵימָא דְּאִית בְּהוֹן עֲצָמוֹת כִּשְׂעוֹרָה — תֵּיפּוּק לֵיהּ מִשּׁוּם עֶצֶם כִּשְׂעוֹרָה! אֶלָּא, דְּאַקְמַח אַקְמוּחֵי.§ "עַל אֵבֶר מִן הַמֵּת וְעַל אֵבֶר מִן הַחַי שֶׁיֵּשׁ עֲלֵיהֶן בָּשָׂר כָּרָאוּי".§ אֵין עֲלֵיהֶן בָּשָׂר כָּרָאוּי מַאי? רַבִּי יוֹחָנָן אָמַר: אאֵין הַנָּזִיר מְגַלֵּחַ עֲלֵיהֶן, רֵישׁ לָקִישׁ אָמַר: הַנָּזִיר מְגַלֵּחַ עֲלֵיהֶן. רַבִּי יוֹחָנָן אָמַר: אֵין הַנָּזִיר מְגַלֵּחַ עֲלֵיהֶן, דְּהָא קָתָנֵי בְּרֵישָׁא: עַל אֵבֶר מִן הַמֵּת, וְעַל אֵבֶר מִן הַחַי (א) וכו', שֶׁיֵּשׁ עֲלֵיהֶן כַּזַּיִת בָּשָׂר — אִין, אֲבָל אֵין עֲלֵיהֶם — לָא. ור' שִׁמְעוֹן בֶּן לָקִישׁ אוֹמֵר: מְגַלֵּחַ, מִדְּלָא קָתָנֵי בְּסֵיפָא. וְרַבִּי יוֹחָנָן אָמַר לָךְ: כָּל הֵיכָא דְּמַשְׁמַע מִכְּלָלָא — לָא קָתָנֵי בְּסֵיפָא. וְהָא חֲצִי קַב עֲצָמוֹת, דְּמַשְׁמַע: חֲצִי קַב עֲצָמוֹת — אִין, רוֹבַע עֲצָמוֹת — לָא, וְקָתָנֵי בְּסֵיפָא רוֹבַע עֲצָמוֹת! הָתָם, אִי לָאו רוֹבַע עֲצָמוֹת הֲוָה אָמֵינָא: אֲפִי' עַל מַגָּעוֹ וְעַל מַשָּׂאוֹ לָא, לְהָכִי אִיצְטְרִיךְ לְמִיתְנֵי רוֹבַע עֲצָמוֹת — דְּעַל אֲהִילָן הוּא דְּאֵין הַנָּזִיר מְגַלֵּחַ. וְהָא חֲצִי לוֹג דָּם, דְּשָׁמְעַתְּ מִינָּהּ: חֲצִי לוֹג דָּם — אִין, רְבִיעִית דָּם — לָא, וְקָתָנֵי בְּסֵיפָא רְבִיעִית דָּם! הָתָם לְאַפּוּקֵי מִדְּרַבִּי עֲקִיבָא, [א] *דַּאֲמַר רַבִּי עֲקִיבָא: רְבִיעִית דָּם הַבָּא מִשְּׁנֵי מֵתִים — מְטַמֵּא בְּאֹהֶל. הַאי אֵבֶר מִן הַמֵּת, הֵיכִי דָּמֵי? אִי דְּאִית בֵּיהּ עֶצֶם כִּשְׂעוֹרָה — מ"ט דְּרַבִּי יוֹחָנָן? וְאִי דְּלֵית בֵּיהּ עֶצֶם כִּשְׂעוֹרָה — מ"ט דְּרֵישׁ לָקִישׁ? אָמַר לָךְ רֵישׁ לָקִישׁ: לְעוֹלָם דְּלֵית בֵּיהּ עֶצֶם כִּשְׂעוֹרָה, ואפ"ה רַחֲמָנָא רַבְּיֵיהּ, דְּתַנְיָא: °"וְכֹל אֲשֶׁר יִגַּע עַל פְּנֵי הַשָּׂדֶה בַּחֲלַל חֶרֶב אוֹ בְמֵת"; (ג) "עַל פְּנֵי הַשָּׂדֶה" — זֶה בהַמַּאֲהִיל עַל פְּנֵי הַמֵּת, "בַּחֲלַל" — גזֶה אֵבֶר מִן הַחַי וְיֵשׁ לוֹ לְהַעֲלוֹת אֲרוּכָה, *ד"חֶרֶב" — ה"ז כֶּחָלָל, "אוֹ בְמֵת" הזֶה אֵבֶר הַנֶּחְלָל מִן הַמֵּת, "אוֹ בְעֶצֶם אָדָם" — וזֶה רוֹבַע עֲצָמוֹת, "אוֹ בְקָבֶר" — זזֶה קֶבֶר סָתוּם.

במדבר יט

דַּאֲמַר

רש"י

חֲצִי קַב עֲצָמוֹת. מִיטַּמֵּא עָלָיו עַל מַגָּעוֹ וְעַל מַשָּׂאוֹ וְעַל אֲהִילוֹ. וְעַל רוֹבַע עֲצָמוֹת – לֹא מִיטַּמֵּא, וַאֲפִי' עַל מַגָּעוֹ וְעַל מַשָּׂאוֹ. וְתֵיפּוּק לֵי' מִשּׁוּם עֶצֶם כִּשְׂעוֹרָה א). וּמַאי אִירְיָא רוֹבַע? אֶלָּא דְּאַקְמַח אַקְמוּחֵי. ג) שֶׁשְּׁחָקָן דַּק הַרְבֵּה, כְּמוֹ קֶמַח שֶׁנִּטְחַן, שֶׁאֵין בּוֹ עֶצֶם כִּשְׂעוֹרָה. וְקמ"ל דְּאִי אִית בֵּיהּ חֲצִי קַב – מִיטַּמֵּא עַל מַגָּעוֹ וְעַל מַשָּׂאוֹ וְעַל אֲהִילוֹ, פָּחוֹת מֵחֲצִי קַב – אֲפִי' עַל מַגָּעוֹ אֵינוֹ מִיטַּמֵּא, לְפִי שֶׁאֵין בּוֹ עֶצֶם כִּשְׂעוֹרָה. וְשֶׁיֵּשׁ עָלָיו בָּשָׂר כָּרָאוּי. ה"מ דְּכִי אֵין עָלָיו בָּשָׂר כָּרָאוּי – שֶׁאֵינוֹ מְגַלֵּחַ. רֵישׁ לָקִישׁ אָמַר נָזִיר מְגַלֵּחַ עָלָיו. מִמַּאי, מִדְּקָא חָשֵׁיב בְּסֵיפָא עַל אֵלּוּ שֶׁאֵין הַנָּזִיר מְגַלֵּחַ אע"פ שֶׁמִּיטַּמֵּא בָּהֶן, וְלָא קָתָנֵי בַּהֲדַיְיהוּ: אֵין עָלָיו בָּשָׂר כָּרָאוּי אֵין הַנָּזִיר מְגַלֵּחַ, ש"מ דְּאע"ג דְּאֵין עָלָיו בָּשָׂר כָּרָאוּי – שֶׁהַנָּזִיר מְגַלֵּחַ עַל (ג) אֲהִילוֹ. וְר' יוֹחָנָן אָמַר לָךְ. כָּל הֵיכָא דְּתָנֵי מִידֵי, (ד) וּמַשְׁמַע לֵיהּ (חַד) מִכְּלָלָא, כְּגוֹן הָכָא דְּתָנֵי בְּרֵישָׁא: אִם יֵשׁ עָלָיו בָּשָׂר כָּרָאוּי מְגַלֵּחַ. אִי לָא. הֲדַר תָּנֵי לָהּ בְּסֵיפָא, הֲוָה אָמֵינָא: אֲפִי' עַל מַגָּעוֹ וְעַל מַשָּׂאוֹ לֹא יְהֵא נָזִיר מְגַלֵּחַ. לְהָכִי תַּנְיֵיהּ – דְּעַל אֲהִילוֹ הוּא דְּאֵין הַנָּזִיר מְגַלֵּחַ, אֲבָל עַל מַגָּעוֹ מְגַלֵּחַ. וּכְגוֹן דְּלָא אַקְמַח אַקְמוּחֵי, וְיֵשׁ בּוֹ עֶצֶם כִּשְׂעוֹרָה. וְאִידָךְ נַמִי דְּקָתָנֵי, כְּגוֹן הַסְּכָכוֹת וְהַפְּרָעוֹת, אע"ג דְּאִיכָּא לְמִשְׁמַע לָהּ מִכְּלָלָא, מִדְּלָא קָתָנֵי בְּרֵישָׁא – לְכִי הֲדַר תָּנֵי לְהוּ, מִשּׁוּם דְּקָא מִיטַּמֵּא בָּהֶן, וְצָרִיךְ הַזָּאָה שְׁלִישִׁי וּשְׁבִיעִי. לְאַפּוּקֵי מדר"ע דְּאָמַר רְבִיעִית דָּם הַבָּא מִשְּׁנֵי מֵתִים מְטַמֵּא בְּאֹהֶל. קמ"ל סֵיפָא, דְּמֵמֵּת אֶחָד בָּעֵינָא לָהּ. הַאי אֵבֶר מִן הַמֵּת. שֶׁאֵין עָלָיו בָּשָׂר כָּרָאוּי. הֵיכִי דָּמֵי אִי דְּאִית בֵּיהּ עֶצֶם כִּשְׂעוֹרָה. אַמַּאי אֵינוֹ מְגַלֵּחַ עַל מַגָּעוֹ, וּמַאי טַעְמָא דְּר' יוֹחָנָן? וְאִי דְּלֵית בֵּיהּ עֶצֶם כִּשְׂעוֹרָה. וְאֵין עָלָיו בָּשָׂר כָּרָאוּי, מַאי טַעְמָא דְּרֵישׁ לָקִישׁ דְּאָמַר מְגַלֵּחַ? וַאֲפִילוּ הָכִי רַבְּיֵיהּ. לְמַגָּע. דְּתַנְיָא כו' עַל פְּנֵי הַשָּׂדֶה זֶה הַמַּאֲהִיל עַל פְּנֵי הַמֵּת. הַמּוּטָל ג) בַּשָּׂדֶה, מִדְּלָא כְּתִיב "יִגַּע בְּמֵת בַּשָּׂדֶה". בַּחֲלַל זֶה אֵבֶר הַנֶּחְלָל מִן הַחַי. הַנִּקְלָץ מִן הַחַי, וְיֵשׁ ד) בּוֹ לַעֲלוֹת אֲרוּכָה. רוֹבַע עֲצָמוֹת. דְּמְטַמֵּא בְּאֹהֶל, כִּדְתְנַן: וְאֹהֶל רוֹבַע עֲצָמוֹת, אֶלָּא שֶׁאֵין הַנָּזִיר מְגַלֵּחַ עַל אֲהִילוֹ. זֶה קֶבֶר סָתוּם. שֶׁאֵין בּוֹ חָלָל טֶפַח ה) בֵּין הַמֵּת וְהַגּוֹלֵל, שֶׁמְּטַמֵּא.

דַּאֲמַר

תורה אור

תוספות

חצי קב עצמות כו' היכי דמי אי דאית בהו עצם כשעורה תיפוק ליה משום עצם כשעורה. ל"ע: מאי קא פריך? הא לענין אהל איירינן, ועצם כשעורה לא מטמא באהל! ואומר ר"י: דסמיך אמאי דבעינן למימר בסמוך, דבתר דתנן ברישא חצי קב, דמשמע: אבל פחות לא, אמאי איצטריך למיתני בסיפא רובע עצמות דאין הנזיר מגלח עליו? ומשני בסמוך: דאייתי למידק דפחות מחצי קב לא מגלח על אהילו, אבל על מגעו ועל משאו מגלח. וא"כ הוי עיקר רבותא דמתניתין לאשמועינן דעל מגעו ועל משאו מגלח. ולכך דייק השתא: פשיטא דעל פחות מחצי קב מגלח על מגעו ועל משאו, ותיפוק ליה משום עצם כשעורה! ומשני: כגון דאקמח אקמוחי, שטחן הדק כקמח או כעפר, דכי האי גוונא לא מטמא משום עצם כשעורה.

אין עליהם בשר כראוי מאי. הא ודאי דעל אהילו לא יגלח, כדקתני במתני' דוקא כשיש עליהם בשר כראוי. אלא במגעו ובמשאו, ובשאין שם עצם כשעורה.

רבי יוחנן אמר אין הנזיר מגלח. דהואיל ואין בו עצם כשעורה. ור"ש בן לקיש אמר: נזיר מגלח על מגעו ועל משאו. ואף כי אין בו עצם כשעורה, וגם אין עליו בשר כראוי, ואינו חשוב אבר לטמא באהל – מ"מ חשוב לטמא במגעו ובמשאו, כדדריש ליה מקראי בסמוך, ורשב"ל אומר: נזיר מגלח, מדלא קתני לה בסיפא גבי "אבל סככות ופרעות": ואבר שאין עליו בשר כראוי אף במגעו ובמשאו לא יגלח – מכלל דמטמא במגעו ובמשאו, וכדדרשי' בסמוך. ור' יוחנן אמר לך: הא קתני ברישא: על אבר מן המת ועל אבר מן החי שיש עליו בשר כראוי, [ולא קתני]: אבל אין עליהם בשר כראוי למגעו ולמשאו מ"מ [מגלח], ומדלא קתני הכי – ש"מ דלא מגלח אפילו על מגעו ועל משאו אי אין שם בשר כראוי – ולא איצטריך תו למיתניי' בסיפא. א] ורשב"ל אומר: כל היכא דשמע מכללא דרישא (אמר מר ד) לא קתני בסיפא? **והא** ברישא תני חצי קב עצמות דמשמע: חצי קב – אין, רובע – לא, ואפילו הכי הדר תנא בסיפא רובע עצמות! התם. אי לא תנא רובע עצמות, ה"א דאפי' על מגעו ועל משאו לא יגלח – להכי איצטריך למיתני רובע עצמות, למימר דעל אהילו דוקא אין הנזיר מגלח, הא על מגעו ועל משאו – הנזיר מגלח. **והא** חצי לוג דם דשמעת מינה: [חצי] לוג דם אין, רביעית לא, וקתני בסיפא רביעית דם! ה"ג. **התם** לאפוקי מדרבי עקיבא ב] (דאמר רביעית דם הבא משני מתים). וה"פ: לאפוקי מר"ע דאמר בשילהי פירקין דעל רביעית דם, דעל מגעו ועל משאו מגלח. **האי** אבר מן המת היכי דמי אי דאית ביה עצם כשעורה מאי טעמא דרבי יוחנן. דאמר: אין הנזיר מגלח על מגעו ועל משאו? ואי דלית ביה עצם כשעורה – מאי טעמא דר"ש בן לקיש? אמר לך ר"ש בן לקיש: לעולם אימא לך דלית ביה עצם כשעורה, ואפי' הכי רחמנא רבייה, דתניא: "וכל אשר יגע על פני השדה בחלל חרב או במת או בעצם אדם או בקבר", "על פני השדה" – זה המאהיל על פני המת, מדלא כתיב ג] "אשר יגע במת", אלא "על" דמשמע דמאהיל מיירי, וכדאמר נמי בפ"ק דשבת (דף יז.): טימאוהו משום כלים המאהילים על המת, רוצה לומר: אפי' אין עליהם. ד]. בחלל – זה אבר מן החי ויש בו כדי להעלות ארוכה. דהכי משמע: אבר שנפל מגוף החי ונחתך. **חרב** הרי הוא כחלל. דכלי מתכות הנוגעים במת נעשים אבי אבות הטומאה כמת עצמו, לטמא אדם הנוגע בו ה] מטמא טומאת שבעה כנוגע במת עצמו, או לטמא אדם הבא באהל אשר החרב בתוכו טומאת שבעה כבא אל אהל המת. או במת – זה אבר הנחלל מן המת. ויש בו בשר כדי להעלות ארוכה, דחשיב כמת עצמו. או בעצם אדם – זה רובע עצמות. שמטמא באהל. והלכה למשה מסיני היא דבעינן רובע, וקרא אסמכתא בעלמא. סתום דאמר מר: טומאה בוקעת ועולה מן הקבר, בוקעת ויורדת מן הקבר – זה קבר סתום. אין לומר דהיינו שאין בו פותח טפח – דההוא הוה טומאה רצוצה, ולא מטמא אלא כנגד גופו של מת. והכא איירינן דהקבר עצמו מטמא אפי' שלא כנגד המת. אלא הכא איירי בקבר סתום בכל רוחותיו, ויש בו פותח טפח בינו למת. דיש חילוק בטומאה רצוצה, שהקבר עצמו מטמא באהל אפילו שלא כנגד המת. והכי איתא בסיפרי: "או בקבר" – זה קבר סתום, שמטמא כל צדדין, אפילו ריקן שבו. ודוקא שיש פותח טפח בין המת לקבר שעליו, אבל אין פותח טפח – אינו מטמא כל צדדין, אלא טומאה בוקעת ועולה כנגדו, דהיינו כנגד המת דוקא. והביא רבינו שמשון נ"ע ראיה מפ"ז דאהלות (מ"א): נפש [אטומה], הנוגע בה מן הצדדין – טהור, מפני שהטומאה בוקעת ועולה בוקעת ויורדת. ואם היה מקום הטומאה טפח על טפח – טמא, מפני שהיא כקבר סתום. והא דאמרי' (ברכות דף יט:): רוב ארונות יש בהן פותח טפח – צריך לומר שאותן הקברים היו פתוחים מן הצד, ואין עליהן דין קבר סתום אם לא שכל הצדדים סתומים, והכי תנן באהלות (פ"ג מ"ז): ביב שהוא קמור תחת הבית, יש בה פותח טפח ובילאתו פותח טפח, טומאה בתוכו – הבית טהור*. **דאמר** מר טומאה בוקעת ועולה. בכדי אייתה, דהא לא איירי בקבר. ועוד: דקבר דהכא מטמא אפילו שלא כנגד הטומאה.

ואילו

פי' הרא"ש

אין עליהם בשר כראוי. וגם אין בו עצם כשעורה ר"י אומר אין הנזיר מגלח עליו אף על מגעו ועל משאו. ור"ל אומר הנזיר מגלח עליו ומקרא מרבי ליה לקמן דמטמא במגע ובמשא הלכך נזיר מגלח עליו ור"י סבר אף במגע ובמשא אינו מטמא: ר"י אמר אין הנזיר מגלח עליו. מדקתני על אבר מן המת שיש עליו בשר כראוי נזיר מגלח על אהלו ולא קתני אין עליו בשר כראוי למגעו ולמשאו אלמא אין הנזיר מגלח עליו. ור"ל אמר מדלא קתני בסיפא בהדי סככות ופרעות לאשמועינן דאבר שאין עליו בשר כראוי דאינו מגלח על מגעו ומשאו אע"ג דמטמא כדדרשי' בסמוך אלמא נזיר מגלח עליו: ור' יוחנן אמר לך כיון דשמעי' ליה מכללא דרישא. מדתנא יש עליהן בשר כראוי לאהלו. ולא תנן אין עליו בשר כראוי למגעו ולמשאו שמעי' ליה ולא אצטריך למתניה בסיפא: ופריך ר"ל וכל היכא דשמעי' מכללא לא תני בסיפא והא חצי קב עצמות וכו' והא חצי לוג דם וכו': ה"ג לאפוקי מדר"ע דאמר רביעית דם נזיר מגלח עליו דקאמר במתני' לקמן (כוותיה) לפני ר' אלעזר דמוכח דנזיר מגלח על רביעית דם מק"ו דעצם כשעורה. וא"ת הא נמי שמעי' ליה מכללא מדלא קתני לה גבי עצם כשעורה. אלמ' דאין הנזיר מגלח על מגעו ומשאו. וי"ל דמכללא לא שמעינן ליה דה"א דשפיר אתיא כר"ע. והא דלא תנייה (הם) [גבי] עצם כשעורה משום דהוי בכלל עצם כשעורה דמיניה אתי בק"ו: על פני השדה זה המאהיל על פני המת דמשמע מגע שהוא באויר על פני השדה והיינו אהל. ואע"ג דבפ' בהמה המקשה דריש רבי ישמעאל מהאי קרא להוציא עובר שבמעי אשה ור"ע דריש ליה לרבות גולל ודופק. נ"ל דהכא דריש מעל פני והתם דריש מהשדה מה שדה שהוא בגלוי להוציא עובר שבמעי אשה ולר"ע לרבות גולל ודופק שמונח על פני השדה: בחלל זה אבר מן החי. דהכי משמע שנתחלל ממקום חבורו: ויש בו כדי להעלות ארוכה. הכי גמירי ליה: חרב הרי הוא כחלל. דכיון דנגעה החרב במת נעשה אבי אבות הטומאה כמת עצמו. ולאו דוקא חרב אלא ה"ה כל כלי מתכות הנוגעים במת לפר"ת. ולר' יצחק מספמפונטי אף כלי שטף כמו שאפרש לקמן בע"ה: או במת זה אבר הנחלל מן המת דלמת שלם לא אצטריך דאפי' חרב שנגעה במת מטמא באהל: או בקבר זה קבר סתום שאין לו פתיחה בפותח טפח ומאהיל עליו אפי' שלא כנגד הטומאה טמא דחשבינן ליה כאילו כולו מלא טומאה ובלבד שיהיה פותח טפח בין המת לגג הקבר אבל אם אין בו פותח טפח הוי טומאה רצוצה ובוקעת ועולה ואינה מטמאה מן הצדדים. והכי תנן פ"ז במס' אהלות נפש אטומה הנוגע בה מן הצדדים טהור מפני שהטומאה בוקעת ועולה בוקעת ויורדת. ואם היה מקום הטומאה טפח על טפח על רום טפח הנוגע מ"מ טמא מפני שהוא כקבר סתום:

עין משפט נר מצוה

מח א מיי' פ"ז מהל' נזירות הלכה ו:

מט ב מיי' פ"א מהל' טומאת מת הלכה א סמג עשין רלח:

נ ג מיי' שם פ"ב הל' ג סמג שם:

נא ד מיי' שם פרק ה הל' ג סמג שם:

נב ה מיי' פ"ב שם הל' ז:

נג ו מיי' שם הלכה ט:

נד ז מיי' שם הל' טו:

מסורת הש"ס

[סנהדרין ד. חולין עב. לעיל לח. מט:]

חולין ג. ע"ש פסחים יד:

[ועי' עוד תוס' ב"ב ק: ד"ה ורומן]

הגהות מהר"ב רנשבורג

א] תד"ה ר"י וכו' למתנייה בסיפא. כאן הס"ד ואח"כ מה"ד ורשב"ל אומר כל היכא דשמעינן מידי מכללא דרישא לא קתני בסיפא כנ"ל: ב] ד"ה התם וכו' מדר"ע דאמר רביעית דם הבא משני מתים. מן דאמר עד מתים נמחק: ג] ד"ה האי וכו' מדלא כתיב אשר. תיבת אשר נמחק ר"ב בשדה: ד] בא"ד רלה לומר אפי' אין עליהם. נ"ב ר"ל אין הכלים על המת ולא המת על הכלים. ס"מ: ה] ד"ה חרב הרי וכו' לטמא אדם הנוגע בו טומאת שבעה וכו' כנ"ל:

הגהות הגר"א

[א] גמ' (דאמר ר"ע כר"ד הבא משני מתים מטמא באהל) תא"מ (וע' תוס'):

נוסחת הריב"ן

א) למטמא במגע ב) ששחקו: ג) על פני השדה: ד) ויש לו. ה) מן

הגהות הב"ח

(א) גמ' ועל אבר מן החי שיש עליהן בשר כראוי אין אבל כנ"ל ותיבת הני' ותיבת כזית נמחק: (ב) שם או במת וגו' על פני השדה וכו' בחלל זה אבר הנחלל מן החי ויש בו להעלות ארוכה: (ג) רש"י ד"ה ריש לקיש וכו' שהנזיר מגלח על מגעו ולא על אהילו: (ד) ד"ה ורבי יוחנן וכו' מידי דמשמע ליה מכללא כנ"ל ותיבת חד נמחק והד"א עם ד"ה ואי לא לא מגלח לא הדר תני לה בסיפא הס"ד ואח"כ מ"ה הוה אמינא וכו' ברישא כי הדר:

דְּאָמַר מָר: אטוּמְאָה בּוֹקַעַת וְעוֹלָה בּוֹקַעַת וְיוֹרֶדֶת. וְאִילּוּ גַּבֵּי נְגִיעָה, אֲמַר רַב יְהוּדָה, תַּנְיָא: (במדבר יט) *°ב"(וְכָל) הַנּוֹגֵעַ בְּעֶצֶם אוֹ בֶחָלָל"; (א) "בְּעֶצֶם" — זֶה עֶצֶם כִּשְׂעוֹרָה, "אוֹ בֶחָלָל" — זֶה אֵבֶר הַנֶּחְלָל מִן הַחַי וְאֵין בּוֹ לְהַעֲלוֹת אֲרוּכָה, "אוֹ בְּמֵת" — זֶה אֵבֶר הַנֶּחְלָל מִן הַמֵּת, "אוֹ בְקָבֶר" — אָמַר ר"ל: גזֶה קֶבֶר שֶׁלִּפְנֵי הַדִּיבּוּר. הַאי אֵבֶר מִן הַמֵּת הֵיכִי דָמֵי? אִי דְּאִית בֵּיהּ עֶצֶם כִּשְׂעוֹרָה — הַיְינוּ הַנּוֹגֵעַ בְּעֶצֶם. אֶלָּא — דְּלֵית בֵּיהּ עֶצֶם כִּשְׂעוֹרָה, וַאֲפִי' הָכִי רַחֲמָנָא רַבְּיֵיהּ! (ב) אָמַר לָךְ ר' יוֹחָנָן: לְעוֹלָם דְּאִית בֵּיהּ, וְאִם אֵינוֹ עִנְיָן לְמַגָּעוֹ — דתְּנֵהוּ עִנְיָן לְמַשָּׂאוֹ.§ "וּמַזֶּה בַּשְּׁלִישִׁי וּבַשְּׁבִיעִי וְסוֹתֵר" וכו'.§ אִיבַּעְיָא לְהוּ: הָא דְּקָתָנֵי "עַד שֶׁיִּטְהַר" — בַּשְּׁבִיעִי קָאֵי, עַד דְּעָבֵיד הֶעֱרֵב שֶׁמֶשׁ, וּמַנִּי — *ר"א הִיא. אוֹ דִילְמָא: בַּשְּׁמִינִי קָאֵי, וּמַאי "עַד שֶׁיִּטְהַר" — עַד שֶׁיָּבִיא קָרְבְּנוֹתָיו, וּמַנִּי — רַבָּנַן הִיא? תָּא שְׁמַע, מִדְּקָתָנֵי סֵיפָא "מַתְחִיל וּמוֹנֶה מִיָּד", הָא רֵישָׁא מַאי "עַד שֶׁיִּטְהַר" — עַד שֶׁיָּבִיא קָרְבְּנוֹתָיו, וּמַנִּי — רַבָּנַן הִיא, דְּאָמְרִי: נְזִירוּת דְּטָהֳרָה עַד שְׁמִינִי לָא חָיְילָא.§ **מתני'** האֲבָל הַסְּכָכוֹת, וְהַפְּרָעוֹת, וּבֵית הַפְּרָס, וְאֶרֶץ הָעַמִּים, וְהַגּוֹלֵל וְהַדּוֹפֵק, וּרְבִיעִית דָּם, וְאֹהֶל, א] וְרוֹבַע עֲצָמוֹת, וְכֵלִים הַנּוֹגְעִים בַּמֵּת, וּבִימֵי סְפָרוֹ וּבִימֵי גְמָרוֹ — עַל אֵלּוּ אֵין הַנָּזִיר מְגַלֵּחַ. ווּמַזֶּה בַּשְּׁלִישִׁי וּבַשְּׁבִיעִי, וְאֵינוֹ

[רש"י]

דְּאָמַר מָר טוּמְאָה בּוֹקַעַת וְעוֹלָה. וְנַעֲשָׂה קֶבֶר כְּגוּפוֹ שֶׁל מֵת עַצְמוֹ, וְהַמְּהַלֵּךְ עָלָיו, אע"פ שֶׁאֵין נוֹגֵעַ אֶלָּא מַאֲהִיל — טָמֵא. וְאִילּוּ גַּבֵּי נְגִיעָה אֲמַר רַב יְהוּדָה תַּנְיָא. דְּעַד כָּאן מַיְירֵי בְּטוּמְאַת אֹהֶל, מִדִּכְתִיב בֵּיהּ "עַל פְּנֵי הַשָּׂדֶה", וּמִכָּאן וְאֵילָךְ בִּנְגִיעָה, דְּהָא הֲדַר בֵּיהּ קְרָא וַאֲמַר "וְכָל הַנּוֹגֵעַ בְּעֶצֶם אוֹ בֶחָלָל אוֹ בְּמֵת אוֹ בְקָבֶר". ה"ג: בְּמֵת זֶה הַמְחוּלָּל מִן הַמֵּת. וְאֵין עָלָיו בָּשָׂר כָּרָאוּי. אוֹ בְקָבֶר אר"ל זֶה קֶבֶר שֶׁלִּפְנֵי הַדִּיבּוּר. כְּלוֹמַר, שֶׁהַגּוֹיִם מְטַמְּאִין בְּמַגָּע, אע"פ שֶׁאֵין מְטַמְּאִין בְּאֹהֶל. כִּדְתַנְיָא:* קִבְרֵי הַגּוֹיִם אֵין מְטַמְּאִין בְּאֹהֶל, אֶלָּא בִּנְגִיעָה. וְכָל שֶׁהָיָה קוֹדֶם הַדִּיבּוּר, קוֹדֶם מַתַּן תּוֹרָה, בֵּין שֶׁל גּוֹיִם בֵּין שֶׁל יִשְׂרָאֵל — קָרֵי לֵיהּ קֶבֶר בֶּן נֹחַ, וְקֶבֶר הַגּוֹיִם לְאַחַר הַדִּיבּוּר א) כְּקוֹדֶם הַדִּיבּוּר, שֶׁאֵין מְטַמְּאִין בְּאֹהֶל, לְפִי שֶׁלֹּא נִיתְּנָה לָהֶם תּוֹרָה. וּמש"ה קָרֵי לֵיהּ קֶבֶר שֶׁלִּפְנֵי הַדִּיבּוּר. וְהַאי אֵבֶר מִן הַמֵּת וּמִן הַחַי שֶׁנֶּחֱלַל הֵיכִי דָמֵי? אִי דְאִית בְּהוּ עֶצֶם כִּשְׂעוֹרָה — הָא אִירְבּוּ לְהוּ מֵ"הַנּוֹגֵעַ בְּעֶצֶם אוֹ בֶחָלָל"! (ג) אֶלָּא לָאו — דְּלֵית בְּהוּ עֶצֶם כִּשְׂעוֹרָה וְלֹא בָּשָׂר כָּרָאוּי, וְקָא מְרַבֵּי לֵיהּ רַחֲמָנָא. הִילְכָּךְ, הוֹאִיל וְאִיתְרַבֵּי לֵיהּ — לֶיהֱוֵי נָזִיר מְגַלֵּחַ עָלָיו: וְרַבִּי יוֹחָנָן אָמַר לָךְ לְעוֹלָם דְּאִית בֵּיהּ. עֶצֶם כִּשְׂעוֹרָה, וְאִם אֵינוֹ עִנְיָן לְמַגָּעוֹ דְּנָפְקָא לֵיהּ מֵ"הַנּוֹגֵעַ בְּעֶצֶם" — תְּנֵהוּ עִנְיָן לְמַשָּׂאוֹ. אֲבָל אִם אֵין ב) הָעֶצֶם כִּשְׂעוֹרָה וְלֹא בָּשָׂר כָּרָאוּי — לְעוֹלָם אֵין טוּמְאָתוֹ כְּלוּם, וְאֵין הַנָּזִיר מְגַלֵּחַ עָלָיו: וְאֵינוֹ מַתְחִיל לִמְנוֹת נְזִירוּת דְּטָהֳרָה עַד שֶׁיִּטְהַר כו'. אִיבַּעְיָא לְהוּ הָא דְּקָתָנֵי עַד שֶׁיִּטְהַר ג) בַּשְּׁבִיעִי קָאֵי. כְּלוֹמַר, עַד דְּעָבֵיד הֶעֱרֵב שֶׁמֶשׁ בַּשְּׁבִיעִי, דְּהַיְינוּ (ד) ד) שְׁבִיעִי וּמֵיעַל שְׁמִינִי. וּמַנִּי ר"א הִיא. דְּאָמַר בְּפֶ' "מִי שֶׁאָמַר הֲרֵינִי נָזִיר מְגַלֵּחַ" (לעיל ד' יח:): מַתְחִיל וּמוֹנֶה מִיָּד, מִשּׁוּם ה) "וְקִדַּשׁ אֶת רֹאשׁוֹ בַּיּוֹם הַהוּא", אע"פ שֶׁלֹּא הֵבִיא קָרְבְּנוֹתָיו. אוֹ דִלְמָא. מַאי "עַד שֶׁיִּטְהַר" דְּקָאָמַר — עַד שֶׁיָּבִיא קָרְבְּנוֹתָיו, דְּפֵרוּשֵׁי קָמְפָרֵשׁ. וּמַנִּי רַבָּנַן הִיא. דִּפְלִיגִי עֲלֵיהּ, וְאָמְרִי דְּאֵין מַתְחִיל לִמְנוֹת עַד שֶׁיָּבִיא אֲשָׁמוֹ, דְּהַיְינוּ לְאַחַר הֲבָאַת קָרְבְּנוֹתָיו. וְכָל זְמַן שֶׁלֹּא הֵבִיא קָרְבְּנוֹתָיו — אֵינוֹ מַתְחִיל. וְאִי אִיכָּא סְפָרִים דִּכְתִיב בְּהוּ: וּמַנִּי ר"ש הִיא — לָאו שַׁבֶּשְׁתָּא הִיא, דְּבָרַיְיתָא תָּנֵי לָהּ לְהָא דְּרַבָּנַן כְּר"ש. מִדְּקָתָנֵי סֵיפָא. אֲבָל הַסְּכָכוֹת כו' מַתְחִיל וּמוֹנֶה מִיָּד מִיּוֹם שְׁבִיעִי, לְפִי שֶׁאֵינוֹ מֵבִיא קָרְבָּן. מִכְּלָל דְּרֵישָׁא — דְּאִית בֵּיהּ קָרְבָּן. מַאי עַד שֶׁיִּטְהַר. דְּקָאָמַר — עַד שֶׁיָּבִיא קָרְבְּנוֹתָיו קָמַשְׁמַע, דְּהַיְינוּ ו) שְׁמִינִי. וּמַנִּי — רַבָּנַן הִיא, דְּאָמְרִי: נְזִירוּת דְּטָהֳרָה עַד יוֹם שְׁמִינִי לָא חָיְילָא. **מתני'** אֲבָל הַסְּכָכוֹת. דְּהַיְינוּ אִילָן הַמֵּיסֵךְ עַל הָאָרֶץ, וְיֵשׁ טוּמְאָה תַּחַת נוֹף (ה) ז) בְּא' מֵהֶן, וְאֵינוֹ יָדוּעַ כְּנֶגֶד מִי. וְכֵן תַּחַת אֲבָנִים הַפְּרוּעוֹת. הַיּוֹצְאוֹת חוּץ מִן הַגָּדֵר, וְטוּמְאָה תַּחַת אַחַת מֵהֶן, וְאֵינוֹ יָדוּעַ לָאָדָם, וְהָלַךְ נָזִיר תַּחְתֵּיהֶן. וּבֵית הַפְּרָס. שָׂדֶה שֶׁנֶּאֱבַד בָּהּ קֶבֶר וְנֶחֱרַשׁ. וְאֶרֶץ הָעַמִּים. שֶׁנָּזַר בָּאָרֶץ, וּבְתוֹךְ יְמֵי נְזִירוּתוֹ יָצָא ח) וְנִכְנַס לְאֶרֶץ הָעַמִּים — אֵין הַנָּזִיר מְגַלֵּחַ. וְאֵין

[תוספות]

ואילו גבי נגיעה תניא וכל הנוגע בעצם או בחלל עצם זו עצם כשעורה בחלל זו אבר הנחלל מן החי ואין בו כדי להעלות ארוכה או במת זה אבר הנחלל מן המת ואין בו כדי להעלות. כולהו קראי וכולהו, דרשות איירי לענין מגע. **או** בקבר רשב"ל **אמר** זה קבר שלפני הדיבור. שקודם מתן תורה. ול"ע: לרבנן דר"ש דאמרי (יבמות ד' סא.): אף קברי גוים מטמאין באהל, דלא דרשינן "אדם אתם" – אתם קרויין אדם וכו', אמאי איצטריך ["או בקבר"]? וי"ל: דר"ש היא. מיהו קשה: ב] דהרי גבי נגיעה מודה ר"ש דקברי גוים מטמאין במגע ובמשא, כדאמר רבינא בפרק "הבא על יבמתו" (שם ד' סא.), ודוחק לומר דלא כרבינא! והריב"א פירש: קבר שלפני הדיבור – גם אותן שמתו ג] קודם מתן תורה, קודם שנאמרה פרשת טומאת מת. דס"ד אמינא "אדם כי ימות באהל" – מפרשה זו ואילך. וכיוצא בזה יש °בפ' בתרא דהוריות (ד' י.) דמצריך פסוק לזב שלפני הדיבור, משום ד] דסד"א "איש איש כי יהיה זב מבשרו" – מכאן ואילך. ה]ומקשינן לר"ש: אמאי הוה רבי בנאה מציין מערת המכפלה בפרק "חזקת הבתים" (ב"ב נח.), והא קודם מתן תורה לר"ש לא מטמא באהל! ובפ"ק דמ"ק (ד' ה.) אמרי' דאין מציינים [על דבר שאינו] מטמא באהל! ואומר הריב"א: דשפיר קרייה "אדם" – אדם הראשון, ואברהם – "האדם הגדול בענקים". א"נ: דקסבר מקבר שלפני הדיבור נרבה קבר ו] שלאחר הדיבור, שלאחר מתן תורה*). **אלא** דלית ביה עצם כשעורה ואפי' הכי מטמא ורחמנא רבייה. כיון שיש בו אבר שלם. ור' יוחנן אמר לך: לעולם דאית ביה כשעורה, ואם אינו ענין למגעו – תנהו ענין למשאו. אם אינו ענין לנוגע, דנפקא ליה מ"הנוגע בעצם" – תנהו לענין משאו, דעצם כשעורה מטמא במשא. וקצת קשה: דא"כ מאי קאמר "או במת" – זה אבר הנחלל מן המת ואית בו [כשעורה]? לימא: זו עצם כשעורה: ואינו מתחיל למנות עד שיטהר ויביא קרבנותיו ואיבעיא ליה עד שיטהר. דמתני' בשביעי קאי, דלאחר שטבל והזה וגלח. ומתחיל מאותו יום למנות נזירות טהרה, ויביא קרבנותיו בשמיני. ומני – ר"א היא, דאמר לעיל פרק "מי שאמר" (ד' יח:): מתחיל ומונה מיד. פירוש: שמתחיל ומונה משביעי, כדפי' שם. או דילמא בשמיני קאי, ומאי "עד שיטהר" – שיביא קרבנותיו, ומני – רבנן היא, דאמרי: "וקדש ראשו ביום ההוא" – ביום הבאת קרבנותיו. **ת"ש** מדקתני מתחיל ומונה מיד בהדי הנך שאין הנזיר מביא קרבן טומאה, ומזה בשלישי ובשביעי, ומתחיל ומונה מיד – דהיינו בשביעי, שהרי אינו זקוק להביא קרבן טומאה. ז] האמר ברישא "עד" דקתני, ולא קתני "מתחיל ומונה מיד" כמו בסיפא, שמע מינה דרישא עד שיטהר ויביא קרבנותיו קאמר, ומני – רבנן היא.

סככות ופרעות. מפ' בגמ' [מאי ניהו]. **בית** הפרס. שדה שנחרש בו קבר, [ועד ק' אמה] חשו חכמים שמא דלדל המחרישה בעצמות, ונשתייר שם עצם כשעורה. וליכא טומאה אלא מדרבנן. **וארץ** העמים. דגזרו בה רבנן טומאה, כדאמר בפ"ק דשבת (ד' טו.). **הגולל** והדופק. פרש"י בפ"ק דכתובות (דף ד:): גולל – זה כיסוי הארון, ודופק – הוא דופן של צדדין. וקשה לר"ת: דאמר בפ' "בהמה המקשה" (חולין עב.) "על פני השדה" – לרבות גולל ודופק, משמע דגלויין הן גולל ודופק, ואלו מכוסין הן! ופר"ת: דגולל הוא המצבה, ודופק – אבנים שהמצבה נשענת בהן. ובמקום אחר מפורש באורך. **). **ורביעית** דם ואהל ורובע עצמות. [אע"פ שמטמאין באהל אין הנזיר מגלח עליהן. ובדין הוא דהוה ליה למתני פחות מחצי לוג דם או פחות מחצי קב, אלא נקט שיעורים המפורשין *בפ"ק דאהלות שהן מטמאין באהל]. **וכלים** הנוגעים במת. ד"כי ימות מת עליו" אמרה תורה, [ובגמ' מפ' באיזו כלים איירי]. **וימי** ספרו וימי גמרו. פי': נזיר שמנה מקצת נזירות, ונצטרע בין ימי גמרו – דהיינו ימי חלוטו שהחליטוהו לטומאה, ובין ימי ספרו – אחר שהוחלט וראה הכהן והנה נרפא הנגע מן הצרוע, ומביא צפורים ומגלח, ונכנס במחנה ישראל, וישב מחוץ לאהלו שבעת ימים – שאסור בתשמיש. וביום [השביעי מגלח], ובשמיני מביא קרבנות צרעתו. ואותן ימים קרויין ימי ספרו, ואין עולין לימי נזירות, ואינן מבטלין את הקודמים. ח] (וכתב בנזיר) ואיצטריך למיתני [ספרו וגמרו], דאי תנא ספרו – ה"א: אבל ימי גמרו, דחמירי – סותר. ואי תנא גמרו – ה"א: אבל ספרו דקיל – עולה. וצריך עיון: דלא ליתני אלא ספרו! וליכא למימר: אבל גמרו סותר – דא"כ מאי נפקא מינה במה שימי ספרו אינו סותר? הרי כבר סתר מטעם ימי גמרו! **על** אלו אין הנזיר מגלח. לא קאי אימי ספרו ואימי גמרו, שהרי [הוא צריך] לגלח בשביל צרעתו, אלא קאי אשארא שאין מגלח כדין נזיר טמא. **ומזה.** בגמ' משמע דלא קאי אכלים הנוגעים במת, דמיירי בכלי עץ, ואין אדם הנוגע בהם צריך הזאה. [וכן לא קאי אימי גמרו ואימי ספרו דאין טעון הזאה], אלא קאי אשארא – ארביעית דם וגולל ודופק. ואינו

*) [עי' תוס' נדה ע: ד"ה ואין נגיב ותוס' יבמות סא. ד"ה ואין ותוס' ע"ז ג. ד"ה כהנים ותוס' סנהדרין נט. ד"ה אלא ותוס' ב"ק לח. ד"ה אלא] **) [עי' בתוס' ברכות יט: ד"ה מדלגין ובשבת קנב: ד"ה על קיסתם ובסוכה כג. ד"ה ולא ובכתובות ד: ד"ה עד ובסנהדרין מז: ד"ה מקיסתום]

פי' הרא"ש

או בקבר אמר ר"ל זה הקבר שלפני הדיבור שקודם מתן תורה דאמר פ' הבא על יבמתו אמר רשב"י קברי גוים אינם מטמאים דכתיב ואתן צאני צאן מרעיתי אדם אתם אתם קרויים אדם כו'. ופריך והא כתיב כל הורג נפש וכל נוגע בחלל תתחטאו ומשני דלמא איקטיל חד מינייהו. רבינא אמר נהי דממעטינהו מטומא' אהל דכתיב אדם כי ימות באהל ממגע וממשא מי ממעטינהו. משמע דלאידך שנוייא דאצטריך לשנויי דלמא איקטיל חד מישראל סבר דאף ממגע ומשא מעטי'. ולדידיה איצט' הכא לרבות קבר שלפני הדיבור דאע"ג דלאו ישראל נינהו מטמאו במגעו דהכא במגע איירי ולמגע רבינהו קרא ולא לאהל. ור' בנאה דהוה מציין מערת המכפלה בפ' ח"ה סבר כרבנן דר"ש דפ"ק דמ"ק אמרי' אין מציינין אלא על קבר שמטמא באהל. וריצב"א היה אומר דשפיר קרויין אדם אדם הראשון ואברהם אדם הגדול בענקים: ואפ"ה רחמנא רבייה כיון דהוי אבר שלם: ואם אינו ענין למגעו תנהו ענין למשאו. צ"ע לר"ל מנ"ל דעצם כשעורה מטמא במשא: עד שיטהר דקתני בז' אחר הזאה וטבילה: ומני ר"א דאמר וקדש את ראשו ביום ההוא ביום תגלחתו שמתחיל ומונה מיד בו ביום. או דלמא בח' ומאי עד שיטהר בהבאת קרבנותיו ומני ר' היא דאמר וקדש את ראשו ביום ההוא ביום הבאת קרבנותיו:

עין משפט נר מצוה

נה א מיי' פ"ג מהלכות טומאת מת הלכה ד ה ו:
נו ב מיי' שם פרק ג הלכה ב:
נז ג מיי' שם פרק א הלכה יג:
נח ד מיי' שם פרק ג הלכה ב:
נט ה מיי' פ"ז מהלכות נזירות הלכה ו:
ס ו מיי' שם הל' ב:

מסורת הש"ס

[אהלות פ"ב מ"א חולין עב.] [נ"ל ועל ועי' תוי"ט כלים פ"א מ"ה ד"ה מטמאה] [יבמות סא.] [לעיל יח:] נ"ל בפ"ב

נוסחת הריב"ן

א) כלפני: ב) בו עצם: ג) א' מתחיל למנות מאי קאמר או עד שיטהר בשביעי קאי: ד) מיפק לעולם: ה) מקום שנאמר וקדש: ו) בשמיני: ז) אחד: ח) יצא לארץ העמים ונכנס אין:

הגהות הב"ח

(א) גמ' או בחלל וגו' בעצם זה: (ב) שם ואפי' הכי רחמנא רבייה וכו' ר' יוחנן אמר לך לעולם: (ג) רש"י ד"ה ואלא אבר וכו' או בחלל למה לי אלא לאו: (ד) ד"ה איבעיא להו וכו' דהיינו שביעי ומיעל שמיני ומני כצ"ל ותיבת ד' נמחק: (ה) ד"ה אבל וכו' תחת נוף אחד מהן:

גליון הש"ס

תוס' ד"ה או בקבר. בפ' בתרא דהוריות וכו' אינו מדוקדק דהתם ממעטינן כי יהיה פרט לפני הדיבור וכו' ע"ש תוס' בנדה דף ע ע"ב:

הגהות מהר"ב רנשבורג

א] מתני' והדופק וכו' ואהל. נ"ב עי' תוי"ט ד"ה ואהל וכו': ב] תוד"ה או וכו' מיהו קשה דהכא גבי נגיעה כתיב ומודה כצ"ל: ג] בא"ד גם אותן שמתו קודם. תיבת קודם נמחק. ונ"ב אחר. א"מ ויעו"ש: ד] בא"ד הדיבור משום דסד"א. תיבות דסד"א נמחק ונ"ב דכתיב כצ"ל ושקטה בזה תמיהת הרב א"מ כנלע"ד ברור ודו"ק (א"ה עי' בדברי מר גיסי הרב המחבר ז"ל בחיבורו הורה גבר. דף ל' ע"ב וע"ג): ה] בא"ד כי יהיה וכו' מכאן ואילך. כאן הס"ד ואח"כ מה"ד ומקשי כצ"ל: ו] בא"ד מקבר שלפני וכו' שלאחר הדיבור שלאחר. ג' תיבות שלאחר הדיבור שלאחר נמחקו. ונ"ב שלפני הדיבור של כצ"ל וכן הוא בנדה דף ע' ע"ב בתוס' ד"ה ואין נגיב מלח וכו' א"מ ויעו"ש: ז] ד"ה ת"ש וכו' קרבן טומאה האמר. תיבת האמר נמחק. ונ"ב הא: ח] ד"ה וימי ספרו וכו' הקודמים וכתב בנזיר. תיבות וכתב בנזיר. ונ"ב וכתב בפירוש נזיר כצ"ל ור"ל שמצאו לאיזה מפרש על נזיר שכתב. א"מ:

עין משפט
נר מצוה

סא א מיי׳ פ״ז מהל׳ נזירות הלכה ז:
סב ב מיי׳ שם הל׳ ט:
סג ג ד מיי׳ שם הלכה ו ופי״ג מהל׳ טומאת מת הלכה ב סמג עשין רלח:
סד ה מיי׳ פ״ז מהל׳ נזירות הלכה ח:

אוְאֵינוֹ סוֹתֵר אֶת הַקּוֹדְמִים, וּמַתְחִיל וּמוֹנֶה מִיָּד, וְקָרְבָּן אֵין לוֹ. בבֶּאֱמֶת אָמְרוּ: יְמֵי הַזָּב וְהַזָּבָה, וִימֵי הֶסְגֵּרוֹ שֶׁל מְצוֹרָע — הֲרֵי אֵלּוּ עוֹלִין לוֹ.§

גמ׳ *וְאֵלּוּ הֵן הַסְּכָכוֹת — גאִילָן הַמֵּיסֵךְ עַל הָאָרֶץ, וּפְרָעוֹת (א) — דהַיּוֹצְאוֹת מִן הַגָּדֵר.§ "וְאֶרֶץ הָעַמִּים".§ אִיבַּעְיָא לְהוּ: °אֶרֶץ הָעַמִּים *מִשּׁוּם אֲוִירָא גָּזְרוּ עָלֶיהָ, אוֹ דִילְמָא *מִשּׁוּם גּוּשָׁא גָּזְרוּ עָלֶיהָ? ת״ש: וּמַזֶּה בַּשְּׁלִישִׁי וּבַשְּׁבִיעִי. וְאִי אָמְרַתְּ מִשּׁוּם אֲוִירָא — הַזָּאָה לָמָּה לִי? אֶלָּא לָאו מִשּׁוּם גּוּשָׁא. לָא. לְעוֹלָם אֵימָא לָךְ מִשּׁוּם אֲוִירָא, וְכִי קָתָנֵי — אַשְּׁאָרָא. הָכִי נַמִי מִסְתַּבְּרָא, מִדְּקָתָנֵי: וְכֵלִים הַנּוֹגְעִים בַּמֵּת; ההָנֵי כֵּלִים בְּנֵי הַזָּאָה אִינּוּן? אֶלָּא שְׁמַע מִינָּהּ — אַשְּׁאָרָא.
לֵימָא

ואינו סותר את הקודמים וגם אין עולין לו למנין נזירותו ומתחיל ומונה מיד. במקום שפסק למנות, כשנטמא, לא יתחיל למנות. שימי טומאה אין עולין לו לימי נזירותו. וגם קרבן, שנזיר טמא מביא חטאת ועולת העוף, ואשם — זה אינו מביא. וקשה לרש״י: דבשלמא כולהון ניחא, דכי נמי אינו סותר הקודמין — אין עולין לו. אלא כלים הנוגעים במת, דאפי׳ כלי שטף קאמר, כדמשמע בגמ׳, וכשנגע בהם הנזיר אינו טמא אלא טומאת ערב, [אמאי] אין עולין לו? **באמת** אמרו ימי הזב והזבה. נזיר שהתחיל למנות ונעשה זב, וימי הסגרו — שפרחה בו צרעת, והסגיר אותו הכהן, ועמד בעיניו או כיהה — עולין לו לימי נזירותו. **אילן** המיסך על הארץ. בפ׳ "דם הנדה" (נדה נז.) אמר דמדאורייתא לאו אהל מעליא, שהענפים רחוקים זה מזה ואין בהם פותח טפח, אף כי יש בודאי כזית מן המת תחת אחת מהן, ומן התורה טהור כי הלך תחת כולן, ורבנן הוא דגזרו טומאה בהולך תחתיו. **ופרעות** אבנים היוצאות מן הגדר. הסמוך לבית הקברות, ויש שם נפל תחת אחת מן האבנים. וגזרו חכמים טומאה למהלך תחת אחת מן האבנים, אף כי ספק טומאה ברה״ר ספקו טהור. ובמס׳ נדה (ג״ז שם) משמע דמהלך על פני כולה טמא בודאי. **ארץ** העמים על אוירא גזרו. כגון מהלך בשידה תיבה ומגדל גדולות יותר ממ׳ סאה, שאין מקבלין טומאה, או על גשר ארץ העמים, או הנכנס בקרון או בספינה. שהחמירו בה יותר מבאהל המת, כדי שלא יצא מארץ לחו״ל. או דלמא משום גושא דוקא — המאהיל על גושא גזרו כמי שמאהיל על המת, מפני מתי מבול או מפני רוב מישראל שנהרגו בחו״ל. אבל הנכנס בשידה תיבה ומגדל, או בקרון או בספינה — לא. והא דמשמע בפ״ק דשבת (ד׳ טו:) דגזרו על גושא ועל אוירא — התם ה״פ: בין לנוגע בגושא, בין מאהיל על גושא בלא שום הפסק לגושא. [אבל] בבא בשידה תיבה ומגדל, שיש הפסק — לא איירי. והקשה הרב ר׳ יעקב מאורליינ״ש: דתנן *בפ״ק דאהלות: ואלו מטמאין במגע ובמשא ולא באהל: ארץ העמים, ובית הפרס כו׳. והכא משמע דפשיטא לן דמטמא באהל כי מאהיל מיהא על גושא בלא הפסק שידה תיבה ומגדל! ותירץ: דהתם מיירי בגושא הבא מארץ העמים לא״י. ור״ת אומר: דהאי נשנית קודם גזרה אחרונה דשבת, דאמר התם (בפ״ק דשבת שם) דמעיקרא לא גזרו על אוירא ולא כלום. ועי״ל: דאינו מטמא עד שיכנס שם ראשו ורובו, כדמשמע בשלהי סוגיין, ולא כשמכניס ידו לבד, דאילו באהל המת מטמא אפי׳ במכניס ידו. **ת״ש** ומזה בג׳ ובז׳ ואי אמרת משום אוירא הזאה ל״ל. דאינו סברא שילטרכו בכה״ג הזאת ג׳ וז׳, הואיל ומטמא אף כי הפסק בינו ובין הגוש, דאינו כלל מענין טומאת אהל המת להצריך הזאה ג׳ וז׳. ומשני: כי קתני — אשארא. ה״נ מסתברא מדקתני וכלים הנוגעים במת הני כלים בני הזאה נינהו. והלא אינו טמא הנוגע בהן רק טומאת ערב, ולא טומאת ז׳! אלא ש״מ אשארא. דמשמע ליה דאפילו בכלי שטף איירי דנגעו במת, דהוו אב הטומאה, והנוגע בהם טמא טומאת ערב כנוגע בטמא מת בעלמא, דלא בעיא הזאה, אלא ש״מ אשארא. וא״ת: וליפני ליה דהני כלים בכלי מתכות מיירי, דאדם הנוגע בהם טמא טומאת ז׳, ובעי הזאה ג׳ וז׳, דחרב כחלל! ואור״ת: דע״כ לא מתוקמא מתני׳ בכלי מתכות, דא״כ הנזיר מגלח, דחרב הרי הוא כחלל. ושלח לו רבינו חיים כהן: "איזה בית אשר תבנו לי" א] דאין נזיר מגלח עליו, ה״ה דכהן מוזהר עליו. ואין לך בית שאין בה שום כלי מתכות שהיה באהל המת, או שום מסמר, כדאמרי׳ במס׳ שמחות (פ״ד הל׳ כא): כל טומאה שהנזיר מגלח עליה — כהן מוזהר עליה. ותו: דבהדיא תניא בתוספתא ובמס׳ אהלות (פ״א) דקחשיב התם ד׳ טומאות במת, כיצד? כלים הנוגעים במת, ואדם בכלים, וכלים באדם — טמאים ז׳, והרביעי, בין אדם בין כלים — טמאין טומאת ערב. וקאמר: בד״א — לתרומה וקדשים, אבל נזיר אין מגלח אלא על המת בלבד. פי׳: למעוטי כלים הנוגעים במת דאיירי בהן, דהא ודאי מגלח על אבר מן החי ואכל הני דתנן במתני׳. וע״כ מתני׳ דהתם בכלי מתכות איירי, דבכלי שטף אי אפשר להיות טמאים ד׳, [אלא] דוקא בכלי מתכות דאמר רחמנא חרב כחלל משכחת להן, כמו שמפורש, אבל כלי שטף אינו כחלל. אלמא, דאין הנזיר מגלח עליהן. והא דלא אוקי מתני׳ בכלי מתכות — משום דבלאו הכי קים ליה דקתני אשארא, דע״כ לאו אכולהו קאי "ומזה בג׳ וז׳", דהא קתני נמי ימי ספרו וימי גמרו, דלאו בני הזאה אינון. ומשמעתין קשה למה שפירש הר״ר יצחק מסימפונ״ט: דמתני׳ דאהלות — בין בכלי מתכות בין בשאר כלים, דכולהו גמרי מכלי מתכות, דאמר חרב הוא כחלל, וה״ה לשאר כלים. דבהדיא אמרי׳ בשמעתין: הנוגע בשאר כלים אינו טמא אלא טומאת ערב! ומיהו, קצת יש לדחות: דהא דפריך הכא בני הזאה נינהו — לאו אכלים הנוגעים במת, אלא אספרו ואגמרו קאי, דבתר הכי, והוי כמו וכו׳ ולא נ״ל. וצ״ע. מהרפ״ש. וה״ר יצחק הביא ראיה מתוספתא דכלים (פ״ו מב״ק): החמת שהיא נתונה בתנור ופיה למעלה מן התנור, ועלם כשעורה כרוך בסיב או בנייר ונתון לתוכה — הוא טהור והתנור טהור. הוא טהור — משום דכרוך בסיב, והתנור טהור — דתוכו ולא תוך תוכו. בא הטהור ואחז בו והעלהו — טמא, לפי שהסיט עלם כשעורה, וטמא את החמת, חזרה החמת וטמאה את התנור. אלמא דהחמת כאדם, ונעשית אב הטומאה לטמא את התנור, ואע״ג דלאו כלי מתכות הוא — משוינן ליה כאדם להיות אב הטומאה כמוהו, שניטמא בעלם, דהוי אבי אבות! ויש לדחות: דהתם משום דיקרב בדיקרב הוא, דהאדם ניטמא במשא דעלם כשעורה, ב] ובשעה שהיה [נושא עלם המת שהוא] אבי אבות — באותה שעה היה נוגע בהחמת, והחמת בתנור. ועוד הביא, מדאמר בספרי: "כל אשר יגע בו הטמא יטמא" למה נאמר? לפי שנאמר "בחלל חרב" בא הכתוב ולימד על החרב שהוא מטמא טומאת שבעה, למדנו לכלים ואדם, כלים ואדם וכלים מנין? ת״ל "וכבסתם בגדיכם ביום השביעי וטהרתם". פי׳: שהבגדים שנוגעין באדם שנוגע במת טמאים ז׳. *והתם בגדים משמע, אף בשאינן כלי מתכות! ואור״ת: דתכשיטי כלי מתכות שפיר מיקרו בגדים, כדכתיב בבגדי כהונה (שמות כח) "אלה הבגדים אשר יעשו" וחשיב ציץ. וכללא דמילתא: כלים במת, וכלים באדם, בכלים (וכלים בכלים) — הרי הן כמו אדם במת. ואדם בכלים ג] וכלים בכלים ואדם באדם — ירדו מעלה אחת. דאילו כלי מתכות במת — הרי הן כמוהו, דחרב כחלל. וגם כלים באדם, כדכתיב (במדבר לא) "וכבסתם בגדיכם". אבל כלים בכלים — לא אשכחן שיעשו כיוצא בהן. וכלים בכלים השלישי — אינו אלא ערב, בין אדם בין כלים (באדם). אבל כלים באדם — הכלים כמו האדם; מה האדם טמא ז׳ — אף [כלים] ד] הנוגע ז׳. וכלים במת — הרי הן כמת, מה המת אבי אבות לטמא אדם וכלים טומאת ז׳ — אף כלי מטמא אדם וכלים טומאת ז׳, ותו לא מידי.

וְאֵין סוֹתֵר אֶת הַקּוֹדְמִין. וְהַאי דִּתְנַן בְּפֶ׳ "הֲרֵינִי נָזִיר מְגַלֵּחַ" (לעיל יט:): מִי שֶׁנָּזַר נְזִירוּת מְרוּבָּה וְהִשְׁלִים נְזִירוּתוֹ וְאַחַר כָּךְ בָּא לָאָרֶץ כו׳, ב״ה אוֹמְרִים: נָזִיר כְּבַתְּחִלָּה, וְסוֹתֵר אֶת הַקּוֹדְמִין — הָתָם הָוֵי טַעְמָא לְפִי שֶׁעָשָׂה נְזִירוּתוֹ בְּח״ל, וְאֵין עִיקַּר נְזִירוּת א) אֶלָּא בְּא״י. אֲבָל כָּאן, שֶׁעָשָׂה (ב) וְאַחַר כָּךְ יָצָא — אֵינוֹ צָרִיךְ לִסְתּוֹר אֶת הַקּוֹדְמִים. ב) וּסְפָרוֹ שֶׁל מְצוֹרָע. דְּהַיְינוּ אַחַר חִלּוּטוֹ הוּא, דְּהַאי קְרָא "וְכִבֶּס בְּגָדָיו" וגו׳ (ויקרא יד) בְּסוֹף יְמֵי חִלּוּטוֹ כְּתִיב, דְּהַיְינוּ כְּשֶׁנִּתְרַפֵּא מִצָּרַעְתּוֹ, כִּדְכְתִיב בְּרֵישָׁא דְּעִנְיָינָא "וְיָצָא הַכֹּהֵן אֶל מִחוּץ לַמַּחֲנֶה וְרָאָה הַכֹּהֵן וְהִנֵּה נִרְפָּא" וגו׳. וְאָז הוּא מְגַלֵּחַ, כִּדְכְתִיב "וְגִילַּח אֶת כָּל שְׂעָרוֹ", וּמַתְחִילִין יְמֵי סְפִירוֹ, וּלְאַחַר יְמֵי סְפִירוֹ מְגַלֵּחַ פַּעַם שֵׁנִית, כִּדְכְתִיב בְּהַהוּא קְרָא גּוּפֵיהּ "וְיָשַׁב מִחוּץ לְאָהֳלוֹ שִׁבְעַת יָמִים", וּכְתִיב "וְהָיָה בַּיּוֹם הַשְּׁבִיעִי יְגַלַּח אֶת כָּל שְׂעָרוֹ" וגו׳. וִימֵי סְפִירוֹ שֶׁל מְצוֹרָע — אוֹתָן יָמִים שֶׁכָּתוּב בָּהֶן "וְכִבֶּס הַמִּטַּהֵר וְגִלַּח אֶת כָּל שְׂעָרוֹ וְרָחַץ בַּמַּיִם וְאַחַר יָבֹא אֶל הַמַּחֲנֶה, וְיָשַׁב מִחוּץ לְאָהֳלוֹ שִׁבְעַת יָמִים", וִימֵי גְמָרוֹ שֶׁל מְצוֹרָע — הַיְינוּ יְמֵי חִלּוּטוֹ, דִּכְתִיב בְּהוּ (שם יג) "בָּדָד יֵשֵׁב מִחוּץ לַמַּחֲנֶה מוֹשָׁבוֹ". ג) אַחַר תִּגְלָחִיּוֹת הַלָּלוּ שֶׁל מְצוֹרָע אֵינוֹ סוֹתֵר אֶת הַקּוֹדְמִין וְאַחַר יַתְחִיל לִמְנוֹת יְמֵי נְזִירוּתוֹ, אֶלָּא לַמָּקוֹם שֶׁפָּסַק יַתְחִיל. וְהוּא שֶׁתְּהֵא נְזִירוּת מְרוּבָּה, כְּדֵי שֶׁיְּהֵא בּוֹ גִּידּוּל שֵׂעָר ל׳ יוֹם לְאַחַר שֶׁנִּתְגַּלֵּחַ בְּתִגְלָחִיּוֹת שְׁתַּיִם שֶׁל מְצוֹרָע, וְאַף אוֹתָן יָמִים שֶׁל סְפָרוֹ וְשֶׁל גְּמָרוֹ אֵין עוֹלִין לוֹ לְמִנְיָן. בֶּאֱמֶת אָמְרוּ. הֲלָכָה הִיא לְמֹשֶׁה מִסִּינַי: יְמֵי הַזָּב וְהַזָּבָה, וִימֵי הֶסְגֵּרוֹ שֶׁל מְצוֹרָע — יָמִים הָרִאשׁוֹנִים שֶׁכָּתוּב בָּהֶן (שם) "וְהִסְגִּיר הַכֹּהֵן שִׁבְעַת יָמִים", וּכְתִי׳ "וְהִסְגִּירוֹ הַכֹּהֵן שִׁבְעַת יָמִים שֵׁנִית" — עוֹלִין לוֹ מִמִּנְיַן יְמֵי נְזִירוּתוֹ. וּלְקַמָּן מְפָרֵשׁ מֵהֵיכָא ד) גָּמֵיר. **גמ׳** אִיבַּעְיָא לְהוּ אֶרֶץ הָעַמִּים מִשּׁוּם **אֲוִירָא.** נַמִי גָּזְרוּ עֲלָהּ. וְהֵיכָא דְּאִיכָּא אֲוִירָא בְּלָא גּוּשָׁא — כְּגוֹן דְּנִכְנַס בָּהּ בְּקָרוֹן אוֹ בִסְפִינָה, שֶׁלֹּא פָּסַע לָאָרֶץ אֶלָּא נִכְנַס ה) בָּהּ בַּאֲוִירָא, (ג) קָלֵיט לֵיהּ טוּמְאָה. **אוֹ דִילְמָא מִשּׁוּם גּוּשָׁא.** דְּטוּמְאָה חֲמוּרָה הוּא דְּגָזְרוּ עֲלֶיהָ, וְלֹא מִשּׁוּם אֲוִירָא דְּהַיְינוּ טוּמְאָה קַלָּה. וְאִם נִכְנַס בָּהּ בְּרַגְלָיו — כְּמַאן דְּנָגַע בְּקֶבֶר דָּמֵי, אֲבָל בְּקָרוֹן לֹא. **וְאִי אָמְרַתְּ מִשּׁוּם אֲוִירָא.** ו) הֵיכָא דְּאִיכָּא אֲוִירָא בְּלָא גּוּשָׁא מִי הָוְיָא לָהּ טוּמְאָה חֲמוּרָה כּוּלֵּי הַאי, דְּתִיבָּעֵי הַזָּאָה שְׁלִישִׁי וּשְׁבִיעִי? וְכִי קָתָנֵי. וּמַזֶּה בִּשְׁלִישִׁי וּשְׁבִיעִי — אַשְּׁאָרָא, אַסְּכָכוֹת וּפְרָעוֹת, וְלָאו אַאֶרֶץ הָעַמִּים. **הָכִי נַמִי מִסְתַּבְּרָא.** דְּלָא אַכּוּלְּהוּ קָאֵי, מִדְּקָתָנֵי כֵּלִים הַנּוֹגְעִים בַּמֵּת. וְהָנֵי כֵּלִים בְּנֵי הַזָּאָה נִינְהוּ. כְּלוֹמַר, וְאִם נוֹגֵעַ נָזִיר בְּכֵלִים הַנּוֹגְעִים בַּמֵּת — צָרִיךְ הַזָּאָה? בִּתְמִיָּה. **אֶלָּא לָאו שְׁמַע מִינָּהּ.** לָאו אַכּוּלְּהוּ קָאֵי, אֶלָּא אַשְּׁאָרָא קָאֵי, אַהָנָךְ [דִּבְנֵי] הַזָּאָה נִינְהוּ.
מַאי

לימא

פי׳ הרא״ש

אילן המסך על הארץ וענפיו מובדלים ויש כזית מת תחת אחד מן הענפים ואין ידוע תחת איזו. וכן פרעות אבנים הבולטות מן הגדר ויש כזית מן המת תחת א׳ מהן ואין ידוע תחת איזו ומיירי שהן רחבות טפח דהכי משמע פ׳ דם הנדה בסופו שהמהלך תחת כולו טמא ודאי אלא שאויר מפסיק ביניהם והלך הנזיר תחת א׳ מהם. ויר׳ לי דמיירי שהאילן עומד ברה״ר וכן האבנים בולטים ברה״ר דספק טומאה ברה״ר טהור וחכמים גזרו עליו טומאה אבל ברה״י הוי טומאה דאורייתא וסותר ומביא קרבן כדמוכח לקמן רפ״ב נזירי׳: משום אוירה גזרו שהאויר יטמא אפילו אינו מאהיל על הנושא כגון הנכנס לה בקרון ובספינה או בשידה תיבה ומגדל שמחזיקים מ׳ סאה שאינן מקבלים טומאה וחוצצין בפני הטומאה: ואי אמרת אוירה גזור הזאה למה לי דכיון דאמרי׳ הנכנס בדבר החוצץ טמא א״כ לא גזרו עליה משום טומאה אלא חומרא בעלמא החמירו עליה כדי שלא יצא אדם מארץ לחו״ל וא״כ הזאה למה לי: אלא לאו משום גושא. שגזרו עליה כמאהיל על המת לפי שאין מציינים בה קברים הוא דבעי הזאה: וכי קתני ומזה אשארא רביעית דם ורובע עצמות וכיוצא בהם: הני כלים בני הזאה נינהו פי׳ אדם הנוגע בכלים בר הזאה הוא בתמיה והלא הכלי אב הטומאה ואדם הנוגע בו ראשון וטמא טומאת ערב:

מסורת הש״ס

נדה נז. תוספתא דאהלות פ״ט אהלת פ״ח מ״כ]

[לעיל כ.]

[לעיל יט:]

נוסחר הריב״ן

א) בחו״ל אבל כאן שעשה נזירותו בארץ ואח״כ: ב) גליון וספירו כו׳: ג) מחוץ למחנה מושבו אין הנזיר מגלח על טומאה זו פעם שלישית לכשיתרפא מצרעתו לאחר תגלחיות שתים של מצורע ואח״כ יתחיל למנות לימי נזירותו כו׳ שתים שמצורע ואף כו׳ לו מן המנין: ד) יליף: ה) נכנס ליה באוירא קליט ליה: ו) וכל היכא כו׳ ושביעי אע״ג שלא הזה נמי הס״ד:

הגהות הב״ח

(א) גמ׳ ופרעת אבנים היוצאות: (ב) רש״י ד״ה ואין סותר וכו׳ אבל כאן שעשה נזירות בארץ ואחר כך יצא וכו׳ הקודמין הס״ד ואח״כ מ״ה וימי ספירו של מצורע וכו׳ וכבס המטהר את בגדיו: (ג) ד״ה איבעיא להו וכו׳ דקליט ליה:

גליון הש״ס

גמ׳ ארץ העמים משום אוירא. עיין לעיל דף כ ע״א: תום׳ ד״ה ת״ש וכו׳ והא דלא אוקי מתני׳ בכלי מתכות. עי׳ בטור פ״ד לחולין דף עא ע״ב ד״ה כי קאמר רבה שאדם נוגע בחרב שנטמא במת דאין לו הזיי׳ ג׳ וז׳: בא״ד ולא נראה לי וצ״ע. עי׳ שבועות ד׳ ט׳ ע״ב תד״ה כדאמר. שם דף מא ע״א ד״ה ותאן דתני. ובגיטין דף פ כ״ב ד״ה זו דברי ר״מ:

הגהות מהר״ב רנשבורג

א] תוד״ה ת״ש וכו׳ אשר תבנו לי דאין. תיבת דאין נמחק. וצ״ב דאב[...] ב] בא״ד דעלם כשעורה אבי אבות ובשעה שהיה נושא עלם וכו׳ מדאמר בספרי לכל כנ״ל: ג] בא״ד וכללא למילתא וכו׳ ואדם בכלים דכלים בכלים כנ״ל ועי׳ א״מ: ד] בא״ד אף כלים הנוגעים באדם ז׳ וכו׳ כנ״ל:

לֵימָא כְּתַנָּאֵי: *הַנִּכְנָס לְאֶרֶץ הָעַמִּים בְּשִׁידָּה תֵּיבָה וּמִגְדָּל, ארַבִּי מְטַמֵּא, וְרַבִּי יוֹסֵי בְּרַבִּי יְהוּדָה מְטַהֵר. מַאי לָאו רַבִּי סָבַר מִשּׁוּם אֲוִירָא, ור' יוֹסֵי בר' יְהוּדָה סָבַר מִשּׁוּם גּוּשָׁא? לָא, דְּכוּלֵּי עָלְמָא מִשּׁוּם גּוּשָׁא, מָר סָבַר: אֹהֶל זָרוּק שְׁמֵיהּ אֹהֶל, וּמָר סָבַר: בלָא שְׁמֵיהּ אֹהֶל. וְהָתַנְיָא, רַבִּי יוֹסֵי בְּרַבִּי יְהוּדָה אוֹמֵר: תֵּיבָה שֶׁהִיא מְלֵאָה כֵּלִים וּזְרָקָהּ עַל פְּנֵי הַמֵּת בְּאֹהֶל – טְמֵאָה, וְאִם הָיְתָה מוּנַּחַת – טְהוֹרָה! אֶלָּא, דְּכוּלֵּי עָלְמָא מִשּׁוּם אֲוִירָא, וּמָר סָבַר: כֵּיוָן *דְּלָא שְׁכִיחָא – לָא גָּזְרוּ בֵּיהּ רַבָּנַן, וּמָר סָבַר: אע"ג דְּלָא שְׁכִיחָא – גָּזְרוּ בֵּיהּ רַבָּנַן. וְהָתַנְיָא: *הַנִּכְנָס לְאֶרֶץ הָעַמִּים בְּשִׁידָּה תֵּיבָה וּמִגְדָּל – טָהוֹר, בְּקָרוֹן וּבִסְפִינָה וּבְאִיסְקַרְיָא – טָמֵא. וְאִיבָּעֵית אֵימָא: הָכָא שֶׁמָּא יוֹצִיא רֹאשׁוֹ וְרוּבּוֹ לְשָׁם פְּלִיגִי. וְהָתַנְיָא, ר' יוֹסֵי בר' יְהוּדָה אוֹמֵר: הַנִּכְנָס לְאֶרֶץ הָעַמִּים בְּשִׁידָּה תֵּיבָה וּמִגְדָּל – טָהוֹר, עַד שֶׁיּוֹצִיא לְשָׁם רֹאשׁוֹ אוֹ רוּבּוֹ. § "וּמַתְחִיל וּמוֹנֶה". § אָמַר רַב חִסְדָּא: ל"ש אֶלָּא בִּנְזִירוּת מוּעֶטֶת, אֲבָל בִּנְזִירוּת מְרוּבָּה – מִיסְלַק נַמִי סָלְקִין לֵיהּ. מְתִיב רַב שֵׁרֶבְיָא: *מַתְחִיל וּמוֹנֶה מִיָּד, וְאֵין מְבַטֵּל בָּהֶן אֶת הַקּוֹדְמִין. בְּמַאי? אִילֵימָא בִּנְזִירוּת מוּעֶטֶת – קָבָעֵי גִּידּוּל שֵׂעָר! אֶלָּא

מַאי לָאו דְּרַבִּי סָבַר מִשּׁוּם אֲוִירָא. גָּזְרוּ עָלֶיהָ, וְאִילּוּ הָכָא כֵּיוָן דְּנִכְנַס א) בַּאֲוִיר מִלְמַעְלָה כְּשֶׁהֵן פְּתוּחִין, אוֹ דֶּרֶךְ פְּתָחִים – הָוֵי טָמֵא, שֶׁהֲרֵי נִכְנַס לַאֲוִיר אֶרֶץ הָעַמִּים. וְר' יוֹסֵי בְּר' יְהוּדָה סָבַר מִשּׁוּם גּוּשָׁא. וְלָא מִשּׁוּם אֲוִירָא, וְכֵיוָן דְּקַרְקָעִית שִׁידָּה תֵּיבָה וּמִגְדָּל מַפְסִיק בֵּינוֹ לְבֵין הַגּוּשָׁא – הָוֵי טָהוֹר. לָא דְּכוּלֵּי עָלְמָא ב) מִשּׁוּם גּוּשָׁא. אֲבָל הָכָא בְּהָא קָמִיפַּלְגִי, דְּרַבִּי דִּמְטַמֵּא קָסָבַר: אֹהֶל זָרוּק לָאו שְׁמֵיהּ אֹהֶל, וְלָא הָוֵי הֶפְסֵק, וּכְמַאן דִּמְהַלֵּךְ מַמָּשׁ עַל גַּבֵּי קַרְקַע דָּמֵי, וְר' יוֹסֵי בְּר' יְהוּדָה סָבַר דִּשְׁמֵיהּ אֹהֶל. וְהָתַנְיָא ר' יוֹסֵי בְּר' יְהוּדָה אָמַר תֵּיבָה מְלֵאָה כֵּלִים וּזְרָקָהּ עַל גַּבֵּי הַמֵּת ג) בְּאֹהֶל טְמֵאָה. וְכָל הַכֵּלִים שֶׁבְּתוֹכָהּ. אַלְמָא קָסָבַר דְּאֹהֶל זָרוּק לָאו שְׁמֵיהּ אֹהֶל, וְלָא הָוֵי מַפְסִיק כְּלָל. וְאִם הָיְתָה מוּנַּחַת טְהוֹרָה. דְּכֵיוָן דִּמְוּנַּחַת הָוְיָא לָהּ כְּאֹהֶל קָבוּעַ, וּמַאֲהֶלֶת בִּפְנֵי הַטּוּמְאָה, וְלָא הָוֵי כְּאֹהֶל זָרוּק. אֶלָּא דְּכוּלֵּי עָלְמָא מִשּׁוּם אֲוִירָא. וְהַיְינוּ טַעְמָא דִּמְטַהֵר ר' יוֹסֵי בְּר' יְהוּדָה – מִשּׁוּם דְּקָסָבַר: כִּי נִכְנַס לְאֶרֶץ הָעַמִּים בְּשִׁידָּה תֵּיבָה וּמִגְדָּל – מִילְּתָא דְּלָא שְׁכִיחָא הִיא, וּמִילְּתָא דְּלָא שְׁכִיחָא – לָא גָּזְרוּ בֵּיהּ רַבָּנַן. וְהָתַנְיָא. דִּמְסַיְּיעָא לֵיהּ. הַנִּכְנָס כו' בְּקָרוֹן וּבִסְפִינָה וּבְאִיסְקַרְיָא. כְּלוֹמַר, בִּסְפִינָה גְּדוֹלָה שֶׁיֵּשׁ בָּהּ אִיסְקַרְיָא. וְקָרֵי לָהּ הָכִי עַל שֵׁם אִיסְקַרְיָא שֶׁבָּהּ, דְּהַיְינוּ תּוֹרֶן, וְקָרוּי א] ד) פוס"ט בְּלַעַ"ז. מִשּׁוּם דְּמִילְּתָא דִּשְׁכִיחָא גָּזְרוּ בָּהּ רַבָּנַן, וְהָא (א) מַתְנִי' ר' יוֹסֵי בְּר' יְהוּדָה הִיא. וְאִיבָּעֵית אֵימָא. דְּכ"ע מִשּׁוּם גּוּשָׁא, וּלְכ"ע נַמִי אֹהֶל זָרוּק שְׁמֵיהּ אֹהֶל, וְהַאי דְּקָא מְטַמֵּא ה) הָכָא – מִשּׁוּם דְּקָסָבַר גְּזֵירָה שֶׁמָּא יוֹצִיא רֹאשׁוֹ וְרוּבּוֹ חוּץ מִשִּׁידָּה תֵּיבָה וּמִגְדָּל, וְר' יוֹסֵי לָא גָּזַר. ו) וְהָתַנְיָא. דִּמְסַיְּיעָא ב] לֵיהּ, דְּר' יוֹסֵי אֵינוֹ מְטַמֵּא עַד שֶׁיּוֹצִיא רֹאשׁוֹ וְרוּבּוֹ. ז) וְהָא דְּתָנֵי ר' יוֹסֵי בְּר"י לְעֵיל זָרַק תֵּיבָה מְלֵאָה כֵּלִים עַל פְּנֵי הַמֵּת טְמֵאָה – לָאו מִשּׁוּם דְּקָסָבַר אֹהֶל זָרוּק לָאו שְׁמֵיהּ אֹהֶל, אֶלָּא כֵּיוָן דְּזוֹרְקָהּ קָא ח) מַפֵּיק לָהּ מִתּוֹרַת אֹהֶל, וּמְשַׁוֵּי לָהּ תּוֹרַת כְּלִי. וּלְעוֹלָם קָסָבַר אֹהֶל זָרוּק שְׁמֵיהּ אֹהֶל, (ב) דְּקָתָנֵי בְּסֵיפָא: וְאִם הָיְתָה מוּנַּחַת – טְהוֹרָה, אע"ג דְּאוֹרְחֵיהּ דְּמִטַּלְטֵל לָהּ. אָמַר רַב חִסְדָּא לֹא שָׁנוּ. דִּימֵי חִלּוּטוֹ אֵין עוֹלִין לוֹ מִן הַמִּנְיָן. אֶלָּא בִּנְזִירוּת מוּעֶטֶת (ג). ט) בִּזְמַן שֶׁקִּבֵּל עָלָיו נְזִירוּת שְׁלֹשִׁים יוֹם, [וְנִצְטָרַע] כְּשֶׁעָשָׂה מֵהֶן עֲשָׂרָה יָמִים, וְנֶחְלַט, שֶׁאֵין הַלָּלוּ יָמִים עוֹלִין לוֹ מִן הַמִּנְיָן. שֶׁאִם אַתָּה אוֹמֵר עוֹלִין לוֹ – לֹא יִשְׁתַּיְּירוּ לוֹ כְּדֵי גִידּוּל שֵׂיעָר לְאַחַר תִּגְלָחִיּוֹת שֶׁל צָרַעַת. אֲבָל בִּנְזִירוּת מְרוּבָּה. שֶׁקִּיבֵּל עָלָיו מֵאָה יוֹם, וְנִצְטָרַע בְּתוֹךְ יְמֵי נְזִירוּתוֹ עַד שֶׁלֹּא עָבְרוּ ל' יוֹם, וְנִתְגַּלֵּחַ בִּשְׁתֵּי תִגְלָחִיּוֹת שֶׁל צָרַעַת, הוֹאִיל וַעֲדַיִין י) נִשְׁתַּיְּירוּ שָׁם ל' יוֹם כְּדֵי גִידּוּל שֵׂיעָר – אַף יְמֵי חִלּוּטוֹ עוֹלִין לוֹ מִן הַמִּנְיָן, וְאֵינוֹ צָרִיךְ לִשְׁמוֹר אֶלָּא ל' יוֹם כְּדֵי גִידּוּל שֵׂיעָר טָהֳרָה לִנְזִירוּת לְאַחַר תִּגְלָחִיּוֹת שֶׁל צָרַעְתּוֹ. מְתִיב רַב שֵׁרֶבְיָא. מִי מָצֵית דָּיְיקַתְּ לְמַתְנִי' דִּבִנְזִירוּת מוּעֶטֶת קָאֵי? וְהָא קָתָנֵי: מַתְחִיל וּמוֹנֶה מִיָּד, וְאֵינוֹ סוֹתֵר אֶת הַקּוֹדְמִין. וּבְאֵיזוֹ נְזִירוּת קָאֵי? אִילֵימָא בִּנְזִירוּת מוּעֶטֶת, שֶׁל שְׁלֹשִׁים יוֹם – וּמִי מָצֵית אָמְרַתְּ דְּאֵינוֹ סוֹתֵר אֶת הַקּוֹדְמִין? וְהָא בָּעֵי גִידּוּל שֵׂיעָר. לְאַחַר כ) תִּגְלַחְתּוֹ מִן הַצָּרַעַת, וְלֵיכָּא, דְּאֵין גִּידּוּל שֵׂיעָר פָּחוֹת מִשְּׁלֹשִׁים יוֹם. אֶלָּא

לימא כתנאי. אי משום אוירא אי משום גושא (ד). ור' יוסי בר' יהודה מטהר. דסבר משום גושא, דכיון שהוא בשידה, ואהל זרוק שמיה אהל, טהור. והתניא • בת"כ: זרק תיבה מלאה כלים על פני המת – טמאה, דהוי אהל זרוק, ולא שמיה אהל. ואם היתה מונחת, שעומדת במקום אחד – טהורה, כיון דאינה זזה ממקומה השתא – הוי אהל קבוע. אלמא דאהל זרוק לא שמיה אהל לר' יוסי בר"י. אבל אם פליגי באוירא וגושא – לא קשיא ליה מידי מהך ברייתא, דאיכא לאוקמא לפלוגתייהו בשידה תיבה המונחת, ואפ"ה א"ר: מטמא משום אוירא. אבל השתא דפליגי באהל זרוק – לא מתוקמא פלוגתייהו במונחת, דא"כ רבי לא הוה מטמא, דאהל מעליא הוא. ומשני: דכ"ע משום אוירא, ואהל זרוק לא שמיה אהל לר' יוסי בר' יהודה, ואפ"ה משום דלא שכיחא ליכנס בשידה תיבה ומגדל לא גזרו לר' יוסי. והתניא – בניחותא וכו'. פירוש אחר: לא, דכ"ע משום גושא, מר סבר: אהל זרוק, שנכנס בשידה שבהמה או אדם מוליכים אותו – שמיה אהל, לחוץ ולהפסיק. וצ"ל דעדיף מטלית המנפנפת, דתנן במס' אהלות (פ"ח מ"ה) דאין אוהלין בפני הטומאה ואין מביאין, והיינו טעמא דהכא עדיף – משום דרגלי האדם או הבהמה הנושאים השידה והתיבה נוגעים בארץ, אבל הטלית מנפנפת באויר. ומר סבר: אהל זרוק לא שמיה אהל, והיינו דאמר "והתניא" בניחותא. וכן בפירוש ר"ח: ר' יוסי בר' יהודה אומר תיבה שהיא מלאה כלים וזרקה על פני המת טמאה, דדמיא לטלית המנפנפת, דאזלה כולה באוירא, ואם היתה מונחת על גבי בהמה או אדם הנושאין אותה – טהורה, דאהל זרוק כה"ג, דרגלי הנושאים נוגעים בארץ – שמיה אהל, לחוץ בפני הטומאה.

ה"ג: ואי בעית אימא דכ"ע משום אוירא גזרו וטעמא דר' יוסי בר' יהודה דמטהר (ה) אף כי נמי גזרו על אוירא – היינו בעומד על הגשר של ארץ העמים, או נכנס בקרון ובספינה, דשכיחי להלך. אבל בשידה תיבה ומגדל – לא שכיח, לא גזרו. ורבי סבר: אע"ג דלא שכיח גזרו. והתניא – בניחותא: הנכנס בארץ העמים בשידה תיבה ומגדל טהור, בקרון ובספינה ובאסקריא – גוט"א בלע"ז, ג] משוט הספינה, וכדאמר בעלמא (תענית דף כא.): אילפא תלא נפשיה באסקריא דמכותא. אלמא אף לר' יוסי בר"י דמטהר בשידה תיבה ומגדל – מודה בקרון ובספינה דטמא, משום אוירא גזרו. ואב"א: הכא שמא יוציא ראשו ורובו לשם, ולכ"ע משום גושא גזרו, ושידה תיבה ומגדל דמטהר ר' יוסי בר"י – משום דסבר אהל זרוק שמיה אהל, ולא גזר שמא יוציא ראשו ורובו לחוץ, דאין פתח שידה תיבה ומגדל נוחה ליכנס ולהוציא, ואין נקל כל כך להוציא ראשו. אבל בקרון ובספינה, מטמא משום דגזר שמא יוציא ראשו ורובו לחוץ בקרון ובספינה ויאהל על הגושא, כי נקל להוציא ראשו ורובו מספינה וקרון. ורבי, דמטמא אפי' בשידה תיבה ומגדל – גזר אפי' בהנך, דלמא יוציא ראשו ורובו לחוץ. והתניא בניחותא, הנכנס לארץ העמים בשידה תיבה ומגדל טהור עד שיוציא ראשו ורובו. מכלל דבקרון ובספינה טמא, אע"פ שלא הוציא ראשו ורובו, דנקל הוא להוציא בקרון ובספינה. והשתא דמייתי בפ' "בכל מערבין" (עירובין ל:) ובמס' חגיגה (דף כה.) מהאי ברייתא דהנכנס לארץ העמים בשידה תיבה ומגדל, דפליגי ר' יוסי בר"י ורבי באהל זרוק אי שמיה אהל אי לא, היינו במאי דבעי למימר בשינויא קמא, דפליגי באהל זרוק. אבל ד] שינויא [בתרא] ליכנס בארץ העמים לא פליגי באהל זרוק, אבל לגבי מת הוא דפליגי בה, כדתניא: ואם היתה מונחת בו – טהורה, דאהל זרוק שמיה אהל, והיא ר' יוסי בר"י. (ו) אבל רבי מטמא, דאהל זרוק לא שמיה אהל. ומתחיל ומונה מיד. כשנטהר מונה ה] [למקום] שהפסיק בתחילת לצרעתו, דימי לצרעתו לא עלו לו מן המנין. אמר רב חסדא לא שנו. דימי ספרו וימי גמרו אין עולים לו למנין נזירותו אלא בנזירות מועטת, של ל' יום, ונצטרע בנתיים, ולאחר שנתרפא וגילח לסוף ימי גמרו, וכשגילח שנית אחר ימי ספרו – אז ודאי אינו יכול לגלח לסוף ל' מתחילת ימי נזירותו, שהרי אין גידול שיער פחות מל' יום, וצריך למנות ל' יום לנזירותו משנתרפא ומספר. אבל בנזירות מרובה. שנדר כל כך ימים, שאחר ימי לצרעתו איכא ל' יום אחר שגילח תגלחת שנית לצרעתו, דשפיר איכא כדי גידול שער מסלק נמי סלקי ליה. מתיב רב שרביא מתחיל ומונה מיד ואינו מבטל הקודמים. אומר ר"י: דהיינו מתני' בודאי, (אף) א) [אך] כי החליף הלשון. אילימא בנזירות מועטת הא בעי גידול שיער. ומאי קאמר אינו מבטל הקודמים? והלא על כרחיה יסתור קודמין! ב) אלא לאו בנזירות מרובה, וקתני: מתחיל ומונה מיד, דשמעינן מתחיל ומונה לאחר ימי ספרו. אלמא: ימי ספרו אין עולין! ו] הוא מותיב לה והוא מפרק לה: בנזירות בת חמשים יום איירי מתני'. והיינו נזירות מועטת כרב חסדא, וה"ק: לא שנו אלא נזירות מועטת, כלומר (אי) שאין לו לעשות רק ימי לצרעתו, ז] כבתחילת ימי נזירות מועטת כגון דיתיב עשרים בנזירות ואיתיליד ביה לצרעת, דמגלח בלצרעתו, והדר יתיב שלשים יומים דנזיר – דהא אית ליה גידול שיער, כלומר, וככה"ג דין הוא שלא יעלו ימי לצרעתו כל עיקר, ודין הוא שלא יבטל הקודמין. שאם ימי גמרו וימי חלוטו יעלו לנזירות שבעה ימים או ארבע (או) עשר ימים כפי מה שיעלו – לריך הוא להוסיף על הנדר, כדי שיהא שם גידול שיער. ובכי האי גוונא איירי מתניתין. ונזירות בת חמשים לאו דווקא, דהוא הדין לנזירות בת ארבעים, היכא

א) גירסת א"מ: ב) שייך לע"ב.

פי' הרא"ש

לא דכ"ע משום גושא ורבי דמטמא סבר דאוהל זרוק. פי' המטלטל ע"י אדם או בהמה הנושאים אותו לאו שמיה אהל לחוץ בפני הטומאה ומר סבר שמיה אהל ועדיף מטלית המנפנפת וספינה שטה ע"פ המים דתנן במסכת אהלות שאין חוצצין בפני הטומאה ולא מביאין דמשום דרגלי האדם או הבהמה הנושאים אותם נוגעים בארץ עדיף טפי: והתניא בניחותא. ר"י בר יהודה או' תיבה שהיא מלאה כלים וזרקה על פני המת טמאה דכיון דזרקה באוהל הוי כטלית המנפנפת ולא שמיה אהל ואם היתה מונחת טהורה פי' מונחת ע"ג בהמה או אדם הנושאים אותה דאוהל זרוק שמיה אהל: ה"ג ואיבעי' אימא דכ"ע משום אוירא ולהכי מטמא [רבי] ר"י בר יהודה סבר דבעומד על הגשר או הנכנס לה בקרון או בספינה הוא דגזרו על אוירא אבל בשידה תיבה ומגדל לא גזור: והתניא בניחותא ומייתי סייעתא דאיכא מאן דמטמא בקרון ובספינה ומטהר בשידה תיבה ומגדל משום מילתא דלא שכיחא הוא: ואבע"א דכ"ע משום גושא. פי' הא דמפליג האי תנא בין שידה תיבה ומגדל לקרון וספינה לאו כדקאמרת דכ"ע משום אוירא והא דמטהר בשידה תיבה ומגדל משו' דמילתא דלא שכיחא לא גזרו רבנן. אלא כ"ע משום גושא והא דמטהר ר"י בר יהודה בשידה תיבה [ומגדל] משום דאוהל זרוק שמיה אהל כדתרצי' לפלוגתיהו לעיל וקרון או ספינה דמטמא משום דגזר שמא יוציא ראשו ורובו לחוץ ויאהיל על הגוש אבל בשידה תיבה ומגדל אין נקל כ"כ לפתוח הדלת להוציא ראשו. והתניא בניחותא הנכנס וכו' טהור עד שיוציא ראשו ורובו לשם אלמא הא דמטמא בקרון או בספינה משום דגזרינן שמא יוציא ראשו ורובו: אמר רב חסדא לא שנו הא דימי גמרו וימי ספרו אין עולין לו לימי נזירותו אלא בנזיר מועטת. שנזר ל' יום ונצטרע משום כל כשיתרפא מצרעתו צריך לגלח לצרעתו ואחר אותה תגלחת צריך לנהוג נזירות עד שיהא שערו ראוי לתגלחת דאין גידול שער פחות מל' יום אבל בנזיר מרובה שאחר ימי צרעתו נשארו עדיין ל' יום מנזיר דאיכא גידול שער מיסלק נמי סלקי ליה: מתיב רב שרביא מתחיל ומונה מיד ואינו מבטל את הקודמים היינו מתני' אלא שהביאה בהפך ואי בנזירות מועטת של ל' יום היכי קאמר דאינו סותר את הקודמים הא בעי גידול שער

סה א ב מיי' פי"א מהל' טומאת מת הלכה ה:

עירובין ל: חגיגה כה. גיטין ח:

[עירובין סג: וש"נ]

[תוספתא דאהלות פי"ח]

[לעיל כח:]

נוסחת הריב"ן

א) אויר: ב) סברי: ג) המת טמאה: ד) מעט בלע"ז ומשום: ה) מטמא רבי הכא: ו) (והתניא וכו' ורובו) ליתא בכ"י: ז) והא דתני לעיל: ח) מסלק לה כו' ומשוי לה כלי דלעיל קסבר כו' וכדקתני סיפא: ט) מועטת שקבל עליו כו' ל' יום דמשמע בשעשה כו' שאין ימים הללו עולין כו' אתה אומר שאינו עולין: י) משתיירים שם כו' גידול שיער לנזירות טהרה לאחר: כ) ימי תגלחתו:

הגהות הב"ח

(א) רש"י ד"ה הנכנס וכו' והא מתניתא רבי יוסי: (ב) ד"ה והתניא וכו' שמיה אהל והיינו דקתני בסיפא: (ג) ד"ה אלא בנזירות מועטת בזמן שקבל וכו' ונחלט שאין ימים הללו עולין: (ד) תוספות ד"ה לימא וכו' אי משום גושא ורבי יוסי בר' יהודה מטהר דסבר דכיון כצ"ל ותיבות משום גושא נמחק: (ה) ד"ה ה"ג ואי וכו' דמטהר סבר אף כי נמי וכו' הנכנס לארץ העמים וכו' דטעמא דמשום וכו' תיבה ומגדל סבר גזרו אפי' כצ"ל והד"א עם ד"ה דבעי וכו' היינו למאי בהאהל זרוק אבל לגבי שינויא בארץ העמים וכו' היתה מונחת טהורה כצ"ל ותיבת בו נמחק: (ו) בא"ד רבי יוסי בר"י היא אבל:

הגהות מהר"ב רנשבורג א] רש"י ד"ה הנכנס וכו' דהיינו תורן וקרוי פוס"ט כו'. נ"ב: ב] ד"ה והתניא דמסייעא ליה. תיבת ליה נמחק: ג] תוד"ה ה"ג וכו' משוט הספינה. תיבת משוט וכו' להספינה נמחק ונ"ב שוט כצ"ל. א"מ ועיש"ש בפירושו: ד] ד"ה והתניא כו' שינויא בתרא ליכנס וכו' א"מ ונ"ב להני שינויי כצ"ל. א"מ: ה] ד"ה ומתחיל וכו' למקום שהפסיק בתחילה נ"ב תיבות אלו למקום שהפסיק בתחילה נמחק ונ"ב במקום שהפסיק לצרעתו. א"מ: ו] ד"ה אילימא וכו' אין עולין. כאן הס"ד ואח"כ מה"ד הוא מותיב לה וכו': ז] בא"ד והיינו נזירות מועטת לרב חסדא וכו' כבתחילה. תיבת כבתחילה נמחק ונ"ב כשבתחילה:

היכא דאיתיליד ביה צרעת עשרה ימים וזה הכלל: נזירות מועטת קרי מקום שאין לו למנות רק ל' יום משהתחיל הצרעת, עד סוף ימי נזירותו. אבל בנזירות מרובה, כלומר כשהתחיל צרעתו היה לו למנות עדיין שלשים וא' יום, או שלשים ושנים ימים לנזירות, וכ"ש יותר, כגון נזירות בת חמשים וא' או יותר, ואיתיליד ביה צרעת בכ' – אז ודאי לא תוכל לומר דכל ימי צרעתו אינן עולים כל עיקר, דמנין הימים העוברים מיהא יעלו לו. כגון מי שנדר חמשים ושלשה, ויתיב עשרים ואיתיליד ביה צרעת*, ב] וארבעה עשר יום – שלשה מימי צרעתו יעלו, ואחד עשר לא יעלו, וצריך הוא למנות על ג] [עשרים] ושלשה ל', יום דפחות לא יהיו לו גידול שער. והיינו דנקט: והדר יתיב שלשים ימים דנזיר. **דהא** אית ליה גידול שער. צריך לומר דה"ק: ועל נזירות מועטת כי האי לא תקשי לך כדאקשת מעיקרא: אילימא בנזירות מועטת – הא בעינן גידול שיער, ויסתור הקודמים – דהא אית ליה גידול שער. **מתיב** רמי בר חמא נזיר שהיה טמא בספק לו, אולי נטמא במת. ומוחלט בספק – אולי הוחלט. ומיירי בנזיר ודאי, אך הוא ספק אם נטמא במת אם לא, וכן הוא ספק אם הוא מצורע מוחלט או לא. הר"ף. *)**אוכל** בקדשים לאחר ששים יום. משום

אֶלָּא לָאו בִּנְזִירוּת מְרוּבָּה, וְקָתָנֵי: מַתְחִיל וּמוֹנֶה מִיָּד! הוּא מוֹתִיב לָהּ, וְהוּא מְפָרֵק לָהּ: בִּנְזִירוּת בַּת חֲמִשִּׁים יוֹם, דְּיָתֵיב עֶשְׂרִין וְאִתְיְלִידָא בֵּיהּ צָרַעַת. מְגַלֵּחַ צָרַעְתּוֹ וַהֲדַר יָתֵיב תְּלָתִין יוֹמִין דְּנָזִיר, דְּהָא אִית לֵיהּ גִּידּוּל שֵׂעָר. מְתִיב רָמִי בַּר חָמָא: *נָזִיר שֶׁהָיָה טָמֵא בְּסָפֵק וּמוּחְלָט בְּסָפֵק – אוֹכֵל

אֶלָּא לָאו בִּנְזִירוּת מְרוּבָּה א) וְקָאָמַר מַתְחִיל וּמוֹנֶה מִיָּד. מֵאוֹתוֹ יוֹם שֶׁעוֹמֵד בּוֹ, וּמַשְׁלִים לְאוֹתָן יָמִים שֶׁלִּפְנֵי חִלּוּטוֹ. אֲבָל יְמֵי חִלּוּטוֹ מִיהָא אֵין עוֹלִין לוֹ. בִּנְזִירוּת בַּת חֲמִשִּׁים יוֹם כו' א] (א). דְּאִי אָמְרַתְּ דְּעוֹלִין – לָא פָּשׁ לֵיהּ כְּדֵי גִּידּוּל שֵׂיעָר לְאַחַר תִּגְלַחַת צָרַעְתּוֹ. הִלְכָּךְ דִּלְבָתַר הָכִי מִיבָּעֵי לֵיהּ לְמֵיתַב תְּלָתִין יוֹמִין מִנָּזִיר, דְּהָא אִית לֵיהּ גִּידּוּל שֵׂיעָר. מְתִיב רָמִי בַּר חָמָא נָזִיר שֶׁהָיָה טָמֵא בְּסָפֵק וּמוּחְלָט בְּסָפֵק. ב) שֶׁנִּטְמָא (ב) בְּסָפֵק בְּיוֹם רִאשׁוֹן שֶׁל נְזִירוּת, וְסָפֵק הוּא לוֹ אִם נֶחְלַט, וְנִרְפָּא בְּיוֹם רִאשׁוֹן שֶׁל נְזִירוּתוֹ. אוֹכֵל

דספק מצורע הוא, ואסור לאכול בקדשים עד שיטהר מספק לצרעתו, ויביא קרבנות מצורע, דמחוסר כפורים אסור לאכול בקדשים. אבל משום נזירות טמא – לא מיתסר בקדשים, אע"ג דצריך נמי להביא קרבן – משום דאין טומאה יוצאה עליו מגופו לא מיקרי מחוסר כפורים, כדאמרינן בפ' "ארבעה מחוסרי כפרה" (כריתות י.) דדוקא במי שטומאתו יוצאה מגופו קרי מחוסר כפורים. כיצד? נזר נזירות שלשים יום, וביום הראשון אירע לו ספק טומאה וספק טומאת צרעת, דספק אם פרחה בו צרעת ממש אם בוהק הוא. והשתא מיהא, בתר דנתרפא לגמרי – מזה ושונה וטובל, ונטהר מספק טומאת מת ד] אפי' לסוף שבעה. בא לו לגלח כדין נזיר טמא או כדין מצורע שנתרפא – אומרים לו להמתין מלגלח עד שלשים יום, [דאימא] נזיר טהור גמור אתה, שלא נטמאת, ונזיר טהור אינו מגלח אלא על הדמים בסוף שלשים יום, כשנגמר נזירותו, כדכתיב "תער לא יעבור על ראשו עד מלאת ימי נזרו". לסוף שלשים יום מגלח. ומשפטי הבאת קרבנותיו מפורש לקמן בפרק "שני נזירים" (דף ס.), שמביא לפרי מצורע שחוטה ומשולחת, וחטאת העוף הבאה על הספק – משום ספק נזיר טמא, ועולת בהמה – משום ספק נזיר טהור. [ואע"פ] שאינו יכול לגלח אלא על אחד מהם – ה] [הא אמרינן] דאם גילח על אחד מהם – יצא, ומתנה עליהם. ועדיין אסור לאכול בקדשים, דשמא מוחלט היה, וטעון עוד תגלחת שנית והבאת קרבנות, [כדכתיב] בפרשת מצורע "והנה נרפא נגע הצרעת, ולקח שתי צפרים, ושחט את הצפור האחת על מים חיים, ושלח את הצפור החיה, וגלח את כל שערו וישב מחוץ לאהלו שבעת ימים, והיה ביום השביעי יגלח ורחץ בשרו במים, וביום השמיני יקח שני כבשים אחד לעולה ואחד לאשם וכבש אחד לחטאת", וזה אי אפשר לגלח סוף שבעה לתגלחת ראשונה – כי אולי אינו מצורע, אבל נזיר טמא היה. וצריך להתחיל ימי נזירותו שלשים יום שנזר, כי אותן שלשים יום שמנה לא עלו לנזירותו, דקרינא ביה "והימים הראשונים יפלו", כיון דמספקא לן בנזיר טמא. ו] ושלשים יום השניים הם ימי נזירות טהרה, וקרינן ביה "תער לא יעבור על ראשו עד מלאת ימי נזרו". לסוף ששים מגלח. ובהך תגלחת שניה ליכא לספוקי בנזיר טמא, דמספק נזיר טמא נפק בתגלחת ראשונה עד סוף ל' יום הראשונים, אבל בנזיר טהור איכא לספוקי, או בתגלחת ימי ספרו של מצורע. ומביא עולת בהמה משום ספק נזיר טהור, כדי לגלח על הדמים, ומתנה עליה. למחרת של יום תגלחתו יביא קרבנות מצורע כדי להתירו לאכול בקדשים. ומביא חטאת העוף, דאילו חטאת בהמה אינו בא על הספק, אך יפקיר נכסיו ויביא חטאת העוף, כדין מצורע עני. ואשם נמי יביא לר"ש דאמר: אשם מצי לאתנויי ביה כשלמים. ולרבנן דר"ש אית להו דאשם אינו מעכבו לאכול בקדשים. ועדיין הוא אסור לשתות יין ולטמאות למתים – דשמא מוחלט היה, ושני תגלחיות הללו שעשה למצורע היו לגמרו ולספרו, ואינו עולה לתגלחת נזיר טהור, כדאמרינן לקמן בפ' "ב' נזירים" (שם). לכך טעון עוד שני תגלחות, אחד לנזיר טמא, ואחד לנזיר טהור. לסוף תשעים יגלח שלישית, ובהך שלישית ליכא לספוקי במצורע כלל כי אם בנזיר טהור או בנזיר טמא. והך תגלחת אי אפשר לגלח אלא עד סוף ל' יום, הרי תשעים יום. דלא מיבעיא בנזירות מועטת, דצריך להמתין ל' משום גידול שער אף לרב חסדא, אלא אף בנזירות מרובה, כדפריש ואזיל – משום דספירא דימי צרעתו אין עולין לו כל עיקר, ודלא כרב חסדא. לכך צריך להמתין לתגלחת שלישית אחר תגלחת שניה כמנין ימי הנזירות ז] (שעבר), אולי נזיר מצורע הוה ולא נזיר טמא. ולסוף תשעים כשמגלח שלישית ליכא לספוקי במצורע כלל, אלא או בנזיר טהור או בנזיר טמא, ויביא עולת בהמה – משום ספק נזיר טהור, ולגלח על הדמים, וחטאת העוף – משום ספק נזיר טמא. ועדיין אסור לשתות יין ולטמא למתים – דשמא מוחלט היה, ונזיר טמא, ועלו לו שנים תגלחיות ראשונות לצרעתו, והשלישית לנזיר טמא – לכך צריך למנות עוד ל' לנזירות טהרה. לסוף ל' יגלח ויביא קרבן טהרה לבד, ומתנה ביה, כדמפרש לקמן בפ' "שני נזירים", ומותר לשתות יין ולטמאות למתים. והיינו דקתני: ושותה יין ומיטמא למתים לאחר ק"כ יום. **ומדקדק** הר"ס: דע"כ צריך לומר שהוא מגלח ביום ל', שאם לא היה מגלח עד יום [שלשים ואחד] כשאר נזיר – א"כ הוה מגלח תגלחת שניה יום ששים ואחד, וא"כ לא היה אוכל בקדשים עד יום ששים ושנים. שהרי אחר תגלחת מצורע היה טובל, ולא היה יכול להביא קרבנותיו עד למחר, כדאמר °לעיל בפ' שלישי (דף יח): גלח בס' – מביא קרבנותיו בס'. אלא ביום ל' מגלח, ומביא אחד מג' קרבנותיו דנזיר טהור, עולה או שלמים, כדי לגלח על הדמים – דאולי נזיר טהור היה. ואע"ג דשאר נזיר אינו מגלח עד שלשים ואחד יום – היינו מדרבנן, דמדאורייתא ביום ל' מצי מגלח, לרב מתנא משום דמקצת היום ככולו, או לבר פדא דמכ"ט יום נשלם הנזירות. והלכך, נזיר זה דעדיין אינו שותה ולא מיטמא למתים – לא העמידו דבריהם, ואוקמה אדאורייתא, ושרי ליה לגלח ביום ל'. מיהו, קשה מתגלחת שלישית, דאינו שותה יין – ואפי' הכי בשלשים ואחד! אלא נראה דמשום אכילת קדשים הקילו בשני תגלחיות ראשונות לכתחילה ביום ל'. מהרפ"ש. ה"ג: ואכתי אינו מביא קרבנות נזיר טמא בו ביום, דכיון שהוא צריך לטבול אחר התגלחת, כדין מצורע שטובל אחר כל התגלחות, ומיחזי כאילו היא טבילת נזיר טמא ביום שביעי, אחר דבנזיר טמא נמי מספקא ליה, דאז אינו מביא עד שמיני. ולכך אינו יכול להביא קרבנות נזיר טמא עד למחרת יום תגלחתו, דהיינו ביום שלשים ואחד. וביום שלשים ואחד מביא חטאת העוף כדין נזיר טמא, דשמא הוא טמא ולא מוחלט. וימנה עוד ל' יום מיום שלשים ואחד שמביא קרבן טומאה, וכדרבנן בפ' ג' (שם) דאמר: הביא חטאתו אע"פ שלא הביא אשמו. מונה ח] יום ששים שהוא יום ל' למניינו ומגלח, כדמפרש. ולמחרת דהיינו יום ששים ואחד מביא קרבן לצרעתו – חטאת העוף כמו מצורע עני, ואם עשיר הוא – מפקיר נכסיו. ומותר לאכול בקדשים, דאשמו אינו מעכב לאכול בקדשים לרבנן, ולר' שמעון דאמר מביאין קדשים לבית הפסול מביא גם אשם, ומתנה כשלמים. וזה ששנינו (זבחים עו.) ר"ש אומר: למחרת מביא אשמו ולוגו, ואומר: אם מצורע הוא – זה אשמו וזה לוגו, ואם לאו – יהא שלמים. ואותו אשם טעון לפון ומתן בהונות כו'. הרי למחרת ששים יום, דהיינו יום ששים ואחד – אוכל בקדשים, דכבר גילח ב' תגלחות אם היה מצורע – כבר נטהר. ומיהא תגלחת שלישית ליכא לפרושי הכי, שהרי אינו טובל אחר התגלחת, כיון שעשו לו ספיקות של מצורע. וצריך לומר דודאי בב' תגלחיות אחרונות אינו מגלח עד יום ל' ואחד ט] (מגלח ל' יום על שלשים ואחד), שמניינו התחיל ביום ששים ואחד. ומביא עולת בהמה לגלח על הדמים, וגם מביא חטאת עוף משום ספק נזיר טמא, כי בתגלחת ראשונה – אולי מוחלט היה, ולא עלו לו לנזירותו. ומתחיל מניינו מיום [ששים] ואחד, ומשלים חמשים ותשעה יום על ששים ואחד שהן מאה ועשרים יום. ומגלח ביום קכ"א שהוא ל' ואחד יום למניינו, ומביא קרבן טהרה לבד, ומותר ביום קכ"א לשתות יין י] ומשלים נזירותו. ויש ליתן טעם בדבר דדוקא בשני תגלחיות ראשונות דאיכא לספוקי בספק מצורע – הקילו להיות ביום ל', אבל בשתים אחרונות שאין עליו עוד ספק מצורע – השווהו לשאר נזיר שמגלח ביום שלשים ואחד, ולכך קאמר: ושותה ביין ומטמא למתים אחר ק"כ יום. **ותני** עלה [בד"א] **בנזירות מועטת דאז די לו בק"כ אבל בנזירות בת שנתה אוכל בקדשים לאחר שתי שנים**. כדפרישית, שממתין מלגלח ראשונה עד שנה, דשמא נזיר טהור היה, ושניה עד שתי שנים – דשמא לא היה מוחלט, אלא נזיר טמא. שלישית עד שלש שנים – דשמא מוחלט היה ולא טמא מת. רביעית עד ארבע שנים – דשמא מוחלט וטמא מת היה, וגילח ראשונה ושניה לצרעתו, שלישית לנזיר טמא, רביעית לנזיר טהור.

*) שייך לדף נו.

ה"ג

שער אחר שג[ילח] לצרעתו וקתני מ[תחיל] ומונה מיד ואינו מ[בטל] את הקודמים אלא [על] הקודמים הוא מ[תחיל] למנות להשלים נזי[רותו:] בנזיר בת נ' יומי א[יירי] מתני'. והיינו נ[זירות] מועטת דרב חסדא [והכי] קאמר לא שנו [אלא] בנזיר מועטת כ[לומר] כשהתחילו ימי צר[עתו] לא נשאר לו [מימי] נזירותו אלא נזיר מו[עטת] דהיינו ל' יום דאין [נזיר] פחות מל' יום: [והדר] יתיב ל' יום להש[לים] נזירותו דהא אית [ליה] גידול שער ולכך דין [הוא] שלא יסתור הקוד[מים] וגם אין עולה לו ד[בעי'] גידול שער. אבל ב[נזיר] מרובה כגון שנדר פ' [יום] ולסוף כ' יום נ[תנגע] ונטהר וגילח לסוף ל' [יום] לנגעו מסלק סלקי [ליה] כיון שנשאר מנזי[רותו] כדי גידול שער ולפע[מים] עולים מקצתן כגון [אם] שהה בנגעו מ' או נ' [יום:] נזיר שהיה טמא ב[ספק] ספק אם נטמא [במת] וספק אם הוא מצ[ורע] מוחלט צ"ע במ[סכת] נגעים היכי משכחת [לה] ספק מוחלט דתנן ר[פ"ק] דנגעים כל ספק נ[געים] טהור חוץ מזה [ועוד] אחר והנך ב' הם טמ[אים] ודאי. ותנן נמי בה[הוא] פרקא כל ספק נ[געים] בתחילה טהור ומש[נשקק] לטומאה ספקו ט[מא:] אוכל בקדשים [אחר] ששים יום אבל [קודם] לכן לא דס' מצורע [הוא] ועד שיביא כפרתו א[סור] לאכול בקדשים [אבל] משום ספק נזיר טמא [לא] מיתסר בקדשים [דלא] מיקרי מחוסרי כ[פרה] ליאסר בקדשים אלא [מי] שטומאה יוצאת [עליו] מגופו כדאי' [פ"ד] מחוסרי כפרה. כיצד [נזיר] ל' יום וביום הרא[שון] אירע לו ס' טומאת [מת] וספק צרעת מזה וש[ונה] וטובל וטהור מטו[מאת] מת בא לו לגלח [כדין] נזיר טמא או כדין מצ[ורע] שנתרפא או' לו ה[מתן] עד ל' יום דשמא [נזיר] טהור הוא ולא מצ[ורע] ונזיר טהור אינו מ[גלח] אלא על הדמים דכ[תיב] תער לא יעבור על ר[אשו] עד מלאת ימי נזרו: ל[סוף] ל' יום מגלח [ספק] תגלחת מצורע ספק [נזיר] טמא ספק נזיר ט[הור] ומביא ב' צפרין [כדין] תגלחת של ימי חל[וטו.] וחטאת העוף הבאה [על] הספק משום ספק [נזיר] טמא ועולת בה[מה] משום ספק נזיר ט[הור] כדי לגלח על הד[מים] (ולמחרת יום תגלח[תו)] דאמרינן אם גילח ע[ל א'] משלשתן יצא ומ[תנה] עליה שאם לא ה[גיע] זמנו לגלח שתהיה ע[ולת] נדבה א) בא לו ל[גלח] שנית אחרי ז' ימי ס[פרו] או' לו המתן שמא [נזיר] טמא היה ולא מצ[ורע] וצריך למנות ל' [יום] לנזירות טהרה. אח[ר ל'] יום מגלח ספק תג[לחת] של ימי ספרו ספק נז[יר] טהור ומביא ע[ולת] בהמה משום ס' [נזיר] טהור כדי לגלח [על] הדמים ולמחרת [יום] תגלחתו מביא ק[רבן] מצורע כדי להת[ירו] בקדשים ומביא חט[את] העוף דחטאת בה[מה] אינה באה על הספ[ק או] יפקיר נכסיו וי[ביא] חטאת העוף כדין מצורע עני. ואשם לר"ש דאמר דמצי לאתנויי בשלמים ולרבנן דר"ש אשם אינו מעכבו מלאכול בקדשים. ועדיין הוא אסור לשתות וליטמא למתים דשמא מוחלט היה ותגלחת מצורע אינו עולה לו לתגלחת נזיר טהור ולא לתגלחת נזיר טמא כדאמר לקמן בפ' ב' נזירים וטעון עוד ב' תגלחות א' לנזיר טמא וא' לנזיר טהור ובתוך ל' א"א לו לגלח דשמא מוחלט היה ולא נזיר טמא ולאחר ל' יום מגלח ס' נזיר טהור וס' נזיר טמא ומביא חטאת העוף לס' נזיר טמא ועולת בהמה לגלח על הדמים ומתנה ועדיין אסור לשתות יין ולטמא למתים דשמא מוחלט וטמא היה ולאחר ל' יום מגלח ומביא קרבן הנזיר טהור ושותה

א) נראה דצ"ל ולמחרת יום תגלחתו מביא חטאת העוף הבא על הספק בא לו כו'.

נ"ל ב' תגלחת מצורע

לקמן נט:

נוסחת הריב"ן

א) וקתני: ב) ומוחלט בספק. ספק הוא לו אם כו' והשאר ליתא:

הגהות הב"ח

(א) רש"י ד"ה בנזירות בת חמשים יום דיתיב עשרים ואתילידא ביה צרעת דמגלח לצרעתו ימי חלוטו אין עולין לו דאי אמרת דעולין וכו' ל' יומין דנזיר: (ב) ד"ה מתיב וכו' שנטמא במת בספק:

גליון הש"ס

תום' ד"ה ומדקדק הר"ס כדאמר לעיל בפ"ג. נ"ל פרק שני דף כד ע"ב:

הגהות מהר"ב רנשבורג

א] רש"י ד"ה בנזירת בת חמשים יום וכו' דיתיב עשרין דאי אמרת וכו' הלכך אין עולין לכבר וכו' כצ"ל: ב] תום' ד"ה (מעבר לדף) הוא מותיב וכו' וארבעה עשר יום מימי לצרעתו ג' יעלו כצ"ל: ג] בא"ד ואחד עשר וכו' וצריך וכו' על עשרים. תיבת עשרים נמחק וצ"ב חמשים ושלשה עוד ל' וכו' כצ"ל: ד] ד"ה אוכל וכו' ונטהר מספק טומאת מת אפי'. נמחק תיבת אפי' וצ"ב אם לסוף וכו' עד שלשים יום דשמא נזיר הוי' כצ"ל: ה] בא"ד ואע"פ שאינו יכול לגלח אלא על הדמים הא אמרינן. תיבת הא אמרינן נמחקו וצ"ב ואמרינן דאם וכו' כצ"ל: ו] בא"ד כיון דמספקא לן בנזיר טמא א"כ שלשים יום וכו' כצ"ל: ז] בא"ד כמנין ימי הנזירות אוכ נזיר וכו' כצ"ל: ח] ד"ה ומדקדק הר"ס וכו' אע"כ שלא הביא אשמו מונה ויום ששים וכו' למנינו מגלח וכו' כצ"ל: ט] בא"ד וצ"ל דודאי וכו' עד יום שלשים ואחד מגלח שלשים יום על שלשים ואחד. מן תיבת מגלח בתרא עד ואחד נמחק. וצ"ב ומגלח יום תשעים ואחד וכו' כצ"ל: י] בא"ד ביום קכ"א לשתות יין והשלים וכו' כצ"ל:

אוֹכֵל בַּקֳּדָשִׁים לְאַחַר שִׁשִּׁים יוֹם, וְשׁוֹתֶה יַיִן וּמִיטַּמֵּא לַמֵּתִים לְאַחַר מֵאָה וְעֶשְׂרִים יוֹם. *וְתָנֵי עֲלָהּ: בַּמֶּה דְּבָרִים אֲמוּרִים — בִּנְזִירוּת מוּעֶטֶת, אֲבָל בִּנְזִירוּת בַּת שָׁנָה — אוֹכֵל בַּקֳּדָשִׁים לְאַחַר שְׁתֵּי שָׁנִים, וְשׁוֹתֶה יַיִן וּמִיטַּמֵּא לַמֵּתִים לְאַחַר אַרְבַּע שָׁנִים. וְאִי סָלְקָא דַּעְתָּךְ סָלְקִין לֵיהּ יוֹמֵי — תִּיסְגֵּי לֵיהּ בְּשָׁלֹשׁ שָׁנִים וּשְׁלֹשִׁים יוֹם! וְעוֹד מְתִיב רַב אַשִׁי: °*אֵין לִי אֶלָּא יְמֵי טוּמְאָה שֶׁאֵין עוֹלִין לוֹ מִן הַמִּנְיָן, יְמֵי חִלּוּטוֹ מִנַּיִן? וְדִין הוּא: יְמֵי טוּמְאָה מְגַלֵּחַ וּמֵבִיא קָרְבָּן, וִימֵי חִלּוּטוֹ מְגַלֵּחַ וּמֵבִיא קָרְבָּן, מַה יְּמֵי טוּמְאָתוֹ אֵין עוֹלִין לוֹ מִן הַמִּנְיָן — אַף יְמֵי חִלּוּטוֹ אֵין עוֹלִין לוֹ מִן הַמִּנְיָן. לֹא, אִם אָמַרְתָּ בִּימֵי טוּמְאָתוֹ — שֶׁכֵּן מְבַטֵּל בָּהֶן אֶת הַקּוֹדְמִים, תֹּאמַר בִּימֵי חִלּוּטוֹ שֶׁאֵין מְבַטֵּל בָּהֶן אֶת הַקּוֹדְמִין! אָמַרְתָּ: קַל וָחוֹמֶר הוּא: וּמַה נָּזִיר בַּקֶּבֶר, שֶׁשְּׂעָרוֹ רָאוּי לְתִגְלַחַת נְזִירוּת — אֵין עוֹלִין לוֹ מִן הַמִּנְיָן. יְמֵי חִלּוּטוֹ, שֶׁאֵין שְׂעָרוֹ רָאוּי לְתִגְלַחַת נְזִירוּת — לֹא כָּל שֶׁכֵּן?! וְאֵין לִי אֶלָּא יְמֵי חִלּוּטוֹ, יְמֵי סְפָרוֹ מִנַּיִן? וְדִין הוּא:

מַה

אוֹכֵל בַּקֳּדָשִׁים לְאַחַר שִׁשִּׁים (א) וְשׁוֹתֶה יַיִן וּמִטַּמֵּא לַמֵּתִים לְאַחַר ק"כ יוֹם. שֶׁאִילּוּ א) הָיָה טָמֵא וַדַּאי וּמוּחְלָט וַדַּאי — הָיָה צָרִיךְ לְגַלֵּחַ לְאַלְתַּר תִּגְלַחַת צָרַעַת, וּבְסוֹף שִׁבְעָה יָמִים דְּתִגְלַחַת לִימֵי סְפָרוֹ מֵבִיא קָרְבַּן צָרַעַת, וְאוֹכֵל בַּקֳּדָשִׁים, וְאַח"כ לִמְנוֹת שִׁבְעָה דְּתִגְלַחַת נְזִירוּת טוּמְאָה, וְאַח"כ לִמְנוֹת שְׁלֹשִׁים דִּנְזִירוּת טָהֳרָה. מִפְּנֵי שֶׁהַצָּרַעַת דּוֹחָה לְתִגְלַחַת דְּנָזִיר, כִּדְתְנַן לְקַמָּן בְּאִידָךְ פִּירְקִין (דף נז.) דְּתִגְלַחַת הַנֶּגַע דּוֹחָה לְתִגְלַחַת הַנָּזִיר בִּזְמַן שֶׁהוּא וַדַּאי, וְלֹא בִּזְמַן שֶׁהוּא סָפֵק. וְנִמְצָא אוֹכֵל בַּקֳּדָשִׁים לְאַחַר שִׁבְעָה יָמִים, וְשׁוֹתֶה יַיִן וּמִיטַּמֵּא לַמֵּתִים לְאַחַר אַרְבָּעִים וְאַרְבָּעָה יוֹם. אֲבָל עַכְשָׁיו שֶׁהוּא טָמֵא מְסֻפָּק וּמוּחְלָט מְסֻפָּק, שֶׁאֵינוֹ יָכוֹל לְגַלֵּחַ תִּגְלַחַת צָרַעַת לְאַלְתַּר, לְפִי שֶׁאֵינָהּ דּוֹחָה לְתִגְלַחַת הַנָּזִיר בִּזְמַן שֶׁהוּא סָפֵק — הִלְכָּךְ שׁוֹהֶא ב) אוֹכֵל בַּקֳּדָשִׁים לְאַחַר שִׁשִּׁים כו'. כֵּיצַד? בָּא לוֹ לְגַלֵּחַ תִּגְלַחַת צָרַעַת לְאַלְתַּר, אוֹמְרִים לוֹ: שֶׁמָּא לֹא הָיִיתָ טָמֵא וְלֹא מוּחְלָט, וְאִי אַתָּה רַשַּׁאי לְגַלֵּחַ עַד שְׁלֹשִׁים יוֹם. בָּא לוֹ לְסוֹף שְׁלֹשִׁים ג) וּבִיקֵּשׁ לִשְׁתּוֹת יַיִן — אוֹמְרִים לוֹ: טָמֵא הָיִיתָ וְלֹא מוּחְלָט, וְתִגְלַחַת רִאשׁוֹנָה שֶׁעָשִׂיתָ הִיא תִּגְלַחַת טוּמְאָה, וְאִי אַתָּה מוּתָּר לְגַלֵּחַ כָּל שְׁלֹשִׁים יוֹם מִפְּנֵי שֶׁחָלָה עָלָיו נְזִירוּת טָהֳרָה. וְעוֹמֵד שְׁלֹשִׁים יוֹם ד) וּמְגַלֵּחַ, הֲרֵי שִׁשִּׁים יוֹם. בָּא לוֹ לִשְׁתּוֹת יַיִן — אוֹמְרִים לוֹ: מוּחְלָט הָיִיתָ וְלֹא טָמֵא, וְהַלָּלוּ שְׁנַיִם תִּגְלָחִיּוֹת שֶׁעָשִׂיתָ — הֵן שְׁתֵּי תִגְלָחִיּוֹת שֶׁל צָרַעַת, וְעַכְשָׁיו צָרִיךְ אַתָּה לְהַתְחִיל לְמִנְיַן נְזִירוּתְךָ. וְעָשָׂה שְׁלֹשִׁים יוֹם וּמְגַלֵּחַ — הֲרֵי תִּשְׁעִים יוֹם. בָּא לוֹ לִשְׁתּוֹת יַיִן — אוֹמְרִים לוֹ: שֶׁמָּא מוּחְלָט וְטָמֵא הָיִיתָ, וּשְׁנֵי תִגְלָחִיּוֹת הָרִאשׁוֹנוֹת הָיוּ לְשֵׁם צָרַעַת, וְהַשְּׁלִישִׁית לְתִגְלַחַת טוּמְאָה, מֵעַכְשָׁיו מַתְחִיל נְזִירוּת טָהֳרָה. וְחוֹזֵר וּמוֹנֶה שְׁלֹשִׁים — וַהֲרֵי הֵן מֵאָה וְעֶשְׂרִים יוֹם וְאַרְבַּע תִּגְלָחִיּוֹת. נִמְצָא אוֹכֵל בַּקֳּדָשִׁים לְאַחַר שִׁשִּׁים יוֹם מִמָּה נַפְשָׁךְ, דְּתִגְלַחַת צָרַעַת וַדַּאי קוֹדֶמֶת, וְכֵיוָן שֶׁהֵבִיא קָרְבַּן צָרַעְתּוֹ — הוּתַּר בַּקֳּדָשִׁים. אֲבָל בַּיַּיִן לֹא הוּתַּר עַד לְאַחַר מֵאָה וְעֶשְׂרִים יוֹם, כְּמוֹ שֶׁפֵּירַשְׁתִּי. וְתָנֵי עֲלָהּ. בַּתּוֹסֶפְתָּא. בַּמֶּה דְּבָרִים אֲמוּרִים בִּנְזִירוּת מוּעֶטֶת אֲבָל בִּנְזִירוּת בַּת שָׁנָה. וְהָיָה טָמֵא בְּסָפֵק וּמוּחְלָט בְּסָפֵק בַּיּוֹם רִאשׁוֹן שֶׁל נְזִירוּת, אוֹכֵל בַּקֳּדָשִׁים לְאַחַר (ב) שְׁנֵי שָׁנִים, דְּשֶׁמָּא לֹא הָיָה טָמֵא וְלֹא מְצוֹרָע. וְאֵינוֹ אוֹכֵל כָּל שָׁנָה רִאשׁוֹנָה עַד סוֹפָהּ. וּבְסוֹף שָׁנָה רִאשׁוֹנָה יֵשׁ לוֹמַר טָמֵא הָיָה וְלֹא מְצוֹרָע, וּמִכָּאן וְאֵילָךְ מַתְחִיל נְזִירוּת טָהֳרָה, וְאֵין מְגַלֵּחַ עַד סוֹף שָׁנָה שֵׁנִית. וַעֲדַיִן יֵשׁ לוֹמַר שֶׁמָּא מְצוֹרָע וְטָמֵא הָיָה, וּשְׁתֵּי תִגְלָחִיּוֹת רִאשׁוֹנוֹת לֹא עָלָה לוֹ אֶלָּא לַצָּרַעַת, וְתִגְלַחַת שְׁלִישִׁית עָלְתָה לוֹ לִנְזִירוּת טוּמְאָה, וּמִכָּאן וְאֵילָךְ מַתְחִיל נְזִירוּת טָהֳרָה, וְאֵינוֹ מְגַלֵּחַ עַד סוֹף שָׁנָה רְבִיעִית. נִמְצָא אוֹכֵל בַּקֳּדָשִׁים לְאַחַר שְׁתֵּי שָׁנִים מִמָּה נַפְשָׁךְ — לְפִי שֶׁכְּבָר גִּילֵּחַ שְׁנֵי תִגְלָחִיּוֹת, וְתִגְלַחַת דְּצָרַעַת קוֹדֶמֶת בכ"מ כִּדְאָמְרַן. וְנִמְצָא שׁוֹתֶה יַיִן וּמִיטַּמֵּא לַמֵּתִים לְאַחַר אַרְבָּעָה שָׁנִים. וְאִי ס"ד. דִּבִנְזִירוּת מְרוּבָּה מִסְלַק סָלְקִי לֵיהּ יְמֵי חִלּוּטוֹ, ה) א] דְּשֶׁהוּי יְמֵי חִלּוּטוֹ עוֹלִין לוֹ לְמִנְיַן נְזִירוּת טָהֳרָה. תִּסְגֵּי לֵיהּ. אֶלָּא מִדְּאֵינוֹ יָכוֹל לִשְׁתּוֹת בַּיַּיִן עַד לְאַחַר אַרְבָּעָה שָׁנִים — ו) ש"מ דַּאֲפִי' בִּנְזִירוּת מְרוּבָּה אֵין יְמֵי חִלּוּטוֹ עוֹלִין לוֹ מִן הַמִּנְיָן, וְקַשְׁיָא לְרַב חִסְדָּא. וְעוֹד מְתִיב רַב אַשִׁי אֵין לִי אֶלָּא יְמֵי טוּמְאָה שֶׁאֵין עוֹלִין לוֹ מִן הַמִּנְיָן. דִּכְתִיב (במדבר ו) "וְכִפֶּר עָלָיו מֵאֲשֶׁר חָטָא עַל הַנָּפֶשׁ, וְקִדַּשׁ אֶת רֹאשׁוֹ בַּיּוֹם הַהוּא", וְאח"כ "וְהִזִּיר לַה' אֶת יְמֵי נִזְרוֹ, וְהַיָּמִים הָרִאשׁוֹנִים יִפְּלוּ", וּמֵעַכְשָׁיו הִתְחִיל לְהַזִּיר לַה' יְמֵי נִזְרוֹ, לְאַחַר שֶׁהֵבִיא כַּפָּרָתוֹ. יְמֵי חִלּוּטוֹ. שֶׁאִם ז) (ג) מְצוֹרָע וּמוּחְלָט בְּתוֹךְ יְמֵי נְזִירוּתוֹ. מִנַּיִן. שֶׁכ"ז שֶׁיְּהֵא מְגַלֵּחַ לֹא (ד) הָיוּ עוֹלִין לוֹ מִן הַמִּנְיָן נְזִירוּת טָהֳרָה. (אֶת הַקּוֹדְמִים). וְהוֹאִיל וִימֵי חִלּוּטוֹ אֵין סוֹתֵר בָּהֶן אֶת הַקּוֹדְמִין, יְהוּ עוֹלִין לוֹ מִן הַמִּנְיָן. נָזִיר בַּקֶּבֶר. שֶׁנָּזַר וְהוּא בְּבֵית הַקְּבָרוֹת, שֶׁשְּׂעָרוֹ רָאוּי לְתִגְלַחַת נָזִיר, כִּדְאָמְרִינַן בַּ"הֲרֵינִי נָזִיר [מְגַלֵּחַ]" (לעיל טז:). אֵין עוֹלִין לוֹ. יְמֵי טוּמְאָתוֹ מִן הַמִּנְיָן, וְאֵין סוֹתֵר בָּהֶן אֶת הַקּוֹדְמִין, לְפִי שֶׁאֵין לוֹ קוֹדְמִין. ח) יְמֵי חִלּוּטוֹ כו'. יְמֵי סְפָרוֹ. אוֹתָן יָמִים שֶׁכָּתוּב בָּהֶן "וְיָשַׁב מִחוּץ לְאָהֳלוֹ שִׁבְעַת יָמִים" (ויקרא יד). מִנַּיִן. שֶׁלֹּא יְהוּ עוֹלִין לוֹ לְמִנְיַן נְזִירוּת טָהֳרָה.

מַה

ה"ג: **אוכל** בקדשים אחר ששים. דהיינו ביום ששים ואחד, דשני תגלחיות ראשונות היו ביום שלשים, דאוקמינן אדאורייתא. ומיהו לפירוש זה אוכל בקדשים ביום ששים גופיה, [כיון] דתגלחת ראשונה שלשים יום — א"כ תגלחת שניה ביום חמשים ותשעה דאורייתא, כדאמרינן לעיל: אם גילח ראשונה ביום שלשים מגלח שניה ביום ששים, ואם גלח שניה ביום ששים חסר אחד — יצא, דהיינו ביום חמשים ותשעה. ובו ביום יטבול, ולמחרתו ביום ששים יביא קרבנותיו ויאכל בקדשים. ונמצא דאוכל בקדשים ביום ששים. ואע"ג דלאחר ששים [אמר] — הכי נמי אמרינן בפרק "שני [נזירים]" (לקמן ס:): אוכל בקדשים אחר שמנה ימים, ורוצה לומר ביום השמיני עצמו. וכן הא דקתני: ושותה יין °לאחר ק"כ — היינו ביום קכ"א, דאע"ג דתגלחת שניה ביום שלשים ואחד ודוק. לשון מהרפ"ש. **ואי** ס"ד סלקו לו ימי חלוטו תסגי ליה [בג' שנים ול' יום]. כלומר, אחר שגילח שנית לצרעתו לקץ שתי שנים, יגלח שלישית לסוף שלשים. ממה נפשך; אם נזיר טהור הוא — כך דינו, שהרי עלו לו ימי צרעתו לשנה של נזירות [לרב חסדא], ואינו צריך להמתין רק שלשים יום גידול שער. ב] (אבל) לגלח תגלחת נזיר טהור אחר תגלחת ל' ימתין שנה לתגלחת רביעית, דשמא מוחלט היה וטמא טמא מת, ושתי תגלחות ראשונות — לצרעתו, ושלישית — לנזיר טמא, ועד שיגלח לתגלחת נזיר טמא אי אפשר לו לחזור ולמנות נזירות טהרה. והיינו דפריך: בשלש שנים ושלשים יום סגי, דכך עולה החשבון. אלא ש"מ — ימי צרעתו אין עולין לו כל עיקר, ולכך לא יגלח שלישית עד סוף שלש שנים, דשמא נזיר טהור הוא ומוחלט היה, וימי צרעתו לא עלו לו, ונמצא שאינו יכול לגלח עד סוף השנה. **ועוד** מתיב רב אשי אין לי אלא ימי טומאתו שאין עולין לו. דכתיב "והימים הראשונים יפלו". ימי חלוטו מנין? ודין הוא, ימי טומאתו מגלח ומביא קרבן — דהיינו אשם נזיר טמא, וימי חלוטו מגלח ומביא קרבן לצרעתו — אשם מצורע. לא אם אמרת בימי טומאתו שכן מבטל בהן את הקודמין אבל ימי חלוטו פשיטא לן דלא יסתרו הקודמין, כדדרשינן לעיל בפרק "שלשה מינין" (דף מד.): "כי טמא נזרו" — למעוטי תגלחת ויין שאינן סותרין. **ומה** נזיר בקבר ששערו ראוי לתגלחת נזירות. שאם אמר "הריני נזיר" כשהיה בבית הקברות — שערו ראוי לתגלחת טהרה, שאינו מגלח ומביא קרבן טומאתו, כדאמרינן לעיל בפרק שלישי (דף טז:), אלא מגלח לסוף שלשים יום בשביל נזירות, ואע"פ כן אין ימי נזירות בבית הקברות עולין לו לנזירותו, אלא כשיוצא יתחיל למנות. ימי חלוטו, שאין שערו ראוי לתגלחת נזירות טהרה, שכן צריך לגלח בשביל צרעתו — אינו דין שלא יעלו לו מן המנין. **ימי** ספרו. לאחר שנתרפא, שהוא מגלח כל שערו ומונה (כל) שבעה ימים, וחוזר ומגלח, ואז הוא נטהר לגמרי — מנין שאותן שבעה אין עולין לו מן המנין? וקלא קשה: דתיתי בק"ו מנזיר בקבר, ששערו ראוי לתגלחת טהרה! *) שכן טעון תגלחת והוו כעין ימי טומאתו. **אבל** ימי הזב והזבה וימי הסגרו של מצורע. אחרי שאין טעונין תגלחת — הרי אלו עולין. אילימא בנזירות מועטת כלומר, שאין לו למנות רק שלשים יום משהתחיל צרעתו עד סוף ימי נזירות — והא בעי גידול שיער, והיכי בעי למימר דימי חלוטו יעלו לו מן המנין לנזירותו, דקתני: תאמר בימי חלוטו אין מבטל בהו הקודמין, ולכך יעלו? והא ביום דתחילת צרעתו לא היה לו למנות אלא שלשים יום, ונתרפא וגלח, בתר גילוחו צריך לחזור ולמנות שלשים יום, דבציר משלשים יום לא הוי גידול שיער! אלא לאו בנזירות מרובה שהיה לו למנות יותר משלשים יום כשנצטרע, וכי גילח לצרעתו יש לו עדיין למנות שלשים יום. ואי ס"ד דאמרינן ימי צרעתו יעלו לו מן המנין — הרי יש לו עדיין גידול שיער שלשים יום, כעין מילתא דרב חסדא ממש, וקאמר תנא קמא דלא סלקי ליה, וקשה לרב חסדא. **רבי** אליעזר אמר משום ר' יהושע כל טומאה מן המת שהנזיר מגלח עליה חייבין על ביאת מקדש וכל טומאה מן המת שאין הנזיר מגלח עליה. כגון גולל ודופק ואהל

*) שייך לע"ב

ושותה יין ומטמא למתים ותני עלה בד"א בנזיר מועטת אז די לו בק"כ ימים אבל בנזירות בת שנה אוכל בקדשים אחר ב' שנים דא"א לגלח ב' תגלחות של ימי חלוטו וימי ספרו אלא אחר ב' שנים כמו בנזיר מועטת אחר ששים יום ושותה יין ומטמא למתים אחר ד' שנים כדין נזיר מועטת אחר ק"כ ימים ואי ס"ד סלקי' ליה ימי חלוטו תסגי ליה בג' שנים ול' יום ואחר שגילח שנית לצרעתו לסוף ב' שנים יגלח תגלחת ג' לאחר ל' יום ממ"נ אם נזיר טמא הוא כך הוא דינו ואפי' אחר ז' ימים לתגלחת היה יכול לגלח ואם נזיר טהור הוא ומוחלט כך הוא דינו שהרי עלו לו ימי צרעתו לשנה של נזירות ואינו צריך להמתין רק ל' יום לגידול שער. ואחר תגלחת שלישית ימתין שנה א' דשמא היה מוחלט וטמא וב' תגלחות הראשונות לצרעתו וג' לנזיר טמא ועד שיגלח ויביא קרבנותיו נזיר טמא א"א לו למנות נזירות טהרה. אלא ש"מ ימי צרעתו אין עולין לו כל (עקר) [עיקר] הלכך א"א לו לגלח תגלחת שלישית עד סוף שנה ג' כי שמא מוחלט ונזיר טהור היה וימי צרעתו לא עלו לו ועוד מתיב רב אשי אין לי אלא ימי טומאה. פי' טומאת מת שאין עולין לו מן המנין דכתיב והימים הראשונים יפלו וכיון דסותר את הקודמים כ"ש שאין עולין לו: ימי טומאתו מגלח ומביא קרבן אשם נזיר: ימי חלוטו מגלח לצרעתו ומביא קרבן מצורע: תאמר בימי חלוטו שאינו מבטל הקודמים כדדרשינן לעיל פ' ג' מינים טמא נזרו למעט תגלחת ויין שאינן סותרים אמרת מה נזיר בקבר ששערו ראוי לתגלחת נזיר שאם קיבל עליו נזירות בבית הקברו' א) אינו ראוי לתגלחת טהרה שאינו מגלח ומביא קרבן טומאה בשביל טומאתו כדאיתא לעיל פ"ג אלא יוצא ומזה ושונה וטובל ומונה טהרה ימי חלוטו שאין שערו ראוי לתגלחת נזיר טהרה שצריך לגלחו לצרעתו אינו דין שלא יעלו לו מן המנין ימי ספרו שבין תגלחת א' לב' מנין שאין עולין לו צ"ע אמאי לא אתי נמי בק"ו מנזיר דקבר שהרי אין שערו ראוי לתגלחת נזיר

א) נ"ל שערו ראוי לתגלחת טהרה. וכ"ה בתוס' ד"ה ומה.

לקמן ס. [תוספתא פ"ו]

ספרי פ' נשא

נוסחת הריב"ן

א) שאילו אם היה טמא כו' לימי ספרו ולהביא קרבן ואוכל בקדשים ואח"כ למנות שבעה ימים לטומאה ואח"כ למנות לנזירות טהרה: ב) מלאכול בקדשים עד לאחר כו' צרעת אחר ז' לאלתר: ג) שלשים יום כו' טמא היית ותגלחת ראשונה שעשית כו': ד) ל' יום אחרים כו' והללו שתי תגלחיות כו' ועושה שלשים יום כו' נזירות טהרה ומונה ל' כו': ה) ימי חלוטו למנין נזירות טהרה תסגי ליה בג' שנים ול' יום דהא הוי גידול שיער לאחר ג' שנים ותהוי ליה ימי חלוטו עולין לו למנין נזירות לטהרה אלא כו': ו) כלומר דאפילו בנזירות מרובה אין עולין לו: ז) שאם היה מצורע מוחלט: ח) אלא ימי חלוטו:

הגהות הב"ח

(א) רש"י ד"ה אוכל וכו' ששים יום ושותה וכו' הלכך שוהא ואינו אוכל בקדשים אלא לאחר ששים: (ב) ד"ה במה דברים וכו' לאחר שתי שנים דשמא וכו' ושתי תגלחיות הראשונות לא עלו לו: (ג) ד"ה ימי חלוטו שאם היה מצורע: (ד) ד"ה מנין וכו' לא יהיו עולין וכו' טהרה הס"ד ואח"כ מה"ד תאמר בימי חלוטו וכו' והואיל וימי חלוטו:

גליון הש"ס

גמ' אין לי אלא ימי טומאה. לעיל דף יז ע"ב: **תום'** ד"ה אוכל בקדשים אחר ששים וכו' לאחר ק"כ יום הייט ביום ק"כ:

הגהות מהר"ב רנשבורג

א] רש"י ד"ה ואי ס"ד וכו' דסהוי. תיבת דסהוי נמחק וצ"ב דתהוי ליה: ב] תוס' ד"ה ואי ס"ד כו' גידול שיער אבל. תיבת אבל נמחק וצ"ב אח"כ לגלח וכו' כצ"ל:

עין משפט
נר מצוה

סו א ב מיי׳ פ״ו מהל׳ טומאת צרעת הלכה יא סמג עשין רלה:
סז ג ד מיי׳ שם הלכה י:
סח ה ו מיי׳ פ״ז מהל׳ נזירות הלכה ט:
סט ז מיי׳ פ״ג מהל׳ ביאת מקדש הלכה יג סמג לאוין סה:
ע ח מיי׳ פ״ג מהלכות מתנות עניים הלכה יא:

מה ימי חלוטו טעון תגלחת – אף ימי ספרו, ומה ימי חלוטו אין עולין לו מן המנין – אף ימי ספרו. יכול אף ימי הסגרו כן? והדין נותן: [א]חלוט מטמא משכב ומושב, [ב]וימי הסגרו מטמא משכב ומושב, אם למדת לימי חלוטו שאין עולין לו מן המנין – אף ימי הסגרו אין עולין לו מן המנין. אמרת: לא, אם אמרת בימי חלוטו – [ג]שכן חלוטו טעון תגלחת ומביא קרבן – לפיכך אין עולין, תאמר בימי הסגרו [ד]שאין טעון תגלחת ואינו מביא קרבן – לפיכך יעלו למנין. מכאן [ה]אמרו: ימי ספרו וימי גמרו – אין עולין לו מן המנין. אבל ימי הזב והזבה, והסגרו של מצורע – הרי אלו עולין לו. קתני מיהת: לא, אם אמרת בימי טומאה שכן מבטל בהן את הקודמין, תאמר בימי חלוטו. במאי? אילימא בנזירות מועטת – הא בעינן גידול שער. אלא לאו – בנזירות מרובה, וקתני: שאין עולין לו מן המנין, אלמא: לא סלקין ליה, יש״מ.§ **מתני׳** אמר רבי אליעזר משום ר׳ יהושע: [ו]כל טומאה מן המת שנזיר מגלח עליה – חייבין עליה על ביאת מקדש, וכל טומאה מן המת שאין הנזיר מגלח עליה – אין חייבין עליה על ביאת מקדש. א״ר מאיר: לא תהא זו קלה מן השרץ.§ **גמ׳** ורבי אליעזר משום רבי יהושע גמר לה? והא משום רבי יהושע בר ממל גמר לה. דתניא, *אמר רבי אליעזר: כשהלכתי לערדסקיא מצאתי את ר׳ יהושע בן פתר ראש שהיה יושב ודן לפני ר״מ בהלכה: כל טומאה מן המת שהנזיר מגלח עליה – חייבין עליה משום ביאת מקדש, וכל טומאה מן המת שאין הנזיר מגלח עליה – אין חייבין עליה משום ביאת מקדש. אמר לו: אל תהא זו קלה משרץ! אמרתי לו: כלום אתה בקי ברבי יהושע בר ממל? אמר לי: הן. כך אמר לי רבי יהושע בר ממל משום רבי יהושע: כל טומאה מן המת שהנזיר מגלח עליה – חייב עליה משום ביאת מקדש, וכל טומאה מן המת שאין הנזיר מגלח עליה – אין חייבין עליה משום ביאת מקדש. הוי, משום רבי יהושע בר ממל גמיר לה! אמרו: שמע מינה, כל שמעתתא דמתאמרה בבי תלתא, קדמאי ובתראי – אמרינן, מציעאי – לא אמרינן. אמר רב נחמן בר יצחק: אף אנן נמי תנינא, *אמר נחום הלבלר: כך מקובלני מרבי מיאשא, שקיבל מאבא, שקיבל מן הזוגות, שקבלו מן הנביאים: הלכה למשה מסיני *[ח]בזורע שבת וחרדל בשנים ושלשה מקומות, שנותן פאה מכל אחד ואחד. ואילו יהושע וכלב לא קחשיב, ש״מ.§ **מתני׳** אר״ע: דנתי לפני רבי אליעזר: מה אם עצם כשעורה שאינו מטמא אדם באהל – הנזיר מגלח על מגעו ועל משאו, רביעית דם שהוא מטמא אדם באהל – אינו דין שיהא הנזיר מגלח על מגעה ועל משאה? אמר לי: מה זה עקיבא?! אין דנין כאן מק״ו. וכשבאתי והרציתי (א) דברים לפני רבי יהושע, אמר לי: יפה אמרת, אלא כן אמרו: הלכה.§

גמ׳

פאה פ״ב מ״ו

(תוספות)

ואהל רובע עצמות, וכלים הנוגעים במת. **לא** תהא זו קלה מן השרץ. דכתיב ביה בהדיא דחייבין עליה על ביאת מקדש.

אמר ר״ע דנתי לפני ר׳ אליעזר כו׳ אמר לי מה זו (ר׳) עקיבא אין דנין כאן ק״ו – ולא פירש לו טעמיה. וטעמא דר׳ אליעזר – שאין דנין ק״ו מהלכה (זו): [אלא] כן [אמרו] הלכה. בגמ׳ מפרש דעצם כשעורה הלכה, ואין דנין ק״ו מהלכה.

ורבי אליעזר משום ר׳ יהושע. סתם, שהוא רבי יהושע בן חנניה גמיר לה? והא משום ר׳ יהושע בן ממל גמר לה! **דתניא** אמר ר׳ אליעזר כשהלכתי לערדסקיא מצאתי ר׳ יהושע בן פתר ראש. כך שם אביו. שהיה יושב ודן לפני ר״מ: כל טומאת מת כו׳. אמר לו [כלום] אתה בקי בר׳ יהושע מן ממל? אמר [לי]: הן, כך א״ר יהושע בן ממל – כל זה מדברי ר׳ אליעזר. אלמא מרבי יהושע בן ממל גמיר ליה.

ש״מ מילתא דמיתאמרא [בבי תלתא] קדמאי ובתראי אמר מיצעי לא אמר. ה״נ ר׳ יהושע בן חנניה אמר לר׳ יהושע בן ממל, ור׳ יהושע בן ממל לר״א. ורבי שסידר המשנה הזכיר רבי אליעזר שהיה אחרון, ורבי יהושע בן חנניה שהוא הראשון, ורבי יהושע בן ממל שהוא האמצעי – לא חש להזכירו. **שקיבל** מן הזוגות. הלל ושמאי, והם קיבלו משמעיה ואבטליון, ומיהודה בן טבאי ושמעון בן שטח, שקיבלו מן הנביאים חגי זכריה ומלאכי, שקבלו הלכה למשה מסיני, בזורע שבת וחרדל (וכו׳) בשנים וג׳ מקומות שחייב בפאה מכל אחד ואחד. כך גירסת הספרים. ולא גרסינן ליה, דהך משנה שנויה במסכת פאה (פ״ג מ״ב) גבי מחלוקת דר׳ עקיבא [במנמר] שדהו ושייר קלחים לחים, ר״ע אומר: פאה מכל א׳ ואחד, וחכמים אומרים: מאחד על הכל. ומודים חכמים בזורע שבת כו׳. והכי גרסינן בפ״ב דפאה (מ״ה): הזורע שדהו ב׳ מיני חטין, פי׳: א] שחמתית ולבנה, [עשאן] גורן אחד – נותן פאה אחת, ב׳ גרנות – ב׳ פאות. מעשה שזרע ר״ש איש המצפה, ובא לפני ר״ג, ועלו ללשכת הגזית, ושאלו לנחום ב] הלכה, ואמר: כך מקובלני מר׳ מיאשא כו׳: שני מיני חטין, עשאן גורן אחד – נותן פאה אחת, שתי גרנות – נותן שתי פאות. ואילו יהושע וכלב האמצעים לא קחשיב.

עלס

(רש״י)

מה ימי חלוטו טעון תגלחת. ולפורין, כדמפרש בהו קרא. גמרו. היינו ימי חלוטו. ימי הסגרו. אלו ימים שהוא מוסגר קודם א) שמוחלט, פעמים י״ד יום. ונטהר בתוך ימי הסגר. שהן עולין לו אותן ימים. אבל ימי הזב כו׳. שאינם טעונין תגלחת, ועוד ב) לא נטמאו בטומאת מת – הרי אלו עולין לו מן המנין. קתני מיהת לא אם אמרת כו׳ תאמר בימי חלוטו. שאין מבטל בהן את הקודמין. במאי? אילימא בנזירות מועטת – והא בעינן גידל שיער! אלא לאו בנזירות מרובה, וקתני: שאין עולין לו מן המנין, וקשיא לרב חסדא. ג) שמע מינה. דמהא תיובתא ש״מ. וא״ת: לוקמה בנזירות חמשים יום כדלעיל! הא לא אפשר, דהא קתני לה דומיא דימי טומאה, דמה להלן פסיקא לן דאין עולין – אף כאן אין עולין. **מתני׳** לא תהא זו קלה מן השרץ. ומה על טומאת השרץ שאין ד) הנזיר מטמא כלום – חייבין עליו משום ביאת מקדש, על טומאה מן המת שהוא טעון הזאה ג׳ וז׳ – אינו דין שיהו חייבין עליה משום ביאת מקדש, ואף ע״פ שאין הנזיר מגלח עליה? **גמ׳** ור׳ אליעזר מר׳ יהושע. סתמא, דהיינו ר׳ יהושע בן חנניה, (ב) ה) הא גמר לה? והא מר׳ יהושע בן ממל כו׳. לערדסקיא. שם מקום. בן פתר ראש. כך שמו. אמרתי לו. לר׳ (ג) מאיר: כלום בקי אתה בר׳ יהושע בן ממל? אמר לי: הן. ואמר לי משום ר׳ יהושע כל טומאה כו׳. אמרו ש״מ כל שמעתתא דמתאמרא בבי תלתא. דשלישי שמע משני ושני מראשון, דהאי מאן דבעי למימר להאי מילתא – לא ו) מצטרכא למימר אלא קמאי ובתראי, ומציעאי לא, כדתנן במתני׳ ר׳ אליעזר ור׳ יהושע, ולא קחשיב ר׳ יהושע בן ממל בהדייהו. אמר נחום הלבלר כך מקובלני מר׳ מיאשא שקיבל מן הזוגות. יוסי בן יועזר ויוסי בן יוחנן, יהושע בן פרחיה ונתאי הארבלי, יהודה בן טבאי ושמעון בן שטח, שמעיה ואבטליון, הלל ושמאי. וזוגות ז) שקיבלו מן הנביאים – חגי זכריה ומלאכי, ונביאים קיבלו הלכה למשה מסיני. ה״ג: ח) הזורע את שדהו שני מיני חטין, אם עשאן גורן אחת – נותן פאה אחת. ט) דהואיל ובשדה אחת זרען, אע״פ שהן שני מינים, הואיל ושניהם מין חטין – אינו חייב אלא פאה אחת, אלא א״כ שם דעתו לחלקן ולעשות מהן שתי גרנות. ואית ספרים דכתיב בהו: הזורע שבת וחרדל, אני״ס בלע״ז, ותו לא. ואנן לא גרסינן לה. ואילו יהושע וכלב. דהוו מציעאי, לא קחשיב. אלמא: דקמאי ובתראי – אמרי׳, ומציעאי – לא אמרינן. ומן הנביאים ואילך קחשיב כולהו כחדא, מפני שהיו מבית שני ואילך. **מתני׳** רביעית דם שהיא מטמאה כו׳ אינו דין שהנזיר מגלח על מגעה ועל משאה. וה״ה דהוה ליה י) למימר על אהילות, דלרבי עקיבא אית ליה האי סברא. אלא משום דלגבי (ד) שעורה דקמייתי ליה מיניה מקל וחומר לא מצי אמר על אהילות – לא אמר נמי גבי רביעית דם. אין דנין כאן מק״ו. ובגמ׳ מפרש (מאי קאמר. אין דנין כאן ק״ו). לפי שאין דנין קל וחומר מהלכה.

גמ׳

פי׳ הרא״ש

אילימא בנזיר מועטת שאין לו למנות רק ל׳ יום מתחלת צרעתו עד סוף נזירותו הא בעי׳ גידול שער. ואמאי אצטריך ליה למילף בק״ו דאין עולי׳ לו אלא לאו בנזיר מרובה שיש לו יותר מל׳ יום משהתחילה א) צרעתו עד סוף ימי נזרו וקתני שאין עולין: ור״א מר׳ יהושע סתם שהוא ר׳ יהושע בן חנניה גמיר לה: מצאתי את רבי יהושע בן פתר הראש כך שם אביו אמר ליה הן אמר לו כך אמר ר׳ יהושע בן ממל: ש״מ כל מלתא דמתאמרא בבי תלתא קדמאי ובתראי אמרינן מציעאי לא אמרינן. שהרי רבי יהושע בן חנניה אמרה לר׳ יהושע בן ממל ור״י בן ממל לר״א ורבי כשסדר המשנה הזכיר לר״י בן חנניה שהוא ראשון ור״א שהיה אחרון ואילו ר״י בן ממל האמצעי לא חש להזכיר: שקבל מן הזוגות וכו׳ בזורע שבת או חרדל בב׳ או ג׳ מקומות שהוא נותן פאה מכל א׳ וא׳. כך כתוב הגרסא בספרים וליתא להך (גזרה) [גירסא] דמשנה זו שנויה בפ״ג דמס׳ פאה גבי מחלוקת דר״ע וחכמים המנמר שדהו ושייר קלחים לחים ר״ע או׳ נותן פאה מכל א׳ ואחד וחכ״א מא׳ על הכל ומודים חכמים לר״ע בזורע שבת או חרדל וכו׳ אבל משנה זו היא שנויה פ״ב דפאה הזורע שדהו (ארבע) [שני] מיני חיטים אם עשאן גורן א׳ נותן פאה א׳ ב׳ גרנות נותן ב׳ פאות מעשה שזרע ר״ש איש המצפה ובא לפני ר״ג ועלו ללשכת הגזית ושאלו אמר נחום הלבלר כך מקובלני מר׳ יאשיה שקבל מאביו שקבל מן הזוגות שקבלו מן הנביאים הלכה למשה מסיני הזורע שדהו וכו׳ ואילו יהושע וכלב לא קאמר אלמא אין קפידא אם מדלג מן האמצעים:

א) אולי צ״ל מתחלת ימי נזירותו.

איבעיא

מסורת הש״ס

הגהות מהר״ב רנשבורג

א] תוס׳ ד״ה שקיבל כו׳ פי׳ שחמתית ולבנה. תיבות שחמתית ולבנה נמחקו. ונ״ב שחרית ולבנה עשאן: ב] בא״ד ושאלו לנחום הלבלר ואמר כצ״ל:

[תוספתא פ״ב ע״ש תוס׳ אהלות פ״ד ע״ש שם ושם איתא ר׳ אלעזר]

נוסחת הריב״ן

א) קודם שהוחלט פעמים שבעה ימים פעמים י״ד יום ונטהר מתוך הסגר כו׳ אותן ימים קודם שנחלט כדמפרשי קראי בס״ד: ב) ועוד שלא: ג) ש״מ כו׳ ש״מ) ליתא בכ״י ד) שאין טעון הזאה ג׳ וז׳ חייבין: ה) קא: ו) אצטריך ליה למימר: ז) קבלו: ח) בפ״ב דפאה: ט) ב׳ גרנות נותן ב׳ פאות: י) דה״ל למיתנא על אהילה דלר״ע כו׳ מאי אמר על אהילו ולפיכך אמר נמי גבי רביעית דם מגע ומשא הכ״ל:

פאה פ״ג מ״ב [נדה נח.]

הגהות הב״ח

(א) במשנה והרציתי הדברים: (ב) רש״י ד״ה ורבי אליעזר וכו׳ ר״י בן חנניה הוא דגמר לה: (ג) ד״ה אמרתי לו לר׳ יהושע בן פתר ראש כלום בקי: (ד) ד״ה רביעית וכו׳ דלגבי עלם כשעורה:

גמ' אִיבַּעְיָא לְהוּ: עֶצֶם כִּשְׂעוֹרָה הֲלָכָה, וּרְבִיעִית דָּם – קַל וָחוֹמֶר, וְאֵין דָּנִין קַל וָחוֹמֶר מֵהֲלָכָה. אוֹ דִּלְמָא: רְבִיעִית דָּם – הֲלָכָה, וְעֶצֶם כִּשְׂעוֹרָה – קַל וָחוֹמֶר, וְאֵין דָּנִין קַל וָחוֹמֶר מֵהֲלָכָה? ת"ש, *עֶצֶם כִּשְׂעוֹרָה הֲלָכָה, וּרְבִיעִית דָּם קַל וָחוֹמֶר, וְאֵין דָּנִין קַל וָחוֹמֶר מֵהֲלָכָה.§

הדרן עלך כהן גדול

שְׁנֵי [א]נְזִירִים שֶׁאָמַר לָהֶן אֶחָד "רָאִיתִי אֶחָד מִכֶּם שֶׁנִּטְמָא, וְאֵינִי יוֹדֵעַ אֵיזֶה מִכֶּם" – מְגַלְּחִין, וּמְבִיאִין קָרְבַּן טוּמְאָה וְקָרְבַּן טָהֳרָה, וְאוֹמֵר: "אִם אֲנִי הוּא טָמֵא – קָרְבַּן טוּמְאָה שֶׁלִּי, וְקָרְבַּן טָהֳרָה שֶׁלְּךָ. וְאִם אֲנִי הוּא הַטָּהוֹר – קָרְבַּן טָהֳרָה שֶׁלִּי, וְקָרְבַּן טוּמְאָה שֶׁלְּךָ". וְסוֹפְרִין שְׁלֹשִׁים יוֹם, וּמְבִיאִין קָרְבַּן טָהֳרָה, וְאוֹמֵר: "אִם אֲנִי הוּא הַטָּמֵא – קָרְבַּן טוּמְאָה שֶׁלִּי, וְקָרְבַּן טָהֳרָה שֶׁלְּךָ, וְזֶה קָרְבַּן טָהֳרָתִי. וְאִם אֲנִי הוּא הַטָּהוֹר – קָרְבַּן טָהֳרָה שֶׁלִּי, וְקָרְבַּן טוּמְאָה שֶׁלְּךָ, וְזֶה קָרְבַּן טָהֳרָתְךָ.§ **גמ'** קָתָנֵי: שְׁנֵי נְזִירִים שֶׁאָמַר לָהֶם "רָאִיתִי אֶחָד מִכֶּם שֶׁנִּטְמָא, וְאֵינִי יוֹדֵעַ אֵיזֶה מִכֶּם", וְאַמַּאי? כָּל סְפֵק טוּמְאָה בִּרְשׁוּת הַיָּחִיד מֵהֵיכָא יָלְפִינַן לַהּ – *[ב]מִסּוֹטָה. מַה סּוֹטָה – בּוֹעֵל וְנִבְעֶלֶת, אַף כָּל סְפֵק טוּמְאָה ברה"י – כְּגוֹן דְּאִיכָּא בֵּי תְּרֵי. אֲבָל הָכָא שְׁנֵי נְזִירִים, וְהַאי דְּקָאֵי גַּבֵּיהוֹן – הָא תְּלָתָא, הֲוָה לֵיהּ סְפֵק טוּמְאָה בִּרְשׁוּת הָרַבִּים, [ג]וְכָל סְפֵק טוּמְאָה בִּרְשׁוּת הָרַבִּים סְפֵיקוֹ טָהוֹר! אֲמַר רַבָּה בַּר רַב הוּנָא: [ד]בְּאוֹמֵר "רָאִיתִי טוּמְאָה שֶׁנִּזְרְקָה בֵּינֵיכֶם". אֲמַר רַב אַשִׁי: דַּיְקָא נַמִי, דְּקָתָנֵי

גמ' אִיבַּעְיָא לְהוּ. א) הַאי דְּקָאָמְרִי בְּמַתְנִי' ר' אֱלִיעֶזֶר וְר' יְהוֹשֻׁעַ דְּאֵין דָּנִין (א) ק"ו, הֵיכִי קָאָמְרִי? מִי אָמְרִינַן: עֶצֶם כִּשְׂעוֹרָה הֲלָכָה לְמֹשֶׁה מִסִּינַי דְּנָזִיר מְגַלֵּחַ עָלָיו, וּרְבִיעִית דָּם קַל וָחוֹמֶר מֵעֶצֶם כִּשְׂעוֹרָה דְּנָזִיר מְגַלֵּחַ עָלָיו, וְאֵין דָּנִין קַל וָחוֹמֶר מֵהֲלָכָה, אִי לָאו בְּמִידֵי דְּתַרְוַיְיהוּ גְּמִירֵי לָהּ מִקְּרָא, אוֹ דִּילְמָא הָכִי קָאָמַר: רְבִיעִית דָּם הֲלָכָה לְמֹשֶׁה מִסִּינַי דְּמְטַמֵּא אֶת הָאָדָם בְּאֹהֶל, וְעֶצֶם כִּשְׂעוֹרָה קַל וָחוֹמֶר, כְּלוֹמַר וּמֵעֶצֶם כִּשְׂעוֹרָה קָא גָּמְרִינַן קַל וָחוֹמֶר דְּבִרְבִיעִית דָּם יְהֵא נָזִיר מְגַלֵּחַ. וְקָאָמַר לֵיהּ: אֵין דָּנִין ק"ו מֵהֲלָכָה, שֶׁאֵין לְמֵידִין קַל וָחוֹמֶר מִמִּידֵי דְּלָא גְּמִירֵי לָהּ אֶלָּא מֵהֲלָכָה, אִי לָאו דְּאָתְיָא לֵיהּ מִן הַמִּקְרָא. ת"ש עֶצֶם כִּשְׂעוֹרָה [הֲלָכָה]. שֶׁהַנָּזִיר מְגַלֵּחַ עָלָיו, וּרְבִיעִית דָּם קַל וָחוֹמֶר, וְאֵין דָּנִין קַל וָחוֹמֶר מֵהֲלָכָה.

הדרן עלך כהן גדול

שְׁנֵי נְזִירִים. שֶׁקִּיבְּלוּ עֲלֵיהֶם נְזִירוּת כְּיַחַד. **שֶׁאָמַר לָהֶן אֶחָד רָאִיתִי אֶת אֶחָד מִכֶּם שֶׁנִּטְמָא.** ה"ז נֶאֱמָן ב) לְהַחֲזִיקוֹ בְּחֶזְקַת טוּמְאָה כָּל זְמַן שֶׁאֵין מַכְחִישִׁין אוֹתוֹ, דְּהָא "אוֹ הוֹדַע אֵלָיו חַטָּאתוֹ" כְּתִיב (ויקרא ד), (אוֹ הוֹדַע אֵלָיו) מִכָּל מָקוֹם. **וְאֵינִי יוֹדֵעַ אֵיזֶה מִכֶּם.** מַשְׁלִימִין לִנְזִירוּתָן, וּמְגַלְּחִין, וּמְבִיאִין קָרְבַּן טוּמְאָה וְקָרְבַּן טָהֳרָה בְּשׁוּתָּפוּת. **וְאוֹמֵר.** אֶחָד מֵהֶן. **אִם אֲנִי הוּא כו'.** וַעֲדַיִין אֵינָן מוּתָּרִין לִשְׁתּוֹת בְּיַיִן, לְפִי שֶׁיָּכוֹל לוֹמַר עַל כָּל אֶחָד ג) שֶׁמָּא טָמֵא הָיָה, וְתִגְלַחְתּוֹ שֶׁגִּילֵּחַ עַכְשָׁיו הִיא תִּגְלַחַת טוּמְאָה. אֶלָּא חוֹזְרִין וְסוֹפְרִין עוֹד שְׁלֹשִׁים יוֹם, ד) וּמְבִיאִין קָרְבַּן טָהֳרָה בִּלְבַד מִן הַשּׁוּתָּפוּת. **וְאוֹמֵר.** אֶחָד מֵהֶם: אִם אֲנִי הוּא הַטָּמֵא – קָרְבַּן טוּמְאָה ה) הָיָה שֶׁלִּי, וְקָרְבַּן טָהֳרָה שֶׁלְּךָ, וְזֶה שֶׁל עַכְשָׁיו קָרְבַּן טָהֳרָה כו'. וּמֵעַכְשָׁיו מוּתָּרִין לִשְׁתּוֹת בְּיַיִן. **גמ' אֲבָל הָכָא.** כֵּיוָן דְּהָווּ תְּלָתָא, שְׁנֵי נְזִירִים וְהַאי דְּקָאֵי גַּבַּיְיהוּ, אע"ג דְּקָיְימִי בִּרה"י, הָוְיָא לֵיהּ ו) סְפֵק טוּמְאָה בִּרה"ר, דִּסְפֵיקוֹ טָהוֹר. **אֲמַר רַבָּה בַּר רַב הוּנָא.** כְּגוֹן דְּקָאֵים א] הָאֶחָד בִּלְבַד, וְאוֹמֵר: רָאִיתִי טוּמְאָה שֶׁנִּזְרְקָה לְבֵינֵיכֶם מִבִּפְנִים, דְּלָא הָווּ לְהוּ אֶלָּא תְּרֵי, ז) (ב) כְּבוֹעֵל וְנִבְעֶלֶת. **דַּיְקָא** נַמִי. דְּלָא קָאֵי בַּהֲדַיְיהוּ, דְּקָאָמַר "וְאֵינִי יוֹדֵעַ", דְּאִילּוּ הֲוָה קָאֵי בַּהֲדַיְיהוּ – אִי אֶפְשָׁר דְּלָא ח) הֲוָה יָדַע. וְקָא

עצם כשעורה הלכה. דנזיר מגלח עליו. דמקרא לא אתי, כדכתיב "על כל נפשות מת לא יבא" – מידי דמיטמא בביאה, ורביעית דם בעי לאגמורי מיניה מק"ו. או דילמא: רביעית דם הלכה – מה שהוא מטמא ב] באהל, דלית להו "נפשות מת" לרביעית דם, דאדרבה משמע דם חצי לוג, שהוא שיעור שתי נפשות, והלכה למשה מסיני הוא דמטמא באהל ברביעית. ועצם כשעורה קל וחומר, כלומר מעצם כשעורה בעי ללמוד שיגלח על אהל רביעית דם. ואין דנין קל וחומר מהלכה. פי': מכח חומר שהוא הלכה למשה מסיני לא נעשה קל וחומר. ת"ש: רביעית דם קל וחומר ועצם כשעורה הלכה.

הדרן עלך כהן גדול

שני נזירים שאמר להם אחד וכו'. צריך לומר שהן שותקין, שאם היו מכחישין אותו – לא היה נאמן, כדאמרי' בקידושין בפ' "האומר" (ד' סה:): עד אחד בהכחשה מי מהימן.

מגלחין ומביאין קרבן טומאה וקרבן טהרה ואומר כו'. לאו דוקא נקט "ואומר", אלא זה יקרב לשם מי שהוא, וזה יקרב לשם מי שהוא. **אם** אני הוא הטמא קרבן טומאה. שנעשה כבר – שלי, וקרבן טהרה שנעשה כבר – שלך, (וזה קרבן טהרתי).

°**וסופרין** שלשים יום ומביאין קרבן. בשותפות, קרבן טומאה – חטאת העוף ועולת העוף. אבל אשם לא מייתי על הספק. ג](וקרבן טומאה בספק) עולת העוף תהא נדבה, וחטאת ספק ולא תאכל. ואשם שאינו מביא אינו מעכבו, כרבנן דפרק ג' (לעיל דף יח:): וחכמים אומרים הביא חטאתו ולא הביא אשמו – מונה. ועדיין אסורין לשתות ביין וליטמאות למתים, ולכך סופרים עוד שלשים יום. **באומר** ראיתי שנזרקה טומאה ביניכם. והוא עומד מרחוק, דהוי ספק טומאה ברשות היחיד. ואם תאמר: אם כן יביא כל אחד קרבן טומאה ודאי, דכל ספק טומאה ברשות היחיד שורפין עליה [תרומה]! ויש לומר: דלא גמירי מסוטה אלא דבר שאפשר להיות כסוטה, דאפשר שנטמאת. אבל הכא לא אפשר לטמאות שניהם, דודאי אחד טהור. ואם תאמר: אם כן, מאי פריך מעיקרא: והא ספק טומאה ברשות הרבים הוא, כלומר ויביאו שניהם קרבן טהרה? והא ספק טומאה ברשות הרבים דמטהרינן, נמי מסוטה גמרינן לה, ולא ילפינן אלא דבר שאפשר להיות, והכא בודאי אחד טמא! ויש לומר: דספק טומאה ברשות הרבים לאו מסוטה גמרינן ליה, אלא כל חד וחד מוקמינן אחזקתיה, וילפינן ליה מקרא פרק קמא דחולין (דף י:) להעמיד כל דבר אחזקתיה, אף על גב דודאי אחד טמא, כיון דלא ידעינן ליה. ואף על גב דבפרק קמא דחולין (ג"ז שם) למאי דקא סלקא דעתיה קאמר התם: הילכתא גמירי לה, ומשמע התם דספק טומאה ברשות הרבים לאו משום חזקה, אלא נגמר מסוטה – במסקנא לא קאי הכי. ובמקום אחר, [בריש מסכת נדה *)] מפורש בארוך. דקתני

א א מיי' פ"ט מהלכות נזירות הלכה יד:

ב ב ג מיי' שם הל' טז ופי"ד מהלכות אבות הטומאה הל' א ופט"ו שם הלכה ח ופט"ז שם הלכה א:

ג ד מיי' פ"ט מהלכות נזירות הלכה טז:

פי' הרא"ש

איבעיא להו עצם כשעורה הלכה. דנזיר מגלח עליו דמקרא לא אתי דכתיב על כל נפשות מת לא יבוא דמשמע דלא הוזהר אלא על דבר שמטמא באהל ורביעית הדם בעי לאגמורי מניה בק"ו וקא"ל ר"א אין כאן ק"ו משום דאין דנין ק"ו מדבר (שאינו) [שהוא] הלכה: או דלמא רביעית דם הלכה מה שהוא מטמא באהל דכתיב על כל נפשות מת דמשמע שיעור ב' נפשות דהיינו ב' רביעים: ועצם כשעורה ק"ו ואתה בא ללמוד רביעית דם מעצם כשעורה מתוך חומרא שיש ברביעית דם שמטמא באהל משא"כ בעצם כשעורה וקא"ל אין דנין ק"ו מהלכה. פי' מתוך חומר אהל שיש ברביעית דם שבא מהלכה:

סליק פירקא

פ"ח ב' נזירים שאמר להם אחד וכו' ומיירי שהם שותקים שאם היו מכחישים אותו לא היה נאמן כדאיתא בקדושין כל האומר דעד א' בהכחשה לא מהימן: מגלחים ומביאים וכו' לאחר שיכלו ל' יום שלהם: אם אני הוא הטמא קרבן טומאה א) שנעשה כבר הוא שלי וקרבן טהרה [שנעשה מכבר] הוא שלך: וסופרים ב) שלשים יום מיום שנדר הב': וקרבן טומאה בספק היינו חטאת העוף הבאה על הספק ואינה נאכלת. מביא חטאת העוף לספק טומאה נזיר ואשם לא מייתי כרבנן דאמרי לעיל הביא חטאתו ולא הביא אשמו מונה. נמצא זה מביא קרבנותיו לחצאי' אם נזיר טהור הוא דעולה ראשונה היתה חובה ועתה הוא מקריב חטאת ושלמים והודו חכמים לדברי בן זומא ולא חשו על מה שהקריב קרבנותיו

דיקא

שבת קלב. פסחים פא:

נוסחת הריב"ן

א) מאי: ב) להחזיקו: ג) אחד ואחד: ד) שלשים יום ואין בכך כלום דנזיר טמא יכול לעשות תגלחת טומאה וקרבן טומאה ואפילו לאחר כמה ימים הס"ד ואח"כ מה"ד ומביאין כו': ה) טומאה דאתמול [ונמגוס הוא]: ו) כספק: ז) כי סוטה דליכא אלא תרי בועל ונבעלת: ח) דלא ידע:

הגהות הב"ח

(א) רש"י ד"ה איבעיא וכו' דנין כאן ק"ו היכי: (ב) ד"ה אמר רבה וכו' אלא תרי הס"ד ותיבות בועל ונבעלת נמחק:

סוטה כח:

גליון הש"ס

תוס' ד"ה וסופרין שלשים יום. ציון זה שייך לקמן דף נט ע"ב:

הגהות מהר"ב רנשבורג

א] רש"י ד"ה אמר רבה וכו' האי בלבד וכו' אלא תרי כסוטה דליכא אלא תרי בועל ונבעלת כצ"ל: ב] תוד"ה עצם וכו' מה שהוא מטמא על כל אדם באהל וכו' כצ"ל א"מ: ג] ד"ה וסופרים וכו' וקרבן טומאה בספק. נ"ב עי' א"מ:

לחצאין: באומר ראיתי שנזרק טומאה ביניכם. שהיה מרוחק מהם ד' אמות דהשתא לא הוו אלא תרי דהו"ל ספק טומאה ברשות היחיד:

א) דיבור זה סובב על סיפא דסופרים ל' יום שניים ומביאין קרבן טהרה וכו'. ב) דבור זה שייך למתני' לקמן (דף נט ע"ב) במה אחד מהן וכו' דהתם מביאין קרבן טומאה מספק וע"ז סובב והולך דברי רבינו ועי' בגליון הש"ס.

254; 259

דְּקָתָנֵי "וְאֵינִי יוֹדֵעַ אֵיזֶה מִכֶּם", ש"מ.§ "מְגַלְּחִין וּמְבִיאִין".§ וְאַמַּאי? דִּילְמָא לָאו טְמֵאִין אִינּוּן, וְקָעָבֵיד הַקָּפָה! אָמַר שְׁמוּאֵל: א בְּאִשָּׁה וְקָטָן. וְלוֹקְמָא בְּגָדוֹל, *וְהַקָּפַת כָּל הָרֹאשׁ לָא שְׁמָהּ הַקָּפָה! מִדְּלָא מוֹקִים לָהּ הָכִי – שְׁמַע מִינָּהּ קָסָבַר שְׁמוּאֵל: ב הַקָּפַת כָּל הָרֹאשׁ שְׁמָהּ הַקָּפָה. מָר זוּטְרָא מַתְנֵי לָהּ לְהָא שְׁמַעְתָּא דִּשְׁמוּאֵל אַסֵּיפָא: *נָזִיר שֶׁהָיָה טָמֵא בְּסָפֵק וּמוּחְלָט בְּסָפֵק – אוֹכֵל בְּקָדָשִׁים לְאַחַר שִׁשִּׁים יוֹם, וּמְגַלֵּחַ ד' תִּגְלָחוֹת. (א) וְהָא קָעָבֵיד הַקָּפָה! אָמַר שְׁמוּאֵל: ג בְּאִשָּׁה וְקָטָן. אָמַר רַב הוּנָא: ד הַמַּקִּיף אֶת הַקָּטָן הֲרֵי הוּא חַיָּיב. א"ל רַב אַדָּא בַּר אַהֲבָה לְרַב הוּנָא: (ב) וְדִידָךְ מַאן מְגַלַּח לְהוֹן? אֲמַר לֵיהּ: חוֹבָה. *תִּקְבְּרִינוּן חוֹבָה לְבָנֶיהָ. כּוּלְּהוּ שְׁנֵי דְּרַב אַדָּא בַּר אַהֲבָה לָא אִקַּיַּים לֵיהּ זַרְעָא לְרַב הוּנָא. מִכְּדִי תַּרְוַיְיהוּ סְבִירָא (ג) הַקָּפַת כָּל הָרֹאשׁ שְׁמָהּ הַקָּפָה, בְּמַאי קָמִיפַּלְגִי? רַב הוּנָא סָבַר: °"לֹא תַקִּפוּ פְּאַת רֹאשְׁכֶם וְלֹא תַשְׁחִית [אֵת] פְּאַת זְקָנֶךָ", *ה כָּל שֶׁיֵּשׁ לוֹ הַשְׁחָתָה – יֵשׁ לוֹ הַקָּפָה, וְהָנֵי נָשֵׁי, הוֹאִיל וְלֵיתְנְהוּ בְּהַשְׁחָתָה – לֵיתְנְהוּ נַמִי בְּהַקָּפָה. וְרַב אַדָּא בַּר אַהֲבָה סָבַר: אֶחָד הַמַּקִּיף וְאֶחָד הַנִּיקָּף בְּמַשְׁמָע. וְאִיתְקַשׁ מַקִּיף לְנִיקָּף; כָּל הֵיכָא דְּנִיקָּף מִיחַיֵּיב – מַקִּיף נַמִי מִיחַיֵּיב, וְהַאי קָטָן הוֹאִיל וְהוּא גּוּפֵיהּ לָאו בַּר עוֹנָשִׁין הוּא דְּמִיחַיֵּיב – מַקִּיף נַמִי לָא מִיחַיֵּיב. לֵימָא הַקָּפַת כָּל הָרֹאשׁ תַּנָּאֵי הִיא, *דְּתָנוּ רַבָּנַן: °"רֹאשׁוֹ", מַה תַּלְמוּד לוֹמַר – לְפִי שֶׁנֶּאֱמַר "לֹא תַקִּפוּ פְּאַת רֹאשְׁכֶם", יָכוֹל

תורה אור: ויקרא יט | שם יד

(ד) וְקָא עָבְרִי א) עַל לָאו דְּהַקָּפָה, דְּתִגְלַחַת אֵינוֹ לְצוֹרֶךְ, וְיֵשׁ בָּהּ מִשּׁוּם לֹא תַקִּיפוּ. אָמַר שְׁמוּאֵל בְּאִשָּׁה וְקָטָן. כְּגוֹן שֶׁהָיוּ שְׁנֵי נְזִירִים הַלָּלוּ שְׁתֵּי נָשִׁים, אוֹ שְׁנֵי קְטַנִּים, דְּלָא מִיחַיְּיבֵי אַהַקָּפָה. אַמַּאי מְגַלֵּחַ. אַרְבַּע תִּגְלָחוֹת? וְהָא קָא עָבַר בְּתַרְתֵּי תִּגְלָחוֹת קַמַּיְיתָא מִשּׁוּם לָאו ד"לֹא תַשְׁחִית אֶת פְּאַת (ה) זְקָנֶךָ", שֶׁכֵּן מְגַלֵּחַ [כָּל] שְׂעָרוֹ, וְאַחִידָךְ מִינַּיְיהוּ קָעָבַר מִשּׁוּם הַקָּפָה! וְהָא קָא עָבֵיד הַשְׁחָתָה גָּרְסִי'. א"ל רַב אַדָּא בַּר אַהֲבָה לְרַב הוּנָא לְדִידָךְ. דְּאָמְרַתְּ דְּהַמַּקִּיף אֶת הַקָּטָן חַיָּיב, ג) קְטַנִּים דְּאִיתְנְהוּ מְגוּלָּחִין כָּל הָרֹאשׁ, כִּדְאוֹרְחַיְיהוּ דְּאִינָשֵׁי דְּקָמְגַלְּחִי לְהוּ כְּדֵי לְהַבְרוֹתָן לְאַחַר הַחוֹלִי, מַאן קָמְגַלַּח לְהוּ? אֲמַר לֵיהּ חוֹבָה. כָּךְ שְׁמָהּ דְּאִשְׁתּוֹ דְּרַב הוּנָא. דְּקָסָבַר רַב הוּנָא דְּאִשָּׁה לָא מִיפַּקְדָא אַלָּאו דְּהַקָּפַת הָרֹאשׁ אַרֹאשׁ אֲחֵרִים כְּלָל. אֲמַר לֵיהּ רַב אַדָּא ד) תִּיקְבְּרִינְהוּ לְבָנֶיהָ. דִּלְדִידָךְ דְּאָמְרַתְּ הַמַּקִּיף אֶת הַקָּטָן חַיָּיב, כִּי מַקֶּפֶת לֵיהּ אִשָּׁה נַמִי חַיֶּיבֶת. אֲבָל לְדִידִי – אֲפִילּוּ גָּדוֹל הַמַּקִּיף אֶת הַקָּטָן פָּטוּר, וְהוּא הַדִּין נַמִי לְאִשָּׁה. וְכֵן בְּגָדוֹל הַמַּקִּיף אֶת הַגָּדוֹל חַיָּיב, וְהוּא הַדִּין לְאִשָּׁה. מִכְּדִי תַּרְוַיְיהוּ סְבִירָא לְהוּ דְּהַקָּפַת כָּל הָרֹאשׁ שְׁמָהּ הַקָּפָה. וְהָא הֲוָה לְהוּ הַקָּפַת כָּל הָרֹאשׁ לְבָנָיו דְּרַב הוּנָא. בְּמַאי פְּלִיגִי. כְּלוֹמַר, מַאי אִיכָּא בֵּינַיְיהוּ, דְּמַאן דְּאָסַר בְּגָדוֹל ה) אַמַּאי שָׁרֵי בְּאִשָּׁה? וְהָנֵי נָשֵׁי הוֹאִיל וְלֵיתְנְהוּ בְּהַשְׁחָתָה. דְּלֵית לְהוּ זָקָן – לֵיתְנְהוּ בְּהַקָּפָה כְּלָל, שֶׁאֲפִילּוּ אִשָּׁה הַמַּקֶּפֶת אֶת הַגָּדוֹל פְּטוּרָה. רַב אַדָּא בַּר אַהֲבָה סָבַר כִּי אֲמַר רַחֲמָנָא לֹא תַקִּיפוּ אֶחָד הַנִּיקָּף וְאֶחָד הַמַּקִּיף בְּמַשְׁמָע. וּלְהָא מִילְּתָא אִיתְקַשׁ נִיקָּף לְמַקִּיף, דְּכָל הֵיכָא דְּנִיקָּף חַיָּיב – מַקִּיף נַמִי חַיָּיב, לָא שְׁנָא אִישׁ וְלָא שְׁנָא אִשָּׁה. וְהַאי קָטָן הוֹאִיל וְהוּא גּוּפֵיהּ לָא מִיחַיֵּיב. מִשּׁוּם דְּלָאו בַּר עוֹנָשִׁין הוּא – דְּמַקִּיף לֵיהּ נַמִי לָא מְחַיֵּיב, וַאֲפִילּוּ אִישׁ. יָכוֹל

דקתני ואיני יודע. דמשמע °שלא נודע לו מעולם, משום דלא הוה בהם, מדלא קתני "שכחתי". **והא** קא עביד הקפה. א][בראש], השחתת הקפה. **[באשה].** בראש האשה, שאינה אסורה בהקפה, דדרשינן בסמוך: כל שאינו בהשחתה אינו בהקפה.

והא קא עביד השחתת זקן. דבספק תגלחת מצורע מגלח זקנו בתער, וקעבר בהשחתת זקן ובהקפת ראש מספק.

המקיף את הקטן חייב. דכי כתיב רחמנא "לא תקיפו פאת" – אף אפאות דקטן אזהר.

ודידך מאן מגלח להון. שראה בנים קטנים מגולחים ראשיהם עם פאותיהם. א"ל חובה – אשתו היתה. ורב הונא לטעמיה, דאמר בסמוך: הנשים מותרות להקיף, דכיון דאינן באיסור דניקף – ליתנהו נמי באיסור דמקיף. **חובה** תקברינהו לבניה. דאיסורא קא עבדא. כולהו שני כו'. כשגגה שיוצאת מלפני השליט.

מכדי תרוייהו סבירא להו הקפת כל הראש שמה הקפה. רב הונא, דאמר: חובה מגלחה להו. אבל האיש היה עובר, אע"פ שמגלח כל ראשם. וכן רב אדא דאמר חובה תקברינהו לבניה – חובה נענשה.

במאי פליגי. מאי טעמייהו.

והני נשי הואיל וליתנהו בהשחתה ליתנהו בהקפה. בין להיות נקפות, בין להקיף אחרים, ואפילו לגדול מותרות. **ורב** אדא בר אהבה סבר אחד המקיף ואחד הניקף במשמע. פשטיה [דקרא] ודאי לניקף אזהר רחמנא, דהא "פאת ראשכם" כתיב, דהיינו הניקף. ומיהו מדקאמר "לא תקיפו" ולא כתיב "לא תוקפו" – הוסב הלאו גם על המקיף, כדי להקיש מקיף לניקף. כלומר, כל היכא דניקף בר חיובא הוא – כל מקיף נמי בר חיובא הוא. והאי קטן, הואיל וגופיה לאו בר עונשין הוא, ולא מיחייב – מקיף ליה נמי לא מיחייב. ואפי' איש שרי לאקופי לקטן. ואין לתמוה מנא ליה להתלמוד דרב אדא בר אהבה סבר מותר לגדול להקיף את הקטן – דמשמע ליה מדקאמר ליה לרב הונא "ודידך מאן מקיף להו" – דמשמע: לדידי אפי' גדול מקיף לקטן, אבל לדידך – מאן מקיף להון? והאי דלטייה היינו לפי סברתו דרב הונא דאסר לגדול להקיף לקטן, ואמר ליה: כיון דאסרת לגדול להקיף לקטן – גם האשה אסורה להקיף לקטן, דלא ס"ל למדרש לרב אדא לדרוש: כל שישנו בהשחתה ישנו בהקפה, לפטור אשה המקפת אחרים. ואע"ג דבקידושין בפ' קמא (דף לה:) דרשינן הכי: כל שישנו בהשחתה ישנו בהקפה כו' לפטור (נשים) הניקפות – בההיא דרשה מודה רב אדא, משום דפשטיה דקרא איירי בניקף. אבל מה שדורש רב הונא נמי "לא תקיפו" אמקיף, מלישנא ד"לא תקיפו" ומקישו להשחתת זקן לפטור האשה המקפת אפי' לגדול – בהא ודאי פליג רב אדא, דלית לן להקיש הקפה להשחתה אלא במאי דאיירי פשטיה דקרא, כגון בניקף. והשתא פליגי בתרתי; רב הונא סבר דאשה שריא להקיף, בין גדול בין קטן, הואיל ואינה בהשחתה אינה בהקפה – בין להיות בהקפה דאיירי ביה פשטיה דקרא, בין להקיף אחרים. ורב אדא סבר: דודאי אשה פטורה מלהיות ניקפת מהקישא דהשחתה, דאיירי ביה פשטיה דקרא. אבל מלישנא ד"לא תקיפו" דדרשינן מיניה לחייב גם המקיף – גם האשה חייבת בההוא, ולא נפטרה מהקישא דהשחתה, כיון דלא איירי ביה פשטיה דקרא, ועוברת בלאו אם הקיפה לגדול. ופליגי נמי בקטן, דרב הונא סבר: גדול המקיף את הקטן חייב, ולא מסתברא ליה לרב הונא למידרש משום דאפקיה קרא בהך לישנא ד"לא תקיפו" דמשמע אמקיף ואניקף, למימר דהיכא דניקף לאו בר חיובא הוא מקיף נמי פטור, דהיינו למיגמר מגברא על גברא – לא משמע ליה. ורב [אדא] סבר: דלהכי אפקיה קרא בהך לישנא, למימר: היכא דניקף לאו בר חיובא – מקיף נמי פטור. הילכך גדול המקיף לקטן פטור. ונראה דקיי"ל כרב הונא, דאשה שריא להקיף קטן, וה"ה לגדול, דסוגיא דהתלמוד כוותיה בפרק קמא דבבא מציעא (דף י:), דקאמר: *מאי בינייהו איש דאמר לאשה "אקיפי לי קטן", וקאמר דהשליח דהיינו האשה לאו בת חיובא היא, אלמא דאשה מותרת להקיף לקטן כרב הונא. ומדנקט נמי אשה ולא איש – משמע נמי דאיש המקיף לקטן חייב, והיינו נמי כרב הונא. והוה מצי למימר התם שהאיש אמר לאשה "אקיפי לי גדול", כיון דסוגיא אזלא כרב הונא – אלא הגדול לא יאבה שמוע לה שתקיפנו, כי הוא יתחייב. אבל קטן לאו בר מחאה הוא, ולאו בר עונשין הוא. וא"ת: ולרב אדא דמקיש מקיף לניקף, וה"ה דנקיש ניקף למקיף – ונימא: כל היכא דמקיף לאו בר חיובא – ניקף נמי פטור, ויהיה מותר להיות ניקף מן הגוי! וי"ל: לרב אדא מקיף לניקף מקשינן, משום דעיקר חיובא דקרא אניקף כתיב "לא תקיפו פאת" – דהיינו פאת דניקף, למימר: היכא דניקף בר חיובא גם המקיף חייב, ואי הניקף לאו בר חיובא הוא – המקיף פטור. אבל כשהניקף בר חיובא, אף אם אין המקיף בר חיובא – אסור, דקרא אתי לאקושי מקיף, דמשתמע מלישנא ד"לא תקיפו" – אניקף, דמשמע מגופיה דפשטיה דקרא. אבל אין סברא להקיש גופיה דקרא, דהיינו הניקף – למקיף, דלא משתמע אלא מלישנא בעלמא "לא תקיפו" ולא מגופיה דקרא. ותדע, דאם לא כן – מצורע אמאי דחי לאו דהקפה? והא אפשר לקיים שתיהם, שיקיפהו קטן ואשה וגוי! אלא שמע מינה כדפרישית. וא"ת: ולרב הונא דלא מקיש מקיף לניקף, ואע"ג דניקף לאו בר חיובא הוא מיחייב מקיף, אם כן המקיף את הגוי לחייב כמו המקיף לקטן! ודוחק לחלק משום דקטן אתי לכלל חיוב, דהשתא מיהא לאו בר חיובא הוא. וטעמא דרב הונא לא תלי בהכי, אלא משום דלא מקיש מקיף לניקף. ונראה להר"ף: דיש לומר הואיל וכתיב "פאת ראשכם" אישראל קאי קרא, ולא אגוי. וכ"ש במקיף את האשה אי מחייב כמו בקטן לרב הונא*. **לפי** שנאמר לא תקיפו יכול אף מצורע כן תלמוד לומר ראשו. קא סלקא דעתך השתא דמן הדין לא איצטריך קרא למדחי לא תעשה דהקפה, דאף לאו השוה בכל קים לן ב] דהקפת כל הראש שמה הקפה.

אמר

ד א מיי' פ"ט מהלכות נזירות הלכה טו:
ה ב מיי' פי"ב מהלכות ע"ז הלכה א סמג לאוין נז טוש"ע י"ד סימן קפא סעיף ב:
ו ג מיי' פ"ט מהלכות נזירות הלכה טו:
ז ד מיי' פי"ב מהלכות ע"ז הלכה ב סמג שם טוש"ע י"ד סי' קפא סעיף ה [וברב אלפס מכות פ"ג ד' רפה. ע"ש]:
ח ה מיי' שם הלכה ב ה טוש"ע שם סעיף ז:

פי' הרא"ש

דיקא נמי דקתני ואיני יודע דמשמע שלא ידע מעולם מדלא קתני ושכחתי איזה מכם טמא אלמא שמרחוק היה (נטמא): באשה שאינה באיסור הקפת ראש. כדאמר בסמוך כל שאינו בהשחתה אינו בהקפה וקטן שהוא מופלא סמוך לאיש: המקיף את הקטן חייב דכתיב לא תקיפו פאת ואף פאת קטן בכלל: ודידך מאן מגלח להו. שהיו רגילין שלא לשייר פאות כשהיו מגלחים ראש הקטנים: א"ל חובה. כך שם אשת רב הונא וס"ל דוקא איש המקיף את הקטן חייב ולא אשה כדמפרש טעמא בסמוך: חובה תקברינהו לבנה. וכי היא רוצה שתקבור את בניה שאינה יראת העונש על שהיא מקפת אותם: הוי כשגגה שיוצאת מלפני השליט וקברה בניה אע"פ שלא קלל אותה: מכדי תרוייהו סברי הקפת כל הראש שמה הקפה. רב הונא דאמר חובה מגלח להו ואבל איש לא. וכן רב אדא דאמר תקברינהו לבנה: במאי קמיפלגי דרב אדא סבר דאיש המקיף קטן פטור מדקאמר ודידך מאן מגלח להו מכלל דלדידיה אפי' איש יכול להקיף את הקטן באיזה סברא נחלקו: הואיל וליתנהו בהשחתה ליתנהו בהקפה. פי' באיסור הקפה כלל ואף להקיף הקטן מותרות. וכן אם הקיפה את הגדול פטורה: ורב אדא סבר. נהי דליתנהו בהקפת ראשן בהקפת ראש אחר איתנהו: אחד המקיף ואחד הניקף במשמע דלא תקיפו: והאי קטן וכו' והאי דקאמר רב אדא חובה תקברינהו לבנה לדבריו דרב הונא קאמר לדידך דלית לך דכי ניקף פטור מקיף נמי פטור דקאמ' המקיף את הקטן חייב. גם חובה יש לירא מעונש דאין חילוק בין איש מקיף קטן לאשה מקפת: דתניא ראשו מה ת"ל. גבי מצורע כתיב וגילח את כל שערו את ראשו ואת זקנו ואת גבות עיניו ואת כל שערו יגלח. והשתא דריש לראשו למיתור דבכלל כל שערו הוא ולקמן דריש זקנו. גבות עיניו דריש א) מפי' היה מביא לכלל ופרט וכלל לרבות כל כנוס שער ונראה:
א) נ"ל וגבות עיניו דריש בפ' הוה מבא קף דף עז ע"א לכלל ופרט וכלל:

[לעיל מה. לקמן נח.]
[לעיל נח: לקמן נט:]
ב"ק פ.
קדושין לה:
[לעיל מא. יבמות ה.]
[נ"ל אי נמי]
(עי' תוס' שבועות ג. ד"ה ועל הזקן)

הגהות מהר"ב רנשבורג

א] תוד"ה והא קא עביד הקפה בזקן בהשחתת הקפה בראש כצ"ל ונ"ב: ב] ד"ה לפי שנאמר וכו' בכל קים לן דלהכי אלא כמ"ד דהקפת כל הראש שמה הקפה כצ"ל ח"מ ויעב"ץ:

נוסחת הדי"ן

א) מספק עלי: ב) משום לאו דהשחתה דלא כו' פאת זקנך שכן מגלח בו שערו ואחידך: ג) חייב גבי כוי דידך הוא דלאחינהו כו': ד) חובה: ה) מאי טעמא שרי.

גליון הש"ס

תוס' ד"ה דקתני כו' שלא נודע לו מעולם. עי' יבמות כג ע"ב תוס' ד"ה ואחותו בכור שור שב:

הגהות הב"ח

(א) גמ' ד' תגלחות אמאי והא קעביד: (ב) שם לדידך מאן מגלח: (ג) שם תרוייהו סבירא להו הקפת: (ד) רש"י מע"ל ד"ה ויקא וכו' ויעב הש"ד ואח"כ מ"ה ונקבעו תוספות על כו': (ה) ד"ה אמאי וכו' זקנך שכן:

ט א מיי' פ"ג מהלכות ציצית הלכה ה סמג עשין כו טוש"ע א"ח סימן ט סעיף ב:
י ב מיי' שם טור שו"ע שם סעיף ג:

יכול אף מצורע כן – ת"ל "ראשו". *ותניא אידך: "ראשו" מה ת"ל? לפי שנאמר גבי נזיר °"תער לא יעבר על ראשו", יכול אף נזיר מצורע כן – ת"ל "ראשו". מאי לאו תנאי היא; למ"ד (א) מנזיר, קסבר: הקפת כל הראש לא שמה הקפה, וכי אתא קרא – למידחי את לא תעשה ועשה. ואידך סבר: הקפת כל הראש שמה הקפה, וכי אתא קרא – למידחי לאו גרידא? אמר רבא: דכ"ע הקפת כל הראש לא שמה הקפה, וכי אתא קרא – כגון שהקיף ולבסוף גילח; כיון דאילו גלחיה בחד זימנא – לא מיחייב, כי הקיף ולבסוף גילח – נמי לא מיחייב. ומי כתב קרא הכי? *והאמר ריש לקיש: כל מקום שאתה מוצא עשה ול"ת, אם אתה יכול לקיים את שניהם – מוטב, ואם לאו – יבוא עשה וידחה את ל"ת! אלא, דכ"ע הקפת כל הראש שמה הקפה. ומאן דמוקים לקרא למידחי ל"ת ועשה – לאו גרידא מנליה? יליף מגדילים. דאמר קרא °"לא תלבש שעטנז", ותניא: "לא תלבש שעטנז" – הא גדילים תעשה לך מהם. ומאן דנפקא ליה מ"ראשו" מ"ט לא נפקא ליה מגדילים? אמר לך: לכדרבא הוא דאתא. *דרבא רמי: כתיב °"ונתנו על ציצת הכנף" (ג) – מין כנף "פתיל תכלת", וכתיב °"צמר ופשתים יחדו", הא כיצד? אצמר ופשתים – פוטרים בין במינן בין שלא במינן, בשאר מינין – במינן פוטרין, שלא במינן – אין פוטרין. והאי תנא דמפיק ל"ראשו" ללאו גרידא, דאתי עשה ודחי את לא תעשה ועשה מנלן? נפקא ליה מ"זקנו". *) דתניא: "זקנו" מה ת"ל? לפי שנא' °"ופאת זקנם לא יגלחו", יכול אף כהן מצורע כן – ת"ל "זקנו". ומאן דמפיק ליה ל"ראשו" לעשה ולא תעשה, לילף מ"זקנו"! וליטעמיך, דקיימא לן בעלמא דלא

*) יבמות ה. [לעיל מ:]

במדבר ו | דברים כב | במדבר טו | דברים כב | ויקרא כא

לעיל מא. יבמות ה. ע"ש | לעיל מא. שבת קלג. יבמות כ: מנחות מ: | שבת כז: מנחות לט: יבמות ד:

יכול אף מצורע. לא יקיף? ת"ל "ראשו". א) יכול אף נזיר מצורע. כשנטהר מצרעתו בתוך ימי נזירותו, לא יעביר תער על ראשו! מאי לאו תנאי היא. דלמ"ד דהאי "ראשו" דכתיב במצורע לא אתיא ב) אלא למדחי לא תעשה דנזיר, ד"לא יעבור תער על ראשו", קסבר: משום לאו דהקפה לא צריך, (ג) דאילו מצורע קעביד הקפת כל הראש דשריא, דהקפת כל הראש לאו שמה הקפה, וכי קאתי קרא – למידחי ג) את לא תעשה ועשה דנזיר; עשה – "קדוש יהיה גדל פרע". ואידך. דמצריך ד) משום "לא תקיפו", קסבר דהקפת כל הראש שמה הקפה. לא דכ"ע לאו שמה הקפה. ומאן דתני ה) לה (ד) מ"וראשו" גבי נזיר – ניחא, ומאן דתני לה גבי הקפה – לאו משום דהיכא דמגלח והדר מקיף, ו) דהא לא איצטריך קרא למישרי, משום דהקפת כל הראש לאו שמה הקפה. אלא כי איצטריך קרא – דמקיף ברישא והדר מגלח. ומי כתיב קרא הכי. כלומר, דכיון דאילו מגלח כוליה בחד זימנא לא מיחייב, משום דהקפת כל הראש לאו שמה הקפה, מי קא כתביה רחמנא לקרא, דאי עביד דרך איסור, דמקיף ז) והדר מגלח – לא מיחייב? והא שפיר עדיף דליגלח כוליה, דקא מוקים עשה דמצורע, ולא קא עבר על לאו ד"לא תקיפו"! דהכי עדיף טפי, כדריש לקיש, דאמר: כל מקום שאתה מוצא עשה – כגון "גדילים תעשה לך", ולא תעשה – "לא תלבש שעטנז". (ה) ח) לקיים את שניהם – דלטלית של צמר ציצית של צמר, ולטלית של פשתן ציצית של פשתן. ואם אי אתה יכול לקיים את שניהן – כגון מילה בצרעת. אלא דכ"ע הקפת כל הראש שמה הקפה. ולמאן דמייתי לה להאי "ראשו" (ו) דמצורע משום "לא תקיפו" – משום דאשמועינן דאתי עשה ודחי ל"ת. ומאן דמוקי לה לקרא בנזיר (ט) ולא בהקפה, קסבר: גבי הקפה לא צריך למיכתב, דאתי עשה ודחי ל"ת. והילכך כי איצטריך קרא – למישרי עשה ול"ת דבנזיר. ולמאן דמוקים ליה לקרא בנזיר למידחי את ל"ת ועשה לאו גרידא מנא ליה. ואי אמרת: לאו כל שכן הוא?! י) ומה עשה ול"ת דחי, ל"ת לא כל שכן?! הא לא איריא, משום דאיכא למיפרך כדלקמן: מה לנזיר שכן ישנו בשאלה, (ז) משום דקיל [כולי האי] אתי עשה ודחי כ) ל"ת שבו, תאמר בשאר לאוין. הילכך נפקא ליה מ"גדילים" כו'. ולמאן דנפקא ליה מראשו. ללאו גרידא, ולא פריך כדפרכינן: מה ללאו דהקפה שכן אינו שוה בכל, דבני אהרן ולא בנות אהרן אמר רחמנא. ומאי טעמא לא משמע ליה מ"גדילים"? ההוא לכדרבא אתי דרבא רמי כתיב ונתנו על ציצית הכנף ל) פתיל. (ח) דהא מייתורא משמע דליהוי ממין כנף פתיל תכלת. וכתיב "צמר ופשתים", וסמיך ליה "גדילים תעשה לך". דבקרא אחרינא כתיב "לא תלבש שעטנז צמר ופשתים", וסמיך ליה "גדילים תעשה לך", דמשמע: מצמר ופשתים תעשה לך גדילים, מהם ולא ממין אחר. הא כיצד? – צמר ופשתים פוטרין כו'. נפקא ליה מ"זקנו". דכתיב גבי מצורע. דתניא: "זקנו" מה ת"ל? והלא שער זקנו בכלל כל שערו הוא. יכול אף כהן מצורע כן ת"ל זקנו. דקאתי עשה דמצורע "וגלח את כל שערו, את ראשו ואת זקנו", וקא דחי עשה ול"ת דכהן; ל"ת – "ופאת זקנם לא יגלחו", עשה – "קדושים יהיו לאלהיהם". ולמאן דמפיק לראשו. מ) גבי נזיר למידחי ל"ת ועשה, לילף מ"זקנו"! אמר לך ולטעמיך. נ) דאמרת (ט) לי לנזיר מכהן הוה ליה למילף, הא דקיי"ל בעלמא דלא אתי עשה כו', אמאי? נילף מכהן והוא מצורע דאתי עשה ודחי ל"ת ועשה, והוא הדין בכל התורה! אלא מכהן לא ילפינן. דאיכא למיפרך: מה לכהן – שכן לאו שאינו שוה בכל ס) כו', תאמר בנזיר שהוא שוה בכל. לכך הוצרך הכתוב "ראשו" גבי נזיר, למידחי את ל"ת ועשה שבו. ואפי' הכי בעלמא לא ילפינן מיניה, כדלקמן: מה לנזיר שכן ישנו בשאלה, תאמר בעלמא שאינו בשאלה. אבל כהן *) מיהא מנזיר גמרינן, הואיל דכהן לאו שאינו שוה בכל הוא, ונזיר שוה בכל. אע"ג דאיתיה בשאלה – אפי' הכי עדיף טפי למילף כהן מנזיר, משום דישנו שוה בכל, ולאו למיגמר נזיר מכהן, דלאו שאינו שוה בכל הוא. ואידך סבירא ליה דנזיר מכהן עדיף טפי, משום דכהן אינו בשאלה, דומיא דשאר מצות, מה שאין כן בנזיר. ולמאן

*) גי' א"מ להאי מ"ד

אמר רבא דכ"ע לא שמיה הקפה וכי איצטריך קרא היכא דהקיף הפאה ולבסוף גילח. אע"ג דאפשר לקיים שניהם, כגון שיגלח כל הראש, אתי עשה ד"וגלח" ודחי ליה. ופריך מדריש לקיש כו'. אלא דכ"ע שמה הקפה, למאן דמוקי ל"ראשו" למילף למידחי לא תעשה ועשה, דהיינו בנזיר דכתיב ביה "תער לא יעבור על ראשו" ו"קדוש יהיה" (י) – משום דלאו גרידא נפקא ליה מגדילים: ומאן דמוקי ראשו ללאו גרידא, מאי טעמא לא נפקא ליה מגדילים? דאילו להקפת כל הראש שמה הקפה – לא אילטריך קרא, דסבירא ליה השתא מסברא ידעינן, דאטו משום דהוסיף לגלח לא יתחייב על הפאות? כי היכי דמאן דמוקי ליה ללאו ועשה דהיינו בנזיר, אית ליה דשמה הקפה מסברא. ולאו כמאי דסלקא דעתך מעיקרא, דבעי קרא לאשמועינן דהקפת כל הראש שמה הקפה.

ציצית הכנף מין כנף. דמשמע: מכל מין שיהא הכנף, הן משירים הן מן כלך וסריקין. וכתיב "צמר ופשתים" וסמיך ליה "גדילים". הא כילד? צמר ופשתים פוטרין בין במינן – כגון צמר לצמר ופשתים לפשתים, בין צמר לכלך וסריקין, שאף הן חייבין לרבא מן התורה. וכן משמע בפרק "במה מדליקין" (שבת דף כז:). שאר מינין במינן פוטרין – כגון כלך לכלך וסריקין לסריקין. שלא במינן אינן פוטרים. אבל כלאים בציצית, דליתי עשה ולידחי לא תעשה – אכתי לא נפקא לן.

והאי תנא דמפיק ליה ראשו ללאו גרידא דאתי עשה ודחי ל"ת ועשה. היכא דאינו שוה בכל, מנליה? נפקא ליה מ"זקנו" כדמפרש והולך. ואין לתמוה: אמאי פשיטא להתלמוד דדחי? (כ) י"ל: דאי ס"ד דלא אתי עשה ודחי ל"ת ועשה בשאינו שוה בכל – אם כן למאן דמפיק "ראשו" ללאו גרידא, ולא דריש גדילים – הא קיימא לן בכל דוכתי דאתי עשה ודחי ל"ת גרידא, אפי' השוה בכל, מנלן? אי מהקפה – שכן אינו שוה בכל, אלא ודאי לגופיה [לא] איצטריך, דאפילו לאו ועשה דחי כשאינו שוה בכל, כדמפרש ואזיל ב"זקנו". ואם כן אייתר לו "ראשו" להקפה, אם אינו ענין לשאינו שוה בכל – תניהו ענין לשוה בכל. ומשום הכי פשיטא לן. וקא בעי מנלן דדחי עשה לא תעשה ועשה כשאינו שוה בכל. דסוגיא דפ"ק דיבמות (דף ה.) ס"ל להתלמוד כסוגיא דידן, דס"ד דקרא ד"ראשו" אתא לאשמועינן היא גופה דהקפת כל הראש שמה הקפה, ולא כמסקנא (ל) בסוגיא דידן דידעינן ליה מסברא, כדפרישית. **נפקא** ליה מזקנו. דכתיב במצורע, מה בא ללמוד? והלא כבר נאמר "וגילח כל שערו": יכול אף כהן מצורע כן. דאית ביה לא תעשה דהשחתה, ועשה ד"קדושים יהיו", והא דכתיב "וגילח כל שערו" – נוקי בנמרטו פיאותיו.

נזיר

פי' הרא"ש

יכול אף מצורע כן. לא יגלח כל ראשו והא דכתיב וגילח את כל שערו נוקי ליה בשאר שער הגוף: ת"ל ראשו לומר דגילוח מצורע דחי לאו דהקפה: וקשיא אידך ראשו מה ת"ל וכו' מאן דמוקי לה בנזי' סבר הקפת כל הראש לא שמה הקפה. הלכך למצורע גרידא לא איצטריך דאין כאן הקפה ומוקי לה בנזיר מצורע דאיכא לאו דלא יעבור ועשה דגדל פרע ואתי עשה דגילוח מצורע ודחי להו: ואידך סבר הקפת כל הראש שמה הקפה. וכיון דאיצטריך קרא למדחי לאו גרידא לא מוקמי' ליה למדחי לאו ועשה: וכי אתא קרא כגון שהקיף ולבסוף גילח. כגון שהקיף תחלה וגילח צדעיו ואח"כ גילח שער ראשו: דכיון דאילו גלחיה בחד זמנא לא מחייב ואפי' אינו מצורע כי נמי הקיף ולבסוף גילח לא מיחייב דאתי קרא דמצורע למדחייה: ומי כתב קרא הכי דכי נמי מצי לגלח בהתר דאתי קרא למישרי לגלח באיסור: והא אמר רשב"ל כל מקום וכו'. לאו גרידא מנ"ל. דאי לא הוה ידע ליה מדוכתא אחרינא לא הוה מוקי קרא לדחייה לאו ועשה: הא גדילים תעשה לך מהם. ואתי עשה דגדילים תעשה לך ודחי לא תלבש שעטנז: ומאן דנפקא ליה מראשו מאי טעמא לא נפקא ליה מגדילים. ונדרוש ראשו ללאו ועשה: דרבא רמי כתיב על ציצית הכנף פתיל דמשמע ממין הכנף יהיה הפתיל וכתיב צמר ופשתים יחדו. גדילים תעשה לך דמשמע דוקא מהם עשה גדילים: הא כיצד צמר ופשתים פוטרים בין במינן בין שלא במינן. אהני הסמיכות ליפות כחן שפוטרים אף שלא במינן. כגון צמר בטלית של פשתן או של משי ופשתים בשל צמר ומשי. אבל שאר מינים אין פוטרים אלא במינן כדמשמע ממין הכנף יהיה הפתיל. והשתא אי לאו דשמעי' מראשו דעשה דמצורע דחי לאו דהקפה לא הוה מוקמי' ליה קרא דגדילים לכדרבא ממש אלא כי דוקיא דרבא צמר לצמר ולמשי אבל לפשתים לא. ופשתים לפשתים ומשי דלא מסתבר למימר דעשה דחי לא תעשה כיון דמצי' לאוקומי לכדוקיא דרבא ולא חוי' בשום דוכתא דעשה דוחה לא תעשה. אבל השתא דגלי קרא דעשה מצי' דחי לאו דהקפה אע"ג דמיניה לא ילפינן בעלמא דאיכא למפרך מה ללאו דהקפה שאינו שוה בכל שאינו נוהג בנשים מ"מ אהני דהשתא דדרשי' גדילים לידחייה דאתי עשה ודוחה לא תעשה: ומנ"ל דמצורע נזיר מגלח ראשו: זקנו מה ת"ל דבכלל כל שערו הוא: לפי שנאמר בכהנים ופאת זקנם לא יגלחו. ת"ל זקנו ובכהנים איכא גם עשה דקדושים תהיו. וה"ה נמי דדחי לאו ועשה דנזיר (דמשמע) [וקשה] היכי בעי למילף נזיר מכהן הא איכא לאקשויי מה ללאו ועשה דהשחתה שאינה שוה בכל שאינו נוהג בנשים תאמר בגילוח נזיר ששוה בכל והכי פריך בסמוך. וי"ל דלפי המסקנא ניחא. והשתא קסבר כיון דבכהן איכא חד קולא שאינו שוה בכל ובנזיר חד קולא שכן ישנו בשאלה א"כ שקולים הם ולמדים זה מזה. ובעלמא לא ילפינן מינייהו משום דקיל:

ומאן

נוסחת הריב"ן

(א) יכול אף נזיר מצורע לא יקיף ת"ל ראשו. יכול אף נזיר כו' כשיטהר: ב) לא תאמר ליה אלא כו' לנזיר דתער לא יעבור על ראשו: ג) למדחי לא תעשה לא יעבור תער ועשה קדוש כו': ד) דמצריך ליה משום: ה) לאו דראשו: ו) מקיף דלא: ז) ואתי מגלח כו' ליגלח ... כו': ח) דהכי ... לקיים: ... לאחיה ... למיפרך כדפרכינן לקמן ... ללאו דהקפה שכן לאו שאינו שוה בכל ... דלאשו דנזיר למדחי ל"ת ועשה שבו כו' תאמר בלאו דעלמא שאינו בשאלה כהן מנזיר גמרינן כו' ונזיר נמי שוה בכל ואע"ג דאיתיה בשאלה כו' ולא למגמר נזיר כו' עדיף ליה למילף משום דכהן:

הגהות הב"ח

(א) גמ' למ"ד דנזיר קסבר: (ב) שם על ציצית הכנף הכנף מין כנף וכתיב צמר ופשתים כצ"ל ותיבות פתיל תכלת נמחק: (ג) רש"י ד"ה מאי לאו וכו' דהקפה לא צריך קרא דאילו וכו' ועשה דנזיר ל"ת תער לא יעבור על ראשו עשה קדוש יהיה: (ד) ד"ה לא דכ"ע וכו' דתני לה להאי ראשו גבי וכו' והדר מקיף דלהא לא איצטריך קרא: (ה) ד"ה ומי כתיב וכו' לא תלבש שעטנז אם אתה יכול לקיים את וכו' של פשתן מוטב ואם אי אתה. נ"ב עיין בפ' ואלו נערות (דף מ.) וכמ"ש התוס' לשם: (ו) ד"ה אלא דכ"ע וכו' ראשו במצורע וכו' ודחי ל"ת ניחא ומאן: (ז) ד"ה ולמאן דמוקים וכו' ומשום דקיל: (ח) ד"ה ההוא וכו' הכנף פתיל דהאי קרא מייתרא ומשמע לציצית: (ט) ד"ה אמר לך ולטעמיך דאמרת לן דנזיר מכהן הוה לן למילף וכו' מה לכהן שכן לאו שאינו שוה בכל וכו' אבל כהן מהא מנזיר גמרינן הואיל וכו' עדיף טפי למילף מנזיר משום דכהן כו' והד"א: (י) תוס' ד"ה אמר רבא וכו' וקדוש יהיה ה"ע משום דלאו וכו' השתא דמסברא וכו' וכי לא יתחייב וכו' שמה הקפה הס"ד ואח"כ מ"ה כתיב על ציצית הכנף וכו' כלך וסריקין הן מצמר וכתיב צמר ופשתים יחדו וסמיך ליה וכו': (כ) ד"ה והאי תנא וכו' להש"ס דדחי די"ל דאי ס"ד וכו' אי מהקפה איכא למיפרך מה להקפה שכן אינו שוה בכל אלא ודאי לגופיה לא איצטריך וכו' ואם אינו ענין וכו' וסוגיא דפ"ק דיבמות ס"ל להש"ס כסוגיא דידן למאי דס"ד דקרא. נ"ב וכן פי' לשם התוס' בד"ה להקפה ועיין פירש"י שם דף ו' ע"א: (ל) בא"ד כמסקנא דסוגיא:

יא א מיי' פ"ז מהלכות נזירות הלכה טו:
יב ב ג ד מיי' פי"ב מהלכות ע"ז הל' ט סמג לאוין סב טוש"ע י"ד סי' קפב סעיף א:

א דְּלָא אָתֵי עֲשֵׂה וְדָחֵי אֶת ל"ת וַעֲשֵׂה, לֵילַף מִכֹּהֵן דְּדָחֵי! אֶלָּא, מִכֹּהֵן לָא יָלְפִינַן; מַה לְּכֹהֵן – שֶׁכֵּן לָאו שֶׁאֵינוֹ שָׁוֶה בַּכֹּל. °נָזִיר מִכֹּהֵן נַמִי לָא יָלֵיף – שֶׁכֵּן לָאו שֶׁאֵינוֹ שָׁוֶה בַּכֹּל. וּמַאן דְּמוֹקֵים לְהַאי "רֹאשׁוֹ" בְּנָזִיר, לָמָּה לִי "זְקָנוֹ"?! מִיבָּעֵי לֵיהּ לְכִדְתַנְיָא: (א) "זְקָנוֹ" מַה ת"ל? לְפִי שֶׁנֶּאֱמַר "וּפְאַת זְקָנָם לֹא יְגַלֵּחוּ", יָכוֹל אַף כֹּהֵן מְצוֹרָע כֵּן – ת"ל "זְקָנוֹ". וּמְנָלַן דְּבְתַעַר? *דְּתַנְיָא: "וּפְאַת זְקָנָם לֹא יְגַלֵּחוּ", יָכוֹל אַף גִּילְּחוֹ בְּמִסְפָּרַיִם יְהֵא חַיָּיב – ת"ל "וְלֹא תַשְׁחִית". אִי לֹא תַשְׁחִית, יָכוֹל לִיקְּטָן בְּמַלְקֵט וּבִרְהִיטְנִי חַיָּיב – ת"ל "וּפְאַת זְקָנָם לֹא יְגַלֵּחוּ", אֵיזוֹ גִּילּוּחַ שֶׁיֵּשׁ בּוֹ הַשְׁחָתָה – הֱוֵי אוֹמֵר זֶה תַּעַר. וּמַאן דְּמַפֵּיק לֵיהּ לְהַאי "רֹאשׁוֹ" לְלָאו גְּרֵידָא, לָמָּה לִי לְמִיכְתַּב "רֹאשׁוֹ" וְלָמָּה לִי לְמִיכְתַּב "זְקָנוֹ"? מַשְׁמַע לְמִידְחֵי לָאו גְּרֵידָא, וּמַשְׁמַע לְמִידְחֵי ל"ת וַעֲשֵׂה, הִילְכָּךְ *שָׁקוּל הוּא, וְיָבוֹאוּ שְׁנֵיהֶן. כֹּהֵן מִנָּזִיר לָא יָלֵיף – שֶׁכֵּן יֶשְׁנוֹ בִּשְׁאֵלָה, נָזִיר מִכֹּהֵן לָא יָלֵיף – שֶׁכֵּן לָאו שֶׁאֵינוֹ שָׁוֶה בַּכֹּל. וּבְעָלְמָא לָא יָלְפִינַן מִינַּיְיהוּ – מִשּׁוּם דְּאִיכָּא לְמִיפְרַךְ כִּדְאֲמַרַן. (ב).§ אָמַר רַב: מֵיקֵל אָדָם כָּל גּוּפוֹ בְּתַעַר. מֵיתִיבֵי: ב הַמַּעֲבִיר בֵּית הַשֶּׁחִי וּבֵית הָעֶרְוָה – הֲרֵי זֶה לוֹקֶה. *ג הָא בְּתַעַר, הָא בְּמִסְפָּרַיִם. וְהָא רַב נַמִי בְּתַעַר קָאָמַר! כְּעֵין תַּעַר. אָמַר רַבִּי חִיָּיא בַּר אַבָּא אָמַר רַבִּי יוֹחָנָן: הַמַּעֲבִיר בֵּית הַשֶּׁחִי וּבֵית הָעֶרְוָה לוֹקֶה. מֵיתִיבֵי: הַעֲבָרַת שֵׂעָר אֵינָהּ מִדִּבְרֵי תוֹרָה אֶלָּא מִדִּבְרֵי סוֹפְרִים! – *°מַאי לוֹקֶה נַמִי דְּקָאָמַר ד – מִדְּרַבָּנַן.
אִיכָּא

ולמאן דמוקים ליה להאי ראשו בנזיר. ויליף כהן מנזיר, א"כ למה לי דכתב רחמנא "זקנו" במצורע? מיבעי ליה. לתגלחת מצורע שיהא בתער ולא במלקט ורהיטני, וכדתניא: א) "זקנם לא יגלחו", יכול אפילו מצורע – תלמוד לומר "זקנו", התיר במצורע מה שאסר הכתוב גבי גילוח זקן, שלא אסר הכתוב אלא בתער שעושה השחתה, אבל במלקט ורהיטני לא. וכדאמרינן בפרק "שלשה מינין" (לעיל מ:) דאי ס"ד עביד במלקט ורהיטני נמי מצוה קעביד – לשתוק קרא מיניה ותו (ג) לא, מדלא כתיב ביה תער – מוטב דליעבד במלקט ורהיטני משום דריש לקיש, דאמר: כל מקום שאתה מוצא וכו'. (ד) ולמאן דמפיק ליה להאי "ראשו" לעשה ול"ת דבנזיר, אילטריך ב) ליה "זקנו" לתגלחת דמצורע בתער. אלא למאן דמפיק ליה להאי "ראשו" ללאו גרידא – למה ליה למיכתב "זקנו" כלל? אי משום עשה ול"ת – ליכתוב רחמנא "ראשו" ותו לא, דהוי משמע דלמידחי לאו גרידא קאתי, לאו ד"לא תקיפו", ומשמע נמי למידרשיה גבי נזיר. דהאי קרא שקול הוא, דלא מסתיים ג) מהיכא קאי, ומשום הכי אית לך למימר שיבואו שניהם ממנו! לעולם אילטריך למיכתב "זקנו" משום למידחי עשה ול"ת דכהן. דאי אמרת דלא ליכתוב "זקנו", וכי אתא "ראשו" למידחי עשה ול"ת דבנזיר הוא דאתא – אכתי ליכא למיגמר מיניה עשה ול"ת דכהן, משום דאיכא למיפרך: מה לנזיר שכן ישנו בשאלה. ואי אמרת נמי דהאי *"ראשו" משום עשה ול"ת דכהן הוא דאתא – אכתי לית לך למילף מיניה עשה ול"ת דבנזיר, משום דאיכא למיפרך כדאמרן. דאי מנזיר איכא למיפרך: מה לנזיר שכן ישנו בשאלה, ואי מכהן – מה לכהן שכן לאו שאינו שוה בכל. הילכך אילטריך ליה "זקנו" לעשה ול"ת דכהן, ו"ראשו" ללאו גרידא. אמר רב מיקל אדם כל גופו בתער. ואין בו משום "לא ילבש גבר שמלת אשה". המעביר שער שבבית השחי. תחת אצילי ידיו. כעין תער. שגוזז במספרים בסמוך לבשר, כעין תער. מיתיבי ד) העברת שער. של כל גופו, כגון שבבית השחי ושבבית הערוה – אינה מדברי תורה. ואת אמרת דלוקה. מאי לוקה. דאמרי, מכות מרדות מדרבנן.
איכא

נזיר מכהן נמי לא יליף שכן לאו שאינו שוה בכל הוא. והשתא הוה מצי למיפרך: אמאי לא [ילפינן] מנזיר דעלמא דאתי עשה ודחי ל"ת ועשה, אפי' שוה בכל. דנזיר שוה בכל הוא! ולמסקנא ניחא, דפרכינן בסמוך: מה לנזיר שכן ישנו בשאלה.

ולמאן דמוקי ראשו בנזיר זקנו למה לי. לחנם פי' התלמוד כן (ה) דכוותיה קיימא. גם לחנם שינה לשונו, דקאמר לעיל דלמאן דמפיק "ראשו" לעשה ול"ת מבעיא ליה לכדתניא, למילף דתגלחת מצורע בתער הוא, דאילו מ"ראשו" דנזיר [לא] נפקא. דסבירא לן כמ"ד פ' "ג' מינין" (לעיל מ.) דנזיר חייב בכל מעבירין, ולהכי איצטריך "זקנו", דאילו השחתת זקן אינה אלא בתער, כדמפרש ואזיל. וצ"ע: כי פריך "זקנו למה לי", אמאי לא משני: וליטעמיך הא (ו) קי"ל דאין עשה דוחה ל"ת ועשה, נילף מנזיר מצורע דדחי. אלא מאי אית לך למימר – מה לנזיר שכן ישנו בשאלה.

ולמאן דמפיק ראשו ללאו גרידא למה לי. (ז) לכתוב "זקנו" לבד, דמשמע בין זקנו דכהן בין זקנו דישראל, ומינה שמעי' (בין) ל"ת גרידא בישראל, ומינה שמעי' ל"ת ועשה (ח) מכהנים, דמקרא מלא דיבר הכתוב! ואע"ג ד"ראשו" נמי מקרא מלא הוא, ולא בעי לאוקומי אלא בראשו גרידא, ולא בראשו דנזיר – שאני התם דשני לאוין הן, לאו דהקפה ולאו דנזיר "תער לא יעבור" – הילכך לא מסתברא ליה למימר כולי האי מקרא מלא, לאוקומי אפילו בראשו דנזיר. אבל השחתת הזקן – הכל לאו אחד הוא, בין דישראל "לא תשחית פאת זקנך" בין דכהנים "ופאת זקנם לא יגלחו". הילכך נראה לומר דמקרא מלא דיבר הכתוב, דעשה דמצורע ד"זקנו" ידחה בין לאו דישראל בין לאו דכהנים, כיון דאזהרה אחת היא.

הר"פ: והשתא מצי לשנויי דאי מ"זקנו" איכא למיפרך שכן לאו שאינו שוה בכל הוא, דליתיה בנשים. (ט) ואיצטריך "ראשו" דאם אינו ענין ללאו שאינו שוה בכל – תניהו ענין לשוה בכל. ונראה דסלקא דעתיה דשקולים הן, ולכך מודה לו דל"ת גרידא השוה בכל כמו ל"ת ועשה שאינו שוה בכל, אלא האריך יותר, דאיידי דבעי לאסוקי הך פירכא – מסיק ואזיל לכולי לגדי דפירכות. ומשני: כהן מנזיר לא יליף, שכן ישנו בשאלה. ונזיר מכהן לא יליף – שכן לאו שאינו שוה בכל. ובעלמא לא ילפינן מינייהו, משום דאיכא למיפרך כדאמרן. וקשה להר"ס: (י) דמאי קאמר "כהן מנזיר לא יליף" כו'? לימא דכהן איצטריך משום תער, דבעינן תער במצורע כדקא אמרינן! וע"ק לו: דקא פריך למ"ד "ראשו" ללאו גרידא, וקמהדר ליה למ"ד "ראשו" לנזיר אתא, מדקאמר: כהן מנזיר לא יליף כו'! לכך נראה להר"ס לפרש: דמשמע ליה השתא, כיון דמסקינן ד"זקנו" אתא לאשמועי' תער, מעתה למאן דאית ליה ד"ראשו" אתא ללאו גרידא – מנלן דנזיר מצורע (כ) מגלח וכהן מצורע? אלא על כרחיך צריך לומר דמקרא מלא דבר הכתוב, דכיון דקרא סתמא כתיב – מיירי בכל ענין, בין שהוא כהן בין שהוא נזיר, ולמה לי למיכתב "זקנו"? ואם תאמר: והא שפיר איצטריך לאשמועינן דתגלחת מצורע בתער! וי"ל, דהכי פריך: למה ליה לתנא דלעיל לאיתויי "זקנו" למילף דכהן מצורע מותר בתגלחת, דקתני "זקנו" מה ת"ל כו'? מ"ראשו" שמעינן, שאפילו נזיר מצורע מגלח ראשו, אע"ג דאיכא לאו ועשה, דקרא סתמא כתיב, (ל) דמיניה משמע שגם כהן מגלח זקנו! דהשתא סבירא ליה דלהאי תנא הם שקולין. ומשני: אין הכי נמי, דודאי סבירא ליה דמקרא מלא דבר הכתוב, ומ"ראשו" גרידא שמעינן שגם נזיר מצורע מגלח ראשו. ואפי' הכי, אי לאו דכתב רחמנא "זקנו" לא הוה שמעינן כהן כדפרישית, שכן ישנו בשאלה. ואי כתב "זקנו" – לא הוה שמעינן נזיר, שכן לאו שאינו שוה בכל. ולפי מסקנא זו, תנא דמוקי "ראשו" ללאו גרידא – ה"ה דשמעינן מיניה לאו ועשה. ומה שהזכיר לאו דהקפה גרידא – לגלות לנו דעתו, דסבר דאי לאו הני קראי ד"ראשו" ו"זקנו" – אפילו לאו גרידא לא הוה ידעינן שיהא עשה דוחה אותו. דקרא דגדילים הוה מוקמינן ליה לכדרבא. ובעלמא לא ילפינן כדאמרן. כלומר, דאיכא למיפרך: מה לכהן שכן לאו שאינו שוה בכל, ומה לנזיר שכן ישנו בשאלה. ואם תאמר: ונילף מתרווייהו במה הצד! ואומר ר"י: דאיכא למיפרך: מה לעשה דמצורע דאיכא שלום בית. וכי האי גוונא אמרינן בפ' "שילוח הקן" (חולין דף קמא.) דסלקא דעתך אמינא עשה דלפרי מצורע לידחי לא תעשה א] ועשה דשילוח הקן, משום שלום בית*. אמר רב מיקל אדם כל גופו בתער מיתיבי כו' הרי זה לוקה. משום "לא ילבש גבר" כדדרשינן בסמוך. לא קשיא, הא בתער הא במספרים. והא רב נמי בתער קאמר! כעין תער. א"ר יוחנן המעביר בית השחי ובית הערוה הרי זה לוקה. מיתיבי העברת תער אינה מדברי תורה אלא מדברי סופרים. והוה מצי לסיועיה מברייתא דלעיל, אלא ניחא ליה לשנויי: מאי לוקה – דרבנן, דלא ליפגלו ברייתות אהדדי. ר' יוחנן אף במספרים אוסר, ומשמע דרבי יוחנן פליג אדרב.
איכא

פי' הרא"ש

ומאן דמוקי ראשו בנזיר זקנו למה לי הוה מצי לשנויי דכהן מנזיר לא אתי שכן ישנו בשאלה כדקאמר בסמוך אלא רעדיפא מיניה קא משני דמיבעי ליה לכדתניא דאינו חייב על השחתת זקן אלא בתער ומדאיצט' זקנו למדחי לאו ועשה דכהן ש"מ דמצורע אינו מגלח אלא בתער דאי מצי לגלוחי בלא תער לא הוה דחי. ומנזיר לא שמעי' ליה דשמא ס"ל כמאן דאמר פ"ג מינים לא יעבור לרבות כל המעבירים: ומאן דאוקי ראשו ללאו גרידא ל"ל למכתב ראשו ולמה לי למכתב זקנו. ליכתוב זקנו דמשמע בין בישראל דאיכא לאו גרידא בין בכהן דאיכא לאו ועשה ולשתוק מראשו: ומשני דלאו שקולים הם דבכל חד מנייהו איכא פירכא ולא ילפי' מהדדי. ובעלמא נמי לא ילפי מינייהו כדאמר דמה לכהן שאינו שוה בכל הילכך לא ילפינן מיניה שידחה עשה ל"ת ועשה: אמר רב מיקל אדם כל גופו בתער אפי' בית השחי ובית הערוה ואין בזה משום לא ילבש גבר שמלת אשה. אבל בפאת זקן וראש לא איירי רב אלא בשאר הגוף קאמר: ה"ז לוקה משום לא ילבש וכו'. כעין תער במספרים סמוך לבשר: מיתיבי העברת שער אינה מדברי תורה אלא מדברי סופרים וקשה לר"י דאמר לוקה. וה"ה דהוה מצי למפרך השתי ברייתות אהדדי ולשנויי כדמשני מאי לוקה כדקתני מכת מרדות:

ה"ז

הגהות מהר"ב רנשבורג

א] תוד"ה הר"ף וכו' דסד"א וכו' דלאו ל"ת. נ"ב אין זה מדוקדק דבחולין לא נזכר מדיוק ... לחיות עשה. וצ"ע:

כי קאמר רב בשאר אברים כך הוא גירסת כל הפוסקים [רב אלפס מסכת ע"ז דף רפב. מיתיבי המעביר בית השחי ובית הערוה הרי זה לוקה כי קאמר רב בשאר אברים אבל בית השחי ובית הערוה לא. ושאר אברים מי שרי והא תניא העברת שיער אינה מדברי תורה אלא מדברי סופרים כי קאמר רב במספרים וכי תניא היא בתער והא רב בתער קאמר אימא כעין תער ע"כ גי' רב אלפס שם ועמש"כ תוס' לקמן נט. ד"ה הכא בכס בעל ה"ג]

לעיל מ: חולין קה: מכות כח.

[ב"ק ג. זבחים ז: ערכין ז:]

גי' א"מ זקנו

[דוגמתו שבת מ. וש"נ]

נוסחת הרב"ן

(א) ופאת זקנם לא יגלחו כו' ת"ל זקנו ומה (ומצורע) שאסר הכתוב גבי גילוח זקן שלא אסר הכתוב אלא בתער שעושה השחתה התיר לך הכתוב גבי מצורע אבל במלקט והרהיטני לא וכדאמר בפ' ג' מינין דאי ס"ד הכי עביד: ב) אילטריך לתגלחת: ג) מהיכא: ד) מיתיבי איסור העברת שער:

גליון הש"ס

גמ' נזיר מכהן נמי לא יליף. עי' לעיל דף מא ע"ב תד"ה ואי כתב: שם מאי לוקה דקאמר. שבת דף ה ע"ב יבמות דף כח חולין דף קמא ע"ב:

[ועי' היטב תוס' יבמות ה. ד"ה שכן]

הגהות הב"ח (א) גמ' מיבעי ליה לכדתניא ופאת זקנם לא יגלחו יכול אף גילחו במספרים כצ"ל ותיבות זקנו מה ת"ל לפי שנאמר ופאת זקנם לא יגלחו יכול אף כהן מצורע כן ת"ל זקנו ומנלן דבתער דתניא נמחק: (ב) שם דאיכא למיפרך כדאמרן. נ"ב בריש יבמות כתבו התוספות ואית דלא גרסי כדאמרן ומפרש דקאי איכא למיפרך אהא דקאמר בתר הכי אמר רב כו' דלמאי דמסיק כעין תער איכא למיפרך כיון דלאו דידהו קל אתי עשה ודחי להו וא"כ ליכא למיגמר מינייהו במה הצד וע"ש בדף ו בד"ה שכן ישנו בשאלה: (ג) רש"י ד"ה מיבעי ליה וכו' לישתוק קרא מיניה ותו מדלא כצ"ל ותיבת לא נמחק: (ד) בא"ד שאתה מוצא וכו' הס"ד ואח"כ מ"ה ומאן דמפיק ליה וכו' דלמאן דמפיק ליה וכו' דלא מסתיים אהיכא קאי: (ה) תוס' ד"ה ולמאן וכו' פי' הש"ס כן דהא י"ל דכוותיה לאידך קיימא גם: (ו) בא"ד הא דקי"ל דאין עשה: (ז) ד"ה ולמאן דמפיק וכו' למה לי למיכתב ראשו ולמה לי למיכתב זקנו ליכתוב זקנו לבד: (ח) בא"ד ל"ת ועשה דנזיר מכהנים דמקרא: (ט) ד"ה הר"ף וכו' דליתיה בנשים להכי אילטריך וכו' דשקולין הן דכך חמור לו ל"ת גרידא: (י) בא"ד וקשה להר"ס דלמאי קאמר וכו' למ"ד ראשו לנזיר הוא דאתא מדקאמר: (כ) בא"ד מנלן דנזיר מצורע וכהן מצורע מגלח אלא על כרחיך: (ל) בא"ד ומיניה משמע נמי שגם כהן:

אִיכָּא דְּאָמְרִי, אָמַר ר' חִיָּיא בַּר אַבָּא אָמַר ר' יוֹחָנָן: הַמַּעֲבִיר בֵּית הַשֶּׁחִי וּבֵית הָעֶרְוָה לוֹקֶה מִשּׁוּם °"לֹא יִלְבַּשׁ גֶּבֶר שִׂמְלַת אִשָּׁה". מֵיתִיבֵי: הַעֲבָרַת שֵׂיעָר אֵינָהּ מִדִּבְרֵי תוֹרָה אֶלָּא מִדִּבְרֵי סוֹפְרִים! הוּא דְּאָמַר כִּי הַאי תַּנָּא, דְּתַנְיָא: הַמַּעֲבִיר בֵּית הַשֶּׁחִי וּבֵית הָעֶרְוָה – הֲרֵי זֶה עוֹבֵר מִשּׁוּם "לֹא יִלְבַּשׁ גֶּבֶר שִׂמְלַת אִשָּׁה". וְתַנָּא קַמָּא, הַאי "לֹא יִלְבַּשׁ גֶּבֶר" מַאי דָּרֵישׁ בֵּיהּ? מִיבָּעֵי לֵיהּ לְכִדְתַנְיָא: °"לֹא יִהְיֶה כְלִי גֶבֶר עַל אִשָּׁה" מַאי ת"ל? אִם שֶׁלֹּא יִלְבַּשׁ אִישׁ שִׂמְלַת אִשָּׁה, וְאִשָּׁה שִׂמְלַת אִישׁ – הֲרֵי כְּבָר נֶאֱמַר "תּוֹעֵבָה הִיא" וְאֵין כָּאן תּוֹעֵבָה. אֶלָּא, שֶׁלֹּא יִלְבַּשׁ אִישׁ שִׂמְלַת אִשָּׁה וְיֵשֵׁב בֵּין הַנָּשִׁים, וְאִשָּׁה שִׂמְלַת אִישׁ וְתֵשֵׁב בֵּין הָאֲנָשִׁים. רַבִּי אֱלִיעֶזֶר בֶּן יַעֲקֹב אוֹמֵר: אמִנַּיִן שֶׁלֹּא תֵּצֵא אִשָּׁה בִּכְלֵי זַיִן לַמִּלְחָמָה – ת"ל "לֹא יִהְיֶה כְלִי גֶבֶר עַל אִשָּׁה וְלֹא יִלְבַּשׁ גֶּבֶר שִׂמְלַת אִשָּׁה" – שֶׁלֹּא יְתַקֵּן אִישׁ בְּתִיקּוּנֵי אִשָּׁה. אָמַר רַב נַחְמָן: בְּנָזִיר מוּתָּר. וְלֵית הִילְכְתָא כְּוָותֵיהּ. אֲמַרוּ לֵיהּ רַבָּנַן לר"ש בַּר אַבָּא: חֲזֵינָא לֵיהּ לְרַבִּי יוֹחָנָן דְּלֵית לֵיהּ. אֲמַר לְהוֹן: מֵחֲמַת זִקְנָה נָשְׁרוּ. הַהוּא דְּאִתְחַיַּיב נְגִידָא קַמֵּיהּ דְּרַבִּי אַמִי, אִיגְּלַאי בֵּית הַשֶּׁחִי, חֲזְיֵיהּ דְּלָא מְגַלַּח. אֲמַר לְהוֹן רַבִּי אַמִי: שִׁיבְקוּהּ, דֵּין מִן חַבְרַיָּא הוּא. בְּעָא מִינֵּיהּ רַב מֵרַבִּי חִיָּיא: מַהוּ לְגַלֵּחַ? אֲמַר לֵיהּ: אָסוּר. אֲמַר לֵיהּ: וְהָא קָא גָּדֵל! א"ל: *בַּר פָּחְתֵי, זְמַן יֵשׁ לוֹ, כָּל זְמַן שֶׁהוּא גָּדֵל נוֹשֵׁר. בְּעָא מִינֵּיהּ רַב מֵרַבִּי חִיָּיא: מַהוּ לָחוֹךְ? אֲמַר לֵיהּ: באָסוּר. בְּבִגְדוֹ מַהוּ? א"ל: גמוּתָּר. אִיכָּא דְּאָמְרִי: בְּעָא מִינֵּיהּ: בִּתְפִלָּה בְּבִגְדוֹ מַאי? א"ל: אָסוּר. דוְלֵית הִילְכְתָא כְּוָותֵיהּ.§

מתני'

רש"י

אִיכָּא דְּאָמְרִי. דִּבְהָדְיָא מְפָרֵשׁ רַבִּי חִיָּיא מִשּׁוּם "לֹא יִלְבַּשׁ גֶּבֶר שִׂמְלַת אִשָּׁה", וְאִשָּׁה דַּרְכָּהּ בְּכָךְ, שֶׁהוּא נִיוּוּל לָהּ כְּשֶׁיֵּשׁ לָהּ שֵׂעָר. וְתַנָּא קַמָּא. דְּסָבַר דְּאֵינָהּ אֶלָּא מִדִּבְרֵי סוֹפְרִים, מַאי דָּרֵישׁ א) בְּהַאי "לֹא יִלְבַּשׁ" (א)? אִם לְלַמֵּד שֶׁלֹּא יִלְבַּשׁ. כְּלוֹמַר, וְאִם אָמַר לְךָ הַכָּתוּב ב) שֶׁלֹּא יִלְבַּשׁ הָאִישׁ שִׂמְלַת אִשָּׁה – לְכָךְ לֹא קְרָאוֹ הַכָּתוּב "תּוֹעֵבָה הִיא". ג) אֶלָּא לָמָּה הוּא בָּא – שֶׁלֹּא יִלְבַּשׁ הָאִישׁ שִׂמְלַת הָאִשָּׁה ד) וְיֵלֵךְ וְיֵשֵׁב בֵּין הַנָּשִׁים, שֶׁיֵּשׁ לָחוּשׁ מִשּׁוּם יִיחוּד. בִּכְלֵי זַיִן לַמִּלְחָמָה. כְּדִמְתַרְגְּמִינַן "לָא יְהֵא תִּיקּוּן זַיִן דִּגְבַר". תַּלְמוּד לוֹמַר לֹא יִהְיֶה כְלִי גֶבֶר עַל אִשָּׁה. וְזֶה שֶׁמָּצִינוּ יָעֵל אֵשֶׁת חֶבֶר הַקֵּינִי, שֶׁלֹּא הֲרָגַתּוּ לְסִיסְרָא בִּכְלֵי זַיִן, אֶלָּא כְּמוֹ שֶׁנֶּאֱמַר °"יָדָהּ לַיָּתֵד תִּשְׁלַחְנָה" (שופטים ה). שֶׁלֹּא יְתַקֵּן אִישׁ בְּתִיקּוּנֵי אִשָּׁה. דְּהָכִי מְתַרְגְּמִינַן לֵיהּ – שֶׁלֹּא יִכְחוֹל וְשֶׁלֹּא יְפַרְכֵּס ה) בְּבִגְדֵי לְבָעוֹנִים שֶׁל אִשָּׁה. חֲזֵינָא לֵיהּ לְר' יוֹחָנָן דְּלֵית לֵיהּ. שֵׂיעָר בְּבֵית הַשֶּׁחִי. אִיגְּלַאי בֵּית הַשֶּׁחִי. כִּי הֲווּ מְשַׁלְּחֵי ו) בְּהֶפְשֵׁט מָאנֵיהּ לְנַגְדֵיהּ. דֵּין מִן חַבְרַיָּא הוּא. דְּיָדַע דְּאָסוּר לְהַעֲבִיר ז) בֵּית הַשֶּׁחִי. מַהוּ לְגַלֵּחַ. בְּמִסְפָּרַיִם בֵּית הַשֶּׁחִי. וְהָא קָא גָּדֵל. וְקָא מְצַעֵר לֵיהּ לְאִינָשׁ. בַּר פָּחְתֵי. בְּנוֹ שֶׁל תַּלְמִיד חָכָם. גְּבוּל יֵשׁ לוֹ. לְאוֹתוֹ שֵׂעָר, כֵּיוָן שֶׁגָּדַל יוֹתֵר מִמַּה שֶּׁאָדָם יָכוֹל ח) לְסוֹבְלוֹ – נוֹשֵׁר מֵאֵלָיו. (נָזִיר) מַהוּ לָחוֹךְ. בְּבֵית הַשֶּׁחִי בְּיָדוֹ, כְּדֵי לְהַעֲבִיר אֶת הַשֵּׂיעָר ט). מַהוּ לָחוֹךְ י) בְּבִגְדוֹ. כְּנֶגֶד בֵּית הַשֶּׁחִי, כְּדֵי שֶׁיְּהֵא נוֹשֵׁר עַל יְדֵי חִיכּוּךְ. א"ל מוּתָּר. הוֹאִיל וְאֵינוֹ נוֹגֵעַ בַּשֵּׂעָר אֶלָּא בְּבִגְדוֹ. אִיכָּא דְּאָמְרִי. הָכִי קָמִיבַּעְיָא לֵיהּ: בִּתְפִלָּה בְּבִגְדוֹ מַאי? כְּלוֹמַר, הַמִּתְפַּלֵּל מַהוּ לָחוֹךְ בְּבִגְדוֹ כְּדֵי שֶׁיִּפְּלוּ כִּנִּים מִמֶּנּוּ, הוֹאִיל וְאֵינוֹ נוֹגֵעַ בִּבְשָׂרוֹ. א"ל אָסוּר וְלֵית הִלְכְתָא כְּוָותֵיהּ. מִשּׁוּם דְּכֵיוָן דְּאֵינוֹ נוֹגֵעַ בִּבְשָׂרוֹ מוּתָּר לָחוֹךְ כְּמוֹ שׁוֹר הַמִּתְחַכֵּךְ בַּכּוֹתֶל (בבא קמא דף מד.).

מתני'

תוספות

איכא דאמרי א"ר יוחנן המעביר בית השחי ובית הערוה הרי זה לוקה משום לא יהיה כלי כו' מיתיבי העברת שער אינה מדברי תורה **אלא** מדברי סופרים. ולא מלי לשנויי דרבי יוחנן נמי מדברי סופרים קאמר, דנסיב ליה לטעמיה מקרא.

הוא דאמר כי האי תנא. והוי מלי לשנויי כאידך ברייתא דלוקה, אלא ניחא ליה לאיתויי תנא דדריש ליה מקרא. דהשתא ברייתא איכא למידחי, דלוקה מדרבנן קאמר. לא יהיה כלי גבר על אשה. ובסיפיה דקרא נמי כתיב "ולא ילבש גבר שמלת אשה" שלא ילבש איש שמלת אשה. כפשטיה דקרא הא לא מלית אמרת דבהכי איירי קרא, דהא כתיב בסיפיה "תועבה היא", ובכי האי גוונא ליכא תועבה. **בנזיר** מותר. להעביר בית השחי ובית הערוה. דקסבר: אחרי שנזיר מעביר כל שער ראשו לא חשיב נוי ותיקון לגבי אותו האיש להעביר בית השחי ובית הערוה. ולית הילכתא כותיה, דאסור אף לנזיר. **חזינא** לרבי יוחנן דלית ליה. פירוש: שער בית השחי. [והוא] גופיה מחייב בהעברתו. ומדלא משני במספרים א) שקלינהו – דלכל הפחות מדברי סופרים אסור לרבי יוחנן אף במספרים.

ההוא גברא דאיתחייב נגידא קמיה דר' אמי. נתחייב מלקות. איגלאי בית השחי וחזייה דלא מגלח. אמר להון רבי אמי שבקוה דין מן חבריא הוא. משמע נמי הכא דמדרבנן נמי אסור אף במספרים בבית השחי ובבית הערוה, אבל לשאר האיברים לא מצינו איסור. (זה הלשון) לזו הגירסא. ובהלכות גדולות בהלכות נזיר: ב) אמר רב מיקל אדם כל גופו בתער. מיתיבי: המעביר בית השחי ובית הערוה הרי זה לוקה. כי קאמר רב – בשאר איברים. ומי שרי? והתניא: העברת שער אינו מדברי תורה אלא מדברי סופרים! ואומר ר"י: דפריך משום דברייתא קתני סתמא בהעברת שער, דמשמע בכל מקום, בין בשאר איברים בין בבית השחי ובבית הערוה, אלמא שאר איברים נמי אסור. ומשני: אלא כי קאמר רב במספרים. ומדקאמר "אלא" משמע דהכי פירושו: לעולם מיירי אף בשער בית השחי ובית הערוה, *דקאמר רב – היינו במספרים כעין תער. **אמר** רבי חייא בר אבא א"ר יוחנן המעביר בית השחי ובית הערוה הרי זה לוקה מיתיבי העברת שער אינו מדברי תורה אלא מדברי סופרים. משמע לן דמיירי אף בשער בית השחי ובית הערוה, מדקאמר סתמא. ומשני: מאי לוקה דקאמר ר' יוחנן – מדרבנן, וכן לוקה דברייתא – היינו מדרבנן. וכפי גירסת הלכות גדולות משמע דאפי' דשאר איברים אסור להעביר שיער. ובהלכה פסוקה דרב יהודאי בהלכות נדה מכתב ה"ר יוסף טוב עלם יש כמו בהלכות שלנו, אך דגורס במסקנא: כי קאמר רב במספרים. ולא גרסינן "אלא". ומשמע דה"פ: רב אמר: מיקל אדם כל גופו בתער – היינו דשאר איברים, כדאוקמינן לה. ובתער דקאמר – דכעין תער, אבל בתער ממש ודאי עובר מדברי סופרים, כדקתני בברייתא. והאי דבעי רב מרבי חייא מהו לגלח – במספרים קמבעיא ליה, והשיב לו דאף במספרים אסור. מדקאמר ליה "והא קא גדיל", כלומר ומצערו, ואי שרי במספרים – יטלנו במספרים. ורב נמי דשרי כל גופו במספרים כעין תער – היינו בשאר איברים, אבל בבית השחי ובבית הערוה אסור במספרים. [ושמא] אף על גב דלא כתוב [בספרים] "אלא", מ"מ הוי פירושו כאילו גרסינן "אלא". והרבה יש בהתלמוד כזה, וחזר להעמיד דברי רב בבית השחי כו' ג).

בעי מיניה רב מרבי חייא מהו לגלח. פי': בית השחי ובית הערוה. אמר ליה אסור. לפי גירסת הספרים שלנו הבעיא בתער ממש, ואסר לו תער, ומספרים שרי. ולפירוש [הלכות גדולות] הבעיא במספרים, ואסר לו אף במספרים. וכן נראה, מדקאמר "והא קא גדיל". ומאי קושיא? יטלנו במספרים! **והא** קא גדיל. והואיל וסופו ליגדל ולצער אותו, אף כשיגלחנו אין זה קרוי תיקון ונוי, שאינו מגלח אלא ליגלל מצערא. **גבול** יש לו. שאינו גדל והולך כשיער הראש, וליכא לצערא. (הכי גרסינן) משמע כשאין אדם מתכוין לנוי אלא ליגלל – דלית ביה משום כלי גבר. ואם כן, המסתכל במראה כדי שלא יתבול בעצמו – שרי. וכן אומר הר"ף שרבו הר"ר שמואל מאויר"א היה מסתפר במראה. **מהו** לחוך ולהתחכך. כדי להשיר שער בית השחי ובית הערוה. אמר ליה: אסור. ולית הילכתא כוותיה.

א) נ"ל שמעינן דלכל. ב) גירסת א"מ זה הלשון אמר רב. ג) [ועי' תוס' יבמות מח. ד"ה לא עשה]

ומי

עין משפט נר מצוה

יג א מיי' פי"ב מהל' עבודת כוכבים הל"י סמג לאוין נא טוש"ע יו"ד סי' קפב סעי' ה:

יד ב ג טוש"ע שם סעי' ג:

טו ד טוש"ע או"ח סי' לב סעי' ז בהג"ה וסי' צז סעי' ג:

פי' הרא"ש

ה"ז לוקה משום לא ילבש וכו' וכיון דקרא מייתי אלמא לוקה מדאורייתא: הרי כבר נאמר בסיפיה דקרא כי תועבה היא הלכך ליכא לפרושי רישיה דקרא הכי דבכה"ג ליכא תועבה אלא ביושב בין הנשים דוגמת אשה כדי לזנות עמהן: ה"ג במילתיה דר"א בן יעקב מנין שלא תצא וכו' ת"ל לא יהיה כלי גבר וכו' ולא ילבש גבר שמלת אשה לא יתקן גבר בתיקוני אתתא. פי' שלא יכחול ולא יפרכס ולא יעבור בית השחי ובית הערוה: [בנזיר מותר]. דכיון דמגלח כל ראשו ביום כלות נזירותו ליכא תקון אשה בהעברת בית השחי ובית הערוה. ולית הלכתא כותיה: חזינן ליה לר' יוחנן דלית ליה בית השחי ובית הערוה. וידע דבמספרים א"א לגלחן כ"כ סמוך לבשר: ההוא דאתחייב ניגודא. מלקות: איגלאי בית השחי. כשהפשיטוהו בגדיו להלקותו: דמן חבריא הוא. וידע דאסור להעביר בית השחי: בעא מניה רב מר' חייא מהו לגלח. אין לפ' דבמספרים בעא מניה דכיון דא"ל ר' חייא אסור היכי אמר רב לעיל דמותר להקל במספרים כעין תער ולא מסתברא למימר דפליג אר' חייא רביה. אלא מהו לגלח בתער: א"ל ר' חייא אסור. והא קא גדיל. ותי' מאי פריך לגלחיה במספרים דר' חייא לא אסר אלא בתער. ופר"ת והא קא גדיל ומצערי ליה והואיל וסופו ליגדל ולצערו אף כשמגלחו אין זה תיקון לנוי אלא להצילו מן הצער. גבול יש לו ואינו גדל כ"כ שיגיע לידי צער: מהו לחוך. להתחכך כדי להשיר שער בית הערוה. א"ל אסור: בבגדו מאי א"ל מותר דבכה"ג שהוא מחכך בגדיו להשירו ליכא תיקון אשה: איכא דאמרי בתפלה בבגדו מאי. כשהוא מתפלל מהו לחכך בבגדו בית השחי ובית הערוה: א"ל אסור ולית הלכתא כותיה:

תורה אור

דברים כב

שם

הגהות הב"ח

(א) רש"י ד"ה ות"ק וכו' לא ילבש הס"ד ואח"כ מ"ה מת"ל אם ללמד שלא:

גליון הש"ס

רש"י ד"ה ת"ל לא יהיה כו' ידה ליתד תשלחנה. וכן הוא בתרגום שם. וכן הוא בילקוט שופטים סימן נו:

[ברכות יג: מג. שבת ג: כט.]

גי' א"מ ובתער

נוסחת הריב"ן

א) ביה בהאי: ב) הכתוב כמשמעו: ג) תועבה היא למה כו': ד) וילך בין הנשים: ה) במיני: ו) משלחי ליה כשהפשיטו בגדיו להלקותו: ז) שיער: ח) לסבול: ט) ע"י חיכוך: י) בבית השחי בבגד כדי כו':

טז א מיי' פ"ט מהל' נזירות הלט"ו:
יז ב מיי' שם פ"ז הלט"ו:
יח ג מיי' שם פ"ט הל' טו ופ"י הל"א:

מתני' מֵת אֶחָד מֵהֶן, אָמַר ר' יְהוֹשֻׁעַ: יְבַקֵּשׁ *אֶחָד מִן הַשּׁוּק שֶׁיִּדּוֹר כְּנֶגְדּוֹ בְּנָזִיר, וְאוֹמֵר: "אִם טָמֵא הָיִיתִי – הֲרֵי אַתָּה נָזִיר מִיָּד, וְאִם טָהוֹר הָיִיתִי – הֲרֵי אַתָּה נָזִיר אַחַר שְׁלֹשִׁים יוֹם". וְסוֹפְרִין שְׁלֹשִׁים, (א) וּמְבִיאִין קָרְבַּן טוּמְאָה וְקָרְבַּן טָהֳרָה, וְאוֹמֵר: "אִם אֲנִי הוּא הַטָּמֵא – קָרְבַּן טוּמְאָה שֶׁלִּי, וְקָרְבַּן טָהֳרָה שֶׁלְּךָ. וְאִם אֲנִי הוּא הַטָּהוֹר – קָרְבַּן טָהֳרָה שֶׁלִּי, וְקָרְבַּן טוּמְאָה בְּסָפֵק". וְסוֹפְרִים שְׁלֹשִׁים יוֹם, וּמְבִיאִין קָרְבַּן טָהֳרָה, וְאוֹמֵר: "אִם אֲנִי (ב) הַטָּמֵא – קָרְבַּן טוּמְאָה שֶׁלִּי וְקָרְבַּן טָהֳרָה שֶׁלְּךָ, וְזֶה קָרְבַּן טָהֳרָתִי. וְאִם אֲנִי הוּא הַטָּהוֹר – קָרְבַּן טָהֳרָה שֶׁלִּי, וְקָרְבַּן טוּמְאָה בְּסָפֵק, וְזֶהוּ קָרְבַּן טָהֳרָתְךָ". אָמַר לוֹ בֶּן זוֹמָא: וּמִי שׁוֹמֵעַ לוֹ שֶׁיִּדּוֹר כְּנֶגְדּוֹ בְּנָזִיר? אאֶלָּא, מֵבִיא חַטַּאת הָעוֹף וְעוֹלַת בְּהֵמָה, וְאוֹמֵר: "אִם טָמֵא הָיִיתִי – הַחַטָּאת מֵחוֹבָתִי, וְהָעוֹלָה נְדָבָה. וְאִם טָהוֹר הָיִיתִי – הָעוֹלָה מֵחוֹבָתִי, וְהַחַטָּאת מִסָּפֵק". וְסוֹפֵר שְׁלֹשִׁים יוֹם, וּמֵבִיא קָרְבַּן טָהֳרָה, וְאוֹמֵר: "אִם טָמֵא הָיִיתִי – הָעוֹלָה הָרִאשׁוֹנָה נְדָבָה, וְזוֹ חוֹבָה. וְאִם טָהוֹר הָיִיתִי – הָעוֹלָה הָרִאשׁוֹנָה חוֹבָה, וְזוֹ נְדָבָה. וְזוֹ שְׁאָר קָרְבָּנִי". אָמַר רַבִּי יְהוֹשֻׁעַ: נִמְצָא זֶה מֵבִיא קָרְבְּנוֹתָיו לַחֲצָאִים. אֲבָל הוֹדוּ לוֹ חֲכָמִים לְבֶן זוֹמָא.§ **גמ'** וְלַיְיתֵי! אָמַר רַב יְהוּדָה אָמַר שְׁמוּאֵל: לֹא אָמַר ר' יְהוֹשֻׁעַ אֶלָּא *לְחַדֵּד בָּהּ אֶת הַתַּלְמִידִים. אָמַר רַב נַחְמָן: מַאי לִיעֲבִיד לֵיהּ רַבִּי יְהוֹשֻׁעַ לְדַקֵּיהּ דְּלָא לִיסְרוּ?§ משנה *נָזִיר שֶׁהָיָה טָמֵא בְּסָפֵק וּמוּחְלָט בְּסָפֵק – אוֹכֵל בְּקָדָשִׁים אַחַר שִׁשִּׁים יוֹם, וְשׁוֹתֶה יַיִן וּמִטַּמֵּא לַמֵּתִים אַחַר מֵאָה וְעֶשְׂרִים יוֹם. בשֶׁתִּגְלַחַת הַנֶּגַע דּוֹחָה תִּגְלַחַת הַנָּזִיר בִּזְמַן שֶׁהוּא וַדַּאי, גאֲבָל בִּזְמַן שֶׁהוּא סָפֵק – אֵינוֹ דּוֹחֶה.§

גמרא

ומי שומע לו. אם [אין] דעתו לידור בנזיר, (לא זה) שידור כנגדו. **מי** שומע לו שידור כנגדו בנזיר. בזה הענין, מספק להיות נזיר. אלא הוא לבדו מביא לסוף שלשים יום חטאת העוף. והוא הדין עולת העוף, ולא חש לפרשה. **ועולת** בהמה. כדי לגלח על אחד מהדמים, ואומר כו'. ואסור לשתות ביין, דשמא היה טמא. וסופר עוד שלשים יום ומביא קרבן טהרה – חטאת ועולה ושלמים. ואם טהור הייתי אומר: העולה הראשונה חובה, דלא סגי בלא עולת חובה בגילוח ראשון, שצריך לכל הפחות לגלח על אחד מהדמים. והשאר – קרבני, החטאת והשלמים. ועולה זו שבאה עכשיו – נדבה.

נמצא מביא קרבנותיו לחצאין. דאם טהור היה – עולה ראשונה חובה, כדפרישית, ובגילוח שני מביא חטאת ושלמים. דכיון דאין נזיר אחר עמו אינו יכול לעשות בענין אחר, שכיון שהוא ספק טמא, ובסוף שלשים אינו רשאי לגלח בלא הבאת קרבנותיו, דתניא בפרק שני (לעיל דף יד:) נזיר שכלו ימיו – [לוקה על הטומאה, ואינו] לוקה על התגלחת.

אבל הודו חכמים לדברי בן זומא. דלא איכפת לו אם מביא לחצאין, והלא לא ימצא אחר שידור כנגדו. **ולייתי**. אדרבי יהושע פריך. כלומר, ויביא לחצאין ומה בכך? ומשני: אין הכי נמי, ולא א"ר יהושע אלא לחדד התלמידים. **אמר** רב נחמן בר יצחק מאי ליעבד ר' יהושע לדקיה דלא ליסרו. לא איתפרש בע"א מאי ליעבד רבי יהושע לדקיה דלא ליסרו. פירוש: לבני מעים שלא יסריחו. דכיון שיבקש אחד שידור כנגדו בנזיר, א"כ לסוף שלשים יום כשמגלחין שניהן – שניהם צריכים להניף החלב, ותגלחת שניהם היא לפני תנופה – א"כ יסריח החלב במה שיאחרו להקטיר אותו עד שתי תגלחיות. דנהי דלא מת אחד מהם כך היא לכולי עלמא שמביאין קרבן טומאה וטהרה – הא ודאי [אי] אפשר לתקנו בע"א. אבל בסיפא דמת אחד ואפשר לתקנו בתקנת [בן זומא] בלא נזירות אחרת, ולא הוה ליה למימר לר' יהושע שידור אחר כנגדו. ובפירוש [אחר] כתוב: לדקיה – לאיברים דעולה, דאינן נקטרות עד אחר תגלחת שניהם. וקשה: דעל העולה אינו עיקר מלות דמים, כי אם מן השלמים. ותו: למה ימתין הכהן מלהקטירם עד אחר התגלחת, וזה לא מצינו. ויותר נראה כדפרישית. [דף נה:] **נזיר** שהה טמא בספק. פירשתי לעיל שילהי פ' "כ"ג"*.
ה"ג

מתני' מֵת אֶחָד מֵהֶן א"ר יְהוֹשֻׁעַ יְבַקֵּשׁ אֶחָד מִן הַשּׁוּק. וִיבַקֵּשׁ מִמֶּנּוּ שֶׁיִּדּוֹר כְּנֶגְדּוֹ לִהְיוֹת נָזִיר כְּמוֹ זֶה שֶׁמֵּת, וְיֹאמַר לוֹ: אִם טָמֵא הָיִיתִי – הֲרֵי אַתָּה נָזִיר מִיָּד, וּלְאַחַר שְׁלֹשִׁים (ג) מוּתָּר אַתָּה לְגַלֵּחַ וְלִשְׁתּוֹת בַּיַּיִן. וְאִם טָהוֹר הָיִיתִי וַחֲבֵרִי טָמֵא – הֲרֵי אַתָּה נָזִיר לְאַחַר שְׁלֹשִׁים יוֹם. **וְסוֹפְרִין שְׁלֹשִׁים יוֹם.** מֵעַכְשָׁיו, וּבְסוֹף שְׁלֹשִׁים מְבִיאִין קָרְבַּן טוּמְאָה וְקָרְבַּן טָהֳרָה בְּשׁוּתָּפוּת, וְיֹאמַר לְאוֹתוֹ שֶׁהֵבִיא מִן הַשּׁוּק: אִם אֲנִי הוּא הַטָּמֵא – הֲרֵי קָרְבַּן טוּמְאָה שֶׁלִּי וְקָרְבַּן טָהֳרָה שֶׁלְּךָ. וְאִם אֲנִי הוּא הַטָּהוֹר, וַעֲדַיִין לֹא חָל א) עָלָיו נְזִירוּת עַד לְאַחַר שְׁלֹשִׁים, כְּדַאֲמַר ב) מִתְּחִלָּה "וְאִם טָהוֹר הָיִיתִי – הֲרֵי אַתָּה נָזִיר לְאַחַר שְׁלֹשִׁים", ג) הֲרֵי קָרְבַּן טָהֳרָה שֶׁלִּי, וְקָרְבַּן טוּמְאָה בְּסָפֵק. וְחַטַּאת הָעוֹף שֶׁמֵּבִיא עַל סְפֵק טוּמְאָה אֵינָהּ נֶאֱכֶלֶת, וְאָזְלָה לִקְבוּרָה, כִּדְאָמְרִינַן בְּפֶרֶק "מִי שֶׁאָמַר הֲרֵינִי נָזִיר" (לעיל דף כט.), אָמַר ר' יוֹסֵי בְּר' יְהוּדָה: מִנַּיִן לְחַטַּאת הָעוֹף הַבָּאָה עַל סָפֵק שֶׁאֵינָהּ נֶאֱכֶלֶת כו'. וְעוֹלַת הָעוֹף, אִי בָּעֵי – מַיְיתֵי לָהּ לְשֵׁם נְדָבָה, וְאִי בָּעֵי – לָא מַיְיתֵי לָהּ כְּלָל, כֵּיוָן דְּדוֹרוֹן בְּעָלְמָא הוּא לָא מְעַכְּבָא. וְאָשָׁם נַמִּי לָא אִיצְטְרִיךְ לְאֵיתוּיֵי, דְּאָשָׁם אֵינוֹ מְעַכְּבוֹ מִכַּפָּרָה, כִּדְאָמְרִינַן בְּפֶרֶק "מִי שֶׁאָמַר הֲרֵינִי נָזִיר מְגַלֵּחַ" (לעיל דף יח:): הֵבִיא חַטָּאתוֹ וְלֹא הֵבִיא אֲשָׁמוֹ – מוֹנֶה. וַעֲדַיִין אֲסוּרִין לִשְׁתּוֹת בַּיַּיִן וְלִיטַּמֵּא לַמֵּתִים, ד) אֲבָל חוֹזְרִין וְסוֹפְרִין שְׁלֹשִׁים יוֹם, וּמְבִיאִין קָרְבַּן טָהֳרָה בְּשׁוּתָּפוּת. **וְאוֹמֵר אִם אֲנִי הוּא.** שֶׁהָיִיתִי טָמֵא – קָרְבַּן טוּמְאָה הָיָה שֶׁלִּי וְקָרְבַּן טָהֳרָה הָיָה שֶׁלְּךָ – זֶה שֶׁל עַכְשָׁיו קָרְבַּן טָהֳרָתִי. וְאִם אֲנִי הוּא הַטָּהוֹר, וְאוֹתוֹ שֶׁמֵּת הָיָה טָמֵא, וְקָרְבַּן טָהֳרָה ה) הָיָה שֶׁלִּי וְקָרְבַּן טוּמְאָה הָיָה בְּסָפֵק – הֲרֵי זֶה קָרְבַּן טָהֳרָתְךָ. וּמִכָּאן וְאֵילָךְ מוּתָּרִים לִשְׁתּוֹת בַּיַּיִן וְלִיטַּמֵּא לַמֵּתִים. **אָמַר לוֹ בֶּן זוֹמָא** מִי שׁוֹמֵעַ לוֹ כו'. אֶלָּא ו) מַשְׁלִים אֶת נְזִירוֹ, וְיָבִיא בְּסָפֵק חַטַּאת הָעוֹף. וְלָאָשָׁם וּלְעוֹלַת הָעוֹף לָא חָיְישִׁינַן, כְּמוֹ שֶׁאָמַרְנוּ. אֶלָּא חַטַּאת הָעוֹף שֶׁהִיא בָּאָה עַל הַסָּפֵק יָבִיא, כְּמוֹ עַל סְפֵק טוּמְאָה, וְיָבִיא עִמָּהּ עוֹלַת בְּהֵמָה. וּשְׁאָר קָרְבְּנוֹת נְזִירוּת טָהֳרָה אֵינוֹ צָרִיךְ לְהָבִיא לְאַלְתַּר אֶלָּא לְאַחַר שְׁלֹשִׁים ז) שְׁנִיִּים, שֶׁהֲרֵי עֲדַיִין אֵינוֹ יָכוֹל לִשְׁתּוֹת בַּיַּיִן וְלִיטַּמֵּא לַמֵּתִים עַד לְאַחַר שְׁלֹשִׁים ח) יוֹם. וּמֵעַכְשָׁיו אוֹמֵר: אִם טָמֵא הָיִיתִי – הַחַטָּאת מְחוּבָתִי שֶׁל קָרְבַּן טוּמְאָה, וְעוֹלָה זוֹ לִנְדָבָה, דְּנָזִיר טָמֵא לָא מַיְיתֵי עוֹלַת בְּהֵמָה. וְאִם טָהוֹר אֲנִי – זוֹ עוֹלָה מְחוּבָתִי, וְהַחַטָּאת בְּסָפֵק וְאֵינָהּ נֶאֱכֶלֶת, וְעוֹלַת בְּהֵמָה קְרֵיבָה לְשֵׁם חוֹבָה. וְחוֹזֵר וְסוֹפֵר שְׁלֹשִׁים יוֹם, וּמֵבִיא קָרְבַּן טָהֳרָה בִּלְבַד, חַטַּאת בְּהֵמָה וְעוֹלַת בְּהֵמָה וּשְׁלָמִים, וְאוֹמֵר: אִם טָמֵא הָיִיתִי – עוֹלָה הָרִאשׁוֹנָה נְדָבָה וְזוֹ חוֹבָה עִם שְׁאָר קָרְבְּנוֹתַי, וְאִם טָהוֹר אֲנִי – הֲרֵי עוֹלַת בְּהֵמָה רִאשׁוֹנָה חוֹבָה, וְזוֹ נְדָבָה, וְאֵלּוּ שְׁאָר קָרְבְּנוֹתַי. **א"ר יְהוֹשֻׁעַ נִמְצֵאת.** אַתָּה אוֹמֵר, שֶׁאִם טָהוֹר הָיָה – שֶׁמֵּבִיא קָרְבְּנוֹתָיו לַחֲצָאִין, שֶׁבְּתִגְלַחַת רִאשׁוֹנָה הֵבִיא קָרְבַּן עוֹלַת בְּהֵמָה, וְעַכְשָׁיו הֵבִיא חַטָּאתוֹ וְזִבְחֵי שְׁלָמִים. **אֲבָל הוֹדוּ חֲכָמִים לְדִבְרֵי בֶּן זוֹמָא.** שֶׁאֵין חוֹשְׁשִׁין אִם הֵבִיא קָרְבְּנוֹתָיו לַחֲצָאִין. וְעוֹד, שֶׁאֵינוֹ מוֹצֵא ט) מִי שֶׁיִּדּוֹר נָזִיר כְּנֶגְדּוֹ. **גמ' וְלַיְיתֵי.** כְּלוֹמַר: י) מַה תְּשׁוּבָה הֵשִׁיב ר' יְהוֹשֻׁעַ (ד) בֶּן לֵוִי לְבֶן זוֹמָא שֶׁזֶּה מֵבִיא קָרְבְּנוֹתָיו לַחֲצָאִין – יָבִיא לַחֲצָאִין, וּמַה בְּכָךְ? **אָמַר רַב יְהוּדָה אָמַר שְׁמוּאֵל.** יוֹדֵעַ הָיָה ר' יְהוֹשֻׁעַ שֶׁאֵין תְּשׁוּבָתוֹ כְּלוּם, וְלֹא אָמַר כָּךְ אֶלָּא כְּדֵי לְחַדֵּד בָּהּ אֶת הַתַּלְמִידִים, שֶׁיְּהוּ נוֹשְׂאִין קַל וָחוֹמֶר בְּעַצְמָן: וּמַה כ) (ה) רַבֵּינוּ שֶׁיּוֹדֵעַ הוּא בְּעַצְמוֹ שֶׁאֵין בִּדְבָרָיו וְלֹא כְּלוּם – מֵשִׁיב דָּבָר שֶׁאֵינוֹ מִשְׁנָה, ק"ו לִשְׁאָר כָּל אָדָם שֶׁיָּכוֹל לְהָשִׁיב עַל דִּבְרֵי רַבּוֹ. וַאֲפִי' יוֹדֵעַ בּוֹ שֶׁאֵין בִּדְבָרָיו וְלֹא כְּלוּם, וּשְׁאָר חֲבֵירָיו יִהְיוּ מַלְעִיגִין עָלָיו – לֹא יִמָּנַע מִלִּשְׁאוֹל כָּל צְרָכוֹ, וְכִדְאָמְרִינַן בְּמַסֶּכֶת נִדָּה (דף כז.): יָתֵיב רַב פָּפָּא כו', וְאַחִיכוּ עֲלֵיהּ. וַאֲמַר *רָבָא: אֲפִילּוּ כִּי הַאי מִילְּתָא נֵימָא אִינִישׁ קַמֵּיהּ רַבֵּיהּ וְלָא לִישְׁתּוֹק, שֶׁנֶּאֱמַר "אִם נָבַלְתָּ בְהִתְנַשֵּׂא", אִם נִבַּלְתָּ עַצְמְךָ עַל דִּבְרֵי תוֹרָה – סוֹפְךָ לְהִתְנַשֵּׂא בָּהּ, "וְאִם זַמּוֹתָ יָד לְפֶה" – וְאִם שָׁתַקְתָּ סוֹפְךָ שֶׁיְּהוּ שׁוֹאֲלִין מִמְּךָ וְאִי אַתָּה יוֹדֵעַ לַהֲשִׁיבוֹ, וְתִתֵּן יָד לַפֶּה. **אָמַר רַב נַחְמָן בַּר יִצְחָק מַה לִיעֲבִיד לֵיהּ ר' יְהוֹשֻׁעַ לְדַקֵּיהּ דְּלָא לִיסְרוּ.** כְּלוֹמַר, ל) רַב נַחְמָן (ו) דְּלָא שְׁמִיעַ לֵיהּ לְהָא דְּאָמְרִינַן דְּלֹא אָמַר רַבִּי יְהוֹשֻׁעַ אֶלָּא לְחַדֵּד אֶת הַתַּלְמִידִים, וְהָכִי קָא מוֹתִיב, וְקָאָמַר: לְדִבְרֵי ר' יְהוֹשֻׁעַ, דְּאָמַר נִמְצָא זֶה מֵבִיא קָרְבְּנוֹתָיו לַחֲצָאִין – מ) מַאי רוֹצֶה לַעֲשׂוֹת בִּבְנֵי מֵעַיִם, כְּדַקֵּי בְהֵמָה, לְהַצְנִיעָן שֶׁלֹּא יַסְרִיחוּ עַד שֶׁיָּבִיא שְׁאָר קָרְבְּנוֹתָיו בְּתִגְלַחַת שְׁנִיָּה? אֶלָּא וַדַּאי מֵבִיא לַחֲצָאִין, וְאֵין בְּכָךְ כְּלוּם. **לְדַקֵּיהּ.** כְּמוֹ דַּקִּים שֶׁבִּבְנֵי מֵעַיִם, וּלְהָכִי נָקַט בְּנֵי מֵעַיִם, נ) שֶׁהֵן מַסְרִיחִין לְפִי שָׁעָה, מַה שֶּׁאֵין כֵּן בַּבָּשָׂר. **מתני'** נָזִיר שֶׁהָיָה טָמֵא בְּסָפֵק כו'. כְּמוֹ שֶׁהִיא מְפוֹרֶשֶׁת לְמַעְלָה בְּפֶרֶק "כֹּהֵן גָּדוֹל וְנָזִיר".
גמ'

פי' הרא"ש

ה"ג ולייתי. לרבי יהושע פריך דאמר נמצא זה מביא קרבנותיו לחצאין ומאי נפקא מיניה ויביאם לחצאין: לחדד בה את התלמידים אה"נ מודה הוא לדברי בן זומא והא דאמר שיבקש א' לידר' כנגדו לא אמ' [אלא] לחדד את התלמידים אם יש בהם משיב כבן זומא הא דקאמר [נמצא זה] מביא קרבנותיו לחצאין ה"ק אם אין אחר נודר כנגדו יצטרך להביא קרבנותיו לחצאין: מאי ליעבד ר' יהושע לדקיה דלא ליסרו. לדקיה היינו המעיים: ולר' יהושע דאמר שידור אחר כנגדו צריך לאחר תנופת החלב עד שיגלחו שניהם ותמצא שיסריחו המעיים. ונהי שאם נטמא א' מהם ואין ידוע איזה הוא צריך לעשות כן התם הא"א לעשות בענין אחר. אבל הכא מוטב שיעשה כבן זומא: ולא נהירא גי' זו דהא אמר' כבר דלא אמרה ר' (ישמעאל) [יהושע] אלא לחדד בה את התלמידים: נזיר שהיה טמא בספק. כולה מפ' לעיל פ' כ"ג:

[ע' תוספות מנחות פח. ד"ה התוסה]

נוסחת הריב"ן

א) חל עליו נזירות כו': ב) כדאמר "יה כו' ג) לאחר שלשים יוכ: ד) וליטמא למתים וחוזרין: ה) וקרבן טהרה שלי וקרבן טומאה בספק: ו) בלא ישלים את נזירותו: ז) לאחר שלשים שהרי כו': ח) לאחר שלשים יום שניים ועכשיו: ט) שאינו מוצא שידור כנגדו: י) בזו התשובה שהשיב ר' יהושע לבן ומה כו': כ) ומה ר' יהושע אע"פ שיודע בעצמו שאין בדבריו כלום ומשיב בו' שאין יכול להשיב לדברי רבו ואפילו יודע הוא שאין בדבריו כלום כו' מלשאול כל לבו כו' ואי אתה יודע להשיב כו': ל) כלומר לרב נחמן לא שמיע ליה להא דלא אמר כו': מ) מביא קרבנותיו לחצאין צריך להצניען שלא בו': נ) לפי שהן

[ברכות לג: וש"נ]

לעיל נה: נז:

הגהות הב"ח

(א) במשנה וסופרין שלשים יום ומביאין: (ב) שם אם אני הוא הטמא: (ג) רש"י ד"ה מת אחד וכו' שלשים יום מותר: (ד) ד"ה ולייתי וכו' ר' יהושע לבן זומא כצ"ל ותיבות בן לוי נמחק: (ה) ד"ה אמר רב יהודה וכו' ומה ר' יהושע שיודע הוא בעצמו: (ו) ד"ד אמר רב נחמן וכו' כלומר רב נחמן לא הוה שמיע ליה:

[לפנינו שם איתא רב פפא]

גמ' תָּנָא:* בד"א — בִּנְזִירוּת מוּעֶטֶת, אאֲבָל בִּנְזִירוּת בַּת שָׁנָה — אוֹכֵל בְּקָדָשִׁים לְאַחַר שְׁתֵּי שָׁנִים, וְשׁוֹתֶה יַיִן וּמִיטַּמֵּא לְמֵתִים לְאַחַר אַרְבַּע שָׁנִים. וְתָנֵי עֲלָהּ: בוּמְגַלֵּחַ אַרְבַּע תִּגְלָחִיּוֹת: גתִּגְלַחַת רִאשׁוֹנָה — מֵבִיא צִפּוֹרִים וְחַטַּאת הָעוֹף וְעוֹלַת בְּהֵמָה, שְׁנִיָּה — מֵבִיא חַטַּאת הָעוֹף וְעוֹלַת בְּהֵמָה, שְׁלִישִׁית — מֵבִיא חַטַּאת הָעוֹף וְעוֹלַת בְּהֵמָה, רְבִיעִית — מֵבִיא קָרְבַּן טָהֳרָה.§ אָמְרַתְּ: תִּגְלַחַת רִאשׁוֹן מֵבִיא וכו'. מִמָּה נַפְשָׁךְ שַׁפִּיר קָמַיְיתֵי; דְּאִי וַדַּאי מְצוֹרָע הוּא וְלָאו טָמֵא הוּא — צִיפּוֹרִין חוֹבָתוֹ, °וְחַטַּאת הָעוֹף סָפֵק — אָזְלָא לִקְבוּרָה, וְעוֹלָה הָוְיָא נְדָבָה. וּלְגַלְּחוֹ *תּוֹךְ שִׁבְעָה אִי אֶפְשָׁר, דְּדִילְמָא לָאו מוּחְלָט הוּא, וְרַחֲמָנָא (במדבר ו) אָמַר °"תַּעַר לֹא יַעֲבֹר עַל רֹאשׁוֹ עַד מְלֹאת". וְאִי לָאו מְצוֹרָע וַדַּאי הֲוֵי, וְהוּא טָמֵא — חַטַּאת הָעוֹף חוֹבָתוֹ, וְצִיפּוֹרִין — אַבָּרַאי קָא מִתְעָבְדִין וְלָא הָוֵי חוּלִּין בָּעֲזָרָה, וְעוֹלַת בְּהֵמָה הָוְיָא נְדָבָה. וְאִי לָאו מְצוֹרָע הוּא וְלָאו טָמֵא הוּא — צִיפּוֹרִין אַבָּרַאי קָא מִתְעָבְדִין, חַטַּאת הָעוֹף לִקְבוּרָה, עוֹלַת בְּהֵמָה הָוְיָא חוֹבָתוֹ. וְהָא בָּעֵי אָשָׁם! — רַבִּי שִׁמְעוֹן הִיא, *דְּאָמַר: מַיְיתֵי וּמַתְנֵי. תִּגְלַחַת שְׁנִיָּה וּשְׁלִישִׁית צִיפּוֹרִין לָא צָרִיךְ — דְּהָא עֲבִיד. מַאי אִיכָּא — דִּילְמָא וַדַּאי מוּחְלָט הוּא, חֲדָא לִסְפֵק סְפָרוֹ, וַחֲדָא לִסְפֵק טוּמְאָתוֹ. תִּגְלַחַת רְבִיעִית מֵבִיא קָרְבַּן טָהֳרָה וּמַתְנֵי, וְאִי

גמ' וְתָנֵי עֲלָהּ וּמְגַלֵּחַ אַרְבַּע תִּגְלָחִיּוֹת. בִּנְזִירוּת מוּעֶטֶת מִשְּׁלֹשִׁים לִשְׁלֹשִׁים, וּבִנְזִירוּת מְרוּבָּה מִשָּׁנָה לְשָׁנָה. תִּגְלַחַת רִאשׁוֹנָה מֵבִיא צִפּוֹרִין. דְּהַיְינוּ לִיפָּרֵי מְצוֹרָע, שֶׁכָּתוּב בָּהֶן "וְלָקַח לַמִּטַּהֵר שְׁתֵּי צִפֳּרִים חַיּוֹת טְהוֹרוֹת". וְחַטַּאת הָעוֹף. דְּקָרְבַּן טוּמְאָה דְּנָזִיר. עוֹלַת בְּהֵמָה. דְּקָרְבַּן טָהֳרָה (תורה אור) דִּנְזִירוּת. מִמָּה נַפְשָׁךְ אִי וַדַּאי מְצוֹרָע הוּא וְלֹא טָמֵא. בְּמֵת, הִילְכָּךְ הָא דְּקָא מַיְיתֵי צִיפּוֹרִים — זוֹ הִיא חוֹבָתוֹ, וְחַטָּאת הָעוֹף דְּקָרְבַּן טוּמְאָה א) בְּנָזִיר הָוֵי סָפֵק, וְאָזְלָא לִקְבוּרָה, מִשּׁוּם דְּדִילְמָא לָאו טָמֵא מֵת הוּא, וְלָא חַזְיָא לְהַקְרָבָה. וְעוֹלָה דְּקָמַיְיתֵי — קָרְבַּן נְדָבָה, דִּילְמָא מְצוֹרָע הוּא, וַעֲדַיִין אֵינוֹ רָאוּי לְתִגְלַחַת טָהֳרָה דִּנְזִירוּת. וּלְגַלְּחוֹ *בְּתוֹךְ שִׁבְעָה. כַּמִּשְׁפָּט שֶׁל מוּחְלָט שֶׁסּוֹפֵר שִׁבְעָה וְאַחַ"כ מְגַלֵּחַ. אִי אֶפְשָׁר דְּדִילְמָא לָאו מוּחְלָט. וְלָאו טָמֵא הוּא, וְהָוֵי נָזִיר טָהוֹר, וְרַחֲמָנָא אָמַר "תַּעַר לֹא יַעֲבוֹר עַל רֹאשׁוֹ". ב) וְאִי לָאו מְצוֹרָע וַדַּאי הוּא וְלָאו טְמֵא מֵת הוּא. אֶלָּא נָזִיר טָהוֹר. לְצִיפּוֹרִין דְּקָמַיְיתֵי — לָא חָיְישִׁינַן, דְּאַבָּרַאי קָא מִיתְעָבְדֵי. וְאִי מִשּׁוּם חַטָּאת הָעוֹף — הָא קָאָזְלָא לִקְבוּרָה, וְעוֹלַת בְּהֵמָה דְּקָמַיְיתֵי — הָוְיָא חוֹבָתוֹ. וְהָא קָבָעֵי אִיתּוּיֵי אָשָׁם מְצוֹרָע בְּתִגְלַחַת שְׁנִיָּה, וְאָשָׁם בִּמְצוֹרָע וַדַּאי מְעַכֵּב בַּאֲכִילָתוֹ, כִּדְקַיְימָא לַן: הֵבִיא כַּפָּרָתוֹ — אוֹכֵל בְּקָדָשִׁים. וְאִילּוּ בְּכָל הָנֵי אַרְבַּע תִּגְלָחִיּוֹת — אַמַּאי לָא תָּנֵי לֵיהּ אָשָׁם? הָא מַנִּי ר' שִׁמְעוֹן הִיא דְּאָמַר מַיְיתֵי וּמַתְנֵי. כִּדְאָמְרִי' בְּפֶרֶק בַּתְרָא דְּמַסֶּכֶת מְנָחוֹת (דף קה.), רַבִּי שִׁמְעוֹן אוֹמֵר: לְמָחֳרָת מֵבִיא אֲשָׁמוֹ וְלוּגּוֹ עִמּוֹ, וְאוֹמֵר: אִם מְצוֹרָע הוּא — זֶה אֲשָׁמוֹ וְזֶה לוּגּוֹ, וְאִם לָאו — אָשָׁם זֶה יְהֵא שַׁלְמֵי נְדָבָה. וְאוֹתוֹ אָשָׁם טָעוּן שְׁחִיטָה בַּצָּפוֹן וּמַתַּן בְּהוֹנוֹת. הָכָא נַמִּי מַיְיתֵי אֲשַׁם מְצוֹרָע וּמַתְנֵי. תִּגְלַחַת ב' וּשְׁלִישִׁית צִפֳּרִים חַיּוֹת אֵינוֹ צָרִיךְ. לְהָבִיא, שֶׁכְּבָר הֵבִיא בְּתִגְלַחַת רִאשׁוֹנָה. מַאי אִיכָּא לְמֵימַר — דְּמִיבַּעְיָא לֵיהּ לְאֵיתוּיֵי, דִּילְמָא מוּחְלָט הוּא וְלָא טָמֵא, וְתִגְלַחַת רִאשׁוֹנָה עָלְתָה לוֹ לִימֵי חִלּוּטוֹ, וְתִגְלַחַת שְׁנִיָּה זוֹ הִיא שֶׁל יְמֵי סְפָרוֹ, וְצָרִיךְ לְהָבִיא קָרְבַּן מְצוֹרָע — לְהָכִי הוּא דְּאָמַר דְּלַיְיתֵי חַטָּאת הָעוֹף ג) בְּתִגְלַחַת שְׁנִיָּה וּבְתִגְלַחַת שְׁלִישִׁית, חֲדָא לִסְפֵק חִלּוּטוֹ וַחֲדָא לִסְפֵק טוּמְאָה דִּנְזִירוּת. דִּבְתִגְלַחַת שְׁנִיָּה אִיכָּא לְמֵימַר שֶׁמָּא מוּחְלָט הוּא, וְחַטָּאת הָעוֹף עוֹלָה לִימֵי סְפָרוֹ. וְאַ"ת: וְהָא בְּחַטַּאת בְּהֵמָה הוּא דְּמִיחַיַּיב וְלָא בְּחַטַּאת הָעוֹף, אִי לָאו דְּלֶיהֱוֵי עָנִי! ד) לְפִי שֶׁאֵין חַטַּאת בְּהֵמָה בָּאָה עַל הַסָּפֵק, ה) לְפִי שֶׁאֵינָהּ נֶאֱכֶלֶת מִסָּפֵק, וְהָוְיָא לָהּ כְּחַטָּאת שֶׁנִּתְכַּפְּרוּ בְּעָלֶיהָ וּמִיתְסַר לְאֵיתוּיֵי, לְפִי שֶׁאֵין מְבִיאִין קָדָשִׁים לְבֵית הַפְּסוּל — תַּקּוּן ו)רַבָּנַן שֶׁיְּהֵא כּוֹתֵב כָּל נְכָסָיו לַאֲחֵרִים, וְהָוֵי עָנִי, וּמֵבִיא חַטַּאת הָעוֹף הַבָּאָה עַל הַסָּפֵק, כִּדְאָמַר בְּפ' "מִי שֶׁאָמַר הֲרֵינִי נָזִיר" (לעיל דף כט.) אַע"פ שֶׁאֵינָהּ נֶאֱכֶלֶת. וְה"נ תָּנֵי עֲלָהּ בַּתּוֹסֶפְתָּא (פ"ו) בַּבָּרַיְיתָא. ז) וּמְפָרְשִׁינַן לָהּ נַמִּי הָכִי בְּפֶרֶק בַּתְרָא דְּמַסֶּכֶת נִדָּה (דף ע.) גַּבֵּי שְׁנֵי מְצוֹרָעִים שֶׁנִּתְעָרְבוּ קָרְבְּנוֹתֵיהֶם וכו'. וְאִי אָמְרַתְּ דְּמוּחְלָט וְטָמֵא הוּא, וּשְׁתֵּי תִּגְלָחִיּוֹת הָרִאשׁוֹנוֹת עוֹלוֹת לוֹ לְתִגְלַחַת חִלּוּטוֹ וִימֵי סְפָרוֹ — הִילְכָּךְ בְּתִגְלַחַת שְׁנִיָּה מִיבָּעֵי לֵיהּ לְאֵיתוּיֵי חַטָּאת הָעוֹף בִּמְקוֹם חַטָּאת בְּהֵמָה שֶׁהָיָה מְחוּיָּיב לְהָבִיא. וְאִידָךְ חַטָּאת הָעוֹף דְּקָמַיְיתֵי בְּתִגְלַחַת שְׁלִישִׁית — תֶּיהֱוֵי לִסְפֵק טוּמְאָה. וְעוֹלַת בְּהֵמָה שֶׁבָּזוֹ וְשֶׁבָּזוֹ — תֶּיהֱוֵי נְדָבָה. וְאִיכָּא נַמִּי לְמֵימַר דְּדִילְמָא לָאו מְצוֹרָע הֲוָה, אֶלָּא נָזִיר טָמֵא, וְתִגְלַחַת רִאשׁוֹנָה עָלְתָה לוֹ לְתִגְלַחַת טוּמְאָה דְּנָזִיר, וְתִגְלַחַת שְׁנִיָּה לְתִגְלַחַת טָהֳרָה. לְכָךְ מֵבִיא עוֹלַת בְּהֵמָה דְּהָוְיָא חוֹבָתוֹ, וְהַחַטָּאת בְּסָפֵק. וּבְתִגְלַחַת רְבִיעִית מֵבִיא קָרְבַּן טָהֳרָה — ח) חַטָּאת דִּבְהֵמָה, וְעוֹלָה וּשְׁלָמִים, וּמַתְנֵי. וְאִם

ה"ג: תגלחת ראשונה מביא צפרים. לספק מוחלט, אחת שחוטה ואחת משולחת, וחטאת העוף לספק נזיר טמא, ועולת בהמה לספק נזיר טהור. ועולת העוף דלא אייתי כדין נזיר טמא ק"ל. ושמא מספק לא הצריכוהו. וכן צריך לומר דשלמים דנזיר טהור לא הצריכוהו, שלא הצריכו לספק נזיר טהור רק קרבן להתירו בתגלחת, וכדאמרי': גילח על א' משלשתן יצא. ה"ג: שניה מביא חטאת העוף. לאו משום דנזירות טומאה יעלה לו למנין שבעה וביום השמיני יתחיל למנות, דבנזיר טמא ליכא לספוקי בתגלחת שניה. אלא משום ספק מוחלט. ואף עולת בהמה — שמא לא היה מוחלט, כי אם נזיר טמא. שלישית מביא חטאת העוף. דאולי היה טמא. ותגלחת של מוחלט לא יעלה לתגלחת לא לנזיר טהור ולא לנזיר טמא, כדפרישית בסמוך. ועולת בהמה — דשמא מוחלט הוא, אך לא טמא. **רביעית.** דליכא לספוקי לא במוחלט עוד, ולא בטמא עוד — מביא קרבן טהרה משלם. **אמרת** • כמו "אמר מר". תגלחת ראשונה מביא צפורין וחטאת העוף ועולת בהמה ממה נפשך; אי ודאי מצורע הוא ולא טמא הוא — הצפורין לחובתו, וחטאת העוף — ספק, אזלא לקבורה, ועולה הוי נדבה. ולגלחו בסוף שבעה, דהיינו תוך שלשים — לא אפשר, דדילמא לאו מוחלט הוא, ורחמנא אמר "תער לא יעבור" כו'. **והא** בעי אשם ר' שמעון היא דאמר מייתי ומתנה. דאמר בפרק "התערובת" (זבחים דף עו.) ובפרק בתרא דנדה (דף ע.) דאשם נמי מתנה בשלמים, אף כי ממעט זמן אכילתן. אי לאו מצורע הוא ובודאי טמא הוא; חטאת העוף — חובתו, צפרים — אבראי, ולא הוו חולין בעזרה, ועולת בהמה הוי נדבה. ואי לאו מצורע הוא ולא טמא הוא; צפרים אבראי קא מתעבדי, וחטאת העוף לקבורה אזלא, ועולת בהמה היא חובתו. **תגלחת** שניה ושלישית צפורים חיים בשביל מוחלט לא צריך, דהא עביד. מאי איכא למימר — דילמא ודאי מוחלט היה, חדא לספק [ספרו] וחדא לספק טומאתו. תגלחת רביעית מביא קרבן טהרה ומתנה. *ספק טמא ומוחלט ודאי אוכל בקדשים לאחר (שייך לע"ב) שמנה ימים. כלומר, ביום השמיני. ו"לאחר" לאו דוקא, שיום ראשון לנזירותו מגלח לחלוטו וישב מחוץ לאהלו שבעת ימים, וביום [השביעי] יגלח, וביום השמיני יביא קרבנות מצורע. ובו ביום מותר לאכול בקדשים. ועתה, אם היה טמא ודאי — יספור ז', ויזה שלישי וז', ויגלח בז'. אבל עתה שהוא ספק — דילמא לאו טמא הוא אלא טהור מוחלט, ולכך לגלחו בתוך שלשים אי אפשר — דילמא לאו טמא הוא, ורחמנא אמר "תער לא יעבור על ראשו עד מלאת". ולכך ימנה שלשים, ויום שמיני עולה לו, וביום שלשים ואחד יגלח כדין כל נזיר שמגלח יום שלשים ואחד, כדאמר בפ' קמא (לעיל דף ה:). הרי ביום שלשים יגלח תגלחת שלישית, דשמא נזיר טמא הוא, והימים הראשונים יפלו, וצריך למנות שלשים יום עוד. וביום שלשים ואחד יגלח תגלחת נזיר טהור. והיינו דקאמר: ושותה יין ומיטמא למתים לאחר ששים ושבעה ימים, דהיינו [יום] ס"ח. זה הכלל: אי אפשר לעשות דין נזירות טומאה ולא נזירות טהרה עד תום ימי חלוטו, ואינו קרוי מחוסר כפורים ליאסר בקדשים אלא בשביל מוחלט, שטומאתו מגופו.

מוחלט ספק טמא ודאי אוכל בקדשים אחר שלשים ושבעה ימים ושותה יין ומיטמא למתים לאחר שבעים וארבעה ימים. מאחר שאינו ודאי מוחלט — לא יגלח שום תגלחת כי אם לסוף ז', אחר הזאה שלישי וז', ומגלח בשביעי, ובשמיני מביא קרבן חטאת העוף *(ונזירות טומאה) (גי' א"מ כנזיר טמא). ואי אפשר לגלח שנית עד שלשים, דשמא אינו מוחלט והשמיני יעלה למנין שלשים. וביום שלשים ואחד יגלח — [שמא] מוחלט הוא. והוו להו הנך שני תגלחיות לחלוטו. והיינו דקאמר: אוכל קדשים לאחר שלשים וז', דהיינו יום ל"ח. וסוף שבעה ימים יגלח שלישית כדין נזיר טמא, ויום ל"ח יעלה לו למנין ז', וביום השמיני יתחיל למנות נזירות טהרה (*לישנא אחרינא) (גי' א"מ שלשים יום) וביום שלשים ואחד יגלח תגלחת נזיר ליטהר. והיינו דקאמר: ושותה יין ומיטמא לאחר ע"ד דהיינו יום ע"ה. **טמא** ודאי מוחלט ודאי אוכל בקדשים לאחר ח' ימים ושותה יין ומיטמא למתים לאחר ארבעים וארבעה ימים. דמאחר שהוא מוחלט ודאי — יום תחילת נזירותו יגלח, וביום שבעה יגלח, וביום שמיני יביא קרבנות מצורע, ובו ביום יהא מותר לאכול בקדשים. והאי "לאחר ח'" — לאו דוקא, אלא ח' עצמו. ובשביל שהוא טמא יספור *ז' (גי' א"מ יום שמיני) על יום שמיני של חלוטו, וביום הז' יגלח, וביום השמיני יביא קרבנות טומאה, ויתחיל למנות נזירות טהרה שלשים *על יום (גי' א"מ יום עם יום שמיני) שמיני. וביום שלשים ואחד יגלח ויביא קרבנות טהרה. והיינו דקאמר: ושותה יין ומיטמא למתים לאחר מ"ד ימים, דהיינו יום מ"ה.

נזיר

עין משפט נר מצוה

יט א ב מיי' פ"י מהל' נזירות הל"א:

כ ג מיי' שם הל"ב ד ה ו ז ח וע"ש בכ"מ:

פי' הרא"ש

אמרת. כמו אמר מר: ר"ש היא דאמר בפ' התערובת ובפ' בתרא דנדה דמייתי אשם ומתני בשלמים ולא חייש על מה שממעט זמן אכילתו ומביא קדשים לבית הפסול: הויא חדא לספק ספרו וחדא לספק טומאתו. פי' חטאת העוף על תגלחת שניה הוי לספק סוף ימי ספרו ושל תגלחת שלישית הוי לספק ימי טומאתו.

מסורת הש"ס

[לעיל ט. תוספתא פ"ו]

גי' א"מ בסוף [וכ"ה בכ"י]

גי' א"מ סוף

זבחים עו. מנחות קה. נדה ע.

נוסחת הריב"ן

א) דקרבן טומאה בנזירות הוי בספק כו' הוא ולא אפשר להקריבה ועולה דקמייתי קרבה נדבה: ב) בכ"י איתא בזה"ל ואי לאו מצורע ודאי הוא אלא טמא מת הוא הלכך האי חטאת העוף דקמייתי זו היא חובתו ולאשם ולעולת העוף לא חיישינן אי לא מייתי להו כיון דלא מעכבי והאי דקמייתי צפרים נמי לא חיישינן דאבראי קא מתעבדי: ועולת בהמה דקמייתי הויא חובתו כ"א ואי לאו מצורע ודאי הוא כו': ג) (בתגלחת שניה כו' לימי ספרו) ליתא בכ"י: ד) כיון דאבראי הוי חטאת העוף הוא דמייתי לפי שאין כו': ה) מפני שאינה כו' דהויא לה כו': ו) תקון ליה רבנן כו' על הספק אע"פ שאינה והשאר ליתא: ז) ומפרש לה בפרק בתרא: ח) מגלם חטאת כו' ומתנה אם ודאי נזיר הוא עכשיו והיה מוחלט וטמא עולה ראשונה שבכולן תגלחיות הן עולת נדבה וזו חובה ושאר קרבנותיו ואם:

גליון הש"ס

גמ' וחטאת העוף כו' לקבורה. ע' סוף תמורה במתני':

כא א מיי׳ פ״י מהל׳ נזירות הל״י:
כב ב מיי׳ שם הל׳ יא:
כג ג מיי׳ שם הלי״ב:
כד ד מיי׳ שם הל״א:

(א) וְאִי וַדַּאי נָזִיר הוּא – עוֹלָה הָרִאשׁוֹנָה חוֹבָה, וְזוֹ נְדָבָה. וְאִם טָמֵא וּמוּחְלָט הוּא – עוֹלָה הָרִאשׁוֹנָה נְדָבָה, וְזוֹ חוֹבָה, וְזֶה שְׁאָר קָרְבָּנוֹ. אטָמֵא סָפֵק וּמוּחְלָט וַדַּאי – אוֹכֵל בְּקָדָשִׁים לְאַחַר שְׁמוֹנָה יָמִים, וְשׁוֹתֶה יַיִן וּמִיטַּמֵּא לְמֵתִים לְאַחַר שִׁשִּׁים וְשִׁבְעָה יָמִים. במוּחְלָט סָפֵק וְטָמֵא וַדַּאי – אוֹכֵל בְּקָדָשִׁים לְאַחַר שְׁלֹשִׁים וְשִׁבְעָה יָמִים, וְשׁוֹתֶה יַיִן וּמִיטַּמֵּא לְמֵתִים לְאַחַר שִׁבְעִים וְאַרְבָּעָה יָמִים. גטָמֵא וַדַּאי וּמוּחְלָט וַדַּאי – אוֹכֵל בְּקָדָשִׁים לְאַחַר שְׁמוֹנָה יָמִים, וְשׁוֹתֶה יַיִן וּמִיטַּמֵּא לְמֵתִים לְאַחַר אַרְבָּעִים וְאַרְבָּעָה יָמִים. *שָׁאֲלוּ תַּלְמִידָיו אֶת ר׳ שִׁמְעוֹן בֶּן יוֹחַי: נָזִיר טָהוֹר וּמְצוֹרָע, מַהוּ שֶׁיְּגַלֵּחַ תִּגְלַחַת אַחַת וְעוֹלָה לוֹ לְכָאן וּלְכָאן? אָמַר לָהֶן: דאֵינוֹ מְגַלֵּחַ. אָמְרוּ לוֹ: לָמָּה? אָמַר לָהֶן: אִילּוּ זֶה לְגַדֵּל וְזֶה לְגַדֵּל, וְזֶה לְהַעֲבִיר וְזֶה לְהַעֲבִיר – יָפֶה אַתֶּם אוֹמְרִים. עַכְשָׁיו, נָזִיר – לְהַעֲבִיר, וּמְצוֹרָע – לְגַדֵּל. וְלֹא תַּעֲלֶה לוֹ לִימֵי חִלּוּטוֹ, וְתַעֲלֶה לוֹ לִימֵי סְפָרוֹ! וְאָמַר לָהֶן: אִילּוּ זֶה לִפְנֵי זְרִיקַת דָּמִים וְזֶה לִפְנֵי זְרִיקַת דָּמִים – יָפֶה אַתֶּם אוֹמְרִים, אֶלָּא (ב) מְצוֹרָע לִפְנֵי זְרִיקַת דָּמִים וְנָזִיר לְאַחַר זְרִיקַת דָּמִים. וְלֹא תַּעֲלֶה לוֹ לִימֵי צָרַעְתּוֹ וּנְזִירוּתוֹ, וְתַעֲלֶה לוֹ לִימֵי צָרַעְתּוֹ וְטוּמְאָתוֹ! אָמַר לָהֶן: אִילּוּ זֶה לִפְנֵי בִּיאַת מַיִם וְזֶה לִפְנֵי בִּיאַת מַיִם – יָפֶה אַתֶּם אוֹמְרִים, אֶלָּא טָמֵא לְאַחַר בִּיאַת מַיִם מְצוֹרָע לִפְנֵי בִּיאַת מַיִם. אָמְרוּ לוֹ: יָפֶה אָמַרְתָּ שֶׁלֹּא תַּעֲלֶה לוֹ לִימֵי סְפָרוֹ וְלִנְזִירוּתוֹ. וְתַעֲלֶה לוֹ לִימֵי חִלּוּטוֹ וְטוּמְאָתוֹ – דְּזֶה לְגַדֵּל וְזֶה לְגַדֵּל הוּא! אָמַר לָהֶן: (ג) נָזִיר טָהוֹר וְהוּא מְצוֹרָע – זֶה לְגַדֵּל וְזֶה לְהַעֲבִיר, וְאִם נָזִיר טָמֵא וְהוּא מְצוֹרָע – זֶה לִפְנֵי בִּיאַת מַיִם וְזֶה לְאַחַר בִּיאַת מַיִם.

תָּנֵי

נזיר טהור ומצורע מהו שיגלח תגלחת אחת ועולה לו לכאן ולכאן אמר להן נזיר להעביר ומצורע לגדל. כלומר נזיר להעביר שער מכל וכל, שאינו צריך עוד לשער שיגדלנו לשום מצוה. אבל תגלחת ראשונה של מצורע – לגדל שער ולגלחו שנית לפני יום הבאת קרבנות. והואיל וחלוקות זו מזו לא יפטרו זו את זו. ולא תעלה לו בימי ספרו. בתמיה, כלומר: תגלחת שניה של מצורע שגם היא להעביר, מדוע לא תעלה לו לתגלחת נזירות טהרה? אמר להן: זה לפני זריקת דמים – תגלחת דמצורע, דכתיב "וביום השביעי יגלח ורחץ במים וטהר וביום השמיני יקח שני כבשים בני שנה". וזו – תגלחת נזיר, לאחר זריקת דמים, כדכתיב "וגלח הנזיר פתח אהל מועד ולקח שער ראש נזרו ונתן על האש אשר תחת זבח השלמים".

ותעלה לימי [צרעתו] וטומאתו לתגלחת נזיר טמא אמר להן טמא לאחר ביאת מים. כדכתיב "וגילח ראשו ביום טהרתו ביום א) השמיני יגלחנו", "ביום טהרתו" משמע לאחר טהרתו. והכי דריש ליה בספרי. ומצורע לפני ביאת מים, דכתיב "וביום השביעי יגלח כל שערו ורחץ את (כל) בשרו במים וטהר". אמרו לו יפה אמרת. כמו לשון אחר הוא בכמה ספרים. ולא גרסינן "בעי רב דימי". וזה לפני ביאת מים. מצורע. וזה לאחר ביאת מים – תגלחת נזיר טמא, כדפרישית. ב) זה לפני זריקת דמים – תגלחת נזיר טהור.

ג) **הני** ד׳ תגלחיות משום מצוה. כלומר כולהון משום מצוה, וצריך תער אף לשלישית. ואפי׳ טמא ודאי ומוחלט ודאי שטעון ארבע תגלחיות, ותגלחת שלישית אינה אלא לנזיר טמא. ולפי דעתי לא מהדר אארבע תגלחיות דמתני׳ דאיירי בספק מוחלט וספק טמא, שאין במשנתינו תגלחת שלא תוכל להסתפק או במוחלט או בנזיר טהור ודאי. מצורע ונזיר טהור נפקא לן מקראי בפ׳ "שלשה מינין" (לעיל דף מא.) דבתער, ונזיר טמא נמי גמרינן לה מנזיר טהור. וסוגיא דהתלמוד הוא דסלקא הכי, ולרמי בר חמא מיבעיא ליה. ובקוצר היה יכול לומר: תגלחת נזיר טמא צריכה תער או אינה צריכה תער, אלא דנקט הני תגלחיות משום דאיירינהו בהו בסוגיין במוחלט ודאי וטמא ודאי דמגלח ארבע תגלחיות. אי אמרת משום איעבורי שער אפי׳ סכייה נשא. וצריך לומר דגילח מקלת השער במספרים או בתער. שאם סך נשא בכל ראשו – תו לא הדר, כדאמרי׳ בפ׳ "החובל" (ב״ק דף פו.), ולא מצי למיעבד תגלחת של טהרה. וה״ה דמצי למיבעי או מגלחו במספרים. תא

א) נ״ל השביעי. ב) עי׳ א״מ. ג) שייך לדף ס״ח.

וְאִם וַדַּאי נָזִיר הָיָה. מִתְּחִילָּה, וְלֹא מוּחְלָט וְלֹא טָמֵא – הֲרֵי עוֹלָה רִאשׁוֹנָה חוֹבָה וְזוֹ נְדָבָה. וְכֵן כּוּלָּן, חוּץ מִן הָרִאשׁוֹנָה. וְאֵלּוּ הֵן שְׁאָר קָרְבְּנוֹתָיו. שֶׁעֲדַיִין לֹא הֵבִיא. וְאִם טָמֵא סָפֵק וּמוּחְלָט וַדַּאי. (ד) בְּיוֹם רִאשׁוֹן שֶׁל נְזִירוּתוֹ, אוֹכֵל בְּקָדָשִׁים לְאַחַר ח׳ יָמִים, שֶׁהִיא תִּגְלַחַת שְׁנִיָּה שֶׁל יְמֵי סְפָרוֹ. שֶׁבִּתְחִילַּת יוֹם רִאשׁוֹן שֶׁל יְמֵי נְזִירוּתוֹ, שֶׁהִיא תְּחִילָּה לִימֵי חִלּוּטוֹ – יְהֵא מְגַלֵּחַ תִּגְלַחַת חִלּוּטוֹ, וּלְסוֹף ז׳ – תִּגְלַחַת הַשֵּׁנִית שֶׁל יְמֵי סְפָרוֹ, כִּדְכְתִיב "וּבַיּוֹם הַשְּׁבִיעִי יְגַלַּח" וגו׳. וּלְמָחָר שֶׁהוּא יוֹם ח׳ יָבִיא קָרְבָּנוֹ, כִּדְכְתִיב "בַּיּוֹם הַשְּׁמִינִי" וגו׳, וְאוֹכֵל בַּקָּדָשִׁים א) כְּשֶׁהֵבִיא כַּפָּרָתוֹ, כִּדְתְנַן: שֶׁתִּגְלַחַת הַנֶּגַע דּוֹחָה לְתִגְלַחַת הַנָּזִיר בִּזְמַן שֶׁהוּא וַדַּאי. וְכֵיוָן שֶׁהֵבִיא קָרְבַּן צָרַעְתּוֹ אוֹכֵל בְּקָדָשִׁים, אֲבָל לִשְׁתּוֹת יַיִן וְלִיטַּמֵּא לְמֵתִים אֵינוֹ יָכוֹל עַד לְאַחַר ס״ז יָמִים. שֶׁאִם בָּא לוֹ לְגַלֵּחַ נְזִירוּת טָהֳרָה לְאַחַר שֶׁעָשָׂה שְׁלֹשִׁים אַחַר ז׳ יְמֵי סְפָרוֹ, יֵשׁ לוֹ לוֹמַר: שֶׁמָּא מוּחְלָט וְטָמֵא הָיָה, וְתִגְלַחַת רִאשׁוֹנָה עָלְתָה לוֹ לִימֵי סְפָרוֹ וְזוֹ שֶׁל עַכְשָׁיו לִימֵי טוּמְאָתוֹ, וַעֲדַיִין צָרִיךְ לִמְנוֹת לוֹ שְׁלֹשִׁים יוֹם לִנְזִירוּת טָהֳרָתוֹ, שֶׁהֵן בִּכְלַל ס״ז יָמִים. וְאַח״כ מוּתָּר לִשְׁתּוֹת בַּיַּיִן. הָכִי גָּרְסִינַן: מוּחְלָט סָפֵק וְטָמֵא וַדַּאי אוֹכֵל בְּקָדָשִׁים לְאַחַר ל״ז וְשׁוֹתֶה בַּיַּיִן וּמִיטַּמֵּא לְמֵתִים לְאַחַר ע״ד. דְּכֵיוָן שֶׁהוּא טָמֵא וַדַּאי – מְגַלֵּחַ לְסוֹף שִׁבְעָה, וּמַתְחִיל וּמוֹנֶה ב) שְׁלֹשִׁים וּמְגַלֵּחַ נְזִירוּת טָהֳרָה. וּכְשֶׁבָּא לוֹ לִשְׁתּוֹת בַּיַּיִן, אוֹמְרִים: ג) שֶׁמָּא מוּחְלָט וְטָמֵא הָיִיתָ וּשְׁתֵּי תִגְלָחִיּוֹת הַלָּלוּ הֵן הֵן שֶׁל יְמֵי חִלּוּטוֹ וְשֶׁל יְמֵי סְפָרוֹ, וַעֲדַיִין אֵי אַתָּה מוּתָּר אֶלָּא בַּאֲכִילַת קָדָשִׁים דְּהַיְינוּ לְאַחַר ל״ז. וְחוֹזֵר וּמוֹנֶה שִׁבְעָה לְתִגְלַחַת טוּמְאָה וְאַח״כ שְׁלֹשִׁים לִנְזִירוּת טָהֳרָה, וְנִמְצָא שׁוֹתֶה בַּיַּיִן וּמִיטַּמֵּא לְמֵתִים לְאַחַר ע״ד יוֹם. טָמֵא וַדַּאי וּמוּחְלָט וַדַּאי. מְגַלֵּחַ לְתִגְלַחַת רִאשׁוֹנָה שֶׁל צָרַעַת עַכְשָׁיו, וּמִכָּאן עַד ז׳ יָמִים לְתִגְלַחַת שְׁנִיָּה, כִּדְתְנַן: שֶׁתִּגְלַחַת הַנֶּגַע דּוֹחָה לְתִגְלַחַת הַנָּזִיר בִּזְמַן שֶׁהוּא וַדַּאי. וְאוֹכֵל (ה) בְּיוֹם ח׳ שֶׁמֵּבִיא ד) קָרְבָּנוֹת בַּקֹּדֶשׁ, וְחוֹזֵר וּמוֹנֶה שִׁבְעָה וּמְגַלֵּחַ נְזִיר טוּמְאָה, וְחוֹזֵר וּמוֹנֶה שְׁלֹשִׁים וּמְגַלֵּחַ נְזִירוּת טָהֳרָה. נִמְצָא שׁוֹתֶה בַּיַּיִן וּמִיטַּמֵּא לְמֵתִים לְאַחַר אַרְבָּעִים וְאַרְבָּעָה יָמִים. שָׁאֲלוּ תַּלְמִידָיו אֶת ר׳ שִׁמְעוֹן בֶּן יוֹחַי. מִפְּנֵי מָה נָזִיר טָהוֹר אֵינוֹ כִּמְצוֹרָע. כְּלוֹמַר, נָזִיר וְהוּא מְצוֹרָע וּבָא לוֹ לְגַלֵּחַ תִּגְלַחַת צָרַעְתּוֹ ה) בַּיּוֹם שֶׁנִּשְׁלְמָה צָרַעְתּוֹ וּבַיּוֹם שֶׁנִּשְׁלְמוּ יְמֵי נְזִירוּתוֹ, מָה טַעַם אֵינָהּ עוֹלָה לוֹ תִּגְלַחַת זוֹ לְכָאן וּלְכָאן? אָמַר לָהֶן. אִם אֵלּוּ שְׁתֵּי תִגְלָחִיּוֹת שָׁווֹת, שֶׁיְּהוּ זוֹ לְגַדֵּל וְזוֹ לְגַדֵּל, אוֹ שְׁתֵּיהֶן לְהַעֲבִיר – יָפֶה אַתֶּם אוֹמְרִים. עַכְשָׁיו הֵיאַךְ [אַתֶּם] אוֹמְרִים שֶׁיְּהוּ עוֹלִין לוֹ לְכָאן וּלְכָאן? שֶׁתִּגְלַחַת נָזִיר הוּא לְהַעֲבִיר, וְתִגְלַחַת מְצוֹרָע לְגַדֵּל – שֶׁמִּכָּאן וְעַד ז׳ יָמִים צָרִיךְ לְגַלֵּחַ תִּגְלַחַת שְׁנִיָּה. אָמְרוּ לוֹ וְלֹא תַּעֲלֶה לוֹ לִימֵי חִלּוּטוֹ. בִּשְׁבִיל שֶׁהוּא לְהַעֲבִיר, וְשֶׁל מְצוֹרָע לְגַדֵּל. אֶלָּא תַּעֲלֶה לוֹ לִימֵי סְפָרוֹ. שֶׁשְּׁתֵּיהֶן לְהַעֲבִיר, שֶׁמִּכָּאן וְאֵילָךְ אֵינָן צְרִיכִין לְגַדֵּל שֵׂעָר (ו) וּכְבָר גָּדַל לוֹ כְּדֵי לָכוֹף רֹאשׁוֹ לְעִיקָּרוֹ. עַכְשָׁיו מְצוֹרָע מְגַלֵּחַ לִפְנֵי זְרִיקַת דָּמִים. שֶׁהֲרֵי בַּיּוֹם הַשְּׁבִיעִי מְגַלֵּחַ וּבַיּוֹם הַשְּׁמִינִי מֵבִיא קָרְבְּנוֹתָיו. וְנָזִיר מְגַלֵּחַ לְאַחַר זְרִיקַת דָּמִים. כִּדְכְתִיב "וְאֶת הָאַיִל יַעֲשֶׂה זֶבַח שְׁלָמִים לַיי׳", וַהֲדַר כְּתִיב "וְגִלַּח הַנָּזִיר" כו׳, הֵיאַךְ אַתֶּם אוֹמְרִים שֶׁיְּהֵא עוֹלֶה לוֹ תִּגְלַחַת א׳ לְכָאן וּלְכָאן? א״ל לֹא תַּעֲלֶה לִימֵי סְפָרוֹ וְנִזְרוֹ. בִּשְׁבִיל שֶׁזֶּה לִפְנֵי זְרִיקַת דָּמִים וְזֶה לְאַחַר זְרִיקַת דָּמִים. אֶלָּא תַּעֲלֶה לוֹ לִימֵי צָרַעְתּוֹ שֶׁל יְמֵי סְפָרוֹ וְטוּמְאָתוֹ! דְּנָזִיר שֶׁנִּטְמָא בְּמֵת וְנִצְטָרַע שֶׁתְּהֵא תִּגְלַחְתּוֹ עוֹלָה לְכָאן וּלְכָאן, דְּזֶה וָזֶה מְגַלֵּחַ לִפְנֵי זְרִיקַת דָּמִים, שֶׁשְּׁנֵיהֶן מְגַלְּחִין בְּז׳ ו) וּמְבִיאִין קָרְבָּן בְּח׳ שֶׁלָּהֶן. אָמַר לָהֶן אִילּוּ שְׁנֵיהֶן מְגַלְּחִין לִפְנֵי בִּיאַת מַיִם יָפֶה אַתֶּם אוֹמְרִים. אֲבָל טָמֵא מְגַלֵּחַ לְאַחַר בִּיאַת מַיִם, כִּדְכְתִיב "וְגִלַּח רֹאשׁוֹ בְּיוֹם טָהֳרָתוֹ", מַשְׁמַע לְאַחַר טָהֳרָה, דִּמְגַלֵּחַ לְאַחַר בִּיאַת מַיִם ז). הָכִי גָּרְסִי׳. אָמְרוּ לוֹ יָפֶה אָמַרְתָּ שֶׁלֹּא תַּעֲלֶה לוֹ (ז) ח) יְמֵי סְפָרוֹ לִימֵי נְזִירוּתוֹ וְתַעֲלֶה לוֹ יְמֵי חִלּוּטוֹ וְלִימֵי טוּמְאָתוֹ שֶׁזֶּה לְגַדֵּל וְזֶה לְגַדֵּל. אָמְרוּ לוֹ: תִּקֵּן הַדָּבָר, שֶׁלֹּא תַּעֲלֶה לוֹ תִּגְלַחַת לִימֵי סְפָרוֹ בִּימֵי נְזִיר טָהֳרָתוֹ, שֶׁמְּצוֹרָע בִּימֵי סְפָרוֹ מְגַלֵּחַ לִפְנֵי זְרִיקַת דָּמִים בַּיּוֹם הַשְּׁבִיעִי, וְנָזִיר מְגַלֵּחַ בְּיוֹם הֲבָאַת קָרְבְּנוֹתָיו לְאַחַר זְרִיקַת דָּמִים. אֲבָל תַּעֲלֶה לוֹ תִּגְלַחַת אַחַת לִימֵי טוּמְאָתוֹ וְלִימֵי חִלּוּטוֹ, שֶׁזֶּה וָזֶה מְגַלְּחִין לְגַדֵּל שֵׂיעָר אַחֵר; מְצוֹרָע בִּימֵי חִלּוּטוֹ מְגַלֵּחַ כְּדֵי לְגַדֵּל שֵׂיעָר ט) אַחֵר, וְנָזִיר טָמֵא מְגַלֵּחַ כְּדֵי לְגַדֵּל שֵׂיעָר אַחֵר שֶׁיְּהֵא מְגַלֵּחַ לִנְזִירוּת טָהֳרָתוֹ. אָמַר לָהֶן. לְכָךְ אֵין עוֹלָה לוֹ תִּגְלַחַת אַחַת מְכוּוָּן לְב׳ תִּגְלָחִיּוֹת, שֶׁאִם נָזִיר טָהוֹר הוּא וְהוּא מְצוֹרָע י) בִּימֵי חִלּוּטוֹ – (ח) מְגַלֵּחַ כְּדֵי לְגַדֵּל, וְנָזִיר לְהַעֲבִיר. וְאִם נָזִיר טָמֵא הוּא וְהוּא מְצוֹרָע, אַע״פ שֶׁשְּׁנֵיהֶן לְגַדֵּל עֲדַיִין אֵין עוֹלָה לָהֶן תִּגְלַחַת אַחַת לְכָאן וּלְכָאן, שֶׁמְּצוֹרָע מְגַלֵּחַ לִפְנֵי בִּיאַת מַיִם. כ) וְכֵן נָזִיר טָהוֹר וּמְצוֹרָע בִּימֵי סְפָרוֹ, אַע״פ שֶׁשְּׁנֵיהֶם לְהַעֲבִיר, הוֹאִיל וּמְצוֹרָע בִּימֵי סְפָרוֹ מְגַלֵּחַ לִפְנֵי זְרִיקַת דָּמִים וְנָזִיר טָהוֹר לְאַחַר זְרִיקַת דָּמִים כְּמוֹ שֶׁמְּפוֹרָשׁ לְמַעְלָה, [וּלְכָךְ] אֵין תִּגְלַחַת אַחַת עוֹלָה לִשְׁתֵּיהֶן.

תָּנֵי

[תוספתא פ״ה ע״ש]

פי׳ הרא״ש

ספק טמא ומוחלט ודאי. אוכל בקדשים לאחר ח׳ ימים כי יום [ראשון] לנזירותו מגלח לחלוטו וישב מחוץ לאהלו ז׳ ימים וביום הז׳ מגלח [פעם] ב׳ ובח׳ מביא קרבנותיו בו ביום ואוכל בקדשים מיד. והאי דקאמר לאחר ח׳ ימים לאו דוקא. ומונה ל׳ יום ויום הח׳ מן המנין וביום ל״א יגלח דכיון שנטהר מצרעתו אינו מגלח אלא עד יום ל״א כשאר נזירים אע״פ שעדיין אינו שותה יין ומטמא למתים דשמא נזיר טמא היה ואותו יום ל״א שהוא יום ל״ח לנזירותו עולה לו לנזי׳ טהרה ומגלח יום ל״א שהוא ס״ח לנזירו׳ והיינו דקאמר ושותה יין ומטמא למתים לאחר ס״ז דהיינו יום ס״ח: מוחלט ספק וטמא ודאי אוכל בקדשים אחר ל״ז ימים. דמאחר שאינו מוחלט ודאי א״א לו לגלח מיד אלא מזה ג׳ וז׳ ומגלח בח׳ ומביא קרבן נזי׳ טמא ומביא צפרים לספק חלוטו: וא״א לו לגלח עד סוף ל׳ דשמא לאו מוחלט הוא. וביום ל׳ דהיינו ל״ז לנזיר׳ מגלח דכיון דיש עליו ספק צרעת מגלח ביום ל׳ כדפי׳ לעיל וביום ל״ח יביא עולת בהמה לספק נזי׳ טהרה וחטאת העוף לספק ואוכל בקדשים בו ביום. ושמא מוחלט הוא והויין הנך ב׳ תגלחות לחלוטו ולספרו ולסוף ז׳ ימים יגלח ג׳ לטומאתו. ויום ל״ח עולה לו למנין השביעי. וביום הח׳ יתחיל למנות נזיר׳ טהרה ומגלח יום ל״א והיינו דקאמר ושותה יין ומטמא למתים אחר ע״ד ימים: טמא ודאי ומוחלט ודאי. אוכל בקדשים לאחר ח׳ ימים דכיון שהוא מוחלט ודאי מגלח ביום הא׳ א) וביום הז׳ מביא נזי׳ טמא ומתחיל בו ביום למנות ל׳ יום ומגלח ביום ל״א. והיינו דקאמר שותה יין ומטמא למתים אחר מ״ד ימים: מפני מה נזיר טהור אינו כמצורע ותעלה תגלחת צרעתו לנזירותו כגון אם נחלט ביום השלמת נזירותו ונתרפא וגילח לצרעתו תעלה לו גם לנזי׳ ובמתני׳ אמרי׳ דצריך ד׳ תגלחות משום דתגלחת צרעתו לא עלתה לו לנזירותו: נזיר להעביר הוא מעביר שערו לגמרי ואינו צריך לגדלו עוד לשם מצוה: ומצורע לגדל בתגלחת ראשונה של מצורע צריך לגדל שערו כדי לגלחו שנית לאחר ימי ספרו. והואיל וחלוקים זה מזה אין עולין של זה לזה: ויעלו לו לימי ספרו שגם הוא להעביר: זה לפני זריקת דמים. גלוח מצורע דכתיב וביום השביעי יגלח ורחץ בשרו במים. וביום השמיני יקח ב׳ כבשים. וזו תגלחת נזי׳ לאחר זריקת דמים דכתיב וגילח הנזיר פתח אהל מועד ולקח את שער ראשו ונתן על האש אשר תחת זבח השלמים: ותעלה לימי טומאתו. לתגלחת נזי׳ טמא: טמא לאחר ביאת מים דכתיב וגלח ראשו ביום טהרתו ביום השביעי יגלחנו. ביום טהרתו משמע אחר טהרתו. והכי דריש לה בספרי: ומצורע לפני ביאת מים דכתיב וביום השביעי יגלח את כל שערו ורוחץ בשרו במים וטהר. יש בספרים לישנא אחרינא עד תנא ר׳ חייא זה לפני ביאת מים וכו׳ כדפי׳ לעיל:

הני

א) נ״ל וביום הז׳ יגלח תגלחת שניה וביום הח׳ יביא קרבנות מצורע וחוזר ומונה ז׳ ומגלח נזירות טומאה ומתחיל כו׳.

נוסחת הריב״ן

א) בקדשים בו ביום כיון שהביא כפרתו: ב) ומונה נזירות טהרה כו׳: ג) אומרים לו שמא כו׳ ואח״כ לנזירות כו׳ ע״ד הס״ד: ד) קרבנותיו כו׳ ומגלח נזירות: ה) תגלחת לצרעתו ביום שנשלמו ימי וכו׳: ו) בשביעי שלהן: ז) ומצורע לפני ביאת מים כדכתיב וביום השביעי יגלח את כל שערו ואח״כ כתיב ורחץ את בשרו וטהר: ח) שלא תעלה לו לימי ספרו ולימי נזירותו ותעלה לו לימי חלוטו כו׳ תגלחת אחת לימי ספרו ולימי נזירות: ט) שיער בעבור גילוח יום שמיני וטמא לא לתשלום נזירות טהרתו הס״ד: י) שמצורע בימי חלוטו: כ) ונזיר טמא לאחר ביאת מים וכן נזיר כ׳ ומצורע מגלח לפני כו׳:

הגהות הב״ח

(א) גמ׳ לאי ודאי נזיר: (ב) שם אלא עכשיו מצורע לפני זריקת: (ג) שם אמר להן אם נזיר טהור: (ד) רש״י ד״ה ואם טמא כו׳ ולאי היה ביום ראשון: (ה) ד״ה טמא ודאי וכו׳ ואוכל בקדשים ביום ח׳ שמביא קרבנות וחוזר כצ״ל: (ו) ד״ה אלא תעלה וכו׳ לכבר גדל: (ז) ד״ה הכי גרסינן אמרו לו יפה אמרת שלא תעלה לו לימי ספירו ולימי נזירותו ותעלה לו לימי חלוטו וכו׳ אמרו לו תקנת הדבר שלא תעלה לו תגלחת אחת לימי ספירו ולימי נזירו: (ח) ד״ה אמר להן וכו׳ בימי חלוטו מצורע מגלח כדי לגדל:

תָּנֵי רַבִּי חִיָּיא: זֶה לִפְנֵי בִּיאַת מַיִם (חַיִּים) וְזֶה לְאַחַר בִּיאַת מַיִם, זֶה לִפְנֵי זְרִיקַת דָּמִים וְזֶה לְאַחַר זְרִיקַת דָּמִים.§ "שֶׁתִּגְלַחַת הַנֶּגַע" וכו'.§ בָּעֵי רָמִי בַּר חָמָא: הָנֵי אַרְבַּע תִּגְלָחִיּוֹת דְּקָאָמַר, מִשּׁוּם מִצְוָה אוֹ מִשּׁוּם אַעְבּוּרֵי שֵׂיעָר טוּמְאָה? לְמַאי נָפְקָא מִינָּהּ — לְעַבּוּרֵי *בְּנָשָׁא. אִי אָמְרַתְּ מִשּׁוּם מִצְוָה — לְעַבּוּרֵי בְּנָשָׁא לָא, וְאִי אָמְרַתְּ מִשּׁוּם אַעְבּוּרֵי שֵׂיעָר טוּמְאָה — אֲפִילּוּ סַכֵּיהּ נָשָׁא נַמִי. מַאי? אֲמַר רָבָא, ת"ש: וּמְגַלֵּחַ אַרְבַּע תִּגְלָחִיּוֹת; אִי סָלְקָא דַּעְתָּךְ מִשּׁוּם עַבּוּרֵי שֵׂיעָר טוּמְאָה — אֲפִילּוּ בְּשָׁלֹשׁ נַמִי סַגְיָא לֵיהּ, שְׁמַע מִינָּהּ: מִשּׁוּם מִצְוָה, שְׁמַע מִינָּהּ.§

הדרן עלך שני נזירים

הַגּוֹיִם [א]אֵין לָהֶם נְזִירוּת, [ב]נָשִׁים וַעֲבָדִים יֵשׁ לָהֶן נְזִירוּת, חוֹמֶר בְּנָשִׁים מִבַּעֲבָדִים: [ג]שֶׁהוּא כּוֹפֶה אֶת עַבְדּוֹ, [ד]וְאֵינוֹ כּוֹפֶה אֶת אִשְׁתּוֹ.§ **גמ'** קָתָנֵי: הַגּוֹיִם אֵין לָהֶם נְזִירוּת. מְנָא הָנֵי מִילֵּי? דְּתָנוּ רַבָּנַן: *°"דַּבֵּר (במדבר ו) אֶל בְּנֵי יִשְׂרָאֵל" — וְלֹא לַגּוֹיִם, "וְאָמַרְתָּ אֲלֵיהֶם" — לְרַבּוֹת אֶת הָעֲבָדִים. לָמָּה לִי קְרָא? הָאָמַרְתְּ: *כָּל מִצְוָה שֶׁהָאִשָּׁה חַיֶּיבֶת בָּהּ עֶבֶד חַיָּיב בָּהּ! אֲמַר רָבָא: שָׁאנֵי הָכָא, *דְּאָמַר קְרָא (שם ל) °"לֶאְסֹר אִסָּר עַל נַפְשׁוֹ" — בְּמִי שֶׁנַּפְשׁוֹ קְנוּיָה לוֹ, יָצָא עֶבֶד שֶׁאֵין נַפְשׁוֹ קְנוּיָה לוֹ; (א) הוֹאִיל וְאֵין נַפְשׁוֹ קְנוּיָה לוֹ, אֵימָא גַּבֵּי נָזִיר נַמִי לָא — קָמַשְׁמַע לָן. אָמַר מָר: "דַּבֵּר אֶל בְּנֵי יִשְׂרָאֵל" — וְלֹא לַגּוֹיִם. וְכָל הֵיכָא דִּכְתִיב "יִשְׂרָאֵל" גּוֹיִם לָא? וְהָא גַּבֵּי עֲרָכִין, דִּכְתִיב (ויקרא כז) °"דַּבֵּר אֶל בְּנֵי יִשְׂרָאֵל", *וְתַנְיָא: בְּנֵי יִשְׂרָאֵל מַעֲרִיכִין, [ה]וְאֵין הַגּוֹיִם מַעֲרִיכִין. יָכוֹל לֹא יִהוּ נֶעֱרָכִין — ת"ל "אִישׁ"! שָׁאנֵי הָכָא, דְּאָמַר קְרָא (במדבר ו) °"לְאָבִיו וּלְאִמּוֹ לֹא יִטַּמָּא" — בְּמִי שֶׁיֵּשׁ לוֹ אָב, יָצָא גּוֹי שֶׁאֵין לוֹ אָב. לְמַאי? אִילֵימָא לְעִנְיַן יְרוּשָּׁה — *וְהָא"ר חִיָּיא בַּר אָבִין א"ר יוֹחָנָן: [ו]גּוֹי יוֹרֵשׁ אֶת אָבִיו דְּבַר תּוֹרָה, שֶׁנֶּאֱמַר (דברים ב) °"כִּי יְרֻשָּׁה לְעֵשָׂו נָתַתִּי אֶת הַר שֵׂעִיר"! אֶלָּא: בְּמִי שֶׁמּוּזְהָר עַל כִּיבּוּד אָבִיו. מִי כְּתִיב "כַּבֵּד אָבִיךָ" גַּבֵּי נָזִיר?! אֶלָּא, אֲמַר קְרָא "לְאָבִיו וּלְאִמּוֹ לֹא יִטַּמָּא" — בְּמִי שֶׁיֵּשׁ לוֹ טוּמְאָה, יָצָא

רש"י

תָּנֵי רַבִּי חִיָּיא. א) טָמֵא וְהוּא מְצוֹרָע אֵין עוֹלִין לוֹ לְכָאן וּלְכָאן, לְפִי שֶׁזֶּה לִפְנֵי בִּיאַת מַיִם וְזֶה לְאַחַר בִּיאַת מַיִם. נָזִיר טָהוֹר וְהוּא מְצוֹרָע נַמִי אֵין עוֹלִין לוֹ לְכָאן וּלְכָאן, שֶׁמְּצוֹרָע מְגַלֵּחַ לִפְנֵי ג) זְרִיקָה וְנָזִיר טָהוֹר לְאַחַר זְרִיקַת דָּמִים. בָּעֵי רָמִי בַּר חָמָא הָנֵי אַרְבַּע תִּגְלָחִיּוֹת. דְּקָאָמַר עֲלָהּ: וּמְגַלֵּחַ ד' תִּגְלָחִיּוֹת, מִי אָמַר מִשּׁוּם מִצְוָה ג) אִיתְנְהוּ, ממ"נ, תַּרְתֵּי קַמָּיְיתָא מִשּׁוּם תַּרְתֵּי תִגְלָחִיּוֹת ד) דְּצָרַעַת, וּשְׁלִישִׁית מִשּׁוּם טוּמְאָה, וּרְבִיעִית מִשּׁוּם ה) נָזִיר דְּטָהֳרָה, וְכוּלָּן בְּתַעַר. אוֹ דִּלְמָא מִשּׁוּם עִבּוּרֵי שֵׂיעָר טוּמְאָה. אִיתְנְהוּ, וַאֲפִילּוּ מַעֲבִיר לָהּ בְּנָשָׁא — שַׁפִּיר דָּמֵי. וְאִי ס"ד מִשּׁוּם עִבּוּרֵי שֵׂיעָר טוּמְאָה. הוּא דִּמְגַלֵּחַ, אֲפִילּוּ בְּג' תִּגְלָחִיּוֹת נַמִי סַגְיָא, דְּכֵיוָן דִּשְׁתֵּי תִגְלָחִיּוֹת שֶׁבִּמְצוֹרָע וּשְׁלִישִׁית שֶׁל נָזִיר טָמֵא אִיכָּא עִבּוּרֵי שֵׂיעָר טוּמְאָה. וְהַאי דַּהֲדַר מְגַלֵּחַ בְּתִגְלַחַת רְבִיעִית — הָא לֵיכָּא עִבּוּרֵי שֵׂיעָר טוּמְאָה, וְאַמַּאי מְגַלֵּחַ? אֶלָּא לָאו ש"מ דְּכוּלְּהוּ אִיתְנְהוּ מִשּׁוּם מִצְוָה לְגַלֵּחַ אַרְבַּע תִּגְלָחִיּוֹת, ש"מ.

הדרן עלך שני נזירים

הַגּוֹיִם אֵין לָהֶם נְזִירוּת. הַגּוֹיִם שֶׁנָּדְרוּ בִּנְזִירוּת — אֵין נְזִירוּת חָלָה עֲלֵיהֶן, וּמוּתָּרִין לְגַלֵּחַ וְלִשְׁתּוֹת יַיִן וְלִיטַּמֵּא לַמֵּתִים. חוֹמֶר בְּנָשִׁים מִבַּעֲבָדִים שֶׁהוּא כּוֹפֶה אֶת עַבְדּוֹ. שֶׁהָעֶבֶד שֶׁנָּדַר בְּנָזִיר — יָכוֹל רַבּוֹ לְכוֹפוֹ לִשְׁתּוֹת בַּיַּיִן, אֲבָל אִשְׁתּוֹ שֶׁנָּדְרָה בְּנָזִיר — אֵינוֹ יָכוֹל לְכוֹפָהּ, (ב) וְכֵיוָן שֶׁנָּדְרָה וְשָׁמַע ו) לָהּ וְלֹא הֵיפֵר לָהּ — שׁוּב אֵינוֹ יָכוֹל לְהָפֵר. **גמ'** קָתָנֵי הַכּוּתִים. אֵין חַיָּיבִין בִּנְזִירוּת, אֲבָל הַנָּשִׁים וְהָעֲבָדִים חַיָּיבִין. דְּת"ר דַּבֵּר אֶל בְּנֵי יִשְׂרָאֵל. "אִישׁ אוֹ אִשָּׁה כִּי יַפְלִיא לִנְדּוֹר נֶדֶר נָזִיר" וגו' ז) — בְּנֵי יִשְׂרָאֵל נוֹדְרִין, וְאֵין הַגּוֹיִם נוֹדְרִין. וְאָמַרְתָּ אֲלֵיהֶם. "אִישׁ אוֹ אִשָּׁה" — לְרַבּוֹת אֶת הָעֲבָדִים, שֶׁיֵּשׁ לָהֶן נְזִירוּת. עֲבָדִים לָמָּה לִי. לְרַבּוּיֵי קְרָא שֶׁיֵּשׁ לָהֶן נְזִירוּת? הָא אָמַרְתְּ. בְּמַסֶּ' *קִדּוּשִׁין: כָּל מִצְוָה שֶׁהָאִשָּׁה חַיֶּיבֶת בָּהּ כו'. וְכֵיוָן שֶׁהָאִשָּׁה חַיֶּיבֶת בִּנְזִירוּת, כִּדְכְתִיב "אִישׁ אוֹ אִשָּׁה" — אִיתְרַבּוּ לְהוּ נַמִי עֲבָדִים. שָׁאנֵי הָכָא. גַּבֵּי נְזִירוּת, דְּאִי לָאו דְּאָתֵי קְרָא אַחֲרִינָא לְרַבּוּיֵי עֲבָדִים — לָא הֲוָאִי אָמֵינָא דַּעֲבָדִים מְחַיְּיבֵי בִּנְזִירוּת, מִשּׁוּם דַּאֲמַר קְרָא גַּבֵּי *נְזִירוּת "לֶאֱסוֹר אִיסָּר" כו', קמ"ל "וְאָמַרְתָּ אֲלֵיהֶם" — לְרַבּוֹת אֶת הָעֲבָדִים. וְאֵין הַגּוֹיִם מַעֲרִיכִין. שֶׁאִם אָמַר "עֶרְכִּי עָלַי" — לֹא אָמַר כְּלוּם. יָכוֹל לֹא יְהוּ נֶעֱרָכִין. שֶׁאִם אָמַר יִשְׂרָאֵל: "עֶרֶךְ (ג) ח) זֶה גּוֹי עָלַי" שֶׁלֹּא יְהוּ בִּדְבָרָיו כְּלוּם. תַּלְמוּד לוֹמַר. "אִישׁ אוֹ אִשָּׁה כִּי יַפְלִיא נֶדֶר בְּעֶרְכְּךָ נְפָשׁוֹת לַה'" — דְּאִיתְנְהוּ בִּכְלַל עֵרֶךְ, וְנוֹתֵן עֶרְכּוֹ כְּפִי שְׁנוֹתָיו שֶׁל גּוֹי. (ד) הָכָא נַמִי גַּבֵּי נְזִירוּת, לֶיהֱווּ גּוֹיִם בְּתוֹרַת נְזִירוּת, דְּאִם אֵינָן נְזִירִין לְהָבִיא קָרְבָּן, דִּכְתִיב "בְּנֵי יִשְׂרָאֵל" — וְלֹא גּוֹיִם, לִיתְהֲנוּ בְּהוּ "אִישׁ" דְּלֶיהֱווּ נְזִירִים, אֲבָל לֹא מְבִיאִין קָרְבָּן, כִּדִלְקַמָּן. שָׁאנֵי הָכָא. גַּבֵּי נָזִיר ט) מַה שֶּׁאֵינוֹ בְּתוֹרַת נָזִיר כְּלָל, דַּאֲמַר קְרָא "לְאָבִיו וּלְאִמּוֹ לֹא יִטַּמָּא" — בְּמִי שֶׁיֵּשׁ לוֹ אָב דִּיבֵּר הַכָּתוּב, שֶׁהוּא חַיָּיב בְּתוֹרַת נָזִיר. יָצָא גּוֹי שֶׁאֵין לוֹ אָב. דְּאֵין אָבוֹת לְגוֹי. לְמַאי הִלְכְתָא. אָמְרַתְּ דְּאֵין אָבוֹת לְגוֹי. אִילֵימָא לְעִנְיַן יְרוּשָּׁה כו' כִּי יְרוּשָּׁה לְעֵשָׂו נָתַתִּי אֶת הַר שֵׂעִיר. לְהוֹרִישָׁהּ לְבָנָיו, אַלְמָא דְּאִית אָבוֹת לְגוֹי לְעִנְיַן יְרוּשָּׁה. אֶלָּא. אֵימָא הָכִי: (ה) לְאִמּוֹ וּלְאָבִיו — בְּמִי שֶׁמּוּזְהָר עַל כִּיבּוּד אָבִיו בָּא לְךָ הַכָּתוּב לוֹמַר שֶׁלֹּא יִטַּמָּא בִּשְׁבִיל נְזִירוּת שֶׁעָלָיו, וְגוֹי הוֹאִיל וְאֵינוֹ בְּכִיבּוּד אָבִיו — אֵין נְזִירוּת חָלָה עָלָיו. י) יָצָא

תוספות

תא שמע ומגלח ארבע תגלחיות ש"מ משום מצוה ש"מ. יש מפרשים דדייק מדכולל אותם ביחד — א"כ דמיין אהדדי, וכולהו בתער, אף השלישית שהיא לספק נזיר טמא. גם יש ספרים כתוב: ואי ס"ד משום עיבורי טומאה אפילו בג' נמי סגי. וקשיא לן: מאי מייתי? והלא בכל התגלחיות יש להסתפק אי במצורע או בנזיר טהור, אף בשלישית! ושמא י"ל: דאע"ג דבתגלחת שלישית איכא לספוקי תגלחת בנזיר טהור שהיא צריכה תער, מ"מ אם לא היתה תגלחת טומאה צריכה תער — משום ספק דנזיר טהור לא היה צריך גילוח, שהרי עדיין לא היה מותר לשתות ביין.

הדרן עלך שני נזירים

הגוים אין להם נזירות. ואין קרבנן קרב, אף על גב דמקבלין מהם נדרים ונדבות. ובגמרא מפרש מנלן. **נשים** ועבדים יש להן נזירות. בגמרא מרבה להן. **כופה** את עבדו. שמוחה על נזירותו. בגמרא מפרש טעמא. **מנהני** מילי. דגוים אין להם נזירות? הלא בשאר נדרים דינן כישראל, כדכתיב "איש איש" – לרבות גוים שנודרים נדרים ונדבות כישראל, והכא נמי נדר הוא. **דת"ר** דבר אל בני ישראל ואמרת אליהם איש או אשה כי יפליא לנדור נדר נזיר להזיר לה' וגו' בני ישראל ולא גוים. שאם קבלו נזירות – אינו כלום, ומותרין לשתות ביין, ואין מביאין קרבנות נזירות עליהם. למה לי קרא לרבות לעבדים והא אמרינן כל מצוה שאשה חייבת עבד חייב בה. כלומר, הא קיימא לן הכי. ובפ"ק *דקדושין (דף כג.) ילפינן לה. **שאני** הכא דקאמר קרא לאסור איסר על נפשו מי שנפשו קנויה לו יצא עבד. ואע"ג דאכתיב לגבי נדרים, מ"מ בפ"ק דנדרים (דף ג.) מקשינן נזירות לנדרים מ"לנדור נדר נזיר להזיר". **והא** גבי ערכין דכתיב בני ישראל ותניא בני ישראל מעריכין. לומר "ערכי עלי", או "ערך פלוני עלי". ואין הגוים מעריכין, אף כי נודרים נדרים ונדבות כישראל. יכול לא יהו נערכים, אם אמר ישראל "ערך גוי עלי" ת"ל "איש", והכא נמי גבי נזיר נימא דאהני מיעוטא דבני ישראל לומר בני ישראל נודרים ומביאין קרבן אבל הגוים אין נודרים ומביאים קרבן. יכול לא יהו נודרים כלל לאסור ביין ובטומאה – ת"ל "איש" דהכי נמי אמר התלמוד בסמוך. **למאי** אילימא לענין ירושה. דסתם מקום שנאמר בו אב לענין ירושה קרוי אביו. **מי** שמוזהר על כיבוד [אב]. אבל גוי לא מוזהר. **מידי** [בנזיר כבד] אביך כתיב. ולעיל כי קאמר לענין ירושה לא פריך הכי, דסתם אב נקרא אב לענין ירושה. ודלמא

פי' הרא"ש

הני ד' תגלחיות דאמרי' משום מצוה כלומר כולהו משום מצוה דאפילו טמא ודאי ומוחלט ודאי היו כולן צריכין תער אפילו תגלחת שלישית שהיה משום טומאה: או משום אעבורי שער שיעביר ממנו שער שהי"ל בשעה שנטמא ובעבורי נשא סגי. וה"ה דמיבעיא ליה לכל תגלחת נזיר טמא וצ"ל דא"נ סגי ליה בעבורי נשא צריך לגלח מקצת ראשו בתער או במספרים שאם היה סך נשא כל ראשו תו לא הדר רבי כדמשמע פ' החובל ולא מצי למעבד תו תגלחת שניה של טהרה וק"ל דמסתברא דאפילו נזיר טהור מצי לעבורי שערו בנשא רק שישייר ב' שערות וצ"ל. דתרי גווני נשא נינהו יש נשא שהשער צומח אח"כ. ואע"ג דבס"פ ג' מינין [אמרינן] דבעי' תער דגמרי' ליה מנזיר טהור הכי נמי סלקא סוגיא דשמעתן הכי רמי בר חמא הוה מספקא ליה ת"ש מגלח ד' תגלחת ואי אמרינן משום עבורי נשא א) בג' סגי מעבר עביר שער שהי"ל בשעה שנטמא ואע"ג דבתגלחת שלישי' איכא לספוקי נמי בתגלחת [נזיר] טהור שהיא צריכה תער מכל מקום אם לא היתה תגלחת טומאה צריכה תער משום ספק נזיר טהור לא היתה צריכה גילוח שהרי עדיין לא יהא מותר לשתות יין ולטמא למתים אלא ש"מ שאף תגלחת נזיר טמא משום מצוה וצרי' תער: סליק פרקא

פ"ט הגוים אין להם נזירות אע"פ שגוים נודרין נדרים ונדבות כישראל אם נדר בנזיר אין עליו תורת נזיר ואין מקבלין ממנו קרבנות נזיר להקריבם ואם בא לימלך אם מותר לשתות ולטמא למתים מתירים לו: שהוא כופה את עבדו כופהו לשתות יין ואינו כופה את אשתו לשתות אם לא שאמר בל' הפרה: ב) שהוא מפיר את נדרי אשתו ובהפרה זו נתבטל הנדר ומותרת לשתות יין אף לאחר שתתאלמן או תתגרש ואינו מיפר את נדרי עבדו אע"פ שכופהו לשתות יין הנדר מיהו קיים ואם נשתחרר משלים את הנזירות ולא נהירא הך פירושא דהיינו סיפא הפר לאשתו הפר עולמית אם לא שנאמר דפרושי קא מפרש ונראה לפרש שהוא מפיר נדרי אשתו ואף אם נתרצה אחר ההפרשה שתקיים את נדרה אין עליה תורת נזיר שכבר נתבטל הנדר ובעבדים אף אם כפהו לשתות יין אם רוצה האדון אח"כ שיקיים נזירותו צריך לקיימו. הפר לעבדו לאו דוקא אלא שכפהו לשתות יין: עבר מכנגד פניו שברח בגמרא מפרש טעמא: **גמ'** דבר אל בני ישראל בנזיר כתיב ולא גוים: הא אמרת כל מצוה שהאשה חייבת וכו' דגמרי' לה לה מאשה: שאני הכא דאמר קרא לאסור אסר על נפשו ואע"ג דהאי קרא בנדרים כתיב בפ"ק דנדרים מקשינן נזירות לנדרים מלנדור נדר נזיר להזיר: ולא הגוים מעריכין שאם אמר ערכי עלי או ערך פלוני עלי לא מחייב יכול לא יהו נערכים אם אמר ישראל ערך גוי זה עלי ת"ל איש הכא נמי גבי נזיר אימא אהני מיעוט דאין הגוים נודרים ומביאין קרבן כישראל ואהני ריבויא דאיש שיש עליהם תורת נזיר שלא לשתות ולטמא למתים: יצא גוי שאין לו אב הלכך אינו בתורת נזיר ליין ולטמא למתים הלכך ליכא למדרש הכא איש לרבוי. ותמיה לי לבני ישראל למה לי דליכא למימר דמהאי קרא לא שמעינן אלא יין וטומאת מתים ואתא בני ישראל למעוטי מקרבנות דלא הוה מסתבר שיביא קרבנות נזיר הואיל ואין עליו תורת נזיר כלל ועוד אי מצי' למדרש האי קרא לחצאין אכתי נימא מי שאין לו אב מטמא למתים ומאיש נרבה שאסור לשתות יין אלא ודאי האי קרא ליכא למידרשיה לחצאין וי"ל דמהאי קרא לא הוה שמעינן מידי אי לאו כתיב בני ישראל אלא בתר דכתיב בני ישראל אתיא הך דרשא לאפוקי מרבויא דאיש: שנאמר ירושה לעשו נתתי את הר שעיר נתן לו להורישו לבניו. מי כתיב כבוד אב לענין נזיר ולעיל לא פריך מי כתיב

עין משפט נר מצוה

א א מיי' פ"ב מהלכות נזירות הלכה טז:
ב ב מיי' שם הלכה יז [ובהרא"ש בפסקיו נדרים פ"י סימן י]:
ג ג מיי' שם הלכה יח:
ד ד טוש"ע י"ד סימן רלד סעיף לט:
ה ה ו מיי' פ"א מהל' ערכין הלכה ו סמג עשין קכח:
ו ז מיי' פ"ו מהלכות נחלות הלכה ט סמג עשין צו טוש"ע ח"מ סי' רפג סעיף א:

מסורת הש"ס

פירוש שם המשיר את השיער

[מנחות עג:]

[חגיגה ד. כריתות ז:]

[לקמן סב:]

ערכין ה:

ל"ל חגיגה ד.

קדושין יח. [ומסיק שם אלא מהכא כי לבני לוטן] ל"ל נדרים

נוסחת הריב"ן

א) נזיר טמא והוא מצורע אין תגלחותיו עולין כו': ב) זריקת דמים: ג) איטן: ד) לצרעת: ה) נזירות לטהרה: ו) ושמע בה: ז) וגו' איש לרבות את העבדים כו' והשאר ליתא: ח) גוי זה: ט) מ"ט ליתנהו בתורת נזיר כו' שהוא בתורת נזיר: י) בכ"י כתוב כאן גליון מי כתיב ככד כלומר קרא לאביו לא משמעע שיהא זקוק לכבודו אבל לעיל לא פריך מי כתיב אביו המורישו דהא פשיטא דעיקר אב הוי לענין ירושה. בתוס' עכ"ל:

הגהות הב"ח

(א) גמ' והואיל ואין נפשו: (ב) רש"י ד"ה חומר וכו' דכיון שנדרה ושמע: (ג) ד"ה יכול לא וכו' ערך עובד כוכבים זה עלי וכו' בדבריו כלום ת"ל איש כי יפליא כנ"ל ותיבות או אשה נמחק: (ד) בא"ד והכא נמי וכו' ולא עובדי כוכבים איתנהו בהו איש: (ה) ד"ה אלא אימא הכי לאביו ולאמו במי שמוזהר:

א) נראה דצ"ל משום עבורי שער בג' תגלחות סגי דבתגלחת הג' סגי לעבורי שער שהי"ל בשעה שנטמא וכו'. ב) שייך למתניתין דלקמן דף סב ע"ב.

ז א מיי' פ"א מהלכות טומאת מת הלכה יג:

תורה אור

יצא גוי [א]שאין לו טומאה. מנלן דלית להו טומאה? דאמר קרא "ואיש אשר יטמא ולא יתחטא ונכרתה הנפש ההיא מתוך הקהל" (במדבר יט) – במי שיש לו קהל, יצא זה שאין לו קהל. ממאי? דלמא כרת הוא דלא מיחייב, אבל איטמויי מיטמו! אמר קרא "והזה הטהור על הטמא" (שם), כל שיש לו טהרה יש לו טומאה, וכל שאין לו טהרה – אין לו טומאה. ואימא: טהרה הוא דלא הויא ליה, טומאה הויא ליה! א"ק "ואיש אשר יטמא ולא יתחטא". רב אחא בר יעקב אמר: שאני הכא, דא"ק "והתנחלתם אותם לבניכם אחריכם" (ויקרא כה), כל שיש לו נחלה – יש לו טומאה, וכל שאין לו נחלה – אין לו טומאה. אי הכי עבדים נמי לא! אלא אמר רבא: בשלמא גבי ערכין, שנאמר "בני ישראל" (שם כז) – *בני ישראל מעריכין, ואין הגוים מעריכין. יכול לא יהו נערכין – ת"ל "איש [א] [איש]". הכא, בני ישראל נוזרין ומביאין קרבן, ואין הגוים נוזרין ומביאין קרבן. יכול אף לא יהו נזירין כלל – ת"ל "איש"? אמרי: אי משום קרבן – לאו מהכא נפקא ליה, אלא מהתם: *"לעולה" – פרט לנזירות, דברי ר' יוסי הגלילי! אימא: בני ישראל נוזרין נזירות עולם, ואין הגוים נוזרים נזירות עולם. יכול לא יהו נזירים – ת"ל "איש"! א"ר יוחנן: מי כתיב נזיר עולם?! אימא: בני ישראל מדירין בניהם בנזיר, ואין הגוים מדירין בניהם בנזיר. יכול לא יהו נזירים – ת"ל "איש"! האמר רבי יוחנן: *הלכה היא בנזיר! אימא: בני ישראל מגלחין על נזירות אביהן, ואין הגוים מגלחין על נזירות אביהן. יכול

[לקמן סב. ערכין ה:] מנחות עג: [לעיל כח: וש"נ]

יצא גוי שאין לו טומאה. שאם נגע במת אינו טמא. דלמא כרת הוא דלא מיחייב. כי נכנס במקדש. אבל איטמויי איטמי. כי נגע במת, כדי לטמא אדם וכלים. והואיל והוא מיטמא – נמצאת אתה אומר שאתה נזירות חלה עליו. כל שיש לו טהרה. (א) בהזאה ובטבילת מקוה, יש לו טומאה, וגוי שאין לו טהרה – אין מקבל טומאה. והא דאמרינן במס' יבמות בפ' "הערל" (דף עא.): ערל מקבל הזאה – כגון ערל ישראל שלא נימול, (א) שמתו אחיו מחמת מילה. אבל ערל גוי לא. וכיון שאין מקבל הזאה – לפיכך אין לו טומאה. ודלמא טהרה הוא דלית ליה. שאם קיבל טומאה, אפילו שהוזה – לא נטהר מטומאתו, ופוסל את הקדשים במגעו. (ב) הא טומאה הויא ליה, שאם נגע במת – שהוא טמא, ומטמא אדם וכלים. אמר קרא [איש אשר] יטמא ולא יתחטא. איתקש טומאה לטהרה, דתרווייהו טומאה וטהרה קמישתעו בחד גברא. והכי משמע: כל מי שאין לו טהרה – אין לו טומאה, וגוי הואיל ואי אפשר לו בטהרה – אין לו טומאה. רב אחא בר יעקב אמר שאני הכא. גבי נזירות; טעמא מאי אימעיטו להו גוים מנזירות – כתיב הכא "לאביו ולאמו לא יטמא", והתם כתיב "והתנחלתם אותם לבניכם אחריכם לרשת אחוזה", כל מי שיש לו נחלה להוריש לבניו את עבדיו דבר לך הכתוב גבי נזיר, שיש לו אב ואם, כדכתיב "לאביו ולאמו" – יש להם טומאה. והני גוים, הואיל ואין להם נחלה כדי להוריש עבדו לבנו, כדכתיב "וגם מבני התושבים הגרים עמכם מהם תקנו", ואמרינן במס' (גיטין דף לח.): אתם קונים מהם ולא הם קונים מכם, ולא הם קונים זה את זה – לא הוי להו טומאה. וכל שאין לו טומאה – אין לו תורת נזירות. אי הכי עבדים נמי. לא ליהוו בתורת נזיר, לפי שאינן בתורת נחלה להוריש לבניהם, דכל מה שקנה עבד קנה רבו. ולא הן קונין זה את זה, דהא לאו ישראל נינהו. אלא אמר רבא בשלמא גבי ערכין. דכתיב "[בני] ישראל" לא מצית למעוטי גוים לגמרי, דהא דכתיב "בני ישראל" – ממעריך בלבד הוא דקממעט להו, כדאמרינן: בני ישראל מעריכין. (ג) אבל לגמרי לא מצית למעוטי להו דלא ליהוו נערכין, דהא הדר כתיב בהו "איש" דמייתי את הגוים דליהוו נערכין. אבל הכא גבי נזירות, ליכא לך למימר דליהוי בכלל נזיר כלל, דהיכי אמרת – בני ישראל נוזרין ומביאין קרבן, ואין הגוים נוזרין ומביאין קרבן, דהאי דכתיב בנזיר "בני ישראל" (ג) קא ממעט להו מקרבן – ומשום מיעוטא דקרבן לא איצטריך למיכתב "בני ישראל", דמהתם נפקא שאין נוזרין ומביאין קרבן, דאמרינן במסכת מנחות בפרק "אלו מנחות נקמצות" (דף עג:): "איש איש מבית ישראל כו' אשר יקריב קרבנו לכל נדריהם ולכל נדבותם" – לרבות את הגוים שנודרים נדרים ונדבות כישראל, דמ"לכל נדריהם ולכל נדבותם" נפקא לרבות עולה ושלמים ועופות ויין ולבונה. א"כ מה ת"ל "לעולה" (ד) דכתיב "אשר יקריבו לה' לעולה" – פרט לנזירות, דאין הגוים מביאין קרבן נזירות, דברי ר' יוסי הגלילי. וכיון דמהתם נפקא שאין מביאין קרבן נזירות, "בני ישראל" דהכא למאי אתא? אלא לומר לך דלא חל עלייהו נזירות כלל. והאי דכתיב בהו "איש" – איידי דכתיב אשה לנורך, כתב נמי איש שלא לנורך. ואימא. דהאי דכתיב "בני ישראל" גבי נזירות – משום דקאתי לאשמועי' דממעט להו לגוים מנזירות עולם, ומיהו בנזירות סתם קאי בלא קרבן, מדכתיב בהו "איש". מי כתיב נזיר עולם. בקרא, (ה) דקאמרת בני ישראל נוזרין נזירות עולם, אבל לא הגוים? והא לא גמרי נזירות עולם אלא מאבשלום, כדאמרינן לעיל בפירקא קמא (דף ד:). והאמר רבי יוחנן. בפירקין דלעיל (דף כח:): הלכה

היא

ודלמא כרת הוא דלא מחייב. ת"ל דקאמר מהני [דלא] תיתי לומר שיהא גוי בכרת, אבל אטמויי מיטמו! אמר קרא והזה הטהור על הטמא כל מי שיש לו טהרה יש לו טומאה וכל שאין לו טהרה אין לו טומאה. וגוי אין לו טהרה, דכתיב "והיתה לעדת בני ישראל למשמרת למי נדה חטאת היא" למשמרת לבני ישראל, ולא לגוים, כפי' הקונטרס. ודלמא טהרה הוא דלא הוי להו הא טומאה אית להו. דהאי "והזה הטהור על הטמא" לא מייתר, דבפ"ק דיומא (דף יד.) מוקמינן ליה למילי אחריני, למתכוין להזות על האדם והזה על הבהמה. ומשני: אמר קרא "אשר יטמא ולא יתחטא", דמייתר "יטמא", דהוה ליה למכתב "אשר לא יתחטא". ועוד י"ל: משום ד"והזה הטהור" לא מיירי בטהרה דחיטוי, אלא מיירי בטהור גמור לפי הפשט, או בטבול יום כדאית' ביבמות (דף עג.). וקרא דממעטינן מיניה גוים מטהרה – היינו מטהרת חיטוי, כדכתיב "לבני ישראל למשמרת למי נדה חטאת היא". להכי אייתי קרא ד"אשר יטמא ולא יתחטא" דמיירי בחיטוי, *וצריך עיון. ואף על גב דאמת הוא דגוי אין לו שום טהרה ואפילו טבילה – מ"מ ניחא ליה לאתויי מחיטוי גופיה, דומיא ד"למשמרת למי נדה חטאת היא" דמיניה ממעטינן גוים, דמיירי בחיטוי. *(ושמא) הא דגוי אין לו טהרה ואפי' טבילה – היינו משום דאיתקש טבילה להזאה, דכתיב "וחטאו ביום השביעי וכבס בגדיו ורחץ במים וטהר".
לשון הר"ף: אמר קרא "אשר יטמא ולא יתחטא" ואיתקש טומאה לטהרה. רב אחא בר יעקב אמר והתנחלתם אותם לבניכם אחריכם. אעבדים קאי. רב אחא בא ליישב דרשא של אביו דלעיל, מי שיש לו אב לענין כל ירושה המפורשת בתור'. וירושת עבדים מפורשת בקרא ד"והתנחלתם" וגוי אינו מוריש עבדו לבניו, שאין לגוי קנין בגוף העבד, כדדרשינן פרק "השולח" (גיטין דף לח.): אתם קונין מהם, ולא הם קונין מכם, ולא הם קונין זה את זה. א"כ כל שיש לו נחלה בעבדים – קרוי אביו, והוי בכלל "לאביו ולאמו לא יטמא", וכל שאין לו נחלה – אינו בכלל טומאה, כלומר בכלל "אביו ואמו לא יטמא". אי הכי עבדים נמי. נמעטו מנזירות מהך דרשא. שכמו כן אין מוריש עבד אחד שניתן לו על מנת שלא יהיה לרבו רשות בו, שאינו קונה אותו, כדפרישית: ולא הם קונים זה מזה. וכ"ת דעבדים איתרבו מ"אליהם" – גוים נמי ליתרבו מ"איש"! וה"ה דאשינויא קמא, דמי שיש לו טהרה יש לו טומאה, פריך. אלא אמר רבא בשלמא גבי ערכין איכא לאוקמי מיעוטא ד"בני ישראל" למעוטי גוים דאין מעריכין, ורבוי ד"איש" לרבות גוים דנערכים. אבל הכא, אי "איש" לרבות גוים לנזירות – א"כ [מאי] ממעט "בני ישראל" דמשמע ולא גוים? וכ"ת: בני ישראל נודרים ומביאין קרבן, ולא הגוים. יכול לא יהו נודרים כלל ליאסר באיסורי נזיר – [ת"ל "איש"] אך לא יביאו קרבן. אי משום קרבן – לאו מהכא נפקא, אלא מהתם "לעולה" – פרט לנזירות, בקרא ד"איש איש" בפרשת אמור דמרבינן מיניה שהגוים נודרין נדבות כישראל, וכתיב בסיפיה דקרא "לעולה" – פרט לנזירות דגוי, דאינו מביא קרבן נזירות. וא"ת: וכיון דגוים אימעיטו לגמרי מנזירות – א"כ למה לי "לעולה" פרט לקרבנות נזירות? [וי"ל]: שלא יביא גוי קרבנות נזירות כדי לפטור ישראל נזיר מקרבנותיו. וצ"ע. ואימא בני ישראל מדירין בניהן בנזיר כו' יכול לא יהו נוזרין ת"ל איש הא איתמר עלה א"ר יוחנן הלכה היא בנזיר. א"כ הלכה לא נשנית אלא לגבי ישראל, אין סברא דליתי מיעוטא למעוטי דבר שאינו אלא הלכה למשה מסיני. *) איש כי יפליא דכתיב בערכין למה לי. לרבויי גוים להיות נערכין, כיון דקיימא לן דגוים נודרים נדרים ונדבות כישראלים [לא הוה] ממעט. אפילו שתק מ"איש" הוה מוקמינן מיעוטא ד"בני ישראל" למעוטי גוים דאין מעריכין, דסברא הוא להשוותם מקרא דנודרין נדבות כישראל לכל מה שיוכל. איש כי יפליא מבעיא ליה לאיתויי מופלא סמוך לאיש. הניחא למ"ד. במסכת נדה (דף מו:) דאורייתא, אלא מאן דאמר רבנן, מאי איכא למימר? לאתויי מופלא סמוך לאיש דגוי. ודבר תימה הוא: דבישראל ליתיה אלא מדרבנן, ובגוים איתיה! ופר"י: דודאי ישראל דלא הוי בכלל "בל יחל" עד דהוי גדול, וכי הוי גדול מיהא איתא ב"בל יחל", הלכך דרשינן: כל דליתיה ב"בל יחל" ליתיה בהפלאה, וכדאמר בפרק ["יוצא דופן"] (שם) וממעטינן מופלא סמוך לאיש דישראל. אבל גוי שאינו ראוי לבא לכלל "בל יחל" – לא שייך למעוטי.

*) שייך לדף סב ע"א

הניחא

פי' הרא"ש

כתיב ירושה לענין נזיר דפשיטא דעיקר אב לענין ירושה הוא: יצא גוי שאין לו טומאה שאם נגע במת אינו מקבל טומאה: מנ"ל שאין לו טומאה: יצא זה שאין לו קהל דקהל גוים לא איקרי קהל: ודלמא כרת הוא דלא מחייב וכי תימא אמאי צריך למעוטי מהאי כרת טפי מכל שאר כריתות שבתורה ושמא אין כאן יתורא דאורחיה דקרא למכתב ונכרתה הנפש ההיא מתוך עמה או מתוך הקהל: וכל שאין לו טהרה אין לו טומאה וגוי אין לו טהרה דכתיב והיתה לבני ישראל למשמרת למי נדה משמע לבני ישראל ולא לגוים. ודלמא טהרה הוא דלא הויא להו הא טומאה הויא להו וקרא דוהזה הטהור לא מייתר דבפ"ק דיומא דריש ליה ר"ע ורבנן לדרשא אחריתי: איש אשר יטמא ולא יתחטא איתקש טומאה לטהרה וקרא יתירא הוא למידרש א"נ בהאי איתקש קבלת טומאה לחטוי ולהיקש לא בעי יתורא: שאני הכא דכתיב והתנחלתם אותם לבניכם אחריכם. רב אחא בר יעקב מהדר אשנויא דלעיל מי שיש לו אב לענין ירושה ופריך ליה מהא דר' יוחנן דאמר גוי יורש את אביו דבר תורה ואתא רב אחא לשנויי הך פירכא ולא קשה להאי שינויא דמי שיש לו אב לכל דין ירושה האמורה בתורה אף לענין להנחיל עבדו לבנו יש לו טומאה וישנו בכלל לאביו ולאמו לא יטמא וגוי אינו בכלל נחלה זו להנחיל עבדו לבנו שהרי אף לעצמו לא היה גוף העבד קנוי כדדרשינן בגיטין פ' השולח אתם קונים מהם ולא הם קונים מכם ולא הם קונים זה מזה הלכך אינו בכלל לאביו ולאמו לא יטמא: א"כ עבדים נמי למעטו מהאי קרא שגם עבד אם נתנו לו עבד ע"מ שאין לרבו רשות [בו] אינו מורישו לבנו כדפרישית ולא הם קונים זה מזה וק"ל דדוקא גבי גוים הוא דאמרינן ולא הם קונים זה מזה מובד יצא מכלל גוי ולכל דיני קנינים דינו כישראל. ונ"ל לפרש דעבדים אינם בכלל שום ירושה ולא יורש אביו ולא מוריש ממונו לבנו דעבד אין לו יורש ולעיל נמי ה"מ למפרך הך פירכא אלא דאיפריך האי שינויא והשתא דאוקמיה רב אחא פריך ליה: אלא אמר רבא גבי ערכין איכא למדרש מיעוטא דבני ישראל (קרי בנייה) [ולקומי רבויא] דאיש אבל גבי נזיר ליכא לקומי תרווייהו כדמפרש ואזיל הלכך מיעוטא דרשינן ומאיש לא מציא לרבוי מידי ושמא אתא לדרשא אחרינא: לעולה פרט לנזיר במנחות פרק ואלו מנחות דרשינן איש איש אשר יקריב קרבן לרבות הגוים שנודרים נדרים ונדבות כישראל לכל נדריהם ולכל נדבותם לרבות עולה ושלמים ועופות יין ולבונה א"כ מה ת"ל לעולה דכתיב אשר יקריבו לה' לעולה פרט לנזיר שאין הגוים מביאים קרבן נזיר דברי ר' יוסי הגלילי: מידי נזיר עולם כתיב. דקרא בכל נזיר איירי: בני ישראל מדירים בניהם כדתנן לעיל האיש מדיר את בנו בנזיר. הא אמר ר' יוחנן הלכה היא בנזיר ולא מסתבר לאוקמי מיעוטא דקרא בדבר שהוא הלכה למשה מסיני: בני ישראל מגלחין על נזירות אביהם אם הפריש אביו מעות לנזירותו ומת הבן מגלח על אותן המעות:

נוסחת הריב"ן

א) מפני שמה כו' וכיון שאין לו טהרה שאין מקבל: ב) ואין הגוים מעריכין אבל כו' דהא הדר כתיב בהו: ג) ולא גוים מקרבן קא ממעט להו אי משום מיעוטא כו' לא איצטריך למכתב הכא בני: ד) לעולה דסיפא דקרא אשר יקריבו כו': ה) דהמא:

הגהות הב"ח

(א) רש"י ד"ה כל שיש לו טהרה כלומר שיש לו טהרה בהזאה ובטבילת: (ב) ד"ה ודלמא וכו' במגעו טומאה הא דהויא ליה כצ"ל ותיבת והא נמחק:

הגהות הגר"א

[א] גמ' ת"ל איש (איש) תז"מ:

גליון הש"ס

תום' ד"ה א"ה עבדים כו' שאינו קונה אותו. ע' יבמות דף סו ע"א ברש"י ד"ה ועבדיו שקנו בתוס' שם ד"ה ועבדים: בא"ד דמי שיש לו טהרה יש לו טומאה. דבריהם תמוהים דבפשוט עבד יש לו טהרה במקוה ומקבל טומאה כמו נשים: תום' ד"ה אימא בני ישראל וכו' למעוטי דבר. עי' זבחים דף ה ע"ב תד"ה ניתק ולע"ק:

יכול לא יהו נְזִירִין – ת"ל "אִישׁ"! הָאִיתְּמַר, א"ר יוֹחָנָן: הֲלָכָה הִיא בְּנָזִיר. [א] אִי הָכִי, °"אִישׁ כִּי יַפְלִא נֶדֶר בְּעֶרְכְּךָ" בַּעֲרָכִין לָמָּה לִי? מִכְּדִי, הָאִיתְקַשׁ עֲרָכִין לִנְדָרִים, דְּאָמַר קְרָא "אִישׁ כִּי יַפְלִא נֶדֶר בְּעֶרְכְּךָ", וְהָתַנְיָא* גַּבֵּי נְדָרִים: "אִישׁ" מַה ת"ל °"אִישׁ (א) אִישׁ" – אלְרַבּוֹת אֶת הַגּוֹיִם שֶׁהֵן נוֹדְרִים נְדָרִים וּנְדָבוֹת כְּיִשְׂרָאֵל. "אִישׁ כִּי יַפְלִא" בַּעֲרָכִין לָמָּה לִי? אֶלָּא, הַאי "אִישׁ" מִיבָּעֵי לֵיהּ לְאִיתוּיֵי *במוּפְלָא סָמוּךְ לְאִישׁ. הָנִיחָא לְמ"ד *גמוּפְלָא סָמוּךְ לְאִישׁ דְּאוֹרַיְיתָא, אֶלָּא לְמ"ד דְּרַבָּנַן, "אִישׁ כִּי יַפְלִיא" לָמָּה לִי? לְאִיתוּיֵי מוּפְלָא סָמוּךְ לְאִישׁ דְּגוֹי. הָנִיחָא *לְמ"ד בְּנֵי יִשְׂרָאֵל נֶעֱרָכִין וְאֵין הַגּוֹיִם נֶעֱרָכִין, יָכוֹל לֹא יְהוּ מַעֲרִיכִין – תַּלְמוּד לוֹמַר "אִישׁ", שַׁפִּיר. אֶלָּא לְמ"ד בְּנֵי יִשְׂרָאֵל מַעֲרִיכִים, וְאֵין הַגּוֹיִם מַעֲרִיכִים, יָכוֹל לֹא יְהוּ נֶעֱרָכִין – ת"ל "אִישׁ", אֲפִי' דתִּינוֹק בֶּן חֹדֶשׁ בַּר עֵירוּכֵי הוּא, "כִּי יַפְלִיא" לָמָּה לִי? א"ר אַדָּא בַּר אַהֲבָה: לְאִיתוּיֵי גּוֹי גָּדוֹל, דאע"ג דְּגָדוֹל הוּא (ב) אֵינוֹ יוֹדֵעַ לְהַפְלוֹת. – אֶלָּא "כִּי יַפְלִיא" דִּכְתַב רַחֲמָנָא גַּבֵּי נְזִירוּת, לָמָּה לִי? מִכְּדִי הָאִיתְקַשׁ נְזִירוּת לִנְדָרִים, "כִּי יַפְלִיא" לָמָּה לִי? לְאִיתוּיֵי יָדַיִם שֶׁאֵינָן מוֹכִיחוֹת. *דְּאִיתְּמַר, יָדַיִם שֶׁאֵינָן מוֹכִיחוֹת; אַבַּיֵּי אָמַר: הָוְיָין יָדַיִם, רָבָא אָמַר: הלָא הָוְיָין יָדַיִם. לְאַבַּיֵּי – נִיחָא, אֶלָּא לְרָבָא מַאי אִיכָּא לְמֵימַר? אֶלָּא, "כִּי יַפְלִיא" מִיבָּעֵי לֵיהּ לִכְדְרַבִּי טַרְפוֹן. *דְּתַנְיָא, רַבִּי יְהוּדָה אוֹמֵר מִשּׁוּם רַבִּי טַרְפוֹן: אֵין אֶחָד מֵהֶן נָזִיר, לְפִי שֶׁלֹּא נִיתְּנָה נְזִירוּת אֶלָּא לְהַפְלָאָה. הָנִיחָא לְרַבִּי טַרְפוֹן, אֶלָּא לְרַבָּנַן מַאי אִיכָּא לְמֵימַר? אֶלָּא, מִיבָּעֵי לֵיהּ *לִכְדְתַנְיָא: *והֶיתֵּר נְדָרִים פּוֹרְחִין בַּאֲוִיר וְאֵין לָהֶן עַל מַה שֶׁיִּסְמוֹכוּ. רַבִּי אֱלִיעֶזֶר אוֹמֵר: *יֵשׁ לָהֶם עַל מַה שֶּׁיִּסְמוֹכוּ, שנא' °"אִישׁ כִּי יַפְלִא" °"כִּי יַפְלִא" שְׁתֵּי פְּעָמִים, אֶחָד הַפְלָאָה לְאִיסּוּר, וְאֶחָד הַפְלָאָה לְהֶיתֵּר.§

מתני'

הִיא בְּנָזִיר, שֶׁהָאָב מַזִּיר אֶת בְּנוֹ בְּנָזִיר. א) הוֹאִיל דְּלָאו מִקְּרָא נָפְקָא – לֵיכָּא לָךְ לְמֵימַר דִּבְנֵי יִשְׂרָאֵל אָתָא לוֹמַר דְּיִשְׂרָאֵל מַדִּירִין אֶת בְּנֵיהֶם בְּנָזִיר וְלֹא הַגּוֹיִם, וְאָתָא "אִישׁ" לְרַבּוֹת אֶת הַגּוֹיִם בְּנָזִיר עַצְמוֹ בְּלֹא קָרְבָּן. אֶלָּא דְּהַאי דִּכְתִיב בְּהוּ יִשְׂרָאֵל – קָא מְמַעֵט לְהוּ מִנְּזִירוּת לְגַמְרֵי. **אִישׁ כִּי יַפְלִיא** דִּכְתַב רַחֲמָנָא גַּבֵּי עֲרָכִין לָמָּה לִי. בִּשְׁלָמָא "אִישׁ" דִּכְתַב גַּבֵּי נָזִיר, אַיְּידֵי דִּכְתִיב "אִשָּׁה" שֶׁהוּא לְצוֹרֶךְ, כָּתַב נַמִי "אִישׁ" שֶׁלֹּא לְצוֹרֶךְ. ב) וְ"אִישׁ" דְּגַבֵּי נְדָרִים – לְרַבּוֹת אֶת הַגּוֹיִם שֶׁיְּהוּ נוֹדְרִין נְדָרִים וּנְדָבוֹת כְּיִשְׂרָאֵל. אֶלָּא "אִישׁ כִּי יַפְלִיא" דִּכְתַב רַחֲמָנָא גַּבֵּי עֲרָכִין, לָמָּה לִי? דְּמִכְּדִי אִיתְקַשׁ עֲרָכִין לִנְדָרִים, דְּאָמַר קְרָא "אִישׁ כִּי יַפְלִיא נֶדֶר בְּעֶרְכְּךָ" דִּבְחַד קְרָא כְּתַבִינְהוּ רַחֲמָנָא, וְתַנְיָא גַּבֵּי נְדָרִים כו', וה"ה לְגַבֵּי עֲרָכִין נַמִי דְּאִיתְרַבּוּ לְהוּ גּוֹיִם שֶׁיְּהוּ נֶעֱרָכִים כְּיִשְׂרָאֵל, אֶלָּא "אִישׁ כִּי יַפְלִיא" לָמָּה לִי? **לְאַתּוּיֵי מוּפְלָא הַסָּמוּךְ לְאִישׁ.** ג) דְּיִשְׂרָאֵל, שֶׁיְּהוּ נוֹדְרִין נְדָרִים. **אֶלָּא לְמ"ד דְּרַבָּנַן הִיא.** ד) דִּנְדָרִים נִבְדָּקִין, "אִישׁ כִּי יַפְלִיא" לָמָּה לִי? **לְאַתּוּיֵי מוּפְלָא הַסָּמוּךְ לְאִישׁ דְּגוֹי.** ה) מִדְּאוֹרַיְיתָא נוֹדְרִין נְדָרִים. וְאַל תִּתְמַהּ מִשּׁוּם דְּבְיִשְׂרָאֵל אֵין מוּפְלָא הַסָּמוּךְ לְאִישׁ נוֹדְרִין נְדָרִים מִן הַתּוֹרָה, שֶׁכֵּן מָצִינוּ בְּכַמָּה מְקוֹמוֹת שֶׁהֶחְמִירָה תּוֹרָה עַל הַגּוֹי, כְּגוֹן בְּשׁוֹרוֹ שֶׁל גּוֹי שֶׁהִזִּיק לְשׁוֹרוֹ שֶׁל יִשְׂרָאֵל, בֵּין תָּם בֵּין מוּעָד – מְשַׁלֵּם נֶזֶק שָׁלֵם, וְשֶׁל יִשְׂרָאֵל שֶׁנָּגַח שֶׁל גּוֹי בֵּין תָּם בֵּין מוּעָד – פָּטוּר (ב"ק דף לח.). **הָנִיחָא לְמַאן דְּאָמַר בְּנֵי יִשְׂרָאֵל נֶעֱרָכִין וְאֵין הַגּוֹיִם נֶעֱרָכִין יָכוֹל לֹא יְהוּ מַעֲרִיכִין ת"ל אִישׁ.** גַּבֵּי נְדָרִים, וְאִיתְקוּשׁ עֲרָכִין לִנְדָרִים ו) – (מִיהוּ) שַׁפִּיר הוּא דְּאָתָא "אִישׁ כִּי יַפְלִיא" לְאִיתוּיֵי מוּפְלָא הַסָּמוּךְ לְאִישׁ דְּגוֹי, דְּיָכוֹל לְהַעֲרִיךְ. **אֶלָּא לְמ"ד** דַּבֵּר אֶל בְּנֵי יִשְׂרָאֵל יִשְׂרָאֵל מַעֲרִיכִין וְאֵין הַגּוֹיִם ז) גְּדוֹלִים מַעֲרִיכִין כְּלָל יָכוֹל לֹא יְהוּ נֶעֱרָכִין ת"ל **אִישׁ.** גַּבֵּי נְדָרִים, אִיתְקַשׁ עֲרָכִין לִנְדָרִים לְהָא מִילְּתָא, שֶׁיְּהוּ ח) גְּדוֹלִים נֶעֱרָכִין. הִלְכָּךְ (ג) ט) דִּלְדִידֵיהּ לָא אָתָא "אִישׁ [כִּי יַפְלִיא" דְּנֶעֱרָכִין] אֶלָּא לְאִיתוּיֵי מוּפְלָא הַסָּמוּךְ לְאִישׁ דְּגוֹי, דְּהָוֵי נֶעֱרָךְ, וְלָא מַצְרִיךְ קְרָא, כֵּיוָן דְּמַשְׁמַע לֵיהּ "אִישׁ" דִּנְדָרִים שֶׁהֵן נֶעֱרָכִין – הָא וַדַּאי פְּשִׁיטָא לֵיהּ, דְּכֵיוָן דִּבְתוֹרַת נֶעֱרָכִין הֵן, דַּאֲפִילּוּ גּוֹי בֶּן חֹדֶשׁ בַּר עֲרוּכֵי הוּא, כְּאוֹתוֹ עֵרֶךְ הָאָמוּר בָּעִנְיָן. **אָמַר רַב אַדָּא בַּר אַהֲבָה כִּי אָתָא הַאי כִּי יַפְלִיא לְאִיתוּיֵי** גּוֹי **גָּדוֹל דְּאע"ג דְּגָדוֹל הוּא** (ד) **אֵינוֹ יוֹדֵעַ לְהַפְלוֹת.** דְּאע"פ דִּבְיִשְׂרָאֵל, כֵּיוָן שֶׁהוּא גָּדוֹל, אע"פ שֶׁאֵינוֹ יוֹדֵעַ לְהַפְלוֹת – דְּבָרָיו קַיָּימִים, כִּדְתְנַן בְּפֶרֶק "יוֹצֵא דוֹפֶן" (נדה דף מה:): לְאַחַר הַזְּמַן, אע"פ שֶׁאֵינוֹ יוֹדֵעַ לְשֵׁם מִי נָדַר – דְּבָרָיו קַיָּימִין. גַּבֵּי גּוֹי מִיהָא אֵינוֹ יָכוֹל לְהַעֲרִיךְ וְלִנְדּוֹר עַד שֶׁיְּהֵא גָּדוֹל וְיוֹדֵעַ לְהַפְלוֹת לְדִבְרֵי הַכֹּל. דְּאִילּוּ לְהַאי תַּנָּא דְּקָאָמַר: יָכוֹל לֹא יְהוּ מַעֲרִיכִין, ת"ל "אִישׁ" גַּבֵּי נְדָרִים, לְרַבּוֹת אֶת הַגּוֹיִם שֶׁיְּהוּ מַעֲרִיכִין – בְּגוֹי גָּדוֹל וְיוֹדֵעַ לְהַפְלוֹת קָאָמַר. אֲבָל בְּגוֹי שֶׁאֵינוֹ יוֹדֵעַ לְהַפְלוֹת – לֹא. וְאִידָךְ תַּנָּא נַמִי, דְּקָאָמַר: וְאֵין הַגּוֹיִם מַעֲרִיכִין – בְּגוֹי גָּדוֹל שֶׁאֵין יוֹדֵעַ לְהַפְלוֹת קָאָמַר, אֲבָל גָּדוֹל וְיוֹדֵעַ לְהַפְלוֹת יָכוֹל לְהַעֲרִיךְ וְלִידּוֹר, דְּאִיתְקוּשׁ עֲרָכִים לִנְדָרִים. וּבְנֶעֱרָכִים הוּא דִּפְלִיגִי, אֲבָל בְּמַעֲרִיכִין דִּבְרֵי הַכֹּל גּוֹי גָּדוֹל שֶׁאֵינוֹ יוֹדֵעַ לְהַפְלוֹת לֹא. י) וְאָתָא הַאי "אִישׁ כִּי יַפְלִיא" לְמַעוּטֵי. וּדְקָאָמַר: יָכוֹל לֹא יְהוּ נֶעֱרָכִין ת"ל "אִישׁ" – לָאו מִדִּיוּקָא דְ"אִישׁ כִּי יַפְלִיא" נָפְקָא, אֶלָּא מֵ"אִישׁ אִישׁ" דִּנְדָרִים נָפְקָא, דְּאִיתְקַשׁ עֲרָכִין לִנְדָרִים. אֶלָּא אַיְּידֵי דְּקָאָמַר אִידָךְ תַּנָּא "תַּלְמוּד לוֹמַר אִישׁ" – קָאָמַר אִיהוּ "תַּלְמוּד לוֹמַר אִישׁ". **אֶלָּא כִּי יַפְלִיא** לְגַבֵּי נָזִיר ל"ל. בִּשְׁלָמָא "אִישׁ", אַיְּידֵי דִּכְתִיב "אִשָּׁה" לְצוֹרֶךְ, כָּתַב נַמִי "אִישׁ" שֶׁלֹּא לְצוֹרֶךְ, כִּדְכְתִיב "אִישׁ אוֹ אִשָּׁה כִּי יַפְלִיא לִנְדּוֹר נֶדֶר" וגו'. וְכֵן "אִישׁ" גַּבֵּי עֲרָכִין יְתֵירָא הוּא, מִשּׁוּם דִּכְתִיב בְּהַהִיא פָּרָשָׁתָא "אִם זָכָר אִם נְקֵבָה", וְאָתָא לֵיהּ לְדְרָשָׁא, דְּבָעִינַן גּוֹי גָּדוֹל שֶׁיּוֹדֵעַ לְהַפְלוֹת. אֶלָּא "כִּי יַפְלִיא" דְּגַבֵּי נְזִירוּת ל"ל? מִכְּדִי **הָא אִיתְקַשׁ** נְזִירוּת לִנְדָרִים. כִּדְכְתִיב "נֶדֶר נָזִיר" וּבִנְדָרִים כְּתִיב "הַפְלָאָה", וְכֵיוָן דְּבִנְדָרִים כְּתִיב הַפְלָאָה, בִּנְזִירוּת ל"ל? כ). **לְאִיתוּיֵי יָדַיִם שֶׁאֵינָן מוֹכִיחוֹת** דְּהָוְיָין יָדַיִם. בֵּין בִּנְזִירוּת בֵּין בִּנְדָרִים. בְּנָזִיר – כְּגוֹן דְּאָמַר "אֱהֵא", וּכְדַאֲמַר לְעֵיל בְּפ"ק (דף ג:) כְּגוֹן שֶׁנָּזִיר עוֹבֵר לְפָנָיו. וּלְגַבֵּי נְדָרִים נַמִי, כְּגוֹן דַּאֲמַר "מוּדְרַנִי מִמְּךָ" דְּאָסוּר שֶׁיֵּהָנֶה מִשֶּׁלּוֹ, וְלָא אָמְרִינַן: (ה) דִּלְמָא "לָא מִשְׁתָּעֵינָא בַּהֲדָךְ" קָאָמַר, וּכְדַאֲמַר בְּפ"ק דִּנְדָרִים (דף ה.). אֶלָּא לְמ"ד לָא הָוְיָין יָדַיִם – מַאי אִיכָּא לְמֵימַר? וּפְלוּגְתָּא דְּאַבַּיֵּי וְרָבָא ל) בְּפ"ק דִּנְדָרִים. הָנִיחָא לְרַבִּי טַרְפוֹן **אֶלָּא לְרַבָּנַן.** דְּאָמְרֵי בְּפִירְקִין דִּלְעֵיל שֶׁכּוּלָּן [נְזִירִים], מַאי אִיכָּא לְמֵימַר? **הֶיתֵּר נְדָרִים פּוֹרְחִין בָּאֲוִיר.** הָעוֹלָם, שֶׁאֵין לָהֶן מִקְרָא מִן הַתּוֹרָה עַל מָה שֶׁיִּסְמוֹכוּ מ). **שֶׁנֶּאֱמַר כִּי יַפְלִיא.** אֶחָד *בְּנָזִיר וְאֶחָד *)בִּנְדָרִים. **אֶחָד הַפְלָאָה לְאִיסּוּר.** שֶׁלֹּא לְבַטֵּל אֶת הַנֶּדֶר כְּשֶׁאֵין בּוֹ חֲרָטָה. **וְאֶחָד הַפְלָאָה לְהֶיתֵּר.** כְּשֶׁיֵּשׁ בּוֹ חֲרָטָה. וּבְמַסֶּכֶת חֲגִיגָה קָאֵי.

מַתְנִי'

*) [נ"ל בנזיר וכ"כ רש"י בחגיגה י.]

הניחא למאן דאמר. בערכין: בני ישראל נערכין ולא גוים, יכול לא יהו מעריכין ת"ל "איש" – ודאי י"ל דאתא "איש" לומר דגוי מופלא סמוך לאיש יכול להעריך. אלא למ"ד: בני ישראל ולא גוים, יכול לא יהו נערכין ת"ל "איש" – ואפילו מבן חדש בר ערוכי הוא *(לגבי) נערך.

לאיתויי גוי גדול. כלומר, לאשמועי' דאע"ג דגדול הוא, אם אינו יודע להפלות – לא הוי נדרו נדר. משא"כ בישראל, דלא בעינן יודע להפלות בגדול. והאי דקאמר: יכול לא יהו נערכין ת"ל "איש" – לאו דווקא, אלא אסמכתא בעלמא. דעיקר קרא אתא לגדול שאינו יודע להפלות, ונערכין – מסברא, מקרא דנודרים נדבות כישראל.

לאיתויי גוי גדול דאע"ג דגדול הוא אם אינו יודע להפלות לא. והשתא הוי "לאתויי" כמו למעוטי, דאשמועינן דהיכא דהגוי אינו יודע להפלות – אין נדרו נדר, אע"ג דגדול הוא. מה שאין כן בישראל, דגדול נדרו נדר אפילו אינו יודע להפלות. וא"ת: והא גבי ערכין קיימינן, ואפי' גוי גדול יודע להפלות אין מעריכין! ויש לומר: דאם אין ענין לערכין – תנהו ענין לנדרים. **איש** כי יפליא דכתיב גבי נזיר למה לי לאיתויי ידים שאין מוכיחות. האי "לאיתויי" נמי הוי כמו למעוטי, וכדדרשינן בפ"ק דנדרים (דף ה:) ידים שאין מוכיחות לא הויין ידים [מ"איש] כי יפליא", מה עיקר נזירות בהפלאה – אף ידות בהפלאה. דאיתמר: ידים שאין מוכיחות, אביי אמר: לא הויין ידים, ורבא אמר: הויין ידים, כך כתוב בספרים. ואומר ר"ת: דגירסא הפוכה היא ומשובשת. ובגירס' דריש מס' נדרים (דף ה:) גרסינן הכי, דגרים איפכא: רבא אמר: לא הויין ידים, אביי אמר: הויין ידים. דאי לאו הכי – אין ליישב מה שגרים בספרים הכא: הניחא לרבא, אלא לאביי מאי איכא למימר. ולמאן דגרים במילתיה דרבא לא הויין ידים – ניחא, וכדדרשינן פ"ק דנדרים מ"כי יפליא" דידים שאין מוכיחות לא הויין ידים. וריב"א מיישב גירסת הספרים דהכא, ו"כי יפליא" יתירא דכתיב ב' פעמים קדריש, ועל זה קאמר: ואין מיעוט אחר מיעוט אלא לרבות. והשתא "לאיתויי" הוי לרבות. וכן משמע במסקנא, דמסיק: אחד הפלאה לאיסור ואחד הפלאה להיתר, ור' יהודה משום רבי טרפון מהפלאה יתירא דריש: אין אחד מהם נזיר, לעיל בפ' "בית שמאי" (דף לד.) תנן לה. **כי** יפליא [כי יפליא ב' פעמים]. אחד בפרשת נזיר ואחד בפרשת נדרים. ומיהו "איש" לא דריש. ושמא אידי דאיצטריך למיכתב "כי יפליא" כתיב נמי "איש".

אומר

פי' הרא"ש

אי הכי איש כי יפליא דכתב רחמנא גבי ערכין למה לי לעיל דדרשינן מיניה לרבות הגוים שנערכין למה לי: מכדי אתקש ערכין לנדרים וכיון דקי"ל דגוים נודרים נדרים ונדבות כישראל ממילא אפילו אי לא כתיב איש הוה מוקמי' מיעוטא דבני ישראל למעוטי גוים שאינן מעריכין ולא למעוטי שאינן נערכין דסברא הוא להשוות ערכין לנדרים בכל מה שנוכל ומיעוטא מוקמי' ליה למאי דמסתבר טפי דהיינו שאינן מעריכין: לאתויי מופלא סמוך לאיש והא דקתני בברייתא יכול לא יהו נערכים ת"ל איש לאו דוקא דמנדרים ילפינן שהגוים נערכים אלא תנא לפום ריהטיה נקט הך דרשא דאי לאו רשמעי' ליה ממקום אחר הוה דרשי' ליה מהאי קרא: הניחא למ"ד מופלא סמוך לאיש דאורייתא פלוגתא היא בנדה פ' יוצא דופן. לאתויי מופלא סמוך לאיש דגוי ואם אינו ענין לערכין דמבני ישראל ממעטי' דאין הגוים מעריכין תנהו ענין לנדרים (וא"ע) [ואף למ"ד] דבישראל לא הוה אלא דרבנן בגוי הוי דאורייתא והיינו טעמא דכיון דישראל אתי לכלל בל יחל כשיהיה גדול לא מרבינן שיהיה נדרו נדר עד דאתי לכלל בל יחל אבל גוי דליתא בבל יחל דקרא ומרבינן ליה מאיש כי יפליא מרבי' אפילו מופלא סמוך לאיש: הניחא למ"ד במסכת ערכין פ"ק בני ישראל נערכים ולא הגוים נערכים יכול לא יהיו מעריכים ת"ל איש וטעמא מפרש התם דמסתבר ליה לאוקומי רבויא למעריך ולא לנערך מידי דהוי אטומטום ואנדרוגינוס דמעריכין ואינם נערכים שפיר דמרבינן גוי מופלא סמוך לאיש דמעריכין אלא למאן דמוקי רבויא לרבויה מופלא סמוך א) (שיסמוכו אלא רמז בעלמא שדרשו חכמים איש כי ידור וכו' הוא אינו מיחל אבל אחרים מוחלין לו) לאיש שנערך אפי' בן (חמשה חדשים) [חודש] בר ערוכי הוא לאתויי גוי גדול שאינו יודע להפלות שאינו מעריך ולפי שכבר דרש מבני ישראל למעט גוים נקט האי לישנא לאתויי גוי ופי' כמו למעוטי כלומר לאתויי גם זה לאותו דין שמיעטנו כבר גוי ותקשה תרי מיעוטי ל"ל תרויין דאי לא כתיב אלא חד מיעוטא הוי מוקמינן ליה בגדול שאינו יודע להפלות אע"פ שאם היה ישראל היה מעריך השתא דגוי הוא אינו מעריך ב) ובכה"ג לא הוה מצי למימר לאתויי מופלא סמוך לאיש דאיצטריך תרי קראי דמחד קרא הוה ממעטי' דוקא מופלא סמוך לאיש משום דסוגיא זו למ"ד מופלא סמוך לאיש דרבנן (ומחד קרא ממעטי' אפילו גוי גדול) והא דקתני יכול לא יהו נערכים לאו דוקא אלא אסמכתא בעלמא הוא ובמסכת נדרים ילפינן דגוי נערך ועיקר קרא אתא לגוי גדול שאינו יודע להפלות וי"מ דאם אינו ענין לערכין דהא אין מעריכין תנהו ענין לנדרים מה שאין כן בישראל דלא בעי' יודע להפלות מכדי הא איתקש נזיר לנדרים ונדרים לערכין ובערכין כתיב כי יפליא וכל מאי דדרשת מניה ה"ה לנדרים דאיתקש לערכין איש כי יפליא לנדור נדר נזיר דכתב [רחמנא גבי נזירות] [למ"ל]. לאתויי ידים שאינן מוכיחות פי' למעוטי וכדדרשינן פ"ק דנדרים מאיש כי יפליא דידים שאינן מוכיחות לא הויין ידים. ה"ג דאתמר ידים שאינן מוכיחות אביי אמר הויין ידים רבא אמר לא הויין ידים לרבא ניחא אלא לאביי מאי איכא למימר וכו' וי"מ לאתויי ידים שאינן מוכיחות דהויין ידים כדתנינן לעיל פ"ק האומר אהא הרי זה נזיר ואוקימנא בשנזיר עובר לפניו ולא אמרינן אהא בתענית קאמר ומייתי מדאיש כי יפליא מרבי' דהפלאה כי האי חשיבי הפלאה: היתר נדרים וכו' אין להם מקרא

אבל

א) כ"ה שייך למטה אחר תיבת אין להם מקרא. ב) ומחד קרא ממעטינן אפילו עובד כוכבים גדול שיודע להפלות וכה"ג כצ"ל.

הגהות הב"ח (א) גמ' מה ת"ל איש לרבות כצ"ל ותיבת איש נמחק: (ב) שם דאע"ג דגדול הוא ואינו יודע להפלות לא אלא כי יפליא: (ג) רש"י ד"ה אלא למ"ד דבר וכו' הלכך לדידיה לא אתא וכו' ולא צריך קרא דכיון דמשמע: (ד) ד"ה אמר רב אדא וכו' ואינו יודע להפלות לא דאע"פ: (ה) ד"ה לאיתויי וכו' ולא אמרינן דלא מישתעינא:

עין משפט נר מצוה

ח א מיי' פ"ג מהלכות מעשה הקרבנות ה"ב:
ט ב מיי' פ"א מהלכות ערכין הלכה טו:
גי' א"מ ועובד כוכבים
י ג מיי' פי"א מהלכות נדרים הלכה ד סמג לאוין רמב:
יא ד מיי' פ"א מהל' ערכין הלכה ג סמג עשין קכח:
יב ה מיי' פ"א מהלכות נדרים הלכה כג סמג לאוין רמב טוש"ע י"ד סימן רו סעיף א:
יג ו מיי' פ"ו מהלכות שבועות הלכה ב:

מסורת הש"ס

חולין יג. מנחות עג: [תמורה ב:]
[תמורה שם]
[לעיל כט: נדה מו:]
ערכין ה:
נדרים ה: [זכור קדושין ה: גיטין פה:]
לעיל לד. וש"נ
[נ"ל לכדתנן]
[חגיגה י.]
[נ"ל בעסקינן וכ"כ רש"י בחגיגה י.]

הגהות הגר"א

[א] גמ' אי הכי וכו' [illegible]

נוסחת הריב"ן

א) והוא' כי לית לך למימר דבני ישראל דכתיב אתא: ב) [illegible] ג) [illegible] ד) דנדרים: ה) למדאורייתא: ו) מיהו מעריכין [illegible] ז) ואין הגוים מעריכין: ח) גוים נערכים: ט) [illegible] י) [illegible] כ) למה לי למכתב הס"ד: ל) דאביי ורבא היא: מ) [illegible]

יד א מיי' פי"א מהלכות נדרים הלכה ח סמג לאוין רמב טוש"ע י"ד סימן רלד סעיף ב וסעיף לג [וברא"ש בפסקיו נדרים פ"י סימן י]:
טו ב מיי' פ"ב מהלכות נזירות הלכה יז יח:
טז ג מיי' פי"ב מהלכות נדרים הלכה ב סמג לאוין רמב טוש"ע י"ד סימן רלד סעיף נה:
יז ד מיי' פ"ב מהלכות נזירות הל' יח טוש"ע י"ד סימן רסז סעיף עב:
יח ה מיי' שם הלכה יז יח ופ"ב מהלכות שבועות הלכה ו:
יט ו מיי' פ"ב מהלכות נזירות הלכה יט וע"ש בכ"מ:
כ ז מיי' פ"ח מהלכות עבדים הלכה יג סמג לאוין קמ טוש"ע י"ד סימן רסז סעיף סד:
כא ח מיי' פ"ב מהלכות נזירות הלכה יט:

מתני' חומר בעבדים מבנשים, א שהוא מפר נדרי אשתו ב ואינו מפר נדרי עבדו. הפר לאשתו – ג הפר עולמית, הפר לעבדו – ד יצא לחירות ומשלים נזירותו.§ גמ' ת"ר: *למה רבו כופו – לנזירות, אבל לא לנדרים *ולערכין. מאי שנא גבי נזיר – *דאמר רחמנא "לאסר אסר על נפשו" (במדבר ל) – במי שנפשו קנויה לו, יצא עבד שאין נפשו קנויה לו. אי הכי אפילו גבי נדרים נמי! אמר רב ששת: הכא במאי עסקינן – כגון שהיה אשכול של ענבים מונח לפניו; גבי נדרים, דכי מיתסר בהאי לא מיתסר באחריני – לא מצי כפי ליה. גבי נזירות, דכי מיתסר בהאי איתסר בכולהו – מצי כפי ליה. וגבי נדרים, מי לא עסקינן דליכא אלא האי אשכול, דאי לא אכיל ליה חליש? אלא אמר (א) רבא: כגון שהיה חרצן מונח לפניו; גבי נדרים בהאי הוא דמיתסר – לא מצי כפי ליה. גבי נזיר, דאיתסר נמי באחריני – מצי כפי ליה. וגבי נדרים, מי לא עסקינן דליכא אלא האי חרצן, דאי לא אכיל ליה חליש? אלא אמר (ב) אביי: ה למה רבו צריך לכפותו – לנזירות, ואין צריך לכפותו לנדרים, ואינו צריך לכפותו לשבועה. מ"ט – דאמר קרא "להרע או להיטיב" (ויקרא ה) מה הטבה רשות – אף הרעה רשות, יצא להרע לאחרים שאין הרשות בידו.§ מתני' עבר מכנגד פניו, ר"מ אומר: ו לא ישתה, ורבי יוסי אומר: ישתה.§ גמ' לימא בדשמואל קמיפלגי, *דאמר שמואל: ז המפקיר עבדו – יצא לחירות, וא"צ גט שיחרור. ר"מ – אית ליה דשמואל, רבי יוסי – לית ליה דשמואל? לא, דכולי עלמא אית להו דשמואל. אלא, מאן דאמר ישתה – סבר: סוף מיהדר הדר ואתי גביה, לישתי חמרא כי היכי דלא ליכחוש. ולמ"ד לא ישתה – סבר: ח ליהוי ליה צערא, כי היכי דליהדר גביה.§

מתני'

חומר בעבדים שאינו מיפר נדרי עבדו. שאף בנזירות מוחה, ונתרצה – שוב לא יכול להתיר כי אם בהתרת חכם דוקא. הפר לעבדו יצא לחירות. שנשתחרר, ואח"כ משלים. היפר לאו דוקא, אלא כלומר מיחה: עבר מכנגד פניו, שברח, רמ"א לא ישתה ור' יוסי אומר ישתה. בגמ' מפרש טעמייהו. למה רבו כופהו לנזירות אבל לא לנדרים ולערכין. כופהו – שמוחה על נזירות. לאסור איסר. בנדרים כתיב. ומיהו, בפ"ק דנדרים (דף ג.) מקשינן נזירות לנדרים. גבי נדרים דכי מיתסר בהאי לא מיתסר באחריני לא מצי כפי ליה. דסברא הוא להעמיד מיעוטא דמי שנפשו קנויה לו דמיתסר בכולהו ומתוך כך מיכחש, ואין *כל כך כדי לעשות מלאכה. ודין הוא שיאמר לנו הכתוב שיעכב עליו מי שנפשו קנויה לו. גבי נדרים נמי מי לא עסקינן דאי לא אכיל חליש לביה. ואפילו הכי קאמר: אבל לא לנדרים ואכתי מאי שנא? כגון שהיה חרצן מונח לפניו. שאין טוב לאכילה. וגבי נדרים נמי מי לא עסקינן שפעמים יחזק לבו גם באכילת חרצן. אי נמי, מי לא עסקינן שאף בשאר דברים טובים שמחזיקין אותו. יצא להרע לאחרים שאין הרשות בידו. ולכך לנדרים, אפי' בלא מחאת הרב – לא חל הנדר כלל. דהיינו הרעת אחרים, שמכחיש כחו ואינו חזק למלאכה. דילפינן נדרים משבועות דכתיב בהן "להרע או להיטיב". אבל נזירות אין להקישן לנדרים. ופירש ה"ר יצחק: משום דאמר בפ"ק (לעיל דף ג:) דנזירות חל ואפי' על דבר שאין הרשות בידו, כגון דאמר "שבועה שאשתה" וחזר ואמר "הריני נזיר", כדדרשינן: לאסור יין מצוה כיין הרשות. אלמא הנזירות חל על דבר שאין הרשות בידו, ולכך יחול נמי נזירות העבד, כל זמן שלא ימחה האדון. אבל ודאי, אם מיחה – לענין זה נדרוש "לאסור איסר על נפשו" – מי שנפשו קנויה לו, שתועיל מחאת הרב. ואם אינו ענין לנדרים, שהרי אינו צריך למחות – תנהו ענין לנזירות. והא דקאמר "אבל לא לערכין" – לא הוי דומיא ד"אבל לא לנדרים", אלא שלא תועיל מחאת הרב לערכין כלל, כי הוא [מה] מפסיד אם אמר העבד "ערכי עלי"? ולכשישתחרר או יתנו לו מתנה על מנת שאין לרבו רשות בו – ישלם להקדש. לימא בדשמואל קמפלגי. דהשתא קס"ד כיון שהעבד ברח מכנגד פניו – מסתמא נתייאש הימנו האדון, והיינו הפקר. ר"מ אית ליה דשמואל, דאמר: אינו צריך גט שיחרור. ולכך לא ישתה, שעתה אינו ברשות רבו, ולא תועיל לו עוד מחאתו. ור' יוסי לית ליה דשמואל, וכיון דלא יצא לחירות – תועיל לו מחאתו. דכ"ע אית להו דשמואל דמפקיר עבדו יצא לחירות ואין צריך גט שיחרור. והאי עבד שברח מכנגד פניו – לא איירי בשנתייאש, ולא חשבינן ליה הפקר. ר"מ סבר: לא ישתה, סבר דאין האדון מקפיד אם יצטער ויתכחש כשאינו אצלו, כי היכי דניהוי ליה צער, ונהדר לגביה – שע"י כן ישוב אצלו כדי לשתות ביין. ור' יוסי סבר: ישתה, קסבר: אין נוח לו לרבו שימנע מן היין, דליכחוש חיליה, ולא יהיה כל כך בעל כח וראוי למלאכה כשישוב אצלו.

נזיר

מתני' חומר בעבדים מבנשים שהוא מיפר נדרי אשתו א). ואי זה חומר בעבדים מבנשים, שאם היפר לאשתו – היפר לה עולמית, ואפילו נתארמלה או נתגרשה מיפר מעליה כל הנזירות לגמרי. אבל בעבדים אינו כן, שכיון שיצא לחירות – משלים לנזירותו שקיבל עליו, ומתחיל ומונה כבתחלה. ואם מנה קצת בפני רבו – משלים את השאר. גמ' למה רבו כופו לנזירות. ב) דהשתא הכי משמע: לאיזה דבר יכול לכוף את עבדו – בזמן שקיבל עליו נזירות לנזיר, אבל לא לנדרים ולא לערכין. שאם הדיר בהנאה מפירות פלוני, או שאמר "ערך פלוני עלי" – אינו יכול לכופו, ונדרו נדר וערכו ערך. וכגון שהקנה לו אחר ע"מ שאין לרבו בהם כלום. מאי שנא גבי נזיר. דיכול לכופו – משום דאמר רחמנא "לאסור איסר" כו'. אי הכי אפילו גבי נדרים נמי. יהא יכול לכופו ולהאכילו בעל כרחו מה שהדיר ממנו, דהאי קרא גבי נדרים ג) קאי! גבי נדרים דכי מיתסר בהאי אשכול לא מיתסר באחרינא לא מצי כפי ליה. משום דלא מכחיש ביה כלל, דאפשר ליה באחריני. דכוותה נמי גבי אשתו כהאי גוונא לא מצי מיפר, משום דלא הוי דברים שיש בהן עינוי נפש. וכדתנן בפ' "אלו נדרים" (נדרים דף עט:): "פירות מדינה זו עלי" – לא יפר, ויביא לה ממדינה אחרת. אבל גבי נזירות, דכי מיתסר בהאי מיתסר באחריני, כדתנן בפ' "הריני נזיר מגרוגרות" (לעיל דף יא.): מזגו לו את הכוס ואמר "הריני נזיר ממנו" – הרי זה נזיר. ד) הכא נמי גבי אשכול, כיון דאמר "הריני נזיר ממנו" – ה"ז נזיר, והוי הפסד לרבו, דהוי כחוש ואינו יכול ליטרח – יכול לכופו, להאכילו בעל כרחו מה שהזיר ממנו. דהאי קרא בנזיר קאי. וגבי נדרים. מדקפסיק ותני "אבל לא לנדרים", מי לא עסקינן דלא איכא אלא האי אשכול למיכל ליה? דאי לא אכיל חליש. והוי דומיא דנזירות, ומאי שנא דהכא כופה והכא אינו כופה? גבי נזירות. ה) (ג) החרצן כי מיתסר – מיתסר נמי באחריני, כדתנן בפרק *"כל כינויי נזירות" (לעיל דף ג.). דלא איכא. מידעם למיכל ליה, אלא האי חרצן? אלא אמר (ד) אביי. הכי קתני: למה רבו צריך לכפותו – לנזירות, שאם נדר בנזיר ואין רבו כופהו – הרי זה אסור ביין כל זמן שאינו כופהו, לפי שאמרה תורה "ואמרת אליהם" – לרבות את העבדים. אבל לענין נדרים ו) וערכין – אינו צריך להפר. וערך אין לו, שאין גופו קנוי לו. וכן בנדרים נמי, אפי' בלא כפייה מותר לשתות ביין ולאכול מכל אוכלין. דאמר קרא להרע או להיטיב מה הטבה רשות אף הרעה רשות יצא נשבע להרע לאחרים ז) שאין הרשות בידו. הכא נמי, כיון דקמכחיש כי לא אכיל ולא שתי, ואיכא הפסד לרבו – לא חיילא עליה שבועה. מתני' עבר מכנגד פניו. שברח מפניו של רבו. גמ' רבי מאיר. דאומר: לא ישתה ביין. אית ליה דשמואל. דאמר: כיון שהפקירו רבו – יצא לחירות. והכא נמי ח) דברח – יצא לחירות, ולא ישתה ביין. וצריך לו להשלים נזירות, כדקתני במתניתין. ורבי יוסי דאמר ישתה – לית ליה דשמואל, דאכתי ברשות רבו קאי, ולאו כל כמיניה שלא לשתות, משום דקמכחיש, ואיכא הרעה לרבו. לא דכולי עלמא אית להו דשמואל. והיכא דהפקירו יצא לחירות. ט) אלא הכא, כיון דלא הפקירו אלא שברח מאליו – לא יצא לחירות כלל, וברשות רביה קאי. והכא בהא קמיפלגי; דלמאן דאמר ישתה קסבר: כיון דמיהדר הדר לרביה – לישתי חמרא בכל היכא דאיתיה, כי היכי דלא ליכחוש, ולא ליהוי פסידא לרביה. ולמאן דאמר לא ישתה קסבר. אע"ג דלאו כמפקיר עבדו דמי – אפילו הכי לא ישתה, משום דקנסינן ליה לעבדיה דליהוי ליה צערא דליהדר גבי דרביה. דאי קאי ליה גביה – כפי ליה למישתי חמרא. והלכך אמרינן ליה דלא לישתי כל זמן שהוא בורח מפני רבו, בשביל שהוא תקנת רבו. ולדברי הכל בתר תקנתיה אזלינן.

מתני'

פי' הרא"ש

אבל לא לערכין ולא לנדרים שמעריך ונודר בעל כרחו של אדון. אי הכי נדרים נמי דעיקר קרא בנדרים כתיב גבי נדרים דכי מתסר (בה אי) [בהאי] לא מתסר באחרים לא מצי כייף ליה דאין האדון מקפיד על זה ונפשו קנויה לו לנדר זה אבל נזיר דכי מיתסר בהאי מיתסר בכולהו כדתנן לעיל פרק הריני נזיר מן הגרוגרות מזגו לו את הכוס ואמר הריני נזיר ה"ז נזיר מצי כייף ליה דאין נפשו קנויה לו לנדר זה דאין האדון רוצה שיחליש כחו ולא יוכל לעשות מלאכה: ואי לא אכיל ליה חליש. ואפילו [הכי] אמר אינו כופהו: כגון שהיה חרצן מונח לפניו וס"ד א) דבמונעה אכילת החרצן לא כחיש חיליה ואפ"ה פריך ליה זמנין דליכא אלא האי חרצן וכחיש חיליה אי לא אכיל ליה: אלא אמר אביי הכי קתני למה רבו [צריך] (יכול) לכופו לנזיר ואין [צריך] (יכול) לכופו לנדרים דאמר קרא גבי שבועת ביטוי יצא להרע לאחרים שאין הרשות בידו שאם נשבע שיכה את פלוני אין השבועה חלה ונדרים איתקש לשבועה דכתיב או השבע שבועה לאסור אסר הלכך בנדרים אין צריך לכופו דלא חל הנדר כלל שהנדר רע לאדונו שמכחיש את כחו ואינו ראוי למלאכה וקרא דלאסור אסר על נפשו דדרשי' מניה מי שנפשו קנויה לו שאינו בבל יחל דברו ואע"פ שנדרו נדר יכול רבו לכופו לעבור על נדרו ואינו עובר בבל יחל אם אינו ענין לנדרים שהרי לא חל הנדר תנהו ענין לנזירות. ותימה נזיר נמי איתקש לנדרים ונילף מניה דלא חלה עליו נזירות כלל וי"ל דשאני נזיר דגלי ביה קרא שחל על דבר שאין הרשות בידו כגון אם אמר שבועה שאשתה יין וחזר ואמר הריני נזיר כדדרשינן מיין [ושכר] לאסור (מת) [יין] מצוה כיין [הרשות] הלכך חלה נמי לנזירות עליו אע"פ שאין הרשות בידו להרע לאדון אבל הרב כופהו משום דלאסור אסר על נפשו אינו ענין לנדרים דלא חל הנדר כלל ותנהו ענין לנזיר לומר אע"ג דחלה עליו נזירות הרב כופהו ואינו עובר משום בל יחל ולערכין אינו יכול לכופו דמה מפסיד האדון אם הוא אומר ערכי עלי אם ישתחרר או יתן לו אחר ע"מ שאין לרבו רשות בו ישלם. לימא בדשמואל קמיפלגי דס"ד דכיון שברח העבד נתייאש הימנו והיינו הפקר ר"מ אית ליה דשמואל דאמר אין צריך גט שחרור וכיון שיצא לחירות צריך להשלים נזירותו לא דכ"ע אית להו דשמואל והכא בשביל שעבר מפניו לא נתייאש ממנו עדיין ומ"ד ישתה משום דמצפה האדון שימצאנו ויחזירנו וניחא ליה שישתה יין כדי שלא ימצא כחוש בשובו ומאן דאמר לא ישתה משום דניחא ליה לאדון שיצטער במניעת היין כדי שימהר לשוב אליו ׳אז ישתה יין:

א) נראה דל"ל וס"ד דבמונע עצמו מאכילת חרצן לא כחיש חיליה.

[תוספתא ספ"ו]
[בתוספתא איתא ולא לשבועות]
[לעיל סא.]

נוסחת הריב"ן

א) שביק להפר לנדר אשתו אבל לא לנדרי עבדו כ"ז שהוא תחתיו ולא יצא לחירות ואיזהו חומר בעבדים וכו': ב) השתא הכי הוא דמשמע כו' נזירות אבל: ג) נדרים כתיב הס"ד: ד) ה"ז נזיר והוי הפסד: ה) גבי נזירות כי מתסר מן החרצן מיתסר: ו) נדרים ושבועות בלא כפייה נמי לא חיילא כלום כו' וערכין אינו צריך להפר דערך אין כו' מכל אוכלין שאסר על נפשיה הס"ד: ז) לאחרים שאין עליו שבועה לפי שאין כו': ח) ה"ג כיון דברח כו' דצריך שישלים נזירותו כדקתני: ט) אבל הכא:

גיטין לח. יבמות מח. קדושין כב:

גי' א"מ הריני נזיר יא.

הגהות הב"ח

(א) גמ' אלא אמר אביי כגון שהיה חרצן: (ב) שם אלא אמר רבא למה רבו: (ג) רש"י ד"ה גבי נזירות כי מיתסר בהאי חרצן מיתסר נמי באחריני כצ"ל: (ד) ד"ה אלא אמר רבא הכי קתני וכו' דערך אין לו:

מתני' אנָזִיר שֶׁגִּילֵּחַ וְנוֹדַע לוֹ שֶׁהוּא טָמֵא, אִם טוּמְאָה יְדוּעָה — סוֹתֵר, וְאִם טוּמְאַת תְּהוֹם — אֵינוֹ סוֹתֵר. אִם עַד שֶׁלֹּא גִּילֵּחַ — בֵּין כָּךְ וּבֵין כָּךְ סוֹתֵר. בכֵּיצַד? יָרַד לִטְבּוֹל בִּמְעָרָה וְנִמְצָא מֵת צָף עַל פִּי הַמְּעָרָה — טָמֵא. נִמְצָא מְשׁוּקָּע בְּקַרְקַע הַמְּעָרָה; יָרַד לְהָקֵר — טָהוֹר, לִיטַּהֵר מִטּוּמְאַת מֵת — טָמֵא, שֶׁחֶזְקַת טָמֵא — טָמֵא, וְחֶזְקַת טָהוֹר — טָהוֹר. שֶׁרַגְלַיִם לַדָּבָר.§ **גמ'** מְנָא הָנֵי מִילֵּי? *אֲמַר ר"א: דְּאָמַר קְרָא °"וְכִי יָמוּת מֵת עָלָיו בְּפֶתַע פִּתְאֹם", "עָלָיו" — בִּמְחוּוֶּרֶת לוֹ. רֵישׁ לָקִישׁ אֲמַר: אָמַר קְרָא °"כִּי יִהְיֶה טָמֵא לָנֶפֶשׁ אוֹ בְדֶרֶךְ רְחֹקָה" — כִּי דֶּרֶךְ, מַה דֶּרֶךְ בְּגָלוּי — אַף כֹּל בְּגָלוּי. וְאֶלָּא *הָדִתְנַן: *גאֵיזוֹהִי טוּמְאַת הַתְּהוֹם — כֹּל שֶׁאֵינוֹ מַכִּירָהּ אֶחָד בְּסוֹף הָעוֹלָם, אֲבָל מַכִּירָהּ אֶחָד בְּסוֹף הָעוֹלָם — אֵין זוֹ טוּמְאַת הַתְּהוֹם. בִּשְׁלָמָא (א) לְמ"ד כִּי דֶּרֶךְ — שַׁפִּיר, אֶלָּא לְמ"ד בִּמְחוּוֶּרֶת לוֹ — כִּי מַכִּירָהּ אֶחָד בְּסוֹף הָעוֹלָם מַאי הָוֵי? וְתוּ, הָא דְּתַנְיָא: *הַמּוֹצֵא מֵת מוּשְׁכָּב לְרָחְבָּהּ שֶׁל דֶּרֶךְ, בִּתְרוּמָה — טָמֵא, בְּנָזִיר וּבַעֲשִׂיַּית פֶּסַח — טָהוֹר, מַאי שְׁנָא? אֶלָּא: טוּמְאַת הַתְּהוֹם דגְּמָרָא גְּמִירִי לָהּ.§ "אִם עַד שֶׁלֹּא גִּילֵּחַ" וכו'.§ מַאן תַּנָּא? א"ר יוֹחָנָן: ר"א* הִיא, דְּאָמַר: *תִּגְלַחַת מְעַכֶּבֶת. בָּעֵי רָמִי בַּר חָמָא: נִטְמָא בְּתוֹךְ מְלֹאת, וְנוֹדַע לוֹ לְאַחַר מְלֹאת, מַהוּ? בָּתַר יְדִיעָה אָזְלִינַן — וִידִיעָה אַחַר מְלֹאת הִיא,* אוֹ לָא? וּלְמַאי — לְמִיסְתַּר אֲמַר

מתני' נזיר שגילח. תגלחת טהרה ביום שלשים ואחד שלו. א) ונודע לו שהוא טמא. בטומאת מת. בין שנטמא בתוך מלאת, בין שנטמא לאחר מלאת ב) לבו ביום, קודם שהביא קרבנותיו ושגילח. אם טומאה ידועה. היתה בשעה שנטמא – ה"ז סותר את הכל. אבל ג) לא נטמא עד לאחר הבאת קרבנותיו, אפילו בטומאה ידועה – אינו סותר אלא ז', כדתנן בפרק "שלשה מינין" (לעיל דף מו.): מי שנזרק עליו אחד מן הדמים כו'. ואוקימנא בגמרא דלדברי הכל ז' סותר ותו לא. ואם עד שלא גילח. נודע לו שנטמא, בין בו ביום בין שנטמא בתוך ימי מלאת. בין כך ובין כך. בין בטומאה ידועה, בין בטומאת התהום – סותר את הכל. כיצד. היא טומאת התהום שאינו סותר? אם נטמא בטומאת מת, וירד לטבול במערה ביום שביעי שלו, ולאחר שיצא ד) מצא לשם מת שהוא צף על פני המים שבפתח המערה, והוא לא הכיר בו כשירד שם לטבול – אין זו טומאת התהום. ה) ואפי' אם לא נודע לו עד לאחר גילוח, ואפילו אם לא ירד לשם לטבול אלא להקר – ה"ז טמא, וסותר את הכל. אבל אם נמצא משוקע בקרקע המערה. ו) שבשעה שנכנס לא היה צף, בזו יש חילוק, פעמים שהוא טהור ופעמים שהוא טמא. כשנכנס לשם, ולא נכנס בה אלא להקר, ונודע לו לאחר גילוח שנמצא לשם מת משוקע כנגד פי המערה – ה"ז טהור, דזו היא טומאת התהום. אבל ירד לשם ליטהר מטומאת המת, ואח"כ נודע לו, ואפילו לאחר גילוח – ה"ז טמא, וסותר את הכל, אע"פ שהיא טומאת התהום. שחזקת טמא טמא. העמידו בחזקת ז) טמא. וחזקת טהור. ח) יורד לשם בחזקת טהור. שרגלים לדבר. כלומר, שהדברים נראין כך, דטהור העמד על חזקתו וטמא על חזקתו, ותיהוי חזקת טהור טהור, וחזקת טמא טמא. גמ' במחוורת לו. בברורה לו, כגון טומאה ידועה – סותר, אבל לא על טומאה שאינה ידועה לו. ור"ל אמר אמר קרא. גבי עושה פסח "כי יהיה טמא לנפש או בדרך רחוקה". כי דרך ט) בגלוי אף טומאה בגלוי. לאפוקי טומאת התהום דלא. והוא הדין לנזיר, דבכל מקום נזיר ועושה פסח כי הדדי נינהו. בשלמא למ"ד כי דרך. דבגלוי, שפיר. דכיון דאחד מכירה בסוף העולם – הוי י) גלוי. אלא למ"ד במחוורת לו כי מכירה אחד בסוף העולם. אמאי הוי טמא? והא אינה מחוורת לו! ותו. בין למ"ד במחוורת לו בין למ"ד כי דרך, כיון דמדאורייתא טומאת התהום הותרה גביה, הא דתניא: המוצא מת מושכב כו', מאי שנא גבי תרומה דהוי טמא, וגבי נזיר ועושה פסח דהוי טהור? אלא טומאת התהום גמרא גמירי לה. דאינה מטמאה, והכי גמירי לה, דלנזיר ועושה פסח בלבד אינה מטמאה. אבל לתרומה – לא גמרינן הילכתא, ומשום הכי הוי טמא. מאן תנא. דאם נודע לו קודם גילוח, אע"פ שהביא קרבנותיו, סותר. א"ר יוחנן ר"א היא דאמר. בפרק "שלשה מינין" (לעיל דף מו.): "ואחר ישתה הנזיר יין" – אחר מעשים כולן, דברי ר"א. כ) דכיון דעדיין לא גילח – כמי שנודע לו בתוך מלאת דמי, וסותר את הכל. דאי לרבנן, כיון שנזרק עליו אחד מן הדמים – שוב אינו סותר. בעי רמי בר חמא נטמא. בטומאת התהום בתוך ימי מלאת, ונודע לו לאחר מלאת, קודם הבאת קרבנותיו וקודם גילוח. מהו בתר ידיעה אזלינן. כלומר, מי אמרינן דהא דגמרינן דטומאת התהום אינה סותרת היכא דידיעה הויא לאחר מלאת, אפילו היכא דנטמא בימי מלאת, או דילמא כיון דנטמא בימי מלאת, אע"ג דנודע לו לאחר מלאת, ואפילו לאחר הבאת קרבנותיו – לא אמרינן דטומאת התהום הותרה לו, וסותר. ולרמי בר חמא דקמיבעיא ליה הכי – ל) לא שמיעא ליה מתני', ואמטו להכי קמיבעיא ליה הכי אי סותר או אינו סותר כלל. אמר

נזיר שגילח. תגלחת טהרה ונודע שהוא טמא. אם טומאה ידועה היא – סותר, ואם טומאת התהום היא, כלומר שנודע לו שבמקום שעבר היתה טומאת התהום. ובגמרא מפרש איזו היא טומאת התהום – שאין אחד בעולם מכירה. והכי הילכתא גמירי לה.

אם עד שלא גילח. נודע לו, בין כך ובין כך סותר, בין בטומאה ידועה בין בטומאת התהום. דכי גמירי טומאת התהום דלא סתרה – דוקא כשנודע לו אחר שגילח, אבל נודע לו קודם שגילח – סותר.

כיצד דין טומאת התהום ירד לטבול במערה בשביל טומאת שרץ, ונמצא כזית מן המת צף על פני המערה, ספק אם היה כזית מן המת בתוך המערה בשעה שטבל והאהיל, או שמא לא היה שם בשעה שטבל – טמא, דספק טומאה ברשות [היחיד] ספקו טמא. ואם נודע לו, אפילו אחר שגילח – טמא, ולא אמרינן אף כי היה כזית מן המת תוך המערה בשעה שטבל – יהא טהור משום טומאת התהום, דכיון שאין שום דבר מכסה עליה – הוה ליה כטומאה ידועה.

משוקע בקרקע המערה. אז ודאי מיקרי שפיר טומאת התהום, ולכן ירד להקר. וליום אחרון שגילח נודע לו אותה טומאה – טהור, משום דטומאת התהום הוא. ליטהר מטומאת מת. אם ירד ליטהר מטומאת המת, ואחר שחזר ומנה ימי נזירותו וגילח נודע לו כשירד למערה היה כזית מהמת משוקע במערה – טמא, שחזקת טמא טמא. דכי גמירי דטומאת התהום דמת הותר – דוקא לאדם שלא היה בחזקת טומאת מת: שחזקת טמא טמא (כלומר) שרגלים לדבר כלומר שטעם גדול י"ל: הואיל והוא בחזקת טומאת מת – לא הותרה טומאת התהום אצלו. והא דנקיט ברישא ירד לטבול, ובסיפא ירד להקר – יש ליתן טעם לדבר. דרישא רבותא קא משמע לן, אף כי ירד לטבול, דמסתמא דקדק ועיין היטב שלא תהא טומאה סביביו, ונמצא מת לף על פי המערה – מ"מ טמא משום ספק טומאה ברה"י. וסיפא רבותא קמ"ל, אף כי ירד להקר, ואין דרכו לבדוק ולדקדק סביביו – מ"מ כי משוקע בקרקע המערה – טהור, משום דהוי טומאת התהום. **במחוורת** לו. אבל בטומאת התהום שאינה מחוורת, ולא הכיר בה אחד בסוף העולם – אז אינו סותר. **רבי** שמעון בן לקיש אמר כי דרך. גבי עושה פסח כתיב "איש איש כי יהיה טמא לנפש או בדרך רחוקה לכם" ומדסמך טמא לנפש לדרך, נאמר כי דרך, וגמרינן נזיר מעושה פסח. אבל בפרק "כילד צולין" (פסחים דף פא: ושם) לא קאמר התלמוד הכי, והכי איתא התם: במחוורת לו. אשכחנא נזיר, עושה פסח מנלן – דכתיב "או בדרך רחוקה" כי דרך כו', משמע התם דלא פליגי, ולא גמירי נזיר מעושה [פסח].

אלא למ"ד במחוורת לו כי מכירה אחד בסוף העולם מאי הוי. ובפ' "כילד צולין" (ג"ז שם) לא קאמר הכי, דקאמר: למ"ד כי דרך – נימא עד דידעי בה כולי עלמא, כי דרך א).

לנזיר ועושה פסח טהור. ומיירי בטומאת התהום, כדפריש' בסמוך. **ומאי** שנא תרומה מנזיר ועושה פסח. בפרק "כילד צולין" (גם זה שם) ליתא האי פירכא, דסוגיא דהתם לית לה דגמירי אהדדי, אלא טומאת התהום גמירי. **מאן** תנא א"ר יוחנן ר"א היא דאמר תגלחת מעכבת. מלשתות ביין. דלרבנן דאמרי דתגלחת אינה מעכבת – א"כ אחר שנזרק הדם אין [עליו] עוד תורת נזיר, וכן שנודע לו עד שלא גילח כמי שגילח. תימה: דבפ' "כילד צולין" (גם זה שם) אמר מר בר רב אשי: טומאת התהום מרצה אפילו נודע לו קודם זריקה. והשתא [אי] אליבא דר"א – אפילו לאחר זריקה סותר, קודם גילוח. ואי אליבא דרבנן – הא קודם זריקה לרבנן מעכבת כקודם גילוח לר"א, דהכא משמע דדבר המעכב סותר לכ"ע! י"ל: דלגבי עושה פסח מיירי, שאין טעון גילוח, ואתיא בין לרבנן בין לר"א, דכיון שנשחט הפסח – א"כ הוי הדם עומד ליזרק, וכל העומד ליזרק כזרוק דמי, ולכך אין סותר, כיון שנשחט. אבל תגלחת – מצוה באפי נפשה היא. ועוד י"ל: דהא דאמרינן התם טומאת התהום מרצה – היינו ע"י ריצוי הציץ, ולכך מרצה אף קודם זריקה, אבל על התגלחת – לא שייך רצוי ציץ. **בעי** *רב חמא ניטמא תוך מלאת. בטומאה ידועה או בטומאת התהום, ונודע לו לאחר מלאת קודם גילוח, לר"א מהו? בתר טומאה אזלינן וסותר שלשים, או בתר ידיעה אזלינן וסותר שבעה. אמר

א) [ועי' תוס' פסחים שם ובמנחות נח: ד"ה ואיכא כתבו שזה מן סוגיות החלוקות]

פי' הרא"ש

נזיר שגילח. הביא קרבנותיו וגילח: אם טומאה ידועה. פי' טומאה שאפשר שהיתה ידועה כגון שלא היה קבר התהום סותר: טומאת התהום כדמפרש בגמ' שאין אחר מכירה בסוף העולם. אע"פ שודאי טמאת' אינו סותר דהלכה היא בנזיר: אם עד שלא גילח וכבר הביא קרבנותיו: בין כך טומאה ידועה ובין כך טומאת התהום סותר. דהא דגמירי דטומאת התהום לא סתרה היינו דוקא היכא דנודע לו אחר גילוח לר"א או אחר קרבנותיו לרבנן: כיצד דין טומאת התהום ירד לטבול במערה. מטומאת שרץ ונמצא כזית מן המת צף על פני המים ספק האהיל עליו ס' לא האהיל עליו טמא דספק טומאה ברה"י ספקו טמא ואם נודע לו ס' זה אם אחר שגלח סותר דהיינו טומאה ידועה ואע"ג דאמרי' בגמ' ספק טומאה צפה טהורה היינו ס' מגע אבל ס' אהל טמא: משוקע בקרקע המערה. במקום שטבל ובודאי נטמא אם נודע לו אחר שגלח טהור ואינו סותר דהיינו טומאת התהום וברישא נקט לטבול לרבותא אע"ג דהטובל מטומא' נזהר מכל דבר המטמא אפ"ה א) טהור ליטהר מטומאת המת. כגון שהיה נזי' טמא וטבל במערה שהיה המת משוקע בה והשלים נזירותו. או טמא מת שטבל ואח"כ קבל עליו נזירות טמא וסותר שחזקת טמא טמא וחזקת טהור טהור שרגלים לדבר. האי רגלים לדבר לאו דוקא דהכי גמירי הלכתא אלא כלומר קצת טעם יש לדבר כיון דבחזקת טומאת מת לא נתנה הלכה לטהרו: מנה"מ דטומאת התהום אינה סותרת עליו: במחוורת לו לאפוקי טומאת התהום שאינה מחוורת: ר"ל אמר כי דרך. גבי פסח כתי' איש כי יהיה טמא לנפש או בדרך רחוקה (טמא) טומאה כי דרך בפ' כ"צ יש סוגייא אחרת דקאמר התם אשכחן נזי' עושה פסח מנ"ל אמר קרא כי דרך. אבל סוגיא דהכא סברא דמר יליף נזי' מפסח ומר יליף פסח מנזיר: כל שאין מכירה א' בסוף העולם פירוש שאפשר (שאדם) [שאין אדם] מכירה: בשלמא למ"ד כי דרך שפיר דכיון דא' מכירה בסוף העולם הויא גלויה כי דרך. ובפסחים קאמר עד דידעי בה כולי עלמא כי דרך. ונזיר ועושה פסח טהור דהוי טומאת התהום כדמפרש לקמן מ"ש כי היכי דילפת נזיר מפסח למר ופסח מנזי' למר הכי נמי לילף כל שאר דבר מנהון. והכי נמי ה"מ למפרך ממתני' דמפלגא בין נודע אחר שגלח לנודע קודם שגלח דאי טעמא מקרא ליכא טעמא לפלוגי. וכן מסיפא ליטהר מטומאת מת טמא. ואי מקרא כיון דודאי נטמא בקבר התהום מה לי היה טמא מה לי היה טהור כיון דמטומאת מת ידועה [כבר טבל] וטיהר: טומאת התהום גמרא גמירי לה. וקראי דמייתי לעיל אסמכתא בעלמא נינהו ודוקא לנז' ועושה פסח גמירי. מאן תנא אר"י ר"א היא דאמר תגלחת מעכבת מלשתות ביין ולרבנן דאמרי אין תגלחת מעכבת משנזרק הדם אין עליו תורת נזי' עוד וכך הוי עד שלא גילח כמו משגלח: בעי רמי בר חמא נטמא תוך מלאת (ז') טומא' ידועה או בקבר התהום ונודע לו אחר מלאת קודם גילוח

א) נראה דחסר כאן וצ"ל אפ"ה טמא משום ספק טומאה ברה"י וסיפא רבותא קמ"ל אף כי ירד להקר וכו' אפ"ה טהור וכ"ה בתוס' בסוד"ה משוקע.

כב א מיי' פ"ו מהל' נזירות הלכ"ו:
כג ב מיי' שם הל"כ:
כד ג מיי' שם הלי"ח:
כה ד מיי' שם הלט"ו:

תורה אור: במדבר ו; שם ט

פסחים פא: ע"ש
[צ"ל הדרתניא]
שם [תוספתא זבין פ"ב]
[פסחים שם תוספתא שם]
[לעיל יז: וש"נ]
גי' ה"מ ולא אלימא למיסתר או לא אמר כו'

נוסחת הריב"ן

א) ואחר שגלח נודע לו: ב) בו ביום: ג) אם לא: ד) שילא משם מלא לי': ה) לאפילו: ו) ובשעה: ז) שהוא טמא: ח) היורד: ט) מה דרך בגלוי אף כל טומאה: י) כגלוי: כ) יכיון: ל) אי למספק כלומר דלא מיבעי ליה הכי אי סותר ז' או כולם אלא הכי קמבעי ליה אי סותר כלל או אינו סותר והס"ד:

הגהות הב"ח

(א) גמ' למ"ד כי דרך שפיר. נ"ב עיין בפסחים דף פ"א:

כו א מיי' פ"ט מהל' נזירות הלי"ח ופ"ו מהל' קרבן פסח הלי"א ופי"ח מהל' אבות הטומאה הל"ג:
כז ב מיי' פ"ו מהל' נזירות הלי"ט:
כח ג מיי' שם הלי"ח:
כט ד מיי' פי"ד מהל' אבות הטומאה הל"ג:

אֲמַר רָבָא, ת"ש: אִם עַד שֶׁלֹּא גִּילֵּחַ — בֵּין כָּךְ וּבֵין כָּךְ סוֹתֵר. הֵיכִי דָּמֵי? אִי דְּאִיתְיְדַע לֵיהּ בְּתוֹךְ מְלֹאת — צְרִיכָא לְמֵימַר? אֶלָּא לָאו — לְאַחַר מְלֹאת, ש"מ. וַעֲדַיִין תִּיבָּעֵי לָךְ: כּוּלּוֹ סוֹתֵר אוֹ שִׁבְעָה סוֹתֵר? לְמַאן? אִילֵימָא לְרַבָּנַן — פְּשִׁיטָא דְּכוּלּוֹ סוֹתֵר, וְאִי לר"א, *כָּל אַחַר מְלֹאת — שִׁבְעָה סוֹתֵר! אֲמַר לָךְ: ה"מ כִּי נִטְמָא אַחַר מְלֹאת, וְהַאי לִפְנֵי מְלֹאת הוּא. אוֹ דִּילְמָא שָׁאנֵי הָכָא, דִּידִיעָה אַחַר מְלֹאת הִיא? וּמִינָּהּ, קָתָנֵי: בֵּין כָּךְ וּבֵין כָּךְ סוֹתֵר, וְלָא קָמִיפַּלְגִי. *ת"ר: [א]הַמּוֹצֵא מֵת מוּטָּל לְרָחְבָּהּ שֶׁל דֶּרֶךְ, לִתְרוּמָה — טָמֵא, וּבְנָזִיר וּבְעוֹשֶׂה פֶּסַח — טָהוֹר. בד"א — שֶׁאֵין לוֹ מָקוֹם לַעֲבוֹר, אֲבָל יֵשׁ לוֹ מָקוֹם לַעֲבוֹר — אַף לִתְרוּמָה טָהוֹר. בד"א — שֶׁמְּצָאוֹ שָׁלֵם, אֲבָל מְשׁוּבָּר אוֹ מְפוֹרָק, אֲפִילּוּ אֵין מָקוֹם לַעֲבוֹר — חָיְישִׁינַן שֶׁמָּא בֵּין פִּרְקִין עָבַר. וּבַקֶּבֶר — אֲפִילּוּ מְשׁוּבָּר וּמְפוֹרָק טָמֵא, מִפְּנֵי שֶׁקֶּבֶר מְצָרְפוֹ. בד"א — בִּמְהַלֵּךְ בְּרַגְלָיו, אֲבָל טָעוּן אוֹ רָכוּב — טָמֵא, לְפִי שֶׁמְּהַלֵּךְ בְּרַגְלָיו אֶפְשָׁר לוֹ שֶׁלֹּא יִגַּע וְשֶׁלֹּא יָסִיט וְשֶׁלֹּא יַאֲהִיל, טָעוּן אוֹ רָכוּב — אִי אֶפְשָׁר שֶׁלֹּא יִגַּע וְשֶׁלֹּא יָסִיט וְשֶׁלֹּא יַאֲהִיל. בד"א — בְּטוּמְאַת הַתְּהוֹם, אֲבָל טוּמְאָה יְדוּעָה — שְׁלָשְׁתָּן טְמֵאִים. וְאֵיזוֹ הִיא טוּמְאַת הַתְּהוֹם — כָּל שֶׁאֵין מַכִּירָהּ אֶחָד בְּסוֹף הָעוֹלָם, מַכִּירָהּ אֶחָד בְּסוֹף הָעוֹלָם — אֵין זוֹ טוּמְאַת הַתְּהוֹם. [ב]הָיָה טָמוּן בְּתֶבֶן אוֹ בִּצְרוֹרוֹת — הֲרֵי זוֹ טוּמְאַת הַתְּהוֹם. בַּמַּיִם וּבָאֲפֵילָה וּבִנְקִיקֵי הַסְּלָעִים — אֵין זוֹ טוּמְאַת הַתְּהוֹם. *[ג]וְלֹא אָמְרוּ טוּמְאַת הַתְּהוֹם אֶלָּא לְמֵת בִּלְבַד. § "כֵּיצַד יָרַד". § צָפָה אֵינָהּ מְטַמְּאָה לְעִנְיַן שֶׁרֶץ, *דְּתַנְיָא: [ד]סְפֵק טוּמְאָה צָפָה, בֵּין בְּכֵלִים בֵּין בַּקַּרְקַע — טְהוֹרָה. ר"ש אוֹמֵר: בְּכֵלִים — טְמֵאָה, בַּקַּרְקַע — טְהוֹרָה. מַאי

אמר רבא ת"ש עד שלא גילח בין כך ובין כך סותר היכי דמי אי דאיתידע ליה תוך מלאת צריכא למימר דסותר. נ"ע: מאי קאמר? הא איצטריך לאשמועי' דיש טומאת התהום שסותר, כגון שנודע לו עד שלא גילח! ונראה לפרש: דמיתורא דמתני' דייק, דמדיוקא דרישא נפקא, מדקתני נודע משגלח.

ועדיין תיבעי לך. התלמוד הולך ומפרש הך פשיטותא דרבא דרך קשיא ותירוץ, ואף בעיא דרמי בר חמא הולך ומפרש הטעם באורך.

ועדיין תיבעי לך כולהו סותר או ז' סותר. ומה היה פשיטותא דרבא? ומשיב: למאן, אי לרבנן — פשיטא דכולהו סותר, כדאמר לעיל בפרק ג' (דף טז.) דאף נטמא אחר מלאת סותר [שלשים] מדרבנן. ואי ר"א — הא אמר: כל אחר מלאת ז' סותר. **הני** מילי. דקאמר ר"א אחר מלאת ז' סותר — כי נטמא אחר מלאת. והא דקא מיבעיא ליה: תוך מלאת הוא, או דילמא שאני הכא, דידיעה לאחר מלאת הוא, והוי כמו נטמא אחר מלאת. והיינו בעיא דרמי בר חמא. ופשיט ליה מיניה, ממתני' גופה, דאוקמינן כר"א, וקתני: אם עד שלא גילח נודע לו — בין כך ובין כך סותר, ולא מפליג בין נטמא קודם מלאת לנטמא לאחר מלאת. ובנטמא אחר מלאת פשיטא לך דאינו סותר כ"א ז' לר"א, והכי נמי כי נטמא לפני מלאת — דאינו סותר כי אם ז'.

לתרומה טמא. כיון שהוא מוטל לרחבה של דרך — אי אפשר לו לעבור כי אם דרך עליו ויאהיל. לנזיר ועושה פסח טהור, דהוי טומאת התהום. בד"א דלתרומה טמא — שאין לו מקום לעבור אם לא דרך אותו מקום שהמת נמצא, אבל יש לו דרך לעבור — טהור אף לתרומה. בד"א לתרומה טמא — שנמצא שלם, אבל משובר ומפורק, אפילו אין לו מקום לעבור — טהור, דשמא בין פרקין עבר, ולא עבר דרך ישר אלא דרך מעוקם, והויא ליה ספק טומאה ברה"ר דספקו טהור. אבל אם נמצא בקבר ועבר דרך עליו, אפי' משובר ומפורק טמא, שהקבר מצרפו ליטמא באהל כדדרשינן, "או בקבר" — לרבות קבר סתום, שהעובר אף כנגד הריקן שבקבר מטמא באהל, כדפרישית לעיל.

במה דברים אמורים. דחיישינן שמא בין פרקין עבר וטהור — במהלך על רגליו, שאפשר שלא יגע ושלא יסיט ושלא יאהיל. אבל טעון משאו או רכוב על גבי בהמה — אינו יכול להלך כל כך זקוף שלא יטה עצמו לצדדין, וטמא. דאין זו ספק טומאה ברה"ר, אלא ודאי ניטמא דהאהיל. **במה** דברים אמורים. דאין לו מקום לעבור דטהור — בטומאת התהום, אבל בטומאה ידועה — [שלשתן טמאים], תרומה ונזיר ועושה פסח, ומפרש ואזיל מאי ניהו טומאה ידועה — דמכיר בה א' בסוף העולם. באפילה ובנקיקי הסלעים. אבל אינו מכוסה.

צפה אינו מטמא לענין שרץ דתניא ספק טומאה צפה בין בכלים. שיש מים בכלי, ושרץ צף על פני המים, ספק נגע בכלי ספק לא נגע. או בקרקע — במים שעל גבי קרקע. ר"ש אומר: בכלי — טמא בקרקע — טהור. ודאי נגע — טמא בכל מקום שהוא שורץ, ספק נגע — דוקא על הארץ טמא אם היא טומאה ברה"י. אבל צפה, שאינה קבוע — לא. א)דמספקא לן אי דוקא על פני המים מטהרינן, או הוא הדין צפה באויר, שזורקה אדם באויר, מטהרינן ממעוטא ד"על הארץ". כתיב

אֲמַר רָבָא ת"ש. מִדְּקָתָנֵי מַתְנִי': אִם נוֹדַע לוֹ עַד שֶׁלֹּא גִּילֵּחַ, בֵּין כָּךְ וּבֵין כָּךְ, בֵּין טוּמְאַת הַתְּהוֹם בֵּין טוּמְאָה יְדוּעָה — סוֹתֵר. וְאוֹקִימְנָא לְמַתְנִי' כְּר"א, וְקָחָזֵינָא מִינָּהּ דְּקָפָסֵיק וְאָמַר: כָּל אֵימַת דְּאִיטַּמֵּי, בֵּין בְּתוֹךְ יְמֵי מְלֹאת בֵּין לְאַחַר יְמֵי מְלֹאת — דְּסוֹתֵר. וּדְאִיתְיְדַע לֵיהּ אֵימַת אִילֵימָא בְּתוֹךְ יְמֵי מְלֹאת צְרִיכָא לְמֵימַר דְּסוֹתֵר. בִּתְמִיָּה. אֶלָּא לָאו שְׁמַע מִינָּהּ דְּאִיתְיְדַע לֵיהּ לְאַחַר מְלֹאת, וְקָאָמַר דְּסוֹתֵר, דְּבָתַר טוּמְאָה דַּהֲוָה בְּתוֹךְ יְמֵי מְלֹאת אָזְלִינַן. וַעֲדַיִין תִּיבָּעֵי לָךְ כֵּיוָן דִּלְאַחַר מְלֹאת קָאֵי, ז' סוֹתֵר וְתוּ לָא. אוֹ דִּילְמָא כֵּיוָן דְּנִיטְמָא בְּתוֹךְ יְמֵי מְלֹאת — סוֹתֵר אֶת כּוּלָּן. וּלְמַאן. קָמִיבַּעְיָא לָךְ? אִי לְרַבָּנַן וְקוֹדֶם הֲבָאַת קָרְבְּנוֹתָיו — פְּשִׁיטָא דְּכוּלָּן סוֹתֵר. וְאִי לר"א. וְקוֹדֶם תִּגְלַחַת, הָא שָׁמְעִי' לֵיהּ דַּאֲמַר בְּפֶרֶק "מִי שֶׁאָמַר הֲרֵינִי נָזִיר מְגַלֵּחַ" (לעיל דף טז:): כָּל לְאַחַר מְלֹאת — ז' סוֹתֵר. אָמַר לָךְ. רָמִי בַּר חָמָא: לְעוֹלָם אַלִּיבָּא דר"א קָמִיבַּעְיָא לִי, וְהָכִי קָמִיבַּעְיָא לִי: הָנֵי מִילֵּי א) דִּלְאַחַר מְלֹאת שִׁבְעָה סוֹתֵר וְתוּ לָא — כִּי נִיטְמָא לְאַחַר מְלֹאת, וְהַאי כֵּיוָן דְּנִיטְמָא לִפְנֵי מְלֹאת מוֹדֵי בַּהּ ר"א ב) דְּבָתַר טוּמְאָה דַּהֲוַת בְּתוֹךְ יְמֵי מְלֹאת אָזְלִינַן. **או דילמא** כֵּיוָן דִּידִיעָה לְאַחַר מְלֹאת הוּא. שֶׁכְּבָר הֵבִיא קָרְבְּנוֹתָיו, ג) וְז' הוּא דְּסוֹתֵר וְתוּ לָא. ה"ג: וּמִינָּהּ הָא דְּקָתָנֵי בֵּין כָּךְ וּבֵין כָּךְ סוֹתֵר וְלָא קָמַפְלִיג ש"מ. כְּלוֹמַר, וְתִיפְשׁוֹט לֵיהּ מִמַּתְנִי' גּוּפֵיהּ, דְּמִדְּקָתָנֵי "בֵּין כָּךְ וּבֵין כָּךְ סוֹתֵר", וְלָא קָמַפְלִיג בֵּין ד) דְּנִיטְמָא קוֹדֶם מְלֹאת בֵּין לְאַחַר מְלֹאת. דְּהָא מַתְנִי' כָּל אֵימַת דְּנִיטְמָא בְּמַשְׁמַע, וְאוֹקִימְנָא לַהּ כְּר"א דַּאֲמַר: כָּל לְאַחַר מְלֹאת ז' סוֹתֵר וְתוּ לָא, ש"מ נַמִי דַּאֲפִילּוּ הֵיכָא דְּנִיטְמָא בְּתוֹךְ מְלֹאת, כֵּיוָן דִּידִיעָה לְאַחַר מְלֹאת הוּא — דְּז' סוֹתֵר וְתוּ לָא. לִישָּׁנָא אַחֲרִינָא: אֲמַר רָבָא ת"ש. וּלְרָבָא לֵית לֵיהּ דְּרַבִּי יוֹחָנָן דְּמוֹקֵים לָהּ לְמַתְנִי' כְּר"א וְלָא כְּרַבָּנַן. דְּקָסָבַר רָבָא מַתְנִי' נַמִי מִיתּוֹקְמָא כְּרַבָּנַן, דְּמוֹדוּ רַבָּנַן גַּבֵּי טוּמְאַת הַתְּהוֹם, דְּאַע"ג דִּבְעָלְמָא תִּגְלַחַת לָא מְעַכְּבָא, לְגַבֵּי טוּמְאַת הַתְּהוֹם חֲשִׁיבָא. שֶׁאִם נוֹדַע לוֹ עַד שֶׁלֹּא גִּילֵּחַ ה) — קָפָסֵיק וְתָנֵי בֵּין דְּנִטְמָא לִפְנֵי מְלֹאת בֵּין לְאַחַר מְלֹאת, דְּאִם נוֹדַע לוֹ לְאַחַר מְלֹאת קוֹדֶם גִּילּוּחַ, אַע"ג דְּהֵבִיא קָרְבְּנוֹתָיו — סוֹתֵר, דְּבָזוֹ מוֹדוּ רַבָּנַן לר"א דְּתִגְלַחַת הָוְיָא חֲשׁוּבָה לְעִנְיַן טוּמְאַת הַתְּהוֹם, וש"מ דְּסוֹתֵר. וַעֲדַיִין תִּיבָּעֵי לָךְ כו'. אָמַר לָךְ רָמִי בַּר חָמָא: לְעוֹלָם אַלִּיבָּא דר"א קָמִיבַּעְיָא לֵיהּ, וְהָכִי קָמִיבַּעְיָא לֵיהּ: ה"מ דַּאֲמַר ר"א דְּאֵינוֹ סוֹתֵר אֶלָּא ז' — הֵיכָא דְּנִטְמָא נַמִי לְאַחַר מְלֹאת, ו) וְהָא כֵּיוָן דְּנִטְמָא לִפְנֵי מְלֹאת — מוֹדֵי לְהוּ לְרַבָּנַן דְּסוֹתֵר אֶת כּוּלָּן, דִּכְמַאן דְּנוֹדַע ז) בְּתוֹךְ מְלֹאת דָּמֵי. אוֹ דִּילְמָא שָׁאנֵי הָכָא, דְּכֵיוָן דִּידִיעָה לֵיתָא אֶלָּא לְאַחַר מְלֹאת — שִׁבְעָה הוּא סוֹתֵר וְתוּ לָא. וּמִינָּהּ — אִיכָּא לְמִישְׁמַע מִינָּהּ, דְּהָא קָתָנֵי "בֵּין כָּךְ וּבֵין כָּךְ סוֹתֵר", וְקָא מַשְׁמַע ח) מַתְנִי': לָא שְׁנָא בֵּין הֵיכָא דְּנִטְמָא לִפְנֵי מְלֹאת לְהֵיכָא דְּנִטְמָא לְאַחַר מְלֹאת, דְּסוֹתֵר אֶת כּוּלָּן, וְלָא מִיפַּלְגִי בַּהּ ר"א וְרַבָּנַן. ש"מ דְּלר"א נַמִי, כֵּיוָן דְּטוּמְאָה הֲוָה בִּימֵי מְלֹאת — דְּסוֹתֵר אֶת הַכֹּל. ת"ר **המוצא** מֵת. טָמוּן בַּדֶּרֶךְ, בְּתֶבֶן אוֹ בִּצְרוֹרוֹת, וּמוּטָּל לְרָחְבּוֹ שֶׁל דֶּרֶךְ וְאֵין לוֹ מָקוֹם לַעֲבוֹר אֶלָּא עָלָיו, וּבְשָׁעָה שֶׁהוֹלֵךְ עָלָיו לֹא הִכִּיר בּוֹ שֶׁהוּא תַּחְתָּיו. לְעִנְיַן ט) אֲכִילַת תְּרוּמָה — טָמֵא, וּבְנָזִיר וְעוֹשֶׂה פֶּסַח — טָהוֹר, וְאֵינוֹ צָרִיךְ לַעֲשׂוֹת פֶּסַח שֵׁנִי. וּבְכָל אֵלּוּ שֶׁאָמְרוּ דִּבְנָזִיר וְעוֹשֶׂה פֶּסַח טָהוֹר — כְּשֶׁנּוֹדַע לוֹ לְאַחַר שֶׁעָשָׂה פִּסְחוֹ, אֲבָל נוֹדַע לוֹ קוֹדֶם שֶׁעָשָׂה פִּסְחוֹ — ה"ז טָמֵא, וְנִדְחֶה לְפֶסַח שֵׁנִי. וְהָכִי מְפוֹרָשׁ עֲלָהּ בַּתּוֹסֶפְתָּא, בְּבָרַיְיתָא דְּמַסֶּכֶת נָזִיר (פ"ו) וְשֶׁל פְּסָחִים (פ"ו). **אבל** יֵשׁ לוֹ מָקוֹם. רָחָב לַעֲבוֹר שֶׁלֹּא עַל הַמֵּת, אַף לְעִנְיַן אֲכִילַת תְּרוּמָה טָהוֹר י). ה"ג: **בד"א** דִּמְהַלֵּךְ בֵּין פְּרָקִין טָהוֹר, בִּמְהַלֵּךְ בְּרַגְלָיו. שֶׁיָּכוֹל לְכַוֵּין וְלִפְסוֹעַ בֵּינְתַיִם, **שלא** יִגַּע כ) וְשֶׁלֹּא יַאֲהִיל. אֲבָל טָעוּן אוֹ רָכוּב — טָמֵא בִּתְרוּמָה, לְפִי שֶׁאִי אֶפְשָׁר כו'. אֲבָל לְנָזִיר וְעוֹשֶׂה פֶּסַח — לְעוֹלָם טָהוֹר, דְּהָכִי גְּמִירִי לָהּ (א) בְּטוּמְאַת הַתְּהוֹם. וְהַאי דִּכְתוּב בִּסְפָרִים ל) "אֲפִילּוּ בְּנָזִיר וְעוֹשֶׂה פֶּסַח טָמֵא" — טָעוּת הוּא. **אבל בטומאה** שֶׁהָיְתָה יְדוּעָה. לְשׁוּם אָדָם. שְׁלָשְׁתָּן טְמֵאִין. וַאֲפִילּוּ נָזִיר וְעוֹשֶׂה פֶּסַח. מ) וְעוֹשֶׂה פֶּסַח שֵׁנִי, וְאַע"פ שֶׁכְּבָר עָשׂוּ פְּסָחִים בְּפֶסַח רִאשׁוֹן. **בתבן או בצרורות.** (ב) שֶׁהִיא טוּמְאַת הַתְּהוֹם, דְּאֶפְשָׁר שֶׁלֹּא הִכִּיר בּוֹ אָדָם מֵעוֹלָם. שֶׁהֲרֵי תֶּבֶן יָכוֹל לְהִתְגַּלְגֵּל עָלָיו ע"י רוּחַ, וּצְרוֹרוֹת עֲשׂוּיִין לְהִתְגַּלְגֵּל מִמָּקוֹם לְמָקוֹם. אֲבָל יַמִּים [וַאֲפֵילָה] וּנְקִיקֵי סְלָעִים, הוֹאִיל וְהֵן תְּלוּלִין נ) — יָכוֹל אָדָם לְהִסְתַּכֵּל בָּהֶן ע"י הַדְּחָק, *וְאֶפְשָׁר שֶׁאָדָם אֶחָד מַכִּיר בָּהֶן, שֶׁהֱלִיךְ בְּתוֹכוֹ, וְאֵין זוֹ טוּמְאַת הַתְּהוֹם. **ולא אמרו.** שֶׁהוּתְּרָה טוּמְאַת הַתְּהוֹם, אֶלָּא לְטוּמְאַת מֵת בִּלְבַד, אֲבָל לְעִנְיַן זָב וְזָבָה לֹא. ה"ג: **צפה אינה מטמאה** לְעִנְיַן שֶׁרֶץ. כְּלוֹמַר, אַע"ג דְּטוּמְאַת מֵת צָפָה מְטַמְּאָה בִּסְפֵק מַגָּע, כִּדְתְנַן: וְנִמְצָא מֵת צָף עַל פְּנֵי הַמַּיִם, לְעִנְיַן שֶׁרֶץ מִיהָא אֵינָהּ חֲשׁוּבָה לְטַמֵּא מִסָּפֵק. שֶׁאִם שֶׁרֶץ צָף עַל פְּנֵי הַמַּיִם, סָפֵק נָגַע בּוֹ סָפֵק לֹא נָגַע בּוֹ — סְפֵקוֹ טָהוֹר. **דתניא ספק טומאה צפה.** כְּלוֹמַר, טוּמְאָה צָפָה וְהוּא סָפֵק אִם נָגַע בָּהּ אִם לֹא נָגַע בָּהּ. **בין.** שֶׁהִיא צָפָה בַּמַּיִם שֶׁבְּכֵלִים, בֵּין בַּמַּיִם שֶׁבַּקַּרְקַע — טְהוֹרָה. כְּתִיב

א) [לכאורה נ"ל ומספקא לן וכו' והוא דיבור בפני עצמו וכן מוכח בתוי"ט ע"ש דלפניו היה דברי תוס' הללו ריש סד.]

פי' הרא"ש

גילות לר"א. א) (חסר כאן בכ"י). אם עד שלא גילח בין כך ובין כך סותר דאוקמי כר"א מיבעיא ליה אם סותרת ל' או ז': אמר רבא ת"ש וכו'. היכי דמי אי דאיתידע ליה תוך מלאת צריך למימר כיון שהטומאה והידיעה היתה תוך מלאת פשיטא דסותר: אלא לאחר מלאת וש"מ דסותר. ואכתי לא גמר רבא פשיטותיה דרבא ומפרש' נמי בעי' דרמי בר חמא: ועדיין תבעי לך כולו סותר או ז' סותר דפי' דמתני' מיבעיא ליה: ושקיל וטרי תלמודא לפ' בעיא דרמי בר חמא. אי לרבנן ונודע לו אחר מלאת קודם הבאת קרבנותיו: פשיטא דכולו סותר מדרבנן כדאמר לעיל פ"ג: ואי לר"א הא אמר כל א' מלאת סותר ז': ה"מ כי נטמא אחר מלאת והאי לפני מלאת הוה. והשתא מפרשה בעיא דרמי בר חמא וממתני' ליכא למפשט: וה"ה דמצי למבעי אליבא דרבנן אי בתר טומאה אזלי' וסתר מן התורה ומביא קרבן טומאה כדין נזי' טמא או בתר ידיעה אזלי' ולא סתר אלא מדרבנן. אלא משום דאוקי' מתני' דאם עד שלא גילח כר"א ומבעיא ליה פירוש דמתני' ג) ופשטא ליה אליבא דר"א וה"ה לרבנן: ומינה מדקתני בין כך ובין כך סותר ולא מיפלגי בין טומאה שבתוך מלאת לטומאה שלאחר מלאת אלא קתני סותר בסתם אלמא דין א' להם דכמו שנודע לו אחר מלאת על טומא' שאחר מלאת אינו סותר אלא ז' ה"ה נודע לו על טומא' שלפני מלאת ש"מ דבתר ידיעה אזלי'. ותקש' הא אמרי' במתני' נזי' שגלח ואח"כ נודע לו שהוא טמא אם טומאה ידועה סותר אלמא בתר טומאה אזלי' וי"ל לתרץ דלא דמי דברישא סבר הביא קרבנותיו בטומאה וע"כ צריך להביא קרבנות אחרי' וצריכי' אנו לילך אחר טומאה דאי אזלי' בתר ידיעה כבר עבר נזירותו אבל אם נטמא אחר מלאת קודם הבאת קרבנותיו לרבנן או קודם גילוח לר"א דאכתי לא פסק נזירותיה הא ודאי אזלי' בתר ידיעה: מוטל ברחבה של דרך. וממלא את כל הדרך ואין לו מקום לעבור אלא א"כ שיאהיל עליו: אבל יש לו מקום לעבור. שאינו ממלא כל רוחב הדרך: אף לתרומה טהור. דספק טומאה ברה"ר ספקו טהור. אבל מצאו משובר לחתיכות או מפורק לאיברים. אפי' אין לו מקום לעבור כגון החצי המת מוטל בצד ימין עד חצי הדרך או רובו וחצי האחר מופלג הימנו מצד שמאלו עד חצי הדרך או רובו וההולך דרך ישרה לפניו א"א שלא יאהיל על חצי האחר אפ"ה טהור שאנו תולי' שעיקם דרכו: בד"א דתלינן שעבר בין הפרקים במהלך:

א) נראה דל"ל ועל הא דתנן במתני' אם עד וכו'. ב) נראה דל"ל ולכן מפרש ליה אליבא דר"א.

[לעיל טז: לגי' מז.]

פסחים פא: [עד סוף הענין]

זבחים כג. [פסחים פ: ע"ש ודף פא:]

תוספתא דטהרות פ"ה [טהרות פ"ד מ"ד]

נוסחת הרב"ן

א) דאמר ר"א דסל לאחר מלאת: ב) דסותר את כולן דבתר כו': ג) ז': ד) היכא דניטמא: ה) כמי שנודע לו קודם הבאת קרבנותיו דמי וסותר והכי אמר רבא ת"ש אם עד שלא גילח וקא פסיק ותני בין שנטמא לפני מלאת כו': ו) האי: ז) דנודע לפני: ח) וקא משמע לן מתני' דל"ש: ט) לענין תרומה: י) טהור שמא בין חיבור הפרקים עבר אבל ואבר עבר ואפילו תרומה טהור הס"ד: כ) יגע ולא יסיט: ל) בספרים אבל טעון או רכוב אפילו כו': מ) פסח ואפי' כבר מקום לעבור כו' שכבר עשו פסחיהן: נ) ויכול אדם:

הגהות הב"ח

(א) רש"י ד"ה ה"ג וכו' גמירי לה הס"ד ואח"כ מ"ה בד"א בטומאת התהום: (ב) ד"ה בתבן או בצרורות הרי הס"ד:

גי' א"מ אי אפשר שאין אדם.

מאי טעמא דת"ק? *א"ר יצחק בר אבודימי: כתיב °"בכל השרץ השרץ" — כל מקום שהוא שורץ, וכתיב "על הארץ", הא כיצד? ודאי מגעו — טמא, ספק מגעו — טהור. ורבי שמעון מ"ט? אמר עולא: כתיב °"אך מעין" וכתיב "יטמא (עד הערב"), הא כיצד? צפה בכלים — טמא, בקרקע — טהור.§ ת"ר: אכל [א] הניטלין והנגררין — ספיקן טמא, מפני שהן כמונחין. בוהנזרקין — ספיקן טהור. חוץ גמן כזית המת, והמאהיל על פני טומאה, וכל דבר שמטמא מלמעלה כלמטה, *לאיתויי זב וזבה. בעי רמי בר חמא: [ב] °מת בכלי, וכלי צף על פני המים, מהו? בתר כלי אזלינן או בתר [ג] מיתא אזלינן? את"ל דבתר כלי אזלינן, [ד] מת על גבי שרץ מהו? כיון דהאי טומאת ערב והאי טומאת שבעה — כמאן דמחתא טומאה בכלי דמיא, או דילמא טומאה סמיכתא היא? ואת"ל הכמאן דמחתא טומאה בכלי דמיא, [ה] וטמא ודאי, שרץ על גבי נבלה ונבלה צפה מהו? כיון דתרוייהו טומאת ערב אינון — טומאה סמיכתא היא, או דילמא האי כזית והאי כעדשה? שרץ על גבי שרץ מהו? הני ודאי חד שיעורא נינהו, או דילמא כיון דמפסקי מהדדי לא? [ו] ואת"ל שרץ על גבי שרץ, וכיון דמפסקי מהדדי — כמאן דמנחא בכלי דמי, שרץ על גבי נבלה שנימוחה מהו? כיון דנימוחה הויא ליה משקה, או דלמא האי אוכלא הוא? ואת"ל זדאוכלא הוא, שרץ ע"ג שכבת זרע מהו? ואת"ל חכיון דמיתעקרא ה"ל כי אוכלא, שרץ ע"ג מי חטאת [ז] ומי חטאת צפין על גבי המים, מהו? לא ידעינן, טתיקו.§

אמר

כתיב אך מעין ובור מקוה מים יהיה טהור וכתיב יטמא (*עד הערב) הא כיצד בכלים טמא. דדוקא דומיא דמעין ובור, שהם מים שעל גבי קרקע. כל הניטלין. אדם עומד במים וחברו היה מטלטל שרץ, [ספק] נגע בו אדם העומד במים. או הנגררין – שהיה חבירו גורר שרץ על פני המים, ספק נגע – ספקו טמא. מפני שהן כמונחין – כיון [שיד] אדם תופס בה אין כאן דין טומאה לפה. והמאהיל על פני הטומאה. כגון אדם ההולך במים, ונמצא כזית מת קבוע במים, ספק עבר הטהור עליו והאהיל על המת. דבשרץ כי האי גוונא טהור, או במת לטומאת מגע. דכך לי [טהרה] לפה וטומאה קבוע כמו טומאה הלפה וטהרה קבוע. מ"מ באהל לא מטהרינן. דבר שהוא מטמא למעלה כלמטה, לאיתויי זב וזבה שמטמא בהיסט. וכן עליונו של זב וזבה (מלמעלה) כלמטה ממשכבו. ואם זב וזבה עוברים במים וכלי אצלם, ספק הסיטו – אין לנו ליטהר משום טומאה לפה, אלא במגע דוקא, דומיא דשרץ. וכן אם מדרסות של זב עובר, ספק דרס – אין לטהר משום טומאה לפה. בעי רמי בר חמא מת בכלי וכלי צף על פני המים מהו בתר כלי אזלינן. והא נח, או דילמא בתר מיא אזלינן והא לא נח. מת ע"ג שרץ מהו, כיון דהאי טומאת ערב והאי טומאת ז' כמי דמחתא בכלי דמיא, או דילמא כיון דהאי טומאה והאי טומאה – א) סמיכתא היא. ואת"ל כמאן דמחתא בכלי ודאי דמיא, שרץ ע"ג נבילה ונבילה לפה על פני המים מהו? כיון דתרוייהו טומאת ערב – טומאה סמיכתא היא, כחדא טומאה עבה, ולא חשיב כמונחת. או דילמא האי כזית והאי כעדשה. שרץ על גבי שרץ מהו? הני ודאי חד שיעורא הוא, או דילמא כיון דמפסקי מהדדי – לא. אם תימצי לומר כיון דמפסקי לא, נבילה שנימוחה מי הוי הך נבילה כי משקה, והוי שרץ שעל גבה כטומאה לפה על פני המים, או דילמא אוכלין הוא? ואת"ל כי אוכלין הויין לה ואינן חשובים משקה, וה"ל כמי שאינו לף על פני המים, והא שרץ על גביו, הואיל כשהנבילה שנימוחה לפה על פני המים כזית והאי בכעדשה – כמאן דמנח דמי. שרץ ע"ג שכבת זרע מהו? מי הויא לה כי משקה? ואת"ל כיון דמתעקר מגופיה לא חשיב משקה, אלא כי אוכלין יש לדונו. שרץ ע"ג מי חטאת – שהיה שם אפר ומים, וע"י האפר הוא עב. ומי חטאת דנקיט, אומר ר"י דהוא הדין דמצי למנקט אפר ומים בעלמא, אי חשיב משקה אי לא, אלא לרבותא נקט, דאע"ג דאיכא למימר: כיון דהאי טומאה והאי טומאה הויא ליה כי טומאה סמיכתא לפה על פני המים, מ"מ כיון דהני מי חטאת הוו להו משקה עליהן, ב) והואיל כי לפה על פני המים.

א) נ"ל והאי טומאה טומאה כו'. יעב"ץ. ב) גי' א"מ והוי.

נזיר

כתיב בכל השרץ השורץ. דמשמע: בכל מקום ששורץ טמא, ואפי' לף. וכתיב "על הארץ", דמשמע דבעינן שיהא מונח על הארץ, ולא לף. הא כיצד ודאי נגע. בטומאה, בכ"מ שהוא, בין במים בין בקרקע – טמא. הא ספק נגע, כגון לאחר שנמצא לף על פני המים – ה"ז טהור, בין שנמצא לף במים שבכלים, או במים שבקרקע דספק מגע לף לעולם טהור. אך מעין ובור מקוה מים יהיה טהור. דמשמע דלפה בקרקע טהור. וכתיב יטמא הא כיצד צפה בכלים. ספיקו טמא, לפה בקרקע – ספיקו טהור. כל הניטלין והנגררין. בין טומאת שרץ בין טומאת נבילה, ובשעת א) זחילתן או גרירתן ספק נגע בהן אדם וכלים. ספיקן טמא. שכל הנגרר והניטל – כמו שהן מונחין דמי, והוי כספק טומאה ברה"י, דספיקו טמא. דגמרי' מסוטה (סוטה דף כח:) דכתיב בה "ונסתרה והיא נטמאה". אבל אם היו נזרקין, ב) דבשעת זריקתן ספק נגע בהן אדם וכלים ספק לא נגע – ספיקו טהור, ג) דלא אמרינן קלוטה כמי שהונחה דמיא, אלא כטומאה לפה דמיא, וספיקו טהור. ה"ג: חוץ מכזית מן המת והמאהיל על פני טומאה שמטמא מלמעלה כלמטה לאיתויי זב וזבה. כלומר, חוץ מכזית מן המת שנזרק ע"ג אדם או טהרות, ובין שנזרק טהרות על כזית מן המת, או האדם עצמו דלג עליו, וספק הוא אם האהיל עליו ד) – שספיקו טמא, לפי שמטמא מלמעלה כלמטה, הואיל והוא מטמא שלא בנגיעה, כגון ע"י אהל. והאי דתני והמאהיל על פני טומאה, דלא צריך למיתני אלא חוץ מכזית מן המת והמאהיל עליו – לאיתויי זב וזבה שמטמא נמי מלמעלה כלמטה באבן מסמא, שאם ישב זב על האבן ה) ועל הכלים ועל האדם שהן בתוך הבור תחת האבן – נטמא האדם והכלים כמו במגע עצמו. וכן אם הזב מלמטה והטהור יושב ו) על אבן מסמא. בעי רמי בר חמא מת בכלי וכלי צף על פני המים. ויודע ודאי שלא האהיל עליו, אבל ספק הוא לו אם נגע אם לא נגע בו. מהו. גבי מתניתין מאי טעמא חיישינן לטומאה לפה – דהתם איכא למיחש שמא האהיל עליו, אבל הכא דידוע הוא לו שלא האהיל עליו, אבל ספק הוא לו אם נגע ז). מי אמרינן בתר כלי אזלינן. וכמאן דמונח על גבי קרקע דמי, וספק מגעו טמא. או בתר מיתא אזלינן. ומת מיהא אזיל ולף על פני המים אגב הכלי, וספיקו טהור. אם תימצי לומר. כיון דמת עצמו לא הוי לף ח) על פני המים הוא, בתר כלי אזלינן, וכמאן דמונח על גבי קרקע דמי, וספק מגעו טמא. מת המונח על גבי השרץ. והשרץ לף על פני המים, מהו? כיון דשרץ טומאת ערב ומת טומאת שבעה – כמאן דמחתא טומאה בכלי דמי, וספק מגעו טמא. או דילמא. הא טומאה עבה ט) סמיכתא היא, והיינו דלף שרץ – כלף מת דמי, י) (מיהא מיהא אזיל ולף על פני המים אגב הכלי, וספק מגעו טהור). ואם תמצא לומר. כיון דהאי טומאת ערב והאי טומאת ז' – כמאן דמחתא בכלי דמי, וספיקו טמא ודאי. שרץ צף ע"ג נבילה. והוא הדין נמי לנבילה ע"ג השרץ. אלא האי דקמיבעיא ליה הכי – דשיעורא דשרץ דהוה כעדשה קאי על שיעורא דנבילה ע"ג שיעורא דשרץ. או דילמא. כיון דהאי בכזית והאי בכעדשה – כמאן דמנח בכלי דמי, וספק מגעו טמא. כ) ואת"ל. דשרץ ונבילה נמי, כיון דהאי שיעוריה בכזית והאי שיעוריה בכעדשה – כמאן דמחתא בכלי דמי, וספק מגעו בשרץ טמא. ואת"ל שרץ ע"ג שרץ כיון דמיפסקי מהדדי כמאן דמנח בכלי דמי. וספק מגעו העליון ע"ג שרץ ספיקו טמא. שרץ ע"ג נבילה שנימוחה מהו. מי אמרינן: כיון דנימוחה – הויא לה משקה, ושרץ לף על גביו, וספק מגעו טהור. דכמאן דלף על פני המים דמי. או דילמא כיון דאוכל הוא. ה"ל כמאן דמונח ל) על גביו, וכמו דמונח ע"ג קרקע דמי, מ) דספק מגעו טמא. ואת"ל. הכא, כיון דאוכלא הוא, ולא שוו שיעורייהו אהדדי, דהאי בכזית והאי בכעדשה, כמאן דמנח ע"ג כלים דמי. שרץ נ) ע"ג שכבת זרע. ושכבת זרע לף על פני המים, מהו? מי אמרינן, הואיל ושכבת זרע לאו אוכלא הוא – ה"ל כמשקה, והוה שרץ לף, וספיקו טהור. ואת"ל כיון שנתעקרה מבשרו של אדם ממש, ולא דמי לשאר משקה שבתוכו, כגון מי רגלים שמכונסין לתוכו – ה"ל שכבת זרע כי אוכלא דסמיך הוא. שרץ צף ע"ג מי חטאת. ומי חטאת עבין הן, מפני אפר פרה שבהן. מי הוי כאוכלא? או דילמא משקה הוי, והוי כשרץ לף, וספיקו טהור. לא ידעינן, תיקו.

אמר

פי' הרא"ש

דתנן ספק טומאה צפה בין בכלים בין בקרקע. משנה היא פ"ד דמסכת טהרות וקתני לעיל מינה אלו ספיקות שטיהרו חכמים וכו' ס' טומאה צפה על פני המים. וקתני בתר הכי ס' טומאה צפה על פני המים פירוש שטהרו חכמים בין במים שבכלים בין במים שעל פני קרקע. כתיב כל השרץ השורץ וכו' דמשמע בכל מקום שהוא שורץ פי' ראוי לשרוץ ואפי' על המים (ש"מ) [מטמא]. וכתיב השרץ השורץ על הארץ דמשמע דוקא על הארץ מטמא: הא כיצד. ודאי נגע בכל מקום טמא אבל ספק נגע על המים טהור: כתיב אך מעיין ובור מקוה מים יהיה טהור דמשמע הנוגע בשרץ שעל פני מי מעין ובור ומקוה טהור: וכתיב בתריה והנוגע בהם יטמא דמשמע בכל מקום: כל הניטלין והנגררין. אם נטל שרץ בידו או גררו בארץ אצל טהרות ס' נגע ס' לא נגע ספקן טמא דלא חשיבה טומאה צפה כיון שהוא ביד האדם: והנזרקין. אם זרקן באויר אצל טהרות אע"פ שבא מכח האדם חשוב טומאה צפה: חוץ מכזית מן המת. שזרקו ס' האהיל על הטהרות טמאים דטהרות טומאה צפה מקראי דכתיב בשרץ גמרי' הלכך לא מטהרי' אלא בטומאת מגע דשייכא בשרץ: והמאהיל ע"פ הטומאה כגון שזרק טהרות ס' האהילו על המת דבכה"ג בס' מגע טהור בין שהטומאה צפה א) דהכי איתא בתוס' דטהרות כשם שטהרו ס' טומא' צפה וכו' כך טהרו וכו' טהרה צפה וכו' כיצד עריבה שהיתה טמאה טומאת מת וככר של תרומה כרוך בסיב או בנייר נתנן בתוכו וירדו גשמים ונתמלאת הרי הוא צף ע"פ המים ס' נגע בה ספק לא נגע ספקו טהור מפני שזה טהרה צפה על פני המים ופליגי בה ר"י ורבנן בפ"ד במס' טהרות דקתני הזורק טומאה ממקום למקום ככר לבין המפתחות מפתח לבין ככרות טהור ר"י אומר ככר לבין המפתחות טמא מפתח לבין ככרות טהור: וכל שהוא מטמא מלמעלה לאתויי זב וזבה. כגון עליונו של זב ותחתונו של זב דמטמאי' בלא נגיעה ספקן טמא דלא טהרו אלא ספק טומאת מגע: מת בכלי וכלי צף ע"פ המים. ויודע הוא שלא האהיל עליו ומספקא ליה אם נגע אם לא נגע וה"ה דה"מ למבעיא שרץ בכלי: בתר כלי אזלי' והרי צף או בתר מת אזלי' והרי הוא מונח. ואת"ל ב) לאו בתר כלי אזלי' והו"ל כמונח: מת על גבי שרץ. וס' נגע במת מי אמרי' כיון דשניהם טמאים חשיב כחד גופא והוי טומאה צפה. או דילמא כיון דאין טומאתם שוה שזה טומאת ערב וזה טומאת ז' הוי כמונח בכלי: שרץ ע"ג נבילה מי אמרי' כיון דשניהם טומאת ערב כחד גופא דמי והוי טומאה צפה: או דילמא כיון דהאי בכעדשה ה"ל כמונח בכלי: שרץ ע"ג שרץ וס' נגע בעליון מהו. הא ודאי טומאתן ושיעורן שוה: או דילמא כיון דמפסקי מהדדי לא: ואת"ל כיון דמפסקי מהדדי לא: שרץ ע"ג נבילה שנימוח מהו כיון דנימוח הו"ל משקה ולא הויא הפסקה בין שרץ למים או דילמא האי אוכל' הוי'. כיון דמאוכל בא חשיבי הפסק:

ואת"ל

א) נראה דצ"ל וכן כשהטהרה צפה דהכי כו'. ב) גירסת רבינו ואת"ל לאו בתר כלי אזלינן והיינו לפי פי' ז"ל דלאו אזלינן בתר כלי מקרי צף ודלא כפי' התוס'.

(התוי"ט פ"ד דטהרות מוחק זה)

ל א מיי' פי"ד מהל' אבות הטומאה הל"ג:

לא ב מיי' שם פט"ו הל' ו:

לב ג מיי' שם פי"ז הל"א:

לג ד ה ו ז ח ט מיי' שם פי"ד הל"ד:

[חולין קכז.]

ויקרא יא

שם

[תוספתא פ"ג דטהרות]

נוסחת הריב"ן

א) ובשעת גרירתן או נטילתן: ב) ובשעת: ג) ולא: ד) ספיקו: ה) שעל: ו) יושב לו על: ז) אם נגע אם לא נגע מהו מי אמרינן כו': ח) לא הוי לף דהא קאי ומונח בכלי הוא בתר כלי: ט) הא טומא' עבה כמו סומכא דרקיעא הס"ד ואח"כ מה"ד סמיכתא: י) דמי מיהא כאילו מת אזיל: כ) ואת"ל שרץ על גבי שרץ כיון דמפסקי מהדדי כמאן דמנחא בכלי דמי וספק מגעו בעליון ספיקו טמא ואת"ל דשרץ ונבילה נמי כו' (ואת"ל שרץ כו' ספיקו טמא) כ"ז ליתא בכי"י: ל) דמונח ליה על גביו וכמאן דמונח: מ) וספק מגעו: נ) שרץ לף:

הגהות הב"ח

(א) רש"י ד"ה שרץ לף וכו' בכזית ולא קאי שיעורא דנבלה:

הגהות הגר"א

[א] גמ' הניטלין. נ"ב בתוספתא (פ"ג דטהרות) הגירסא הנתלין (וכ"ה ברמב"ם): [ב] שם מת. נ"ל שרץ (וכ"ה ברמב"ם. דס"ל דלפה אינה אלא לענין שרץ בלבד כפשטות הגמ' דלא כרש"י ותוס'): [ג] שם מיתא. נ"ל מיא (וכ"ה בתוס'): [ד] שם מת ע"ג שרץ. נ"ל שרץ ע"ג מת (וכ"ה ברמב"ם וכנ"ל): [ה] שם (וטמא) חז"מ (וכן ליתא בדפו"י): [ו] שם (ואת"ל שרץ ע"ג שרץ כיון דמפסקי מהדדי כמאן דמנחא בכלי דמי) תא"מ (ובאמת הבעיא שאח"ז לא תליא כלל באת"ל אך מהרמב"ם משמע דגרים האת"ל להיפך ע"ש): [ז] שם (ומי חטאת צפין ע"ג המים) תא"מ (דמיותר הוא וכמו שלא הזכיר בהבעיות שמקודם):

גליון הש"ס

גמ' מת בכלי וכלי צף על פני המים. כעין זה שבת דף ה ע"ב:

לד א מיי' פ"ו מהל' קרבן פסח הלי"א:
לה ב מיי' פ"א מהל' מחוסרי כפרה הל"א:
לו ג מיי' פ"ט מהל' טומאת מת הל"ג:

אָמַר רַב הַמְנוּנָא: נָזִיר וְעוֹשֵׂה פֶסַח שֶׁהָלְכוּ בְּקֶבֶר הַתְּהוֹם בַּשְּׁבִיעִי שֶׁלָּהֶן — טְהוֹרִים. מ"ט — דְּלָא אַלִּימָא טוּמְאַת הַתְּהוֹם לְמִיסְתַּר. מְתִיב רָבָא: יָרַד לִיטָּהֵר מִטּוּמְאַת הַמֵּת — טָמֵא, שֶׁחֶזְקַת טָמֵא — טָמֵא, שֶׁחֶזְקַת טָהוֹר — טָהוֹר! א"ל: מוֹדֵינָא לָךְ בְּנָזִיר, שֶׁמְּחוּסַּר תִּגְלַחַת. א"ל רָבָא: אַף אֲנָא מוֹדֵינָא לָךְ א בְּעוֹשֵׂה פֶסַח, דְּלָא מְחוּסָּר וְלָא כְלוּם. א"ל אַבַּיֵי: וְהָא מְחוּסַּר הֶעֱרֵב שֶׁמֶשׁ! א"ל: *שִׁמְשָׁא מִמֵּילָא עָרְבָא. וְאַף אַבַּיֵי הֲדַר בֵּיהּ. דְּתַנְיָא: ב יוֹם מְלֹאת — תָּבִיא, תּוֹךְ מְלֹאת — לֹא תָּבִיא. יָכוֹל לֹא תָּבִיא עַל לֵידָה שֶׁלִּפְנֵי מְלֹאת, אֲבָל תָּבִיא עַל לֵידָה שֶׁלְּאַחַר מְלֹאת, וְתִיפָּטֵר מִשְׁתֵּיהֶן — ת"ל °"וּבִמְלֹאת יְמֵי טָהֳרָהּ", בְּיוֹם מְלֹאת — תָּבִיא, תּוֹךְ מְלֹאת — לֹא תָּבִיא. אָמַר רַב כָּהֲנָא: שָׁאנֵי הָכָא דִּמְחַסְּרָא קָרְבָּן, הָתָם נַמִי מְחַסְּרָא הֶעֱרֵב שֶׁמֶשׁ! א"ל אַבַּיֵי: שִׁמְשָׁא מִמֵּילָא עָרְבָא.§ (ויקרא יב)

מתני' * ג הַמּוֹצֵא מֵת *בַּתְּחִילָּה, מוּשְׁכָּב כְּדַרְכּוֹ — נוֹטְלוֹ וְאֶת *תְּפוּסָתוֹ, שְׁנַיִם — נוֹטְלָן וְאֶת תְּפוּסָתָן. מָצָא שְׁלֹשָׁה, אִם יֵשׁ בֵּין זֶה לָזֶה מד' אַמּוֹת וְעַד שְׁמוֹנֶה — הֲרֵי זוֹ שְׁכוּנַת קְבָרוֹת.

בּוֹדֵק

נזיר ועושה פסח שהלכו בקבר התהום בשביעי שלהן טהורים מאי טעמא לא אלימא טומאת התהום למיסתר מתיב רבא ירד ליטהר מטומאת מת טמא שחזקת טמא טמא. אלמא: היכא דאתחזק בטומאתו – לא מטהרינן בטומאת התהום. **אמר** ליה מודינא לך בנזיר דמחוסר תגלחת.

פי': תגלחת טומאה. ומתני' איירי הכא דמחוסר תגלחת, שהרי אף טבילה הוא מחוסר, שהרי הוא ירד לטבול, וכ"ש תגלחת שאחריה. ורב המנונא מיירי בשביעי אחר שגילח. דנהי דמחוסר הערב שמש – בהאי לא קרינן ליה בחזקת טמא, כדמפרש ואזיל. א"ל: אף אנא מודינא לך בנזיר ועושה פסח דלא מחוסר ולא כלום, כלומר, ואחר שטבל ואחר שגילח, אמר ליה אביי: והא מחוסר הערב שמש! א"ל: שמשא ממילא ערבא. ואף אביי הדר ביה, והודה דשימשא ממילא ערבא, ולא חשיב חסרון. **דתניא** יום מלאת תביא תוך מלאת לא תביא. האי יום מלאת לאו דוקא, אלא כלומר חזרה וילדה יום פ"א – תביא ב' קרבנות. תוך מלאת, שחזרה וילדה שנית תוך ימי לידה ראשונה – לא תביא רק קרבן א'. יכול לא תביא על לידה שלפני מלאת, אבל תביא על לידה של אחר מלאת, כגון שילדה בשניה ביום ס"ד ללידה ראשונה, וחזרה וילדה ביום ס"ד ללידה שניה, שהיא תוך מלאת של לידה שניה ולאחר מלאת של לידה ראשונה – ת"ל "ביום מלאת", דכל תוך מלאת, בין ללידה *)שניה הנפטרת בקרבן של ראשונה – אינה מביאה אלא קרבן אחד. ואמר רב כהנא: היינו טעמא – דמחסרא קרבן. כלומר, משום הכי מיפטרא בקרבן אחד – לפי שמחוסרת קרבן של לידה, ולא יצא עליה שעה שראויה להביא קרבן של לידה ראשונה. ד"בכל קדש לא תגע ואל המקדש לא תבא עד מלאת ימי טהרה", והואיל וילדה שנית – לא תוכל להביא קרבן של ראשונה עד מלאת לידה שניה. והואיל ולא הספיקה למלאות לידה שניה עד שילדה שלישית, ולכך דין הוא שתיפטר היא בקרבן אחד. **התם** נמי מחוסר הערב שמש. כמו והוינן בה: התם, בלידה שלאחר מלאת, אמאי תביא קרבן ללידה שניה? הא מחסרא הערב שמש. כלומר, מי לא עסקינן באשה שלא טבלה לסוף שבועיים כל עיקר? הרי אף לאחר שמונים אינה ראויה להביא קרבן לידה ראשונה, ואפ"ה מביאה קרבן על לידה שלאחר מלאת. **אמר** אביי שימשא ממילא ערבא. כלומר, לא מיבעיא חסרון הטבילה שאינו חשוב חסרון, שהרי מקוה לפניו ובידו ליטבול. אלא אף הערב שמש שאינו בידו – לא קחשיב חסרון, דשימשא ממילא ערבא. ואית דמפרשי: האי דמיחסרא הערב שמש – מטבילה דרבנן בסוף [פ"א], כדאמר בפרק "חומר בקודש" (חגיגה דף כא.). ולא נהירא, חדא: דמדאורייתא אמרי'. ותו, הא לא בעי הערב שמש, דקתני התם דמחוסר כיפורים צריך טבילה לקודש, והתם דייק: טבילה – אין, הערב שמש – לא, אמילי אחרינא א). **בתחלה.** שלא נודע לו כי קבור שם בקבר. **כדרכו**. בגמ' מפרש מאי נקטיה. **נוטלו**. נהי דקבר הידוע אמרינן בפרק "נגמר הדין" (סנהדרין דף מז:) אסור לפנותו – התם הוא דוקא בשנודע בו לדעת שנשאר קבור שם. אבל בנמצא אמרינן התם מותר ליטלו, מאחר שלא נודע הקבר לבני אדם – נכון לומר כי לאקראי נקבר שם. **תפוסתו**. מפ' בגמ'. **מצא** שלשה אם יש בין זה לזה מד' אמות ועד שמונה ה"ז שכונת קברות. כלומר, דאיגלאי מילתא כיון דמשכחא תלתא כי בית הקברות היה שם, ולכך אסור ליטלן ולפנותו. גם צריך לבדוק הימנו ולהלן עשרים אמה, כי בודאי שבית הקברות היה שם. ורגילים היו לקבור במערות, כדאמרי' בשלהי "המוכר פירות". והתם מפורש להך לישנא דהאי תנא סבר דתוכה של מערה ד' אמות על שמונה כר"ש דברייתא. והך שלשה לאו תוך ארבע אמות אשכחינהו, כדמוכח התם, דרוחב הכוך אמה ובין כוך לכוך אמה, ואלי אמה מקום פנוי סמוך לכותל המערה לשני כתלים – הרי תוך ד' אמות שני כוכין. ודקאמר מארבע עד שמונה – הכי קאמר: השלשה מונחין כפי סדר הראוי לקבור שלשה מתים במערה שרחבה ד' אמות וארכה שמונה אמות, מהן לרחבה שני כוכין, והשלישי לא יהיה מרוחק יותר מן ב) אמה ואלי, שכן המשפט המערה שרחבה ארבעה וארכה שמונה. כך תירץ ר"ת. ולא כפי' רשב"ם, שפירש תוך הארבע אמות שלשה כוכין, דהא ליתא כדפרישית. מארבע אמות עד שמונה. ל"ג: כהלין מטה וקוברין. דגבי אלר הקבר הוא דמיתני, בפרק "המוכר פירות".

בודק

א) [ועי' תוס' חגיגה כא. ד"ה האונן]. ב) גי' א"מ חלי אמה.

[בהלכות כתב התי"ט שבנוסחת מהר"ס נמחק תיבת בתחילה]

*) גי' א"מ ראשונה בין ללידה שניה וכו':

אָמַר רַב הַמְנוּנָא נָזִיר וְעוֹשֵׂה פֶּסַח. שֶׁנִּטְמְאוּ בְּטוּמְאַת מֵת, וְהוּזָּה עֲלֵיהֶן בַּג' וּבַשְּׁבִיעִי, וְהָלְכוּ בְּקֶבֶר הַתְּהוֹם בַּשְּׁבִיעִי שֶׁלָּהֶן, וְלֹא נוֹדַע לְעוֹשֵׂה פֶסַח עַד שֶׁעָשָׂה פִּסְחוֹ, וְלַנָּזִיר עַד שֶׁמָּנָה נְזִירוּתוֹ וְגִילַּח לִנְזִירוּת טָהֳרָה. טְהוֹרִים. וְאע"ג דְּנִטְמְאוּ בַּשְּׁבִיעִי שֶׁלָּהֶן. דְּלָא אַלִּימָא א) הָךְ טוּמְאַת הַתְּהוֹם לְמִיסְתַּר, הוֹאִיל וּכְבָר עָבַר וְנִטְהַר לִכְשֶׁנִּטְמָא בְּטוּמְאַת הַתְּהוֹם. מְתִיב רָבָא יָרַד. לִטְבּוֹל וְלִיטָּהֵר מִטּוּמְאַת הַמֵּת, וְנִמְצָא מֵת מְשׁוּקָּע בְּקַרְקַע הַמְּעָרָה – טָמֵא, שֶׁחֶזְקַת טָמֵא טָמֵא. וְהָכָא נַמִי, כֵּיוָן דַּהֲוֵי בְּחֶזְקַת טָמֵא בַּשְּׁבִיעִי שֶׁלּוֹ ב) כְּשֶׁנִּטְמָא בְּקֶבֶר הַתְּהוֹם, לְפִי שֶׁעֲדַיִין לֹא גִּילַּח תִּגְלַחַת טוּמְאָה דִּנְזִירוּת, וְלֹא הֶעֱרִיב שִׁמְשׁוֹ, דְּתִגְלַחַת לְאַחַר בִּיאַת מַיִם הוּא, כִּדְאָמְרִי' לְעֵיל בְּפֶרֶק ["שְׁלֹשָׁה מִינִין"] (דף מד:), ג) לוֹקְמִינֵיהּ נַמִי עַל חֶזְקָתוֹ וְלֶהֱוֵי טָמֵא! אֲמַר לֵיהּ מוֹדֵינָא לָךְ בְּנָזִיר. דְּכֵיוָן דְּנִטְמָא בְּיוֹם שְׁבִיעִי שֶׁלּוֹ קוֹדֶם תִּגְלַחַת, דְּטָמֵא, וַאֲפִי' כִּי לֹא נוֹדַע לוֹ עַד לְאַחַר גִּילּוּחַ דְּטָהֳרָה, ד) מִשּׁוּם דִּמְחוּסַּר תִּגְלַחַת טוּמְאָה כִּי נִטְמָא בְּקֶבֶר הַתְּהוֹם. דְּלָא מְחוּסָּר וְלָא כְּלוּם. וַהֲוֵי בְּחֶזְקַת טָהוֹר ה) כִּי נִטְמָא בְּקֶבֶר הַתְּהוֹם, וּמִסְּפֵיקָא לָא מַחְתִּינַן לֵיהּ טוּמְאָה, כִּדְתְנַן: שֶׁחֶזְקַת טָהוֹר טָהוֹר. א"ל. עוֹשֵׂה פֶּסַח נַמִי בְּיוֹם ז' שֶׁלּוֹ ו) קָא מְחוּסַּר הֶעֱרֵב שֶׁמֶשׁ, וְקָאָמַר דְּחֶזְקַת טָמֵא טָמֵא! מִמֵּילָא עָרְבָא. וּכְלָא מְחוּסָּר וְלָא כְלוּם דָּמֵי. וְאַף אַבַּיֵי חֲדַר בֵּיהּ. ז) דַּאֲמַר: הֶעֱרֵב שֶׁמֶשׁ לָאו חִסָּרוֹן הוּא, דְּשִׁימְשָׁא מִמֵּילָא עָרְבָא. דְּתַנְיָא "וּבִמְלֹאת יְמֵי טָהֳרָהּ לְבֵן אוֹ לְבַת" וגו'. יוֹם מְלֹאת תָּבִיא. אִם חָזְרָה וְהִפִּילָה בְּיוֹם מְלֹאת לְזָכָר, דְּהַיְינוּ בְּיוֹם אַרְבָּעִים וְאֶחָד לְזָכָר, וְיוֹם פ"א לִנְקֵבָה – תָּבִיא שְׁתֵּי קָרְבָּנוֹת. אֲבָל עַל אוֹתוֹ שֶׁיָּלְדָה בְּתוֹךְ מְלֹאת – לֹא תָּבִיא, דְּאָמַר קְרָא "זֹאת תּוֹרַת הַיּוֹלֶדֶת" – הַתּוֹרָה רִיבְּתָה עַל כַּמָּה וְלָדוֹת שֶׁיֵּשׁ לָהּ בְּתוֹךְ יְמֵי לֵידָה, שֶׁמְּבִיאָה קָרְבָּן א' וְאוֹכֶלֶת בַּקֳּדָשִׁים, וְאֵין *הַשִּׁיּוּר עָלֶיהָ חוֹבָה. יָכוֹל לֹא תָּבִיא כו' אֲבָל תָּבִיא עַל שֶׁלְּאַחַר מְלֹאת. שֶׁאִם יָלְדָה נְקֵבָה בְּתוֹךְ שְׁמוֹנִים, ח) וּלְאַחַר שֶׁעָבְרוּ פ' דְּרִאשׁוֹנָה חָזְרָה וְיָלְדָה נְקֵבָה בְּתוֹךְ שְׁמוֹנִים שֶׁל שְׁנִיָּה, יָכוֹל שֶׁתָּבִיא קָרְבָּן עַל הָרִאשׁוֹנָה וְעַל הַשְּׁלִישִׁית, לְפִי שֶׁהוּא לְאַחַר ט) מְלֹאת שֶׁל רִאשׁוֹנָה? ת"ל וּבִמְלֹאת. דְּמַשְׁמַע: כָּל זְמַן שֶׁיָּלְדָה בְּיוֹם מְלֹאת, בְּשָׁעָה שֶׁרְאוּיָה לְהָבִיא בָּהּ קָרְבָּן – תִּתְחַיֵּיב בְּקָרְבָּן עַל שְׁתֵּיהֶן, אֲבָל תּוֹךְ מְלֹאת – לֹא תָּבִיא. וְזוֹ, הוֹאִיל וְהִיא בְּתוֹךְ מְלֹאת שֶׁל שְׁנִיָּה – לֹא תָּבִיא. אָמַר רַב כָּהֲנָא. כְּלוֹמַר, וַאֲמַר רַב כָּהֲנָא עֲלָהּ דְּהַהִיא: שָׁאנֵי הָכָא בְּלֵידָה י) דִּלְאַחַר מְלֹאת, מ"ט לָא מְחַיְּיבָא לְאֵיתוּיֵי עֲלָהּ קָרְבָּן – מִשּׁוּם דִּמְחַסְּרָא קָרְבָּן, דְּכָל חֲדָא וַחֲדָא דְּמִתְיַלְּדָא לָהּ הָוְיָא בְּשָׁעָה שֶׁאֵינָהּ רְאוּיָה לְהָבִיא בָּהּ קָרְבָּן. וּמוֹתְבִינַן עֲלָהּ דְּהַהִיא: הָתָם נַמִי בְּיוֹם מְלֹאת לְפ"א, אַמַּאי מַיְיתָא קָרְבָּן? הָא מְחַסְּרָא הֶעֱרֵב שֶׁמֶשׁ, שֶׁהֲרֵי הִיא צְרִיכָה לִהְיוֹת חוֹזֶרֶת וְטוֹבֶלֶת בּוֹ בַּיּוֹם אע"פ שֶׁכְּבָר טָבְלָה לְבַסּוֹף י"ד כ) מֵחֲמַת לֵידָה, כְּדֵי לְהַתִּירָהּ לֶאֱכוֹל בַּקֳּדָשִׁים. כִּדְתְנַן בְּמַסֶּכֶת חֲגִיגָה בְּפֶרֶק "חוֹמֶר בַּקּוֹדֶשׁ" (דף כא.) שֶׁהָאוֹנֵן וְהַמְחוּסַּר כִּפּוּרִים צְרִיכִין טְבִילָה לַקּוֹדֶשׁ, וּצְרִיכִין הֶעֱרֵב שֶׁמֶשׁ, דְּהַיְינוּ טְבוּל יוֹם אָרוֹךְ, שֶׁאע"פ שֶׁטָּבְלָה לְסוֹף י"ד – אֵינָהּ אוֹכֶלֶת בַּקֳּדָשִׁים עַד סוֹף פ"א, וּצְרִיכָה הֶעֱרֵב שֶׁמֶשׁ. אָמַר אַבַּיֵי. הָאֵיךְ חִסָּרוֹן דְּמֵיעַל שִׁימְשָׁא לָאו שְׁמֵיהּ חִסָּרוֹן, דְּשִׁימְשָׁא מִמֵּילָא עָרְבָא, וְהָוֵי לָהּ שָׁעָה הָרְאוּיָה לְהָבִיא בָּהּ קָרְבָּן. מש"ה אֲמַר דְּבְיוֹם מְלֹאת תָּבִיא. וְהָא מִילְּתָא דְּאַבַּיֵי וְרַב כָּהֲנָא לָא שְׁמִיעָא לַן הֵיכָא אִיתָא. מתני' הַמּוֹצֵא מֵת מוּשְׁכָּב כְּדַרְכּוֹ ל). [וְלֹא] יוֹשֵׁב, וְלֹא רֹאשׁוֹ בֵּין יַרְכוֹתָיו, וְלֹא הָרוּג. נוֹטְלוֹ וְאֶת תְּפוּסָתוֹ. מ) וּמְפַנּוֹ לְמָקוֹם אַחֵר. וְאֵינוֹ חוֹשֵׁשׁ שֶׁיֵּשׁ כָּאן בַּמָּקוֹם הַזֶּה שׁוּם מֵת אַחֵר, וּמוּתָּר לוֹ לְהַלֵּךְ בְּכ"מ. וְכֵן אִם מָצָא שְׁנַיִם. אֲבָל אִם מָצָא שְׁלֹשָׁה, אִם יֵשׁ בֵּין זֶה לָזֶה מֵאַרְבַּע וְעַד ח', אִם יֵשׁ בֵּין רִאשׁוֹן נ) לַשֵּׁנִי מִתְּחִילַּת אַרְבַּע לְסוֹף אַרְבַּע, דְּהַיְינוּ לְרוֹחַב הַמְּעָרָה, אוֹ שֶׁהֵן מוּשְׁכָּבִין בְּתוֹךְ שְׁמוֹנֶה ס) בְּמִדַּת אוֹרֶךְ הַמְּעָרָה, שֶׁהָאֶחָד בִּתְחִילַּת אֶחָד וְהַשְּׁלִישִׁי בְּסוֹף ח', דְּהָכִי קָא מוֹקִים לָהּ אַלִּיבָּא דְּרַבָּנַן וְר"ש בְּפֶ' "הַמּוֹכֵר פֵּירוֹת" (ב"ב קב.). ה"ז שְׁכוּנַת קְבָרוֹת. וְקָנוּ מְקוֹמָן. וְאע"פ שֶׁאֵין שָׁם כָּרָאוּי, כִּדְגָרְסִי' הָתָם שֶׁנִּפְתַּח לְתוֹכוֹ ע) כּוּכִין שֶׁשּׁוֹכְבִין מִיכָּן לְאוֹרֶךְ הַמְּעָרָה, דְּאִיתְרַמּוּיֵי אִיתְרְמִי, דְּלֹא הִסְפִּיקוּ לִקְבּוֹר שָׁם אֶלָּא הַלָּלוּ [שְׁלֹשָׁה] מֵתִים, וְהוֹאִיל וְזוֹ שְׁכוּנַת קְבָרוֹת – יֵשׁ לָחוּשׁ שֶׁמָּא נַעֲשׂוּ כָּאן שְׁתֵּי מְעָרוֹת, אַחַת מִכָּאן וְאַחַת מִכָּאן, וְחָצֵר בָּאֶמְצַע שֶׁהוּא שֵׁשׁ עַל שֵׁשׁ. וְצָרִיךְ

תורה אור

[פסחים לג:]

ב"ב דף קא: אהלות פט"ז מ"ג [במשנה שבמשניות ובן בערוך איתא תבוסתו ובן גירסת הרמב"ם והר"ב ועיין תוי"ט]

נ"ל השאר

פי' הרא"ש

ואת"ל הא אוכל' הוי' שרץ ע"ג שכבת זרע מהו ואת"ל כיון דמתעקרא שנעקרה מן הגוף הוי' כי אוכל': שרץ על מי חטאת ומי חטאת צפין ע"פ המים. מי אמרי' הא ודאי משקה הוא וטומאה סמיכתא היא שגם מי חטאת מטמאים או דילמא כיון דאפר מעורב בהן והוא קצת עב הוי כי אוכלא: אמר רב המנונא נזיר ועושה פסח שהלכו בקבר התהום בז' שלהן. כגון נזיר שנטמא והזה ושנה וטבל ובו ביום עבר על קבר התהום ולא נודע לו עד שהשלים נזירותו והביא קרבנותיו אינו סותר: מתיב רבא ליטהר מטמא מת טמא. אלמא טומאת התהום סותרת כל ז'. א"ל אביי מודינא לך בנזי' שמחוסר תגלחת. הלכך אפי' טבל כיון דמחוסר תגלחת סותר ובהכי איירי מתני'. אבל רב המנונא איירי אחר שטבל וגילח ופסקה הימנו טומאת נזי' וה"ה דה"מ לשנויי מתני' בשלא טבל אלא רבותא טפי אשמועי' דאפי' טבל כל זמן שלא גלח סותר: א"ל רבא אף אנא מודינא לך בעושה פסח דלא מחוסר ולא כלום. רבא פריך לאביי דאמר דמודה רב המנונא במחוסר תגלחת סותר ואיהו איירי בשגילח. וקא"ל רבא אף אנא מודינא בעושה פסח דלא מחוסר מידי. וא"כ מאי קמ"ל דרב (כהנא) [המנונא] מלתא דפשיטא היא כיון שגלח וטבל הנזי' ועושה פסח דתו לא סתר. וה"ה דהמ"ל כיון שגילח מאי למימרא אלא נקט עושה פסח דלא מחסר מידי בתר טבילה:

א"ל אביי מחוסר הערב שמש. והיינו רבותיה דרב (כהנא) [המנונא] דאפ"ה קרו ביה חזקת טהור טהור והשיב לו רבא דאין זו רבותא דשמשא ממילא ערבא. כן נ"ל לקיים גירסת הספרים כי ראיתי שמחקוה כל המפרשים: ואף אביי הדר ביה. מהאי דקאמר מחוסר הערב שמש: דתניא יום מלאת תביא. פי' יולדת נקבה שהפילה יום פ"א תביא ב' קרבנות: תוך מלאת לא תביא אם הפילה תוך פ"א לא תביא כדדרשי' במס' נדה (דף מ) זאת תורת היולדת מלמד שמביאה קרבן א' על לידות הרבה: יכול תביא קרבן א' על לידה שלאחר מלאת ת"ל זאת: יכול לא תביא על לידה שלפני מלאת כדקאמר שאינה מביאה אלא קרבן א' על לידה של תוך מלאת: אבל תביא על לידה שלאחר מלאת. כגון שילדה נקבה והפילה נקבה אחרת תוך פ' וחזרה והפילה ולד שלישי תוך פ' לשניה שהוא אחר מלאת של הראשונה וה"פ יכול לא תביא על לידה שלפני מלאת לראשון אבל תביא על לידה שלאחר מלאת לראשון אע"פ שהוא תוך מלאת לשני: ת"ל ובמלאת דמשמע דוקא יום מלאת תביא אבל על של תוך מלאת לא תביא והאי נמי תוך מלאת של השני הוא. ופ"ב דכריתות פליגי בה ר"י ורבנן דתניא התם ר"י אומר מביאה על הראשונה ואינה מביאה על השניה מביאה על השלישית ואינה מביאה על הרביעית והך ברייתא דרבנן כר' יהודה: אמר רב כהנא שאני הכא דמחוסר קרבן. כלומר מה טעם אינה מביאה על השלישית הואיל והוי אחר מלאת של ראשון וקאמר רב כהנא משום שלא הגיע השעה שתוכל להביא קרבן על הראשון הלכך הוי בתוך מלאת לראשון: התם נמי הא מיחסר הערב שמש פירוש המפלת יום פ"א דקי"ל דמביאה ב' קרבנות דאף אור לשמונים וא' מחייבי בה ב' קרבנות ואמאי הא מחוסר הערב שמש. תימה מאי הערב שמש שייך הכא והלא היא טובלת אחר שבועיים ונקראת טבולת יום ארוך ואסורה בתרומה עד אור לפ"א והוו הערב שמש שלה. וי"ל מי לא עסקי' שאחרה טבילתה עד יום פ"א וצריך אז הערב שמש ואינה מביאה כפרתה עד למחר ואפ"ה קי"ל דבכל ענין אם הפילה יום פ"א מביאה ב' קרבנות ואע"ג דמחסר הערב שמש: ומשני אביי דשמשא ממילא ערבא ולא מקרי חסרון וכיון שמה שמחוסר הערב שמש לא מקרי חסרון גם מה שאינה יכולה להביא קרבנות בלילה עד למחר זמן מידי דהוה אמפלת אור לפ"א ואי תיקשי לך ע"כ פלוג ביום פ"א שאם הפילה קודם שטבלה מחוסר מעשה היא א) ומביאה קרבן א' והה"נ אחר שטבלה נמי מחוסרת הערב שמש דלא פלוג דמתוך דמחוסר טבילה לא מקרי מחוסר מעשה כיון דבידה ליטבול מידי דהוי אילדה אחר מלאת קודם שהביאה קרבנותיה. דכיון דבידה להביאם הוי כאילו הביאתם: וי"מ והא מחוסר הערב שמש דכי נמי טבלה קודם צריך לטבול שנית יום פ"א כדתנן במס' חגיגה פ' חומר בקודש אונן ומחוסר כפורים צריך טבילה להקדש

א) דברי רבינו אינו מובן ואולי דט"ס נפל בדברי רבינו וצ"ע.

נוסחת הריב"ן

א) טומאת התהום למיסתר הס"ד ואח"כ מה"ד מתיב: ב) ונטמא בקבר התהום ועדיין לא: ג) מוקמינן ליה על: ד) דטהרה אבל לעושה פסח דלא מחוסר ולא כלום וכו' בחזקת טהור: ה) ונטמא בקבר התהום ומספיקא לא: ו) שלו לא אלימא למחסר דלא מחוסר ולא כלום הס"ד ואח"כ מה"ד והא מחוסר הערב שמש ונימא דהוי בחזקת טמא הס"ד ואח"כ מה"ד שמשא ממילא ערבא וכמאן דלא מחוסר ולא כלום דמי הס"ד: ז) ולמחר: ח) שמונים של ראשונה: ט) פ' של: י) כגון דקדמה: כ) מטומאת לידה: ל) כדרכו בתחלה שלא היה יודע מעולם לאיש ולמאן מושכב כדרכו לא יושב כו': מ) ומפנהו למקום אחר כו' ומותר לו להלוך: נ) לשני מתחלת: ס) במדת אורך כו' בתחלת א' והשלישי בסוף ח' כדאמר בבבא בתרא דהכא מוקים לה אליבא דר"ש: ע) לתוכו שמונה כוכין כו' שמא נעשו שם שתי:

בודק הימנו ולהלן עשרים אמה, מצא אחד בסוף עשרים אמה — בודק הימנו ולהלן עשרים אמה, שרגלים לדבר, שאילו תחילה מצאו — נוטלו ואת תפוסתו.§ **גמ'** אמר רב יהודה: מצא — [א]פרט למצוי, מת — [ב]פרט להרוג, מושכב — [ג]פרט ליושב, כדרכו — [ד]פרט לשראשו מונח בין ירכותיו. תני עולא בר חנינא: *[ה]מת שחסר — אין לו תפוסה, ולא שכונת קברות. וכל הני, מ"ט לא? אמרינן [ו]דילמא גוי הוא.§ [ז]מצא שנים, ראשו של זה בצד מרגלותיו של זה, וראשו של זה בצד מרגלותיו של זה — אין להן תפוסה, ולא שכונת קברות. [ח]מצא שלשה, האחד ידוע ושנים תחילה, או *שנים תחילה ושנים ידועים — *אין להם תפוסה, ואין להם שכונת קברות. מעשה ברבי ישבב שבדק ומצא שנים ידועין ואחד תחילה, וביקש לעשותן שכונת קברות. אמר לו ר"ע: כל שיגעת — לריק יגעת, לא אמרו שכונת קברות אלא לג' [א] ידועין, או לשלשה תחילה.§ "נוטלן ואת תפוסתן".§ *היכי דמי תפוסה? אמר רב יהודה: אמר קרא °"ונשאתני ממצרים"* — טול עמי. וכמה שיעור תפוסה? [ט]פירש רבי אלעזר א) [ב] (ברבי צדוק): נוטל עפר תיחוח, וחופר בבתולה ג' אצבעות. מיתיבי: וכמה שיעור תפוסה? פירש רבי אלעזר ברבי צדוק: [ג] נוטל את הקיסמין ואת הקססות, וזורק את הוודאין, ומניח את הספיקות, והשאר מצטרף [ד] לרוב בנינו של מת, ולרובע עצמות, למלא תרווד רקב! הוא דאמר כי האי תנא, דתניא: וכמה שיעור תפוסה? א"ר יוחנן משום בן עזאי: נוטל עפר תיחוח וחופר בבתולה שלש אצבעות.§ "בודק הימנו".§

אמר

תורה אור: °ברא' מז

[עי' ר"ש פי"ז מאהלות מ"ג [ובמס' שמחות פ"ד ה"ט]; גי' ר"ש ש]

א) [טעות הדפוס ועי' תוס' ד"ה כמה]

רש"י

וצריך שיהא בודק ממנו ולהלן עשרים אמה. שהיא כמנין שני מערות והחצר שביניהם. והתם א) מתרגם לה רב ששת בריה דרב אידי אליבא דר"ש, דאמר פותח בה שתי מערות של ב) שש על שמונה, דחדא מנייהו בנפלי. ואידך מוקים לה כרבנן, דאמרי: שאין אורך המערה אלא ד' אמות על ו' אמות, ותמני סרי הוא דהויין. וקא מוקים לה דחדא מנייהו באלכסונה, והויין להו עשרים. והתם פרישית לכולה ג) מילתא דמתניתין דהכא. חזר ומצא אחד *בתוך עשרים בודק ממנו ולהלן עשרים אמה. משום דאיכא למימר שכונת קברות היא זו. שרגלים לדבר. שהיא שכונת קברות, מדאשכח ג' בתוך כ' אמה, שיש בין זה לזה מד' אמות ועד ח', ועכשיו מצא אחד ד) בתוך כ'. ולא אמרינן אתרמויי איתרמי, דלא נקבר שם אלא ה) אחד. שאילו זה יחידי, אם מצאו מתחילה — היה רשאי לפנותו למקום אחר, ונוטלו ואת תפוסתו. אבל עכשיו שמצא ג' בתוך כ', ואחד בסוף עשרים — יש לומר שהיא שכונת קברות.

גמ' אמר רב יהודה מצא פרט למצוי. דהא דתנן: מצא ג' מתים מושכבין כדרכן, דקנו מקומן ויש להן שכונת קברות — פרט למצוי. שאם היה יודע ו) קודם לכן שאחד מהן נקבר לשם — אין זו שכונת קברות, ונוטלן ואת תפוסתן, ומותר לו לפנותן למקום אחר, שלא קנו ז) מקומן. מת פרט להרוג. שאם מצא א' מגוייד, או שלשתן מגויידין — אמרינן דהכי איתרמי, שנהרגו לשם ונקברו ח) שם שלא בבית הקברות, ולא מחזקינן ליה ט) כשכונת קברות, אלא נוטלן ואת תפוסתן. מושכב פרט ליושב. שאם מצאן יושבין, הואיל ואין מושכבין כשאר מתים — נוטלן ואת תפוסתן. כדרכו פרט לראשו מונח לו בין ירכותיו. שאם מצא אחד מהם ראשו מונח לו בין ירכותיו — אמרינן דהכי איתרמי, שנזרק לשם. מת שחסר אין לו תפוסה. י) שנוטלו בלא תפוסתו. ולא שכונת קברות. שאם חסר א' כ) מאותן ג' — אין להם שכונת קברות, ל) דלא קנו מקומן. וכל הני מאי טעמא לא. הוי שכונת קברות? בשלמא א' מצוי מ) — דהכי הוא דגמירי, דבעי' שלשה ידועין או שלשה שמצאן תחילה, כדאמרינן לקמן. אלא כי מצאן אחד הרוג, או יושב, או ראשו מונחת לו בין ירכותיו, או חסר, נ) הואיל ושלשתן מצאם תחילה שיש להן שכונת קברות, מ"ט (א)? דילמא גוי הוא. ס) ואיקבר להכא. וגוי אינו עולה מן המנין, ולא פש להו ע) להכא אלא תרי. ותנן: מצא שנים — נוטלן ואת תפוסתן, משום הכי לא קנו מקומן. ראשו של זה בצד מרגלותיו של זה אין להם תפוסה. דגוים הם שנקברים פ) בכך. וכן אם הן ג', וב' מהן נקברים כענין הזה — אין להם שכונת קברות. א'. מהללו ג' מתים ידוע כבר, וב' מהן צ) שמצאו עכשיו תחילה, או אחד מהן עכשיו תחילה הוא מצוי. וביקש לעשותן שכונת קברות. דקנו מקומן. אלא לג' ידועין או לג' שמצאן תחילה. שלא היו ידועין קודם לכן, דהכי הוא דגמירי. אבל באידך גיסא — לא. ממצרים. מעפר מצרים טול עמי. נוטל עפר תיחוח. שנעשה מחמת הדם שיצא ממנו, ומחמת מוהל שיצא מן המת. וחופר. בבתולת קרקע ג' אצבעות, דאמרינן כשיעור ג' אצבעות נבלע בקרקע. נוטל את הקיסמין ק). של נסרים שנעשו מן הארון כשהרקיבו. ואמרי לה — קיסמין של עצי בשמים, כדכתיב באסא בדברי הימים (ב' טז) "וישכיבוהו במשכב אשר מלא בשמים". ואת הקססות. קוזזות של אדמה שנדבקו מן הדם ומן המוהל, שקורין בליסטי"ט בלע"ז. וזורק את הוודאין. דבר שהוא ודאי לו שאינו מן המת, שלא יחוש להן משום טומאה. ומניח את הספיקות. שיהא מפנן למקום ר) אחד, דחוששין להן משום טומאה. והשאר. דברים שהן מן המת, וקיסמין, מצטרפין לרוב בנייני של מת ש) דאהל. ולרובע עצמות למלא תרווד רקב. ודקא אמר לעיל בפרק "כהן גדול ונזיר" (דף נא.): נקבר בארון של עץ אין לו רקב — הני מילי בעיניה, אבל (לא) לאיצטרופי לאחריני שנקברו ערומים בארון של שיש ת) — מצטרף.

אמר

א) גי' א"מ לחוץ: ב) ולישאר שם בקברם. כצ"ל. ג) [ב"ק סט.] ד) גירסת א"מ וי"מ קססות. ה) נ"ל ואת פריה:
ו) גירסת א"מ אם ולאי: ז) [ועי' תוס' כתובות ח. ד"ה רב וכו']:

תוספות

בודק הימנו ולהלן כ' אמה. בפרק "המוכר פירות" (ב"ב דף קב.) פריך: עשרים ותרתין הויין, לשתי מערות ששה עשר, וחצר הקבר אמרינן התם: לר"ש ורבנן שש אמה! ומשני: בנפלים, שרגילות הוא כשאחת מן המערות גדולות השניה של נפלים, ולכך בשנית סגי בארבע על שש. ואיכא דמוקי התם למתני' (דהתם ומתני') דהכא כרבנן, דאמרי: תוכה של מערה ארבע על שש. ופריך: תמני סרי הויין! ומשני: שבדק מערה ראשונה באלכסון, ולחפש ולבדוק היטב, ומה שהוא מתעקס עולה לשתי אמות.

מצא א' בסוף כ' בודק הימנו ולהלן עשרים שרגלים לדבר שאילמלי בתחילה מצאו נוטלו ואת תפוסתו. אבל עתה שמצא כבר ג' מתים, אף כשמצא אחד יש לחוש לשכונת הקברות, וצריך לבדוק עד עשרים. **מצא** פרט למצוי. פ' ר"י: שאם היה ידוע — לא יהא נוטלו, כדאמרינן בפרק "נגמר הדין" (סנהדרין דף מז:): [קבר הנמצא — מותר לפנותו], קבר הידוע — אסור לפנותו. והא דאמרינן התם: פינה מקומו טהור, והכא משמע דיש לו תפוסה — אמר ר"י דהתם לא בתפוסה איירי. דתפוסה היינו לצד הקרקע בעומק, אבל התם בטומאה דרבנן איירי, דמדרבנן מטמינן א) לתוך כל הקבר לד' רוחות. אבל רשב"ס פירש: פרט למצוי — דהיינו א' ידוע ושנים בתחילה דבסמוך. וקשיא לשיטתו: דא"כ בחנם נקט "המוצא", דהוא הדין לשלשתן ידועין, דיש לו שכונת קברות.

פרט להרוג. כדאמרינן בסמוך: דמת שחסר אין לו תפוסה ואין לו שכונת קברות. מת שחסר אין לו שכונת קברות. קשה להבין למה, ושמא הלכה למשה מסיני הוא.

גוי הוא. דישראל אין קוברין אותו בענין זה.

אחד ידוע ושנים הוא מוצא עתה בתחילה אין לו שכונת קברות. רשב"ס פי': הלכה למשה מסיני הוא. ור"י פי' טעם בדבר: דאין לנו [לומר] שכונת קברות, ובית הקברות היה. הואיל ונקברו שם ג' מתים, כיון דא' נודע תחילה, אי איתא דאין דעתו היה לפנותם ב) ולישאם שם [לקברו], כי היכי דידוע לנו האחד — יהיו ידועים לנו אותם שעמו. ולא אמרו שכונת קברות אלא או [לשלשה] ידועים, או לשלשה תחילה. **כמה** שיעור תפוסה פי' ר' אלעזר. הוא ר"א בן פדת, שהוא אמורא, נוטל עפר תיחוח וחופר בקרקע בתולה שלש אצבעות. בירושלמי מפרש שמוהל המת יורד בקרקע עד ג' אצבעות. **מיתיבי** כמה שיעור תפוסה פירש ר' אלעזר ברבי צדוק נוטל את הקיסמין. פי': מן הארון של שיש שנכתת. ואת הקססות — י"א: כמו ג) קוזזות אדמה. וזורק את הוודאים — פירוש: מה שודאי לן שאינו מן המת. ומניח את הספיקות — מה שהוא מסופק אם היו מן המת אם לאו, מניח במקום המוצנע [ה] שלא יטמאו עושי טהרות. והשאר — שהוא ברור לו שהוא מן המת. מצטרפין לרוב בנין או לרוב מנין ולרובע — רובע הקב לטמא באהל. ולמלא תרווד רקב. ד) כמו: יין קוסס (ב"ב דף צז:) — מיני קיהוי ובשמים שמשימין בארון. וקשה: דא"כ אין לו רקב, דנעשה גלגלין, מידי דהוה אנקבר בארון עץ! דאף שערו העומד ליגזז איבעיא לן פ' "כ"ג" (לעיל דף נא.) אי נעשה גלגלין. עוד מפרש: קססות — היינו לשון דבר בלוי, כמו ה) "ופריו יקוסס" (יחזקאל יז). אלמא תפוסה לר"א ברבי לדוק אינו זקוק ליטול עפר, דאין לו לחפור בקרקע בתולה, כי ו) אסורה ודאי המת וספיקו.

הוא דאמר כי האי תנא דתניא כמה שיעור תפוסה פי' ר' יוחנן. לאו היינו ר' יוחנן האמורא, אלא רבי יוחנן בן נורי ז).

אמר

עין משפט נר מצוה

לז א מיי' פ"ט מהל' טומאת מת הל"ו:
לח ב ג ד מיי' שם הל' ג:
לט ה מיי' שם הל"ה:
מ ו ז מיי' שם הל"ט:
מא ח מיי' שם הל"ו וע"ש בכ"מ:
מב ט מיי' שם הל"ח:

מסורת הש"ס

נ"ל בסוף

[לעיל נא: ע"ש]

נוסחת הריב"ן

א) מפרש: ב) של ח' על שמונה וחד"א מינייהו כו' מוקים לה אליבא דרבנן כו' אלא ד' אמות כו': ג) לכולה מתני': ד) בסוף כ': ה) אלא זה: ו) יודע זה קודם: ז) קנו את: ח) ונקברו במקומן: ט) בשכונת: י) ונוטלו: כ) אחד מהן אין: ל) ולא קנו: מ) הכי הוא: נ) (הואיל כו' קברות) כתא בכ"י: ס) לאתרמי איקבר כו': ע) ולא פש בהו אלא: פ) כך וכן אם הי': צ) נמצאו: ק) הקיסמין נשרו מן הארון כשהרקיבו: ר) אחר: ש) לאהל ורבע כו': ת) מצטרפין:

[נ"ל ממצרים טול עמי כך גירסת הערוך בע' תבס וגי' הירקוט מקרקע מצרים טול עמי וז"ל הרב ברטנורה דכתיב ונשאתני ממצרים וקברתני בקבורתם שאין צריך לומר ממצרים אלא הכי קאמר מעפר של מצרים טול עמי וכתב התוספות יום טוב לא נמצא כתוב שנקבר בתחילה במצרים והרמב"ם כתב דאסמכתא הוא]

הגהות הב"ח

(א) רש"י ד"ה וכל הני וכו' קברות כ"ע לא דילמא כצ"ל והד"א:

הגהות הגר"א

[א] גמ' ידועין או לשלשה תא"מ נ"ב בתוספתא (פט"ז דאהלות) ל"ג לה וע"ש שאמרו בא' ודאי ב' תחלה אין להם שכונת קברות ה"ש המוצא (וע' א"ר אהלות פט"ז): [ב] שם בר' לדוק תא"מ: [ג] שם נוטל כו'. נ"ב גירסת התוספתא (פ"ב דאהלות) בורר את הצרורות ואת הקסמין ונוטל את הודאי ומניח את הספק והו עפר קברות מלא תרווד ועוד: [ד] שם והשאר מצטרף למלא תרווד רקב עפר קברות כצ"ל (וע' א"ר אהלות פ"ב): [ה] תוס' ד"ה מיתיבי כו' מניח במקום המוצנע. נ"ב אבל בתוספתא מפרש שהספק מצטרף עם השאר דהיינו הרקב כמלא תרווד ועוד עפר קברות ועפט"ז דאהלות:

פי' הרא"ש

להקדש וצריכה הערב שמש. וליתא להך פירושא דכל טבילה דרבנן לא בעיא הערב שמש ואחר הבאת קרבנותי' אוכלת בתרומ': המוצא מת בתחי' שלא היה יודע שהיה שם קבר: מושכב כדרכו. בגמ' מפ' למעוטי מאי: נוטלו ואת תפוסתו. מותר לפנותו משם ולקוברו במקום אחר ונוטל מן העפר של הקבר עמו כשיעור המפורש בגמ' והוא נקרא תפוסה. וכן אם מצא ב': מצא ג' אם יש בין זה לזה מד' אמות ועד ח' פי' מקבר ראשון עד ג' אין פחות מד"א ולא יותר מח': ה"ז שכונת קברות. וניכר שלשם קבורה נתנום שמה ואסור לפנותם משם ואפי' א' אם היה יודע שלשם קבורה נתנו שם היה אסור לפנותו אלא שבא' או ב' אנו תולין שלא נקברו שם אלא לפי שעה והיה דעתם לפנותם או נקברו בשדה בלא רשות הבעלים ולא קנו מקומם אבל כשהם ג' מוכח שזה המקום מיוחד לקבר כי אורך המערה הוא ח' ורחב המערה ד' אמות: כמלא מטה וקובריה לא גרסי' הכא דבפ' המוכר תנן גבי חצר ו' על ו' כמלא מטה וקובריה אבל לענין שיעור מערה לא שייך למתני שיעור זה: ובודק ממנו ולהלן כ' אמות דהיינו שיעור אורך ב' מערות והחצר ובפ' המוכר פריך אי לימא כר"ש א) דאמרי אורך המערה ו' והחצר ו' י"ח הויין ומוקי לה כרבנן וכגון דבדק באלכסון וא"נ כר"ש ובנפלים. ותימה אמאי לא פריך [מיניה] וביה מדקתני עד ח' אלמא אורך המערה ח' א"כ כ"ב הויין. וי"ל דשמא ס"ל שהחצר אינה רחבה כ"א ד' על ד': ובודק הימנו ולהלן כ' אמה. מן הדרום לצפון וכן מהמזרח למערב דמספקא לן איזהו רוחב המערה ומרוחב המערה ואילך צריך לבדוק כ' אמה. וכן צריך לבדוק מצד א' כ' אמה מן הצפון לדרום ומן המערב למזרח דמספקא לן לאיזה צד היו החצר והמערה הב'. וי"מ שאין צריך לבדוק אלא מצד א' שהיו רגילים להכנים ראש המת תחילה לכוך ורגליו לצד חלל המערה הלכך אין צריך לבדוק אלא לצד רגלי המתים: מצא א' בסוף כ' בודק ממנו ולהלן כ' אמה שרגלים לדבר שזו השדה עשויה לקברים והיו בה ג' מערות אחרות ומשום רגלים לדבר תנא כל הני משניות הכא וכולן שנויות במקומן ואגב גררא תנינהו הכא: אמר רב יהודה המוצא פרט למצוי. פרשב"ם פרט לידוע שאם א' מהם ידוע וב' תחלה אין להם שכונה: מת פרט להרוג שאין לו תפוסה ולא שכונה משום דכחסר דמי והכי גמירי: מושכב פרט ליושב [כדרכו] פרט לשראשו מונח בין ירכותיו. דדלמא גוים נינהו כיון שלא נקברו כדין: ראשו של זה בצד מרגלותיו של זה. אין דרך ישראל לקבור כך מתיהם. א' ידוע וב' תחילה פי' שהיה ידוע הקבר אבל אין ידוע אם נקבר שם לשם קבר או לפי שעה והיה דעתם לפנותו: ושנים תחילה שלא ידעו שהיו קבורים שם אלא עתה מתחלה מצאום או א' תחילה וב' ידועים יש להם תפיסה. אם בא ליטלם משם: ואין להם שכונה. ויכול לפנותם משם כיון שלא היו שלשתן מענין א' אין תולין שנקברו שם לשם קבר שהרי נמצאו ב' שאינם ידועים וכן ב' ידועים וא' תחלה אבל כשלשתן ידועים או תחילה אז אנו תולין שלשם קבורה הונחו שם: היכי דמי תפוסה. פי' היכי חזי' שצריך ליטול עמו: ממצרים טול עמי מעפר הארץ מיתורא דמצרים קדריש: וחופר בבתולה ג' אצבעות. מפ' בירושלמי שמוהל המת נכנס בקרקע ג' אצבעות: א"ר אלעזר נוטל עפר תיחוח ה"ג ול"ג ר"א בר צדוק אלא ר' אלעזר אמורא הוא דפריש ליה [וקא מקשה ליה] מר"א בר צדוק וקאמר הוא דאמר כי האי תנא: הקיסמין. קוצץ עצים של הארון. ואת הקססות כמו קוזות אדמה: וי"מ שהיו נותנים בארון מיני ב) קיסמות כמו מקבל עליו עשר קוססות למאה דפ' המוכר פירות. אלו נוטלן וגונזן. שלא יטמאו הנוגעים בהם קסמים משום גולל ודופק וקוססות שנבלע בהם מוהל המת

א) נראה דצ"ל דאמר דאורך המערה ח' והחצר ו' עשרין ותרתין הויין ואי רבנן דאמרי כו'. ב) נ"ל מיני קיהוי ובשמים קססות כמו כו'.

מג א מיי' פ"ט מהל' טומאת מת הל"ג:
מד ב מיי' פ"ו מהל' טומאת צרעת הל"ב:
מה ג מיי' שם הל"ט:
מו ד מיי' שם פ"ב הל"ג סמג עשין רלח:
מז ה מיי' שם הל"ט:
מח ו מיי' פ"ב מהל' מחוסרי כפרה הל"ב סמג עשין ריח ריט:
מט ז מיי' שם הל"ח:
נ ח מיי' פ"ג מהל' מטמאי משכב ומושב הל"ב והל' יב והל' יד:
נא ט מיי' פ"ו מהל' רוצח ושמירת נפש הל"ה:

אמר רבא בדק ומלא גם השני ופנה בדק ואשכח, ובדק עוד ומלא ג' – לא [האי] מפני לגבי ב', דאיגלאי מילתא שבמתכוון קברוהו כדי (לא) ליטאר [שם]. ולא הני תרי מפנה לגבי חד – א"נ שיפנה שנים ויחזיר לגבי חד, אלא השלישי למקום שהיה בו קבר. ואית דגרסי הכא: ומשוי להו שכונת קברות.

פי': שהיה בודק משם ולהלן עשרים אמה. **איכא** דאמרי כיון שניתן רשות לפנות. שכבר פינה קודם שידע שהשלשה הם, אף השלישי מפנה למקום שירצה, דבאחד לא נתקן שכונת קברות. וקשה קשה: אם הלכה היא, ושמא כל זה מן ההלכה! ולישוינהו שכונת קברות. ומשני: אמר ר"ש בן לקיש: עילא מצאו וטיהרו כל א"י, ואין להחזיק טומאה ולהחמיר.

בדק מכ' אמה ולא מצא מאי. דלאחד מן הרוחות, מי אמרי' כי היכי דלרוח זה לא מצא – לא יהא זה זקוק לבדוק לשאר הרוחות, מדברוח זו ליכא או לא?

אמר רב משרשיא שכונת קברות. כלומר, שכונת קברות של שלשה שנמצאו כבר – יש לו, אבל לא יצטרך יותר לבדוק. מאי טעמא – עילא מצאו וטיהרו את א"י. אית דמפרשי: בדק ולא מצא מאי – מהו שיהא *לחפור בעומק עד שיגיע לסלע או לבתולה. **כל** ספק נגעים בתחילה עד שלא נזקק לטומאה טהור. דאוקמיה אחזקתיה. ובמסכת נגעים (פ"ה מ"ד) מפרש: כיצד? שנים שבאו אצל כהן, בזה בהרת כגרים ובזה בהרת כסלע לסוף שבוע בזה כסלע ובזה כסלע, ואינו יודע [איזה מהן] פשה טהור: משנזקק לטומאה. התם מפרש: כיצד? שנים באו אצל כהן, בזה כסלע ובזה כגרים, לסוף שבוע בזה כסלע ועוד, ובזה [כסלע] ועוד – טמאין. לסוף בזה ובזה כסלע, ואינו יודע איזה מהם כיהה – שניהם טמאים, עד *שיחזיק לשניהם להיות כגרים, דכל חד אוקמיה בחזקת טומאה.

מנא הני מילי. דעד שלא נזקק לטומאה ספק נגעים להקל? אמר קרא "לטהרו" (*אומר) הואיל דפתח הכתוב בטהרה תחילה.

אי הכי אפי' משנזקק לטומאה נמי. דהא לא איצטריך קרא לעד שלא נזקק לטומאה דתיפוק ליה לאוקמיה אחזקתיה, אלא לנזקק לטומאה. פר"ת: אלא אי איתמר דרב (הונא) אדר' יהושע איתמר, דמטהר אפילו נזקק לטומאה. אבל מתני' [דהכא] – נאמר בין נזקק בין לא נזקק, מסברא, דאוקמיה אחזקתיה. **ורבי** יהושע אומר כיהה מאי כיהה וטיהר ודלמא כיהה וטמא. ותימה: דא"כ היינו ת"ק! ופי' הר"ר יהודה מקורבייל: ודילמא כיהה וטמא – ובא לחלוק על ת"ק. שתנא קמא [מטמאו] מספק, ור' יהושע בא לומר שהוא ודאי מנורע. ומשני לך: דכיהה וטיהר לגמרי, דאמר קרא "לטהרו או לטמאו" הואיל ופתח בטהרה תחילה. לעולם לא נאמרה במנורע אלא טהור גמור או טמא גמור.

בשבעה דרכים בודקין את הזב עד שלא נזקק [לזיבה]. כמו בראיה ראשונה או שניה: במאכל ובמשתה, במשא ובקפיצה במראה. שראה איש ואשה נזקקין זה לזה. וכן משמע במס' זבין (פ"ב מ"ב), דפליג רבי יהודה, ואמר: אפי' ראה בהמה חיה ועוף נזקקין זה לזה מהרהר. משנזקק לטומאה. כמו בראיה שלישית לרבנן, פרק "בנות כותים" (נדה דף לה.) דמחייבי קרבן. אבל רביעית לר"א, ליסתור מה שספר – אין בודקין אותו, דהא "מבשרו" ולא מחמת אונסו לא קאי אלא אשתים לרבנן, או אשלישית לר"א.

אונסו. כמו מאכל ומשתה. והנך שבע דאמרינן שמרגילין זיבות, טמא משנזקק לטומאה. ספקו ושכבת זרעו. מפ' בגמ'. **רבי** נחמיה פוטר שרגלים לדבר. דחולה הוא, הואיל והיקל ממה שהיה. איידי דתנא "שרגלים לדבר" נקטי' הכא. **מנה"מ** א"ר [נתן] דאמר קרא "והזב" את זובו לזכר ולנקבה. "והזב" – ראיה ראשונה, "את זובו" – ראיה שניה, "לזכר ולנקבה" – שלישית, אקשיה רחמנא לנקבה, ונקבה מטמאה באונס. **רבי** אלעזר אומר בשלישית בודקין אותו ברביעית אין בודקין אותו. מ"ט דר"א דלית ליה דרשה דאמרינן, אלא באתים קמיפלגי, ר"א דריש: "הזב" – חדא, "את" – תרתי, "זובו" – תלתא, ברביעית אקשייה לנקבה. ובפרק "בנות כותים" (נדה דף לה.) מפרש ליה התלמוד טפי.

אמר

אמר רבא: בדק ופנה, בדק ופנה, בדק ואשכח – לא האי מפני ליה גבי הנך תרי, ולא הני תרי לגבי האי חד. איכא דאמרי, אמר רבא: כיון שנתנה רשות לפנות – מפנה להון. ולישוינהו שכונת קברות! *אמר ריש לקיש: עילא מצאו וטיהרו ארץ ישראל.§ בדק מעשרים אמה ולא מצא, מאי? אמר רב מנשיא בר ירמיה אמר רב: [א]שכונת קברות. מאי טעמא? אמר ר"ל: עילא מצאו וטיהרו את ארץ ישראל.§ **מתני'** *[ב]כל ספק נגעים בתחילה טהור – עד שלא נזקק לטומאה. [ג]משנזקק לטומאה – ספקו טמא.§ **גמ'** מנא הני מילי? אמר רב יהודה אמר רב: אמר קרא °"לטהרו או לטמאו", הואיל ופתח [בו] הכתוב בטהרה תחילה. אי הכי, אפילו משנזקק לטומאה נמי ספקו טהור! אלא, כי איתמר דרב יהודה אמר רב – אהא איתמר: *[ד]אם בהרת קדמה לשער לבן – טמא, ואם שער לבן קודם לבהרת – טהור. [ה]ספק – טמא. ור' יהושע אמר: כיהה. מאי כיהה? אמר רב *יהודה: כיהה וטהור. ודילמא כיהה וטמא? אמר רב יהודה אמר רב: אמר קרא "לטהרו או לטמאו" – הואיל ופתח בו הכתוב בטהרה תחילה.§ **מתני'** *[ו]בשבעה דרכים בודקין את הזב עד שלא נזקק לזיבה: במאכל, ובמשתה, במשא, ובקפיצה, ובחולי, ובמראה, ובהירהור. [ז]משנזקק לזיבה – אין בודקין אותו. [ח]אונסו, וספיקו, ושכבת זרעו – טמאים, שרגלים לדבר. *[ט]המכה את חבירו ואמדוהו למיתה והיקל ממה שהיה, לאחר מכאן הכביד ומת – חייב, ר' נחמיה אומר: פטור, שרגלים לדבר.§ **גמ'** מנא הני מילי. אמר רבי נתן: אמר קרא °"והזב את זובו" – לראיה שלישית איתקש לנקיבה. והתניא, *רבי *אלעזר אומר: בשלישית – בודקין אותו, ברביעית – אין בודקין אותו! אלא *באתים קמיפלגי, רבי אליעזר דריש אתים *ורבנן לא דרשי אתים.§ "אונסו וספיקו".

אמר

ויקרא יג | שם טו | תורה אור

אמר רבא בדק ופנה. בדק ומלא מת ופינהו ממקומו, כדתנן: נוטלו ואת תפוסתו. בדק ופנה. נמי לשני, כדתנן: מלא שנים נוטלן ואת תפוסתן. ולבתר הכי בדק ואשכח, שמלא שלישי א) – לא מפני ליה גבי הנך קמאי. ולא הנך תרי. מפני להון גבי חד. דמחזקינן ב) בשכונת קברות. ה"ג: ג) אמר רבא כיון שניתנה רשות לפנותן מפני להו ולישוינהו שכונת קברות אמר ר"ל עילא מצאו וטיהרו את א"י בדק מכ' אמה ולא מצא מאי אמר רב מנשיא בר ירמיה אמר רב ד) ששת שכונת קברות. וה"פ: אמר רבא: כיון שניתנה רשות לפנות להן כשמלא את השנים, כדתנן: מלא שנים – נוטלן ואת תפוסתן, מפני להו להאי ג'. ה) ואמאי מפני להו? לישוינהו שכונת קברות, שיחזרו למקומן ויחזיקו לאותו מקום כאילו עדיין יש שם מערות אחרות סביבותיו, ולא יכנסו עושי טהרות לשם, כדי שלא יאהילו על הטומאה! אמר ר"ל עילא. כלומר, כשניתנה רשות לפנות כשלא מלא אלא אחד ושנים, כי הדר ומלא להך שלישי – מפני ו) להו גבייהו, כדי לטהר את המקום הזה, שלא להחזיקו שיש מערות סביבותיה, שיהו כהנים ועושי ז) פסח מותרים להלך לשם. קתני בודק ממנו ולהלן ואם בדק ולא מצא מאי. מי אמרינן: כיון דלא מלא אלא הנך ג' – אתרמויי אתרמו דאיתקבור להכא, ולא קנו מקומן, או דלמא כיון דג' הן – מחזקינן ליה בשכונת קברות, ואסור לפנותן. אמר רב מנשיא אמר רב ה"ז שכונת קברות מ"ט אמר ר"ל עילא מצאו וטיהרו את א"י. נלע של מתים מלאו, דמתרגמינן (בראשית ג): נלע = עילא. וטיהרו את א"י. כלומר, אע"פ ח) שאין כאן אלא הללו ג' קברים – אמרינן: זו היא שכונת קברות של עיר, ושאר סביבות העיר טהור ט). י) ה"ג: ספק טמא ר' יהושע אומר כיהה.

מתני' בז' דרכים בודקים הזב עד שלא נזקק לטומאה. עד שלא ראה ג' ראיות. באכילה ובשתיה. מחמת רוב אכילה ושתיה. כ) הדרכים האמורים כאן מביאים האדם לידי זיבה. ובמראה. שראה אשה או ד"א, ל) ונפחד מחמתו. והוי אונס, ואמר מר (נדה דף לה.): "מבשרו" – ולא מחמת אונסו. משנזקק לזיבה. שכבר ראה *) ראיה – שוב אין בודקין אותו. שרגלים לדבר. שלא מ) בא מחמת אונסו, אלא מחמת זיבה ממש. אונסו וספיקו ושכבת זרעו. הכל טמאים מחמת זיבה, דאי אפשר להם בלא לחלוחי זיבה. ורבי נחמיה פוטר שרגלים לדבר. שלא נ) בא מחמת המכה, הואיל ומתחילה היקל ממה שהיה. **גמ'** מנה"מ. דמשנזקק לטומאת זיבה שוב אין בודקין אותו. א"ר נתן אמר קרא "והזב את זובו. לזכר ולנקבה" אחר שאמר הכתוב שתי זיבות "זב זובו". הקיש הכתוב זכר לנקבה לראיה שלישית, לומר לך: מה נקבה דלא כתיב בה "מבשרה", ואפילו מאונסה הויא ס) טמאה – אף זכר, כיון שראה ב' פעמים שנזקק לטומאת ז', אפי' ראה את השלישית באונס, כיון דחזא ב' פעמים שלא באונס ע) – הוי טמא, ומייתי קרבן. ר"א אומר בשלישית בודקין אותו. מפני הקרבן, שאם ראה פ) ב' ראיות מחמת זיבות ואת השלישית באונס – אינו מביא קרבן. ברביעית אין בודקין אותו. כלומר, צ) כיון שראה שלש שלא באונס, וראה את הרביעית בתוך ימי ספרו, ואפי' אם היא באונס – אין בודקין אותו אם מחמת אונסו היא, אלא ק) סותרין את הכל, כדמפרש במסכת נדה בפ' "בנות כותים" (דף לה.). ר"א דריש אתים. "הזב" – חדא, "את" – תרתי, "זובו" – תלתא, ולרביעית איתקש לנקיבה, דמטמאה אפי' באונס.

*) נ"א ב' ראיות [וכ"ה בכ"י]

לא

כתובות כ:
נגעים פ"ה מ"ד
סנהדרין פז: נדה יט. ב"מ פו. כתובות עה: נגעים פ"ד מ"ח
קדושין כ: זבים פ"ב מ"ב
[סנהדרין עח. ע"ש]
[נ"ל רבי אליעזר]
[נדה לה.]
[פסחים כב: וש"נ]
נ"ל זקוק לחפור
נ"ל שיחזור
נדה לה. ע"ש
גי' א"מ או לטמאו

נוסחת הריב"ן

א) שלישי דאילו אם מתחלה מלא שלשתן לא היה רשאי לפנותן מפני שנעשה שכונת קברות לא מאי שלישי מפני ליה כו': ב) דמחזקינן ליה: ג) ה"ג ר"ד אמר רב: ד) אמר רב שכונת: ה) שלישי גבייהו ואמאי כו' שיחזרם למקומן ויחזיק אותו מקום: ו) מפני ליה: ז) ועושי טהרות: ח) שלא מצאו א"א: ט) טהור דאמרינן ליכא שכונת קברות אחריני הכא אלא הך שכונת קברות מפי המורה הס"ד: י) בכ"י איתא הכי עד שלא נזקק לטומאת נגעים דספק טהור ה"ג ספק טמא רבי יהושע כיהה מאי כיהה אמר רבה כיהה וטיהר: כ) וטעינת משוי יותר מדאי וכל הדרכים כו': ל) ונתפחד מחמת חרדה ושותת זיבה והוי אונס: מ) שלא מחמת אונסו בא אלא: נ) שלא מחמת ור' ממה שהיה מפי המורה הס"ד: ס) הויא זיבה: ע) זב הוי ומייתי קרבן: פ) שאם ראה את השלישית באונס: צ) לאחר שראה: ק) סותר את:

פי' הרא"ש

המת וזורק את הודאי' דבר ידוע שאינו מן המת וגם אינו מטמא והשאר מצטרפין לרוב בניינו ומניינו: ולרובע הקב עצמות ולמלא תרווד רקב. כגון שנקבר המת ערום בארון של שיש ונפתח הארון מתחתיו ויצא מרקבותו דרך הפתח העפר שתחת הארון מתחתיו הוא ספק אם מעפר הארץ הוא או מרקביבות המת והנמצא בתוך הארון הוא או מרקביבות המת והנמצא בתוך הארון הוא ודאי ומצטרף כולו יחד כמלא תרווד: אמר רבא בדק ופנה ובדק ופנה בדק ואשכח. כדין נמצא קבר א' ופנהו משם ולא הוה יודע שהיה שם קבר א' ושוב בדק ומצא אחר ופנהו משם ושוב מצא קבר ג': לא האי מפני גבי הנך אין יכול לפנות הג' מכאן כי הוברר הדבר (שאינן) [שהן] שכונת קברות: ולא הנך תרי לגבי האי חד. גם לא חייבוהו חכמים לחזור הב' למקומם כיון שבשעה שפינם משם לא היה ידוע שהיה שכונת קברות. איכא דאמרי כיון שנתנה רשות לפנות מפני להון פי' שברשות פינם כל זמן שלא מצא הג' מפנה גם הג' משם: ולישוינהו שכונת קברות. השתא מיהא איגליא מלתא דהויא שכונת קברות ולמה יפנה הג': אמר ר"ל עילא מצאו. א"י בעלילה מועטת ובסברא קטנה טהרו ארץ ישראל משום כהנים ועושי טהרות והכא נמי כיון שברשות פינם הב' התירו לפנות גם הג' ולא דמי לקבר הידוע דאסור לפנותו דאין כאן ידיעה ודאית: בדק כ' אמה ולא מצא. בתוך כ' שום מת מי אמרי' לא בדק שפיר וצריך עוד לבדוק עד קרקע בתולה: אמר רב ששת ה"ז שכונת קברות. אין לטמא אלא ג' הראשונים שמצא ואין צריך לבדוק עוד. וק"ל דבפ' ט"ז דאהלות בתר הך משנה תנן הבודק בודק אמה ומניח אמה עד שהוא מגיע לסלע או לקרקע בתולה. אלמא מתחלה צריך לבדוק עד קרקע בתולה. ועוד דלשון ה"ז שכו' קברות לא משמע כהאי פי' עוד מפ' בדק כ' אמה ולא מצא מהו שהצריכו לבדוק עוד כ' אמה מרוח אחרת מי אמרי' כיון דלא אשכח מהאי גיסא אידך גיסא נמי ליכא או דלמא צריך מיהא לבדוק ה"ז שכונת קברות וא"צ עוד לבדוק. א) וגם על פי הק"מ דלדברי המפרשים שא"צ לבדוק רק מרגלי המת ואילך ליכא למיבעיא מידי ולדברי המפרשים שאין הכר ברגלי המת פשיטא דצריך לבדוק מב' צדדים דהי מנייהו מפקת. ואמאי פשט ליה דא"צ ועוד שהרי זו שכונת קברות לא משמע גם כפי' זה. ונ"ל לפרש בדק ולא מצא מאי ומיבעיא ליה אם מותר לפנות ג' מכאן דקודם בדיקה חיישי' שמא מערות הוו כאן מתוקנים לקברים וכיון דבדק ולא מצא הוברר הדבר שאין כאן שכונת קברות דאין דרך לקבור מתים אלא במקום המיוחד לקברים הרבה: ה"ז שכונת קברות ופשטא ליה כיון דג' הם מחזקי' ליה שכונת קברות אע"פ שלא מצא יותר. ול"ג הכא מאי טעמא אמר ר"ל עילא מצאו וכו': כל ספק נגעים בתחילה טהור וכו' בפ"ה דמסכת נגעים מ"ד
א) נראה דל"ל וגם על פי' זה יש להקשות לדברי המפרשי' כו'.
לה

אֲמַר רָבָא: לָא תֵּימָא סָפֵק חֲזָא סָפֵק לָא חֲזָא. אֶלָּא וַדַּאי חֲזָא, סָפֵק מֵחֲמַת שִׁכְבַת זֶרַע סָפֵק מֵחֲמַת רְאִיָּה, כֵּיוָן שֶׁנִּזְקַק לְטוּמְאָה — סְפֵיקוֹ טָמֵא.§ "שִׁכְבַת זַרְעוֹ טְמֵאָה".§ לְמַאי? אִילֵימָא לְמַגָּע, מִי גָּרַע מִשִּׁכְבַת זֶרַע דְּטָהוֹר? אֶלָּא זַרְעוֹ שֶׁל זָב מְטַמֵּא בְּמַשָּׂא. מַאן שָׁמְעַתְּ לְהָא דְּאָמַר שִׁכְבַת זֶרַע שֶׁל זָב מְטַמֵּא בְּמַשָּׂא? אִילֵימָא הַאי תַּנָּא, דְּתַנְיָא, *רַבִּי אֱלִיעֶזֶר אוֹמֵר: שִׁכְבַת זַרְעוֹ שֶׁל זָב אֵינוֹ מְטַמֵּא בְּמַשָּׂא, וְרַבִּי יְהוֹשֻׁעַ אוֹמֵר: [א]מְטַמֵּא בְּמַשָּׂא, לְפִי *שֶׁאִי אֶפְשָׁר לָהּ בְּלֹא צִיחְצוּחֵי זִיבָה. אֲפִי' רַבִּי יְהוֹשֻׁעַ לָא אֲמַר אֶלָּא מִשּׁוּם צִיחְצוּחֵי זִיבָה, אֲבָל בְּעֵינֵיהּ — לָא אֲמַר! אֶלָּא אָמַר רַב אַדָּא בַּר אַהֲבָה: לוֹמַר שֶׁאֵין תּוֹלִין בָּהּ. סְבַר רַב פָּפָּא קַמֵּיהּ דְּרָבָא לְמֵימַר: אַיְּדֵי חוּלְשָׁא הוּא דַּחֲזֵי. א"ל רָבָא: *וְהָתְנַן, [ב]גֵּר שֶׁנִּתְגַּיֵּיר — מְטַמֵּא מִיָּד בְּזִיבָה! א"ל: אֵין לְךָ חוֹלִי גָּדוֹל מִזֶּה. אֶלָּא, תַּנָּאֵי הִיא. דְּתַנְיָא: שִׁכְבַת זֶרַע שֶׁל זָב מְטַמֵּא בְּמַשָּׂא כׇּל מֵעֵת לְעֵת, ור' יוֹסֵי אוֹמֵר: יוֹמוֹ. בְּמַאי קָמִיפַּלְגִי — בְּדִשְׁמוּאֵל. דִּשְׁמוּאֵל רָמֵי: א] כְּתִיב °"כִּי יִהְיֶה בְךָ אִישׁ אֲשֶׁר לֹא יִהְיֶה טָהוֹר מִקְּרֵה לָיְלָה" וּכְתִיב "לִפְנוֹת עֶרֶב יִרְחַץ בַּמָּיִם"; מ"ד מֵעֵת לְעֵת — דָּיֵיק מִ"לִּפְנוֹת עֶרֶב", וְאִידָךְ דָּיֵיק "מִקְּרֵה לָיְלָה" ומ"ד מִ"לִּפְנוֹת עֶרֶב", הָכְתִיב "מִקְּרֵה לָיְלָה"! א"ל: אוֹרְחָא דְּקֶרִי לְמֵתְיָא בְּלֵילְיָא.§ **מתני'** [ג]נָזִיר הָיָה שְׁמוּאֵל, כְּדִבְרֵי ר' נְהוֹרַאי, שֶׁנֶּא' °"וּמוֹרָה לֹא יַעֲלֶה עַל רֹאשׁוֹ"; נֶאֱמַר בְּשִׁמְשׁוֹן °"וּמוֹרָה" וְנֶאֱמַר בִּשְׁמוּאֵל "וּמוֹרָה", מַה מּוֹרָה הָאֲמוּרָה בְּשִׁמְשׁוֹן — נָזִיר, אַף מוֹרָה הָאֲמוּרָה בִּשְׁמוּאֵל — נָזִיר. א"ר יוֹסֵי: וַהֲלֹא אֵין מוֹרָה אֶלָּא שֶׁל בָּשָׂר וָדָם! א"ל רַבִּי נְהוֹרַאי: וַהֲלֹא כְּבָר נֶאֱמַר °"וַיֹּאמֶר שְׁמוּאֵל אֵיךְ אֵלֵךְ וְשָׁמַע שָׁאוּל וַהֲרָגָנִי" — שֶׁכְּבָר הָיָה עָלָיו מוֹרָא שֶׁל בָּשָׂר וָדָם.§ **גמ'** *א"ל רַב לְחִיָּיא בְּרֵיהּ: חֲטוֹף

דברים כג | שמואל א א | שופטים יג | שמואל א טז | תורה אור

לָא תֵּימָא. דְּהַאי סְפֵיקוֹ דְּקָאָמַר שֶׁמְּטַמֵּא, דְּקָא בָּעֵי לְמֵימַר סָפֵק חֲזָא סָפֵק לָא חֲזָא, דְּמִכׇּל מָקוֹם לָא מוֹקְמִינַן עֲלֵיהּ טוּמְאָה לָא לְעִנְיַן חִיּוּב קׇרְבָּן וְלָא לְעִנְיַן סְתִירָה אִם כְּבָר הִתְחִיל לִמְנוֹת יְמֵי סְפָרוֹ, כְּדִכְתִיב "וְסָפַר לוֹ שִׁבְעַת יָמִים לְטׇהֳרָתוֹ". אֶלָּא וַדַּאי חֲזָא, וּמִיהוּ סָפֵק מֵחֲמַת שִׁכְבַת זֶרַע. **מִי גָּרַע.** שִׁכְבַת זֶרַע דְּזָב מִשִּׁכְבַת זֶרַע דְּטָהוֹר, דְּטָמֵא בְּמַגָּע, כִּדְאָמַר מָר (נדה דף מג.): *"וְאִישׁ אֲשֶׁר תֵּצֵא מִמֶּנּוּ שִׁכְבַת זָרַע" (ויקרא כב) "אוֹ" — לְרַבּוֹת אֶת הַנּוֹגֵעַ. **אֶלָּא אָמַר רַב אַדָּא בַּר אַהֲבָה.** מַאי הָא דְּקָאָמַר דְּשִׁכְבַת זַרְעוֹ טְמֵאָה — לוֹמַר שֶׁאֵין תּוֹלִין בָּהּ, דִּלְאַחַר שֶׁנִּזְקַק לְטוּמְאָה אִם רָאָה קֶרִי א) וְרָאָה זִיבָה — אֵין אוֹתָהּ זִיבָה כְּקֶרִי, כִּי הַהִיא דִּתְנַן בְּמַסֶּ' זָבִין (פ"ב מ"ג): הָרוֹאֶה קֶרִי — אֵינוֹ מְטַמֵּא בְּזִיבָה כׇּל מֵעֵת לְעֵת. **סָבַר רַב פָּפָּא** קַמֵּיהּ **דְּרָבָא** לְמֵימַר. הַיְינוּ טַעְמָא דְּאֵין תּוֹלִין אֶת הַזִּיבָה בְּשִׁכְבַת זֶרַע — דְּאָמְרִינַן: אַיְּדֵי חוּלְשָׁא שֶׁנֶּחֱלַשׁ מִזִּיבָה רִאשׁוֹנָה, ב) שֶׁכְּבָר נִזְקַק לְטוּמְאַת זִיבָה — חֲזָא נַמִּי לְהָךְ זִיבָה, וְלָא מֵחֲמַת קֶרִי. אֲבָל הֵיכָא דְּלָא נִזְקַק לְטוּמְאָה, וְרָאָה קֶרִי — הַיְינוּ טַעְמָא דְּתָלֵינַן אֶת הַזִּיבָה בְּקֶרִי, וְאֵינוֹ מְטַמֵּא כׇּל מֵעֵת לְעֵת — מִשּׁוּם דְּלָאו ע"י חוּלְשָׁא הוּא דַּחֲזָא, דְּהָא אַכַּתִּי לָא נִזְקַק לְזִיבָה. **א"ל רָבָא וְהָא תְּנַן.** בְּמַסֶּ' זָבִין:* גּוֹי שֶׁרָאָה קֶרִי וְנִתְגַּיֵּיר — מְטַמֵּא בְּזִיבָה מִיָּד. וְתָנֵי עֲלָהּ בְּבָרַיְיתָא: (גּוֹי שֶׁרָאָה קֶרִי וְנִתְגַּיֵּיר — מְטַמֵּא בְּזִיבָה מִיָּד) בד"א — בִּזְמַן שֶׁנִּתְגַּיֵּיר מָהוּל. וְהָא הָכָא דְּלֵיכָּא חוּלְשָׁא, וַאפ"ה לָא תָּלֵינַן אֶת הַזִּיבָה בְּקֶרִי, וְהָוֵי טָמֵא מִיָּד! א"ל: כֵּיוָן דִּמְקַבֵּל עָלָיו עוֹל מִצְוֹת — אֵין לְךָ חוֹלִי גָּדוֹל מִזֶּה. וְלָא חוֹלִי מַמָּשׁ קָאָמַר, דְּאִי חוֹלִי מַמָּשׁ — לָא הָוֵי מְטַמֵּא בְּזִיבָה, שֶׁזּוֹ אֶחָד ג) מִז' דְּרָכִים שֶׁבּוֹדְקִין בָּהֶן אֶת הַזָּב שֶׁשָּׁנִינוּ בְּמִשְׁנָתֵינוּ. אֶלָּא מֵחֲמַת חוּלְשָׁא ד) בְּעָלְמָא הוּא דַּחֲזָא, שֶׁכֵּן זִיבָה בָּאָה מִבָּשָׂר מֵת, וְלָא מֵחֲמַת קֶרִי. **אֶלָּא תַּנָּאֵי הִיא.** אַדִּלְעֵיל קָאֵי. דְּהָא דְּדָחֵינַן לְעֵיל: מַאן שָׁמְעַתְּ לֵיהּ דְּקָאָמַר שִׁכְבַת זַרְעוֹ מְטַמֵּא בְּמַשָּׂא רַבִּי יְהוֹשֻׁעַ הִיא, וַאֲמַר עֲלָהּ: וַאֲפִי' רַבִּי יְהוֹשֻׁעַ לָא אָמַר אֶלָּא מֵחֲמַת זִיבָה — אִיכָּא תַּנָּאֵי אַחֲרִינֵי דְּאָמְרִי ה) דְּלֵיכָּא טַעְמָא מִשּׁוּם לִיכְלוּכֵי זִיבָה, אֶלָּא שֶׁכָּךְ גְּזֵירַת הַכָּתוּב. דְּתַנְיָא: שִׁכְבַת זֶרַע שֶׁל זָב מְטַמֵּא ו) מֵעֵת לְעֵת לְאַחַר שֶׁרָאָה זִיבָה ז) מְטַמֵּא בְּמַשָּׂא. ר' יוֹסֵי אוֹמֵר יוֹמוֹ בִּלְבַד. שֶׁרָאָה בּוֹ זִיבָה, אִם רָאָה קֶרִי — תּוֹלִין אֶת הַקֶּרִי בְּזִיבָה, וּמְטַמֵּא בְּמַשָּׂא אוֹתוֹ הַיּוֹם בִּלְבַד, אֲבָל מִכָּאן וּלְהַבָּא — לֹא. וְלָאו מִשּׁוּם דִּסְבִירָא לֵיהּ דְּאִי אֶפְשָׁר בְּלֹא לִיכְלוּכֵי זִיבָה, אֶלָּא שֶׁכָּךְ גְּזֵירַת הַכָּתוּב. ח) וּבְכִי הַאי דִּשְׁמוּאֵל קָמִיפַּלְגִי. דִּשְׁמוּאֵל רָמֵי: כְּתִיב "כִּי יִהְיֶה בְךָ אִישׁ אֲשֶׁר לֹא יִהְיֶה טָהוֹר מִקְּרֵה לַיְלָה וְיָצָא אֶל מִחוּץ לַמַּחֲנֶה וְרָחַץ בַּמַּיִם אֶת כׇּל בְּשָׂרוֹ", *אַלְמָא מִדְּקַשֵּׁי ט) בְּדִיבּוּרֵיהּ — ש"מ דִּבְטוּמְאַת קֶרִי קָאָמַר. מ"ד י) כׇּל מֵעֵת לְעֵת. מְטַמֵּא שִׁכְבַת זֶרַע שֶׁל זָב, דָּיֵיק מִ"לִּפְנוֹת עֶרֶב", דְּמַשְׁמַע ב' עֲרָבִים. "לִפְנוֹת" — חַד עֶרֶב מַשְׁמַע, כִּדְכְתִיב "כִּי פָנָה הַיּוֹם" (ירמיהו ו), וְהַאי דִּכְתִיב "עֶרֶב" — הַיְינוּ נַמִּי עֶרֶב אַחֲרִינָא, וְהָוֵי מַשְׁמַע (א) כ) דִּכְתִיב בֵּיהּ מֵעֶרֶב וְעַד עֶרֶב, לוֹמַר לָךְ: מֵעֶרֶב וְעַד עֶרֶב מְטַמֵּא שִׁכְבַת זֶרַע שֶׁל זָב בְּמַשָּׂא. דְּה"נ תַּנְיָא לָהּ בְּסִיפְרָא: "וְהָיָה לִפְנוֹת עֶרֶב יִרְחַץ בַּמָּיִם" — מְלַמֵּד שֶׁהַקֶּרִי פּוֹטֵר בְּזִיבָה מֵעֵת לְעֵת. **וְאִידָךְ** דָּיֵיק מִ"מִּקְּרֵה לַיְלָה". דְּמַשְׁמַע: עַד לַיְלָה מְטַמֵּא בְּמַשָּׂא כִּי זִיבָה, דְּהַיְינוּ יוֹמוֹ. **אוֹרְחֵיהּ** דְּקֶרִי **דְּאָתְיָא בְּלֵילְיָא.** כְּשֶׁמְּהַרְהֵר עַל ל) מִשְׁכָּבוֹ, וְדִבֵּר הַכָּתוּב בַּהוֹוֶה. **מתני'** כְּדִבְרֵי רַבִּי נְהוֹרַאי. כָּךְ דִּבְרֵי רַבִּי נְהוֹרַאי. מַה מּוֹרָה הָאֲמוּרָה בְּשִׁמְשׁוֹן נָזִיר. דִּכְתִיב "כִּי נְזִיר אֱלֹהִים יִהְיֶה הַנַּעַר מִן הַבֶּטֶן" (שופטים יג). גמ'

אמר רבא לא תימא ספק חזא ספק לא חזא אלא ודאי חזא ספק מחמת זרע ספק מחמת ראיה וכיון דנזקק לטומאה ספקו טמא. פר"י: כדאמרינן בפ' "המפלת" (נדה דף כב.): זיבה דפתיכא ביה שכבת זרע — לא סתרה אלא יום אחד, זיבה דלא פתיכא ביה שכבת זרע — סתרה שבעה. ורבא איירי כגון שבדק עצמו ומצא שכבת זרע וגם זיבה על הבגד, ולא נודע אם באה הזיבה לבדה והשכבת זרע לבד ויסתור שבע, או פתך בה זיבה, שבאו יחד, ולא יסתור רק יום אחד.

ושכבת זרע למאי אילימא למגע. דמשנזקק לטומאה יטמא לשכבת זרע במגע. פשיטא, מי גרע משכבת זרע דטהור בעלמא, ואפי' לא נזקק נמי! אלא למשא, דשכבת זרע דטהור בעלמא אינו מטמא במשא, וכשנזקק לטומאה — מטמא במשא.

אילימא האי תנא דתניא כו' אפילו רבי יהושע לא קאמר אלא בצחצוחי זיבה אבל בעיניה לא. ושכבת זרע דמתני' משמע דאף בעיניה. אלא אמר רב אדא בר אהבה לומר שאין תולין בה. דבמסכת זבין (פ"ב מ"ג) תנן: הרואה קרי — [אינו מטמא בזיבה] כל מעת לעת, שהקרי פוטר זיבה הבא לאחריה כל מעת לעת. אבל משנזקק לטומאה — אז לא תפטור השכבת זרע את הזיבה הבא אחריה.

סבר רב פפא קמיה דרבא למימר איידי חולשא הוא דחזא. כלומר, להכי אמרינן דקרי פוטר זיבה הבא אחריו כל מעת לעת — דאיכא למיחש שמא מחמת חלישות נתרוקן מן השכבת זרע הוא דחזא, וקרי כאן: "מבשרו" — ולא מחמת אונסו. אבל משנזקק לטומאה אונס — לא פוטר. והיינו נמי טעמא דרב אדא בר אהבה. **אמר** ליה רבא [והא תנן] גר שנתגייר מטמא בזיבה [מיד]. ה"ג: ולמאי? הא אין לך חולי גדול מזה. פר"י: גר שראה קרי קודם שנתגייר, ונתגייר וראה זיבה — מטמא בזיבה, ולא תפטור קרי את הזיבה. ואם כדברי רב אדא ורב פפא, דטעמא דקרי פוטר בזיבה הבא אחריו משום חולשא — גבי גר נמי נימא הכי, דאין לך חולי גדול מזה, דכי היכי דבדקינן אותו — לפטור בקרי, דמה לי קרי שראה כשהוא גוי, מה לי שראה כשהוא ישראל! **אלא** תנאי [היא] כלומר דרב אדא ורב פפא ליתא. דודאי טעמא דקרי לאו משום חולשא, אלא משום גזירת הכתוב. דדרשינן בספרי: "והיה לפנות ערב ירחץ במים" — מלמד שהקרי פוטר זיבה כל מעת לעת. ולכך ל"ש נזקק ול"ש לא נזקק, אמרי' דקרי פוטר זיבה הבאה אחריו מעת לעת. ושכבת זרע דמתני' לאו בזיבה איירי, כדאמר רב אדא בר אהבה, אלא כדאמר מעיקרא — למשא. והני תנאי א) של זב דאמרי דקרי של זב מטמא במשא מעת לעת — כלומר, כשראה קרי תוך מעת לעת שראה בזיבה. **רבי** יוסי אומר כו'. וא"ת: ולייתי מתני' דמסכת כלים (פ"א מ"ג): למעלה מהם רוקו של זב ושכבת זרעו שמטמא במשא. ובפרק "כיצד הרגל" (ב"ק דף כה.) מייתי לה! [וי"ל]: שרגלים לדבר דמתני' מיירי דוקא שכבת זרע שרואה סמוך לזיבות, (והתם בעי לאתויי שיטמא במשא כל ז'). **במאי** קמיפלגי בדשמואל דשמואל רמי כתיב כי יהיה בך איש אשר לא יהיה טהור. שהוא זב מקרה לילה, כלומר שאם ראה קרי תוך ב) (היום) אחר שראה הזיבה ג) טמאה משאו לקרי. וכתיב "לפנות ערב" — אף אחר שפנה הערב, והיינו עד מעת לעת, וכדדרשינן נמי בספרי כדפרישי' לעיל, דמשמע מעת לעת. מ"ד מעת לעת דייק מ"לפנות ערב", ומ"ד יומו — דייק מ"לילה". ואידך, הא דכתיב לילה — משום דאורחיה דקרי למיתיא בלילה. ונראה לומר דאידך דורש ד) "לפנות ערב" כדדרשינן בסיפרי, דקרי פוטר זיבה של אחריה כל מעת לעת. **מה** מורה האמור בשמשון נזיר. דכתיב "נזיר אלהים יהיה הנער מן הבטן". חטוף

פי' הרא"ש

לה: עד שלא נזקק לטומאה כיצד שנים שבאו אצל כהן בזה בהרת כגרים ובזה כסלע בסוף שבוע בזה כסלע ובזה כסלע ואין ידוע באיזה מהם פשתה בין באיש א' בין בב' אנשים טהור. ואע"ג בודאי א' מהם טמא וכ"ש באיש א' בודאי אותו האיש שיש בו נגע טמא אפ"ה טהור: ובת"כ דריש ליה מקרא וטמא אותו את הודאי הוא מטמא פי' נגע שהוא ודאי מטמא ולא קאי אגברא ואינו מטמא את הספק: משנזקק לטומא' ספקו טמא. כיצד ב' שבאו אצל כהן בזה בהרת כגרים ובזה כסלע בסוף שבוע בזה כסלע ועוד ובזה כסלע ועוד שניהם טמאים עד שיחזרו להיות כגרים. ובת"כ דריש ליה מקרא וטהר אותו את הודאי הוא מטהר ואינו מטהר את הספק: מה"מ דספק נגעים להקל: הואיל ופתח בו הכתוב בטהרה תחילה. מזה יש ללמוד דכל ספק מקלינן ביה לטהרו: אי הכי דמהאי קרא ילפת ליה. אפי' נזקק לטומאה נמי דגזרת הכתוב הוא: אלא כי אתמר דרב יהודה אהא אתמר והך קרא אתא לדרשא אחרינא והא דמיפלגי במתני' בין נזקק לטומאה ובין לא נזקק מקראי דת"כ דריש ליה כדפרי' במתני': אם בהרת קודמת לשער לבן טמא. דכתיב והיא הפכה שער לבן דבעי' שהבהרת מהפכתו ללבן: ספק טמא ור' יהושע אומר כיהה. פי' טהור כמו והנה כהה הנגע: ודילמא כיהה וטמא כלומר מ"ט דר' יהושע דמטהר דילמא ראוי להיות טמא והוי כמו מה"מ אלא שלשון נזיר משונה: בשבעה דרכים בודקים את הזב. שאם ראה מחמת אונס טהור דדרשי' מבשרו ולא מחמת אונסו. עד שלא נזקק לטומאה דהיינו כשרואה ראיה שניה שבה יגמור לטמא משכב ומושב אבל ראיה ראשונה מטמאה באונס טומאת ערב כדין בעל קרי כדדרשי פ' בנות כותים זאת תורת הזב ואשר תצא ממנו ש"ז. ראיה ראשונה של זב איתקש לבעל קרי ומצטרפי' עם השניה אפי' היתה באונס: במאכל אם אכל דברים המביאים לידי זיבה כדמפרש פ"ק דיומא א) ר"ג בש' בי"י בריבוי שתיה במשא כבד שנשא במראה ראה אשה אפי' לא הרהר ובהרהור אפי' לא ראה ואם אירע לו א' מאלו הז' קודם שראה ראיה שניה שלא באונס: אין בודקין אותו ואף אם ראה שלישית באונס נעשה זב לקרבן וכן הרביעית סותרת אפי' באונס: ספקו ושכבת זרעו. מפרש בגמ' שרגלים לדבר שלא באתה הראיה מחמת האונס כיון שכבר נעשה זב: מה"מ דבשלישית אין בודקין אותו: דאמר קרא והזב את זובו לזכר ולנקבה הזוב חדא וזובו תרי לזכר עד כאן יש לו דין זכר שאינו מטמא באונס מכאן ואילך ולנקבה יש לו דין נקבה ומטמא באונס כדאיתא [בפ'] בנות כותים כי יזוב זוב דמה הרי אונס אמור ומה אני מקיים דמה מחמת עצמה ולא מחמת ולד: והא דתניא ר"א אומר בשלישית בודקי' אותו. ובראיית אונס אינו נעשה זב לקרבן. ברבייעת אין בודקין אותו וסותרת אפי' באונס במאי קמיפלגי. ר"א דורש את וג' ראיות יש דין זכר: אמר רבא לא תימא ספק חזא ספק לא חזא דהא ודאי לא מטמאי'. אלא ודאי ס' מחמת ש"ז ס' מחמת ראיה כגון שבדק בעד ומצא עליו זיבה וקרי ואינו יודע אם ראה כל אחד בפני עצמו וסותר ז' או אם ראה שתיהם בבת אחת ואינו סותר אלא יומו כדאיתא פ' המפלת זיבה דפתיכא ביה שכבת זרע לא סתרה אלא יומא. וי"מ ספק מחמת ש"ז פירוש ספק אם ראה ש"ז תחילה וטיפת זיבה הבאה אח"כ אינה מטמאה כדתנן פ"ב דמס' זבים הרואה קרי אינו מטמא בזיבה מעת לעת ספק אם טיפת זיבה יצאת תחילה ועד שלא נזקק הקרי מטהר הזיבה משום דהוי אונס שניזדעזעו איבריו ונתרוקן גופו ונחלש והוי כחולי: משנזקק לטומאה אפי' אונס נטמא. וק' לפי זה מאי קאמר מחמת [ספק] ש"ז אפי' ודאי מחמת ש"ז טמא. ועוד לרב אדא בר אהבה דמפרש שכבת זרעו לענין שאין תולין היינו ספקו: מי גרע מש"ז דטהור דמטמא במגע ואפי' ר' יהושע לא קאמר אלא משום צחצוחי זיבה אבל בעינא לא ומתני' קתני מטמא במשא מטעם ש"ז ולא משום זיבה ואפי' איכא בלא צחצוחי זיבה: אמר רב אדא בר אהבה לומר שאין תולין בה. פי' אם ראה זיבה אחר קרי אין תולין שמחמת הקרי בא הזיבה והא דתנן דקרי מטהר הזיבה מעת לעת משום דמחמת חולשא דקרי חזי. ולכך משנזקק לטומאה דמטמ' באונס טמא: א"ל רבא והתנן גר שראה קרי ונתגייר מטמא בזיבה מעת לעת ר' יוסי אומר יומו: ובתוס' מוקי לה בנתגייר מהול דאי לאו הכי כל זמן שמצטער מחמת [המילה] אינו מטמא בזיבה: ה"ג ואין לך חולי גדול מזה. פירוש ואי אמרת דטעם דקרי מטהר בזיבה משום חולשא מה לי ישראל מה לי גר אדרבה טפי חולשא איכא בגר שהכנים עצמו לדאגת המצות

א) נ"ל דלאין מאכילין אותו לא תגב"י ולא גב"ס: במשתה. בריבוי שתיה וכו'.

נב א מיי' פ"ו מהל' מטמאי משכב ומושב הל"ד:
נג ב מיי' פ"ב מהל' מחוסרי כפרה הל"ד:
נד ג מיי' פ"ב מהל' מזורות הל"ו:

נ"ל או איש | [ב"ק כה.] | [נדה כב.] | זבים פ"ב מ"ג ע"ש | שם | ברכות נג: | גי' א"מ בשמו הל"ל אלא מדקני כו'

הגהות הב"ח

(א) רש"י ד"ה מ"ד כל מעת וכו' וכו' והוי משמע כאלו כתוב ביה:

הגהות מהר"ב רנשבורג

א] גמ' דשמואל רמי כתיב כי יהיה בך איש גו'. עי' שיטה מקובצת:

נוסחת הריב"ן

א) וחזר וראה: ב) דכבר שמקק: ג) מז' אחד מן הדרכים: ד) חולשא הוא: ה) דלא הוי טעמא: ו) מטמאה כל מעת לעת כו': ז) שראה זיבה של קרי מטמאה במשא מעת לעת: ח) וחכמי דשמואל: ט) מדקני קרא בדבוריה: י) בכ"י כתוב בזה"ל גליון פי' מתוס' איש אשר לא יהיה טהור מקרה לילה דמשמע אשר לא יהיה טהור מקרה ממה א"כ לילה מיותר לומר דעד לילה הוא מטמא הקרי כזוב לטמא במשא ותו לא וזהו יומו: כ) כדכתיב מערב ועד ערב ולומר לך דמערב ועד ערב כו' וה"נ תניא לה בספרי: ל) מטתו:

א) נ"ל היא דתניא ש"ז של זב: ב) גי' א"מ מע"ל: ג) גי' א"מ הזיבה טומאת משא לקרי: ד) [במ"ג פ"ב דזבים ס"ל לר' יוסי דאינו פוטר קרי לזיבה של אחריה אלא יומו והניח התוי"ט הדבר הזה בתמיה רבה ומיישב קושית תוספת באופן אחר ע"ש ועי' א"מ]:

נה א טוש"ע או"ח סי' רא סעי' ד:
נו ב מיי' פ"א מהל' ברכות הלי"א:

חטוף • מהר לברך שתהא זריז ונשכר: גוליירין מתגרין וגבורים מנצחין. הפרשים הבאים אחרי כן, ושם נצחון המלחמה על הפרשים הגומרין.

אחד המברך ואחד העונה אמן. נוטל שכר, אלא שממהרין למברך תחילה ליתן שכר, ולהכי אמרינן ליה חטוף ובריך.

הדרן עלך הכותים אין להם נזירות וסליקא לה מסכת נזיר

[א]חֲטוֹף וּבְרִיךְ. וְכֵן א"ל רַב הוּנָא לְרַבָּה בְּרֵיהּ: חֲטוֹף וּבְרִיךְ. לְמֵימְרָא דִּמְבָרֵךְ עֲדִיף? *וְהָתַנְיָא, רַבִּי יוֹסֵי אוֹמֵר: גָּדוֹל הָעוֹנֶה "אָמֵן" יוֹתֵר מִן הַמְבָרֵךְ. וא"ל רַבִּי נְהוֹרַאי: הַשָּׁמַיִם! כָּךְ הוּא. תֵּדַע, שֶׁהֲרֵי גּוּלְיָירִים מִתְגָּרִין בַּמִּלְחָמָה וְגִבּוֹרִים נוֹצְחִין! תַּנָּאֵי הִיא, *דְּתַנְיָא: [ב]אֶחָד הַמְבָרֵךְ וְאֶחָד הָעוֹנֶה "אָמֵן" בְּמַשְׁמַע, אֶלָּא שֶׁמְּמַהֲרִין לַמְבָרֵךְ תְּחִילָּה. *אָמַר רַבִּי אֶלְעָזָר א"ר חֲנִינָא: תַּלְמִידֵי חֲכָמִים מַרְבִּים שָׁלוֹם בָּעוֹלָם, שֶׁנֶּאֱמַר °"וְכָל בָּנַיִךְ לִמּוּדֵי ה' וְרַב שְׁלוֹם בָּנָיִךְ" (א).*§

ישעיהו נד

הדרן עלך הכותים אין להם נזירות וסליקא לה מסכת נזיר

גמ' חֲטוֹף. חֲטוֹף כּוֹס שֶׁל בְּרָכָה וּבָרֵיךְ בִּרְכַּת זִימּוּן, שֶׁתְּהֵא א) מְקַיֵּים לְבָרֵךְ עַל הַכּוֹס בִּרְכַּת ג) זִימּוּן. הַשָּׁמַיִם כָּךְ הוּא. בִּשְׁבוּעָה, עַל שֵׁם "וַיָּרֶם יְמִינוֹ אֶל הַשָּׁמַיִם וַיִּשָּׁבַע בְּחֵי הָעוֹלָם" (דניאל יב). כָּךְ הוּא, שֶׁהָעוֹנֶה אָמֵן גָּדוֹל מִן הַמְבָרֵךְ. וְתֵדַע. שֶׁהוּא כָּךְ. שֶׁהֲרֵי גּוּלְיָירִין. חַלָּשִׁין, מִתְגָּרִין בַּמִּלְחָמָה תְּחִלָּה, וְאַחַר כָּךְ גִּבּוֹרִים בָּאִין וְנוֹצְחִין. אַף כָּאן, הָעוֹנֶה אָמֵן בָּא לְאַחַר הַמְבָרֵךְ, וּמְנַצֵּחַ. לוֹמַר שֶׁהָעוֹנֶה אָמֵן מְשׁוּבָּח מִן הַמְבָרֵךְ. תַּנָּאֵי הִיא. דְּאִיכָּא לְמ"ד ג) דְּעוֹנֶה אָמֵן מְשׁוּבָּח מִן הַמְבָרֵךְ, וְאִית דְּאָמַר שֶׁהַמְבָרֵךְ מְשׁוּבָּח. א' הָעוֹנֶה וְאֶחָד הַמְבָרֵךְ בְּמַשְׁמַע. דִּקְרָא שֶׁנֶּאֱמַר (תהלים לד) "גַּדְּלוּ לַה' אִתִּי" – בְּרָכָה, "וּנְרוֹמְמָה שְׁמוֹ יַחְדָּיו" – אָמֵן. אֶלָּא שֶׁמְּמַהֲרִין לַמְבָרֵךְ תְּחִילָּה. לִיתֵּן ד) שָׂכָר.

הדרן עלך הכותים אין להם נזירות וסליקא לה מסכת נזיר

תורה אור

ברכות נג:

ג"ז שם

ברכות סד. יבמות קכב: כריתות כח: תמיד לב: [בברכות שם. איתא אל תקרי בניך אלא בונך]

הגהות הב"ח

(א) גמ' ורב שלום בניך אל תקרא בכך אלא וכו':

נוסחת הריב"ן

א) מקדים: ב) המזון: ג) (דעונה כו' ואית דאמר ליתא בכ"י: ד) שכרו:

יומם יצוה ה' חסדו ובלילה שירה. והיינו אני יהודה ובני יוסף הולכים לאור תורה ונר מצוה ושם טוב בהשארות בכל הש"ס נהגה גם אחר הילדות והשחרות עד זקנה וגם בשיבה דשנים ורעננים נעסוק במכתב אלהים החרות בכל פרק ופרק נאמר הדרן עלך וכן עתה ביום א' ד' בתשרי רע"ד בגמר פ' הכותים אין להם נזירות:

אנוש יצדק ידכה וישוח. יזכה בעמל כמחכה יקו אור אל יחזיר שכינתו שוכן בציון על תוכן יבאר הוא הכן במסכת נזיר איש גר אנכי בארץ חמו"ע

(כן כתוב בסוף הכ"י המפרש על נזיר).

פי' הרא"ש

המצות. אלא תנאי היא כלומר טעמא דקרי מטהר זיבה לאו משום חולשא אלא גזירת הכתוב היא ודוקא בישראל ולא בגר כמו שאפרש לקמן ושינויא דרב אדא בר אהבה ליתא דאפי' משנזקק לטומאת קרי מטהר הזיבה וש"ז דמתני' (דאמר) [מפרש] לה רבא שמטמא במשא ולא כר' יהושע אלא כהני תנאי: כתיב איש אשר לא יהיה טהור מקרה לילה דמשמע אשר לא יהיה טהור בסתם כלומר שהוא טמא טומאה אחרת היוצא מגופו דומיא דקרי ומאי ניהו זיבה ומקרה משמע ש"ז שראה הקרי אחר הזיבה וכתיב לילה מיותר אלא ש"מ דלילה שאחר הזיבה יש לטיפת קרי דין זיבה ומטמא במשא. ות"ק דייק מלפנות ערב דעד שיפנה היום דהיינו מעת לעת יש לה דין זיבה. ובספרי קתני והיה לפנות ערב מלמד שהקרי מטהר הזיבה מעת לעת. ודריש קרא גם למפרע דזיבה הבאה מעת לעת של קרי אין לה דין זיבה ולא דריש יומו ודוקא בישראל שקריו [טמא] אבל גוי [שקריו] טהור אינו מטהר הזיבה. א"ל אורחיה דקרי דמייתי בלילה ולא מייתר לדרשא. ומאן דאמר יומו סבר דלפנות ערב בשביל הערב שמש נקט דאפי' טבל מבע"י לא נטהר לגמרי עד לפנות ערב ורו"ש פירש במס' זבים דטעמא דקרי מטהר בזיבה משום חולשא וגר שראה קרי נתגייר אפי' ראה זיבה קודם שנתגייר מטמא בזיבה מיד משום דזיבות גוי לא שמיה זיבה ומה שראה עתה היא ראיה ראשונה שלו ומטמא באונס ואם יראה ראיה שניה אחר מעת לעת נעשה זב. וא"א לקיים פירושו לפי סוגיא דשמעתא אלא משמע לומר לתלמודא דלישניה דמטמא בזיבה מיד משום דנעשה זב גמור מיד אם ראה ב' ראיות בתוך מעת לעת הלכך ליכא לפרושי משום חולשא אלא מגזירת הכתוב: מה מרה האמורה בשמשון נזיר דכתיב כי נזיר אלהים יהיה הנער: אין מורה אלא של בשר ודם שלא תהא מורת ואימת בשר ודם עליו: חטוף כוס של ברכה וכן כל ברכות אל יקדמך אחר גוליירון וכו' וכן גמר הברכה היא עניית אמן:

הדרן עלך מס' נזיר והדרן עלן מס' נזיר וסליקא וכו'

The following קדיש *requires the presence of a* מנין.

יִתְגַּדַּל וְיִתְקַדַּשׁ שְׁמֵהּ רַבָּא
בְּעָלְמָא דְּהוּא עָתִיד לְאִתְחַדָּתָא
וּלְאַחֲיָאָה מֵתַיָּא, וּלְאַסָּקָא יָתְהוֹן לְחַיֵּי עָלְמָא
וּלְמִבְנֵא קַרְתָּא דִירוּשְׁלֵם, וּלְשַׁכְלָלָא הֵיכְלֵהּ בְּגַוַּהּ
וּלְמֶעְקַר פָּלְחָנָא נֻכְרָאָה מֵאַרְעָא
וְלַאֲתָבָא פָּלְחָנָא דִשְׁמַיָּא לְאַתְרֵהּ
וְיַמְלִיךְ קֻדְשָׁא בְּרִיךְ הוּא בְּמַלְכוּתֵהּ וִיקָרֵהּ
(נוסח ספרד: וְיַצְמַח פּוּרְקָנֵהּ וִיקָרֵב מְשִׁיחֵהּ)
בְּחַיֵּיכוֹן וּבְיוֹמֵיכוֹן וּבְחַיֵּי דְכָל בֵּית יִשְׂרָאֵל
בַּעֲגָלָא וּבִזְמַן קָרִיב, וְאִמְרוּ אָמֵן.

יְהֵא שְׁמֵהּ רַבָּא מְבָרַךְ לְעָלַם וּלְעָלְמֵי עָלְמַיָּא.

יִתְבָּרַךְ וְיִשְׁתַּבַּח וְיִתְפָּאַר וְיִתְרוֹמַם וְיִתְנַשֵּׂא
וְיִתְהַדָּר וְיִתְעַלֶּה וְיִתְהַלָּל
שְׁמֵהּ דְּקֻדְשָׁא בְּרִיךְ הוּא
לְעֵלָּא מִן כָּל בִּרְכָתָא
/בעשרת ימי תשובה: לְעֵלָּא לְעֵלָּא מִכָּל בִּרְכָתָא/
וְשִׁירָתָא, תֻּשְׁבְּחָתָא וְנֶחֱמָתָא, דַּאֲמִירָן בְּעָלְמָא
וְאִמְרוּ אָמֵן. (קהל: אָמֵן)

עַל יִשְׂרָאֵל וְעַל רַבָּנָן
וְעַל תַּלְמִידֵיהוֹן וְעַל כָּל תַּלְמִידֵי תַלְמִידֵיהוֹן
וְעַל כָּל מָאן דְּעָסְקִין בְּאוֹרַיְתָא
דִּי בְּאַתְרָא (בארץ ישראל: קַדִּישָׁא) הָדֵין, וְדִי בְּכָל אֲתַר וַאֲתַר
יְהֵא לְהוֹן וּלְכוֹן שְׁלָמָא רַבָּא
חִנָּא וְחִסְדָּא, וְרַחֲמֵי, וְחַיֵּי אֲרִיכֵי, וּמְזוֹנֵי רְוִיחֵי
וּפֻרְקָנָא מִן קֳדָם אֲבוּהוֹן דִּי בִשְׁמַיָּא
וְאִמְרוּ אָמֵן.

יְהֵא שְׁלָמָא רַבָּא מִן שְׁמַיָּא
וְחַיִּים (טוֹבִים) עָלֵינוּ וְעַל כָּל יִשְׂרָאֵל
וְאִמְרוּ אָמֵן.

Bow, take three steps back, as if taking leave of the Divine Presence, then bow, first left, then right, then center, while saying:

עֹשֶׂה שָׁלוֹם/ בעשרת ימי תשובה: הַשָּׁלוֹם/ בִּמְרוֹמָיו
הוּא יַעֲשֶׂה בְרַחֲמָיו שָׁלוֹם, עָלֵינוּ וְעַל כָּל יִשְׂרָאֵל
וְאִמְרוּ אָמֵן.

The following Kaddish requires the presence of a minyan.

Magnified and sanctified may His great name be,
in the world that will in future be renewed,
reviving the dead and raising them up to eternal life.
He will rebuild the city of Jerusalem
and in it re-establish His Temple.
He will remove alien worship from the earth
and restore to its place the worship of Heaven.
Then the Holy One, blessed be He,
will reign in His sovereignty and splendor.
May it be in your lifetime and in your days,
(*Nusaḥ Sepharad:* make His salvation flourish,
and hasten His messiah,)
and in the lifetime of all the House of Israel,
swiftly and soon – and say: Amen.

May His great name be blessed for ever and all time.

Blessed and praised,
glorified and exalted,
raised and honored,
uplifted and lauded
be the name of the Holy One,
blessed be He,
beyond any blessing,
song, praise and consolation uttered in the world –
and say: Amen.

To Israel, to the teachers,
their disciples and their disciples' disciples,
and to all who engage in the study of Torah,
in this (*in Israel add:* holy) place or elsewhere,
may there come to them and you great peace,
grace, kindness and compassion,
long life, ample sustenance and deliverance,
from their Father in Heaven –
and say: Amen.

May there be great peace from heaven,
and (good) life for us and all Israel –
and say: Amen.

Bow, take three steps back, as if taking leave of the Divine Presence, then bow, first left, then right, then center, while saying:

May He who makes peace in His high places,
in His compassion make peace for us and all Israel –
and say: Amen.